The Age of Sultan Süleyman the Magnificent

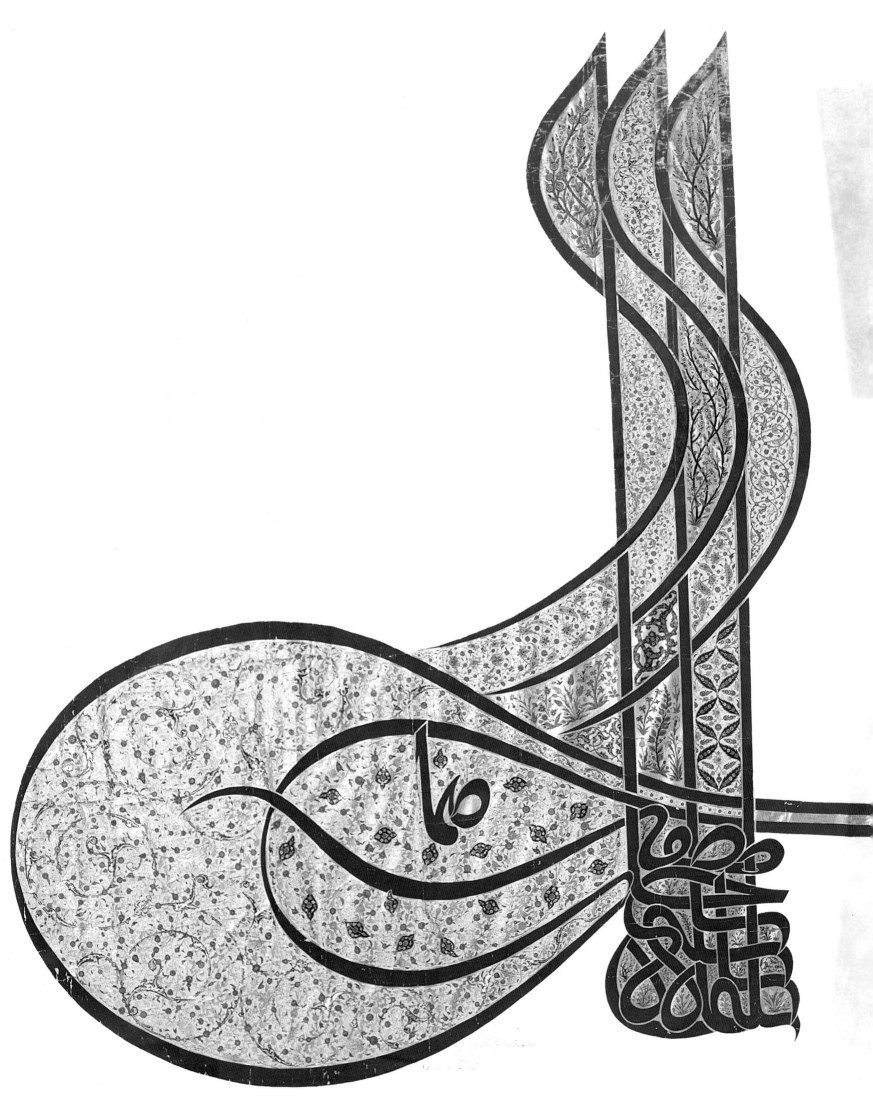

Esin Atıl

The Age of
Sultan Süleyman
the Magnificent

National Gallery of Art, Washington
Harry N. Abrams, Inc., New York

This exhibition is made possible by Philip Morris Companies Inc.

Exhibition Dates
National Gallery of Art, Washington, 25 January-17 May 1987
The Art Institute of Chicago, 14 June-7 September 1987
The Metropolitan Museum of Art, New York, 4 October 1987-17 January 1988

Cover design by Zeki Fındıkoğlu

Frontispiece: Illuminated tuğra of Sultan Süleyman, c. 1550 (İstanbul, Topkapı Sarayı Müzesi, G.Y. 1400)

Designed by Melanie B. Ness
Edited by Jane Sweeney

The text type is Meridien, set by VIP Systems, Inc., Alexandria, Virginia
Printed on 128 gsm Gardamatt manufactured by Cartiere del Garda
Printed and bound in Italy by Amilcare Pizzi, S.p.A., Milan

The clothbound edition is published by Harry N. Abrams, Inc., New York

Library of Congress Cataloging-in-Publication Data
Atıl, Esin
The age of Sultan Süleyman the Magnificent.
Bibliography: p.
Includes index.
1. Art, Ottoman—Exhibitions. 2. Turkey—Civilization—16th
century—Exhibitions. 3. Süleyman I, Sultan of the Turks,
1494 or 1495-1566—Art patronage—Exhibitions. National Gallery of Art (U.S.)
II. Title.
N7165.A85 1987 709' .561'0740153 86-19179
ISBN 0-89468-098-6 (paper)
ISBN 0-8109-1855-2 (cloth)

Contents

gift (D. Epstein) 9-89

Among the sixteen states founded throughout history by the Turks, the Ottoman Empire, which survived for more than six centuries (1299–1922), has a distinct place in world history. Works of art from one of the most glorious periods of the Ottoman Empire will be displayed for the first time in the United States during the exhibition *The Age of Sultan Süleyman the Magnificent.*

Throughout history, Anatolia has actually and constantly assumed the role of being a bridge between east and west. As a result of this historical fact, the culture and civilization of the Ottoman period reflect a synthesis of the cultures of east and west. During the reign of Sultan Süleyman I, known as "Süleyman the Magnificent," who ruled between 1520 and 1566, the Ottoman Empire became one of the leading states of the world, not only in political and military arenas, but also in cultural and social fields.

It is my belief that this exhibition, which contains some valuable samples of artifacts of only one period of the long history of our country that possesses many richnesses, will draw the attention and appreciation of the American public, and will contribute to the creation of a bridge of culture between the Turkish and American nations. Furthermore, I hope that the exhibition will be an opportunity for those American friends who have not so far been able to visit our country to see at least some small portion of the artistic and cultural legacy of Turkey.

While extending my thanks to those who contributed to the preparation of this exhibition, I would also like to send to the American people my best wishes for their success and happiness.

President of the
Republic of Turkey

THE WHITE HOUSE
WASHINGTON

The generous loan by the Republic of Turkey of a splendid collection of objects from the reign of Sultan Süleyman I is a most welcome event, and one in which Nancy and I take great personal interest.

Süleyman, known also as the Lawgiver, played a leading role in the diplomatic affairs of the sixteenth century. The twentieth-century globe may be a more complicated map than the one Süleyman studied, but the continuing value of international friendship is one he would recognize and endorse.

It is in the spirit of such friendship that I hope each of you will view the exhibition, remembering the good faith and trust the Turkish people have shown by sharing their national treasures with us.

Ronald Reagan

Foreword

The richness of the sixteenth century in European art is such that we tend to forget how much was happening in other parts of the world. This first comprehensive exhibition of Turkish art devoted to the most celebrated period of Ottoman history, the reign of Sultan Süleyman the Magnificent, reminds us of the great civilization that flourished at the eastern end of the Mediterranean.

Süleyman is known as "the Lawgiver" in Turkey for his far-reaching influence on civil law. Some of his acts were models for the legal codes of many countries, including our own. Thus the sultan's likeness appears in the chamber of the United States House of Representatives, joining the images of great leaders such as Hammurabi, Moses, Solon, and Jefferson, whose thinking helped to shape our constitution.

A brilliant jurist, Süleyman was also a discerning collector, a significant patron, and an accomplished poet. He, as well as his wife, daughter, sons, and court officials, commissioned many architectural monuments and literary and historical texts. The sophisticated patronage of Süleyman and his court nurtured the high standards and creativity that came to typify Ottoman art of the sixteenth century. *The Age of Sultan Süleyman the Magnificent*, with more than two hundred judiciously chosen works of art, includes manuscripts (with examples of Süleyman's own poetry) as well as jeweled vessels, silks, painted ceramics, and other sumptuous objects created in the imperial studios under the guidelines established by the sultan. This system of centralized court workshops permitted the dissemination of high standards throughout the empire. These workshops were crucial not only for the spread of favored themes from the capital to provincial centers, but also for fostering a synthesis of European and Islamic styles with Turkish ones.

We are indebted to the Turkish government for its enthusiastic response in lending to us under its new law that allows national treasures to leave the country on a temporary basis. Kenan Evren, the president of the Republic of Turkey; Turgut Özal, the prime minister; Mesut Yılmaz, the state minister for information; Vahit Halefoğlu, the minister of foreign affairs; Mükerrem Taşcıoğlu, the minister of culture and tourism; Şükrü Elekdağ, the ambassador of the Republic of Turkey; M. Oluş Arık, deputy minister of culture and tourism; Erdoğan Sanalan, general director of cultural affairs in the Ministry of Foreign Affairs; Nurettin Yardımcı, general director of antiquities and museums in the Ministry of Culture and Tourism; and other Turkish officials and their staffs have helped bring this exhibition to fruition with the same spirit of patronage of the arts demonstrated by Süleyman himself. In addition, we would like to thank Robert Strausz-Hupé, the United States ambassador to Turkey, and his staff, who have energetically promoted this cultural exchange. We are also grateful to the public institutions and private collectors who have entrusted us with these magnificent objects. A list of their names follows this Foreword.

We would like to take this opportunity to express our profound gratitude to Philip Morris Companies Inc., whose generous financial support has made this exhibition possible. A leader in corporate support of the arts for more than a quarter of a century, Philip Morris has achieved a most distinguished record of sponsoring significant cultural events in this country and abroad. We wish to thank in particular Hamish Maxwell, chairman and chief executive officer, R. William Murray, president, Philip Morris International, and Walter Thoma, president, Philip Morris Europe EEMA Region, for offering the patronage of their corporation for the enlightenment and enjoyment of American audiences. In addition, this exhibition is supported by a United States Government indemnity from the Federal Council on the Arts and the Humanities.

Many individuals in Chicago, New York, and Washington deserve thanks for their work on the exhibition. Special gratitude is due the following staff at the National Gallery: D. Dodge Thompson, chief, exhibition programs; Gaillard Ravenel, chief, and Mark Leithauser, deputy chief of design and installation; Elizabeth A. Croog, associate secretary, general counsel; and Joseph J. Krakora, external affairs officer. At the Art Institute of Chicago, Jack V. Sewell, curator of oriental and classical art, Katharine C. Lee, assistant director, and Dorothy Schroeder, assistant to the director, have been instrumental in mounting the exhibition. At the Metropolitan Museum of Art in the department of Islamic art, Stuart Cary Welch, special consultant in charge, and Carolyn Kane; Mahrukh Tarapor and John McDonald, office of the director; and Emily Rafferty, vice president for development, have rendered invaluable assistance in making the exhibition a reality.

Above all, thanks go to Esin Atıl, and to the Smithsonian Institution for allowing her to act as our guest curator, thereby bringing her vision and enthusiasm to this venture. Dr. Atıl's connoisseurship and scholarship have combined to produce an exhibition and catalogue that invite us to explore and savor *The Age of Sultan Süleyman the Magnificent*.

J. Carter Brown
Director, National Gallery of Art

James N. Wood
Director, The Art Institute of Chicago

Philippe de Montebello
Director, The Metropolitan Museum of Art

Acknowledgments

The idea for this project was born over a decade ago when I was working on the impact of the nakkaşhane on the decorative vocabulary of Ottoman art. I found I wanted to share my findings with a wide audience, in the form of an exhibition. At that time the antiquities laws of Turkey prohibited the loan of objects, and so I became involved with other exhibitions and publications, hoping that one day the project would be realized. The delay in the change of Turkey's antiquities laws was most fortuitous, since in the interval I was able to focus on a particular period and concentrate on the patronage of a remarkable man, Sultan Süleyman the Magnificent, during whose reign the characteristic features of Turkish art were formulated.

I owe a debt of gratitude to many friends and colleagues who shared my enthusiasm and encouraged the project during all these years. This undertaking could not have been possible without the support of the government of Turkey and the efforts of the Turkish officials mentioned in the Foreword. In addition, I would like to personally acknowledge the assistance of Aytuğ İzat, Nimet Berkok, Mehmet Yılmaz, and Nilüfer Ertan in the Ministry of Culture and Tourism; Erdoğan Aytun in the Ministry of Foreign Affairs; and Aydan Karahan, Murat Ersavcı, Ferit Ergin, and Cem Tarhan in the Embassy of the Republic of Turkey in Washington.

The majority of the works of art in the exhibition belong to the Topkapı Palace Museum, where they have been meticulously preserved since the day they were created. I am grateful to Kemal Çığ, Afif Duruçay, and Sabahattin Batur, the former directors; to Sabahattin Türkoğlu, the present director; and to the members of the curatorial staff for allowing me to spend many months researching their collections and for accommodating my endless requests. I am also grateful to the directors and staffs of the Museum of Turkish and Islamic Arts, the Library of the University of İstanbul, and the İstanbul Archaeological Museum, particularly to Nazan Tapan-Ölçer and Erol Pakin. Above all, I want to acknowledge Filiz Çağman, my collaborator for the project in the Topkapı Palace, for her unrelenting efforts, cheerful assistance, and critical guidance through all these years.

Other friends and colleagues in western Asia, Europe, and the United States were most supportive when I approached them for the loan of their precious objects. I thank the following for their generosity in facilitating my research: Leopoldine Arz and Gary Vikan in Baltimore; Vishakha Desai and Jean-Michel Tuchscherer in Boston; Kjeld von Folsach in Copenhagen; Elsie Holmes Peck in Detroit; David James in Dublin; Sheikha Hussa al-Sabah in Kuwait; Princess Esra Jah, J. Michael Rogers, and Oliver Watson in London; S. Cary Welch in New York; Marthe Bernus-Taylor in Paris; Rifaat Sheikh al-Ard in Riyadh; and Christian Beaufort-Spontin and Angela Völker in Vienna. A special thanks goes to the late Edwin Binney, 3rd, for his generous and enthusiastic endorsement.

I would also like to thank David Alexander for encouraging me to include a larger selection of ceremonial arms and armor; Hüsamettin Aksu, Ludvik Kalus, Anatol Ivanov, and Mohamed U. Zakariya for translating and verifying inscriptions; Reha Günay for taking the photographs of the objects in the Turkish collections; Zeki Fındıkoğlu for designing the cover and drawing the reconstructions of fragmentary textiles; Alan Fisher for reading the chapter on the historical setting; Walter B. Denny for reading the entire text and giving constructive suggestions; and Nurhan Atasoy, Ülkü Bates, John Carswell, Talat S. Halman, and Louise W. Mackie for providing references as well as encouragement.

My tenure as guest curator at the National Gallery of Art was the most pleasant and memorable part of the project. The generous support and hospitality of the director, J. Carter Brown, and his staff were extremely gratifying, enabling the exhibition and its related activities to be successfully realized. I am particularly grateful to D. Dodge Thompson, Chief of Exhibition Programs, and the members of his department; and to those who worked on the production of the book: Melanie B. Ness, the designer; Jane Sweeney, the editor; and Maryrose Smyth, my invaluable assistant.

This publication, which is the result of years of research, is dedicated to these and other friends and associates who shared my enthusiasm and optimism, gave me moral support and encouragement, and assisted me in my studies by providing me references and information.

Esin Atıl

Lenders to the Exhibition

Baltimore, The Walters Art Gallery

Boston, Museum of Fine Arts

Cambridge, Mass., Harvard University Art Museums

The Art Institute of Chicago

The Cleveland Museum of Art

Copenhagen, The David Collection

The Detroit Institute of Arts

Dublin, The Chester Beatty Library

Ecouen, Musée de la Renaissance

İstanbul, Arkeoloji Müzesi, Çinili Köşk

İstanbul Üniversite Kütüphanesi

İstanbul, Topkapı Sarayı Müzesi

İstanbul, Türk ve İslam Eserleri Müzesi

Kuwait National Museum

London, The British Museum

London, Princess Esra Jah Collection

London, Victoria and Albert Museum

Los Angeles County Museum of Art

New York, The Metropolitan Museum of Art

Paris, Musée des Arts Décoratifs

Paris, Musée du Louvre

Private collection

Riyadh, Rifaat Sheikh al-Ard Collection

Vienna, Kunsthistorisches Museum

Vienna, Österreichisches Museum für Angewandte Kunst

Washington, The Textile Museum

Note to the Reader

All Turkish names, places, and titles are spelled according to official modern Turkish orthography. Modern Turkish transliteration is also used for Arabic and Persian words within a Turkish context. Non-Turkish names of individuals and cities or regions outside the boundaries of the Republic of Turkey follow English spelling. When a Turkish term appears for the first time in the text, it is italicized and followed by a translation or explanation. Terms used frequently are listed in the Glossary.

The following is a guide to the pronunciation of Turkish words:

c   pronounced "j" as in "John"
ç   pronounced "ch" as in "chair"
ğ   soft guttural, lengthens the vowel preceding it
ı   pronounced somewhat like "e" as in "open"
j   pronounced like the French "j" as in "Jacques"
ö   pronounced like the French "eu" as in "peu"
ş   pronounced "sh" as in "shall"
ü   pronounced like the French "u" as in "lune"

The Turkish system of alphabetization is used in the Shortened References and Select Bibliography. A letter with diacritical marks is alphabetized after the same letter without the marks; for instance c falls before ç.

The word *bin*, meaning "son of," frequently a part of a name, is abbreviated as b., as in Süleyman b. Selim.

All dates, with the exception of those in colophons and inscriptions, are given in the Gregorian calendar. When a year in the Islamic calendar, which is based on lunar months, goes beyond the Christian year in which it began, both years are given, separated by a slash, as in 1557/1558.

Numerals in bold type refer to colorplates as well as catalogue numbers.

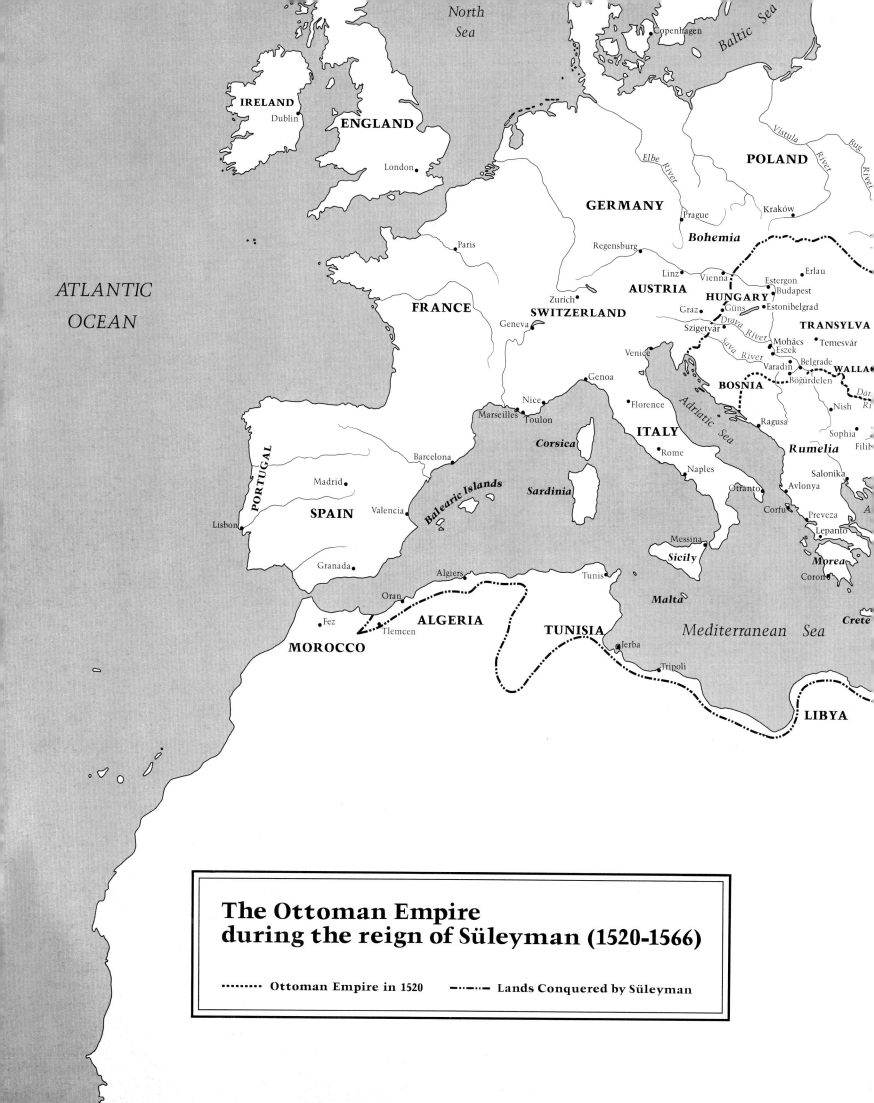

The Ottoman Empire
during the reign of Süleyman (1520-1566)

········ Ottoman Empire in 1520 ·—··—·· Lands Conquered by Süleyman

Introduction

The age of Sultan Süleyman the Magnificent was not only the zenith of Ottoman political and economic expansion, but also an era when the strong demands of imperial patronage were met by a highly energetic and innovative response, bursting into an unprecedented explosion in the arts. During Süleyman's long and dynamic reign the court studios employed hundreds of artists with diverse backgrounds and traditions who synthesized the existing modes, formulated new forms, themes, and techniques, and helped to create an indigenous artistic expression that reflected the cultural vitality of the empire. The evolution of this artistic expression and the establishment of the classical Ottoman style owed much to the personal involvement and support of the sultan, whose high sense of aesthetics and refined connoisseurship left a distinguished mark on Turkish art and architecture.

Patronage has always been the essential ingredient of cultural development and Süleyman was a most magnanimous patron, scrutinizing the works of his artists and generously rewarding them for outstanding performances. His persistent interest provided the artists with tremendous stimulation, compelling them to excel beyond expectation and to produce splendid works of art that glorified their benefactor. The highly centralized administrative structure of the state was also applied to artistic production, which was undertaken by societies created to respond to the specific needs of the palace. The most influential of these societies was the *nakkaşhane* (imperial painting studio), which formulated the decorative themes and designs that were first employed on manuscripts and then transmitted to various court arts, from architectural decoration and furnishings to metalwork, textiles, and ceramics. The nakkaşhane was the creative brain of the Ottoman court style, which spread to all parts of the empire, from the central Islamic lands and northern Africa to the Balkans, and had a profound influence on its neighboring cultures.

The most conspicuous feature of Ottoman art is the joyful representation of nature, depicting fantastic or realistic flora in perpetual growth. This theme, executed in styles that reflected a mystical approach as well as a more naturalistic one, is easily comprehensible and appreciable by all peoples at all times, transcending time and place. Rendered in an impeccable technique with virtuosic use of form, color, and design on diverse materials, this intrinsic quality was largely responsible for the far-flung and long-lasting impact of Ottoman art, both at home and abroad. It highlights the essence of nature—its beauty and perpetuity—and presents it in a most delightful manner, totally devoid of dogmatic or didactic implications. The universal message of Ottoman art reflects its ecumenical culture, which endured the changes of time, its potency and aesthetic appeal as valid today as the day it was initiated.

The vast and powerful empire inherited by Süleyman provided the proper setting for the cultural explosion that took place. His dynamism in political and judicial spheres was matched by the exuberant creativity of the artists of his court.

Historical Setting

The Turks began moving westward from their original homeland in central Asia after the second half of the eighth century and established independent states in Afghanistan, eastern Iran, and northern India. The most significant migration occurred in the eleventh century when the Seljuks arrived in the central Islamic lands, dominated Iran, Iraq, and Syria, and expanded into Anatolia. The Seljuk rule in Anatolia survived until the turn of the fourteenth century, at which time it disintegrated and the region became divided among a number of Turkish emirates.

The northwestern corner of Anatolia was claimed by Osman (1299?–1324?), the leader of one of the emirates who founded the Osmanlı, or Ottoman, dynasty in which the rule passed from father to son or to the eldest male in the family until 1922, at which date the sultanate was abolished and a year later replaced by the Republic of Turkey. During the

Detail, **42a**

17

formative years of the Ottoman state Osman's descendants took Bursa (Brusa), which became the first capital; then they moved into İznik (Nicaea), and İzmit (Nicomedia), crossed the Dardanelles into Thrace, and entered Edirne (Adrianople), which was chosen as the second capital. The Ottomans soon extended their rule into central, northeastern, and southwestern Anatolia as well as into Macedonia, Bulgaria, Serbia, and Romania.

The emirate of Osman became a world-renowned empire during the reign of Mehmed II (1451–1480). In 1453 Mehmed, known as the Conqueror, captured Constantinople, the capital of the Byzantine Empire, moved his court there, and founded the Topkapı Palace, which became the administrative seat of the state. He then undertook systematic campaigns to expand his realm and to form a protective ring around his new capital, now called İstanbul. In the west his armies swept through Greece, Albania, and Yugoslavia, infiltrating the Balkans as far as Belgrade. His navy overpowered the Venetians, captured several islands in the Aegean, and landed at Otranto, the tip of the Italian peninsula. In Anatolia he put an end to the Greek rule in Trabzon (Trebizond), wiped out the remaining Turkish emirates in the south, and inflicted serious defeats upon the Mamluks, who were ruling in Syria and Egypt. The Crimea was annexed together with regions bordering the Sea of Azov. The Ottomans were now the rulers of Anatolia and the eastern Balkans, controlling these lands from their court in İstanbul.

After a brief period of consolidation under Bayezid II (1480–1512), the expansion of the Ottoman frontiers continued with the ensuing sultans. Selim I (1512–1520) campaigned in the south and southeast; he captured Azerbaijan and the Safavid capital of Tabriz; then he defeated the Mamluks at Maj Dabiq and Cairo, incorporating into his empire Syria, Palestine, and Egypt as well as the Hijaz. The Ottoman sultan was now the protector of Islam and the guardian of Mecca, Medina, and Jerusalem, the three holy cities of the Islamic world; he also ruled over the renowned cultural centers of Damascus and Cairo. The Ottomans were firmly entrenched in the strategic lands linking three continents (Asia, Africa, and Europe) and dominated the surrounding seas.

This powerful and vast empire was inherited by Süleyman I (1520–1566), the tenth ruler of the house of Osman. He was the Ottoman sultan with the longest rule—forty-six years—and the one who more than doubled the extent of his realm.[1] At the time of his death the Ottoman Empire included in the west Greece, Albania, Bulgaria, Yugoslavia, Romania, Hungary, and parts of Czechoslovakia, stretching up to Vienna, the capital of the Habsburg Empire; in the north it incorporated the Crimea and the provinces between the Don and the Dnieper rivers; in the east and southeast its boundaries touched the Caspian Sea, ruling over parts of Georgia, Azerbaijan, western Iran, the central Islamic lands, and the regions along the Arabian Gulf and the Red Sea; in the south it

Fig. 1. Portrait of Sultan Süleyman attributed to Titian, c. 1530 (Vienna, Kunsthistorisches Museum, 2429)

claimed Egypt, Sudan, Somalia, Ethiopia, Libya, Tunisia, Algeria, and part of Morocco. The Black Sea, Arabian Gulf, Red Sea, and a major portion of the Mediterranean were controlled by the Ottoman navy.

In Turkish history Süleyman is known as Kanuni, the Lawgiver, in reference to his legislative acts, which helped to form the basis of many national constitutions; in Europe his honorific is the Great or the Magnificent due to his outstanding political and cultural achievements. He was a brilliant military strategist and statesman, and an acclaimed legislator who determined the administrative, fiscal, military, and social laws that regulated his state and its subjects. Although the şeriat (Islamic jurisprudence based on the Koran) was the law of the empire, the Ottoman sultans reserved the right to issue decrees on matters not covered in Islamic traditions. These decrees, called fermans, became the kanuns (sultanic laws) of the empire. Süleyman issued hundreds of decrees that covered every subject from landrights, taxation, concessions given to foreign merchants, war declarations, peace treaties, and investiture of titles to endowments of social and charitable institutions.[2]

Süleyman had been superbly trained for the sultanate, having been in charge of the sancaks (provincial districts) of Bolu, Kefe (Kaffa), and Manisa since he was fifteen, following the

18

Louis II, the king of Hungary (1516–1526), who was related by marriage to the Habsburgs. Another adversary was Tahmasp (1524–1576), the second ruler of the Safavid dynasty of Iran. Among his allies were the kings of France, Francis I (1515–1547) and Henry II (1547–1559); John Zápolya, the prince of Transylvania installed as the king of Hungary (1526–1540) by the sultan; and the rulers of Poland and the Crimea.

Europe in the sixteenth century was torn by constant battles between the Habsburgs, headed by Charles V, and the French, led by Francis I. England, ruled by Henry VIII, and the Italian states of Venice, Genoa, and Florence were constantly changing sides, deeply involved with protecting their own interests. Europe was also divided between the followers of Martin Luther, who were aided by the French, and those of the pope, who were helped by the Habsburgs. Süleyman took advantage of this rivalry to expand his realm; he formed an alliance with the French and supported the Lutherans and Calvinists against the papal forces. By his relentless pressure on the Habsburgs and the papacy he successfully maintained the political disunity in Europe and not only achieved his territorial ambitions but was also instrumental in the growth of Protestantism. Although a number of regions were annexed by his descendants who extended the Ottoman rule into Poland in the west and the Caucasus in the east, the lands conquered by Süleyman formed the core of the Ottoman Empire for centuries to come.

Fig. 2. Marble bust of Sultan Süleyman by Joseph Kiselewski, 1949–1950 (Washington, U.S. Capitol)

Ottoman tradition in which princes, accompanied by their tutors, were sent at an early age to serve as governors in the provinces to acquire experience in administrative and military affairs. The sultan fought on both western and eastern fronts, personally leading over a dozen campaigns against the Habsburgs, who controlled most of Europe, and the Safavids, who ruled Iran. One of Süleyman's first acts was to take the city of Belgrade, which had resisted a number of Ottoman attacks, and another was to capture Rhodes from the troublesome Knights of Saint John. He annexed Hungary and besieged Vienna; he recaptured Tabriz and took Baghdad, adding Iraq and western Iran to his empire. His fleets, led by the celebrated Barbaros Hayreddin Paşa, were able to defeat the combined forces of Europe in the Mediterranean; his other admirals challenged the Portuguese in the Indian Ocean.

Born in an age of kings, powerful and influential men destined to shape the world, Süleyman was by far the most dynamic. His military victories, inherited and acquired wealth, and patronage of art and architecture were unmatched by his allies or his adversaries. Süleyman's rivals were such luminaries as Charles V, the head of the Habsburgs, who served as the king of Spain (1516–1550) and the Holy Roman Emperor (1521–1557); Ferdinand, the archduke of Austria who replaced his brother Charles V as emperor (1558–1564); and

Süleyman the Sultan

Süleyman was born to Selim and Hafsa on 6 November 1494 in Trabzon, where his father was serving as governor.[3] The prince lived there until 1509, at which date he was given the sancak of Bolu in northwestern Anatolia to govern; a few months later he was sent to Kefe in the Crimea, where he held the same post for three years. After his father ascended the Ottoman throne on 24 April 1512 he was asked to reside in İstanbul while the sultan was fighting in Anatolia. The following year Süleyman was appointed governor of Manisa. When Selim I was campaigning against the Safavids and Mamluks in 1514 and 1516–1517, Süleyman was asked to serve as regent and move to Edirne to protect the western flanks of the empire. He was back in Manisa by the time his father died on 22 September 1520. The crown prince arrived in İstanbul on 30 September and his accession ceremonies took place the following day. Since he did not have any living brothers, he was the only heir to the sultanate.

When Süleyman I ascended the Ottoman throne at the age of twenty-six he inherited a vast empire run by an efficient system established by his forefathers. The Ottoman state was governed by a central administration headed by the sultan, who was the supreme ruler of the empire, the commander in

Fig. 3. Procession of Sultan Süleyman in the At Meydanı, woodcut after
Pieter Coecke van Aelst, dated 1553 (New York, The Metropolitan Museum
of Art, 28.85.7a-b)

chief of the armed forces, and the protector of Islam. The
grand vezir represented his executive authority and held the
highest post among the administrators, who were responsible
for political and financial affairs. The *şeyhülislam* (leader or
chief enforcer of Islam) represented the sultan's religious authority and headed the ulema (learned men), who were in
charge of religious, judicial, and educational affairs. The sultan was assisted by the Divan-ı Hümayun (Imperial Council
of Ministers), which represented both sectors. The sultan's
primary responsibility was the enforcement of law and justice, and the Divan-ı Hümayun functioned as a supreme
court where complaints and grievances from subjects were re-
viewed, national and international policies discussed, and administrative procedures formulated.

The Ottoman system of recruitment and training of administrative and military personnel was unique and formed the
core of the central administration.[4] Although a few officials
were the sons of administrators, the majority had been recruited through the *devşirme* system in which non-Muslim
boys were taken from the rural areas in the Christian provinces and trained to serve the state. The largest group was absorbed into the army, particularly the Janissary Corps, while
others were sent either to the provincial courts or to the Topkapı Palace to receive training. They became important palace
officers, military commanders, and governors, and the most
able and enterprising ones rose to the rank of grand vezir.

Almost all the grand vezirs of the empire had risen from
the devşirme ranks and many married royal princesses.
Among them were the celebrated grand vezirs of Süleyman:

İbrahim, who married the sultan's sister Hadice; Rüstem, who
married his only daughter Mihrimah; and Sokollu Mehmed,
who married his granddaughter Esmahan and held the same
post under his son, Selim II, and grandson, Murad III. This
system enabled the sultan to have a fresh supply of highly
trained and totally dedicated administrators and military personnel whose loyalty to the sovereign was unquestionable;
having no allegiance to region or family, their sole existence
was devoted to serving the state.

The Topkapı Palace, founded by Mehmed II in 1459, was
conceived from the beginning as the administrative and educational center of the state and designed as a fortified structure with high walls and massive gates leading into three
consecutive courtyards.[5] It occupied the northern tip of the
peninsula overlooking the Golden Horn, Bosporus, and Sea
of Marmara, providing a magnificent vista of İstanbul.
Thought to have been staffed by close to twenty thousand
men, four or five thousand of whom resided on the premises,
this vast palace proclaimed Ottoman power and dominance
over the city that had been chosen as the capital by all its
previous rulers. Originally called the New Palace, it later
came to be known as the Topkapı (Cannon Gate) Palace after
one of its gates.

The palace was administered by three institutions, the Birun (Outer Service), the Enderun (Inner Service), and the
Harem, the latter having developed during the reign of Süleyman. The plan of the Topkapı Palace clearly reflects its organizational structure. The first courtyard,[6] open to the public,
was reserved for the Birun, which included officers in charge

of maintenance, supplies, the mint, the arsenal, the kitchens, and the stables as well as tutors, physicians, standard-bearers, gatekeepers, gardeners, guards, architects, and artisans employed by the palace.

The second courtyard, open only to those who had official business in the palace, contained chambers for the Divan-ı Hümayun, the grand vezir, and his staff. It also included the imperial kitchens, which provided meals for the residents, and the imperial stables, where the sultan's horses and riding equipment were kept.

The third courtyard was the inner sanctum of the palace and housed the staff of the Enderun School, whose primary responsibility was to train the novices chosen from the devşirme boys. The novices were subjected to a rigid education and advanced according to their capabilities and competence. Upon graduating they were assigned as pages to various imperial chambers, the highest of which were the Hazine (Treasury), Kiler (Pantry), Seferli Oda (Campaign Room), and Has Oda (Royal Room). In time they were promoted to join the ranks of Enderun officers. Some of them were later sent to head departments in the Birun, others were given commissions in the provinces or in the military forces. Included in the third courtyard were the Arz Odası (Reception Room), where dignitaries and foreign envoys were received; the Hazine, where the sultan's private collection of rare and precious objects was kept; the Has Oda, which functioned as the Throne Room;[7] and facilities for the Enderun staff.

The Harem (literally meaning "sacred place") was the private domain of the sultan, where members of his family resided. Originally women and children were housed in the Old Palace situated in the center of the city and not allowed into the Topkapı Palace. They began to reside in the Topkapı Palace after the 1550s and the Harem grew to include over 360 chambers with suites for the *valide sultan* (queen mother), *hasekis* (favorites), *şehzades* (princes), eunuchs, tutors, and a large number of attendants and servants.

Although the Harem was not a formal part of Ottoman administration, it was organized in a fashion similar to the Enderun School. At the top was the valide sultan, whose son was the reigning sultan; she was by far the most powerful woman and frequently advised the sultan on household as well as national and international affairs. Below her were the hasekis, who had produced male offspring. Most of the women in the Harem were of slave origin who had been captured, purchased, or given as gifts; they were trained either in the İstanbul palace or in the provincial courts and presented to the sultan. In some ways their lives resembled those of the devşirme children; they received an excellent education and could advance in rank. Many were married off to governors and commanders; they could divorce their husbands, return to the palace, or be married to other officials, if they so desired. Some enterprising individuals established their own charitable institutions and sponsored architectural complexes.

Hürrem and Mihrimah, the wife and daughter of Süleyman, were among the most energetic patrons.

Royal marriages had been performed during the early years of the empire in order to form alliances with the neighboring states, but this practice was abandoned by the fifteenth century. Süleyman was one of the very few sultans to officially take a wife, marrying Hürrem shortly after his accession. Hürrem, thought to have been of Ukranian or other Slavic descent, may have met Süleyman when he was in Kefe and attracted his attention with her amiable outlook and intelligence. Süleyman adored his wife and remained loyal to her throughout his life. Before meeting her, Süleyman's haseki had been Gülbahar, who had given birth to Mustafa in 1515.[8] After their marriage Hürrem produced five sons and a daughter: Mehmed (1521–1543), the sultan's favorite and chosen heir apparent; Abdullah (1522–1526), who died at the age of four; Mihrimah (1522–1578), his only daughter, who married in 1539 the grand vezir Rüstem Paşa; Selim (1527–1574), who succeeded him in 1566, being the only living son at the time; Bayezid (1525–1561), accused of inciting a civil war and executed with his sons after fleeing to the Safavid court; and Cihangir (1531–1553), a crippled and sensitive child. Süleyman was very supportive of his children; he assigned sancaks to his sons, gave them military commands during campaigns, and appointed them as regents while he was engaged in battles along the frontiers.

The history of Süleyman's reign was tightly woven with international politics, and the sultan became an important protagonist in European affairs shortly after his accession. Charles V, the Habsburg king of Spain, and Francis I, the Va-

Fig. 4. Portrait of Emperor Charles V by Titian (detail), dated 1548 (Munich, Alte Pinakothek, 632)

Fig. 5. Portrait of King Francis I attributed to Jean Clouet (detail), c. 1535 (Paris, Musée du Louvre, 5247)

lois king of France, had been fighting over the crown of the Holy Roman Empire. When Charles V was elected emperor in 1521 war broke out between the two rivals and Europe became divided. Süleyman used this dispute to his advantage, launched his first western campaign, and marched into Hungary, which was allied with the Habsburgs and was causing disturbances in the western provinces. He entered Belgrade on 29 August 1521, securing the Ottoman lands along the Danube River.

The sultan's second campaign was directed against Rhodes, which was controlled by the Knights of Saint John, who had settled there in 1308 following their expulsion from Palestine. The formidable fortress of Rhodes fell on 21 December 1522 after a long and fierce battle that involved both the Ottoman army and navy. Thus the last Christian stronghold in Anatolia was captured and the Aegean Sea was secured.

The spectacular conquests of Belgrade and Rhodes within the first two years of Süleyman's reign sent shock waves throughout Europe. Both fortresses had been formerly impenetrable to the Ottomans and had withstood previous attacks by his forefathers. The young sultan proved to be a more able commander, moving swiftly to remove obstacles to his ultimate control of eastern Europe and the Mediterranean.

Süleyman was soon drawn deeper into European affairs and formed an alliance with the French; it became the first of a series of political, commercial, and cultural relations. Francis I, who had been defeated and imprisoned by Charles V, sent a letter to Süleyman in 1525, requesting his assistance. The sultan, quick to realize the benefits of a Franco-Ottoman alliance, marched into Hungary in the spring of the following

year. Louis II and his entire forces were annihilated within two hours during the Battle of Mohács on 29 August 1526. Süleyman installed as king of Hungary John Zápolya, the ruler of Transylvania who had joined the Ottoman army against the Habsburgs.

When the sultan returned to İstanbul Ferdinand, the archduke of Austria who claimed to be the rightful heir to the throne of Hungary, captured Budapest and expelled Zápolya. Süleyman was forced to march into Hungary and reinstall Zápolya. He then continued on to Vienna, the capital of Austria, and besieged the city for two weeks between 26 September and 16 October 1529. Because winter was approaching and his heavy artillery had been late in arriving, Süleyman lifted the siege and headed home.

The conflict over Hungary was resumed when Ferdinand and Süleyman could not resolve their differences through diplomatic channels and the Habsburgs besieged Budapest again. During the 1532 campaign in Austria Süleyman's most notable conquest was the capture of Güns. The following year the two rulers signed a treaty, which provided a brief halt in Habsburg-Ottoman hostilities.

The sultan was then free to devote attention to the problems in the Mediterranean and in the east. While he was campaigning in Austria, Andrea Doria, a Genoese admiral who had shifted his alliance from Francis I to Charles V, had attacked several Ottoman ports in Algeria and Greece, capturing the fortress of Coron in the Morea (Peloponnisos), to the great embarrassment of the Ottomans. Upon returning to İstanbul, the sultan summoned to the capital Barbaros Hayreddin Paşa, a sixty-three-year-old veteran seaman, and requested him to command the naval forces. Under his leader-

Fig. 6. Portrait of Archduke Ferdinand, engraving by Bartholemeus Beham, dated 1531 (Vienna, Österreische Nationalbibliothek, 503.533-B)

ship the Ottoman navy sailed from one victory to another. His first task was to capture Coron and Tunis; then he undertook systematic raids on the coastal towns of Italy and Spain.

Assured that the Mediterranean was in good hands, Süleyman embarked on his next offensive, moving this time against the Safavids in the east. During the campaign of 1534–1536 the Ottomans captured Tabriz and then Baghdad, annexing parts of Azerbaijan and Iraq. Meanwhile the sultan had concluded a treaty with the French to join forces in attacking the Habsburgs in the Mediterranean. In the spring of 1537 Süleyman moved into Albania and Greece and besieged the fortress on the island of Corfu as a prelude to the invasion of Italy. The fortress held out and he was forced to lift the siege.

The following year the sultan embarked on his eighth campaign, which resulted in the annexation of southern Moldavia. While he was preoccupied in the Balkans the greatest Ottoman victory at sea took place. On 28 September 1538 Barbaros Hayreddin confronted at Preveza Andrea Doria, who commanded the six-hundred-vessel armada that included the combined forces of the Holy Roman Empire, the papacy, the Italian states of Venice, Genoa, and Florence, in addition to ships supplied by Portugal and the Knights of Malta. Within five hours Barbaros Hayreddin emerged as the victor, inflicting such a devastating blow to the Europeans that they could not recover for three decades and terminating their hopes to contain Ottoman supremacy in the Mediterranean. This was the greatest age for the Ottoman navy, its daring captains claiming major Mediterranean ports and vying with the Portuguese in the Indian Ocean. The period between 1520 and 1540 was one of continual victories for Süleyman.

The conflict over the supremacy of Hungary resumed when John Zápolya died in 1540 and left an infant son on the throne. Ferdinand, quick to take advantage of the situation, moved in and besieged Budapest. Süleyman was compelled to secure Budapest by formally annexing Hungary, which in 1541 became a province controlled by an Ottoman governor.

Another siege of Budapest by the Austrians forced the sultan to embark on his tenth campaign in 1543. Meanwhile Barbaros Hayreddin, sent to aid the French in Marseilles, was attacking Nice and other ports on the Mediterranean. Süleyman once again asserted his sovereignty over Budapest and went on to conquer Peç (Pécs), Estergon (Esztergom), and Estonibelgrad (Székesfehérvár). In 1547 he signed a five-year peace treaty with the Habsburgs in which Ferdinand was allowed to keep a portion of Hungary, paying in return a yearly tribute. The same year the Franco-Ottoman alliance was renewed by Henry II, who had succeeded Francis I and was convinced that his monarchy would survive against Charles V only with the sultan's support.

Charles V in return had allied himself with Tahmasp, the Safavid ruler of Iran, forcing Süleyman to curtail his campaigns in order not to fight on both fronts. After signing the peace treaty with the Habsburgs, Süleyman was free to confront the Safavids, who had taken Tabriz and were ravaging Georgia. During this campaign, which took place in 1548–1549, the Ottomans advanced into Hamadan and Isfahan, and recaptured Tabriz, Van, and most of Georgia. As soon as Süleyman withdrew his forces and returned to İstanbul, Tahmasp began attacking Erzurum and Van, forcing the sultan to launch yet another confrontation with the Safavids.

The third war with Iran, lasting from 1553 to 1555, resulted in the conquest of Nahçivan (Nakhichevan) and Revan (Yerevan). Süleyman decided to spend the winter of 1555 in Amasya. There peace treaties with the Habsburgs and Safavids were signed; by the former, its delegation headed by Baron Ogier Ghiselin de Busbecq,[9] a six-month cease-fire was obtained, and by the latter the Ottoman-Safavid boundaries were determined.

During these years Süleyman lost two of his sons. Şehzade Mustafa, his eldest son, was accused of plotting to depose him to take over the sultanate and was killed by the royal executioners when he came to see his father near Konya in the fall of 1553. Cihangir, Süleyman's frail youngest son, died shortly after.

Although battles continued on the western front in the ensuing years, the Habsburgs ceased to be a major threat after the death of Charles V, and Süleyman did not lead an imperial campaign for some ten years. He was made desolate by the death of his beloved wife Hürrem in 1558, and torn by the feud between his sons, Bayezid and Selim, which developed into a civil war by the spring of 1559. The battle of Konya resulted in the defeat of Bayezid, who fled with his four sons to the court of Tahmasp, where Bayezid was held for ransom and eventually sold to the Ottomans. In 1561 Bayezid and his sons were delivered to an Ottoman delegation in Kazvin and were promptly executed.

The following year an eight-year peace treaty was signed with Ferdinand, who was now the emperor of the Holy Roman Empire, having succeeded Charles V. In 1565 the Ottoman navy attempted to capture Malta, the domain of the Knights of Saint John since their expulsion from Rhodes in 1522. The attack, led by Turgud Reis, who lost his life in the battle, was unsuccessful and was repelled by the knights.

The same year problems developed on the Austrian-Ottoman frontier and Süleyman decided to lead his army once again, leaving İstanbul on May 1566. This was his seventh attempt to secure Hungary, a struggle that had begun within a year of his accession to the throne. The Ottoman forces arrived at Szigetvár on 6 August and besieged the fortress for a month. Süleyman was seriously ill when he embarked on his campaign and could barely ride his horse. During the siege of the fortress he lay sick in his tent; he died on the eve of 7 September, a few hours before Szigetvár fell. The grand vezir Sokollu Mehmed Paşa felt that the announcement of his death would be detrimental to state security unless the new sultan was present. He had an officer who resembled Süleyman impersonate the sultan and stalled for more than forty days in Szigetvár, moving out only when he was assured that Selim had arrived at Belgrade and was ready to take over. The army finally arrived in İstanbul in November and Süleyman's body was laid to rest behind the Süleymaniye Mosque, next to the mausoleum of Hürrem.

Süleyman must have known that Szigetvár would be his last campaign. He was seventy-two years old at the time, ailing, and had not led the army for more than ten years, but he insisted on commanding the Ottoman forces himself. If he wanted to die on the field as a true *gazi* (warrior of the faith), his wish was fulfilled.

Süleyman, who gave so much to his world—in legislative acts, international prestige, expansion of the frontiers, glorious conquests, increased national wealth, patronage of the arts—died alone, having lost his beloved wife and favorite sons. He was truly a sultan who served the state, devoting his life and sacrificing those of his loved ones for the welfare of the empire. It was extraordinary that he found time to indulge in the arts and to support the activities of the artists.

Süleyman the Patron

The reign of Süleyman was the golden age of Ottoman culture, which flourished under the sultan's personal involvement and ardent support. Süleyman was by training a goldsmith, following the tradition of the Ottoman house that every ruler had to have a practical trade. He spoke Arabic, Persian, and Çağatay (Eastern Turkish), and was an accomplished poet, writing in Persian and Turkish under the pseudonym Muhibbi, meaning "beloved friend" or "affectionate lover." In addition he was a great patron of art and architecture, which during his long and glorious reign reached the most innovative and productive level in Ottoman history. The members of his court also supported and practiced the arts; many excelled in writing poetry, literature, and history, and several became celebrated calligraphers and painters.

The age of Süleyman was renowned for the construction of monumental architecture, with the sultan, his family, and high administrative officials commissioning one spectacular complex after another. It was also a most prolific period for the production of religious, literary, and historical manuscripts, their bookbindings, calligraphy, illuminations, and illustrations outstanding as works of art. The high aesthetic and technical achievements of these artists were matched by the goldsmiths, jewelers, arms and armor makers, woodworkers, cloth makers, embroiderers, rug weavers, and potters, who produced the most exquisite pieces for Süleyman. The imperial studios employed hundreds of men from all parts of the empire, their origins as diverse as the lands ruled by the sultan. This period saw the synthesis of European, Is-

lamic, and Turkish traditions, giving birth to an artistic vocabulary that was unique to the Ottoman world.

It was an age of giants among architects and artists, including Sinan, the master of monumental buildings and complexes; Haydar Reis, who used the pseudonym Nigari, the portraitist; Nasuh, known as Matrakçı, the initiator of the topographic genre of painting; Piri Reis, the cartographer and author of naval guides; Şahkulu, the creator of exquisite drawings; Kara Memi, the illuminator of imperial manuscripts; and Osman, the master of illustrated histories.

Süleyman's reign is probably best known for its prolific activities in literature and history. The greatest intellects of the sixteenth century belonged to the ulema, the most renowned member of which was Ebussuud (1490–1575), who served as şeyhülislam for close to three decades and issued thousands of *fetvas* (responses to legal questions in accordance with Islamic jurisprudence) as well as sanctioning the opening of the first Turkish coffeehouses and performances of the Karagöz shadow theater. The central administration also produced famous scholars, authors, and artists, including Nasuh (died 1564?), an officer in the Enderun who was a mathematician, swordsman, inventor of athletic games, historian, and illustrator; Ahmed Feridun Paşa (died 1583), commander, governor, and member of the Divan-ı Hümayun who was known for his histories, one of which describes Süleyman's last campaign at Szigetvár; Mustafa Ali (1541–1599), the statesman and historian who wrote an account of the artists; and Piri Reis (1465?–1554) and Haydar Reis (1492?–1572), both naval officers who practiced writing and painting.

Poetry was by far the most popular of the court arts, encouraged and practiced by the sultan and his sons as well as his grand vezirs (İbrahim and Rüstem in particular) and other members of the court. Süleyman belongs to a long list of poet sultans, including Mehmed II, Bayezid II, Selim I, Selim II, and Murad III.

The sultan's passion for poetry was matched only by his zeal for sponsoring art and architecture. During his reign İstanbul became a bustling metropolis with flocks of merchants and artisans arriving daily to reap its bounty. The city was enhanced with the construction of religious, charitable, and social establishments designed and built by Sinan (1490?–1588), under whom Ottoman architecture reached its greatest monumentality. Appointed the royal architect by Süleyman, Sinan was responsible for over three hundred monuments scattered throughout the empire;[10] he continued to work for the succeeding sultans, achieving his ambition of building the largest and highest dome in Ottoman history with the Selimiye Mosque in Edirne, completed in 1575.

Fig. 7. Portrait of Sultan Süleyman with the Süleymaniye Mosque in the background (detail), engraving by Melchior Lorichs, dated 1559 (London, The British Museum, 1848 11-25 24)

TF̄M
COSTIT:
A
SVLT:
SOLEIM:

Sinan's most spectacular complex was built for Süleyman between 1550 and 1557. Called the Süleymaniye, it consisted of over a dozen buildings arranged around a mosque and included four *medreses* (universities), a college of medicine, elementary and secondary schools, a hospital, hospice, *imaret* (soup kitchen), bath, shops, cemetery, and mausoleums for the sultan and his wife, together with residences for students, staff, and caretakers. The mosque is a most impressive structure, its central dome hovering over scores of smaller domes that cascade to the ground. The edifice was decorated with tiles, carved stonework, inlaid woodwork, stained glass window panels, pile rugs, and thousands of glass lamps.[11]

In addition, Süleyman commissioned Sinan to build a medrese in memory of his father, Selim I, as well as mosques and attached buildings to commemorate his sons, Mehmed and Cihangir. His daughter Mihrimah employed the architect as did his wife Hürrem, who was in fact the first to hire him. In 1538/1539 Sinan constructed for her a complex in the Aksaray district of İstanbul, and later he designed a large and most remarkable bath, with separate units for men and women, facing the At Meydanı outside the Topkapı Palace. Sinan was also commissioned by such dignitaries as the grand vezirs İbrahim, Rüstem, and Sokollu Mehmed to build for them similar compounds.

Süleyman sponsored a number of other building activities, including waterworks and bridges in İstanbul and elsewhere; constructed a complex in Damascus; restored the Dome of the Rock in Jerusalem; and renovated and redecorated the Kaaba in Mecca. He also endowed several religious and charitable institutions in Hürrem's name and assigned the income from several towns and villages to maintain them.

The sultan was deeply involved with educational and artistic activities of the state despite his heavy commitments to administrative, judicial, military, and diplomatic tasks. He personally supervised the curricula in the universities; he expanded studies in mathematics and medicine, projecting the need for future engineers and physicians. He scrutinized the activities of the writers and artists, studying their works with care. He is said to have read overnight Ali Çelebi's *Hümayunname* (Book of kings), the Turkish translation of the classical Arabic book on princely behavior; he carefully went over some thirty thousand verses of his own biography, the *Süleymanname* (Book of Süleyman), which was written in Persian verse. He took time to inspect the works of the artists and he rewarded them.

The flourishing artistic activities in İstanbul created a need for competent artists and craftsmen, and they came from all corners of the empire to seek employment in the most glorious of all capitals. Some joined the artisans' guilds in the city, while others were admitted into the Ehl-i Hiref (Community of the Talented), which was formally attached to the Birun and included men of all trades, from calligraphers to cobblers, whose duty it was to serve the palace.

The Ehl-i Hiref was structured and administered in the same manner as the other bureaus of the state. Its members were the elite and by far the most influential, although there existed a large number of other artists and craftsmen practicing in the capital.[12] Artists also resided in provincial centers, some of which specialized in the production of particular wares; for instance, Bursa was prolific in the manufacture of textiles, İznik supplied most of the state's need for ceramics and tiles, and Uşak was the center of rug weaving. No doubt artisans were employed in all the major cities of the empire to supply local needs.

Since Ottoman art was highly centralized, the designs created for the court soon spread all over the empire. These designs originated from the nakkaşhane, which formulated the decorative vocabulary of the age. The heterogeneous nature of this society led to an extremely energetic artistic production, its members experimenting with newly formulated themes and concepts and showing a total open-mindedness to innovative ideas. The artists reinterpreted existing themes and created fresh approaches to surface decoration.

They revitalized the traditional floral scrolls with undulating branches bearing *hatayi* blossoms and buds or *rumi* leaves. The hatayi blossom, which resembles a stylized lotus rendered in profile, took its name from Hatay, meaning eastern or central Asia, where this motif was thought to have originated. The word rumi, applied to a stylized split leaf, referred to Rum, that is, to the lands of the Eastern Roman Empire, more specifically to Anatolia, where it was popularly employed in Seljuk art. Both the hatayi and rumi, used in the Islamic world since the thirteenth century, became a major ingredient in Ottoman decoration. Other traditional motifs included cloud bands with thin bands of scrolling cloud formations, also employed in other Islamic courts; and the *çintemani* pattern, which consisted of a series of triple balls, often accompanied with a pair of wavy lines, representing the spots and stripes of leopard and tiger skins. Its origin and meaning are not well-enough known, but the pattern had talismanic implications and symbolized imperial power among the Turkish tribes.

The two most innovative design concepts that evolved during the reign of Süleyman were the *saz* style and the naturalistic genre. The saz style, abstracted from drawings that recreated an enchanted forest inhabited by mythical creatures, was applied to scrolls with compound hatayis and long feathery leaves impregnated with additional florals, twisting, turning, intersecting, and piercing one another in a turbulent manner. The naturalistic genre, in contrast, represented peaceful paradise gardens with a profusion of realistic flora, depicting flowering fruit trees and bunches of roses, tulips, carnations, hyacinths, and other spring flowers.

These three approaches to decorative arts were formulated in the nakkaşhane and flourished in the mid-sixteenth century. The traditional mode was eventually superseded by the saz style, which together with the naturalistic genre came to identify the court arts of Süleyman's era. The naturalistic genre, which had a more popular appeal than the esoteric saz style, had a stronger impact on Turkish art and survived much longer.

NOTES

1. The extent of the lands under direct control of the Ottomans at the death of Süleyman is generally accepted as being 877,800 square miles, which included 462,700 square miles in Asia, 224,100 square miles in Europe, and 191,000 square miles in Africa. In addition, the Ottomans controlled the tributary states in Moldavia, Walachia, and Crimea with a total of some 350,000 square miles. Pitcher 1972, 134–135.

2. For a study of Süleyman's legislation see İnalcık 1969.

3. Some sources give 27 April 1495 as the birth date of Süleyman. The earlier date used here is accepted by most historians. There seems to be some confusion about Hafsa's origin as well. Some historians state that she was the daughter of Mengili Giray Han, the ruler of the Crimean Tatars. Others mention that Ayşe, another wife of Selim I, was the Crimean princess and give as Hafsa's father a man named Abdülmümin or Abdülhay, an unknown person, suggesting that she was of slave origin.

4. This system was employed to a certain extent by a number of earlier Islamic states, including the Abbasid caliphates and Mamluk sultanates.

5. For an architectural study of the palace see Eldem and Akozan 1982. The fourth courtyard and a major portion of the Harem were built after Süleyman's reign.

6. Only a few of the original buildings of the first courtyard survive today. They include the Çinili Köşk (Tiled Pavilion), built in 1472; the Alay Köşkü (Procession Pavilion), completely refurbished in the nineteenth century; and the sixth-century Byzantine church of Aya Irene, which was converted into the imperial arsenal.

7. This chamber also housed the Mukaddes Emanetler (Sacred Trusts)—including the mantle, bow, and standard of the Prophet Muhammed, the swords of the first four caliphs, and the earliest Koran attributed to the third orthodox caliph, Osman—brought back from Egypt by Selim I when he assumed the caliphate and became the spiritual leader of Islam.

8. Very little is known about the sultan's other offspring. Historians mention Mahmud (1512–1521) and Murad (1519–1521) in addition to two unknown daughters (one died in 1521) whose mothers were not recorded.

9. The letters of Busbecq, who was in the Ottoman court between 1554 and 1562, vividly describe his impressions of İstanbul, cities and towns on route to Amasya, and meetings with the sultan. They are translated into English in Forster 1968. Busbecq was accompanied by Melchior Lorichs, an artist who executed various vistas of the capital and studies of Ottoman figures, including portraits of Süleyman. See Fischer 1962 and Eyice 1970 for a study of his works. The drawings and engravings of Lorichs were published several times. Most of his works appear in Oberhummer 1902.

10. For the works of Sinan see Goodwin 1971, 196–284; Sözen 1975; Kuran 1978; and Bates 1980, 102–123.

11. The list of artists and the expenses of the Süleymaniye Complex are published in Barkan 1972–1979. See also Rogers 1982. The endowment is studied in Kürkçüoğlu 1962. For the Korans commissioned for the mosque see Appendix 2b.

12. Evliya Çelebi listed hundreds of artisans and craftsmen working in the city. See Danışman 1969–1971, 2:207–334.

The Nakkaşhane

The reign of Süleyman was a most creative period in Ottoman art, during which an indigenous decorative vocabulary was established. Without doubt the phenomenal burst of energy seen in the artistic production of the age owed much to the efforts of the nakkaşhane members who formulated the themes and concepts that came to characterize Ottoman decorative arts and set the standards for their high technical and aesthetic achievements.

All the arts and crafts required by the state were undertaken by the Ehl-i Hiref, which consisted of a number of societies that represented a variety of professions, including calligraphers, painters, bookbinders, goldsmiths, jewelers, woodworkers, weavers, tailors, hatmakers, and boot makers, as well as such unlikely occupations as surgeons and wrestlers. Each society was organized in similar fashion with a chief, deputy chief, group of masters, and apprentices. The members were paid daily wages by the state, which were duly recorded in payroll registers drawn four times a year.[1] Some projects required special personnel and expenditures, which were also carefully registered in the ledgers.[2] Salaries and advancement in rank followed a predetermined system, but the artists were given additional raises and bonuses when they performed exceptional tasks. Master artists presented gifts to the sultan during *bayram* (religious holiday) celebrations—and received in return cash bonuses as well as such awards of honor as brocaded-satin or velvet *kaftans* (robes).

Since the courts in the provincial capitals followed the same structure as that in İstanbul, they also retained a similar group of artists and craftsmen. The Ehl-i Hiref in the sancaks of the şehzades included the same mixture of professions. Documents dating from Süleyman's tenure as governor in Kefe and Manisa indicate that he had a large staff of artists in his court; they included hatmakers, furriers, halbard makers, bow makers, goldsmiths, saddlers, and musicians.[3] There are also notations in the registers that state some artists from the İstanbul Ehl-i Hiref were transferred to other palaces, such as

those in Edirne or in the sancaks of the princes.

One of the groups in the Ehl-i Hiref was called the Cemaat-i Nakkaşan (Society of Painters) and comprised artists whose duty was to decorate the manuscripts commissioned for the imperial libraries. They produced tens of thousands of books on religious, historical, literary, and scientific subjects, the best of which were housed in the Hazine of the palace, while others were distributed to various other departments or presented to the educational institutions of the endowments. These artists also provided designs used by other craftsmen, such as weavers, potters, stone carvers, and wall painters. The term *nakkaş* (plural *nakkaşan*) was all-encompassing and was applied to men who created decorative themes; they could apply their talents to the illumination of manuscripts, at which time they were called *müzehhib*; or to the illustration of texts, becoming *ressam* or *musavvir*, that is, painters who represented figures and settings. It is surprising that there was no term to distinguish paintings from drawings, which were rendered with both bold and delicate brushstrokes and shaded with washes and tints.

There were other men who practiced the art of painting in addition to those employed in the nakkaşhane. Some belonged to the guilds of illuminators, decorators, and painters in the capital and other major centers; others were individuals who indulged in this art form while involved with other professions. Evliya Çelebi, a famous traveler who wrote extensively about the life in the Ottoman world during the first quarter of the seventeenth century, listed hundreds of artisans and craftsmen in İstanbul, some of whom were illuminators and painters.[4] He mentioned that there were one thousand nakkaş who worked in one hundred shops.[5] Their main headquarters was above the Arslanhane, a building that once stood on the north side of the first courtyard of the Topkapı Palace. The ressam guild was relatively small, with four shops and forty members. There was also a group called *falcıyan* (fortune-tellers), who used paintings to predict the future.

Members of the central administration also tried their hand at painting; several were extremely proficient and either illustrated their own texts or collaborated with other writers. The most renowned of these were Piri Reis, a naval captain, and Nasuh, an official in the Enderun, both of whom helped to establish the tradition of documentary painting with their topographic illustrations and maritime atlases. This tradition not only influenced the nakkaşhane's future but became one of the characteristic features of Ottoman art. Another talented naval officer was Nigari, who became a major force in promoting the indigenous art of portraiture.[6]

Although not all nakkaşhane documents from the reign of Süleyman have survived, there exist six payroll registers dated between 1526 and 1566 in addition to a number of ledgers that record the gifts exchanged between the sultan and the artists. The earliest payroll register of the nakkaş-hane, which is undated, lists forty-one members headed by Şahkulu. Since it includes the same men as another register dated 1526, it must have been drawn about the same time. The 1526 document gives detailed information on the origins of the artists and explains how and when they entered the nakkaşhane, enabling us to reconstruct the history, the organizational structure, and the heterogeneous nature of the society. Ten of the artists had come either from Iran or were the sons of Iranian masters; in addition, there were two Circassians, an Albanian, and a Moldavian. Nine of the men had registered during the reign of Bayezid II and thirteen had arrived during the reign of Selim I.

The next register, drawn in 1545, shows that an internal division took place, separating the fifty-nine-member society into two corps: the Rumiyan and the Aceman. The former, once again headed by Şahkulu, had forty-four men and included four Bosnians, three Austrians, two Circassians, and one each from Albania, Moldavia, and Rumelia. The latter contained fifteen artists, of whom ten were from Tabriz and one from Isfahan. It appears that the Aceman corps was exclusively made up of artists from Iran while the Rumiyan included all others.

The separation of the society into the same two corps continued in 1557 and 1558. Of the two documents bearing these dates, one appears to be incomplete and lists only the Rumiyan group, which had thirty-four members headed by Mehmed Şah, who was recorded as having come from Tabriz and was a member of the Aceman in 1545. His corps included several Albanians, Bosnians, and Hungarians as well as individuals from Austria, Circassia, Georgia, and Moldavia.

The second document with the same dates covers a twelve-month period and lists thirty-nine members: twenty-six were in the Rumiyan corps, headed by Kara Memi, and thirteen were in the Aceman corps. The former included several Bosnians and one man each from Albania, Georgia, and Moldavia; the latter, made up primarily of artists from Tabriz, also had members from Hungary and Isfahan together with a man of undetermined European origin, called Freng (Frank).

The document of 1566 shows the same two divisions and records thirty-seven men. The thirty-one-member Rumiyan group was headed by Mehmed Sinan and contained six Bosnians and individuals from Albania, Georgia, Hungary, and Moldavia. The Aceman included one European and four artists from Tabriz; among them was Mehmed Şah, who had been the head of the Rumiyan corps in 1557/1558.

The next two registers, dated 1596, show a different structure: the 124 to 129 members were equally divided into masters and apprentices within a single corps. The director, called the sernakkaşan (head of the painters), was followed by the kethüda (lieutenant) and the serbölük (chief of the corps). Almost all of the members appear to be native artists, with the exception of a few individuals whose names indicate they were originally from Albania, Bosnia, Europe, and Georgia.

Information compiled from other sources indicates that the first recorded chief of the nakkaşhane was Hasan b. Abdül-celil, also known as Hasan Çelebi, who was listed as the ser-nakkaşan or nakkaşbaşı (head painter) in 1510 and held this position through the 1540s.[7] Şahkulu, whose name was listed first in the payroll register of 1526, became the serbölük of the Rumiyan corps in 1545. Mehmed Şah emerged as the serbölük of the same corps in 1557/1558; the nakkaşbaşı during these years was Kara Memi. Kara Memi was replaced in 1566 by Mehmed Sinan, who was not previously recorded in the registers.

The documents summarized above suggest that the nakkaş-hane was already established during the reign of Bayezid II and supplemented by artists from Tabriz brought by Selim I. Around the 1540s it was divided into two corps: the first, called the Rumiyan, included mostly men from Anatolia and the western provinces of the empire; the second, named the Aceman, was primarily made up of Iranians. This separation, which continued through the 1560s, was by no means exclusive, as some westerners could work in the Aceman group and certain Tabrizi artists, for instance Mehmed Şah, could be assigned to the Rumiyan corps. The reason for separating the painters into two divisions is not known.

The hierarchy within the nakkaşhane as well as the wages are not clear; for instance, Şahkulu's salary in 1526 was lower than that of a man who ranked below him but higher than that of the nakkaşbaşı, Hasan b. Abdülcelil. It appears that these registers recorded the retainer fees paid to the artists, who were given additional wages or bonuses upon the completion of special projects. For example, Kara Memi's daily wage was 16.5 akçes (silver coins) in 1545 and rose to 25.5 akçes in 1557–1558; however, he received an additional 6,000 akçes for illuminating a Koran during these years.

The duties of a nakkaş varied, and the term was applied to both illustrators and illuminators. The training in the nakkaş-hane obviously prepared the men to undertake different projects, and they were given the opportunity to practice more than one form of art.

Membership was drawn from all corners of the empire, although from the 1520s to the 1560s it appears to have relied heavily on masters from Tabriz or on their trainees. These artists either emigrated to the Ottoman capital from Iran after the fall of the Akkoyunlu state in 1501 or came as a part of Selim I's booty after the 1514 conquest of Tabriz. Although it is thought that Selim I transported a thousand artists, craftsmen, scholars, and poets to the capital, the registers record only thirteen men who entered the painting studio during his reign. A related document lists sixteen painters and adds a note stating that there were twenty-three others just as talented.[8] Of these sixteen names, eleven are mentioned in various documents and payroll registers. It is possible that the others entered different societies of the Ehl-i Hiref or joined the local guilds.

Artists listed as Tabrizi in the registers obviously included painters from Herat who had been taken to Tabriz after the fall of the Timurid Empire. Selim I also brought with him Bedi üz-Zaman, the last Timurid sultan held captive by the Safavids, and his retinue of court artists and scholars.[9] It should be noted that Selim I must have also brought Syrian and Egyptian artists to İstanbul after the defeat of the Mamluks in 1517. The last Mamluk court in Cairo had just begun to sponsor major illustrated manuscripts, which appear to have been produced by artists trained in the Akkoyunlu schools of Tabriz and Shiraz.[10] Once in İstanbul they joined their former colleagues and their individual styles became absorbed by the nakkaşhane.

Although the archival documents provide information on the structure of the nakkaşhane and its membership, the styles of the vast majority of the individuals and their contribution to the development of Ottoman painting are not known. Many painters cannot be identified with the existing works since most of the manuscripts have no colophons and the few that do record only the names of the calligraphers. Many texts were illustrated by the combined efforts of several artists, who either produced single paintings or collaborated with colleagues; therefore their identity was lost within the overall production. Even when the hands of individuals can be determined in a series of illustrations, they still remain anonymous.

There are, fortunately, four exceptions: Bayram b. Derviş, Şahkulu, Kara Memi, and Osman, each of whom represents a different tradition practiced in the court studio. Bayram, known as the illuminator of a Koran (see 8), reveals a conservative and traditional mode. He was a highly competent artist with great technical facility and probably was the best in his league.

Şahkulu, on the other hand, was a revolutionary painter and the creator of the saz style, which came to be identified with the high court art of the age. He was a virtuoso of saz drawings that represented a fantastic world filled with hatayis and twisting leaves, frequently inhabited by ferocious *senmurvs* (fantastic birds resembling phoenixes), *chilins* (four-legged mythical creatures), lions and dragons as well as placid *peris* (angelic female spirits or fairies). Although at best only two drawings datable to the 1540s and 1550s (see figs. 8 and 9) can be properly assigned to his hand, he was the indisputable master of this sophisticated style, which reveals mystic tendencies. The inherent symbolism of these works must have been intellectually stimulating to Süleyman, since saz drawings were incorporated into albums compiled for him; they reflect his personal taste as well as his interest in mysticism, which is also evident in his own poetry. The floral themes that evolved from drawings executed in this style became the most distinct characteristics of Ottoman decorative arts. Saz style drawings ceased to be produced after the end of the sixteenth century although the decorative theme survived much longer, having an exuberant revival in the first half of the 1700s.

Kara Memi, another exceptionally innovative artist, formulated a totally different concept of decoration, the naturalistic genre in which a profusion of spring flowers and trees joyfully re-create paradise gardens. The representation of such flowers as roses, tulips, carnations, and hyacinths (which symbolized sacred and profane love, abundance, or perpetuity) in addition to blossoming fruit trees (called *bahar*, which also means "spring") and cypresses (symbols of the ascension of the soul into heaven) reflects yet another mystical trend, rendered in a different idiom. The elements of this genre, more easily comprehended than the saz themes, immediately spread to the other media and continued to be a significant feature in Ottoman decorative arts for centuries to come. Kara Memi, whose name is mentioned in two manuscripts produced in the 1550s and the 1560s (see **14** and **26**), established this genre, which coexisted with the saz style of decoration initiated by Şahkulu in the second quarter of the sixteenth century.

Osman represents yet another revolutionary trend in the nakkaşhane, that of illustrated histories. He was an exceptional artist who could portray the psychological interaction between the protagonists while remaining true to the documentation of the events within their proper settings. He and his assistants worked primarily with Lokman, the official court biographer, producing hundreds of paintings that re-created the lives and achievements of the sultans and recorded in detail their glorious campaigns, festive events, ceremonial activities, and private lives (see **42** and **43**). Osman, who flourished between the 1560s and the 1590s, is not only mentioned in the manuscripts of the period, but also portrayed in two of them. His style, which dominated the nakkaşhane until the second quarter of the seventeenth century, owed much to the anonymous master of the *Süleymanname*, written by the court biographer Arifi (see **41**), the first illustrated history in the Ottoman court that realistically documented the events, personages, and settings of the age.[11]

The term nakkaşhane appears to denote the society of

Fig. 8. (above) Drawing after a dragon made by Şahkulu, first quarter sixteenth century (İstanbul, Topkapı Sarayı Müzesi, H. 2154, fol. 2a)

Fig. 9. (right) Flying peri attributed to Şahkulu, c. 1550 (Washington, Freer Gallery of Art, 37.7)

painters rather than an actual building where all the artists worked. There was, however, a nakkaşhane building outside the Topkapı Palace in the eighteenth century, as illustrated in the *Surname-i Vehbi* (Festival book of Vehbi), dated around 1720.[12] This painting shows a two-story structure situated on the main road encircling the palace, presumably next to the Alay Köşkü, where the sultans viewed processions.

It is recorded that famous calligraphers such as Şeyh Hamdullah were given quarters in the palace and that Süleyman himself liked watching Şahkulu work. The sultan also ordered the construction of a special building to be used by Arifi's calligraphers and painters after reading and approving his text.[13] Lokman, the court historian who followed Arifi, mentions that the nakkaşhane building was situated on the right of the first courtyard of the palace, placing it approximately in the same area as the one described by Evliya Çelebi, who states that the artists worked above the Arslanhane, a building long since destroyed. It is possible that the structure represented in the eighteenth-century manuscript replaced an older one dating from Süleyman's reign.

Since membership in the nakkaşhane reached well over one hundred men at times, the structure was probably used as the headquarters of the society with only a few resident artists, the majority of the men sharing studios with fellow painters, working at home, or, as mentioned by Evliya Çelebi, in their own shops. The nakkaşhane building must have functioned as a meeting place where the members discussed

new projects, received their assignments, showed their drafts to the nakkaşbaşı, and turned in their finished works to be compiled into the volumes. Here they would have had access to reference materials and consulted with the authors and calligraphers.

As observed in the registers, there were a number of established families in which the profession was passed from father to son; there were as well many newcomers who arrived from such distant lands as Bosnia and Georgia. The artists represented different traditions and approaches to book decoration, their heterogeneous backgrounds resulting in a phenomenally energetic output.

The nakkaşhane members were assigned a variety of tasks, including illuminating and illustrating diverse texts. They also decorated the *tuğras* (monograms) affixed to the sultan's fermans; embellished the *vakfiyes* (endowment documents) that recorded the terms for religious, charitable, and social institutions; worked on the illuminations of religious texts transcribed by contemporary or past calligraphers; illustrated literary and historical texts composed by living authors as well as by classical poets; produced single paintings and drawings; and compiled albums for the imperial libraries. In addition they executed designs that were used as cartoons and transferred to other techniques, such as wall paintings, metalwork, textiles, rugs, tiles, and ceramic vessels.[14]

The tuğras (see **1–5**), drawn by the *tuğrakeş* (executor of tuğras), were beautifully adorned with both the traditional and the newly developed saz scrolls or the sprays of naturalistic flowers. The same combination of decorative elements appears in the illuminations of religious texts, including pilgrimage documents and guides (see **22** and **23**), which were illustrated with topographic renderings of the monuments and sites based on eyewitness accounts. The nakkaşhane also refurbished the texts of the esteemed calligraphers of the past, such as Yakut and Abdullah Sayrafi (see **13** and **14**), carefully preserving the scripts and pasting them on folios embellished with contemporary decorative themes.

It is the paintings in the literary manuscripts produced between the 1520s and 1550s that best reflect the heterogeneous or eclectic nature of the nakkaşhane, revealing both local and foreign influences. Although a number of works show a conglomeration of several traditions, three styles of painting can be identified. The first reveals the impact of the late-fifteenth-century Timurid school of Herat, which appears in unadulterated form in several volumes (see **31**), while in others it is blended with the style associated with the Akkoyunlu court of Tabriz. Some of the paintings produced in the İstanbul nakkaşhane are indistinguishable from those made in the Safavid capital of Tabriz (see **32**), since both relied heavily on the Timurid and Akkoyunlu schools during their formative years in the early decades of the sixteenth century.

The second style reflects a newly developed local tradition, which was also influenced by the figure types and compositional schemes established in Timurid Herat. Characterized by a decorative approach and limited pictorial cycle, it dominated the literary manuscripts until the 1550s (see **28** and **29**). Its disappearance coincided with the rise of illustrated histories, which overshadowed the production of literary texts after the middle of the sixteenth century, showing a change in taste and interest.

The third style, found in literary manuscripts, developed from within the nakkaşhane. Inspired by the influx of outsiders, it nevertheless retained its own identity and shows an acute awareness of local figures and settings, incorporating them into the scenes (see **33** and **34**). This type of localization can also be observed in the manuscripts produced in the last Mamluk court in which classical texts were illustrated with native ceremonial settings and architectural features.

One foreign tradition that seems to have been lost within the nakkaşhane is that of eastern Europe. According to the payroll registers, there were a substantial number of Bosnians and several Hungarians, Austrians, Moldavians, and Albanians. Since the styles of painting practiced in these regions are not well-known, the contributions of these artists are not as clearly visible as those of the painters from Herat and Tabriz. Ottoman painting was basically an extension of the Islamic tradition, and European elements brought into the nakkaşhane were soon obscured and absorbed. One could hypothesize that the illusionistic settings with fields and cities placed in the background, the modeling and drapery used with some

of the figures, and certain features such as European types of costumes, architecture, and sailing vessels, as well as the maritime atlas and topographic genres, were developed by these artists. On the other hand a number of these features existed as early as the 1490s and many were formulated by non-nakkaşhane artists, such as Piri Reis, Nasuh, and Nigari.

The fusion of the tremendous energy of the imperial painting studio with the traditions practiced by its members and outside artists resulted in the creation of the most characteristic Ottoman genre, that of illustrated histories (see **37** and **41–43**). This genre, which glorified the reign of the sultans, can be observed in some manuscripts produced for other Turkic dynasties, including the Timurids and the Mughals, but its persistence through the centuries with such a voluminous production was unique to the Ottoman Empire.

The two major ingredients of illustrated histories, documentation of the settings and portrayal of historical personages, were definitely influenced by the paintings of three men who worked outside the nakkaşhane. The topographic and maritime scenes of Piri Reis (see **35** and **36**) and Nasuh (see **38–40**) are not mere maps, but exquisitely rendered paintings with great artistic merit. Inspired to some extent by contemporary European examples, their works established the concept of depicting geographical and architectural settings. Nigari's interest in portraying the physical and at times even the psychological characteristics of his subjects (figs. 10 and 11) also influenced the nakkaşhane artists. Although Ottoman portraiture was initiated during the reign of Mehmed II, who invited such Italian artists as Gentile Bellini and Costanza da Ferrara to his court, the impact of these Europeans was short-lived and negligible.[15] Nigari's portraits, on the other hand, were the product of a new local tradition. The nakkaşhane artists absorbed these elements and employed them in their pictorial narratives of historical works, which became the major preoccupation of the studio after the 1550s.

A second and equally significant indigenous tradition is found in tinted drawings incorporated into albums. The evolution of the Ottoman saz style is clearly observed in the representations of elaborately intertwining flora, engulfing fantastic creatures such as dragons and peris (see **45–49**). The blossoms and leaves abstracted from these drawings came to characterize the decorative vocabulary of the age. The mystical and shamanistic concept of an enchanted forest inhabited by spirits hidden among the rocks and trees was of central Asian origin and frequently represented in fifteenth-century drawings. It continued to be popular in the Timurid and Akkoyunlu courts and was passed on to the Ottoman and Safavid artists. The Ottomans, however, transformed it into a unique theme, which was employed in such diverse techniques as stone carving and weaving.

The decorative vocabulary of the nakkaşhane was extremely rich and diversified. In addition to the saz style the artists employed both the traditional floral scrolls, rumis, and

Fig. 10. Portrait of Sultan Süleyman by Nigari, c. 1560 (İstanbul, Topkapı Sarayı Müzesi, H. 2134/8)

Fig. 11. Portrait of Sultan Selim II by Nigari, c. 1570 (İstanbul, Topkapı Sarayı Müzesi, H. 2134/3)

cloud bands and the indigenous çintemani patterns, spiral vines, and sprays of naturalistic flowers. The çintemani pattern, using triple balls and double wavy lines alone or in combination, was applied to a variety of media, including textiles and ceramics. The spiral scroll, which evolved around 1520, was generally rendered in blue with delicate blossoms; it was used in manuscript illuminations as well as in a group of ceramics. The most original theme of the age was the naturalistic genre with clearly identifiable spring flowers. The delight in representing a garden in perpetual bloom made its appearance in the 1540s and soon spread to all the decorative arts. The aristocratic saz style coexisted with the joyous and colorful naturalistic genre, each representing a different approach to decoration and yet each in its own way highly characteristic of Ottoman aesthetics.

The Ehl-i Hiref also included the Cemaat-i Katiban (Society of Calligraphers), whose duties were to transcribe the texts. These men, listed in payroll registers and other documents, were scribes who worked alone or in groups, churning out one volume after another. Very little is known about most of them; though several recorded their names in the colophons of a few manuscripts, they are identified only by these examples. On the other hand, the lives and works of certain celebrated master calligraphers, such as Şeyh Hamdullah and Ahmed Karahisari, are well documented. These artists were not members of the *katiban* society, but held a special status in the court; they were highly respected for their art, which was primarily devoted to copying the Koran.

Ottoman calligraphers practiced the traditional Arabic scripts established by the great Yakut in the thirteenth century as well as the Persian types, and in addition they developed their own individual styles. Yakut's *aklam-ı sitte* (six scripts that included *sülüs, nesih, muhakkak, reyhani, tevkii,* and *rikaa*) was revolutionized by Şeyh Hamdullah and Ahmed Karahisari, both of whom established their own schools of writing. Hamdullah was renowned for his impeccable nesih (see **7**); Karahisari came to be known for his *celi,* a large script employed in architectural inscriptions (fig. 12), and for his *müselsel*, a style of writing in which the letters are joined together (see **9–11**). Hamdullah used nesih in his Korans while Karahisari employed several styles, contrasting the larger scripts with the smaller ones.

The katiban also employed the Persian styles of *divani, nastalik,* (which they called *talik*), and *siyakat.* Divani, applied to transcribing fermans, soon developed into a characteristic Ottoman style. Talik was generally used in literary texts and at times rendered in *kaatı,* that is, in découpage with the letters cut out of colored papers and pasted on folios tinted with contrasting tones (see **18** and **30**). Siyakat, reserved for archival documents, came to be an Ottoman code or shorthand, today decipherable only by specialists. The calligraphers also wrote in *gubari,* a minuscule script generally used in the tiny volumes called sancak Korans, which were suspended from banners (see **17** and **21**).

Although the names of over a hundred katiban are known,[16] only a handful can be identified with actual works. These include Abdullah b. İlyas and Mehmed Tahir, who transcribed Korans in nesih and gubari; Abdülhayf Ali and Mehmed b. Gazanfer, who practised kaatı; and Pir Ahmed b. İskender, Şahsuvar Selimi, and Mehmed Şerif, the talik masters who worked on literary texts and the collected poems of Selim I and Süleyman. One should add to this list Nasuh, who not only illustrated his own texts but also transcribed them in a fairly good nesih.

The payroll registers and other documents pertaining to the Ehl-i Hiref also list the members of the Cemaat-i Mücellidan (Society of Bookbinders).[17] A remarkable family headed by the patriarch Ahmed, who was recorded as being an imperial master at the time of his death in 1518, dominated the society of the bookbinders for over a century. Ahmed's four sons, Mustafa, Hasan, Hüseyin, and Mehmed, are listed in the registers dated between 1526 and 1566; Mehmed b. Ahmed was the head of the society between 1545 and 1566 and his descendants continued the tradition well into the second quarter of the seventeenth century. Another master bookbinder, Hürrem-i Rum, was employed between 1545 and 1596; his son also worked in the imperial society. A third master, Ahmed Kamil, active between 1545 and 1558, was also followed by sons. As with those of the painters, the works of the bookbinders remain anonymous, although the most spectacular examples must have been produced by Mehmed b. Ahmed, who was the head of the society for over two decades.

The bookbinders, whose society constituted eight to twelve men between 1526 and 1566, were considerably more family-oriented and homogeneous than the nakkaşan, with only one Bosnian, Austrian, or Circassian enrolled at a time. Most of their works follow the traditional Islamic format with stamped and gilded leather exteriors and filigree interiors. Some of these are exquisitely decorated and display superb technique, in which the field is deeply recessed and the mo-

tifs rendered in considerable relief. The best examples, made for the Korans of Karahisari and for the collected poems and illustrated histories of the sultan (see **27**), were obviously by the hand of the chief bookbinder, Mehmed b. Ahmed.

There are also lacquered bookbindings that must have been painted by nakkaşhane artists (see **18a** and **33b**). Some are decorated with the same themes used in manuscript illuminations, while others show pictorial scenes related to the illustrations in literary texts.[18] At times the lacquer was applied to both the exterior and interior surfaces; at others it was used only on the doublures. An interesting collaboration between the two societies appears in several examples, which have stamped and gilded areas set apart by lacquered fields.

The decorative themes and techniques of early sixteenth-century Ottoman bindings are extremely close to those produced in Herat and Tabriz, reflecting the conservatism of the tradition. Examples dating after 1530 can generally be distinguished by their saz scrolls, naturalistic blossoms, and çintemani patterns.

Some bookbindings were made of precious materials, frequently employing jade plaques inlaid with gold and encrusted with such stones as emeralds and rubies (see **9**, **20**, and **21**). Produced by the Cemaat-i Zergeran (Society of Goldsmiths) in collaboration with the Cemaat-i Hakkakin (Society of Gemstone Carvers), these are truly dazzling and were made exclusively for Korans, with one exception: the binding of the *Divan-ı Muradi,* the collected poems of Murad III, which is inscribed with the name of the maker, Mehmed, and dated 1588.[19] The tradition of precious materials used in the court will be discussed in the next chapter.

The chronological sequence and the stylistic development of these jeweled Koran bindings cannot be properly determined since they are not dated and the majority are sepa-

Fig. 12. Circular panel from the Süleymaniye Mosque, composed by Ahmed Karahisari, c. 1557

rated from their manuscripts. The few that still retain their original texts have no colophons, with the exception of the rare hexagonal example that encloses a sancak Koran transcribed in 1570/1571 (see **21**). This Koran provides the key for dating not only the jeweled gold and jade bindings, but also those containers and vessels that employ the same materials and techniques.

The experimentation that took place during the age of Süleyman is clearly evident in a unique tortoiseshell binding made for an imperial album (see **49**). Employing the technique and materials applied to later furnishings and to such architectural components as doors and shutters, it proves that the tradition of using thin plaques of tortoiseshell underlaid with gold leaf was established in the 1560s.

Tuğras, Fermans, and Vakfiyes

The most outstanding symbol of the Ottoman sultan's authority was his imperial tuğra, which was affixed to all official documents, including fermans, vakfiyes, and correspondence; it was also carved on his seals and stamped on the coins minted during his reign. Each sultan chose his personal tuğra immediately after his accession and used the same format throughout his life.

Since the word tuğra is of Oğuz Turkish origin, it is thought that the tradition of validating documents with the ruler's name or signature was practiced as early as the ninth or tenth century, and passed on to later Turkish dynasties, including the Seljuks and the Mamluks. Although the use of a tuğra was an ancient practice, the type devised by the Ottomans was unique and remained unchanged for some six hundred years.

The Ottoman tuğra (fig. 13) has four basic components: the *sere*, the lower portion with stacked letters bearing the name of the owner; the *tuğ*, three vertical projections at the top joined by S-shaped strokes; the *beyze*, two concentric circular extensions on the left, the inner one called *küçük* (small) beyze and the outer *büyük* (large) beyze; and the *kol*, a curved stroke extending from the sere into the beyze. With the exception of two strokes added to balance the tuğ, all four components were integral parts of the name, composed of letters rendered in a highly elaborate and decorative manner.

The earliest Ottoman tuğra belongs to Sultan Orhan and is dated 1324, the first year of his reign. The sere reads "Orhan bin Osman"; the tuğ and the beyze had not yet evolved. In the tuğras of the ensuing sultans the title *Han* was added as well as the phrase "el-muzaffer daima" (the eternally victorious), which led to the development of the tuğ, beyze, and kol. The most harmonious use of the basic components appear in the tuğras of Süleyman (fig. 14), which read "Süleymanşah bin Şelimşah Han el-muzaffer daima." It is this for-

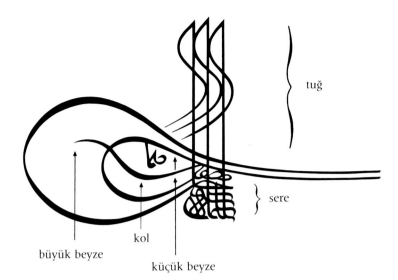

Fig. 13. The components of the Ottoman tuğra

mat, with obvious changes in the sere to accommodate the name of each new sultan, that became the prototype for future Ottoman tuğras.

It has been pointed out that the word *şah* following both Süleyman and Selim was not a title but part of their names. Selim I's tuğras as şehzade and sultan read "Selimşah," which appears to be his complete name, similar to those of his brothers, Şahınşah and Alemşah. The tuğras of Süleyman's sons, Bayezid and Mehmed, give the name of their father as "Süleymanşah." Selim II, however, used only "Selim" on his tuğras as a şehzade, but employed "Selimşah" after he became sultan, most likely to conform the wording with that of his father. The word *şah* denoting a title appears in the tuğra of Murad III, which reads "Şah Murad bin Selimşah. . . ."[20] This word, both as a title and as part of the name, disappears from the tuğras after Murad III.

In the Ottoman court it was the *nişancı*, the chancellor in the Divan-ı Hümayun, who was responsible for affixing the sultan's tuğra on documents. After the contents of the documents were checked and approved, they were given to the nişancı, who centered the tuğra at the top. In later periods he was assisted by a tuğrakeş who was chosen for his expertise in rendering the complicated letters.

Tuğras were also used by şehzades assigned to sancaks; they had their own nişancıs in their courts, and many retained the same format after ascending the throne. The tuğras of Süleyman drawn when he served as governor in the 1510s are identical to those he used after he became sultan.[21] The same consistency appears in the tuğras of his father and his son, Selim I and Selim II.[22] A related type was used by the şeyhülislams, grand vezirs, vezirs, and governors when validating their documents. These signatures are similar to those used by the sultans and şehzades, except that they are gener-

Fig. 14. The reading of Sultan Süleyman's tuğra

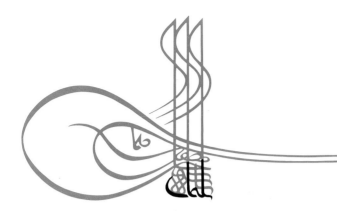

Süleyman

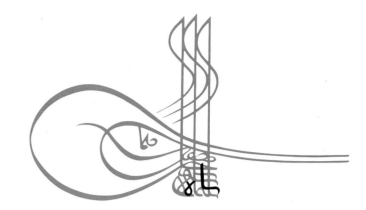

şah

bin

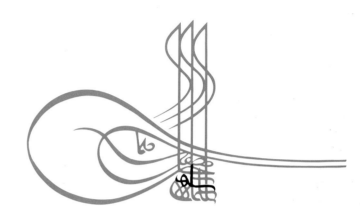

Selim

şah

han

el-muzaffer daima

(decorative strokes completing the design)

ally placed sideways on the documents and frequently have a single beyze.

The Ottoman tuğra was used as the coat of arms of the dynasty after the eighteenth century and was employed on such official items as postage stamps, flags, ships, and government buildings. The format of the tuğra was also later applied to writing Koranic verses, prayers, and names of individuals.

The tuğras of Süleyman are of two different types. The first is the simple tuğra; rendered in gold or black, it appears on the majority of his official correspondence and fermans. The execution of simple tuğras is utilitarian at best, indicating that these were drawn by the nişancı himself. Although not all the persons who held that post during Süleyman's long reign are known, one individual, Celalzade Mustafa Paşa, called Koca (Great) Nişancı, is documented. This official, renowned for his histories of Selim I and Süleyman, served first on the staff of the grand vezir İbrahim Paşa. He later became the head of the secretaries in the Divan-ı Hümayun and was appointed nişancı in 1534/1535; he retired in 1556/1557; he was reappointed in 1566 and died a year later.

The nişancıs were chosen for their knowledge of the şeriat and kanuns and for their experience in writing and codifying laws. It was not mandatory for them to be expert calligraphers, as can be observed in the majority of Süleyman's tuğras, which are drawn accurately but simply.

The second type of tuğra is expertly rendered and decorated, revealing the hand of a master tuğrakeş who was assisted by an illuminator. There are scores of these illuminated versions that appear at the top of fermans transcribed in divani script, frequently written in gold, blue, and black. The format of the tuğras is consistent, with the same proportions used for the sere, tuğ, beyze, and kol; the letters are rendered in blue and outlined in gold; and the interstices between the letters are decorated with a profusion of naturalistic flora and scrolls composed of rumis, hatayis, and cloud bands frequently overlaid by additional floral motifs. Each unit bears a different design; some are on a plain ground, while others are placed on a gold ground. Blue and gold dominate, with touches of red usually applied to the blossoms and buds. The illuminators took advantage of the spacious büyük beyze and filled it with several different types of scrolls that float above one another, interact, and create a vibrant three-dimensional composition.

Illuminated tuğras from Süleyman's reign are very important in determining the development of the artistic vocabulary of the age. Even though a number of examples, particularly those in American and European collections, have been separated from the fermans, those in Turkish collections are datable and thus help to provide a chronological sequence of decorative motifs. It is perhaps not surprising that the majority of these illuminated tuğras were affixed to documents that validated endowments of land and property for charitable foundations established by the royal family.

There also exist rare oversize tuğras that reveal consummate integration between the efforts of the tuğrakeş and the illuminator. The earliest example belongs to Süleyman and was rendered in dark blue outlined with gold on polished paper (1). Its majestic format (158 by 240 centimeters, or more than 62 by 94 inches), harmonious interplay of vertical and horizontal components, and diversity of decorative motifs that fill the voids between the strokes indicate that a master tuğrakeş drew the tuğra and a talented artist was assigned to decorate it. The piece was most likely produced in 1550, shortly after the appearance of the naturalistic genre.

Each unit of the tuğra contains an independent design, its colors contrasting with and accentuating those in the adjacent zones. The decoration alternates between stylized and naturalistic themes that are repeated, thus creating a flowing movement. The overall composition recalls a musical score, visually recalling the rhythm and harmony of a fugue.

The sere, where the sultan's name is written, is decorated with rumi scrolls, blossoming fruit trees, and clusters of tulips, carnations, hyacinths, and roses. The tuğ contains naturalistic flowers and trees, stylized floral and rumi scrolls, and cartouches composed of leaves overlaid by blossoms. The büyük beyze reveals a most refined design with three superimposed scrolls showing a profusion of hatayi blossoms and buds, cloud bands, rumis, and leaves; the küçük beyze has two superimposed scrolls accented by rumi cartouches.

This spectacular example belongs to a limited series of oversize tuğras executed for Süleyman, Murad III, and Ahmed I, the latter signed by Hasan Paşa.[23] The reason for the production of these majestic tuğras is yet to be properly understood. It has been suggested that they were made to commemorate a specific event, but this is dubious since there is no reference to such an occasion on the panels. Another suggestion was that they hung in the Divan-ı Hümayun chambers, but this too is not convincing. What is possible, however, is that they hung in the chamber where the nişancı or the tuğrakeş worked, providing them with proper models.

One of the earliest illuminated tuğras of Süleyman (2) is unfortunately undated, for the end of the document has been lost; its stylistic features, however, suggest that it was produced in the 1530s.[24] This example, drawn in blue with gold outlines, has spiral scrolls with blue flowers in the küçük beyze; a scroll with gold rumis and blossoms, accentuated by three blue cartouches filled with cloud bands, appears in the büyük beyze. Enclosing it is a triangular formation composed of spiral scrolls sprinkled with cloud bands. The design of the scrolls is identical to that employed on a group of blue-and-turquoise painted ceramics popularly called Golden Horn ware, since several pieces were found on the site of the Golden Horn (Haliç) in İstanbul (see **178** and **179**). This ware, thought to have been inspired by the decorative themes used on Süleyman's tuğras, is dated to the second quarter of the sixteenth century.

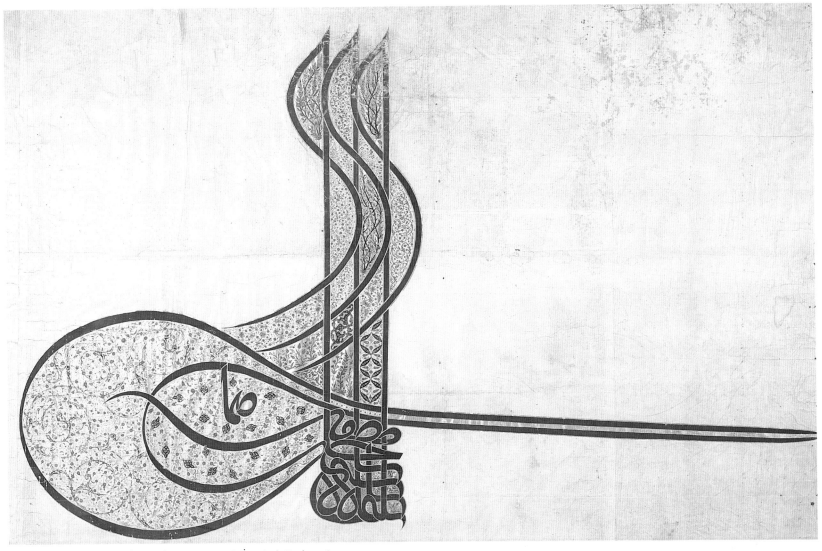

1. Illuminated tuğra of Sultan Süleyman, c. 1550 (İstanbul, Topkapı Sarayı Müzesi, G.Y. 1400)

The document, which is written in a scroll format like all Ottoman fermans, is devoted to the allocation of lands under the sancak of Vize in Thrace; it is transcribed in divani, the traditional script for imperial edicts. The first line, which is found in all Ottoman tuğras and generally rendered in gold, begins with the marks called *nişan-ı şerife alişan* (reading from right to left, it consists of a single dot, three dots forming a triangle, and a vertical stroke) and contains the formulaic *methiye*, which praises the sultan and concludes with the words "it is his order that." In this example the first line was rendered in blue whereas the text was written in black and gold; the letters were sprinkled with gold. The practice of sprinkling gold dust on texts while the ink was still wet was par-

ticularly favored in illuminated official documents.

The scroll that encloses the tuğra and creates a triangular formation is an unusual feature for Süleyman's reign. The illuminations of the tuğras of his predecessor and immediate followers are limited to the areas between the letters and do not enclose the entire piece. Finials extending from the tuğ and arms of the beyze began to appear in the seventeenth century and became more and more elaborate until they totally engulfed the tuğra. The overly-decorated examples coexisted with the simple calligraphic types and those that restricted the illumination to the parts of the tuğra itself.

The illuminated tuğra that characterizes the age of Süleyman was firmly established in the 1550s. There are numerous

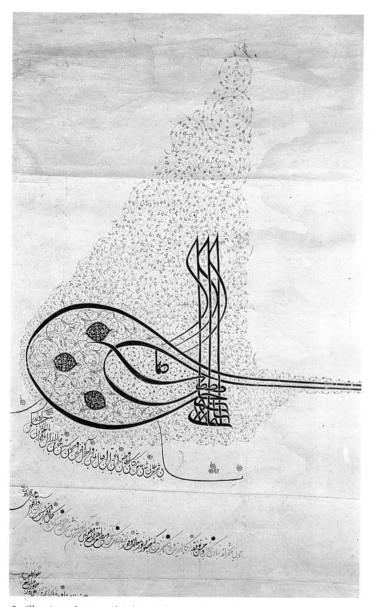

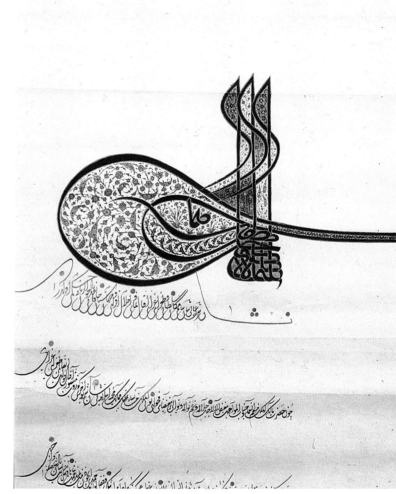

3. Illuminated tuğra of Sultan Süleyman from a ferman dated 1552 (İstanbul, Topkapı Sarayı Müzesi, E. 7816/2)

2. Illuminated tuğra of Sultan Süleyman from a ferman, c. 1530–1540 (İstanbul, Türk ve İslam Eserleri Müzesi, 2238)

examples of this type in Turkish, European, and American collections. Although each example shows minor variations in the choice of designs filling the areas between the letters, there is a considerable amount of standardization in the selection and placement of the decorative themes.

The most beautifully illuminated tuğras are found on a series of eleven fermans in the archives of the Topkapı Palace.[25] Dated between 1550 and 1555, they contain allocations of property to support Hürrem Sultan's endowment in Jerusalem. Belonging to a type of document called *mülkname* (property deed), they list the names of villages and orchards in Jerusalem, Gaza, Ramla, and Tripoli whose rents and other revenues were assigned to the imaret endowed by Hürrem Sultan. In these documents she is called "the mother of Şeh-

zade Selim," who was her oldest living son at the time and the heir presumptive. These fermans issued by Süleyman for his wife's endowments contain his most elaborate tuğras.

Possibly the most refined example in the series is the tuğra (3) on the document dated 1552. It is also decorated with the characteristic themes found on the examples illuminated after the 1550s. The letters are drawn in blue and outlined in gold; gold is also used in the background of the sere, the three alternating semicircular units in the tuğ, the triangular area with four compartments joining the tuğ with the beyze, and in the long arms on the right. The büyük beyze is filled with two superimposed spiral scrolls, one bearing blue blossoms and the other gold hatayis and leaves overlaid with sprays of flowers. The latter exemplifies the saz style of decoration with

4. Illuminated tuğra of Sultan Süleyman, c. 1555–1560 (New York, The Metropolitan Museum of Art, 38.149.1)

elaborate compound blossoms and twisting feathery leaves embellished with floral motifs intersecting and overlapping one another.

The lower half of the küçük beyze contains a braid composed of black and gold rumis with red or blue triple dots sprinkled in the interstices. The upper half of the same section reveals six bunches of blue, red, and yellow carnations, tulips, hatayis, and other blossoms growing from clusters of leaves. The gold units of the tuğ have either floral scrolls or sprays of blossoms; one bears cloud bands flanking a flower. The remaining compartments of the tuğ are embellished with red carnations, blue blossoms, and cloud bands. Cloud bands also fill the arm extending to the right.

The designs and themes filling the three units of the

beyze—combining spiral scrolls, braids, and floral sprays rendered in the saz style, traditional mode, and naturalistic genre—were employed in many of the tuğras made for Süleyman as well as for his followers. Gold applied to the background for the sere and to alternating units of the tuğ also reappears in imperial tuğras until the middle of the seventeenth century.[26]

The standard established by the tuğra on the document dated 1552 enables us to date similar examples removed from the fermans, including the one in the Metropolitan Museum of Art (4), which must have been produced in the late 1550s. The büyük beyze here has a more intricate design, its superimposed blue and gold scrolls painted with ultimate refinement. The blue scroll contains hatayis with tiny red buds en-

41

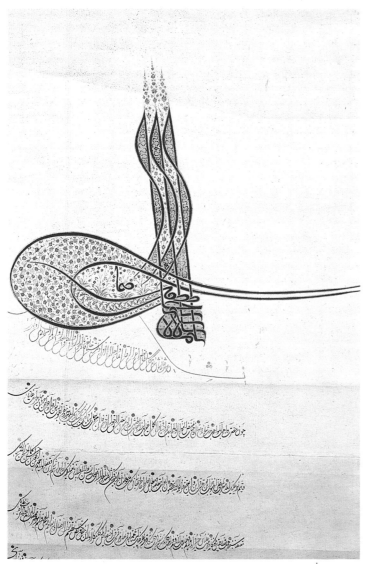

5. Illuminated tuğra of Sultan Selim II from a ferman, dated 1569 (İstanbul, Türk ve İslam Eserleri Müzesi, 4125)

semicircular units as well as on the same triangular section with four compartments found in the 1552 tuğra. These areas are filled with floral scrolls and blossoming fruit trees painted in pink, red, blue, and green. The remaining portions have either red and blue floral motifs, or triple gold dots overlaid with blue rumis, similar to the design used in the beyze. The long arm on the right contains black and blue cloud bands.

The format and decoration of Süleyman's imperial tuğras were copied in those made for his son and heir, Selim II. One of the outstanding examples from Selim's reign (5) appears on a mülkname that assigns the income from several districts in Thrace to a village in the same region. The document drawn in 1569 in İstanbul is written in gold, blue, and black on polished and gold-speckled paper. Its tuğra has a sere similar to the ones described earlier except here it is further enhanced by triple red dots. The büyük beyze with blue and gold spiral scrolls accentuated with red, and the upper portion of the küçük beyze with naturalistic red and blue carnations, also follow the decoration of Süleyman's tuğras. Although the lower portion of the küçük beyze is filled with a similar rumi braid, the motifs in this example are painted blue, red, and gold. The tuğ section shows a further variation: gold is used as the background in the three upper and three middle semicircular units as well as in the lower triangular compartments, which are filled with black and red cloud bands with an occasional blossom. The remaining areas reveal sprays of blue hatayis with red carnations that project from the voids above the tuğ. This type of projection was also seen in at least one tuğra dating from the 1550s and became more popular in the ensuing years.

Unfortunately the artists who executed the tuğras on these fermans cannot be identified. There is no record of a tuğrakeş who worked during Süleyman's reign and the nakkaşhane documents do not offer clues on the painters who might have illuminated them. Since the same impeccable technique and combination of stylized and naturalistic motifs are found in illuminated manuscripts signed by Kara Memi (see 14 and 26), this artist must have worked on a number of tuğras dating between the 1540s and 1560s, including the oversize demonstration piece. Kara Memi, who originated the naturalistic genre with delicate sprays of tulips and carnations, established a prototype for future illuminators of tuğras and possibly even supervised an atelier in which other men were trained to follow in his steps.

Kara Memi's distinctive style appears on several other documents, including a bound volume that contains the deed of endowment pertaining to the architectural complex commissioned by Hürrem Sultan in the Aksaray district of İstanbul. The deed was established to support the mosque, imaret, and medrese built for her by Sinan in 1538/1539. The *Vakfiye* of Hürrem Sultan was prepared in 1540, signed in the presence of witnesses, and validated by Süleyman's tuğra. The volume opens with an illuminated double *serlevha* (title page) in

closed by green leaves growing at their tips. The gold scroll, one of the best renditions of the saz style, is composed of hatayis also sprouting buds and leaves intermingled with large feathery leaves overlaid with sprays of pink and blue flowers. The lower half of the küçük beyze has a more complex design, a double scroll of gold and black rumis interspersed with blue cloud bands with touches of pink. The upper portion contains four sprays of blue and red carnations with gold leaves and stems.

The tuğ employs gold in the two upper and three lower

6. Illuminated serlevha from the *Vakfiye* of Hürrem Sultan transcribed in 1540 (İstanbul, Türk ve İslam Eserleri Müzesi, 2191, fols. 1b—2a)

which areas painted in gold and blue, each overlaid with polychrome blossoms and rumis, are delicately balanced (6). Blue spiral scrolls with hatayi blossoms appear behind the gold text, repeating the design found on the tuğras of the sultan. Blue hatayis accompanied by red carnations are also used on the finials.

The text states that the *vakıf* (endowment) is to be supported by revenue obtained from lands assigned to Hürrem Sultan and lists in detail the salaries of the staff, outlines their duties and responsibilities, specifies the types of meals to be distributed, assigns the Babüssaade Ağası (chief official in charge of the Enderun) as the overseer of the vakıf, and names the trustee.[27] The vakfiye was prepared with great care and foresight, making sure that the activities of the complex were properly and judiciously handled for centuries to come. It is typical of scores of documents issued by Süleyman to protect and maintain the religious, charitable, and social institutions established in the endowments.

43

Religious Manuscripts

Similar to other Islamic societies, the Ottomans regarded calligraphy as the noblest of all the arts. To copy the Koran was considered an act of piety and devotion, and the persons who performed this task with the highest degree of perfection became the most celebrated artists, respected and honored by sultans. Throughout Islamic history the veneration of the holy book led to the development of both calligraphy and illumination, which also benefited the production of secular manuscripts, setting high standards for the aesthetics and connoisseurship of the art of the book.

In the Ottoman world the development of calligraphy was particularly energetic, each new generation of artists mastering and perfecting the older traditions and periodically revitalizing and revolutionizing the established styles. Calligraphers continued to surpass their predecessors and reach new heights until well into the nineteenth century.

The men who practiced calligraphy belonged to several different groups. First there were the salaried copyists, the katiban, who were either a part of the Ehl-i Hiref and worked in the capital or provincial courts or belonged to the staff of administrators. These men were prolific, turning out one manuscript after another, copying them alone or with their associates. The majority of the manuscripts, particularly the illustrated ones, were the products of these copyists, most of whom were not named in them or in the biographical dictionaries of the artists.

The second group of calligraphers practiced this form of art for personal pleasure and included sultans, şehzades, grand vezirs, şeyhülislams, and other officials. Some of them excelled in their hobbies and became highly respected calligraphers, including Bayezid II and his son Korkud, both of whom were trained by Şeyh Hamdullah.

The third group constituted the great masters, men who taught and practiced calligraphy as an act of devotion. These men were not salaried, but generously rewarded for their services by the sultans and received ample stipends and benefits.[28] Two of the most renowned master calligraphers in history, Şeyh Hamdullah and Ahmed Karahisari, worked in the sixteenth century, each a revolutionary artist with a markedly different style.

Şeyh Hamdullah, born in Amasya in 1429(?), was the son of a şeyh (spiritual leader) of the Sühreverdi order of dervishes, Mustafa Dede, who had come from Bukhara. Hamdullah studied calligraphy with Hayreddin Maraşi, a student of Abdullah Sayrafi, himself a student of the celebrated Yakut el-Mustasimi, who had established the canonical forms for the six styles of Arabic script. Similar to other Ottoman calligraphers, Hamdullah practiced all six styles, but it was for his sülüs and nesih that he came to be renowned.

He tutored Bayezid II while the latter was serving as governor in Amasya. Upon ascending the throne in 1481, Bayezid invited his teacher to İstanbul and assigned him a studio in the palace. According to tradition, Bayezid so greatly admired the calligrapher that he used to sit long hours holding his inkwell and watching him work. During the course of one such session the sultan asked him whether Yakut's six styles could be improved. Hamdullah disappeared for forty days and when he returned to the palace he had totally revolutionized Yakut's scripts, establishing his own school of writing.

A legend in his own lifetime, Hamdullah is thought to have written close to fifty Korans and hundreds of volumes containing collections of prayers, selections from the Koran, and calligraphic verses and exercises. In addition, he composed the inscriptions on the entrance portal and the mihrab of the Mosque of Sultan Bayezid II, those over the entrance in the mosques of Davut Paşa and Firuz Ağa, and that on the Edirnekapı, one of the main gates of the capital. He was also a great swimmer, archer, and hunter: he swam across the treacherous Bosporus from Saray Burnu to Üsküdar; he was made the leader of the archers at Ok Meydanı, which earned him the title Şeyh; and he was an expert in hawking. A man of many talents, Hamdullah was also a tailor and is said to have made a kaftan for Bayezid II.

When Bayezid II was overthrown by his son Selim in 1512, Hamdullah was extremely disillusioned and retired to his estate at Alemdağ in Üsküdar. After Süleyman ascended the throne he invited Hamdullah back to the palace and asked him to write a Koran. Hamdullah declined, saying he was too old, and suggested that one of his students undertake the task. The calligrapher, who was more than ninety years old at the time, died two months later. He trained many students and inspired followers who immortalized his style for centuries to come. Hamdullah's family produced a dozen calligraphers, each carrying the tradition of the great master.

Hamdullah's mature style is observed in a Koran transcribed in İstanbul in 1495/1496. Although it bears no dedication, the manuscript, which is of exceptional quality, must have been produced for Bayezid II. The volume follows a traditional format with an illuminated double frontispiece preceding an illuminated double serlevha that contains the first verses. The illuminations are extremely refined, using three different tones of gold, and light and dark shades of red, blue, and green. The decorative repertoire is characteristic for the period and includes rumis, cloud bands, floral scrolls, and sprays of blossoms. The text, written in fourteen lines of nesih per page, is embellished with illuminated chapter headings, marginal ornaments, and verse stops (7). The chapter headings are conceived as long and narrow panels enclosing oval cartouches with the titles written in white ink. Each heading employs a different color scheme and composition, and contrasts the design in oval cartouches with the corner spandrels of the panels.

Hamdullah's nesih in this work indeed befits his reputation. His calligraphy shows extreme control and exactitude as well as an effortless and gentle flow. The elongation and exaggeration of certain letters help to create a rhythmic pattern that enhances the movement of the script. The work of such a master calligrapher required the assistance of the most highly qualified illuminator of the court. Although this artist is anonymous, he must have been well regarded to be called upon to decorate a volume of the great Şeyh Hamdullah.

Among manuscripts produced during the early years of Süleyman's reign is a unique Koran that provides not only the date and the name of the calligrapher but also identifies the illuminator, who is listed in the payroll registers.[29] This Koran, dedicated to Süleyman, was transcribed in 1523/1524 by Abdullah b. İlyas and decorated by Bayram b. Derviş Şir, who is called ''nakkaş.'' The calligrapher, whose name is found only in this work, appears to have been a follower of the Şeyh

Hamdullah school and his nesih script is closely related to the style established by the master.

Bayram, the illuminator, is recorded in the register of 1526 as having entered the nakkaşhane during the reign of Bayezid II; the same document states that his sons Ali and Mehmed were also working in the studio, the latter having joined in 1499. Bayram must have been a fairly well-established master in the 1520s. A later document states that Bayram died on 5 November 1558, at which time he must have been close to ninety years old.

Similar to Hamdullah's Koran, this manuscript contains an illuminated double frontispiece and an illuminated double serlevha with the opening verses. The decoration of the frontispiece is dazzling, employing several tones of gold highlighted by deep blue and touches of polychrome pigments

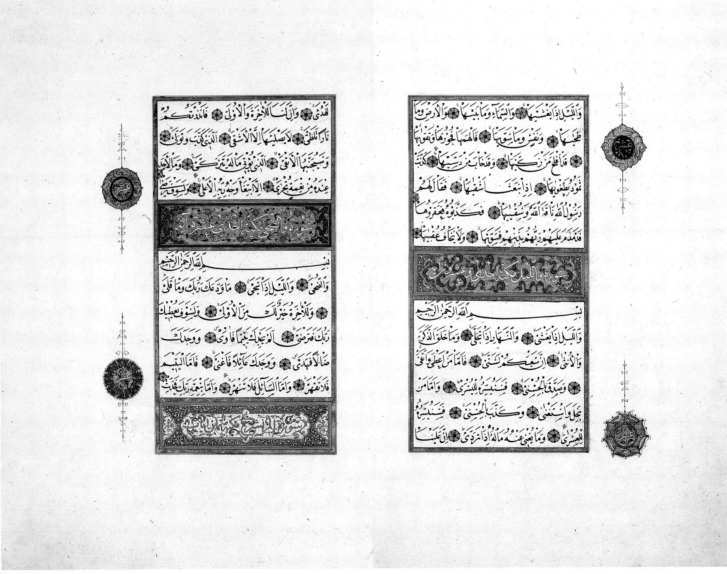

7. Illuminated folios from a Koran transcribed by Şeyh Hamdullah in 1495/1496 (İstanbul, Topkapı Sarayı Müzesi, E.H. 72, fols. 327b–328a)

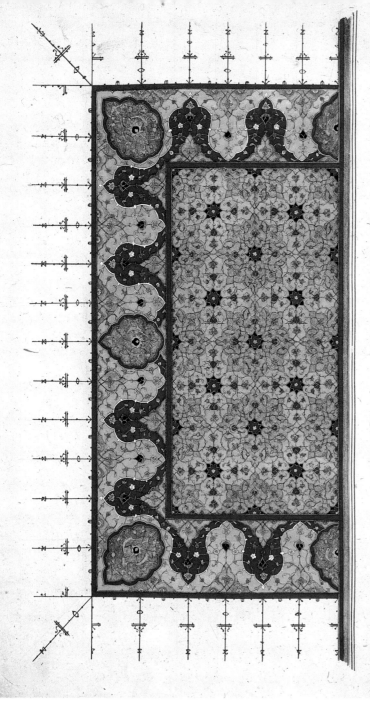
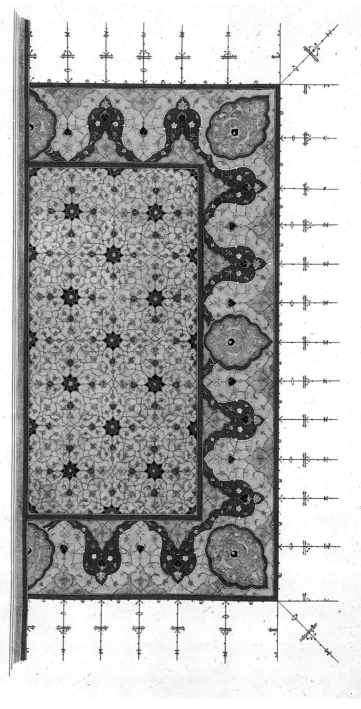

8. Frontispiece from a Koran illuminated by Bayram b. Derviş in 1523/1524 and dedicated to Sultan Süleyman (İstanbul, Topkapı Sarayı Müzesi, E.H. 58, fols. 1b–2a)

(8). A wide frame with reciprocal arches, accented by oval medallions, encloses the central field, which contains a geometric pattern composed of eight-pointed stars interspersed with crosses. Both the frame and central field are decorated with layered rumi and hatayi scrolls, which create a fine mesh over the entire surface.

Bayram's illuminations reveal a conservative style, employing traditional compositions and decorative elements. Produced at the height of his career, they also reflect a refined and restrained execution. The illuminator must have worked on a number of other manuscripts, possibly even on the Ko-

ran transcribed by Hamdullah discussed above.

The 1523/1524 Koran, dedicated to Süleyman a few years after his accession, was obviously produced with extreme care by the best talents in the court and was considered to be of such high quality that its calligrapher and illuminator were honored by being mentioned in the colophon. Its outstanding binding was also the work of an imperial master, whose name, unfortunately, was not recorded.

Manuscripts in the Topkapı Palace collections were periodically repaired and their bindings restored or replaced. One such example is the Koran copied in 1546/1547. Its original binding was removed in the seventeenth century and replaced by a gem-encrusted gold cover; recently this too was removed. The volume now has a modern binding made by using older stamps. The rebinding of the manuscript a century after it was produced indicates the importance given to the work that was transcribed by Ahmed Karahisari, a giant in the history of calligraphy.

The artist, whose given name was Ahmed Şemseddin, was born in 1469(?) in the town of Karahisar (now called Afyonkarahisar), which he appended to his name. Known not only as Şemseddin (the star of religion) but also as Şemsül-hat (the star of calligraphy), Ahmed Karahisari was a brilliant calligrapher who broke from the traditions of the past and the schools of Yakut and Hamdullah.

Karahisari began his career studying the aklam-ı sitte of Yakut with Asadullah Kirmani, a famous calligrapher from Kirman; it is not known whether he went to Kirman to work with the master or if Asadullah had moved to Anatolia. The date of Karahisari's arrival in İstanbul is also not known, but he was probably an established master by the time Süleyman ascended the throne. Karahisari worked primarily for Süleyman, producing Korans, collections of prayers, and albums of calligraphic exercises. He also worked on architectural inscriptions, the most famous examples being the circular panels around the mihrab (see fig. 12) and the large frieze encircling the dome of the Süleymaniye Mosque, which appear to have been his last works, since he died in 1556.

Critics of calligraphy, who frequently compare his style with that of Hamdullah, state that although Hamdullah outranked him in the perfection of forming individual letters and devising line lengths, Karahisari was unequaled in his overall compositions of the pages and was the greatest calligrapher of the celi style of writing. Like other Ottoman calligraphers, he preferred sülüs and nesih, but also practiced the other scripts. The artistry of Karahisari does not lie in his performance of the established styles but in his unique compositions, applied both to Korans and to individual folios bound into albums.

The double serlevha at the beginning of his Koran dated 1546/1547 contains one of the most magnificent illuminations created during Süleyman's reign (9a); the layout and decorative panels surrounding the text show the hand of a master painter who combined both traditional and innovative themes. The artist, identified as Kara Memi, not only relied on the established repertoire of rumis, hatayi scrolls, and cloud bands, but also represented naturalistic flora that revolutionized the decorative vocabulary of the age.

The most striking examples of the naturalistic genre appear in the two pairs of oval panels flanking the text, each representing a luxuriant spray of polychrome blossoms growing from a cluster of leaves placed on a deep blue ground. This particular theme, which made its appearance in the 1540s, was reemployed on a number of other manuscripts, including the *Süleymanname* of Arifi dated 1558,[30] a copy of the *Divan-ı*

Muhibbi illuminated by Kara Memi in 1566, and an album of calligraphy compiled around 1560 (see **26** and **49b**). The same composition and color scheme were used on tile panels, such as those in the Mausoleum of Hürrem Sultan, built after her death in 1558; on the facade of the Sünnet Odası in the Topkapı Palace, obviously removed from a building decorated in the mid-sixteenth century; on the portico of Rüstem Paşa's mosque constructed in 1561; and the chamber built in 1574/1575 by Murad III in the Harem (see **210**). The design was also adopted by weavers and employed on kaftans and prayer rugs. Kara Memi, who had tremendous impact on the decorative arts of the age, was sufficiently esteemed to have been entrusted with the task of decorating this important Koran.

Karahisari's mastery of the art of calligraphy is clearly demonstrated in the serlevha: gold sülüs appears immediately above and below the text, which is rendered in black nesih; the illuminated panels at the top and bottom contain white tevkii on a gold ground. The remaining folios, written in nesih, use white sülüs for the chapter headings while the prayer added at the conclusion of the text is once again rendered in gold sülüs. The last four pages of the manuscript contain additional prayers, which may date from the seventeenth century, when the manuscript was rebound.

The structure of this binding (**9b**) combines gem-encrusted gold panels with a type of brocaded silk called *seraser* over a pasteboard core. This fabric, woven with silver and/or gold threads, was generally reserved for imperial kaftans and furnishings (see **119** and **156**). The core is covered on the exterior and interior with silver seraser; the exterior is decorated with gold plaques that constitute the central medallion, axial pendants, corner quadrants, thin bands defining the frame, and the cartouches of the frame. These plaques, secured to the core with gold nails, were produced from molds and represent floral scrolls rendered in high relief with ring matting applied to the sunken grounds. The flowers are embellished with ruby and turquoise centers set into plain collars; four pearls appear around the large ruby in the central medallions. The technique of execution and style of decoration recall two other works dating from the second half of the seventeenth century: a mirror and a clock, the latter signed by an artist named Şahin, who may have also produced this binding.[31]

Karahisari's most exciting works appear in a collection of religious texts that includes the Enam Suresi (the chapter entitled Cattle) from the Koran, selections from the Hadis (Traditions), and the famous *Kaside-i Burda* (Ode to the Prophet's mantle). His signature appears in the middle of the manuscript as well as at the end, where he mentioned that he was

overleaf

9a. Illuminated serlevha from a Koran transcribed by Ahmed Karahisari in 1546/1547 (İstanbul, Topkapı Sarayı Müzesi, Y.Y. 999, fols. 1b–2a)

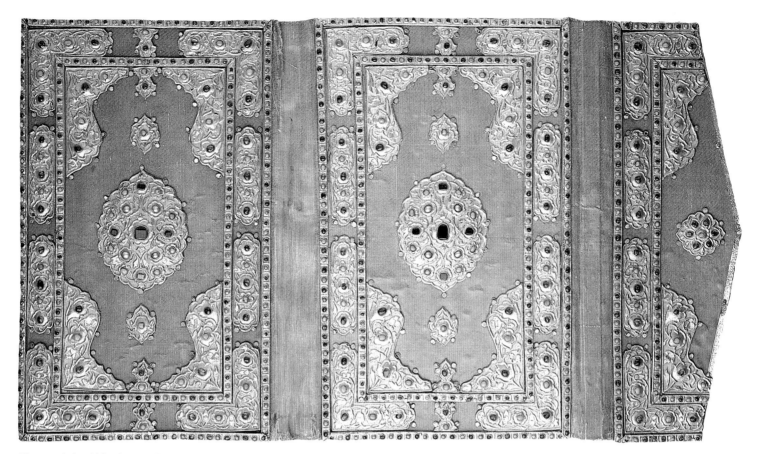

9b. Jeweled gold binding made for the Koran transcribed by Ahmed Karahisari in 1546/1547, second half seventeenth century (İstanbul, Topkapı Sarayı Müzesi, 2/2097)

the student of Asadullah Kirmani. The undated volume is written in a combination of large and small scripts that characterize Karahisari's style.

The double frontispiece contains the two best-known examples of his work (10). Pasted into the folios, they must have been executed as separate studies in the 1540s and incorporated into the volume. The example on the left is a tour de force, the phrase "el-hamd ül-i v'aliy ül-hamid" (praise be to the praiseworthy), executed in sülüs without once lifting the pen. This form of writing, called müselsel, presented a tremendous challenge to calligraphers. The letters are outlined in black and filled with two different decorative schemes: the central ones have a floral scroll bearing tiny eight-petaled blossoms composed of minute black and gold dots, while those at the beginning and end are rendered in gold.

The folio on the right contains three other calligraphic masterpieces. On the top is the phrase "el-hamd ül-illah" (praise to God), written in black *kufi* (angular script) in a form called

makili (checkerboard or squared). The phrase, repeated four times, is embellished with gold. Below it is the most revolutionary execution of the *besmele*, the phrase that appears at the beginning of each Koranic chapter: "bismillah ir-rahman ir-rahim" (usually translated "in the name of God, the Merciful, the Compassionate"). Written once again in müselsel sülüs, in black ink with gold diacritics, it demonstrates the genius of Karahisari. At the bottom is another makili kufi inscription rendered in gold, containing the besmele together with a verse from the Koran.

Another collection of Karahisari's calligraphy appears in an album dated 1552/1553 that includes alphabetic exercises written in alternating gold and black sülüs and nesih. The folios are composed sideways and in facing pairs with the backs left blank. The pair at the beginning (11) contains prayers rendered in two lines of sülüs with a line of nesih in between, a format followed throughout the manuscript. The first page has black sülüs on the top, black nesih in the middle, followed by another black line in gubari (which appears

50

10. Frontispiece from a collection of religious texts transcribed by Ahmed Karahisari c. 1540–1550 (İstanbul, Türk ve İslam Eserleri Müzesi, 1443, fols. 1b–2a)

only on this folio), and gold sülüs at the bottom. The following page repeats the same design, except that the gold and black sülüs lines are reversed.

The binding of this album reveals an interesting technique: the exterior, covered with reddish-brown leather, has a central medallion and four corner quadrants that are stamped with gold and decorated with saz scrolls, the motifs of which were cut out of black or dark brown leather and applied to these areas. The binding also bears a noteworthy label added to the manuscript when it was in the library of Ahmed III. It describes the contents of the volume and concludes with a phrase that is translated ''protect it from worms,'' a highly significant precaution issued by a conscientious conservator.

Karahisari conceived the layout and began the transcription of possibly the most spectacular Koran in the history of Islam. The large volume (62 by 41 centimeters, or about 24 by 16 inches, with 298 folios) is thought to have been finished after

11. Two folios from an album of calligraphy transcribed by Ahmed Karahisari in 1552/1553 (İstanbul, Topkapı Sarayı Müzesi, A. 3654, fols. 1b–2a)

his death by his student and adopted son, Hasan, who in reverence to his master did not put his name on the manuscript. The volume's expenses were recorded in detail in documents dated between 1584 and 1586, which list the costs and amounts of paper, pigments, gold leaf, and burnishing utensils purchased for the artists. Later documents, dated between 1590 and 1593, record the amount of blue pigment and liquid gold purchased for the illuminated serlevha as well as the expenses of the gold-stamped bookbinding.[32] The same documents also state that Karahisari died in 1556 before completing the transcription. Nevertheless, the monumental work is known as the Koran of Karahisari. The volume, which was assigned to the Has Oda, was superbly designed and executed, carefully documented, and highly revered throughout the centuries.

Hasan (known as Çerkes Hasan, Hasan b. Abdullah, Hasan b. Ahmed Karahisari, or Hasan Çelebi), who finished the transcription of the great Koran, was a Circassian slave in the service of Karahisari. The master freed him, adopted him as his son, and taught him his art. Hasan worked on the celi inscriptions on the Süleymaniye Mosque and executed those in the Selimiye Mosque in Edirne. It is said that while he was working in the Selimiye, a piece of lime fell into his eye and, without realizing what he was doing, he washed out both eyes with the water in which he had been rinsing his lime covered brushes. Totally blinded in one eye and seriously handicapped in the other, he was forced to retire and was assigned a lifetime pension by Selim II.

The calligrapher, who died in 1594, closely followed the tradition established by his master, as can be observed in his collection of daily prayers, called *Evrad el-Usbu*. The volume, transcribed in 1566/1567 and dedicated to Selim II, is written in alternating large and small scripts with illuminated rectangular panels flanking the blocks of small script. Illuminations also appear on the double-folio *zahriye* (dedication) at the beginning, on the serlevha, and on headings for the seven prayers; the margins of the folios are gold-speckled.

The serlevha (12) contains the title executed in white tevkii on the right folio; the text below has two blocks of three lines of nesih, each followed by a line of sülüs or muhakkak. The first and last lines on the facing folio are in muhakkak with the central one rendered in white sülüs and placed on an illuminated panel; between them are the same two blocks of nesih seen on the first folio. The illuminations, similar to those of the large Koran of Karahisari, contain both naturalistic and stylized motifs and may have been executed by the artists who worked on that volume.

The illuminators were also assigned to work on Korans transcribed by the great calligraphers of the past, including Yakut el-Mustasimi, Abdullah Sayrafi, and Argun Kamili, which were preserved in the palace libraries. Periodically these volumes would be restored and embellished. This practice was particularly noticeable during the reign of Süleyman when older manuscripts were decorated and rebound in the court studios.

One such example is the second part of a thirty-volume Koran transcribed by Yakut el-Mustasimi in 1282/1283, which was refurbished in the mid-sixteenth century. Yakut, who established the canons that formed the basis of calligraphic styles for centuries to come, was born in Amasya and entered the services of the caliph of Baghdad, el-Mustasim (1242–1258), whose name he adopted as his honorific. Thought to have died in 1298 or 1299, he is reputed to have written 1001 Korans. Although the figure appears exaggerated, Yakut was prolific. A large number of his Korans are kept in the Topkapı Palace and other collections; an equal number of fraudulent imitations bear his name, which attests to his reputation and popularity.

The text of the 1283/1284 Koran of Yakut, written in mu-hakkak, was carefully cut out and pasted on new sheets and

the volume was rebound in gold-stamped leather covers with filigree doublures, following the style of the mid-sixteenth century. Each line of text was enclosed by a contour band, the field was painted gold and decorated with floral scrolls, and gold drawings with hatayi scrolls were applied to the margins of the folios.

The double serlevha (13) is the most elaborate section of the manuscript. The horizontal and vertical panels enclosing the text and the wide frame composed of reciprocal arches are beautifully designed and integrated into the composition. The artist was not only an expert painter but also a designer of illuminated folios.

The same meticulous care is found in the decoration of another Koran that was transcribed in nesih by Abdullah Sayrafi, a master from Tabriz thought to have written some three dozen Korans. This calligrapher, who died in 1342, had studied with Yakut and was renowned for his nesih script. The

12. Illuminated serlevha from a book of prayers transcribed by Hasan b. Ahmed Karahisari in 1566/1567 and dedicated to Sultan Selim II (İstanbul, Topkapı Sarayı Müzesi, E.H. 1077, fols. 2b–3a)

13. Illuminated serlevha from a Koran transcribed by Yakut el-Mustasimi in 1282/1283 and illuminated mid-sixteenth century (İstanbul, Topkapı Sarayı Müzesi, E.H. 227, fols. 1b−2a)

text of Sayrafi's Koran was cut out and pasted onto new sheets. Each line was enclosed by a contour band and the field decorated with floral scrolls; chapter headings and double folios with the text at the beginning and end were illuminated. Illuminated folios with additional Koranic verses were appended to the front and back.

A notation on the flyleaf in the front of the book provides a most unusual documentation on the artists who refurbished the volume and the person who commissioned the decoration. It states that the Koran transcribed by Abdullah Sayrafi in 1344/1345 was illuminated by Kara Mehmed Çelebi in 1554/1555 and bound by Mehmed Çelebi in 1555/1556; the appended folios, chapter headings, and verse indicators in the margins were written by Hasan ''veled-i (son of) Ahmed el-Karahisari'' in 1556/1557; and the volume, prepared for the treasury of Rüstem Paşa, was delivered by Hüseyin Çelebi, the head of his household.

The patron of the work, Rüstem Paşa, served as Süley-

man's grand vezir twice (1544-1553 and 1555-1561) and was married to the sultan's daughter, Mihrimah. Both Rüstem and Mihrimah were enthusiastic patrons of the arts, particularly of architecture, commissioning Sinan to build for them several complexes. Blamed for the execution of Şehzade Mustafa, Rüstem was expelled in 1553 but reinstated two years later. He appears to have commissioned the decoration of Sayrafi's Koran immediately after his reappointment and employed the best artists of the court to celebrate his return to favor and to demonstrate his restored power.

The illuminations of the appended folios as well as those of opening and closing verses reveal great finesse. The concluding pair of text folios (14) are enclosed by a wide blue and gold frame with hatayi scrolls filling its reciprocal arches. Chapter headings are written in gold sülüs and placed against a blue ground densely covered with gold scrolls bearing polychrome florals or gold rumis. The colophon, which appears on the lower left, follows the same format. This portion, writ-

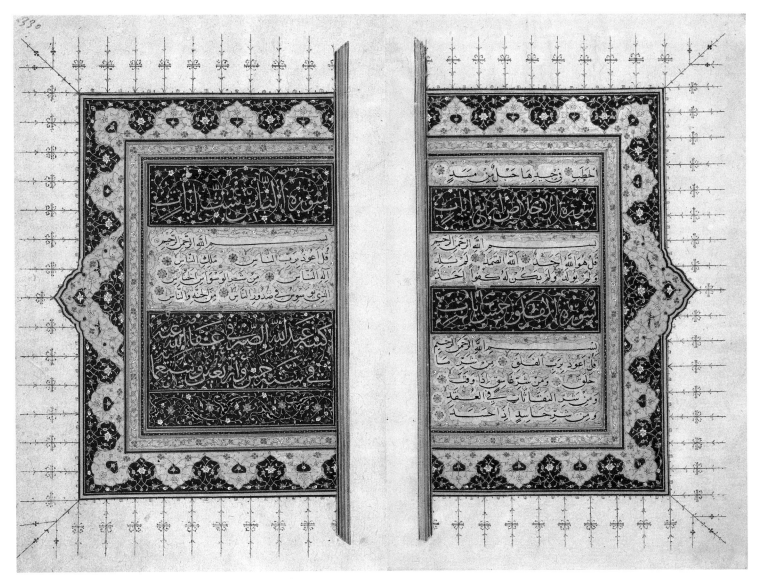

14. Two folios from a Koran transcribed by Abdullah Sayrafi in 1344/1345 and illuminated by Kara Memi in 1554/1555 (İstanbul, Topkapı Sarayı Müzesi, E.H. 49, fols. 329b–330a)

ten in a larger script (rikaa) must have been added by Hasan, the student and adopted son of Ahmed Karahisari (see **12**), who was also responsible for the chapter headings. The illuminations, made by Kara Memi, called Kara Mehmed Çelebi in the notation, harmonize with Hasan's calligraphy and enrich the folios.

Kara Memi, whose name is recorded in one other manuscript, the *Divan-ı Muhibbi* dated February/March 1566 (see **26**), is also listed in the payroll registers. In 1545 he was identified as Mehmed-i Siyah, Memi being a shortened version of Mehmed and Siyah (black) another way of defining Kara (dark); two apprentices, Mustafa b. Yusuf and Hamza of Austria, were named also. In 1557–1558 he was called nakkaşbaşı and had an apprentice by the name of Nebi. Since his name does not appear in the register drawn between July and October 1566, the artist's last work may have been the *Divan-ı Muhibbi*. He appears as Kara Mehmed in a document related to the palace expenses accrued between 1552/1553

and 1555/1556. Here he is listed as having illuminated a Koran for the Süleymaniye Mosque, receiving the highest wage.[33] The artist was also discussed in Mustafa Ali's *Menakıb-ı Hünerveran* (Legends of the talented), a biography of the artists. Mustafa Ali called him a "müzehhib," the greatest student of Şahkulu, and the master of Süleyman's nakkaşhane. With the exception of Mustafa Ali's brief account and the listings in the documents, not much is known about his life. We do not know where he came from and when he started his apprenticeship with Şahkulu. Kara Memi is, nevertheless, among the very few artists of the nakkaşhane whose style can be identified by existing works.

Analysis of his signed and dated works indicates that Kara Memi was indeed the master of Süleyman's nakkaşhane. His naturalistic themes appear in manuscripts produced between the 1540s and 1560s, and no doubt his apprentices and students continued the tradition. If one artist can be credited with the most significant contribution to Ottoman decorative arts, then it is Kara Memi, whose impact is still visible today.

The binding of Sayrafi's Koran made by Mehmed Çelebi, who was listed as Mehmed b. Ahmed in the payroll registers, is unfortunately lost, the manuscript having been rebound in recent times. This would have been the only identifiable work of the master, who entered the society of the bookbinders before 1526 and became its chief between 1545 and 1566. As the head of the mücellidan, Mehmed must have produced most of the bindings found on imperial manuscripts in addition to those on the refurbished volumes.[34]

It was during the reign of Süleyman that the classical Ottoman type of bookbinding evolved. Ottoman bindings were not limited to examples with stamped and gilded covers, frequently with filigree doublures, but also included lacquered and embroidered examples as well as those executed in precious materials, such as in jade and gold, encrusted with gems. The decorative theme identified with bookbindings of the age is the saz scroll with a profusion of hatayi blossoms and buds accompanied by feathery leaves, at times enhanced by rumis and cloud bands. This style, which appeared on bookbindings produced around 1550, incorporated the earlier Ottoman traditions as well as those identified with the late-fifteenth-century school of Herat.

The evolution of the classical style of Ottoman bookbinding

15. Stamped and gilded leather binding from a Tefsir transcribed in 1519
(İstanbul, Topkapı Sarayı Müzesi, A. 21)

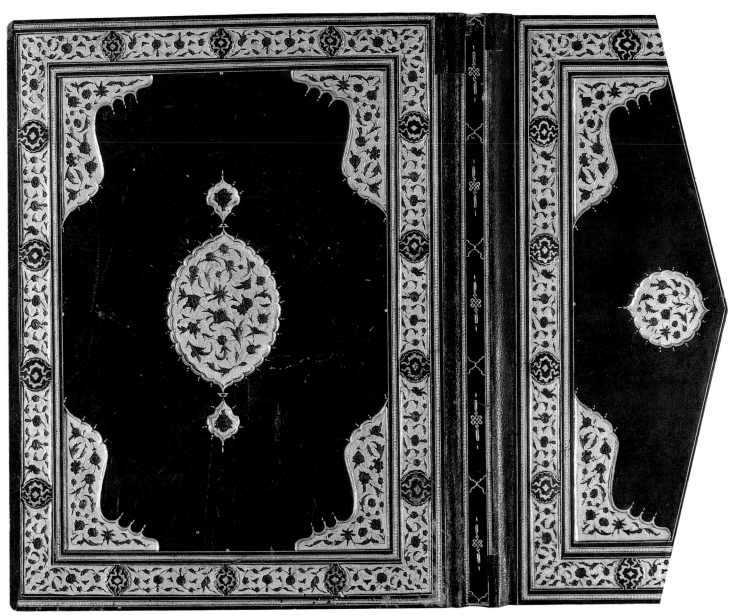

16. Stamped and gilded leather binding from a Koran transcribed by Argun Kamili in 1306/1307 and bound mid-sixteenth century (İstanbul, Topkapı Sarayı Müzesi, E.H. 222)

is observed on the covers of a Persian interpretation of the Koran, the *Tefsir-i Mevahıb-ı Aliye*.[35] The exterior (15), covered with light-brown leather, has an overall design with rumi and hatayi scrolls executed in relief and enclosed by a border filled with raised floral motifs. The background of the field is stamped with gold; the rumi scroll is reserved in the natural tone of the leather, whereas the hatayi scroll is rendered in silver with touches of off-white pigment applied to the blossoms. Gold is also used as background of the border with some of the floral motifs rendered in reserve. The gold-stamped ground reveals an effect not unlike ring matting found in metalwork, due to the texture of the leather. The combination of these two types of scrolls dates back to the bookbindings and other works of art made in Timurid Herat.

The interior of the binding is also Herat-inspired, with intersecting filigree medallions that have contrasting grounds. In the center is an eight-lobed medallion from which circles and polygons evolve; these units are painted in gold, green, and dark and light blue and overlaid with brown leather rumis and hatayis. The wide border with a dark blue ground has filigree leather floral scrolls and cloud bands, the latter painted gold.

Saz scrolls characteristic of classical Ottoman bookbindings appear on a copy of the Koran transcribed by Argun Kamili in 1306/1307 and refurbished in Süleyman's court around 1550. The calligrapher, a famous student of Yakut known for his muhakkak and sülüs scripts, was born to Turkish and Arab parents in eastern Iraq and lived in Baghdad until his death in 1343. The text of his Koran was cut out and pasted onto new sheets; illuminations were added to the serlevha, chapter headings, and the field surrounding the text; then the work was rebound.

The exterior of the bookbinding (16), covered with dark brown leather, has a central medallion with axial pendants,

17. Stamped and gilded leather binding from a small Koran, mid-sixteenth century (İstanbul, Topkapı Sarayı Müzesi, E.H. 522)

he died in 1543.[36] Both the exterior and interior covers are lacquered—painted on leather over pasteboard cores and finished with a heavy coating of lacquer. The designs used are both highly traditional and innovative, indicating not only the coexistence of diverse modes but also the virtuosity of the

18a. Lacquered binding (exterior) from a Hadis transcribed by Abdülhayf Ali c. 1540 and dedicated to Şehzade Mehmed (İstanbul, Topkapı Sarayı Müzesi, E.H. 2851)

corner quadrants, and a border filled with saz scrolls, similar to that of Karahisari's album of calligraphy dated 1552/1553. The border is further accented by a series of ovals in relief and decorated with cloud bands, both stamped with gold.

The doublures, covered with reddish-brown leather, are composed of a central medallion with superimposed hatayi and rumi scrolls executed in leather filigree placed on a blue ground. The combination of the newly devised saz scrolls on the exterior and the traditional hatayis and rumis on the interior is frequently employed on bookbindings made in the mid-sixteenth century.

Saz scrolls were employed on a great number of bindings, including one made for a tiny volume of the Koran (5.7 by 5 centimeters, or about 2 inches square). Known as sancak Korans, these manuscripts, protected by metal, leather, or fabric-covered boxes, were hung on banners or standards used during campaigns. Written in gubari enclosed by circular frames, the work has a reddish-brown leather cover. The exterior (17) is decorated with saz scrolls that are painted black and stand in relief against the recessed gold-stamped ground. The scroll is conceived as a fragment of a larger design, framed by a thin gold braid that intersects the motifs, showing a deviation from the classical format, with self-contained compositions filling the central medallions and corner quadrants. The doublures are simply designed with a series of gold dots framed by a braid.

An entirely different technique and decorative vocabulary are employed on a volume containing the Persian translation of the forty Hadis. Made for Şehzade Mehmed, the work must have been completed and presented to the prince before

painter who excelled in both styles (**18a**).

The exterior follows the traditional format with a central medallion and corner quadrants. The field is painted black and embellished with gold hatayi scrolls; the color scheme is reversed in the central medallion and corner quadrants, which have black cloud bands placed against a gold ground.

The decorative elements, delicate execution, alternating use of black and gold, and overall restraint can be traced to late-fifteenth-century examples made in Herat.

The interior, in contrast, is revolutionary, bursting with life and color. The design is painted sideways and shows an incredible array of naturalistic blossoms and trees spring-

Interior, **18a**

59

18b. Illuminated serlevha from a Hadis transcribed by Abdülhayf Ali c. 1540 and dedicated to Şehzade Mehmed (İstanbul, Topkapı Sarayı Müzesi, E.H. 2851, fols. 1b–2a)

ing from clusters of leaves. The flowers, painted in polychrome pigments on a gold ground, include tulips, carnations, hyacinths, violets, irises, and narcissi amid rosebushes and blossoming fruit trees. The panels are encircled by thin black bands and framed by red borders embellished with gold hatayi scrolls.

The theme of a paradise garden filled with eternally blooming spring flowers, commemorating the exuberance, beauty, and perpetuity of nature, makes its first datable appearance in this work. The love of flowers and gardens and the delight in being surrounded by representations of naturalistic flora, perhaps the most distinct features of Ottoman culture, are expertly demonstrated on the doublures of this bookbinding.

The text, written in tevkii and talik, was executed in the kaatı technique by a calligrapher named Abdülhayf Ali. This laborious technique is a type of découpage in which the let-

ters are cut from colored papers and pasted on folios with contrasting hues. Ali used cream, white, and blue papers for his text, and dark beige and varying tones of pinks for the folios, some of which are gold-speckled and marbled. As seen in the illuminated serlevha (18b), a line of tevkii alternates with four lines of talik, some of which are written diagonally, leaving triangular units in the corners for the illuminator. Kara Memi, who is thought to have painted the covers, must also have worked on the illuminations of the text.

The illuminations employ hatayi scrolls, rumis, and sprays of blossoms, the most elaborate of which appear in the finials around the headings. Here we see Kara Memi's characteristic tulips, carnations, hyacinths, roses, and violets rendered in red and interspersed with blue hatayis.

A similar combination employing a different technique is found on the covers of an undated Koran made in the second

60

half of the sixteenth century. The exterior, covered with black sharkskin, is embroidered with gold and blue with certain elements defined in black (19). The central medallion with pendants and the corner quadrants have tulips, hyacinths, and five-petaled blossoms rendered in blue on a gold ground; the field and the wide border show scrolls bearing hatayis, tulips, and hyacinths, embroidered in gold and blue on the black leather ground. The spine, devoid of decoration, appears to have been restored. The fore-edge flap, however, is original and displays a series of lozenges composed of serrated leaves with hatayi blossoms placed in the interstices. The doublures, covered with reddish-brown leather, are decorated with gold-stamped medallions and spandrels containing saz scrolls, identical to the exterior covers of Karahisari's 1552/1553 album.

The use of sharkskin on the exterior of the binding is unusual and deserves comment. This fine-grained and highly durable leather was made from the skins of sharks and rays; it was first used in eastern Asia and then spread to the Ottoman world, whence it was transmitted to Europe. An item of luxury, it was frequently dyed green and applied to the handles of imperial swords (to provide a good grip) and covered containers of precious objects. Known as shagreen in English, the word was applied both to real sharkskin and to its imitations in which other skins were soaked and wrapped tightly with seeds to simulate the granular texture found in the original. The word itself appears to be of Turkish origin, deriving from *sağrı*, which referred to the underpart of a horse from which a small piece of skin was taken to make the imitation sharkskin; the French pronounced it ''*chagrin*'' and the English changed it to "shagreen," obviously influenced by its green color.

Only a few examples of sixteenth-century Ottoman sharkskin have come to light. These include the bookbinding described above, a large rectangular box (see **140**), and a tankard. Since all three display the same technique of decoration and choice of motifs, they must have been contemporary and produced in one workshop. Further research in the storage rooms of imperial collections may reveal other examples and prove that the material was more widely used in the court than previously assumed.

A second noteworthy aspect of this bookbinding is the technique of its decoration. Embroidery was popularly used to embellish such leather objects as boots, slippers, shoes, containers, quivers, and bow cases. Items for the court were made with colored silk and gold metallic threads, sometimes wrapped around silk cores to give them additional strength. Stitches resemble those employed on linen, velvet, and satin. Other sixteenth-century examples of embroidered leather bookbindings are not known to have survived; there exists, however, a unique embroidered satin bookbinding made for Mustafa Ali's *Nusretname* (Book of victories), which was completed in 1584.[37]

Another group of bookbindings has been preserved in relatively large number, though few are datable and their chronology is yet to be determined. Fashioned in jade and encrusted with gold and gems, they reflect the taste for precious and luxurious items that is observed in all imperial collections, whether Ottoman, Safavid, Romanov, or Habsburg. Produced by the court goldsmiths and jewelers, these bookbindings were made almost exclusively for Korans,[38] the only known exception being the one found on the *Divan-ı Muradi* made in 1588 by Mehmed, the head of the society of goldsmiths.[39] Although the payroll registers from the reign of Süleyman list a large number of goldsmiths, gemstone cutters, and inlayers,[40] only Mehmed is known to have signed and dated a few of his pieces.

One of the earliest and technically most interesting of all the gold bindings in the Hazine of the Topkapı Palace has been removed from its original Koran (**20**). The exterior con-

19. Embroidered sharkskin binding from a Koran, second half sixteenth century (İstanbul Üniversite Kütüphanesi, A. 6570)

61

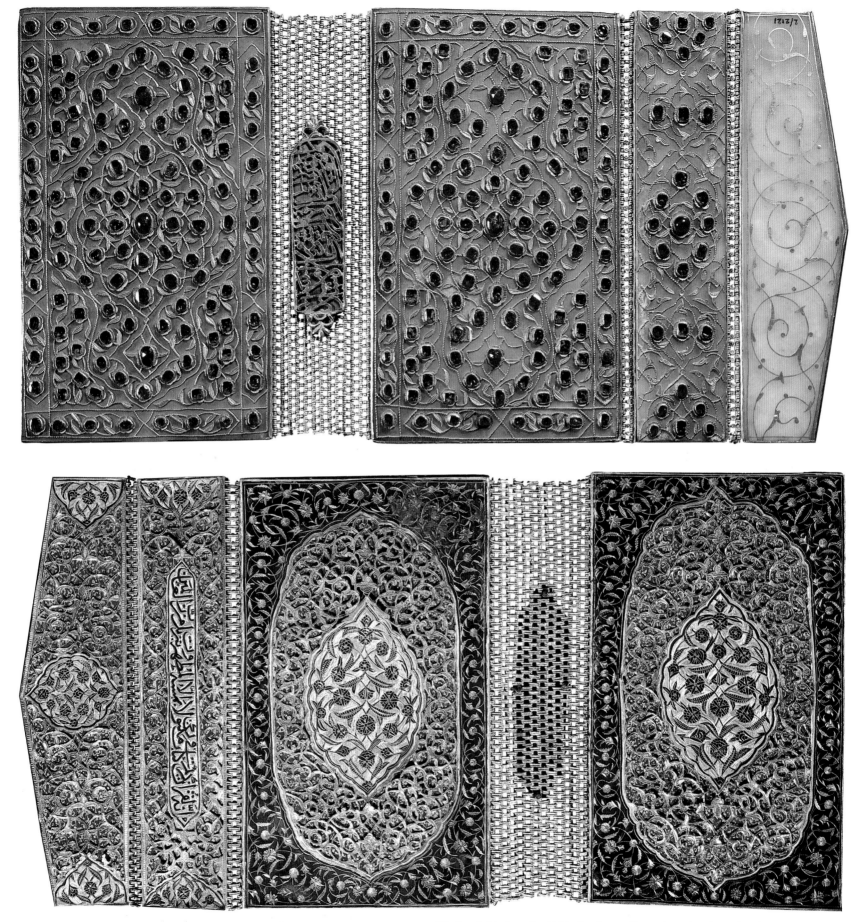

20. Jeweled jade and gold binding from a Koran (exterior above, interior below), second half sixteenth century (İstanbul, Topkapı Sarayı Müzesi, 2/2121)

tains pale-green jade plaques inlaid with twisted gold wires that define the central medallion with pendants, the corner quadrants, and the borders. These areas as well as the field are filled by similarly constructed scrolls that bear leaves and blossoms with gem-encrusted centers: emeralds in the spandrels and rubies in the other units. The fore-edge flap, with a large central medallion flanked by two pairs of smaller ones, has emeralds applied to the central blossoms of the four lateral panels and rubies in the remaining ones. The flexible spine, constructed of a series of gold chains, bears a cartouche with a filigree inscription placed on a red-enameled ground; the cartouche, which appears to have been added in the eighteenth century, states that the work is the vakıf of Eyüb Paşa, an otherwise unidentified person. The flap has a simple gold-inlaid rumi scroll. Gold chains fasten all four components of the binding, enabling the covers to move freely.

The inlay technique on the jade panels was employed on a number of other bindings: twisted gold wire was embedded into grooves carved into the jade, as were the leaves and six-petaled blossoms, both of which have chased details; the centers of the blossoms contain raised ring collars, which hold the gems above the surface and create a relief effect. The gems vary in size, with the largest ones applied to the centers of the units; they are not faceted, but cabochon-cut.

The interior, constructed of gold, is the most complex portion of the binding and reveals several different techniques. The front and back covers have central oval plaques decorated with saz scrolls, inlaid with niello, and placed on a minutely hatched ground. Enclosing each plaque is a second oval with filigree rumi scrolls lined with blue paper embellished with gold florals. The remaining portion of the covers has saz scrolls on a background inlaid with niello. Both the nielloed and plain gold motifs are enhanced by additional chasing. The flap displays similar elements with medallions bearing nielloed saz scrolls placed on a filigree rumi field lined with blue paper. The fore-edge flap has a gold cartouche with an inscription inlaid with niello containing the popular verse from the Koran that pertains to the divine revelation of the holy book: "Certainly it is an honored Koran, in a book that is protected, none shall touch it save the purified, [it is] a revelation from the Lord of the worlds."

It has been suggested that the exterior and interior portions of the covers were made by different artists and that the interior is one of the earliest examples attributed to Mehmed, the chief goldsmith. Mehmed, who is listed as Mehmed Bosna in the 1596 and 1605 payroll registers,[41] appears to have originated from Bosnia and entered the society of goldsmiths around 1570. Attributed to him are such masterpieces as the imperial gold and jade canteen (see 54), the crown presented to Stephen Bocskay in 1605 by Ahmed I (now in the Treasury of Vienna), and the decorative elements added to several sacred swords associated with the Prophet Muhammed. His style combines delicately chased and repoussé rumi and saz

scrolls, filigree, and niello inlay, displaying a virtuosity seldom attempted even by master goldsmiths.

The Topkapı Palace owns a number of similar jade and gold Koran bindings encrusted with gems, some including filigree panels and nielloed sections.[42] Several have been removed from the manuscripts and those that are intact are not dated. An exception is a hexagonal sancak Koran with a jade binding (21), its colophon stating that it was transcribed in 1570/1571 by Mehmed Tahir. The technique and style of decoration of its binding are identical to the one described above. The covers are made of jade plaques inlaid with gold and set with emeralds and rubies; gold chains are used on the spine and the binding closes like a box, held by a clasp that has three blossoms. Emeralds appear in the center of the covers, in two of the small blossoms in the surrounding scroll, and in the outer buds of the clasp. The remaining flowers are set with rubies.

The interior, covered with reddish-brown leather, has a large medallion enclosing a gold-stamped scroll. The underside of the clasp is gold and chased with a central cypress tree flanked by tulips and carnations. The text, transcribed in gubari, has an illuminated serlevha, chapter headings, and verse stops. The name of the same calligrapher appears in a calligraphic sample incorporated into the famous album compiled for Murad III. This folio, written in talik in 1553/1554, is the only other known example signed by Mehmed Tahir.[43]

The bookbinders, calligraphers, and illuminators of the court also produced other types of religious manuscripts, including texts devoted to the description of pilgrimage routes and sites that served as illustrated guides to the holy cities. The earliest in the series is the *Futuh el-Harameyn* of Muhyi Lari (died 1526), who wrote the guide in Persian verse and dedicated it in 1506 to the sultan of Gujerat, Muzaffer b. Mahmud (1511–1526), who in turn is thought to have presented it to the Safavid ruler, Ismail.

The first illustrated version of this text was produced in Süleyman's court around 1540 and contains thirteen topographic scenes, beginning with the representation of the Mescid-i Haram (Sacred Mosque) enclosing the Kaaba in Mecca (22). On the lower right is the entrance gate to the compound leading into a large courtyard surrounded by two rows of colonnades with oil lamps hanging between the columns. Four minarets appear at the corners of the courtyard, which is filled with several small structures and minbars; in the center is the Kaaba, enclosed by a circular arcade.

The other paintings in the text depict the sites around Mecca, the tomb of the Prophet and the Mescid-i Nebi (Mosque of the Prophet) in Medina, the plain of Arafat, and other areas visited by the pilgrims. The scenes, shown both in bird's-eye view and in elevation, accurately depict the sites and the buildings, their style recalling the topographic paintings of Nasuh, which must have inspired the painter. The artist not only followed the text, but appears to have used his

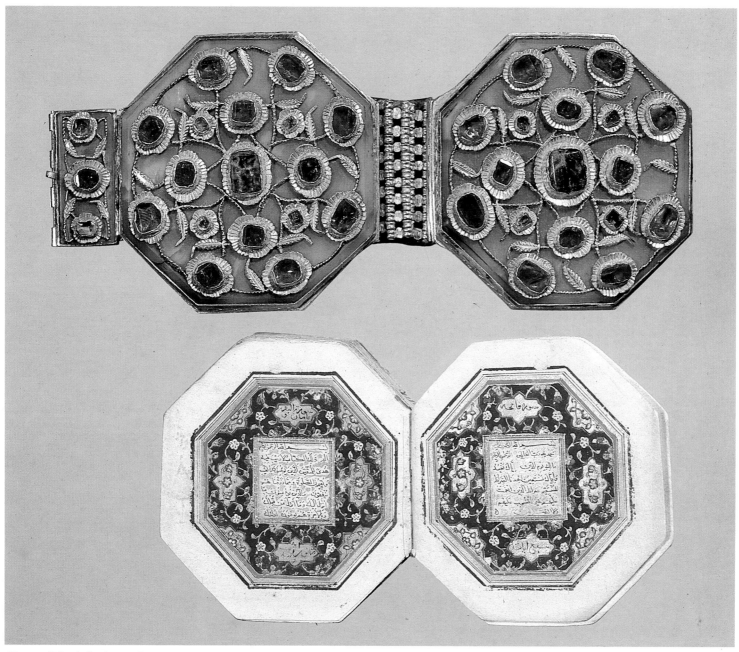

21. Jeweled jade binding and Koran transcribed by Mehmed Tahir in 1570/
1571 (İstanbul, Topkapı Sarayı Müzesi, 2/2896)

personal experience in representing these regions. He was an
expert draftsman and painter, executing architectural details
with care and using brilliant colors to enliven the scenes. The
paintings in the *Futuh el-Harameyn* were repeated in a number of contemporary and later examples.[44] Illustrated copies
of this and similar texts were produced into the nineteenth
century, continuing to be in demand both for their literary
and their practical values.

The same genre of painting is found on a pilgrimage scroll
made in honor of Şehzade Mehmed. When the prince died in
1543, Süleyman asked Hacı Piri b. Seyyid Ahmed to perform

the pilgrimage in his son's memory. This gentleman under-
took the pious task and prepared the scroll known as *Hac
Vekaletnamesi*, which was transcribed in 1544/1545 by Ebu
Fadl Sincari and signed by several witnesses.

The document contains fifteen topographic scenes: they
describe the Mescid-i Haram in Mecca and the sites in the
vicinity of the city visited by pilgrims; depict the mountains,
rivers, fountains, wells, mosques, and tombs around the
countryside; show the Mescid-i Nebi in Medina and the important places around that city; and conclude with the Aksa
Mosque and the Dome of the Rock in Jerusalem. Each scene

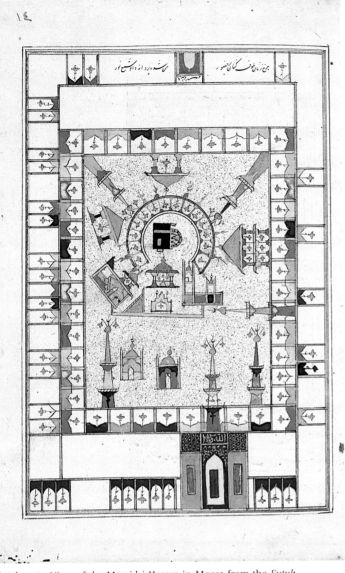

22 (above). View of the Mescid-i Haram in Mecca from the *Futuh el-Harameyn* of Muhyi Lari, c. 1540 (İstanbul, Topkapı Sarayı Müzesi, R. 917, fol. 14a)

23 (right). View of the Aksa Mosque and the Dome of the Rock in Jerusalem from a pilgrimage scroll prepared in 1544/1545 for Şehzade Mehmed (İstanbul, Topkapı Sarayı Müzesi, H. 1812)

is enclosed by bands of sülüs inscriptions containing Koranic verses. The entire scroll reads like a filmstrip tracing the route taken during the pilgrimage, representing all the major monuments and identifying them with tiny notations.

The view of Jerusalem (23) depicts the Dome of the Rock in the center of a ten-sided courtyard with five entrance gates. The domed monument, decorated with rumi scrolls, rises over the famous rock, which has a lamp suspended over it. Two structures, identified as Mahkeme-i Davud (Court of David) and Mirac Kümbedi (Tomb of the Miraj, or Prophet Muhammed's Journey to Heaven), flank the monument,

while a third appears above. The platform around the courtyard contains four minarets placed in the corners; two domed mausoleums, known as İsa and Musa Kümbedi (Tombs of Jesus and Moses), appear at the foreground; a circular pond and an arched structure with scales, symbolizing justice, is placed in the background. The arcaded building with a minbar and mihrab on the very top represents the Aksa Mosque.

Although the paintings are rendered with great charm, their execution is not as refined as the scenes in other works describing the pilgrimage sites, such as the *Futuh el-Harameyn*. Where the scroll was made is a matter of speculation; it is possible that the entire work was produced in Mecca, since it bears the signatures of the guides to the Haram; it is also feasible that the scenes were sketched during the pilgrimage and finished when Hacı Piri returned to İstanbul.[45]

Literary Manuscripts

The majority of the illustrated manuscripts produced during the reign of Süleyman are devoted to literary subjects. These volumes—bound, transcribed, illuminated, and/or illustrated by the court artists—reveal diversified styles and include copies of both classical and Turkish texts and contemporary works. The majority are collections of poetry, which was particularly favored in the court and practiced by the sultan, members of his family, and high officials. The sultan's personal involvement with this art form no doubt stimulated the energetic production of literary manuscripts.

Interest in illustrated literary works had already been observed during the reign of Mehmed II, beginning in Edirne in the 1450s. Two of the earliest manuscripts, the *Dilsizname* (Book of the mute) of Badi ed-Din et-Tebrizi (dated 1455/ 1456)[46] and the *Külliyat-ı Katibi* (c. 1460–1480),[47] show the emergence of a local school of painting that incorporated Ottoman figure types with the stylistic features found in the Akkoyunlu manuscripts made in Shiraz. The same tradition continued in İstanbul under the patronage of Bayezid II, producing between 1490 and 1510 over a dozen volumes that included the *Kelile ve Dimne, Hamse-i Dihlevi*, and several copies of the *Hüsrev ve Şirin* composed by both Hatifi and Şeyhi, and the *İskendername* (Book of İskender, or Alexander the Great) of Uzun Firdevsi and Ahmedi.[48]

A number of paintings in these volumes incorporate unusual architectural settings and employ panoramic vistas, suggesting that the artists were not only inspired by the buildings in the capital but also by European traditions of representation. These features are particularly noticeable in the 1498 *Hamse-i Dihlevi*[49] and the 1499 copy of Hatifi's *Timurname* (Book of Timur).[50]

The development of the local style of painting was overshadowed by the influx of artists from Herat and Tabriz, who arrived in the nakkaşhane in 1514 as a result of the eastern campaigns of Selim I and were immediately put to work. The paintings in two manuscripts produced during the reign of Selim I are representative of the emergence of a new tradition and reflect the style of Timurid Herat: the *Mantık et-Tayr* (Language of the birds) of Attar[51] and the *Yusuf ve Züleyha* of Hamdi,[52] both dated 1515. The latter, the earliest illustrated copy of Hamdi's work, contains an interesting colophon that states that one person was responsible for transcribing, illustrating, collating, and binding the manuscript; although proud of his many talents, the artist has not given his name.

The illustrations of the manuscripts dated between the 1520s and 1540s are highly eclectic, their styles as varied as the backgrounds of the men employed in the nakkaşhane. Some were made by artists trained in the Timurid and Akkoyunlu traditions of Herat and Tabriz; others were painted by those who followed the school of İstanbul; and a number show the combined efforts of painters practicing different

24. Folio from the *Divan-ı Muhibbi* written by Sultan Süleyman, mid-sixteenth century (İstanbul, Topkapı Sarayı Müzesi, H. 1132, fol. 94a)

styles. Some of the manuscripts produced in İstanbul are indistinguishable from those made in Herat and Tabriz, with the same tradition followed in all three courts. The artists in the nakkaşhane also had at their disposal a vast repertoire of fifteenth- and early sixteenth-century manuscripts produced in Herat, Tabriz, Baghdad, and Cairo that had been incorporated into the palace libraries.

During the political turbulence caused by the rise of the Safavids, several rulers had sought the protection of the Ottomans and came to İstanbul with their retinues and treasures, which included artists and valuable manuscripts. One of them was the last Akkoyunlu sultan, Alvand, who fled to the Ottoman court when his capital, Tabriz, fell to the Safavids in 1501. Another was the last Timurid sultan, Bedi üz-Zaman, who had escaped to Tabriz when his capital, Herat, was overrun by the Uzbeks in 1507, but was held captive by the Safavids when they conquered that city in 1510. Freed by Selim I and invited to join the İstanbul court, Bedi üz-Zaman arrived in 1514 with his artists and treasury.[53]

Other artists and libraries were taken as booty and brought to İstanbul during Selim I's campaigns in Iran, Syria, and Egypt. Although his glorious victories led to exaggerated figures, there is no doubt that a substantial group of new painters joined the nakkaşhane and important works came to the palace libraries as a result of his campaigns. The earliest illustrated version of the Turkish translation of Firdausi's *Şahname* (Book of kings), made in 1511 in Cairo for the last Mamluk sultan Kansu el-Gavri, was part of his booty.[54]

Artists and books continued to arrive at the court, both voluntarily and involuntarily. Süleyman's campaigns to Iraq, Iran, and Hungary resulted in similar enrichment of the nak-kaşhane and palace collections, the most notable example being the library of Matthias Corvinus taken to İstanbul after the conquest of Budapest in 1526.[55] The conglomeration of such diverse traditions resulted in a burst of creativity that was felt in all the arts, and its most profound impact was upon the production of literary manuscripts.

The nakkaşhane produced exquisite volumes, copying the works of such famous classical poets as Nevai, Nizami, Arifi, Hafiz, Sadi, Jami, and Firdausi, as well as those composed by contemporary or near-contemporary writers, such as Fuzuli, Ulvi, Hamdi, Musa Abdi, and Fethullah Arif, known as Arifi. The most carefully executed volumes were copies of the *Di-van-ı Muhibbi*, the collected poems of Süleyman composed both in Persian and Turkish. Süleyman's odes (*gazels*) reveal a rare combination of lyricism and mysticism as well as humility and sincerity, as exemplified by his most frequently quoted verses:

Halk içinde muteber bir nesne yok devlet gibi
Olmaya devlet cihanda bir nefes sıhhat gibi.
Saltanat dedikleri ancak cihan kavgasıdır;
Olmaya baht-ü saadet, dünyada vahdet gibi.

The people think of wealth and power as the greatest fate,
But in this world a spell of good health is the best state.
What men call sovereignty is worldly strife and constant war;
Worship of God is the highest throne, the happiest estate.[56]

There has yet to be a critical study of the sultan's poetry.

Several copies of Süleyman's poems were produced by court artists, and there is also a volume written in his own hand (24). It shows a rapid and efficient execution of talik, with corrections, insertions, and deletions added to the text, indicating that this was a draft version that he later gave to the copyists. Two of the most elaborate versions were transcribed by Mehmed Şerif, an artist from Tabriz who specialized in copying the poems of the sultans, including those written by Mehmed II, Bayezid II, and Selim I.[57]

One of Mehmed Şerif's transcriptions, dated 1565/1566, has a superb binding richly stamped with two tones of gold and decorated with saz scrolls and cloud bands. The text is written diagonally with illuminated triangular panels fitted into the upper and lower corners. Each folio is elaborately decorated with gold marginal drawings that represent naturalistic sprays of tulips, roses, carnations, narcissi, irises, and hyacinths in addition to date palms, cypresses, and blossoming fruit trees and bouquets of flowers in vases.

The headings for the two sections that contain the Turkish and Persian poems (25) have delicate marginal drawings with

25. Illuminated serlevha from the *Divan-ı Muhibbi* transcribed by Mehmed Şerif in 1565/1566 (İstanbul, Topkapı Sarayı Müzesi, R. 738 mük., fols. 39b–40a)

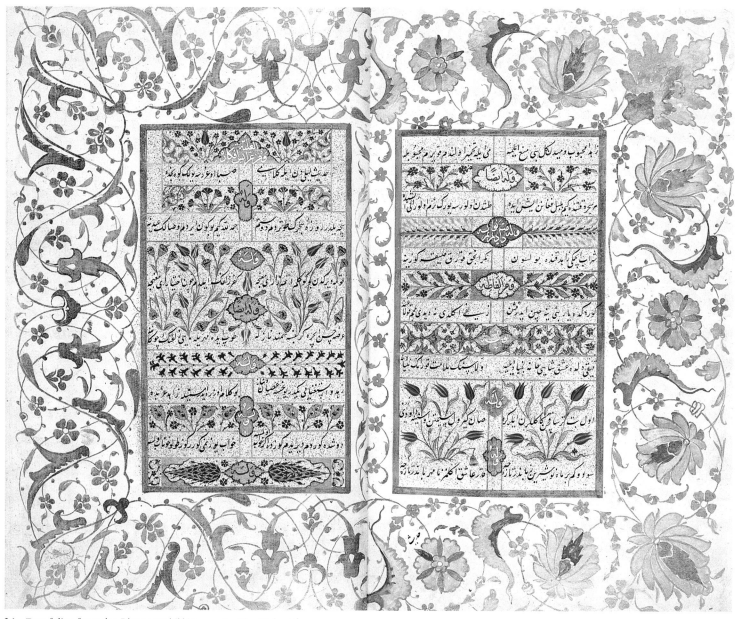

26. Two folios from the *Divan-ı Muhibbi* transcribed by Mehmed Şerif and illuminated by Kara Memi in 1566 (İstanbul Üniversite Kütüphanesi, T. 5467, fols. 359b–360a)

large hatayi blossoms and fan-shaped leaves (recalling those of the plane tree), superimposed with additional floral elements. The drawings, rendered in gold, are enhanced by soft blue and green tints. This volume appears to have been unfinished and contains several empty folios. The last three odes are in the sultan's hand; he must have composed these shortly before his death and had them appended to the volume.

A second copy of the *Divan-ı Muhibbi*, transcribed by Mehmed Şerif in February/March 1566, was illuminated by Kara Memi. This work, the most spectacular copy of the sultan's poems, bears a different layout and decorative repertoire. The text is written horizontally with the lines separated by illuminated panels. Kara Memi's exquisite designs appear on each folio, from the first to the last, and show a great diversity of themes. The volume is extremely important for establishing not only the artist's style, but also for identifying the full range of the artistic vocabulary of the age. It is an encyclopedia, combining every conceivable feature associated with the traditional mode, saz style, and naturalistic genre. The designs reveal an incredible finesse and unmatched virtuosity both in their harmonious composition and execution. They must have awed all illuminators who sought inspiration from the volume.

Kara Memi's skillful combination of stylized and naturalistic elements is visible throughout the manuscript. The double

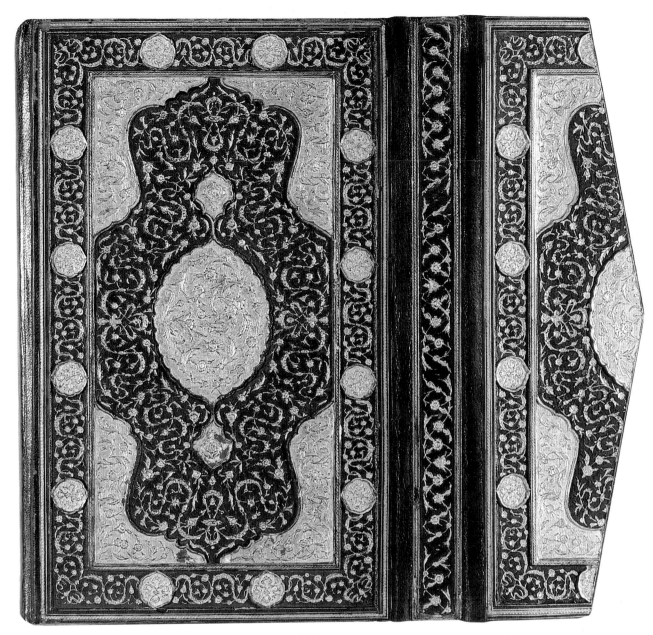

27. Stamped and gilded leather binding from the *Divan-ı Muhibbi*, c. 1560 (İstanbul, Türk ve İslam Eserleri Müzesi, 1962)

folios in the beginning of the volume have superimposed spiral scrolls bearing blue hatayis and gold rumis enclosing the dedication medallions, identical to the design used on the sultan's tuğras. The double serlevha that follows has the characteristic blue oval cartouches filled with blossoming fruit trees used on several contemporary manuscripts, including the 1545/1546 Koran of Karahisari (see **9a**), the 1558 *Süleymanname* of Arifi, and the album compiled around 1560 (see **49b**).

The verses on the ensuing folios (**26**) are either separated by illuminated panels or have floral sprays growing under them, almost engulfing the letters; the margins bear gold drawings tinted with pastel colors. The decoration overwhelms the text. The panels between the text of a typical folio may contain sprays of morning glories, narcissi, tulips, carnations, roses, and hyacinths as well as cypresses, blossoming fruit trees, ivy vines, and saz leaves overlaid with blossoms, while the margins might be decorated with rumi or hatayi scrolls, stylized designs, and çintemani patterns.

This volume, which was completed some six months before the death of the sultan, was the last work of Kara Memi. Since the artist is not mentioned in the payroll register of July–October 1566, he probably died shortly after finishing the decoration of his patron's poems.

The binding of the work, which has been removed, must have been just as outstanding as the illuminations. It would have been comparable to the cover of the 1565/1566 copy as well as the one on an undated version of the same text, the latter being among the masterpieces of Ottoman bookbinding. The exterior (**27**), covered with black leather, has a gold-stamped central medallion with pendants, corner quad-

28a. Sultan Selim I in his library (left) and riding with his court (right) from the *Divan-ı Selimi* transcribed by Şahsuvar Selimi c. 1520 (İstanbul Üniversite Kütüphanesi, F. 1330, fols. 27b–28a)

28b. Two folios from the *Divan-ı Selimi* transcribed by Şahsuvar Selimi c. 1520 (İstanbul Üniversite Kütüphanesi, F. 1330, fols. 25b–26a)

rants, and small roundels accenting the frame. The field, as well as the frame, is decorated with gold hatayi scrolls and cloud bands placed on the black ground. The central medallion and quadrants have gold saz designs stamped onto the gold background; the same technique is used in the roundels of the frame, which contain gold cloud bands. The combination of gold and black and the use of two tones of gold create a sumptuous effect. The gold-ground areas are rendered in slight relief and decorated with large motifs, which produce a contrast with the recessed black-ground areas and their minute scrolls.

The interior, covered with reddish-brown leather, has a gold frame bearing a black hatayi scroll. The central medallion and corner quadrants have filigree rumi and hatayi scrolls lined with blue paper. The contrast of the boldness of the exterior with the delicacy of the interior is a characteristic of the imperial bookbindings produced for the sultan. The poems of Süleyman, transcribed and illuminated by the masters of the court, must also have been bound by the chief bookbinder, Mehmed b. Ahmed, who was the head of the society at that time.

Although the *Divan-ı Muhibbi* was reproduced a number of times during Süleyman's reign,[58] there is only a single version of the *Divan-ı Selimi*, the collected poems of his father, Selim. The manuscript, datable to the 1520s, was illustrated by two double-folio paintings.

The first pair (**28a**), conceived as two separate scenes, is united by a frame composed of overlapping motifs recalling fat rumis or cloud bands overlaid with floral scrolls. The left half represents Selim I, distinguished by his long mustache, seated in a pavilion and accompanied by two youths, one of whom holds a book. The chamber, its walls covered with hexagonal tiles, has three windows that open into a garden. Above the side windows are compartmented niches with bowls, jugs, and tankards bearing flowers; between the niches is a geometric panel that might represent a stained-glass window. To the right is either the entrance facade of the chamber or that of an adjacent structure with an attendant guarding it. The right half of the double folio represents Selim I riding in a landscape, with an attendant walking in front of his horse. Four additional riders appear behind the hills in the background.

The other pair of folios shows a hunting scene spread across both halves, once again united by a frame composed of cartouches bearing floral scrolls and rumis. The pages are almost mirror images of one another, with a rider in the foreground, a second in the center, and a pair of figures flanking the hills in the background. The figures use swords and bows and arrows to hunt such game as lions, leopards, mountain goats, gazelles, and hares.

The composition of both the interior and exterior scenes, the postures of the figures, and the decorative elements indicate that these paintings were made by the same artist who worked on the 1515 *Mantık et-Tayr*. Both works show the strong impact of Herat with their limited repertoire of subject matter—courtly entertainments and hunts—and highly decorative approach to illustration. Although stylistically the paintings are closely related to the school of Herat, certain features are purely Ottoman. These include vessels with tulips, roses, and other blossoms decorating the niches of the sultan's chamber; the çintemani-patterned robe on one of the riders accompanying the sultan; and figures with large voluminous turbans, delicately painted features, and long drooping black mustaches.

This decorative style, which made its appearance immediately after the conquest of Tabriz, dominated the literary manuscripts of the court until the 1550s. It is last seen in the 1558 *Süleymanname*, which contains the anonymous artist's only historical paintings. He was truly a nakkaş, a decorator in the broadest sense, who also worked on the pairs of small panels inserted into the text (**28b**). These represent facing, conversing angels, and in rare cases floral motifs or animals.

The *Divan-ı Selimi* was transcribed by a calligrapher named Şahsuvar, who has appended the word "Selimi" to his name, presumably in honor of his patron. This artist, who must have come to the court during the reign of Selim I, has not left other signed works. He not only copied the poems of his patron in the text blocks, but also placed select verses in the margins, writing them diagonally between the beautifully rendered gold drawings. The margins are thus an equally important part of the manuscript, combining text and decoration.

The hand of the same painter is found in the illustrations of a similarly ornate copy of the collected poems of Ali Şir Nevai, the famous statesman and poet of Herat, who wrote in Çağatay, the native tongue of the Timurids. Datable to the 1530s, the manuscript contains an exceptional binding executed by another master. Its stamped and gilded central medallion and spandrels are decorated with saz scrolls, while the lacquered field shows a symmetrical group of flying angels bearing bowls of fruits and long-necked wine bottles. These fantastic creatures with large swooping wings, headdresses made of leaves, and long fluttering ribbons tied to their torsos resemble the examples found in drawings attributed to Şahkulu and his followers. The saz style, applied both to the flora and to the creatures inhabiting an enchanted forest, is explicitly represented on this bookbinding.

The illustrations in the *Divan-ı Nevai* represent such courtly themes as hunts and princely entertainments, and are enclosed by gold marginal drawings. The scenes are highly decorative with a few participants placed against intricately painted settings. One of them (**29**) shows a pair of polo players galloping toward the ball in the center of the folio while figures, silhouetted against the gold sky, observe. The scene is divided into three horizontal planes by gently rolling hills that define the foreground, the middle ground, and the background; each plane is painted a different color and embellished with clusters of flowers or floating clouds. This formulaic division characterizes the compositions of the master, who places his active figures in the first two planes, reserving the last for the spectators and commentators. His forte appears to be the representation of hunters or polo players mounted on horses drawn in various positions.

Another manuscript in which the same style of painting appears is the *Guy ve Çevgan* (Polo ball and mallet) of Arifi, transcribed in 1539/1540 by Mehmed b. Gazanfer in kaatı talik. The work is a masterpiece of kaatı writing, its folios

29. Polo players from the *Divan-ı Nevai*, c. 1530–1540 (Istanbul, Topkapı Sarayı Müzesi, R. 804, fol. 89b)

embellished with gold-speckled margins, marbled papers, or stenciled designs.

The illuminated double serlevha (**30**) is remarkably well designed and executed. Above and below the almost square text panels of each half are large rectangular bands, the whole encircled by a wide frame composed of reciprocal arches filled with floral scrolls. The composition extends into the margins by a series of finials enhanced by cloud bands and hatayi scrolls. The boldness of the blue and gold that predominate in these units creates a contrast to the delicacy of the text panels. The text, rendered in alternating white and gold, is pasted on pink and beige grounds with rectangular panels inserted into the text. These panels, painted white and gold, have arched units, echoing both the color scheme of the text and the design of the frame.

Although most literary texts produced in the nakkaşhane combine the style of Herat with that of local origin, there are several works that are almost identical to those made in the former Timurid capital. One of the manuscripts displaying a pure Herati style is the *Divan-ı Jami*, datable to 1520. The work contains an unusual lacquered binding decorated with angels, and its stamped and gilded doublures show rumi and floral scrolls. The exterior has been badly damaged with only the flap retaining parts of the original painting.

Its illustrations have the same formulaic compositions discussed earlier; they depict either an enthroned prince entertained in a pavilion or a garden, or show such outdoor activities as hunting parties or polo games. The paintings merely adorn the text and display no innovation. Their significance lies in masterfully embellishing the surfaces and varying the placement and groupings of the figures, while adhering to the traditional mode of representation.

This concept of book decoration is clearly demonstrated in the double frontispiece (**31**), which represents a polo game on the left and the entertainment of a prince on the right, following the same composition and stylistic features observed in manuscripts produced during Herat in the 1480s and 1490s, particularly in copies of the poems of Nevai.[59] The decorative style of Timurid Herat was also influential in the Safavid capital, and several manuscripts produced in Tabriz in the 1510s and 1520s reveal a similar development.

A more typical style associated with Safavid Tabriz incorporated Akkoyunlu and Timurid elements and flourished in the first quarter of the sixteenth century. This early Safavid court style is also observed in contemporary manuscripts produced in the İstanbul nakkaşhane, obviously executed by artists practicing the same traditions. The most beautiful paintings of this group are found in a copy of Firdausi's *Şahname*, datable to 1520–1530. This exquisite manuscript, bound with a stamped and gilded cover with filigree doublures, contains two pairs of illuminated serlevhas for the introduction and the text and a dedicatory medallion, which unfortunately was left empty. Its double frontispiece shows a hunting scene on

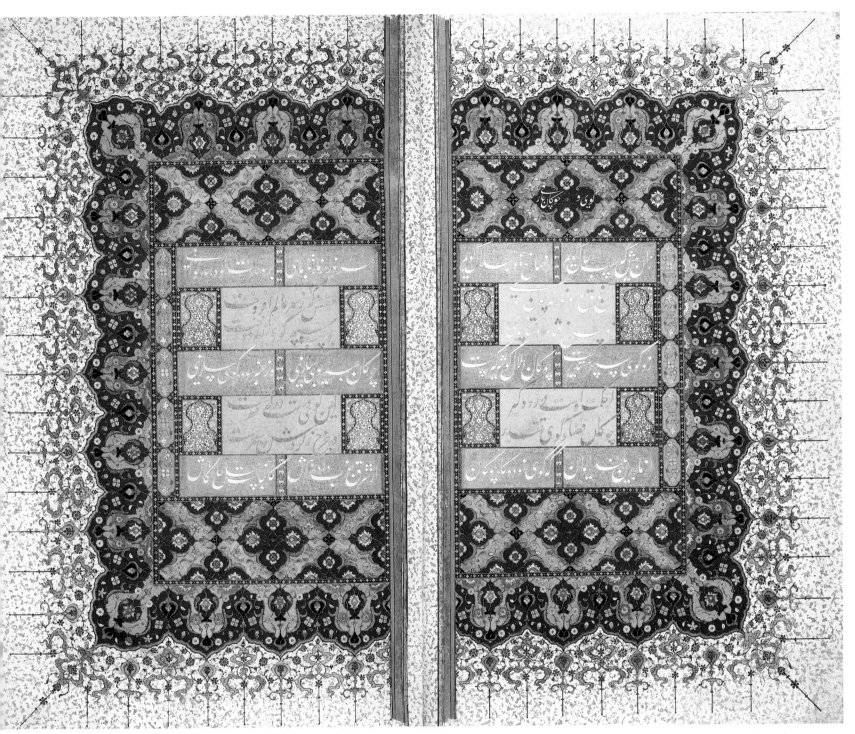

30. Illuminated serlevha from the *Guy ve Çevgan* of Arifi transcribed by
Mehmed b. Gazanfer in 1539/1540 (İstanbul, Topkapı Sarayı Müzesi, H. 845,
fols. 1b−2a)

31. Polo game (left) and entertainment of a prince (right) from the *Divan-ı Jami*, c. 1520 (İstanbul, Topkapı Sarayı Müzesi, H. 987, fols. 1b−2a)

the left and an enthroned prince on the right, following the traditional formula. It is intricately composed, with numerous figures actively participating in the two events.

The volume contains fifty-seven paintings, which reveal the hands of at least four artists. The majority appear to have been made by the painter who represented the court of Gayumars, the first ruler of Iran. This scene (32), framed by an arch composed of craggy rocks, shows Gayumars at the top with a lion crouched at his feet; attired in a robe decorated with five-petaled rosettes instead of his usual leopard-skin outfit, he sits on a bench covered with a tiger skin. Pairs of seated and standing figures line the edges of the scene; in the center are attendants with bowls of food and men training wild animals. The landscape is filled with clusters of leaves and flowers, blossoming trees, tufts of grass, and rocks; also included are several lions and sheep, and a solitary fox and gazelle. Some of the figures feed the animals or pet them. One raises a stick to a lion that cowers and holds its head

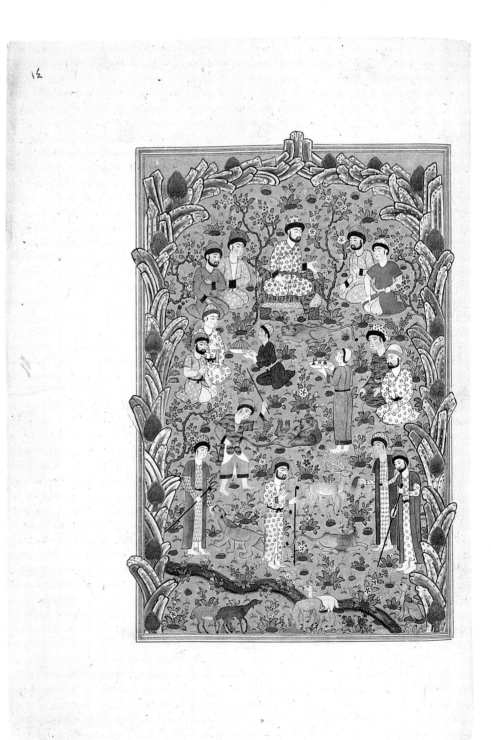

32. Court of Gayumars from the *Şahname* of Firdausi, c. 1520–1530 (İstanbul, Topkapı Sarayı Müzesi, H. 1499, fol. 14a)

only the direct importation of the styles of Herat and Tabriz, but also their absorption into the local traditions. One such localization was observed in the decorative style of the master of the *Divan-ı Selimi* and copies of the works of Nevai and Arifi. A second and far more indigenous style is found in the sixteen paintings of the *Hamse-i Nevai*, transcribed by Piri Ahmed b. İskender in 1530/1531. A work of imperial quality, it continues the interest established in the 1498 *Hamse-i Dihlevi* by incorporating local architectural settings into the scenes. Several figure types recall those found in the illustrations of the 1515 *Yusuf ve Züleyha* of Hamdi, indicating the persistent impact of Herat.

33a (left). Capture of Ferhad by Hüsrev from the *Hamse-i Nevai* transcribed in 1530/1531 (İstanbul, Topkapı Sarayı Müzesi, H. 802, fol. 99a)

33b (above). Lacquered binding from the *Hamse-i Nevai* transcribed in 1530/1531 (İstanbul, Topkapı Sarayı Müzesi, H. 802)

with its front paws, adding an unexpected but delightful, whimsical touch to the scene.

The depiction of the peaceable kingdom of Gayumars, who befriended and domesticated animals, frequently appears in sixteenth-century manuscripts. Its most spectacular version was made by a Tabrizi artist for a copy of the *Şahname* produced for Tahmasp between 1520 and 1540 and presented to Selim II in 1568.[60]

Manuscripts produced in the 1520s and 1530s show not

The illustrations of the *Hamse-i Nevai* appear to have been produced by two or possibly three artists. The majority belong to the hand of the painter who executed the scene representing the capture of Ferhad by Hüsrev's men (**33a**). Hüsrev, seated in his tent on the lower left, is being informed of the defeat of Ferhad by his messengers, who point to the men in the upper right carrying his fatally wounded rival. Another figure in the background enacts the cruel battle by throwing rocks and crushing the head of an enemy. The composition of the scene—with a group of tents in the foreground, the action taking place in the center, and a fortress placed in the background—became the prototype for the siege scenes frequently depicted in illustrated Ottoman histories. Other paintings in the work include domed and arcaded structures and pavilions with gardens or courtyards, attempting to re-create specific architectural settings.

The manuscript's lacquered cover (33b) is decorated with saz scrolls rendered in slight relief and painted red and gold on the black leather ground. The scrolls, which spring from the cluster of leaves placed in the center of the lower edge, represent the perfected form of this style. They bear compound hatayis and sprays of blossoms intermingled with undulating leaves that pierce or overlap the floral motifs, creating a highly dynamic composition. The blossoms and leaves are overlaid with additional flora or sprout other floral elements. This style of exuberant decoration was also employed by the potters and weavers, as seen in the tiles, brocaded silks, and pile rugs produced for the court. The indication of the point of origin of the scroll, a directional feature frequently employed on textiles and ceramics, is noteworthy.

The 1530/1531 *Hamse-i Nevai* establishes the terminus a quo for the fully developed saz scroll that had a tremendous impact on the other imperial arts. It also establishes the date in which an indigenous Ottoman painting style began to emerge, synthesizing the traditions of artists trained in Herat and Tabriz with those of local origin and creating a characteristic court style.

The ultimate development and refinement of this style is found in the three paintings of the *Ravzat el-Uşak* (Garden of lovers) of Arifi. The author was the *şahnameci* (official court biographer) and wrote for Süleyman the *Şahname-i Al-i Osman* (Book of kings of the Ottoman house), a five-volume history of the Ottoman sultans. Arifi, whose contribution to the genre of illustrated history will be discussed later, collaborated with a particular group of painters, one of whom was selected to illustrate his only literary work.

Datable to 1560, the volume contains three paintings that represent original and diverse subjects, indicating that a highly innovative artist composed them. The first (34) depicts a princely couple in a courtyard with the lady pondering her reflection in a pool. The domed two-story structure in the background, with narrow entrance, arched balcony, stained-glass windows, and colonnaded facade, exhibits the same architectural features found in the representation of the Topkapı Palace in the *Süleymanname*, the fifth volume in Arifi's voluminous history (see **41a–41d**). It is clear that the artist has used as his setting one of the courtyards of the sultan's palace. Other realistic details include accessories worn by the protagonists, such as the ivory-handled dagger tucked into the belt of the prince, the embroidered cap of the lady, and the jeweled belts worn by both figures, examples of which exist in the imperial collections (see **92**, **93**, and **76–78**). The

34. Royal couple in a courtyard from the *Ravzat el-Uşak* of Arifi, c. 1560 (Cambridge, Mass., Harvard University Art Museums, fol. 23a)

depiction of a mirror-image reflection is most unusual and rarely employed in Islamic painting.[61]

The interest in representing realistic settings is clearly demonstrated in the remaining illustrations. One of them, possibly the earliest scene from everyday life in Ottoman art, re-creates a typical butcher's shop.[62] The other shows a fox dressed as a half-naked dervish walking in a landscape, with a cluster of buildings in the background that resemble the types used to represent eastern European cities in historical manuscripts.[63] The anonymous painter of the *Ravzat el-Uşak* applied the same refined execution, documentary realism, and original compositions he employed in the illustrations of Arifi's historical works, indicating that the classical style of Ottoman painting was firmly established after the 1550s.

The illustrations of literary works produced between 1520 and 1560 reveal both the heterogeneous nature of the nakkaş-hane and the gradual development of the classical style of painting. As previously discussed, some manuscripts were illustrated by artists who followed the traditions of Herat and Tabriz, while others were executed by painters who absorbed these traditions and blended them with the preexisting Ottoman styles.

There is yet another group of painters, who remained oblivious to changes taking place in the nakkaşhane and formulated their own styles. They worked on contemporary Turkish texts that had not been previously illustrated and were free to create their own pictorial cycles. The paintings in such manuscripts as Musa Abdi's *Camaspname* (Book of Camasp) dated 1527,[64] a copy of the *Tercüme-i Şahname* (Translation of the book of kings) of c. 1530,[65] Fuzuli's *Hadikat üs-Sueda* (Garden of the fortunates)[66] of c. 1550, and Şeyhi's *Hüsrev ve Şirin* of c. 1560[67] lack the structured composition and refined execution of nakkaşhane products, but nevertheless display originality.

There also exist works that were partially illustrated when they arrived at the court and were later completed in the nakkaşhane. The most interesting of these is a copy of the *Hamse-i Nizami*, which was begun in the 1450s at the Kara-koyunlu court at Shiraz, was continued after 1510 in the Safavid court at Tabriz, and was finished in the 1530s or 1540s in İstanbul.[68]

Illustrated Histories

The classical style of Ottoman painting evolved from the tradition of illustrated histories, which became firmly established in the 1560s. This tradition, which visually re-created the personages and the settings of the events with documentary realism, was initiated not by court artists but by members of the administration, such as Piri Reis, Nasuh, and Nigari. It was, however, adapted and taken to its ultimate height by the nakkaşhane painters.

Chronicles recording the activities of the state had been produced since the formative years of the Ottoman Empire. In addition, the sultans had established the post of the şahna-meci, whose specific duty was to document the lives and achievements of the rulers. Historians were extremely prolific during Süleyman's reign, writing voluminous texts devoted to universal histories, past and present accounts of the Ottoman dynasty, biographies of individual sultans, and descriptions of specific campaigns and political events. There were also geo-graphical and maritime studies written by travelers and naval commanders.

One of these was Piri Reis, a famous captain in the imperial navy and the nephew of the renowned admiral Kemal Reis, with whom he sailed on many campaigns in the Mediterranean. Piri Reis retired to Gelibolu when his uncle died in 1511, but was recalled to duty by Selim I during the 1517 campaign to Egypt. He continued working for Süleyman and joined the sultan during the 1522 campaign to Rhodes. He was later given the command of the Egyptian fleet and was active in the Red Sea, Arabian Gulf, and Indian Ocean. Accused of taking bribes to lift the siege of Hormuz and thus failing to capture that important fortress from the Portuguese, he was executed upon returning to Egypt in 1554. Piri Reis, who obviously led a very colorful and controversial life, was also a man of diverse talents who was best known for his cartographic studies and naval charts.

The most renowned of his cartographic works is a parchment (deerskin) map of the Atlantic Ocean (**35**) that shows the western shores of Europe and Africa and the eastern parts of Central and South America. The work is the surviving half of a larger map representing the world.[69] Produced in Gelibolu in 1513 and presented to Selim I in Cairo in 1517, it bears a long inscription on the lower left that lists the sources used to represent different regions. Piri Reis consulted more than thirty maps: twenty were made by ancient cartographers dating from the period of Alexander the Great, eight were drawn by Muslim mapmakers, four others were produced by the Portuguese, and one was made by Christopher Columbus. For the depiction of the Antilles and the coastal regions of the New World he relied on a copy of the map by Columbus.[70] He also checked the Portuguese maps of South America and obtained information from a Spanish prisoner who had participated in Columbus' three voyages to the New World.

Piri Reis' map includes wind roses and scales of nautical distances, as well as commentaries and illustrations. It is not only a major cartographic document that compiles early and contemporary sources, but also a fascinating painting, with vignettes and anecdotes. Ships sail on the seas or rest in ports; landmasses are filled with mountains, rivers, fortresses, and figures of seated kings, elephants, ostriches, llamas, parrots, monkeys, and monstrous or fantastic creatures. One amusing vignette appears on the upper portion, showing figures building a fire on an island, their ship anchored close by. According to the inscription, this is the tale of sailors who mistook a whale for an island and lit a fire on its back; when the whale's skin started burning, it dove into the sea and the men hurried back to their ship.

Since the map was published in 1929 scholarly controversies and hypotheses have developed concerning the identifica-

35. Parchment map made by Piri Reis in 1513 (İstanbul, Topkapı Sarayı Müzesi, R. 1633 mük.)

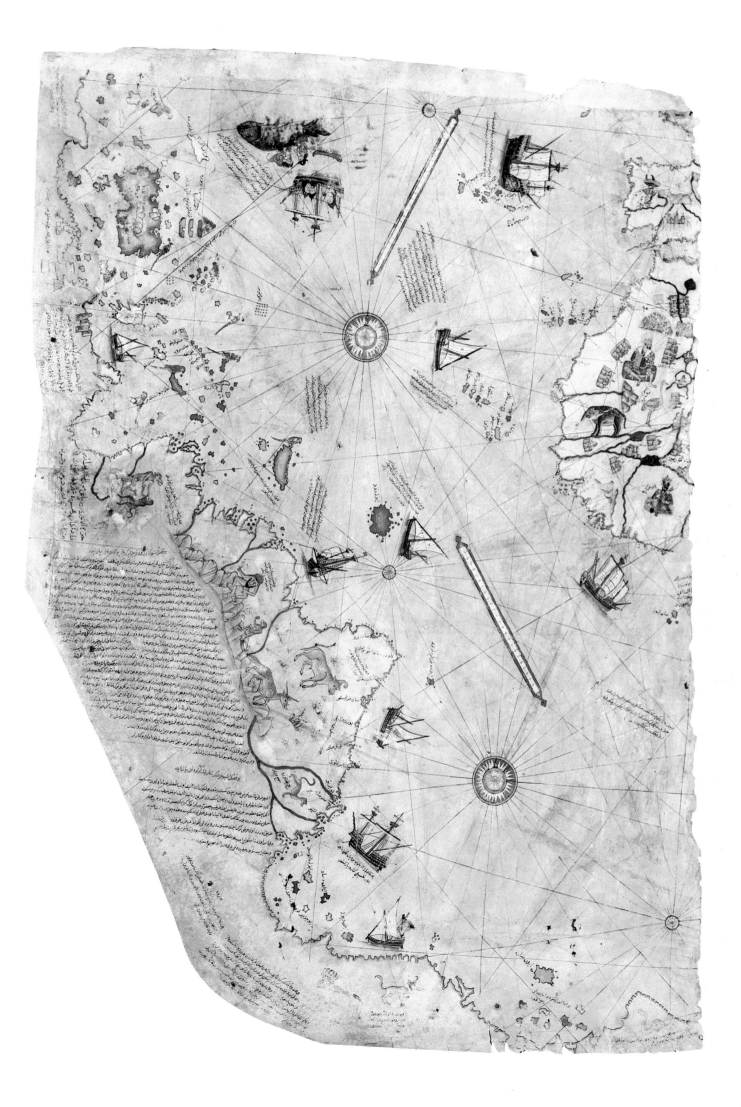

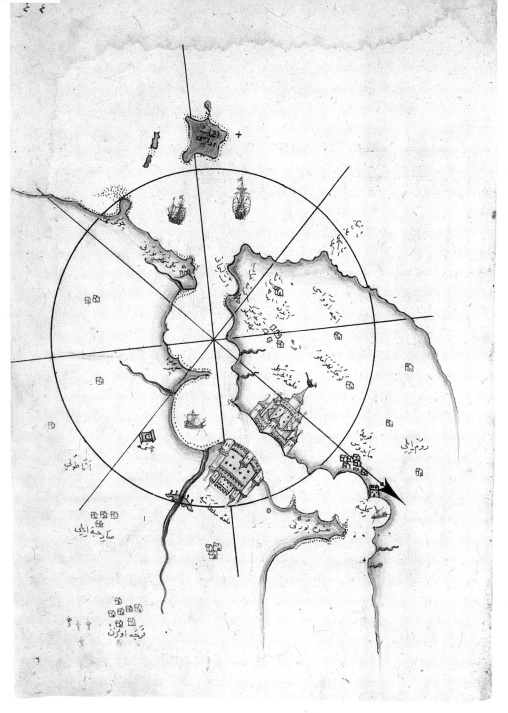

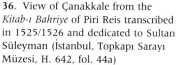

36. View of Çanakkale from the *Kitab-ı Bahriye* of Piri Reis transcribed in 1525/1526 and dedicated to Sultan Süleyman (İstanbul, Topkapı Sarayı Müzesi, H. 642, fol. 44a)

tion of the ancient sources used by Piri Reis and his remarkable accuracy in representing areas thought to be unknown at the time he made the map. Questions have been raised about the depiction of Antarctica as a land mass without ice, a continent not known even to exist before 1818; and the accurate charting of other remote geographic regions, which required the use of special instruments, invented centuries later, to calculate the curvature of the earth. Speculations on how Piri Reis and the ancient cartographers whose works he consulted could describe areas not confirmed until the twentieth century even led to such extreme theories as the one put forth by Erich von Daniken in *Chariots of the Gods*, attributing the map to extraterrestrials. In addition to its cartographic signifi-

cance the work is an important document of the development of illustrated histories, showing the earliest example of the topographical and maritime atlas genres that were more fully developed a generation later by Nasuh.

Some figures, such as seated kings and roaming animals, resemble those found in early sixteenth-century manuscripts produced in the nakkaşhane, while others are related to the strange creatures depicted in the fifteenth-century Mamluk or Akkoyunlu copies of the *Acaib al-Mahlukat* (Marvels of creation) of el-Kazvini. The models for the ships, however, are not found in Ottoman or other Islamic manuscripts; these as well as some architectural and figural elements appear to have been derived from European illustrated maps or naval guides.[71] Obviously Piri Reis researched not only cartographic sources, but also illustrated manuscripts and charts to produce his unique map.

Piri Reis' most popular work was the naval guide to the Mediterranean entitled the *Kitab-ı Bahriye* (Book of the mariner), which was written in 1521 and revised four years later.[72] The earliest illustrated copy of the revised version was transcribed in 1525/1526 and dedicated to Süleyman. The work has a stamped and gilded leather binding decorated with saz scrolls that may be the earliest appearance of this design on bookbindings. It is, however, feasible that the text was bound in the court several years after it was presented to the sultan.

The text, compiled by Piri Reis and written down by Muradi, a contemporary historian, has 215 charts that illustrate various Mediterranean ports and harbors on the continental coasts and the islands.[73] As exemplified by the first scene in the work, which represents Çanakkale (**36**), the strait between the Sea of Marmara and the Aegean (also known as the Dardanelles), the illustrations are very graphic. Bold lines define the landmasses that have softly tinted shores, and tiny red dots indicate shallow coastal waters, a feature also observed on his map of the Americas. Minuscule ships sail around the waters or lie anchored in the harbors.

Protecting the narrowest portion of the strait are two impressive fortresses with several towers and crenellated walls; a large bird perches on the peaked tip of the highest roof. The folio is sprinkled with smaller fortresses, landmarks, farmhouses, bridges, and villages with clusters of houses, each site and region identified by fine script. The structures are tinted with pastel colors as is the large island on the top of the page, inscribed Eşek Adası (Donkey Island). Similar to all the illustrations in the book, there is a large eight-spoked wind rose placed over the scene, the arm with an arrow on the lower right pointing north.

It is tempting to assign all the charts in this volume to Piri Reis, who must have also written the notations; the text, on the other hand, appears to have been transcribed by a calligrapher and shows a different hand. Piri Reis' charts were copied in later versions of the *Kitab-ı Bahriye*, which was produced until the nineteenth century. Some of the later illustrations are more elaborately painted though they remain essentially faithful to the cartographer's originals.[74]

The tradition of illustrated histories, which flourished in the second quarter of the sixteenth century, began with the *Şahname* of Melik Ümmü, an unknown historian who wrote about the reign of Bayezid II. The only illustrated version of this work, completed around 1500, shows the impact of the Akkoyunlu school of Shiraz, and relies on formulaic enthronement and battle scenes. The next in the series, devoted to the reign of Selim I, is the *Selimname* (Book of Selim) of Şükrü Bitlisi, written in Turkish verse and presented to Süleyman around 1525. The work opens with a double frontis-

piece of which only the left half remains. In it the author, sitting under a tent, is accompanied by two calligraphers; the right half must have shown Selim I and his court. The remaining twenty-three illustrations begin the pictorial narration with the enthronement of Selim and conclude it with his death. Executed by two similar hands, they reveal influences from Herat and possibly even Cairo. This is the first work that attempts to document historical events, showing the figures in identifiable garments, as in the scene representing the 1514 Battle of Çaldıran (**37**), in which the Safavids were defeated and Tabriz conquered.

The painting, divided in half by a hill, represents on the left the Safavids, who wear tapered turbans with tall batons; opposite are the Ottomans with their more rounded turbans, accompanied by a group of janissaries holding spears. Standing

37. Sultan Selim I at the Battle of Çaldıran from the *Selimname* of Şükrü Bitlisi, c. 1525 (İstanbul, Topkapı Sarayı Müzesi, H. 1597-1598, fol. 113a)

between the two armies in the center of the folio is the victorious Selim I, pointing to both groups. The moment depicted here is not very clear; the scene appears to represent the surrender of the Safavids, with their commander expressing bewilderment by biting his index finger, a traditional Islamic gesture of astonishment and awe.

The following group of manuscripts, composed in Turkish prose by Nasuh el-Silahi el-Matraki, known as Matrakçı Nasuh, are unique in conception. Transcribed and illustrated by the author, they depict the cities and ports conquered by the Ottomans with extreme realism, showing a firsthand knowledge of those sites. The paintings are devoid of human figures and represent the flowering of the topographic and maritime atlas genres.

Nasuh, born in the town of Visoka in Bosnia, was educated in the Enderun and rose to the rank of officer during the reign of Bayezid II, retaining this position until his death, which is thought to have taken place in 1564. A man of many talents, he wrote prolifically on history, mathematics, and swordsmanship. An expert swordsman himself, he earned the honorific "el-Silahi." As observed in his manuscripts, he also was a competent calligrapher as well as an extremely talented draftsman and painter. He came to be known as "el-Matraki" or "Matrakçı" after inventing the game of *matrak* (played by throwing sticks) during the 1530 festival organized to celebrate the circumcision of Süleyman's three sons, Mustafa, Mehmed, and Selim. Nasuh left numerous works of history, which include translation of Tabari's *Universal History* from Arabic into Turkish, biographies of Bayezid II and Selim I, and detailed eyewitness accounts of

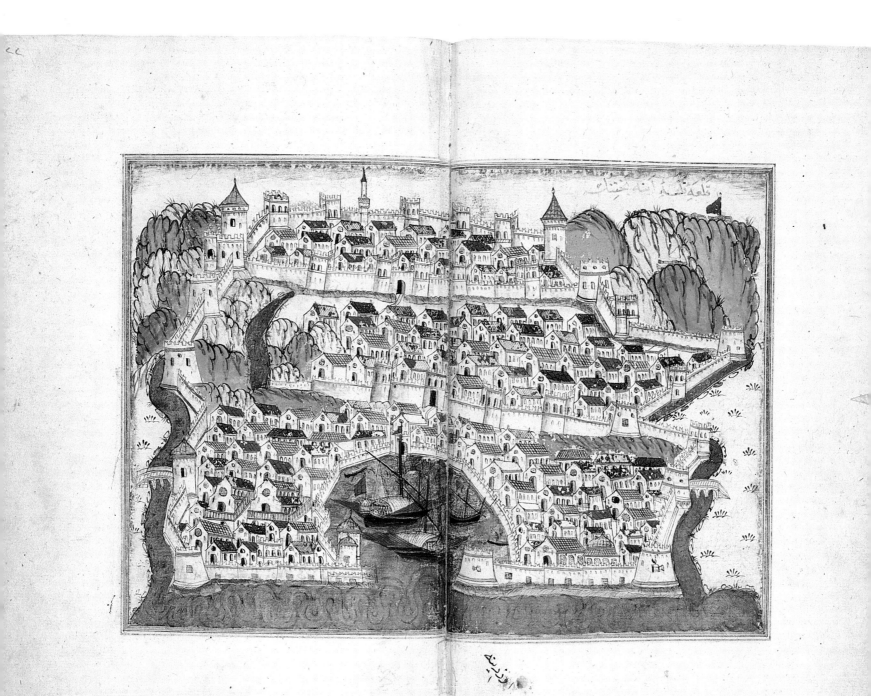

38 (left). View of Lepanto from the *Tarih-i Sultan Bayezid* of Matrakcı Nasuh, c. 1540 (İstanbul, Topkapı Sarayı Müzesi, R. 1272, fols. 21b–22a)

Detail, 38 (above)

the campaigns of Süleyman between 1520 and 1560.

Nasuh's *Tarih-i Sultan Bayezid* (History of Sultan Bayezid), completed around 1540, narrates the events involving Bayezid II and his brother Cem in the 1480s and 1490s. It is illustrated with ten paintings, which depict a number of fortified ports such as Coron and Lepanto, the latter called İnebahtı in Turkish. The representation of Lepanto, spread to double folios (38), shows the city protected by high walls between massive towers. Waterways with bridges appear outside the walls or cut through the city and flow into the sea. In the center are several ships at anchor in a harbor guarded by two massive towers. The city is divided into three districts, each enclosed by walls and densely packed with a variety of buildings; many have sloping roofs, although some have belfries or domes. Mountains appearing in the background and within the walled enclosure suggest that the region was considerably rugged.

In Nasuh's depiction the city of Lepanto, with its natural and manmade fortifications, is most impressive and appears impenetrable. Conquered by the Ottomans in 1499, it was zealously guarded through the centuries because its strategic location and safe harbor were essential for the defense of the Mediterranean.

Nasuh's most elaborate work is the *Beyan-ı Menazil-i Sefer-i Irakeyn* (Descriptions of the halting stations during the Irakeyn campaign), originally entitled *Mecmu-i Menazil*. It is devoted to Süleyman's 1534–1536 campaign to Iraq and Iran, called the two Iraqs, or the Irakeyn, in Turkish (Irak-ı Acem with its capital at Hamadan and Irak-ı Arab with its capital at Baghdad). Completed around 1537, the work contains 128 paintings that depict the cities and sites where the army halted. It is almost a traveler's guide to these regions, representing their geographic conditions, mountains and rivers, flora and fauna, and all the major monuments in the towns.

The first painting in the volume shows İstanbul (**39a**), where the campaign originated. Spread to double folios, it places the section then called İstanbul on the right and Galata on the left, separated by the Golden Horn and surrounded by the Bosporus and the Sea of Marmara. A small portion of Üsküdar appears on the upper left, next to the famous Kız Kulesi, the lighthouse also known as the Tower of Leander.

The representation of İstanbul, with its monuments rendered both frontally and from the air, is the most magnificent painting in the volume. It is also the earliest known Ottoman illustration of the capital. This extraordinary painting represents the surrounding rivers, hills, gardens, and orchards as well as all the major structures, each carefully and accurately drawn. The Galata section is enclosed by walls and towers, the largest being the famous Galata Tower built by the Genoese in the fourteenth century. Foreign diplomatic and commercial missions were located in this area, which is subdivided into districts by additional fortifications.

The İstanbul section, also enclosed by walls and towers, is much larger and more densely filled with all types of structures. The Topkapı Palace with its own fortified walls appears at the top; the painter has clearly identified the three courtyards and their entrance gates. Other structures around the Topkapı Palace include the Aya Sofya (Hagia Sophia), the sixth-century Byzantine church converted into a mosque after the conquest of İstanbul; and the At Meydanı, the hippodrome, with its ancient obelisks, colonnades, and serpentine column. Below are the Covered Bazaar, the Aqueduct of Valens, the complex built by Bayezid II, the Old Palace enclosed by a wall, and the Mosque of Mehmed II. The districts of the city and their monuments are explicitly illustrated, including the Yedikule quarter on the lower right with its famous seven-towered fortress.[75]

39a. View of İstanbul from the *Beyan-ı Menazil-i Sefer-i Irakeyn* of Matrakçı Nasuh, c. 1537 (İstanbul Üniversite Kütüphanesi, T. 5964, fols. 8b–9a)

Nasuh showed the same care in documenting the other cities, as observed in the double-folio depiction of Sultaniye in northwestern Iran (**39b**). The city, founded by the Ilkhanid ruler Oljeitu (1304–1317) to rival Tabriz, was heavily built up during the fourteenth century and later abandoned. Only two of the monuments of this great center remain today—the Mausoleum of Oljeitu and the tomb complex of Çelebioğlu dated to the 1330s, both of which are in ruins.

Nasuh's painting, therefore, is of great importance, representing Sultaniye as it appeared in the 1530s. The area around the former Ilkhanid capital has beautifully drawn trees and flowers with many birds and wild animals. Several rivers flow through the city, which has three major buildings in addition to a number of smaller flat-roofed residences. In the center of the folio on the right is a magnificent structure, which is several stories high and has a towering dome enclosed by eight small minarets. Behind it is a small hexagonal building with two minarets flanking its more modest dome. Opposite is another religious edifice with a large entrance portal flanked by minarets at one side and a three-story domed unit at the other.

The largest building with its splendid decoration is obviously the famous Mausoleum of Oljeitu, characterized by the unusual minarets springing from the base of its dome. The one on the left must be the tomb complex built by Çelebioğlu. The other domed building cannot be identified.

It appears that even in the sixteenth century Sultaniye was neglected; most of its legendary buildings were destroyed by an earthquake and its walls crumbled. The city was occupied by villagers living in unpretentious huts, with only three monuments still standing as vestiges of its great past.

Nasuh's third manuscript, entitled the *Tarih-i Feth-i Siklos, Estergon ve Estonibelgrad* (History of the conquest of Siklós, Esztergom, and Székesfehérvár), also called the *Süleymanname*, describes Süleyman's 1543 campaign to Hungary in the first part and Barbaros Hayreddin Paşa's activities in the Mediterranean of the same date in the second part. The work, completed around 1545, contains representations of ports such as Toulon, Marseilles, Nice, and Genoa.

The view of Genoa (**40**) is masterfully composed with a fleet of ships breezing by in the foreground, their curved sails creating a lively movement. The city, protected by high walls, has an inner harbor in which two galleons are anchored. As in the representation of Lepanto, the city is packed with buildings with pitched roofs and domes. An inner tower with heavy fortifications appears in the background; a number of other structures, including monasteries, castles, lighthouses, and watchtowers, appear outside the walls. The suburbs are separated by rivers, which are crossed by bridges. The buildings are rendered in pale tones highlighted by occasional red roofs, contrasting with the colorful hills and meadows and the silvery waters.

The ships are particularly well drawn, their types recalling

39b (above). View of Sultaniye from the *Beyan-ı Menazil-i Sefer-i Irakeyn* of Matrakcı Nasuh, c. 1537 (İstanbul Üniversite Kütüphanesi, T. 5964, fols. 32b–33a)

40 (right). View of Genoa from the *Tarih-i Feth-i Siklos, Estergon, ve Estonibelgrad* of Matrakcı Nasuh, c. 1545 (İstanbul, Topkapı Sarayı Müzesi, H. 1608, fols. 32b–33a)

those employed in Piri Reis' works. Different models appear to have been used to represent the two fleets; the galleons in the harbor, based on European prototypes, appear to belong to the Genoese, while those sailing in the foreground reveal a native style and presumably depict the Ottoman armada, led by Barbaros Hayreddin Paşa's flagship. The contrast between softly rounded hills, angular structures, and rhythmically curved sails is most effective.

Nasuh's unique style, combining documentary depiction with masterful compositions, had a long-lasting impact on Ottoman painting, particularly on the tradition of illustrated histories. Another person whose paintings influenced the nakkaşhane artists was Haydar Reis, who signed his works Nigari. A naval officer by profession, Nigari was a learned

man, his home in the Galata section of İstanbul the gathering place of scholars and writers. He practiced poetry, wrote about the victories of the grand admiral Sinan Paşa, and frequently included couplets on his paintings. Nigari's strength was portraiture, and his representations of Süleyman, Selim II, and Barbaros Hayreddin were painted from life on single sheets (see figs. 10 and 11). The artist appears to have been self-taught, formulating his own style and technique. His figures are large, boldly painted, and placed on a dark green ground. His paintings are not as refined as those of the nakkaşhane artists and lack their technical perfection; the sheets are not polished, the pigments are irregularly applied and have started to flake. Nevertheless, Nigari promoted the genre of portraiture, continuing the tradition begun in the 1480s by

Mehmed II, who had invited several Italian artists to his court, including Gentile Bellini and Costanza da Ferrara,[76] whose styles had a brief impact on the works of their Turkish contemporaries.

Nigari's portraits are purely in the Ottoman tradition, showing no vestiges of these earlier works. Although he made copies of European portraits—such as his versions of portraits of Francis I and Charles V by Clouet and Cranach—his own style remained untouched by European traditions.[77]

The genre of documentary painting established by Nasuh and the interest in portraiture promoted by Nigari were soon absorbed into the repertoire of the artists of the nakkaşhane, who were themselves beginning to formulate indigenous styles in the 1530s, as observed in the works of Nevai discussed earlier. The synthesis that took place made its initial

appearance in a most appropriate manuscript, the official biography of the sultan, the *Süleymanname* of Arifi.

Arifi (died 1561/1562) was the first şahnameci whose works were illustrated, and set a precedent for future court biographers by employing an exclusive group of artists. His text, written in Persian verse following the meter of Firdausi's *Şahname*, was also used as a model in later years. The post of the şahnameci, established by Mehmed II, gained considerable importance after the reign of Süleyman and was occupied by such great historians as Lokman, Talikizade, and Nadiri, whose works were profusely illustrated both by nakkaşhane and non-nakkaşhane artists.

Arifi was formerly in the service of Elkas Mirza, the brother of Tahmasp and the governor of Shirvan, and came to İstanbul in 1547 when his master fled to the Ottoman capital after

41a. Siege of Belgrade from the *Süleymanname* of Arifi transcribed in 1558
(İstanbul, Topkapı Sarayı Müzesi, H. 1517, fols. 108b−109a)

an unsuccessful insurrection against the Safavid ruler. Arifi was appointed şahnameci by Süleyman, who asked him to write a history of the Ottoman dynasty. The poet conceived the *Şahname-i Al-i Osman* as a five-volume set, beginning with the creation of man and ending with the biography of the sultan. The first and last volumes in the series, the *Anbiyaname* (Book of Prophets) and the *Süleymanname*, were both transcribed in 1558; volumes two and three are missing; and only the first half of volume four, which is devoted to the rise of the Ottomans and the early sultans, remains.

A document listing the expenses of an "imperial şahname," drawn between 1552/1553 and 1555/1556, itemizes the costs of paper, ink, gold leaf, pigments, and other materials ordered for the work, lists the salaries of the scribes and painters, and concludes with the amount paid to the carpenters, who constructed partitions for the scribes in the *derhane* (residence or studio) of Fethullah Çelebi, the şahnameci. This document must be related to Arifi's *Şahname-i Al-i Osman*, possibly to the lost sections, since it mentions as the chief calligrapher Mustafa, whose name does not appear in the colophons of the remaining volumes.[78]

The *Süleymanname* is the most spectacular work in the series, its binding, illuminations, and illustrations produced by the best talents in the court. The binding, stamped and heavily gilded, is attributed to Mehmed b. Ahmed, the head of the bookbinders; the illuminations, revealing the same naturalistic themes observed in the 1546/1547 Koran of Karahisari and the 1566 *Divan-ı Muhibbi*, must have been executed by Kara Memi, the head of the nakkaşhane. The same care is observed in the selection of the painters employed to illustrate its sixty-five scenes (four spread onto double folios). The scenes show the hands of two major and three minor artists, each selected for his expertise and background.

The master of the *Süleymanname*, who executed the majority of the illustrations, was a most innovative artist. This painter worked primarily with Arifi and also illustrated the *Anbiyaname*; the 1557/1558 *Futuhat-ı Cemile* (Admirable conquests), an account of the 1551–1552 campaigns in Hungary and Transylvania undertaken by vezirs Ahmed and Mehmed Paşas;[79] and the historian's only literary work, the *Ravzat el-Uşak* (see **34**).

The second major painter of the *Süleymanname* was the doyen of the studio. His decorative style, first seen in 1515 in *Mantık et-Tayr*, dominated the illustrated literary manuscripts through the 1550s, as observed in the collected poems of Selim I, Nevai, and Arifi discussed above. The same painter worked on the second volume in the series, which, together with the *Süleymanname*, was his last contribution. Two of the minor artists, one specializing in the representation of the Safavids and the other that of the Europeans, worked with the master of the *Süleymanname*. The fifth artist produced only two scenes, which were extremely formulaic in style and subject matter.

The master of the *Süleymanname* devised the compositions for accession ceremonies, sieges of fortresses, and receptions in pavilions and tents that became the prototypes for later paintings. He was the first to apply Nasuh's topographic genre to the representation of the Topkapı Palace and other architectural structures, placing his protagonists within realistic settings. He was also the first to portray identifiable personages, who are attired in their characteristic garments and placed in the scenes according to court protocol.

One of his double-folio paintings represents the siege of Belgrade (**41a**), Süleyman's first campaign undertaken in 1521. On the left half is the Ottoman camp with the sultan seated in his tent, accompanied by his vezirs, commanders, and Has Oda officials, watching with great apprehension the assault on the Hungarian capital. Opposite is the city of Belgrade, crowded with pitched roofs, belfries, and domes, with its flags flying valiantly from the towers. A group of residents, soldiers, and monks have gathered in the church, praying for deliverance from the Ottomans while fire consumes the outer tower, throwing its defenders into panic. The scene not only documents the event, but also portrays the emotional responses of the participants. The majestic stillness and self-assurance that prevails in the Ottoman camp is contrasted by the commotion and desperation of the Hungarians.

Another double folio executed by the same painter depicts the Battle of Mohács (**41b**), which took place in 1526 and resulted in the annexation of Hungary to the Ottoman Empire. The artist re-created the fervor and excitement of this great Ottoman victory while at the same time identifying the protagonists, describing the terrain, and documenting the battle tactics. Süleyman, mounted on a horse, appears in the center of the right half, surrounded by his personal guards. The janissaries, who are neatly lined up in front of him, fire their cannons and rifles at the enemy, encouraged by the music of the imperial military band, which stands at his back.

The left half is full of action and shows several fighting warriors. Enemy forces retreating and regrouping in a disorganized fashion contrast with the regimentation and discipline of the sultan's army depicted on the opposite folio. The two halves of the scene are united by the field and the rivers that flow across the plain and the pool in the foreground. The banks are lined with bodies of dead horses and soldiers. In the foreground are many Hungarians who were drowned in the swamps while trying to escape, trapped by their heavy armor.

One of the paintings in the *Süleymanname* depicts the sultan conversing with Barbaros Hayreddin Paşa under the arcades of a pavilion overlooking a lovely garden in the third courtyard of the Topkapı Palace (**41c**). Süleyman, who invited the formidable seaman to İstanbul to discuss the reformation of the Ottoman naval forces, has allowed his guest to be seated in his presence, ordinarily a privilege granted only to members of the royal family. A sense of intimacy and privacy permeates the scene despite the presence of the sultan's personal attendants and guards. Süleyman is portrayed as a youthful monarch benefiting from the experience of the old man, whose skin is wrinkled and beard pure white.

The representation of Barbaros Hayreddin is remarkably similar to the portrait executed by Nigari; it either was based on Nigari's work or was another life study. The painter also shows care in depicting the secondary figures, who can be

easily identified through their garments and placement in the scene. The two on the left belong to the Has Oda, those opposite are pages, while the group below represents the imperial gatekeepers.

Vezirs, members of the Has Oda, and two separate corps of guards (*solaks* and *peyks*) accompany the sultan during his visit to Kasr-ı Şirin (**41d**), named after the ruins of an ancient palace thought to have been built by the legendary king Hüs-

41b. Battle of Mohács from the *Süleymanname* of Arifi transcribed in 1558 (İstanbul, Topkapı Sarayı Müzesi, H. 1517, fols. 219b–220a)

41c. Sultan Süleyman with Barbaros Hayreddin Paşa from the *Süleymanname* of Arifi transcribed in 1558 (İstanbul, Topkapı Sarayı Müzesi, H. 1517, fol. 360a)

41d. Sultan Süleyman arriving at Kasr-ı Şirin from the *Süleymanname* of Arifi transcribed in 1558 (İstanbul, Topkapı Sarayı Müzesi, H. 1517, fol. 367a)

rev (Khosrau) for his beloved Şirin (Shirin). The group rides through a lush meadow and approaches a fabulous palace, its facade and dome covered with tiles, bricks, and stone. The composition recalls the scenes depicting Hüsrev approaching Şirin's castle, frequently employed in fifteenth- and early-sixteenth-century copies of Nizami's work produced in the Timurid, Safavid, and Ottoman courts.

The anonymous master of the *Süleymanname* must have trained Osman, a highly prolific artist who started working in the nakkaşhane in the 1560s and produced hundreds of paintings during the next three decades. His distinct style appears in the *Nüzhet el-Esrar el-Ahbar der Sefer-i Sigetvar* (Chronicle of the Szigetvár campaign) written in 1568/1569 by Ahmed Feridun Paşa, a celebrated vezir, commander, and governor who took part in the Szigetvár campaign and was

later married to one of the sultan's granddaughters. The work, devoted to the last campaign of Süleyman directed against the Hungarian fortress of Szigetvár in 1566, describes in detail the events leading up to the death of Süleyman and concludes with the accession ceremonies of Selim II.

The paintings are very much in the spirit of the chronicle, visually documenting the last campaign of the sultan. One of the scenes represents Süleyman receiving Stephen Zápolya, his vassal in Transylvania (**42a**). Stephen's father, John, had been crowned king of Hungary by Süleyman. Hungary was annexed after John's death in 1541 and Stephen, then an infant, was made the ruler of Transylvania, a tributary state of the Ottomans.

When Süleyman stopped in Belgrade en route to Szigetvár, Stephen, now a mature man, came to pay his respects to the

91

42a. Sultan Süleyman receiving Stephen Zápolya from the *Nuzhet el-Esrar el-Ahbar der Sefer-i Sigetvar* of Ahmed Feridun Paşa transcribed in 1568/1569 (İstanbul, Topkapı Sarayı Müzesi, H. 1339, fol. 16b)

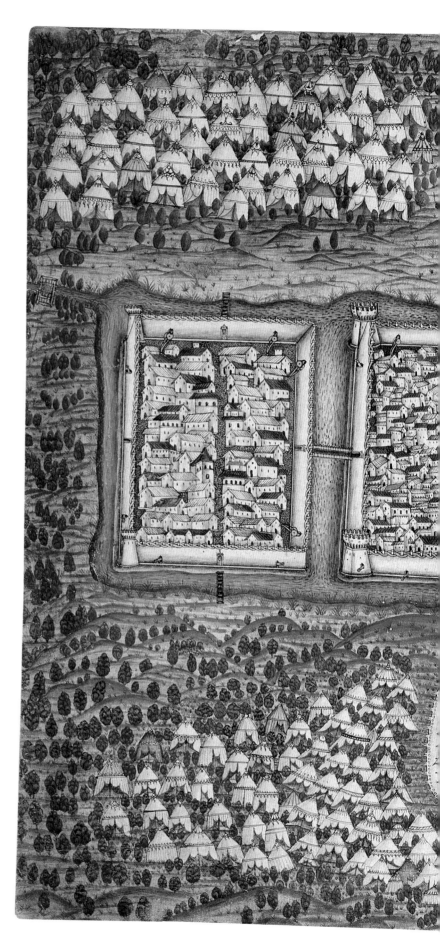

sultan. Süleyman, clearly showing his advanced years and ill health, is enthroned under an elaborate tent, flanked by his vezirs and personal attendants. Spread on the ground is a large carpet or textile with a central medallion adorned by the same saz scrolls and rumis used to decorate bookbindings. Stephen kneels in front of the sultan, holding his hat in his hand. Members of his retinue stand at the edge of the scene, also with their hats in their hands; one of them places his hand over his heart and bows, demonstrating his deep respect for the sultan.

The scene is at once ceremonial and emotional, dominated by the stoical presence of the ailing sultan. The figures surrounding him project a feeling of sadness and fatalism, as if having a premonition that he would not return from this campaign. The artist who injected such pathos and poignancy into a static composition representing a routine activity was indeed a master.

The representation of the fortress of Szigetvár (42b) dis-

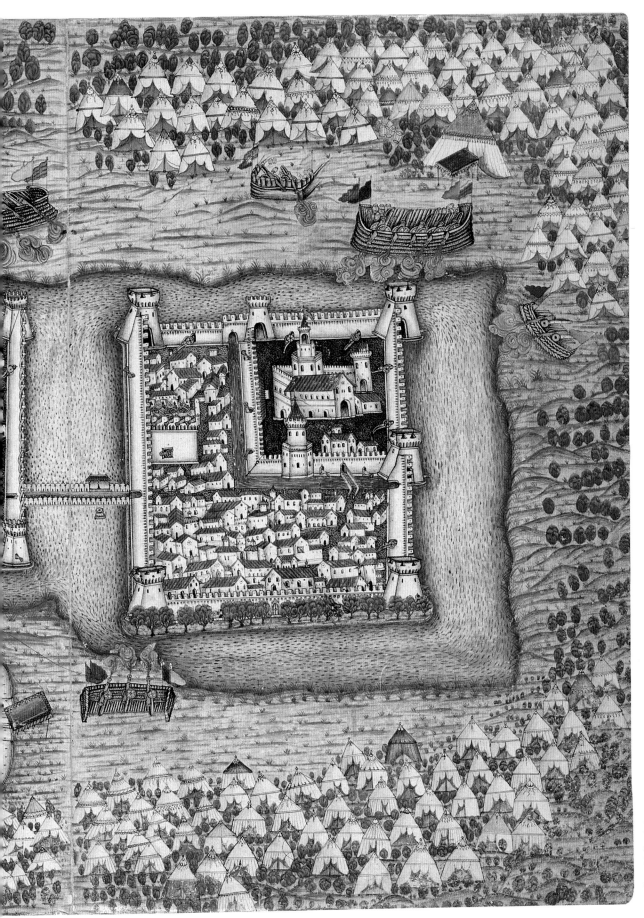

42b. View of Szigetvár from the *Nuzhet el-Esrar el-Ahbar der Sefer-i Sigetvar* of Ahmed Feridun Paşa transcribed in 1568/1569 (İstanbul, Topkapı Sarayı Müzesi, H. 1339, fols. 32b–33a)

plays yet other features of the artist: his great sense of composition, crisp draftsmanship, and ability to create a panoramic scene on a mere double folio. The fortress, constructed as three independent enclosures connected by bridges and surrounded by a moat, is heavily fortified with additional walls protecting the inner city on the right of the largest enclosure. The Ottomans have besieged the fortress, which is totally engulfed by their tents and strategically placed barricades, with cannons firing at its walls.

The imperial tent, in a group of other tents bounded by a fence, appears in the center of the foreground. It has a canopy over the entrance, which is flanked by two towers, resembling the first gate of the Topkapı Palace. Another large tent, also with a canopy over its entrance, is placed on the upper right; it most likely belonged to the grand vezir Sokollu Mehmed Paşa, who was the second in command. The representation of Szigetvár, crammed with red-roofed buildings, recalls the topographical scenes of Nasuh and shows the persistence of that tradition.

Osman's style also appears in the *Tarih-i Sultan Süleyman* written by Lokman, who served as the şahnameci between 1569 and 1595 and worked exclusively with this painter and his assistants. The manuscript, completed in 1579/1580, was conceived as the final chapter of Arifi's *Süleymanname*, using the same meter and concluding with the death of the sultan.

One of the paintings represents Süleyman praying at the Mausoleum of Eyüb Ensari (**43a**). Eyüb Ensari, a revered martyr, was the Prophet Muhammed's companion and standard-bearer who died during the first Arab siege of the city in the 670s. A mosque with dependencies was built near his tomb by Mehmed II after the conquest of İstanbul and the district, called Eyüb Sultan, became the burial site of many famous people, including Ahmed Feridun Paşa, the author of the Szigetvár chronicle. To the Ottomans the Mausoleum of Eyüb Ensari was one of the most important pilgrimage sites after Mecca, Medina, and Jerusalem. It was also where the sultans girded themselves with the sword of Osman, the founder of the dynasty, as part of their accession ceremonies.

In the painting Süleyman stands with his hands held in prayer in front of the domed mausoleum, which has an arched doorway; inside is a mosque lamp suspended over an open *rahle* (folding bookstand). The sultan is joined by several vezirs and attendants including three members of the Has Oda, one carrying his sword and another holding his *matara* (canteen). A large candlestick placed on a stand appears on the right, behind which is a religious dignitary, possibly the şeyhülislam. Imperial guards and horses wait outside the high wall enclosing the structure.

This painting, which contains the earliest representation of the Mausoleum of Eyüb Ensari, depicts in detail the personal regalia of the sultan—his sword and matara—and specific tomb furnishings—mosque lamp, rahle, and candlestick. The artist's careful representation of these items enables us to

43a. Sultan Süleyman praying at the Mausoleum of Eyüb Ensari from the *Tarih-i Sultan Süleyman* of Lokman transcribed in 1579/1580 (Dublin, The Chester Beatty Library, MS. 413, fol. 38a)

identify and date some existing objects.

The illustrations in the *Tarih-i Sultan Süleyman* also represent the ailing sultan, supported by his grand vezir, leading his men to Szigetvár and the siege and fall of the fortress; events following his death on the eve of 7 September 1566; and the return of the armed forces to Belgrade. The latter scene (**43b**), spread to double folios, shows various regiments proceeding slowly and silently through mountainous terrain, bearing in their midst the carriage containing Süleyman's coffin, which is identified by a solitary imperial turban, the symbol of his rank. In the foreground an officer leads the sultan's riderless horse, followed by the grand vezir Sokollu Mehmed Paşa and a group of commanders. Cavalrymen, flag bearers, the military band, janissaries, and other corps move in an orderly fashion, displaying the full majesty and legendary discipline of the Ottoman forces. A solemn and somber mood prevails over the scene, expressing dignified control over the sorrow and despair felt by the men at the loss of their beloved sultan and leader.

The same sobriety is observed in the following double folio (**43c**), the left half of which represents the new sultan, Selim

43b (above). Army marching with Sultan Süleyman's coffin from the *Tarih-i Sultan Süleyman* of Lokman transcribed in 1579/1580 (Dublin, The Chester Beatty Library, MS. 413, fols. 113b-114a)

43c (below). Sultan Selim I praying outside Belgrade from the *Tarih-i Sultan Süleyman* of Lokman transcribed in 1579/1580 (Dublin, The Chester Beatty Library, MS. 413, fols. 116b-117a)

43d. Burial of Sultan Süleyman from the *Tarih-i Sultan Süleyman* of Lokman transcribed in 1579/1580 (Dublin, The Chester Beatty Library, MS. 413, fol. 115b)

spread over the sarcophagus or stored in cupboards. Legend has it that Süleyman wanted to be buried with this casket, which was contrary to religious practice. As the ulema were discussing how to comply with the wishes of the sultan, the casket fell down and its contents spilled out. It contained the şeyhülislam's fetvas, which answered legal questions in accordance with the şeriat. This anecdote illustrates the importance Süleyman gave to conforming his sultanic laws with the established canons of Islamic jurisprudence.

The funeral procession moves along the walls of the Süleymaniye Mosque, heading toward the sanctuary where the ceremony was held. In the background is the courtyard behind the mosque where figures dig a grave under a large tent erected next to the Mausoleum of Hürrem Sultan, who had died in 1558. On the far right is the residence of the caretaker of the tombs. This painting not only contains the earliest representation of these buildings, but indicates that the Mausoleum of Süleyman was not constructed before his death. The structure, built by Sinan, the imperial architect responsible for the Süleymaniye Complex and many other imperial buildings in the capital, appears to have been already designed and its site determined, but erected after 1566. Süleyman's body was placed in the grave and the mausoleum built over it soon after. The monumental Süleymaniye Mosque is also represented in the manuscript, its structural components and hovering central dome shown in detail.

The *Tarih-i Sultan Süleyman*, which reveals the collaboration of Lokman and Osman, initiated a series of spectacular manuscripts written by the şahnameci and illustrated by the painter. Osman, at times assisted by his brother-in-law Ali and members of his studio, produced hundreds of scenes that constitute the corpus of classical Ottoman painting, his style continuing to leave a pronounced mark on the artists of the nakkaşhane until the middle of the seventeenth century. Listed in the payroll registers dated between 1566 and 1596, mentioned in several manuscripts, and praised in a number of others, the artist was also portrayed in two versions of the *Şahname-i Selim Han*. The first painting in the copy dated 1581 represents Şemseddin Ahmed Karabağı, a renowned scholar in the court, discussing the work with Lokman, Osman, Ali, and the calligrapher, İlyas Katib.[80] There also exists an undated version, thought to have been completed around 1575, which includes a similar scene.[81]

This work, devoted to the reign of Selim II, appears to be Lokman's earliest endeavor, composed before the *Tarih-i Sultan Süleyman*. The şahnameci also wrote the two-volume biography of Murad III, entitled the *Şahınşahname* (Book of the king of kings);[82] another two-volume work called the *Hünername* (Book of achievements), which covers the history of the Ottoman dynasty in the first part and the life of Süleyman in the second;[83] a genealogy of the Ottoman sultans illustrated with their portraits, the *Kıyafet el-İnsaniye fi Şemail-i Osmaniye* (General appearances and dispositions of the Ottomans);[84]

II, leading the prayer for his deceased father outside Belgrade after he formally took over the sultanate and rode there to meet his father's cortege in October. The participants, attired in dark garments, gather in groups and hold up their hands in prayer. Even the horses are depicted in arrested movement, their heads bowed in silence. Selim, clearly despondent over the death of his father, stands with a religious dignitary next to the carriage with the body, which is protected by a large canopy. The opposite folio shows the imperial tents set up outside the city of Belgrade.

The next scene takes place in İstanbul, where Süleyman's body was finally laid to rest the following month (**43d**). Süleyman's coffin bearing his large turban is carried in the foreground, led by the şeyhülislam Ebussuud Efendi, who performed the last religious rites. It is preceded by a man holding on his head a golden casket that contained the personal possessions of the sultan. According to Ottoman tradition, personal garments, accessories, and other items belonging to the deceased were kept in their mausoleums, either

and a universal history, the *Zübdet üt-Tevarih* (Cream of histories).[85] This prolific şahnameci, who composed both in Turkish and Persian, was also responsible for the voluminous *Surname* (Book of festivals), which narrates the 1582 fete organized for the circumcision of the son of Murad III.[86]

Lokman was followed by Talikizade, who held the post of the şahnameci until 1600, working primarily with Hasan, a famous statesman with a remarkable talent for painting.[87] The last of the great court biographers was Nadiri, who chose as his painter another member of the administration, Ahmed Nakşi.[88]

The tradition of illustrated histories, which was established during the reign of Süleyman and flourished under the patronage of his followers, lost its impetus after the middle of the seventeenth century. Although there were sporadic attempts to re-create the lives and activities of the sultans in later periods, the energetic output observed in the second half of the sixteenth century was never equaled.

As observed in the manuscripts described above, the legacy of Süleyman went far beyond his age. He was the only Ottoman sultan whose reign was so profusely documented by writers and painters, and whose personal and ceremonial activities and political and social achievements were recorded in such detail and so gloriously preserved.

Single Paintings, Drawings, and Albums

Although the primary duty of the artists of the nakkaşhane was to illuminate and illustrate religious, literary, and historical texts, their energies were not totally consumed by the production of manuscripts. They also executed single paintings and drawings that were free from the restrictions of the texts. These individual studies were so highly regarded that they were later incorporated into imperial albums.

Compilation of the works of esteemed calligraphers and painters into albums was a special form of art; single sheets were organized in a predetermined sequence and pasted onto the pages alone or in groups; the margins were carefully designed and decorated to enhance the contents; and finally the folios were compiled and the volume was bound.

The interest in album making appears as early as the fifteenth century, as observed in a group known as the "Fatih Albums" housed in the Topkapı Palace. These volumes, however, are almost scrapbooks with illustrations chosen at random and pasted on the pages; their contents range from eastern and central Asian themes and fourteenth- and fifteenth-century Islamic manuscript illustrations to European prints.[89]

The majority of Ottoman albums produced between the sixteenth and nineteenth centuries were carefully prepared; some were appended with a number of new folios and rebound at a later time. Several sixteenth-century examples are truly imperial in quality, each folio a work of art. Two of the most spectacular ones were compiled for Süleyman around 1560 and for Murad III in 1572/1573. The same interest in making imperial albums existed in Safavid and Mughal courts; some albums are preserved in the Topkapı Palace. Not all the single paintings and drawings produced in the nakkaşhane were intended for albums. Some paintings were meant to be studied as individual works, others were sketches that were later considered for albums.

One of the single examples is a fairly large painting that represents the city of Lepanto (**44**) and must have been used as a topographic map of the region.[90] Executed in the style initiated by Nasuh, it depicts the city situated at the mouth of the Gulf of Corinth (an inlet of the Ionian Sea) with two fortresses guarding the narrow entrance to the strait on the left. Several ships are anchored in the port; in one of them a group of sailors hoists the sails and prepares the ship to leave. In the center is the main fortress surrounded by high walls and towers, divided into several districts also supplied with fortified enclosures. At the lower portion is a circular inner harbor, protected by additional towers and a heavy chain barricading its entrance. Inside the walls are mosques, fountains, a large bath surrounded by a garden, and a number of residential and administrative buildings. The hills outside the compound are sprinkled with villages, some of which have their own mosques and hospices with courtyards. Careful attention was given to documenting the water supply of the city, with a large aqueduct and several waterwheels represented on the right. Major gates, towers, and buildings are identified by inscriptions.

In contrast to Nasuh's paintings in the *Tarih-i Sultan Bayezid* (see **38**), this example is more schematic. It also contains human figures. In addition to the sailors in the ship, there is a courtly personage holding a hawk who walks on a bridge connecting the inner fortress with the villages on the left; above is an archer aiming at unseen prey and a janissary firing his gun toward an unidentified target on the right.

The contents of the albums produced during the reign of Süleyman are extremely valuable for the development of the saz style, which coexisted with the genre of historical painting and flourished in the 1550s. The word *saz* was recently identified as being of ancient Turkish origin and applied to an enchanted forest filled with fantastic spirits.[91] The themes employed in album drawings are closely related to the original definition of the word and represent an imaginary world filled with composite blossoms growing amid highly exaggerated leaves, frequently inhabited by peris and dragons. The stylized floral elements abstracted from these drawings became the most characteristic decorative feature of the age and were applied to all Ottoman arts. The ingredients of the saz style, which had its roots in the fifteenth-century traditions of both Timurid Herat and Akkoyunlu Tabriz, also left an impact on early-sixteenth-century Safavid art. In the Ottoman world it was formulated into a major decorative style and

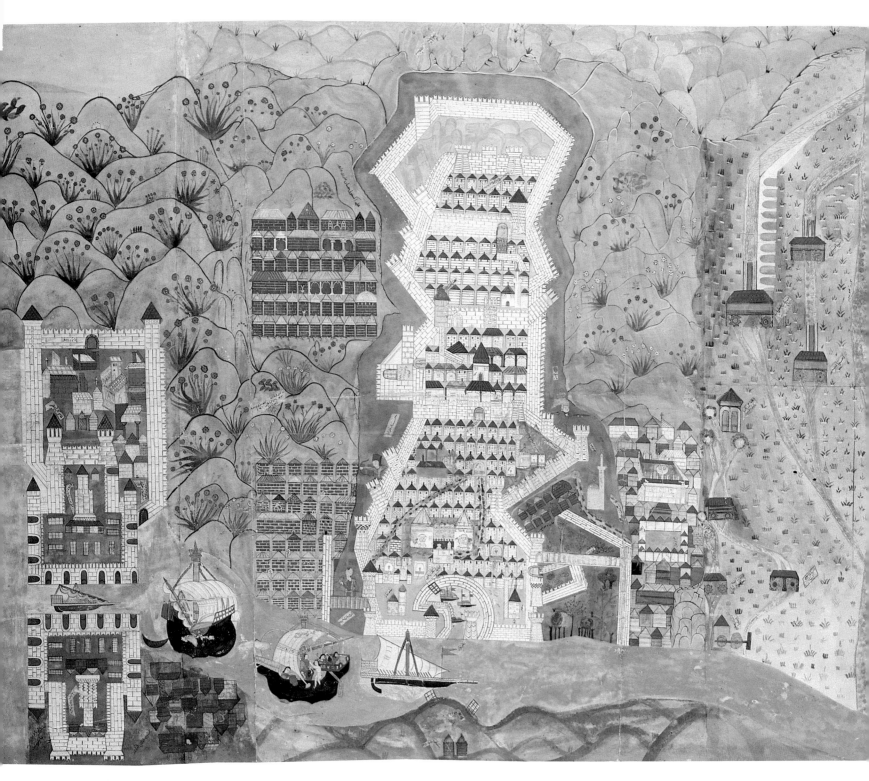

widely applied, becoming a distinct characteristic of the period.[92]

The development of this style of decoration is observed in the drawings incorporated into several sixteenth-century albums.[93] They reveal similar technique, employing bold black calligraphic brushstrokes to define the major elements, soft delicate lines to render the details, and washes to produce volume and texture; select areas are highlighted with gold or silver and tinted with pastel colors. Many contain almost mi-

croscopic details, displaying remarkable virtuosity.[94] Produced until the end of the sixteenth century, their execution varies: some are extremely dynamic and original in composition, others are more stylized and derivative.

One of the mid-sixteenth-century albums combines samples of calligraphy and paintings with saz style drawings, and includes a representation of a bunch of leaves drawn on gold-speckled paper and enhanced by touches of gold (45a). The leaves spring from the lower left, sweep across the sheet,

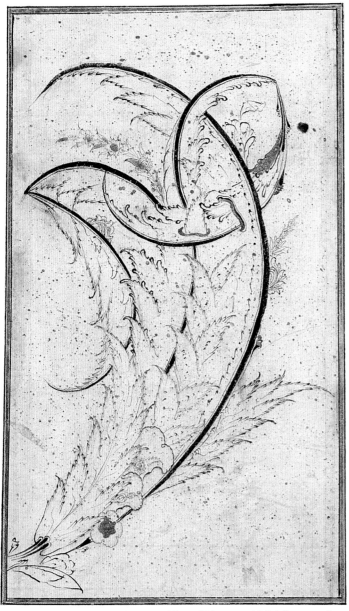

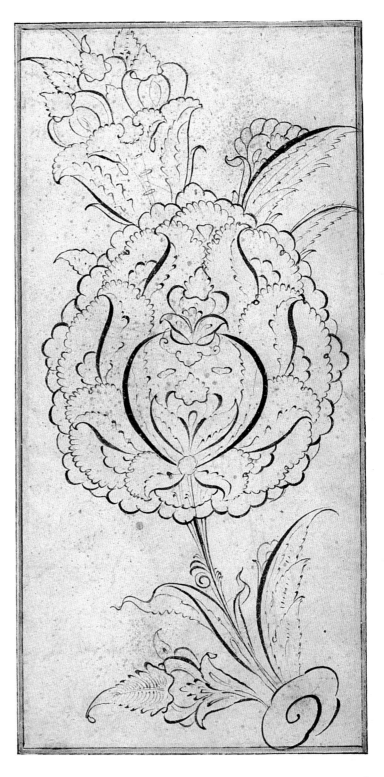

45a and **45b**. Saz leaves (above) and hatayi blossoms (right) from an album, mid-sixteenth century (İstanbul, Topkapı Sarayı Müzesi, H. 2147, fols. 22b and 23a)

44 (left). View of Lepanto, mid-sixteenth century (İstanbul, Topkapı Sarayı Müzesi, 17/348)

twist, turn, and pierce themselves in a manner aptly termed as "suicidal."[95] The strength of the bold brushstrokes defining the main design elements and the delicacy of the feathery-edged secondary features indicate great skill on the part of the artist. The drawing is disturbing, since one does not expect such harshness, even cruelty, from a spray of leaves; on the other hand, its execution is extremely lyrical and sensitive. The combination of strength and lyricism creates a powerful visual impact.

Another folio from the same album represents a compound hatayi (**45b**), a second essential ingredient of the saz style. Also drawn on gold-speckled paper, the blossom springs from a spiral scroll placed on the right, its stem flanked by smaller leaves and buds. The large stylized blossom, overlaid with additional petals and buds, has yet another pod growing from its top, itself composed of a multitude of petals and buds. The main components of the design are rendered once again with bold brushstrokes, while delicate lines define the curves of

45c. Floral composition with senmurv and chilin from an album, mid-sixteenth century (İstanbul, Topkapı Sarayı Müzesi, H. 2147, fol. 21a)

the petals. In contrast to the severe, suicidal tendency of the previous example, the artist here depicted perpetual and multiplying growth, full of life and rejuvenation.

Saz leaves and blossoms were frequently combined with fantastic creatures, such as chilins and senmurvs, whose origins can be traced to eastern or central Asian art. One of the drawings (**45c**) shows a chilin and a senmurv about to attack one another in a dreamlike landscape also occupied by a large saz leaf that sprouts hatayi blossoms and buds from its edges and twists across the sheet, piercing itself. The senmurv swoops toward the chilin, which rushes to meet it, their imminent clash briefly forestalled by the leaf. Both the animals and the floral motifs are rendered with bold and delicate strokes, highlighted with gold, and tinted with washes of gray and blue. The whole effect is one of a unified composition where all living entities are treated alike.

A more intense confrontation appears in yet another tinted drawing (**45d**) from the same album, in which the next two ingredients of the saz repertoire, the lion and the dragon, make their appearance. The equally matched creatures are engaged in a life-and-death combat, testing their strength by locking their jaws on each other, totally oblivious to the dense floral scroll engulfing them. The scroll, growing from a cluster of leaves on the lower right, bears the same type of leaves and blossoms described above, with at least nine birds hidden in the foliage. Sketchy cloud formations above and below suggest that this timeless battle takes place in a physical setting equally undefined.

A folio removed from another imperial album (**46**) displays the most masterful rendition of this theme and is possibly the largest as well as the earliest of Ottoman dragon drawings. It represents a ferocious beast, its body entangled in foliage, its claws tearing the leaves and branches while launching an attack on a creature that appears to be a part of the flora. The same zoomorphic transformation occurs with the head of a lion that evolves from a branch and clamps its jaws onto the neck of the dragon. The sprays of flowers, compound blossoms, and feathery leaves that break, pierce, twist, intersect, or overlap one another are extremely well-executed, creating a beautifully balanced composition that fuses the foliage with the creatures.

In spite of its vicious and terrifying aspect, there is a feeling of awe and even majesty in the representation of the dragon, which is engaged in endless combat with the spirits of its environment. The symbolism of scenes such as this one is not clearly understood, but one feels the impact of a strong mystical and shamanistic tradition that was preoccupied with the eternal struggle of supernatural forces.

The drawing belongs to a large group of dragons collected in the İstanbul albums, singular examples of which are presently in American and European museums. Two of these offer clues in identifying the name of an artist. The first is a badly damaged drawing (see fig. 8) that bears the seal of Şah-

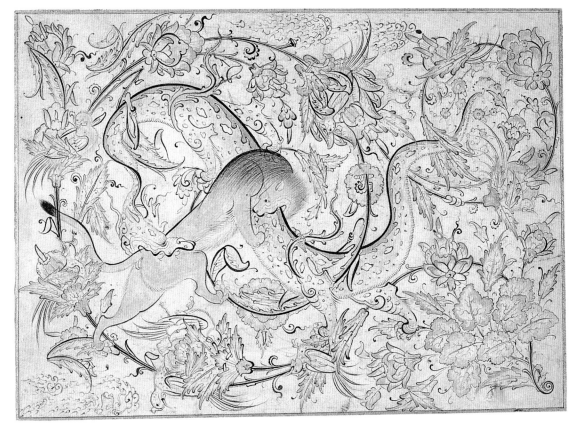

45d. Combat between dragon and lion from an album, mid-sixteenth century (İstanbul, Topkapı Sarayı Müzesi, H. 2147, fol. 32b)

46. Dragon in foliage from an album, mid-sixteenth century (The Cleveland Museum of Art, 44.492)

kulu and the notation: "This dragon is the work of master Şahkulu, the Rumi." The sketch, in the so-called Behram Mirza Album, has a preface written in 1544/1545 by Dost Muhammed, who might have been responsible for the notation. It appears to be the earliest datable drawing of Şahkulu. Even though too faint to determine the artist's style, it nevertheless establishes a date for his dragon drawings.

The second dragon, in the Metropolitan Museum of Art, bears another later notation that states the work was by Şahkulu. Although this drawing belongs stylistically to the last quarter of the sixteenth century and is not as refined as the others in the series, it is significant in attempting to identify the dragon theme with Şahkulu.[96]

The name of Şahkulu appears on one other drawing (see fig. 9), that of a flying peri holding a long-necked bottle and a stemmed cup, also removed from an imperial album. This example, now in the Freer Gallery of Art, is superbly detailed, its execution befiting the reputation of the master.[97]

Şahkulu, recorded in the payroll register of 1526 as "Şahkulu-i Bağdadi," must have originated from Baghdad. The document states that he was exiled from Tabriz, most likely around 1501 when Ismail took over in Iran. Şahkulu, whose name means the "servant (or slave) of the şah," was probably in the service of the Akkoyunlu sultan and left Iran when the Safavids defeated his patron. He first lived in Amasya and then moved to İstanbul, joining the nakkaşhane between December 1520 and January 1521. He drew the highest salary in the society in 1526, was made serbölük in 1545, and is mentioned in a document dated 1555/1556 as having died before he could be given the bayram gifts from the sultan. Another document datable to 1545 states that he gave a representation of a peri on paper to the sultan.

Mustafa Ali, in his biography of the artists completed in 1586, wrote that Şahkulu was trained in Tabriz by a master named Aka Mirak, an artist who later joined the Safavid court.[98] According to Mustafa Ali, when Şahkulu came to the court soon after Süleyman's accession, he was given an independent studio; the sultan used to watch him work there and frequently rewarded him with gifts. Mustafa Ali also insinuated that the artist was ill-mannered, had a nasty temperament, and frequently feuded with his colleagues. Şahkulu, identified with drawings of dragons and peris, must have been the master who executed the Cleveland example, which shows the same refined technique as his work in the Freer.

The last ingredient of the saz style is the peri, which counteracts the ferocious stalking dragon and represents the idyllic tranquility of the enchanted forest. The peri is also an integral part of this world, blending with its leaves and blossoms, as observed on a composite page (**47**) from an album in İstanbul. Constructed of four separate fragments pasted together, the right portion contains the head of a female who has long locks of black hair falling to her shoulders and wears an elaborate hat made of large blue and red tinted leaves. The figure,

47. Composite page with saz leaves and peri from an album, mid-sixteenth century (İstanbul, Topkapı Sarayı Müzesi, H. 2168, fol. 10b)

which emerges from a bunch of saz leaves with tiny birds perched on its tips, is almost a personification of a blossom. This portion of the folio is painted on silk, whereas the other fragments are on paper. Saz leaves overlap blossoms on the left panel, while a more delicate rendition of the leaf design occupies the horizontal piece added to the top. These fragments, enhanced with touches of gold and yellow, green, and blue tints, are skillfully united with the drawing on silk by extending and joining the floral elements.

Another İstanbul album is filled with single paintings and drawings, many of which represent angels who either fly or sit in an undefined space, although at times they are shown in a landscape or have carpets spread under them. The peris have pairs of swooping wings and frequently wear crowns or hats made of long feathery leaves, short-sleeved tunics over long sleeves and skirts, jeweled belts, and flowing ribbons tied to their torsos. They hold in their hands musical instru-

ments, long-necked wine bottles and cups, bunches of flowers, or peacocks, offering the delights of paradise.

A typical example (48a), pasted below an illuminated panel
with a verse of poetry, depicts the fantastic creature flying
over a landscape while playing a lute. The landscape is rendered in full color and represents trees interspersed with clusters of flowers and bushes. The figure, executed in bold outlines, is delicately detailed with washes, touches of gold, and
pink tints applied to select areas. She wears the outfit characteristic of the peris: the feathery hat surmounted by leaves
and infinitesimally decorated double-tiered tunic over a long
skirt. Spiral scrolls bearing blossoms embellish the neck of her
undergarment, the cuffs of her tunic, and the long knotted
ribbon tied to her chest; a larger version of the same scroll
appears on the long sleeves and lower tier of her tunic; the
cloud collar enclosing the shoulders of her tunic has a similar
scroll with birds, and her skirt shows cranes flying amid
cloud bands. She wears jeweled earrings, rings, and a belt

48a. Peri with a lute from an album, mid-sixteenth century (İstanbul,
Topkapı Sarayı Müzesi, H. 2162, fol. 9a)

48b. Seated peri attributed to Velican from an album, second half sixteenth
century (İstanbul, Topkapı Sarayı Müzesi, H. 2162, fol. 8b)

composed of plaques and fastened with a large scalloped buckle; a circular container hangs at the side. This type of belt,
which can be traced to fifteenth-century Timurid paintings,
was a common accessory in the Ottoman court: examples
made in mother-of-pearl and ivory inlaid with gold and gems
were worn by men and women alike.

Displaying extremely refined execution, this representation
is the work of a master. Its style recalls that of the Freer peri
bearing the name of Şahkulu, suggesting that it may have
been made by him or by one of his close followers, possibly
Kara Memi, his famous student.

The same album contains a slightly later drawing of another peri (48b) bearing the inscription "kalem-i [pen of]
Velican." The posture of the figure, who sits in three-quarter

103

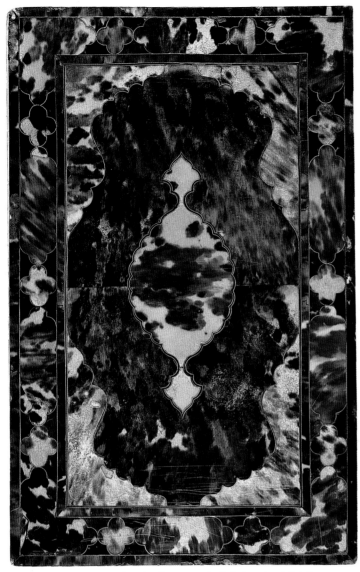

49a. Tortoiseshell and silver binding (exterior left, interior right) from an album, c. 1560 (İstanbul Üniversite Kütüphanesi, F. 1426)

view with one knee tucked under and the other bent up, echoing the movement of the drooped and raised wings, was copied in a number of other examples. The peri is bareheaded and sports a topknot, the characteristic hairstyle of these creatures. She sits in a relaxed manner, hovering in space with sketchy clouds appearing overhead. The figure is modeled with washes and fine lines that suggest volume; her wings are extremely well drawn and delicately detailed, as are her garments and floating ribbons. Although rendered carefully with touches of gold, the drawing reflects a slight mannerism in brushstrokes, particularly in the hem of the garment and the curves of the ribbons.

The inscription giving the name of Velican appears to be a later attribution, with the same wording and style of writing found on several album drawings. A number of other draw-

ings are inscribed simply "Velican," written in a different hand at a later time.[99] One example, however, a study of hatayi blossoms and buds with the name hidden among the foliage, seems to bear an authentic signature.[100] Even though it is difficult to determine how many of the drawings attributed to Velican were actually by his hand, the artist appears to have been renowned for his drawings and recognized as a master of the saz style.

Velican, recorded in the payroll registers of 1596 and mentioned in the documents relating to the 1584/1585 volume of the *Hünername* as being one of its illustrators, was a student of Siyavuş the Georgian, a painter in the Safavid court. Velican, who must have come to İstanbul in the 1570s, was the last practitioner of the saz style, which lost favor in the Ottoman court after 1600.

Two saz-style drawings were also incorporated in an album prepared around 1560, presumably for Süleyman. This remarkable collection contains samples of calligraphy executed by renowned Iranians, each page exquisitely illuminated by a master of the nakkaşhane.

The volume was bound with a unique tortoiseshell cover with stamped and gilded leather doublures (49a). The design of the exterior follows the traditional format of a central medallion with axial pendants, corner quadrants, and a wide frame enclosed by thin bands filled with alternating ovoid and quatrefoil cartouches. These areas are outlined with silver strips and lined with gold leaf, and thus differentiated from the field. Tortoiseshell cut in paper-thin plaques and lined with gold leaf was frequently used in furnishings, doors, and cupboards.[101] The employment of this material and technique

on a bookbinding is, however, most unusual. The doublures, lined in brownish-red leather, have the same format as the exterior, with highly refined saz scrolls filling the gold-stamped areas. Another unusual feature of the album is the polychrome saz scrolls painted on its flyleaves, which were traditionally either left blank or made from marbled paper.

The first pair of folios (49b) contains the Fatiha Suresi, the opening chapter of the Koran, written in six lines of talik by Şah Mahmud Nişapuri, a renowned calligrapher who worked in Tabriz. He was so highly regarded that the Safavid ruler Ismail is rumored to have hidden him together with Behzad when Tabriz was captured by Selim I, considering both men his most valued treasures. Although there is little truth to this story, Şah Mahmud, who died in 1545, was equally revered in the Ottoman court; his calligraphic works were collected

49b. Frontispiece transcribed by Şah Mahmud Nişapuri c. 1530–1540 from an album illuminated c. 1560 (İstanbul Üniversite Kütüphanesi, F. 1426, fols. 2b–3a)

and bound into imperial albums. His best writings were assembled in this volume, their high esteem clearly reflected in the exquisite decorations enclosing his texts.

It is interesting to note that both halves of the double frontispiece contain the same seven verses from the Fatiha Suresi, but the lines in each folio show a different number of words. The signature of the calligrapher is a part of the last line of the version on the left. Şah Mahmud obviously executed them as a demonstration of his expertise in talik, which was seldom used in the transcription of the Koran.

The verses, pasted on the folios, are framed by a wide band with blue and gold reciprocal arches; its semicircular head and tail extensions are filled with blossoming fruit tree branches that spring from a cluster of leaves and are painted in polychrome on a deep-blue ground. The latter theme is characteristic of Kara Memi, who must have executed all the illuminations in this manuscript. The artist's naturalistic style also appears in margins with delicate red tulips interspersed with blue finials that extend to the gold hatayi scrolls and cloud bands encircling the edges of the folios.

The decorative themes found on the opening folios were fully exploited throughout the manuscript, each page showing an original layout and design (**49c** and **49d**). The text, pasted horizontally, vertically, or diagonally on the folios, allows ample space for the illuminator, whose repertoire included both his unique naturalistic genre and the saz style initiated by his former master, Şahkulu. Sprays of naturalistic flowers and trees contrast with stylized scrolls of rumis, cloud bands, hatayis, and leaves, each panel employing a different color scheme. The margins are tinted in various tones and

49c and **49d**. Two folios transcribed by Şah Mahmud Nişapuri c. 1530–1540 from an album illuminated c. 1560 (İstanbul Üniversite Kütüphanesi, F. 1426, fols. 22b and 27a)

embellished with gold drawings, frequently saz scrolls.

Near the conclusion of the volume are two calligraphic exercises: one is in the form of a lion, the other composed of large letters enclosing a minuscule script. The folio that follows them contains a remarkable kaatı garden executed in colored papers and pasted together, creating a three-dimensional painting. This technique, first observed in calligraphy, appears to have been applied to a pictorial representation by the middle of the sixteenth century.[102] The floral elements are layered and stand in relief, protected by a transparent sheet covering the surface and sides. It is difficult to determine whether the calligraphic exercises were produced in the Ottoman or the Safavid court; the kaatı garden, on the other hand, is of local origin, decorated with spring flowers and trees.

Pasted on the last pair of facing folios are two tinted drawings with typical saz themes. On the left (**49e**) is a ferocious dragon stalking through dense foliage that it rips apart with its claws. The sinuous curve of its back, accentuated by a thick black line, is almost calligraphic in execution. Its flaming wings that spring from both front and back legs are rendered in silver and gold, while soft strokes and washes re-create the scaly body. The exuberant foliage growing from clusters contains feathery leaves overlapping and piercing the blossoms, and hatayis sprouting additional flowers and buds. The drawing was cropped around the edges and pasted sideways on the page. It is enclosed by blue and gold frames using the same dimensions as the one on the facing folio and placed on gold-speckled pink paper.

The drawing on the right (**49f**) depicts a spray of hatayi

49e and **49f**. Dragon (left) and hatayi blossoms (right) from an album, mid-sixteenth century (İstanbul Üniversite Kütüphanesi, F. 1426, fols. 48a and 47b)

Kaatı garden (detail) from album **49**, mid-sixteenth century (İstanbul
Üniversite Kütüphanesi, F. 1426, fol.47a)

blossoms with pods and leaves, tinted pink and blue. Since it was rendered on a sheet smaller than that of the dragon, an attempt was made to enlarge it by adding a wide pink border decorated with a scroll composed of twisting feathery leaves interspersed with blossoms and pods. The execution of this border is as refined as the central unit and stylistically almost identical. The margins of this folio are also gold-speckled and the same color as the one opposite it.

It is highly possible that these two drawings were executed by Şahkulu, who died a few years before the compilation of the album. Kara Memi appears to have mastered his mentor's style, as observed in the decorations of the folios. It seems logical that this imperial album, produced during the last years of Süleyman's reign, would contain not only the works of the great Iranian calligraphers but also those of the masters of his own nakkaşhane.

NOTES

1. The painters and bookbinders mentioned in the registers and other documents published in Meriç 1953, 1954, and 1963 together with those in Barkan 1979 and in an unpublished register of 1566 are compiled in Appendix 3. The 1526 register is published in its entirety in Uzunçarşılı 1986.

2. For two documents related to the expenses of manuscripts commissioned by the palace between 1552/1553 and 1555/1556 see Appendix 2.

3. Uluçay 1970, 237–249.

4. See Danışman 1969–1971, 2:207–334.

5. Danışman 1969–1971, 2:287–290.

6. Later Enderun members who became renowned painters include Hasan Paşa, a famous statesman, who illustrated several official histories in 1570–1610 (Akalay 1979; and Atıl 1980, 198 and 203–206, ills. 97–101). Another dignitary was Ahmed Nakşi, an astronomer and the official timekeeper of the Süleymaniye Mosque, who illustrated both literary and historical manuscripts during the first quarter of the seventeenth century (Atıl 1978a; and Atıl 1980, 212–215, ill. 110 and pls. 30 and 31). Working in the early eighteenth century was Abdülcelil Çelebi, known as Levni, thought to be also an Enderun graduate (Atıl 1980, 218–222, ills. 117–122, pls. 32 and 33).

7. The registers list several Hasans, three of them called Çelebi, an honorific title, which makes the identification of the nakkaşbaşı difficult. One Hasan Çelebi was the father of an artist named Hüseyin and died during the reign of Selim I; another was Büyük (Elder) Hasan Çelebi, presumably Hasan b. Mehmed; a third was Küçük (Younger) Hasan Çelebi, or Hasan b. Abdülcelil. See Appendix 3.

8. This document is partially published in Meriç 1953, no. LXXIV. In addition to the painters there were four musicians and eighteen others listed under *müteferrika*, a term that included calligraphers, goldsmiths, metalworkers, tile makers, and glassmakers.

9. Celalzade Mustafa (Koca Nişancı) mentioned in his *Selimname* that on 13 September 1514 Bedi üz-Zaman arrived in İstanbul with his entire court of scholars and artists (Topkapı Palace Museum, H. 1415, fol. 107a; Karatay 1961b, no. 635). The painters in Bedi üz-Zaman's retinue must have been responsible for the strong impact of Herat found in Ottoman paintings. This influence is described in Çağman 1978.

10. The flowering of the late Mamluk school of painting is discusssed in Atıl 1984.

11. For a study of the illustrations in this work see Atıl 1986.

12. Reproduced in Atıl 1980, ill. 120.

13. Woodhead 1983, 159–161 and 179, quoting from Aşık Çelebi. See also Appendix 2A.

14. For a study of cartoons and their application to other arts see Denny 1981.

15. For paintings produced during the reign of Mehmed II see Atıl 1973b.

16. For a study of the calligraphers of the age see Derman 1970.

17. See Appendix 3.

18. For a study of sixteenth-century lacquer Ottoman bookbindings and their prototypes see Tanındı 1984.

19. Works of this master goldsmith as well as the techniques and styles employed in the society are discussed in Çağman 1984. For the cover of the *Divan-ı Muradi* see Çağman 1984, figs. 1 and 2; Atıl 1980, ill. 107; and İstanbul 1983, E. 201.

20. See Umur 1980, 41 and 42.

21. Umur 1980, figs. 115–117.

22. Umur 1980, figs. 109–114 and 125–131; for the tuğras of Şehzades Mehmed and Bayezid see Umur 1980, figs. 123 and 124.

23. İstanbul 1983, E. 193. In addition, there is a large undecorated tuğra of Selim II in the Topkapı Palace Archives and possibly two more illuminated but damaged examples dating from the seventeenth century in the Topkapı Palace Library.

24. A group of similar tuğras on documents dated between 1531 and 1535 in Italian collections is published in Bombaci 1965, figs. 5 and 6.

25. These are numbered E. 7816/1 to E. 7816/11.

26. See, for instance, the tuğras of Süleyman published in Berlin 1982, no. 99; Binney 1979, no. 8; Riyadh 1985, no. 29, dated 1565; *Sanat* 1982, 78; Sertoğlu 1975, 21, 23, and 25. For the tuğras of Selim II see Umur 1980, fig. 126. See also Umur 1980, figs. 135, 142, and 150 for those of Murad III, Mehmed III, and Ahmed I.

27. See Appendix 1.

28. Hamdullah's retainer was recorded as 30 akçes a day, while that of Karahisari was 15 to 16 akçes.

29. The names of three other illuminators, Hasan b. Abdullah, Fazullah b. Arab, and Mehmed b. İlyas, appear in the colophons of Korans in the Topkapı Palace. Hasan b. Abdullah illuminated a Koran transcribed in 1503/1504 by Şeyh Hamdullah (Karatay 1962–1967, no. 800; and Yağmurlu 1973, fig. 18); Fazullah b. Arab illuminated two copies of the Enam Suresi in 1506/1507 (Karatay 1962–1969, nos. 806 and 807; and Yağmurlu 1973, no. XVIII); and Mehmed b. İlyas worked on a Koran dated 1547/1548 (Karatay 1962–1969, no. 818; Yağmurlu 1973, fig. 25; and Demiriz 1977). These artists are not listed in the payroll registers, with the possible exception of Fazullah b. Arab, who may be the Fazullah mentioned in 1505. See Appendix 3A.

30. For the illuminated serlevha of the *Süleymanname* see Atıl 1986, 88 and 89.

31. These are published in İstanbul 1983, E. 265 and 268.

32. These documents are published in Meriç 1953, no. CXV; see also İstanbul 1983, E. 192.

33. See Appendix 2B.

34. It is not possible to determine when the Korans of Yakut and Sayrafi entered the Topkapı Palace. They may have been in the collection for a long time or arrived during Süleyman's reign. A number of historians, including Arifi, the author of the *Süleymanname*, describe the gifts presented to the sultan on various occasions. Among those sent to the court by Elkas Mirza, a Safavid prince who joined the sultan's campaign to Iran in 1548–1549, were Korans transcribed by these very two calligraphers, presumably taken as booty when Elkas advanced with the Ottoman army as far as Isfahan. Since the Topkapı Palace owns several manuscripts by Yakut and Sayrafi, many of which were decorated and rebound in later years, the volumes sent by Elkas cannot be properly identified.

35. This text, also known as *Tefsir-i Hüseyni*, was composed by Hüseyin el-Kaşifi. The earliest copy, transcribed by the author in 1494, is in the Topkapı Palace (Karatay 1961a, no. 4).

36. Another contemporary work with a lacquered binding, a copy of the *Divan-ı Babur*, appears to have also been produced for Şehzade Mehmed, whose seal is found in the manuscript. For this and other lacquered bindings dating from Süleyman's reign see Tanındı 1984.

37. Reproduced in Atıl 1980, ill. 106; and İstanbul 1983, E. 124.

38. The Topkapı Palace owns over forty of these bindings dating between the sixteenth and nineteenth centuries; substantially more examples are listed in palace inventories. See Çağman 1984, 54, n. 12.

39. Reproduced in Atıl 1980, ill. 107; and İstanbul 1983, E. 201. See Çağman 1984, where this piece and other works by the same artist are analyzed. The tradition of using jeweled bindings for religious texts also existed in Europe and Iran. The Safavids used jeweled gold covers on secular manuscripts as well, for example, on the famous *Şahname* of Tahmasp (Çağman 1984, 54). At times Ottomans applied gems and pearls to leather bindings, including the c. 1535–1540 copy of the *Divan-ı Babur* (Tanındı 1984, fig. 15) and a Koran dated 1583 (İstanbul 1983, E. 183), both in the Topkapı Palace.

40. Çağman 1984 mentions that the societies included ninety men in 1526, sixty-nine men in 1558–1559, fifty-eight men in 1566.

41. Since there are no payroll registers dated between 1566 and 1596, it is not possible to determine exactly when Mehmed started working at the court. His name is not listed in the 1606 register, which indicates that he died shortly after 1605.

42. See, for instance, Çığ 1971, pls. XXXIII and XXXIV; İstanbul 1983, E. 199–202 and 204; Çağman 1984, figs. 8 and 9; and Frankfurt 1985, vol. 2, no. 1/86.

43. Duda 1983, pl. 350.

44. There is an undated copy in İstanbul made a few years later (Karatay 1961a, no. 771); another volume dated 1582 in London (Titley 1981, no. 50); and a slightly later version in the Binney Collection (Binney 1979, no. 100; and Frankfurt 1985, vol. 2, no. 1/17b).

45. Islamic pilgrimage documents prepared in scroll format seem to have existed since the eleventh or twelfth century. Among the earliest illustrated versions is an example dated 1285, now in the Museum of Turkish and Islamic Arts. Many of the pre-Ottoman scrolls came to İstanbul from the Great Mosque in Damascus. See Tanındı 1983a, 409 and 410, n. 12.

46. Stchoukine 1967.

47. Çağman 1974–1975.

48. These manuscripts are discussed in Grube 1981.

49. Stchoukine 1966, pl. IV; and Atıl 1980, ill. 70.

50. Sotheby's 1985c, no. 408.

51. Atıl 1980, pl. 17; and İstanbul 1983, E. 55.

52. Söylemezoğlu 1974.

53. It should also be noted that another group of artists had fled Tabriz when the Safavids captured the city and took up residence in Amasya before joining the nakkaşhane in İstanbul. Included among them was Şahkulu of Baghdad, who will be discussed later. See also note 8 above.

54. Atıl 1984, pls. 6 and 8–13.

55. For a study of this library see Berkovits 1964. See also Atıl 1986, 77, n. 42.

56. Halman 1979, 10.

57. Derman 1970, 283.

58. In addition to these versions discussed here, there is an unpublished copy in the İstanbul University Library, T. 1976, datable to the 1560s.

59. This style and its Ottoman counterparts are discussed in Çağman 1978.

60. Dickson and Welch 1981; Ahmed Feridun Paşa in his account of the Szigetvár campaign discusses the presentation of the manuscript to Selim II and describes its binding and paintings (TSM, H. 1339, fol. 246b).

61. Reflecting pools appear in thirteenth- and fourteenth-century Mamluk manuscripts of the *Kelile ve Dimne* (Atıl 1981a, 22) as well as in sixteenth-century Turkish translations of the same work, entitled the *Hümayunname*, which may have provided the impetus for this scene.

62. Binney 1979, no. 13; and Atıl 1986, fig. 40.

63. Binney 1979, no. 13; and Atıl 1986, fig. 41.

64. Stchoukine 1966, pl. IX; and Titley 1981, no. 1.

65. Atıl 1980, ill. 75.

66. Binney 1979, no. 9.

67. Çığ 1959, no. 5.

68. Stchoukine 1972 and Akalay 1973.

69. The Topkapı Palace owns another fragmentary parchment map made by Piri Reis that shows only the North and Central American coasts and bears the date 1528/1529 (Selen 1937).

70. The original maps used by Columbus are now lost. The earliest copy appears to have been made c. 1500 by Juan de la Cosa, who took part in the 1492 expedition; another, made c. 1525 by Alessandro Zorzi, was based on a map brought to Italy in 1506 by Columbus' brother Bartholomew.

71. The same style of painting is found in maps made in the first decade of the sixteenth century (Hapgood 1979, figs. 86, 89, 92, 99, and 104). One of these, dated c. 1502, appears to contain what would have been included in the missing half of Piri Reis' world map (Hapgood 1979, figs. 99 and 104).

72. Both versions were first published in Kahle 1926 and 1929; see Soucek 1973 for the latest study.

73. Piri Reis also discussed the New World in this book and mentioned that the earth is a sphere, a revolutionary concept for the time (Adıvar 1970, 68).

74. Over thirty copies of this text are known to exist. Since many are undated and their illustrations are careful copies of those in the original, it is difficult to determine their chronological sequence.

75. These monuments are clearly identified in Denny 1970.

76. See Atıl 1973b.

77. Binney 1979, no. 12. For an early study of Nigari's life and works see Ünver 1946; the artist's other works are published in Binney 1979, no. 11; Atıl 1980, ills. 85−87; Welch and Welch 1982, no. 6; İstanbul 1983, E. 69; and Atıl 1986, fig. 20. These include a hunting scene and the portraits of Süleyman, Barbaros Hayreddin Paşa, and Selim II in the Topkapı Palace; another portrait of Selim II in the Sadruddin Aga Khan Collection in Geneva; a group portrait with several dignitaries accompanying a person identified as Cenab Paşa, and copies of the portraits of Francis I and Charles V in the Edwin Binney, 3rd Collection. The portraits of Barbaros Hayreddin, Francis I, and Cenab Paşa bear inscriptions that include the name Nigari or Haydar.

78. For a study of this work see Atıl 1986. The document is translated in Appendix 2A.

79. Fehér 1976, pls. XXIX, XXX, XXXII−XXXIV, and XXXVI; and Atıl 1986, figs. 37 and 38.

80. See Çağman 1973; and Atıl 1980, ill. 93. Upon the completion of the manuscript Lokman received a bonus of 10,000 akçes; the salaries of Osman and Ali were raised by two akçes and the same increase was given to the calligrapher, illuminator, and bookbinder. This document, dated 1581, is published in Çağman 1973, 415.

81. See Meredith-Owens 1962; Titley 1981, no. 49; and Frankfurt 1985, vol. 2, no. 1/16a.

82. Volume 1, dated 1581, is in the İstanbul University Library; volume 2, completed between 1592 and 1597, is in the Topkapı Palace (Stchoukine 1966, no. 45; and İstanbul 1983, E. 173 and 187 with full bibliography).

83. The first volume was completed in 1584/1585 and the second in 1587/1588. Both are in the Topkapı Palace. The first volume was published in Anafarta 1969. For a complete bibliography see İstanbul 1983, E. 184.

84. There exist several versions of this text, some of which were appended to include the later sultans. The earlier volumes, dated between 1579 and 1589, are in the İstanbul University Library (two copies), the Topkapı Palace (three copies), and the British Library. See Atasoy 1972 and Titley 1981, no. 46.

85. Also called the *Silsilename* (Book of genealogy), there exist three copies of this work produced between 1583 and 1588; they are in the Museum of Turkish and Islamic Arts, the Chester Beatty Library, and the Topkapı Palace. These manuscripts are published in Minorsky 1958, no. 414; Renda 1973 and 1976; Atıl 1980, ill. 103; and İstanbul 1983, E. 180.

86. See Atıl 1980, pl. 25; and İstanbul 1983, E. 174 and 175 with complete bibliography.

87. The works of this fascinating man are discussed in Akalay 1979. See also Atıl 1980, ills. 97−101; and İstanbul 1983, E. 188−190 and 193.

88. See Atıl 1978 for a discussion of his style. See also Atıl 1980, pls. 30 and 31; and İstanbul 1983, E. 196.

89. These albums are discussed in *Islamic Art* 1981. There is a similar collection in Berlin, known as the "Diez Album," published in İpşiroğlu 1964.

90. Another example in the Topkapı Palace shows Belgrade. See *Sanat* 1982, 81.

91. Banu Mahir, "Osmanlı Resim Sanatında 'Saz' Üslubu," Ph.D. diss., University of İstanbul, 1984, discusses the origin and development of this style.

92. This style is expertly analyzed in Denny 1983. See also Grube 1962a, 1962c, and 1962d; and S. C. Welch 1972 for earlier studies.

93. The earliest examples appear in the so-called Behram Mirza Album in İstanbul, its preface written by Dost Muhammed in 1544/1545.

94. The most exquisite ones, showing the ultimate perfection of this style, are in the album compiled for Murad III in 1572/1573. This album, which is in Vienna, is published in Duda 1983, 109−160 and figs. 348−397.

95. This term was coined by Walter B. Denny. See Denny 1983.

96. Grube 1962b, no. 78; S. C. Welch 1972, fig. 2; and London 1976, no. 627. For a recent study of Şahkulu see Mahir 1986 where his style and works are analyzed and dragons attributed to him illustrated in figs. 1-9.

97. See Atıl 1986, fig. 7; see also Atıl 1986, 52, n. 46 for other references. For this and other peris attributed to Şahkulu see Mahir 1986, figs. 10-15.

98. Dickson and Welch 1981, 95−117.

99. See, for instance, the drawings of a hatayi blossom and saz leaf, and a European man from another İstanbul album published in İstanbul 1983, E. 177 and 178.

100. Denny 1983, pl. 17.

101. See, for instance, the c. 1578 door from the Harem published in İstanbul 1983, E. 150; and a pair of panels thought to have been made for the Azhar Mosque in Cairo in the late 1590s, illustrated in Riyadh 1985, no. 78; and Sotheby's 1985a, no. 137.

102. It is also found in the album of Murad III. See Duda 1983, fig. 361.

The Sultan's Treasury

The most splendid and the least studied Ottoman works of art are those made for the Hazine, the treasury of the sultans. The collection in the Topkapı Palace includes ceremonial and personal items produced by court artists as well as luxurious and exotic pieces, sharing in the concept of *Schatzkammer* and *Kunstkammer* (treasure and art cabinets) observed in many great Asian and European empires, combining the accumulation of treasures with patronage of the arts. The sultans' passion for objects made of precious materials was perhaps second only to their enthusiasm for illustrated manuscripts. The desire to be surrounded by rare and valuable items and the personal pleasure in using luxurious pieces have been the prerogatives of kings throughout history.

The Ottoman treasury was established by Mehmed II, who transformed the state into a formidable empire and founded the imperial institutions that reflected its majesty. Through his campaigns he not only acquired what was left of the royal collections of the Byzantines and Akkoyunlus, but also claimed the silver and gold mines in the Balkans, adding them to the rich copper supplies of Anatolia. The state now possessed a treasury with a group of rare and precious objects and had its own rich mines that not only increased the national wealth, but supplied the raw materials for the production of new pieces.

The Hazine was enriched by Bayezid II, known for his fascination with silver objects, and by Selim I, who added Safavid and Mamluk treasuries after the conquest of Tabriz and the annexation of Syria and Egypt. Selim I also founded an assay office, which controlled the weight of the precious metals used in the objects and stamped them with the sultan's seal. Each sultan inspected the treasury immediately upon his accession to the throne and locked the chamber with his seal. The Hazine was the personal property of the sultans, and one of the four highest Enderun offices was responsible for maintaining its security and preparing its inventories. The earliest record of the treasury, dated 1505, lists large quantities of sil-

ver and gold items, some of which were stated as having come from Europe. Subsequent inventories show vast numbers of precious objects of which only a small percentage appears to have survived.[1]

The Hazine of the Topkapı Palace today contains more than six hundred objects, most of which are displayed in the pavilion built by Mehmed II in the third courtyard of the complex. It incorporates items from the sultans' original collection as well as objects from other sections of the palace. The original collection was housed in the building known as the İç Hazine (Inner Treasury, thus distinguishing it from the state treasury), situated next to the grand vezir's chamber in the second courtyard of the palace. Other valuable objects were kept in different parts of the palace: the sultans' riding equipment was in the Raht Hazinesi (Treasury of the Stables), a structure to the left of the second courtyard; his arms and armor belonged to the Cebehane (Arsenal), the church of Aya İrene (Hagia Eirene) which was converted into an armory in the first courtyard when the palace was built; and the most valued items were reserved for the Has Oda in the third courtyard, later called the Hırka-i Saadet Odası (Chamber of the Holy Mantle), since it housed the sacred mantle of the Prophet Muhammed together with his other relics, swords of the orthodox caliphs, and donations to the Kaaba, such as locks and keys. Most of the holy swords and the sacred items were decorated and protected in jewel-encrusted gold cases in the sixteenth century. The İç Hazine and the Has Oda also contained manuscripts, which were later transferred to the library when the palace became a museum.[2]

Although the inventories of the Hazine are fairly extensive, only a very few items mentioned in the documents can be properly identified with existing pieces. Descriptions in the ledgers are either too general and could apply to more than one piece, or they pertain to items that appear to have been replaced, recycled, or lost. The contents of the treasury fluctuated through the centuries: pieces were added to or removed from the collection. The sultans acquired new objects by various means. Many were commissioned from artists who belonged to the Ehl-i Hiref; others were presented as gifts, received as tribute, taken as booty during campaigns, confiscated from officials for reasons ranging from treason to disgraceful conduct, or purchased from local guilds and foreign markets.

One of the foreign purchases is thought to be a gem-encrusted gold helmet made for Süleyman by a Venetian artist named Luigi Caorlini in 1532, said to cost more than 100,000 ducats.[3] Its payment and transportation were said to have been handled by the grand vezir İbrahim Paşa. Süleyman allegedly used the helmet only once, during a reception of the Austrian delegation. There is no record in the Ottoman archives related to this piece, nor is there mention of its having arrived in İstanbul. There is, however, a figure wearing a fantastic helmet constructed of four tiers of crowns surmounted by a large plume in an engraving made in 1532 by an anonymous Venetian,[4] which was copied in 1535 by Agostino Veneziano,[5] who inscribed it with Süleyman's name (fig. 15). This fanciful headgear presumably represents the Venetian helmet made for Süleyman; whether it was actually made and purchased by the sultan is highly speculative.

The sultans' Hazine was also enriched by gifts from foreign rulers, heads of tributary states, ambassadors, and subjects, including members of the administration and the artisans. Lists of gifts presented during accession ceremonies, official receptions, bayram celebrations, and other festive events provide an insight into the wealth accumulated by the court.[6]

Objects in the Hazine were, on the other hand, pilfered throughout its history. Frequently the sultans themselves were forced to melt down the silver and gold objects to convert them to currency for their military campaigns and other expenditures. Some pieces were destroyed to create new ones, reusing the metals and the gems; others were given to esteemed officials and to members of the royal family on special occasions or sent to heads of foreign states as diplomatic gifts.

One of the most impressive gifts was a crown sent by Ahmed I to Stephen Bocskay, the ruler of Transylvania appointed king of Hungary by the sultan. The crown, made of gold and encrusted with gems and pearls, was taken to Budapest by the grand vezir Lala Mehmed Paşa and placed on Bocskay's head in 1605.[7] Later confiscated by the Habsburgs, it is now in Vienna. Since the Ottoman sultans did not wear crowns or display such symbols of imperial power as the scepters and orbs used by European monarchs, its creation was just as extraordinary as the Venetian helmet supposedly made for Süleyman.

Over the centuries the sultans also sent substantial numbers of precious gifts to the Kaaba in Mecca and to the tomb of the Prophet in Medina. In addition they presented valuable items to the mausoleums of their predecessors, family members, and revered spiritual leaders, particularly to that of Eyüb Ensari. These gifts included silver and gold lamps, chande-

Fig. 15. Sultan Süleyman wearing the Venetian helmet, engraving by Agostino Veneziano, dated 1535 (London, The British Museum, 1859-8-6-307)

liers, decorative hangings, and chests as well as inlaid wood Koran stands and boxes. Objects in the *türbes* (mausoleums) included the garments and accessories of the deceased, such as kaftans, handkerchiefs, belts, and turban ornaments, which were laid on top of the symbolic sarcophagus (the body having been deposited in the earth underneath according to Islamic law). Gifts were either placed around the chamber or stored in the cupboards built into the walls. When Turkish national museums were established the items in the türbes were transferred to these collections. Although a few were salvaged from the mausoleums of Hürrem Sultan, Şehzade Mehmed, and Selim II, nothing was left in the tomb of Süleyman, which must have contained the most outstanding pieces. Valuable objects were also lost during fires, earthquakes, and civil disorders that periodically plagued the city and the palace.

Although the core of the Hazine in the Topkapı Palace comprises objects made in the court, there are as well extremely valuable items representing the imperial traditions of the Timurids, Safavids, and Mughals, as well as those of Asian and European origin, including Chinese porcelain, German clocks, and Russian bibelots, some of which were gifts, while others were taken as booty or confiscated.[8]

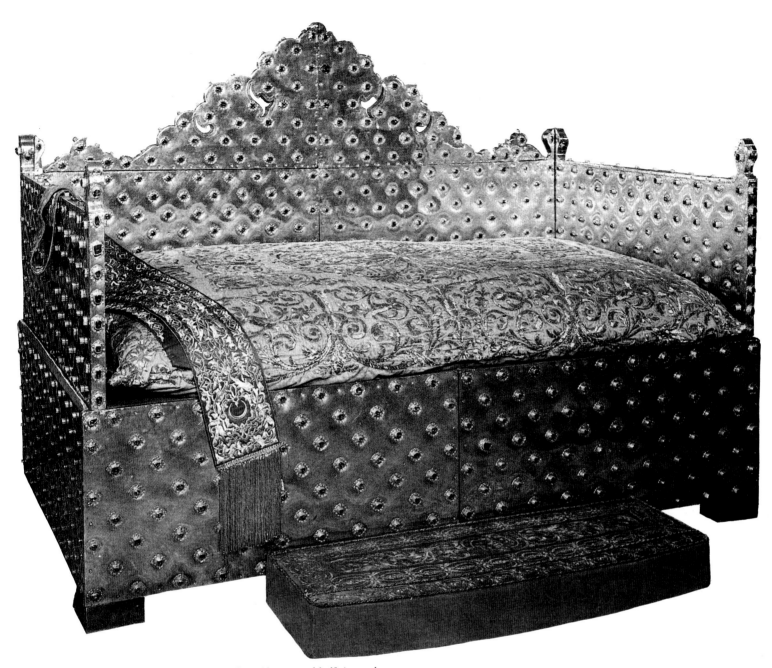

Fig. 16. Gold ceremonial throne encrusted with peridot, second half sixteenth century (İstanbul, Topkapı Sarayı Müzesi, 2/2825)

Ottoman objects are also found in European collections, including the collection of the Habsburg emperors, now in the Kunsthistorisches Museum in Vienna. A large and varied group of arms and armor, dating from the sixteenth and seventeenth centuries, is owned by the Waffensammlung section of the museum. Some of these were presented as gifts, others taken as booty during the long Habsburg-Ottoman wars. An equally impressive collection in the Wawel Castle in Kraków contains the incredibly rich arms and armor and other items confiscated by John III Sobieski, the king of Poland who led the surprise attack in which the Ottomans were defeated dur-

ing the second siege of Vienna in 1683. In fact, many European treasuries—including those in Germany, France, Italy, Sweden, and Denmark—contain a representative group of Ottoman arms and armor together with objects for personal use, reflecting the prolific production of the sultans' workshops.

The objects housed in the Topkapı Palace and other imperial collections indicate that the artists produced a variety of ceremonial objects as well as functional pieces for daily use. The most striking ceremonial item is the famous gold throne (fig. 16), popularly called the Bayram Tahtı (throne used dur-

Fig. 17. Inlaid wood throne made for Ahmed I by Sedefkar Mehmed Ağa, c. 1610 (İstanbul, Topkapı Sarayı Müzesi, 2/1652)

ing bayram celebrations) because it was traditionally placed in front of the gate leading into the third courtyard of the palace during religious holidays. Made of ten interlocking pieces, it has a wood core faced with gold plaques, which are encrusted with 954 large pieces of peridot set into gold petal mounts with high collars affixed to the core by a series of gold nails.[9] The throne is traditionally said to be the one described in an inventory dated 1585, and made for Murad III by two artists named İbrahim and Derviş.

The sultans traveled with their portable thrones, and several manuscript illustrations represent the rulers seated in gem-encrusted gold examples during campaigns and activities taking place outside the palace. Süleyman himself is enthroned on a similar piece in the paintings of the 1558 *Süleymanname*. There must have been a number of such thrones, which were destroyed and/or reworked through the years. It is, therefore, not possible to positively identify the gold throne in the palace as the one listed in the 1585 inventory. The piece could very well date from Süleyman's reign, since it shows the understated grandeur found on other objects made for him, such as a silver plate and an ivory mirror (see **50** and **73**). The use of peridot, a relatively inexpensive gem today, suggests that it was considered an unusual stone at the time. Peridot (called *zeberced* in Turkish) comes from the island of Zebirged in the Red Sea and must have been brought from Egypt shortly after its conquest by Selim I. Its first appearance in the court must have been unusual enough to warrant its use on the gold throne.

Extremely few Ottoman thrones are in existence. In addition to the gold example, there are two other portable ones, both made of inlaid wood. One of them has the same shape as the Bayram Tahtı, but is considerably smaller (see **107**). Datable to the mid-sixteenth century, it is inlaid with ebony, ivory, and mother-of-pearl. The other has a domical canopy surmounted by a gold clock and is inlaid with mother-of-pearl and tortoiseshell and encrusted with gems (fig. 17). It was made for Ahmed I in the 1610s by Sedefkar (inlayer of mother-of-pearl) Mehmed Ağa, a remarkable man who not only also produced the inlaid wood *kursi* (lectern) and doors of the Mosque of Sultan Ahmed, but was also the building's chief architect.[10]

Official Ottoman thrones appear to have been the large platform types with canopies, built into the chambers. There are two of these structures in the Topkapı Palace, one of which is in the Arz Odası, where foreign dignitaries, heads of state, and high officials were received. It was refurbished later, but the lacquered dome of the canopy, representing a combat between a dragon and a senmurv, dates from the end of the sixteenth century.[11] The other built-in throne is in the Has Oda; it too was refurbished in later years and the present one, covered with gilded silver, was made in the second quarter of the seventeenth century by Evliya Çelebi's father, Derviş Mehmed, who was the chief goldsmith at the time.

Precious Objects

Although it is not possible to perceive the full scope of the Hazine during Süleyman's reign, its contents must have been in keeping with the power and wealth of his empire. Both Selim I and Süleyman were goldsmiths by training and therefore gave particular attention to the promotion of this tradition. Evliya Çelebi, himself a goldsmith and the son of a renowned master, mentioned that Süleyman learned the technique while residing in Trabzon (as did Selim I); the sultan supported the guild of the goldsmiths and endowed it with a fountain, mosque, bath, and compound with workshops arranged around a court.[12]

The payroll registers of the Ehl-i Hiref dating from Süleyman's reign indicate that a large group of men were involved with metalworking and jewelry. The artists belonged to diverse societies, the specific wares of which are at times difficult to identify. The Cemaat-i Zergeran (also called *kuyumcu*) constituted the goldsmiths, silversmiths, and possibly also those who worked with zinc; the Cemaat-i Hakkakin were the gemstone carvers; the Cemaat-i Zernişani were the gold inlayers; and the Cemaat-i Sikkezan produced metal stamps for striking coins as well as assay marks on silver and gold objects. In addition there were the *kazgancı* (casters and kettle makers), who appear to have worked with copper alloys, such as brass and bronze; the *kündekari*, woodworkers who also carved and cut ivory, mother-of-pearl, and tortoiseshell and inlaid them on wooden objects; the *küftci*, who produced gold wire from sheet metal and used it for inlays; and the *çıkrıkcı*, who seem to have produced vessels by spinning them on a lathe.

In the earliest payroll register of the Ehl-i Hiref drawn in 1526, the section pertaining to the goldsmiths and jewelers includes ninety artists, of whom fifty-eight belonged to the society of goldsmiths, nine to the society of gemstone carvers, and twenty-two to the society of gold inlayers.[13] There was also one *foyeger* (foil maker), which indicates that some gems were placed on colored foils. A number of artisans were themselves the sons of masters. Several were transferred from Edirne, indicating that the former capital was active in the production of gem-encrusted and gold-inlaid metalwork. All three societies were headed by men exiled from Tabriz, presumably in 1501 when the Akkoyunlu Empire fell, and who had been living in Amasya before joining the İstanbul studios, as had Şahkulu, the head of the nakkaşan.

The fifty-eight-member *zergeran* (goldsmiths) had thirty-four masters and twenty-four apprentices, three of whom were listed as *sikkezan* (stamp makers), headed by Hoca Mercan Tebrizi, who had come via Amasya. This register, which gives the backgrounds of the artists and the dates they entered the studio, indicates that six of the men had been employed by Bayezid II, seven by Selim I, and forty-five by Süleyman, who certainly enlarged the society. About half of the

membership was of local origin; the largest group of outsiders came from the Balkan provinces, particularly from Bosnia. There were also men from Russia, Albania, Walachia, Herzegovina, Bulgaria, Macedonia, and Croatia. In addition to the chief, a couple of others had arrived from Tabriz via Amasya; there are also three Tabrizis whose names are recorded in a document listing the artists transported by Selim I after his conquest of Tabriz.[14]

Among the nine *hakkakin* (gemstone carvers) listed in 1526, one had joined the studio during the reign of Bayezid II, three were added by Selim I, and five by Süleyman. The hakkakin included five masters and four apprentices; its head was Şirim or Şirin Horasani (from Khorasan), who, similar to his colleagues in charge of the nakkaşan and zergeran, had come to İstanbul via Amasya. One half of the group were native artists and the remaining men were from the Balkans. One of them, a diamond cutter, came from Egypt and was registered during the reign of Selim I.

The list of *zernişani* (gold inlayers) also indicates that the society was active under Bayezid II; it grew during the reigns of Selim I, who added twelve men, and Süleyman, who added nine. The group, consisting of nine masters and thirteen apprentices, was headed by İsmail Tebrizi, and included many local artists, a number of Circassians, and a few from the Balkans; there were also men from Georgia and Tabriz.

The portion of the payroll register of 1545 pertaining to these societies has not yet come to light, but the document covering a twelve-month period between 1557 and 1558 shows that the goldsmiths and jewelers had been reduced to sixty-nine men. The society of goldsmiths was divided into two corps, the Rumiyan and the Aceman, similar to that observed in the Cemaat-i Nakkaşan. There were thirty-seven men in the Rumiyan group, headed by Ahmed Gürci (Georgian), who was listed in 1526 as having been brought from Georgia by Süleyman; seven members were in the Aceman corps, headed by Hüseyin, possibly the Hüseyin Horasani or Hüseyin Çerkes (Circassian) mentioned in 1526. The gemstone carvers were reduced in number to six members, as were the gold inlayers to fourteen. However, there was an independent society for the stamp makers; it had five members.

The last register drawn during the reign of Süleyman is dated 1566. It included thirty-nine goldsmiths, once again separated into Rumiyan, which constituted ninety percent of the society, with a small corps of Aceman. It also lists four gemstone carvers, eight gold inlayers, and seven stamp makers.

There is a gap of thirty years in the payroll registers before the appearance of the next register, which is dated 1596. The membership in the Ehl-i Hiref had risen considerably, the goldsmiths alone numbering 110 men. As also observed in the nakkaşhane's enrollment, the Ehl-i Hiref in these years employed the largest number of men in the history of the Ottoman Empire. The goldsmiths, abolishing the separation into the Rumiyan and Aceman corps, were equally divided into masters and apprentices, and headed by Mehmed Bosna (Bosnia), the only artist whose works are identifiable.[15]

Mehmed, who headed the seventy-eight-member goldsmiths 1605, is not mentioned in the register drawn the next year, suggesting that he was no longer living in 1606.[16] It is not known when Mehmed registered in the society of the goldsmiths, since the documents between 1566 and 1596 are missing. He was, however, an established master and the head of the group when he made the gold bookbinding for the collected poems of Murad III in 1588, which he signed "Usta [master] Mehmed serzergeran [chief goldsmith]." His signature appears on two other works produced for Murad III: a casket made for the Prophet's mantle dated 1592/1593 and a lock and key made for the Kaaba in 1593/1594. The artist is thought to have started working in the court during the reign of Selim II in the 1570s, his last work being the crown presented to Stephen Bocskay in 1605.

The payroll registers indicate that precious objects had been sponsored by the court since the reign of Bayezid II and that the artists were organized according to technique. Selim I promoted the artists, who were further supported by Süleyman. Even though there was a decrease in membership in the three major societies—goldsmiths, gemstone carvers, and gold inlayers—between 1526 and 1566, many more groups evolved during these years, dividing the Ehl-i Hiref into even more highly specialized departments.

The documents reveal that Süleyman rewarded his court artists with cash bonuses and, occasionally, kaftans. One of these ledgers, drawn around 1535, lists 149 men who received a total 225,450 akçes (each averaging 1,500 akçes, the equivalent of four to six months' salary) in addition to more than thirty garments.[17] Another document lists 104,400 akçes and ten garments presented to 76 artists during the twelve-month period between 1555 and 1556.[18] The artists in return gave their best to the sultan, offering him their most beautifully made wares.[19]

The artists combined a variety of techniques and materials when producing their pieces, obviously collaborating with their colleagues in other societies. Silver, gold, and zinc (called *tutya*) were the favored metals for imperial wares, which were shaped by casting, hammering from sheet, or spinning. Their surface decoration was produced by working both sides (chased and incised on the front and repoussé from the back) and the backgrounds of the motifs were enhanced by hatching, crosshatching, or ring matting, using chisels or circular punches. Frequently the pieces were gilded; inlaid with gold, niello, and enamels; and encrusted with gems. Some were further embellished with filigree panels, gold-inlaid and gem-encrusted jade plaques or rock-crystal components lined with illuminated paper sheets, indicating collaboration with painters. Since the metalworkers made the stamps used on leather bookbindings, they also participated in the production of manuscripts.

Although silver and gold had been fashioned into objects since antiquity, the use of zinc was unusual. It was employed in Safavid Iran during the early sixteenth century, as observed in a group of elaborate, gold-inlaid and gem-encrusted bottles, jugs, and bowls brought back from Tabriz by Selim I.[20] The production of zinc vessels seems to have stopped in Iran after 1514, and the fascination with this metal disappeared as quickly as it appeared. In the Ottoman court the same tradition, obviously inspired by the Safavid examples, survived until the mid-seventeenth century.[21] The material, mined in India and China, must have arrived in western Asia around 1500 and been thought rare and exotic enough to be fashioned into court objects. Since zinc lacks strength and tarnishes easily, its novelty eventually wore off. The metal was better suited for producing brass by combining it with copper.

Copper and copper alloys, that is brass and bronze, were generally reserved for more prosaic objects, and were frequently employed in architectural decorations, such as doors, fireplaces, and domes. Using the same techniques as those applied to precious metals, they were also tinned and gilded. Tinning, which produced a protective coating against the poisonous effects of copper, was also a decorative feature, attempting to simulate silver. Gilded copper (called *tombak*) was extremely widespread and primarily an aesthetic preference, simulating gold.

Inlaid brasses, which were popular in the thirteenth and fourteenth centuries throughout the Islamic world, appear to have lost favor in later years. Only one silver-inlaid brass vessel is known to have been produced for the Ottoman court, a bowl made for Murad II in the fifteenth century.[22] The shape, style of decoration, and technique of the piece indicate it was manufactured in Mamluk Syria or Egypt, possibly as a gift to the sultan.[23]

Gemstone carvers fashioned jade, rock crystal, and other materials (including amber, jet, and chalcedony) into objects, and cut turquoise, emerald, ruby, and other stones for encrustation.[24] The gems were frequently left in their natural state or cabochon-cut, sometimes rose-cut, grouped according to size, and affixed to the pieces. Pearls, coral, diamonds, and other gems such as amethysts and sapphires were seldom used in the sixteenth century, the Ottoman taste of the period showing a strong preference for bluish-green, red, and green stones. In some cases transparent gems, such as diamonds, were placed over red or green foils to produce a desired color. The primary purpose of encrusting objects with gems was to create a coloristic effect; faceting, light refraction, and physical perfection of the gemstones were totally ignored. The overall effect is not unlike manuscript illumination or enameling, producing a brilliant and colorful surface.

Both the goldsmiths and gemstone carvers worked closely with the gold inlayers who created elaborate scrolls bearing leaves and blossoms. The artists employed two distinct types of inlay, one flush with the surface and the other rendered in high relief. In the first type, frequently observed in rumi scrolls decorating jade objects, thin pieces of gold were applied to shallow grooves, and the inlay lay flush with the surface. In the second, more complicated type, a scroll with branches bearing leaves and blossoms was carved into the jade; then twisted gold wire was applied to the branches and pre-cut gold pieces to the leaves. The blossoms were composed of scalloped gold settings representing petals, each with a raised central collar holding a gemstone. The leaves and petals were further enhanced with chased lines and striations. The entire scroll stood above the surface, with the blossoms resembling corollate flowers with jeweled centers. These two types of inlay, both indigenous to the Ottoman world, were frequently combined on the same piece, and were applied to metalwork as well as jade, rock crystal, and porcelain.

Several different metalwork styles appear to have coexisted at the court. One group includes objects without surface decoration, relying on the elegance and simplicity of their forms. This concept is not found in other Islamic societies and appears to be unique to the Ottomans.[25] Included in it are cups, bowls, bottles, and candlesticks made of silver, brass, or copper.

A related group is decorated with chased and repoussé designs rendered in relief, employing the decorative repertoire of the age. Although some of the themes recall those found on fifteenth-century Timurid objects, they are essentially based on the designs formulated in the nakkaşhane, which were used on a variety of other contemporary arts, such as ceramics and architectural decoration. Many items in this group were made of silver, and a number were gilded. Examples produced in the late fifteenth and early sixteenth centuries are decorated with rumi and hatayi scrolls, while those made after the second quarter of the sixteenth century frequently show the saz style that was ubiquitous in all Ottoman decorative media. One of the earliest pieces embellished with rumis and hatayis is a silver chandelier from the Mosque of Mehmed II[26] datable to the 1480s; another is a gilded silver bowl, its rim decorated with animals, bearing the stamp of Bayezid II.[27] The latter has a most unusual shape, with scalloped and fluted walls and a movable central disc. This particular shape as well as the style of animals decorating the rim recall eastern European examples. The bowl was most likely produced by one of the artists from the Balkans listed in the document of 1526 as having been registered during the reign of Bayezid II.[28] This artist combined his native traditions with the decorative features of the Ottoman court.[29] The same combination of rumi and hatayi scrolls appears on a silver plate made for Süleyman (see 50) and a series of single-handled gilded silver jugs, a few of which have the stamp of either Selim I or Süleyman (see 51 and 52). The shape of the jugs with dragon-headed handles is directly related to late-fifteenth-century Timurid examples, but the decoration is

purely in the Ottoman style. Also included in this group are brass and gilded copper items revealing the same surface interest.[30] The saz style, which developed in the nakkaşhane in the second quarter of the sixteenth century, was popularly employed by the metalworkers. The naturalistic genre was not as widespread and was used on a limited number of objects, mostly arms and armor.

The most exquisite silver and gold objects were produced in the third quarter of the sixteenth century and decorated with saz scrolls, at times inlaid with niello. Frequently the silver was gilded, and in rare cases the pieces were enameled. Among the outstanding examples are a small gilded silver bowl with enameled motifs;[31] a jade and gold bookbinding (see 20), a ceremonial canteen (see 54), and the handle and scabbard of one of the Prophet's swords attributed to Mehmed, the chief goldsmith; and the bookbinding, casket, and Kaaba lock and key signed by the same artist. Mehmed's style masterfully combines refined metalworking with gem encrustation, striking a perfect harmony between the arts of the goldsmith and the lapidary.

Although a number of imperial items, such as the canteen and sword carried by the Has Oda officials, had ceremonial significance, they were basically functional objects for use by the sultans, as were the thrones. Even such pieces as locks and keys for the Kaaba, which represented the sultans' suzerainty over the holy sites in the Hijaz, had practical uses. Perhaps the only nonfunctional and purely decorative items were the elaborate spherical ornaments that were suspended from ceilings—even above portable and built-in thrones—and employed in both secular and religious settings, such as reception chambers and mausoleums.

The majority of the Hazine items was for daily use and included jugs and tankards for drinking; canteens for carrying purified water; bowls, plates, and trays for serving food; ewers and bottles for dispensing liquids; boxes for jewels and other treasured items; and pen boxes. The sultan's table was set with silver, gold, and porcelain pieces, the latter of which had been collected since the fifteenth century. Acquired by purchase, as booty and gifts, but mostly through confiscation, the Chinese porcelain collection during Süleyman's reign was quite extensive and was kept in the kitchens with the other cooking and serving pieces.

Some porcelain vessels were restored by adding metal rims, caps, and handles (see 70); others were changed to serve the sultans' needs (see 71). For example, vases or ewers were made into canteens by adding a pair of spouts, and pieces dating from different periods were combined to create covered bowls and incense burners. Certain examples were embellished with gold and silver fittings and encrusted with gems (see 68 and 69), following the techniques employed on jade and rock-crystal objects. Most of the decorated pieces were Yüan and Ming dynasty blue-and-whites, although white ware and celadons were also refurbished.[32]

50. Silver plate stamped with the seal of Sultan Süleyman, second quarter sixteenth century (İstanbul, Topkapı Sarayı Müzesi, 23/1625)

The sultans did not wear jewelry in the manner of other Asian and European monarchs; their accessories were limited to jeweled mother-of-pearl and ivory belts (see **76–78**) and gold turban ornaments (see **79–83**). The Ottoman turban, yards of fine cloth wrapped around an inner cap, was embellished with a *sorguç,* which held plumes. This ornament was stuck into the turban and secured by hooks attached to chains. Both women and men wore these decorative belts and turban ornaments, the ones for the ladies being smaller and more delicate.

Another personal accessory used by both sexes was the hand-held mirror, of which there are several dating from Süleyman's reign (see **72–74**). Some were made of iron, inlaid or overlaid with gold, and had polished metal faces; others were of carved ivory with glass mirrors. One of them was made in 1543 by an artist named Gani (see **73**), who must have been the most prominent member of the ivory carvers.

His name appears only on this example, but the members of his society produced many buckles and plaques for belts and handles for daggers that they presented to the sultans during bayrams. Documents enumerating these gifts distinguish walrus tusk *(balıkdişi)* from elephant tusk *(fildişi),* indicating that the difference between the two materials was clearly known at the time.

There are a very few silver objects that have survived from the reign of Süleyman. These include a unique plate, a group of jugs with dragon-shaped handles, and several small items such as archer's rings.[33] The sultan's collection must have included many more silver vessels, probably melted down in later years to produce currency needed by the state.

The only silver piece made for Süleyman that remains in the Topkapı Palace is a small silver plate with a slightly raised, rounded, and grooved rim (**50**). The central mark and a series of concentric rings at the back indicate that it was produced by spinning. The rim was gilded front and back; the central medallion was engraved with two superimposed scrolls radiating from a central blossom, with ring matting filling the background. One of the scrolls bears hatayi blossoms and buds while the other contains composite rumis, their intersecting volutes enhancing the circular shape of the piece. This understated and yet striking example, which contrasts decorated and plain concentric zones, accentuated by a thin band of gilding, bears the seal of Süleyman stamped on the outer section.

The decorative themes used in the central medallion were employed on a group of contemporary blue-and-white ceramics, some of which have the same shape and concentric zones. The same hatayi and rumi scrolls are found on bookbindings and illuminations dating from the first quarter of the sixteenth century, at which time they must have entered the repertoire of the metalworkers and the potters.

These decorative elements appear on a series of single-handled silver jugs, all of which are in collections outside Turkey. The shapes of these jugs are based on late-fifteenth-century silver- and/or gold-inlaid Timurid brasses, several of which are in the İstanbul museums. Most of these pieces must have arrived in the court after the conquest of Tabriz, either brought by Bedi üz-Zaman, the last sultan of Herat, or taken as booty from the Safavids. The same shape was previously used on a jade vessel made for Ulugh Bey in the second quarter of the fifteenth century as well as on early-sixteenth-century Safavid objects, including several inlaid brasses and a unique gold-inlaid black stone piece made for Ismail and brought from Tabriz by Selim I.[34] It is also found in zinc, rock-crystal, jade, and other stone examples made in the Ottoman court as well as in contemporary ceramics. In addition, it was copied in fifteenth- and sixteenth-century Chinese blue-and-white porcelain, presumably made for the Islamic courts.

The fact that the jug was produced in such diverse materials and techniques indicates that it was extremely functional. The Turkish word still used to identify objects with this shape is *maşrapa*, a drinking vessel. The size of the jugs (four to five inches high) also confirms its usage, large enough to contain a single serving.

Ottoman jugs differ from the Timurid and Safavid examples in both material and technique. There are some six or seven silver pieces that were cast and decorated in relief with the characteristic hatayi and rumi scrolls executed in repoussé with chased details; ring matting was applied to the background and the pieces were gilded.[35] They all have a single handle in the shape of a dragon, its head attached to the rim and its curved or fan-shaped tail to the swelling portion of the body. The handle, cast separately, was soldered onto the piece. Some examples have domical lids with raised knobs, also cast and soldered.

Although the shapes of Ottoman jugs point to western

Asian prototypes, the techniques of production and decoration reflect another source, that of eastern Europe. These features must have been transmitted by artists recorded in the payroll registers as having originated from Bosnia and other parts of the Balkans, who applied their native techniques to produce traditional Islamic shapes and decorated these objects with the style formulated in the Ottoman court.[36]

The shapes, proportions, and decorative features of these jugs are fairly consistent: a high and straight neck, with a slightly flaring and molded rim, is joined to the bulbous body with a thick ring; the rim, the band between the neck and thick body, and the high, splayed foot are plain, whereas the neck and body are decorated; inside the foot ring is a central blossom executed in relief. Decoration hidden inside the foot ring, observed only when the piece is raised, is an Islamic feature dating back to the eleventh century.

One of the earliest examples in the series is in the Victoria and Albert Museum (**51**). The body was cast, its decoration produced by repoussé, and the details of the motifs and the ring matting in the background applied by chasing and punching from the front. The neck bears a rumi braid; the body contains two densely composed superimposed scrolls creating cartouches, one with rumis and the other with ha-

51. Gilded silver jug with lid, second quarter sixteenth century (London, Victoria and Albert Museum, 158-1894)

121

52. Gilded silver jug stamped with the seal of Sultan Selim I (?), second quarter sixteenth century (London, Princess Esra Jah Collection)

tayis; inside the foot ring is a multipetaled blossom. The dragon on the handle is decorated with a floral cartouche, its tail fanning out with pierced rumis.

The lid with a crenellated edge, added in the seventeenth century, is attached to the handle with a chain. On the rim of the jug is zigzag scraping, possibly to remove some silver for testing; on the handle is a stamp, which is illegible.

A second, slightly smaller jug without a lid (52) bears a combination of rumi and hatayi scrolls on both the neck and body; those on the neck show rumis and buds, whereas the ones on the body have composite leaves and blossoms. The scrolls contain elements larger than those on the Victoria and Albert piece, and create overlapping S-shaped volutes instead of intersecting one another to form cartouches. The dragon handle is also less elaborate, with a simple split-leaf terminal. Stamped on the rim is a seal that has been tentatively identified as that of Selim I.

Assay marks on metal objects are very difficult to read, since the stamping was frequently irregular and registered only a portion of the inscription. In addition some sultans had the same name, thus making it impossible to distinguish "Süleyman b. Selim" from "Selim b. Süleyman" when only part of the seal is visible on the objects. The stylistic features of this jug date it to the second quarter of the sixteenth century, since it bears the same elaborate floral motifs found in tuğras of the period. A similar style of decoration appears on a lidded jug in the Hermitage, which contains in its foot ring

a stamp belonging to either Selim I or Süleyman.[37]

Scrolls with the rumis, hatayis, and cloud bands used in manuscript illuminations produced in the nakkaşhane were also applied to gilded copper and brass objects. One of the earliest of these is a single-handled tankard (53).

This type of drinking vessel, called *hanap*, was popular in the second half of the sixteenth century and produced in gem-encrusted jade and underglaze-painted ceramics; it was also copied in Hungary, as in the famous metal example from Eger.[38] The vessel, whose shape most likely derives from European models, is thought to have been used for *boza*, a milky drink made from fermented millet. One of the earliest in the series is this example, which may have been based on gold or gilded silver models that have not survived.

The tankard is decorated with a tripartite composition. In the center of the body are three lobed oblongs linked to two trefoils formed by pairs of large rumis that extend from the rim and the base. The oblongs enclose incised inscriptions that repeat in Arabic "everlasting glory and prosperity," a benediction used on Islamic metalwork since the eleventh century. Scrolls with hatayis, leaves, and other blossoms fill the trefoils between the rumis. Large lobed ovals linked to two-lobed lozenges extending from the rim and base appear between the oblongs. The ovals enclose a central cypress tree

53. Gilded copper-alloy tankard, second quarter sixteenth century (Baltimore, The Walters Art Gallery, 54.512)

54. Jeweled gold canteen, second half sixteenth century (İstanbul, Topkapı Sarayı Müzesi, 2/3825)

flanked by a pair of floral sprays growing from a cluster of leaves placed at the bottom; floral elements fill the lozenges. The interstices are densely packed with scrolls bearing hatayis, six-petaled blossoms, and saz leaves superimposed by cloud bands, with ring matting applied to the background. Ring matting is used in the background of the main units, except in the inscribed oblongs, which are left blank. At the base is a band embellished with a scroll bearing blossoms, leaves, and cypress trees, separated from the body by a thin braid. The broken hinge at the top of the handle indicates that the tankard once had a lid.[39]

Although the decorative repertoire of the tankard is derived from contemporary nakkaşhane designs, the wording of the

inscriptions reflects a much older metalwork tradition. These cartouches, which recall the panels with headings in manuscripts, are notably plain, particularly when compared with the density of decorative motifs used in the surrounding areas. It is possible that the prosaic inscriptions were an afterthought and these cartouches were originally intended to have more elaborate designs, such as applied filigree panels or enameled designs.

Objects produced in gold datable to Süleyman's reign are almost as rare as those made in silver, obviously only the most prized pieces having escaped conversion into currency. One of these is a spectacular gem-encrusted gold matara used for carrying the sultan's drinking water (**54**). Its flattened bul-

123

bous body tapers toward the short cylindrical neck and rests on a high splayed foot; on one side is a small curved spout terminating in a dragon head, while two additional dragon heads project from the shoulders, one holding in its mouth a large pearl and the other an emerald. The domical lid, surmounted by a large ruby, has two gold chains connected to the shoulders by the pair of rings that also attach to the gold mesh handle.

The piece, encrusted with gold palmettes, pale-green jade plaques, and gems, is vibrantly articulated. The surfaces are further embellished with chased and incised floral scrolls with ring matting applied to the sunken backgrounds, enhancing the multilayered effect.

Both the flattened front and back have an oval jade plaque affixed to the center and a series of double palmettes that encircles the outer edges. The jade plaques are decorated with twisted wire scrolls bearing leaves and flowers with high central collars holding gems; in the center of each plaque is a large emerald rising from a multipetaled blossom. Gems set into both the recessed areas and the raised palmettes show a different setting: the flowers rise to create truncated forms, with the stones set into their apex. The sides of the canteen, superimposed with gold medallions, also have similarly decorated jade plaques as well as truncated gem settings in both the recessed and raised areas. The same mounts appear on the neck, spout, and foot.

The lid, on the other hand, shows yet another setting: the stones are encased in straight-sided geometric mounts with squares used on the outer zone, triangles in the inner zone, and a high circular one for the large central stone. The lid extends into the neck with a gold cylindrical cone, chased with medallions and inlaid with niello.

Most of the gems used on the matara appear to be emeralds and rubies, although there are also lavender, purple, and colorless stones, which may be amethysts, almandites, sapphires, or diamonds. Almost all the gems are unfaceted, with the largest ones used in the apex of the lid, in the centers of the jade plaques, in the blossoms encircling these units, and on the spout; medium and small examples are sprinkled

around. A few stones, including the large one on the lid and several on the foot and body, are rose-cut.

Such diversity is explained partially by a notation inscribed on the head of the dragon with the pearl: "640 *dirhems*," the weight of the piece (almost two kilos, or four and a half pounds), and "*tecdid*," which means refurbished (unfortunately, the date of the refurbishing is not mentioned). The lid and the rose-cut gems must date from the time the canteen was repaired, a decade or so after it was made.

The jade plaques used on the matara are embellished in the same manner as those used on Koran bindings (see **20** and **21**), one of which has a manuscript transcribed in 1570/1571, indicating that the technique of decoration was established by that date. Identical lobed oval plaques[40] were used on arms and armor and horse trappings, and the same technique was applied to jade objects.

Similar canteens appear in manuscript illustrations representing Süleyman and Selim II, who are accompanied by a pair of Has Oda officials, one carrying the sultan's sword, the other his matara. The earliest depiction of a gem-encrusted gold example is in the account of the Szigetvár campaign by Ahmed Feridun Paşa, dated 1568/1569. An almost identical canteen is found in the *Tarih-i Sultan Süleyman* of Lokman, dated 1579/1580, in the scene showing Süleyman's visit to the Mausoleum of Eyüb Ensari (see **43a**). This type of jeweled canteen appears to have been used after the mid-sixteenth century and, together with the sword, represented the sultan's imperial authority. Although an attendant carrying a sword was an integral part of a ruler's retinue in all Islamic dynasties, the use and display of the canteen was a tradition unique to the Ottomans.[41] The shape of the matara can be traced to leather examples made in central Asia as far back as the fifth century B.C., such as those found in the Pazyryk barrow graves. A later leather canteen with appliquéd decoration was presented by Murad III to the Habsburg emperor Rudolph II (see **105**), which indicates the same material was used in the Ottoman court.

Another ceremonial gold piece with a practical use is a padlock commissioned for the Kaaba by Süleyman (**55**). Its shape follows the traditional locks made for the sanctuary: a thin and long cylindrical shackle attached to a shorter but wider octagonal barrel, surmounted by a lobed, arch-shaped

55. Gold-sheathed Kaaba lock made for Sultan Süleyman 1565/1566 (İstanbul, Topkapı Sarayı Müzesi, 2/2274)

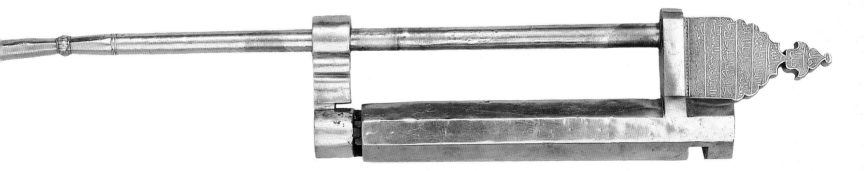

headpiece that terminates in a palmette. The lock, made of silver sheathed with gold, has a steel or iron interior mechanism. Its key seems to be missing.

The headpiece and the finial bear an eight-line inscription that states the lock was made for the Kaaba by Süleyman in 1565/1566.[42] Saz leaves, either overlapping blossoms or superimposed by floral sprays, appear around the letters, together with occasional knots. Horizontal bars separate the lines of text, and ring matting appears in background.

The padlock commissioned by Süleyman belongs to an extensive collection of similar pieces housed in the Topkapı Palace. Many are locks and keys to the Kaaba donated by Ottoman sultans as well as by the rulers of earlier Islamic dynasties, including the Mamluks, who were the overseers of Mecca.[43] After Selim I overthrew the Mamluks, the Ottoman sultans became the protectors of the holy cities and periodically sent keys to the Kaaba to assert their suzerainty and reconfirm their role as guardians of Islam. Most of these locks and keys are dated and some are signed by the makers, including the one made for Murad III in 1593/1594 by the chief goldsmith Mehmed, which is the most elaborate example in the series.[44] Similar symbolic pieces were made for fortresses and cities.

Ottoman silversmiths and goldsmiths must have also produced the zinc vessels that were popular during the sixteenth century. These examples were inspired by the Safavid tradition, and the earlier pieces may have been made by Tabrizi artists. Safavid tutyas included large bottles and bowls, frequently decorated with animals and inscriptions, whereas the Ottoman examples show a preference for jugs with floral compositions. Large versions, called *güğüm*, used as ewers, and cups and plates were produced also.[45]

One of the earliest examples in the series of Ottoman zinc vessels is a lidded jug decorated with gold filigree cartouches and floral scrolls set with emeralds, rubies, turquoises, and pearls (**56**). The pearls on this piece indicate that it closely followed the Iranian models and was among the first to be produced in İstanbul. The settings for the stones are also in the Safavid style, with five-prong claws to hold the gems.

The jug's neck contains six filigreed oval cartouches set with rubies and turquoises, their backgrounds painted moss-green in an attempt to distinguish these areas from the surrounding field, which is filled with scrolls bearing leaves and blossoms encrusted with gems and pearls. The body follows the same decorative scheme, employing larger filigreed panels. The cartouches of the neck and body are placed on alternating axes, a feature commonly found on Ottoman and Safavid metalwork.

The decoration of the flat lid, which has three cartouches, is identical to that of the neck, except that gold cloud bands executed in relief encircle the edge, reflecting the Ottoman

56 (above) and 57 (below). Jeweled zinc jugs with lids, second quarter sixteenth century (İstanbul, Topkapı Sarayı Müzesi, 2/2873 and 2/2856)

court tradition. The high knob is surmounted by a large turquoise. The handle, also inlaid with a gold scroll bearing gem-studded blossoms, has a small trefoil thumb rest, a vestige from much earlier examples. The foot is encircled by a boldly executed gold braid.

A second tutya jug with a similar shape has a domical lid and higher neck (57). Its decoration is slightly different, employing gold-outlined lobed oval medallions filled with twisting branches bearing leaves and gem-centered blossoms; the surrounding areas combine two gold scrolls, one with gemencrusted flowers and the other with delicately incised rumis. The stones, set in prongs as well as in high plain collars, include rubies and turquoises, with diamonds employed only in the centers of the medallions on the body.

The neck contains four ovals alternating with a pair of half medallions placed at the upper and lower edges. Inside is a gold filter decorated with hatayi and rumi scrolls set with gems. The design used on the neck reappears on the body; here, however, the interstices between the ovals are further embellished with gold cloud bands.

The lid, which has three medallions, repeats the decoration found on the neck; its flattened edge bears a floral scroll, while its high knob is set with a peridot. The handle, again decorated with a floral scroll, has a gilded silver underside, presumably to strengthen the tutya. A gilded silver chain hangs between the knob and the thick ring on the handle, which also functions as a thumb rest. The low foot contains a gold scroll with leaves.

The entire surface of the jug is ring matted, with the exception of thin bands defining the rim, neck, and body. This texturing is also found on other tutya vessels, at times applied to the main panels to distinguish them from the field. The metal, which has oxidized to a dull dark gray, originally had a bright silvery tone and must have looked sumptuous with its gold inlays and colorful gems.

The artists produced similar vessels by carving rock crystal and other stones such as chalcedony and obsidian. Rock crystal, a colorless transparent material, was frequently combined with gold components, set with gems, and lined with painted paper sheets.

One of the earliest rock-crystal jugs made in the Ottoman court is also the only piece in this material that shows no embellishment (58). This simple and perfectly proportioned vessel has a large S-shaped handle carved from another piece and attached to the rim and swelling shoulders by rivets and adhesives. The handle, an abstracted form of the dragon-shaped examples found on silver vessels, terminates with a curved leaf, the tip of which is chipped. Both the neck and body are carved with a series of vertically placed oblong panels that have trefoil heads; those on the neck also have trefoils at their bases while the ones on the body terminate with inverted rounded arches. The panels are framed with bands executed in relief; a series of moldings appears around

58. Rock-crystal jug, second quarter sixteenth century (İstanbul, Topkapı Sarayı Müzesi, 2/467)

the rim, neck, body, and foot. The simplicity of the piece recalls the plain metal objects that also rely on the elegance of their forms and harmony of their proportions.

Ottoman rock crystal was usually more elaborately decorated, as exemplified by a rectangular pen box that has a high lid with sloping sides (59). Five panels of rock crystal compose the top and sides of the lid, and the same number, the sides and bottom of the base. The lid panels are joined by gold bands with scalloped edges incised with saz leaves and blossoms and set with natural emeralds and rubies mounted in slightly articulated high collars. The base panels are joined in similar fashion, except that gems are omitted along the edge of the opening; this portion, as well as the shallow feet, is decorated with incised leaves.

The side panels of both the lid and base are carved with a series of reciprocal trefoils, resembling the design applied to manuscript illuminations. Each trefoil contains a gold flower with raised scalloped petals and a high central collar holding either an emerald or a ruby; tiny gold leaves or blossoms are inlaid into the adjacent units. The flowers on the lid create a central medallion flanked by two half medallions with large emeralds placed in their cores. The lid is attached to the base by hinges and kept from falling back when opened by a chain joining it to the base.

The interior contains three glass compartments framed in the same manner as the exterior panels. The smaller compart-

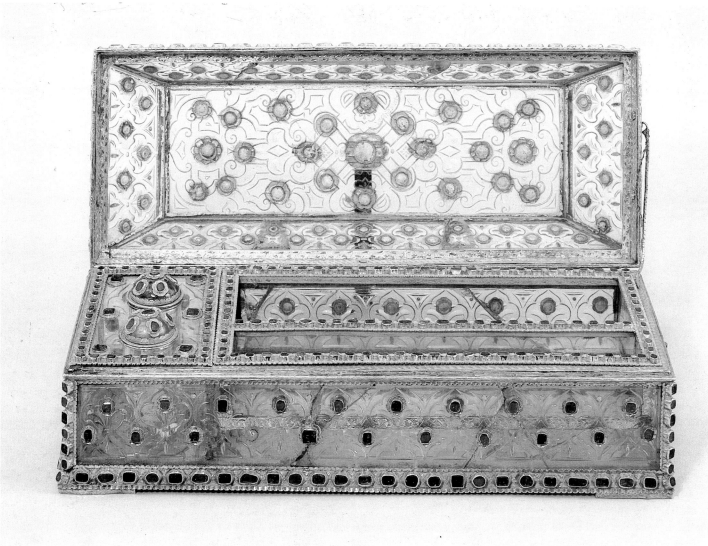

59. Jeweled rock-crystal and gold pen box, second half sixteenth century (İstanbul, Topkapı Sarayı Müzesi, 2/479)

ment on the left is covered and set with two cylindrical containers; the lids of these containers are decorated with ruby-centered blossoms, while the other flowers on the cover have emerald cores. On the right are two oblong sections. The division of the interior follows the traditional format of Islamic pen boxes with cylindrical containers used for ink and sand, and the long rectangular units for pens and other writing implements.

A second matara in the Hazine of the Topkapı Palace is made of rock crystal and fitted with a gold head and foot (**60**). The octagonal rock-crystal body is decorated with reciprocal ogival medallions formed by twisted gold wire and set with rubies and emeralds. The settings show a variation from the types discussed above: the blossoms have striated petals and contain high square collars that enclose the gems, overlapping their edges. Since the settings follow the shape of the

stones, some of these collars are rectangular or ovoid. In addition to vertical faceting, the rock crystal contains horizontal fluting that counterbalances the verticality of the body and relates it to the bands of rubies encircling the head and foot.

The gold circular head dips in the center and flares at the sides with a pair of extended spouts. One of the spouts has a lid, attached by a chain to another chain looped through the prominent ring rising in the center, which serves as the handle; the lid for the second spout is missing. Each side of the gold head is decorated with a central semicircular band executed in relief and embedded with rubies. The remaining areas are sprinkled with gold squares enveloping rubies and occasional emeralds, with a ring of diamonds surrounding the large ruby in the core of the semicircular band. The surface is decorated with saz leaves and blossoms on a ring-matted ground. The same settings and goldwork appear on the oc-

128

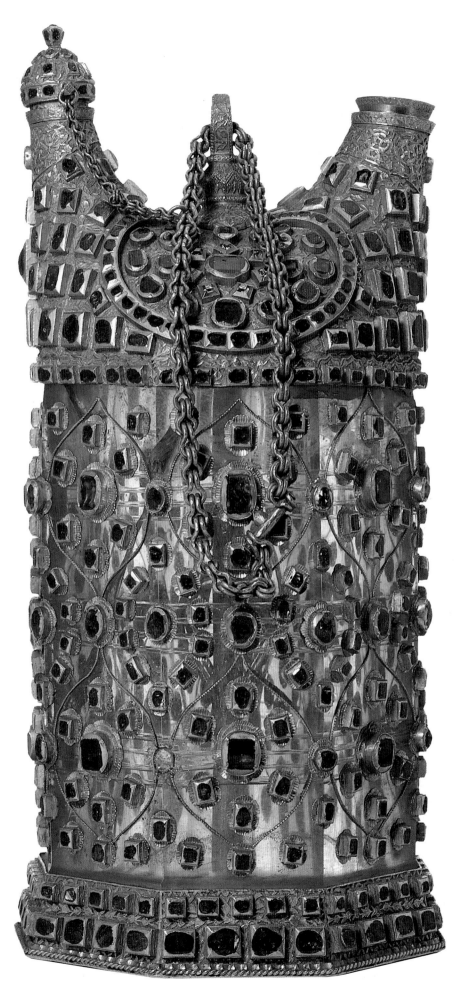

60. Jeweled rock-crystal and
gold canteen, second half
sixteenth century (İstanbul,
Topkapı Sarayı Müzesi, 2/484)

tagonal foot decorated with two rows of rubies.

The canteen has a rod inside, secured to the foot as well as to the top, which was designed to relieve stress when the piece was carried by its chain handles. The combination of divergent forms, techniques, and decorative themes reflects the virtuosity of the artist who has created a true showpiece. The square gold mounts for the gems recall those used on the lid of the other canteen (see **54**), which may have been repaired by the same artist.

A group of objects has rock-crystal panels lined with painted paper sheets created by the nakkaşhane artists. One large jug (**61**), its body containing eight ovoid panels with squared tops, is embedded with emeralds and rubies set in the same striated petal mounts with high square centers as the rock-crystal canteen (see **60**). The fairly thick panels are faceted and have sloping sides. They stand in relief, encased in gold frames, similar to the gems. Under each panel is a dark-blue paper painted with white, pink, and gold flowers. The rest of the piece is executed in gold and encrusted with rows of rubies set into high plain collars.

The metal parts are decorated with floral scrolls placed against a background filled with vertical rows of minute horizontal lines, creating an unusual texture. The handle is shaped as a double-headed dragon; one head, baring its teeth, is attached to the rim, and the other, emitting from its mouth flames represented by a scalloped semicircle filled with rumis, is affixed to the body. Inside the foot ring is a circular design radiating from a central star and creating a series of large petals.

Damage has destroyed the harmony of the jug's proportions. It was crushed at one time and the body has caved in over the foot, giving it a squat appearance.

The same workshop appears to have produced the rock-crystal pen box (**62**), which has rounded edges and a flat lid composed of oval and circular plaques joined by smaller concave-sided pieces. Placed under the components of the lid and sides of the base are white paper sheets painted with red, blue, and gold blossoms and gold rumis. The plaques are framed with gold bands embellished with emeralds set into high round collars, the sunken ground incised with floral motifs. Similar bands encircle the edges of the lid and the base. The rock-crystal plaques are also set with rubies and emeralds in petaled mounts, identical to those on the rock-crystal jug (see **61**). The gems in the medallions and ovals are sparsely placed, showing more of the paper lining, thus creating a contrast with the surrounding zones.

The underside of the lid and the interior of the base are lined with gold sheet. The interior is fitted with a nielloed panel placed on the left, decorated with rumi and hatayi scrolls and set with gems; inserted into this panel are three cylindrical containers for inks. The longer section for pens on the right, incised with large floral scrolls, is divided into two by a central bar and has a small caster for sprinkling sand.

61. Jeweled rock-crystal and gold jug with lid, second half sixteenth century (İstanbul, Topkapı Sarayı Müzesi, 2/8)

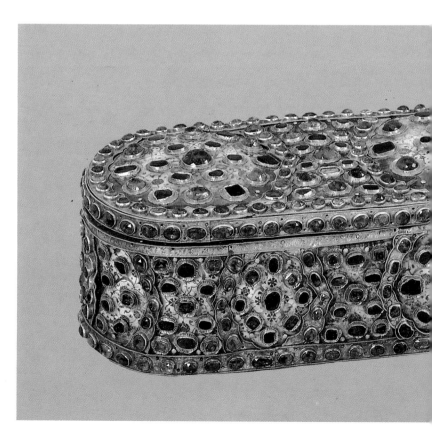

62 (above and below). Jeweled rock-crystal and gold pen box, second half sixteenth century (İstanbul, Topkapı Sarayı Müzesi, 2/22)

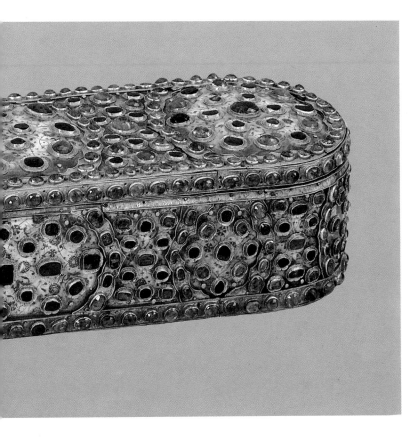

This section is attached by a chain to the lid and can be lifted out; under it is a large compartment for storing documents, its sides decorated with painted designs. The underside of the base is covered with gold and incised with medallions.

Some of the gems are left in their natural state, the larger ones are cabochon-cut, and others, particularly the emeralds on the framing bands, are rose-cut. The faceting of the stones points to the second half of the sixteenth century, when Ottoman jewelers began to cut gems.

An even more popular material in the court was jade, the color of which ranged from pale to dark green. All the jade objects in the Hazine are made of nephrite, presumably brought in large quantities from Turkestan, which had large deposits of it and supplied both eastern and western Asia.[46]

Among the earliest Ottoman jade objects is a pair of small boxes with sliding lids. The dark-green jade plaques used for the lid and sides of the base have an overall pattern of gold blossoms. In their cores either rubies or turquoises are held with prongs, as they are set on the tutya jugs (see **56** and **57**). Sprinkled between the gems are tiny gold roundels. The plaques are held together by nielloed gilded silver brackets and rest on four dragon-shaped legs.

131

63. Jeweled jade box, second quarter sixteenth century (İstanbul, Topkapı Sarayı Müzesi, 2/2085)

The lid, neck, body, and foot of the jug are inlaid with scrolls made of twisted gold wire bearing delicately incised leaves and blossoms, in the center of which are rubies and lavender-colored stones, possibly amethysts. The piece has a dragon-shaped handle; the open-mouthed head of the creature is attached to the rim, and the tail, terminating in floral motifs, to the body. The head and tail of the dragon are inlaid with leaves and ruby-centered blossoms; its body is decorated with gold leaves, which reappear on the rim of the jug. Inside the neck is an exquisitely rendered gold filter. In the center of the filter is a small medallion composed of nielloed rumis, set with a large turquoise, enclosed by a circular inscription written in sülüs and interspersed with saz leaves and blossoms; enclosing the inscription is a nielloed braid and a pierced saz scroll, which is also repeated on the inner walls of the rim.

A different technique appears on the underside of the lid. The circular collar that fits into the neck is executed in gold

The boxes show slight variations in size and in the construction of their brackets. One of them (63) has gilded silver brackets framing the sides and the base, with a pair of palmette-shaped braces securing the plaques.[47] The brackets are decorated with rumi braids placed on a nielloed ground and encrusted with gems set into plain collars; turquoises are used on the vertical brackets at the sides, while rubies appear along the base and in the braces. The lid has a similarly decorated clasp, which fastens to a loop at the side. The legs of the box, also made of gilded silver, are arched-back dragons, their tails and heads used as supports. The dragons face out, their open mouths showing tiny teeth, recalling those on the handles of the gilded silver jugs as well as the ones on the slighly later gold and rock-crystal and black stone examples (see 51, 52, 61, and 64). This box, most likely made to store such precious items as jewels or gemstone seals, can be dated to the same period as the gilded silver and tutya jugs, that is, to the second quarter of the sixteenth century.

The characteristic Ottoman techniques applied to jades and other hard stones appear in a gem-encrusted jug (64) that combines the traditional Timurid shape with the court style of decoration. The piece is carved from an unusual black material, called "Herat stone" in the Topkapı Palace records. The stone is too black to be jade, but as hard and sturdy. It is possible that the material is quartz, possibly black-stained chalcedony (known as black onyx) or obsidian.[48] The same stone can be seen in one other example, the famous jug bearing Ismail's name. Similar to tutya, this material enjoyed brief popularity in the Safavid court and was considered a novelty when it first appeared there during the early sixteenth century. A piece of this stone must have arrived in İstanbul and been worked on by the gemstone carvers in the second half of the sixteenth century, judging from its decorative style.

64. Jeweled black stone jug with lid, second half sixteenth century (İstanbul, Topkapı Sarayı Müzesi, 2/3831)

Detail of filter, 64

65. Jeweled jade cup, second half sixteenth century (Paris, Musée du Louvre, M.R. 202)

66. Jeweled jade tankard with lid, second half sixteenth century (İstanbul, Topkapı Sarayı Müzesi, 2/3832)

with incised scrolls decorating the inner side; the outer side is enameled and shows sprays of carnations, tulips, hyacinths, and leaves rendered in blue, gold, yellow, and white. Enameling also appears on the thin band around the rim of the lid, which is decorated with gold and white strokes, and on the lower edge of the foot, which has a pierced frieze of blue and green tulips, framed by narrow gold bands incised with minute floral scrolls. Inside the foot ring is a gold-inlaid six-pointed star filled with floral motifs.

This jug displays several extraordinary features, the most outstanding of which is enameling. This technique was rarely used in the sixteenth century and its appearance on such discreet areas of the jug suggests that it had a limited appeal. A second feature is the representation of naturalistic flowers, which were unusual in metalwork and carved stones. The pleasant surprises hidden in the neck and under the foot are also noteworthy, particularly the inscription on the filter, which contains a Koranic verse related to pure and holy water in paradise.

Scrolls composed of twisted wire and gem-encrusted blossoms with striated petals and leaves were the most common types of decoration applied to jade. Executed in relief, they coexisted with another technique in which the gold inlay was embedded into the jade, lay flush with the surface, and almost always represented rumi scrolls. This combination of styles, also observed in bookbindings, appears on a small dark-green jade cup (65). Its outer walls are decorated in relief with four oval medallions interspersed with half medallions placed on the rim, each containing blossoms set with rubies. The interstices are filled with the flat rumi scrolls.

A number of examples displaying these two techniques were in the past identified erroneously as Indian.[49] Their decoration is indigenous to the Ottoman world, popularly employed on diverse items produced for the court from the mid-sixteenth to the end of the seventeenth century.

Jade was also fashioned into such pieces as cylindrical tankards, a shape also used in metalwork and ceramics (see 53 and 205). One such example (66), made of the palest green nephrite, has a lid with a high knob set with a large stone and a handle with an articulated contour. The lid, body, and handle are decorated with the twisted wire scrolls bearing striated leaves and blossoms encrusted with gems set into high collars, using the same technique described above. The scrolls are organized into medallions defined by twisted wire: the lid has a large circular medallion encircled by a band, and the body contains upper and lower horizontal bands enclosing a wide central zone accentuated by three oval medallions. A gold zigzag band encircles the rim.

The interior of the tankard is lined with gold sheet; gold filigree panels decorated with rumi scrolls are affixed to the underside of the lid and to the bottom of the body. The stones include green emeralds and peridots, red rubies, and lavender-colored gems, which appear to be amethysts. Many are left in their natural state; others, particularly the rubies in the centers of the medallions, are rose-cut, similar to those found on the rock-crystal pen box (see 62). The only part of the object that employs the flat inlay technique is the high knob on the lid, which is decorated with a vine bearing leaves, showing an abbreviated version of the rumi scroll.

67 (above). Jeweled jasper pen case, second half sixteenth century (İstanbul, Topkapı Sarayı Müzesi, 2/2111)

68 (below). Jeweled blue-and-white porcelain pen box, fifteenth-century Chinese ware decorated second half sixteenth century (İstanbul, Topkapı Sarayı Müzesi, 2/894)

Among the more unusual objects in the Hazine is a thin and long pen case with rounded edges (67), made of a translucent pale green stone called *balgami*, which appears to be jasper (green chalcedony). The piece has a sliding lid set into a gold frame; inside is a cylindrical inkwell carved out of the same material and space for a few pens. The lid and the exterior walls are embellished with gold scrolls that bear multipetaled hatayi blossoms and buds rendered in profile with delicate, incised lines applied to their petals. Their centers are encrusted with natural emeralds and rubies set into high collars. The gold frame around the upper edge is incised with a series of diagonally placed leaves and strokes, creating a double zigzag pattern. The cap of the inkwell contains a blossom,

rendered in ruby-red enamel, holding an emerald.

This example is not only made out of an unusual material, but also employs enameling and hatayi blossom mounts, indicating that several different styles of decoration coexisted in the court studios.

Gold-inlaid and gem-encrusted pieces were so popular in the second half of the sixteenth century that the same techniques were applied to Chinese porcelain, particularly to select examples of Ming dynasty white or blue-and-white ware. One of these pieces was a fifteenth-century blue-and-white pen box (68), its shape based on the rectangular Islamic examples with rounded edges.

The top of the lid and the sides of the base were originally

underglaze-painted with floral vines reminiscent of the hatayi scrolls used in the court; hence, inlaying the branches with twisted gold wire and enhancing the flowers with rubies followed the practice and taste of the age. Gold wire was also applied over the lines encircling the panels of the lid and the base, and a few additional flowers were placed on the bands around the lid and along the edge. The top of the lid was further embellished with gold leaves, and a large cartouche, set with rubies and emeralds, adorns the front of the base.

The interior was adapted to serve an Ottoman calligrapher and was appropriately decorated. The panel on the left is covered with the palest green jade and inlaid flush with rumis; a gold inkwell with an emerald on its lid is inserted in the center. Next to it are two other cylindrical gold containers: one has a pierced jade cover and the other contains a gold lid encrusted with emeralds. A gold blossom set with an emerald appears before the section for pens. The underside of the lid shows a different technique of decoration: it contains a central medallion and corner cartouches composed of rumis and hatayi sprays, painted in gold and polychrome pigments. The lid is attached to the body by a pair of gold hinges and supported by a gold chain, following the Ottoman format.

The Chinese produced several blue-and-white pen boxes in the fifteenth century, themselves adapting the Islamic shape to hold their inks, paints, and brushes. Its readaptation to suit the needs of an Islamic calligrapher is an interesting cross-cultural transaction.

Another adaptation is a covered container for which two different mid-sixteenth-century Chinese bowls were used to create a new piece (69). The bowls have plain white exteriors; the interior of the one used as the lid has a central medallion depicting a landscape painted in blue, while the cavetto is carved; the interior of the base shows a symmetrically composed blossom amid leaves, also in blue. The rims of the bowls were cut down to fit together, and the edge of the lid was encased by a crenellated gold frame, incised with diagonal leaves and strokes. In addition, the foot of the bowl used as the lid was replaced by a large rock-crystal dome and framed with the same gold band. Placed under the dome is a paper sheet painted with blue and gold flowers, similar to the technique used in the rock-crystal jug and pen box (see 61 and 62). Surmounting the dome is a large rock-crystal knob, its finial broken off. The knob as well as the dome were riveted to the porcelain body.

The decoration on the rock-crystal components follows the same technical features used on all carved stone vessels, employing twisted gold wire, leaves, and emerald- and ruby-encrusted blossoms. The dome contains three oval medallions filled with floral scrolls, with sprays of additional blossoms placed in the interstices. The lid shows a different decorative scheme and has five units composed of large leaves overlaid with blossoms, enclosing a central floral spray. The serrate-edged leaves are outlined in twisted gold wire, while the

69. Jeweled covered white porcelain bowl with rock-crystal dome, made of two mid-sixteenth-century Chinese bowls decorated second half sixteenth century (İstanbul, Topkapı Sarayı Müzesi, 15/2767)

flowers are shaped as hatayis and contain emerald or ruby cores, identical to those found on the jasper pen case (see 67). The base is similarly decorated but has six of these units. The piece is further embellished by gold-painted designs applied around the foot as well as to the blue florals inside the base. The paint has flaked off and only a portion of the design is visible.

The goldwork on the rock-crystal and porcelain components of the covered bowl combines two different traditions: formulaic flowers in the rock-crystal section and the saz style in the porcelain. Leaves overlaid with blossoms translate the theme found in saz drawings and grow from a central source, a feature popularly employed in the other arts. Floral sprays flanked by large leaves, frequently used in ceramics and textiles, also seem to have influenced the goldsmiths, as observed on this piece.

The decoration applied to some Chinese vessels was minimal, at times necessitated by restoration efforts. One of the most elegant white porcelain ewers dating from the early fifteenth century was refurbished by adding a metal rim and lid

(**70**). The ewer, decorated with an *an-hua* (hidden) hibiscus scroll rendered so delicately that it is barely visible to the naked eye, has a curving handle with a ring at the top used to attach the lid and a flaring spout connected to the neck by a thick scroll.[50]

The beauty of the ewer's shape and decoration was obviously appreciated in the sixteenth century, since an effort was made to preserve it after its rim was broken and lid lost. The rim was not restored to its original height but was encased by an articulated gold frame incised with saz flowers and encrusted with lavender-colored stones set into plain high collars. The same band encircles the edge of the gold lid, which is surmounted by a large turquoise. The surface is incised with saz leaves and blossoms and decorated with three ovals created by the gems. The lid, whose shape resembles the helmets of the age, tapers toward the top and is lined with silver.

Another Chinese vessel, a molded celadon dating from the late fourteenth or early fifteenth century (**71**), was most likely also an ewer that lost its handle, spout, and parts of its rim. It

70. White porcelain ewer with jeweled gold lid, early-fifteenth-century Chinese ware refurbished second half sixteenth century (İstanbul, Topkapı Sarayı Müzesi, 15/2944)

71. Celadon canteen with gilded silver components, late-14th- or early-15th-century Chinese ware refurbished second half sixteenth century (İstanbul, Topkapı Sarayı Müzesi, 15/668)

was restored with gilded silver components and converted into a double-spouted canteen. The placement of the spouts followed that of the original appendages and appears slightly askew. Each side of the flattened body contains a medallion with a different design: one shows a crane diving down from the clouds and the other, a bird flying over waves. Floral motifs fill the remaining areas.

The refurbishing consisted of fitting the neck with a wide lobed band, a lid surmounted by a large coral knob, and two curving spouts joined to the body with large plaques, their lips decorated with petals. The spouts and lid have chains attached to a palmette, which contains a hook used for hanging the vessel. The edges of the rim and lid are incised with a series of vertical panels filled with horizontal lines, creating a texture not unlike the one used on the rock-crystal and gold jug (see **61**). The surfaces of the remaining metal components are decorated with angular striations and multipetaled blossoms superimposed with six spokes, resembling the flowers used on a gold Koran binding.[51] The artist who refurbished

137

72. Jeweled and gold-inlaid steel mirror with jade handle, second quarter sixteenth century (İstanbul, Topkapı Sarayı Müzesi, 2/1801)

this piece employed the decorative repertoire of the second half of the sixteenth century to convert a broken vessel into a typical Ottoman matara.[52]

The precious objects discussed above were used by the sultans during official and ceremonial activities as well as on a daily basis when dining or writing. Another group of equally sumptuous but more personal pieces, including hand mirrors, belts, and turban ornaments, belonged to their wardrobes. Produced in gold, steel, ivory, and mother-of-pearl, they were inlaid with precious metals and set with gems.

One of the earliest Ottoman mirrors is a circular example (72) made of blackened steel, inlaid with gold, set with rubies and turquoises, and attached to an octagonal dark green jade handle. The back has a large medallion with gold-inlaid cartouches bearing cloud bands executed in reserve; the interstices are filled with gold-inlaid rumi scrolls. In the center is a six-pointed star with a ruby core, surrounded by ovoid cartouches. The band encircling the medallion contains six lines from a Persian poem, written in gold-inlaid talik and separated by rumis executed in reserve. The lobes on the edge are embellished with gold rumis. Turquoise stones are set just beyond the points of the central star, while turquoises or emeralds appear between the verses.

The verses are from a mystical poem in which the mirror is compared to the beloved. By looking at the beloved a person sees himself, just as he sees his reflection in the mirror.

The face of the mirror is framed by a gold band decorated with reserved rumis, alternately set with rubies and turquoises. The large reflective surface in the center is metal, probably bronze, which is now oxidized. The head is attached to the jade handle with a gold palmette and faceted ring, embellished with nielloed rumis and gems. The handle terminates with a fluted knob, at the end of which is a blossom.

The stones, both natural and cabochon-cut, are set into round collars and are held by prongs, a feature seen on other early-sixteenth-century pieces (see 56, 57, and 63). The decoration of the mirror demonstrates the influence of the nakkaşhane; almost identical designs were used on lacquered bookbindings dating between 1520 and 1540 (see 18a). They, in turn, were influenced by late-fifteenth-century examples produced in Herat.

There is a similar gold-inlaid steel mirror in the Metropolitan Museum of Art that appears to have been produced in the same workshop.[53] It has an ivory handle and a metal face. The back contains a central medallion with a radiating design composed of floral scrolls and rumis, encircled by a band with the same elements.

Another mirror in the Topkapı Palace (73), made for Süleyman by an artist named Gani in 1543/1544, employs different materials, techniques, and style of decoration. It is constructed of three pieces of deeply carved ivory; two superimposed panels are used on the back and one on the face, affixed to an ebony core with a series of gold nails worked into the design. The ebony handle is fluted, with the grooves in the center placed diagonally, producing a twisted effect; a ribbed ring joins it to the ivory stem of the head, and a ribbed elongated globe appears at the end.

The lobed ovoid head rising to a palmette finial has a continuous inscription around the edge, written in sülüs and placed over a scroll with hatayi blossoms and leaves. Attached to its center is the second smaller lobed oval, its border filled with saz scrolls and cloud bands. This plaque, which is higher than the first, has a raised central panel deco-

73. Carved ivory mirror with ebony handle made for Sultan Süleyman by Gani in 1543/1544 (İstanbul, Topkapı Sarayı Müzesi, 2/2893)

74. Carved ivory mirror, second quarter sixteenth century (İstanbul, Topkapı Sarayı Müzesi, 2/1804)

rated with two superimposed scrolls, one bearing composite hatayis and the other elaborate rumis. Black organic material is inlaid into the grooved band that encircles the outer and inner plaques and forms occasional loops; the loops on the inner plaque are set with gold nails.

The face of the mirror has an ivory frame inlaid with gold twisted wire, which outlines the scallops and bands around the edge, and defines the rumis decorating the finial and stem. Set into the frame is a glass mirror, which has a crack; its metallic backing is oxidized and slightly damaged.

The mirror, its back constructed of several superimposed planes each carved in layers, displays an extraordinarily vi-

brant articulation. The ivory is almost an intricate lace, with scrolls weaving in and out, passing over and under one another, harmoniously blending with the curves of the letters.

The Turkish poem around the edge is in the nature of an invocation, imploring the Creator to keep the beholder's beautiful face perpetually radiant, to preserve the mirror "as long as the world revolves," and to accept the prayers. The inscription on the stem states that the piece was made during the reign of "Sultan Süleyman Şah" and gives the name of the maker and the date. The splendid and understated elegance of the mirror is unsurpassed.

A second ivory mirror executed with equal delicacy (74)

139

bears no dedication. It has a circular head decorated with two deeply carved superimposed scrolls, one in the saz style with hatayis and peonies, the other with large rumis. The scrolls radiate from a central multipetaled rosette embellished with a six-petaled gold blossom set with turquoise. The sides of the mirror are decorated with similar saz scrolls, while a rumi braid frames the face, which is now empty. The glass insert must have shattered and been removed.

The handle, which is also ivory, is unusual in design. It is hollow, pierced with long, thin openings, and originally enclosed an ivory chain, which was broken and is now mostly lost. The knob at the end is also pierced, its tip decorated with a swirling petal design.

These two mirrors, one produced for Süleyman and the other made either for him or for another member of the royal family, possibly his wife, were set with glass, which is the earliest occurrence of this material on mirrors in the Ottoman world. There is no evidence that glass mirrors were used elsewhere in the palace, such as on walls or in frames. Since they appear only on small hand-held examples, one can assume that reflective glass was a rarity at the time.

Ottoman glassmakers in the sixteenth century were primarily involved with supplying the needs of architectural decoration—making colorless or stained glass window panes, oil lamps, and other lighting fixtures—in addition to producing simple bottles, vases, and drinking vessels for public consumption, hardly any of which have survived. Some of the artists were employed by the imperial society of the *camger* (glassmakers); others belonged to local guilds and made stained glass windows as well as large blown glass bottles, as can be seen in the illustration of the procession of the guildsmen during the 1582 festival in Lokman's *Surname*.[54] It has been suggested that high-quality glass vessels as well as mirrors were imported from Europe, particularly from Venice, while domestic production served more prosaic needs.[55]

Mirrors were considered valuable enough to be presented to the sultan during bayrams. Among the gifts he received during these celebrations were jeweled mirrors produced by goldsmiths and gold inlayers as well as ivory examples made by the kündekari. The kündekari, in addition, gave ivory belt plaques, dagger handles, combs, and archer's rings, some of which were identified in the registers as having been made from walrus tusks.[56]

The same delicate scrolls used on the two mirrors described above appear on an ivory belt buckle (75) with a curved and lobed panel at the front and a plain bar at the back, through which a strip of leather or fabric would have been threaded. The front panel, framed by grooved bands, is carved with exquisite saz scrolls bearing compound hatayis, buds, and feathery leaves that overlay and intersect, intermingled with cloud bands that form cartouches in the center and at the sides. The densely packed scrolls, rendered in high relief with extremely refined details, appear to float over the surface, casting a

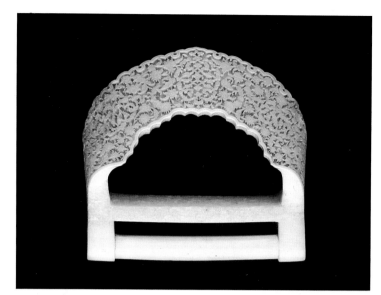

75. Carved ivory buckle, second quarter sixteenth century (Kuwait National Museum, LNS 46 I)

shadow on the deeply recessed field, which is lost in the background, creating almost a filigree effect.

The buckle would have been attached to an equally magnificent strip, heavily brocaded or embroidered, possibly also embellished with gems or with additional carved ivory pieces.[57] Belts were also made of series of linked ivory plaques, frequently inlaid with black organic material and gold, and set with gems. The Hazine of the Topkapı Palace contains a number of these complete belts as well as individual plaques and buckles.

One of the ivory belts in the Hazine (76) is constructed of four long and three short plaques linked together by series of interlocking tiny pieces that provide flexibility. The plaques have trefoil lobes on their upper and lower edges; in the center of each is a raised smaller unit with the same shape, creating a stepped effect. The belt fastens with a series of loops held together with a draw pin.

The surfaces of the plaques as well as their sides are incised with minute floral scrolls with occasional rumi palmettes and filled with black material; placed over them are gold-inlaid scrolls with leaves, buds, and blossoms with ruby or turquoise cores held with prongs. The ivory has been waxed or covered with a thin coat of lacquer, producing a shimmering surface. The style of the mounts for the gems suggests that the piece was made in the second quarter of the sixteenth century.

Another similarly decorated belt (77) was found in the Mausoleum of Selim II and dates from the mid-sixteenth century. It is constructed of four square ivory plaques with circular medallions rising in their centers; the plaques are attached by hinges to narrow strips that are linked to a series of small pieces arranged in five rows of threes and fours. The belt fastens with loops held by a draw pin.

140

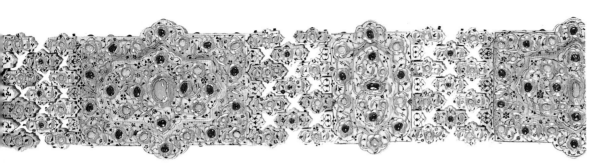

76. Jeweled ivory belt (detail), second quarter sixteenth century (İstanbul, Topkapı Sarayı Müzesi, 2/539)

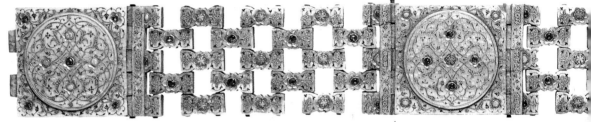

77. Jeweled ivory belt (detail), mid-sixteenth century (İstanbul, Türk ve İslam Eserleri Müzesi, 482)

78. Gold-inlaid mother-of-pearl belt (detail), mid-sixteenth century (İstanbul, Topkapı Sarayı Müzesi, 2/575)

The surfaces as well as the sides of the plaques are decorated with black-inlaid floral scrolls superimposed with gold-inlaid rumi scrolls with niello applied to the large leaves. Set into the rumi scrolls are blossoms with plain round collars holding rubies and turquoises. Most of the turquoise stones are carved into six-petaled florets, which is unusual in Ottoman lapidary art. Similar to the previous example, the ivory has been treated to create a shiny surface. The belt, only 65.5 centimeters (25⅞ inches) long, either must have been worn by a slender person or is missing some of its parts.

A group of six other belts in the Topkapı Palace employs mother-of-pearl embedded into gilded silver plaques shaped as polygons or as ovals alternating with concave-sided pieces,

affixed to leather strips covered with silk fabric. The existence of a series of identical examples indicates that they were worn by a particular group, possibly by personal attendants of the sultan (Has Oda officials or pages) or the ladies in the Harem. Both men and women used similar accessories, and it would be difficult to identify their specific owners.

One of the belts (78) has an oblong buckle with a clasp, and contains a series of oval medallions alternating with concave-sided pieces affixed to a leather strip covered with red silk. The tongue does not contain plaques, and was meant to slide under the buckle. The plaques are carved with hatayi scrolls inlaid with black; the fifth and the last ovals from the buckle have a different design, with tulips in the scrolls. Set

141

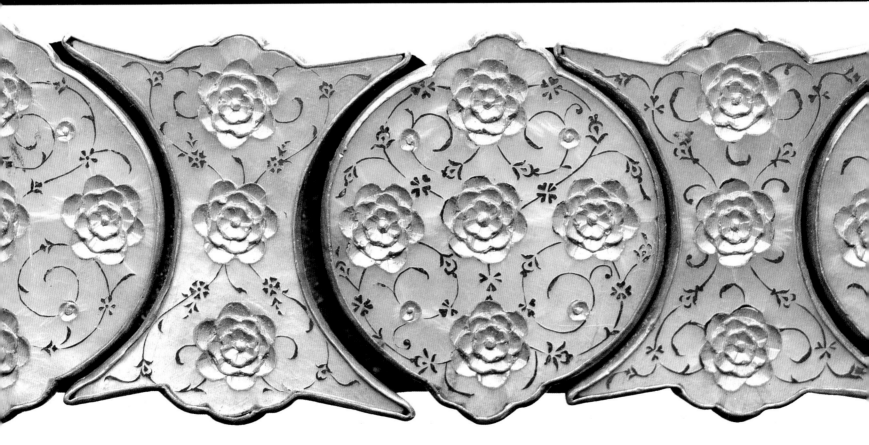

Details, 77 (above) and 78 (below)

over the scrolls are multipetaled gold blossoms resembling roses or peonies. The belt also has loops used for attaching small containers or pendants, as seen in the drawings of the period (see **48a**).

Other belts dating from the second half of the sixteenth century are elaborately decorated and heavily encrusted with gems. A group found in the Mausoleum of Ahmed I indicates that peridot was a favored gem. In some belts the gems are affixed to gilded silver plaques attached to leather strips covered with dark red velvet or brocaded silks, the contrasting textures creating a colorful effect.

Both carved ivory and mother-of-pearl were very popular in the first half of the sixteenth century and were used on a number of objects. In addition to mirrors and belts, ivory, at times dyed green, was employed on hilts of swords and daggers, inlaid into woodwork, and fashioned into finials for furnishings, banners, and tents. It was rarely used for objects in the round.[58] Mother-of-pearl was also employed on woodwork and made into plaques decorating horse trappings, arms and armor, and riding equipment, generally inlaid with gold and encrusted with gems.

The decorative accessories worn by the sultans were limited to jeweled kaftan fastenings (of which none survive from the sixteenth century), belts made of rare and precious materials, and gold turban ornaments called sorguç, which were basically pins with sockets holding the plumes of rare birds, stuck into turbans and fastened by chains. Sixteenth-century examples of these turban ornaments are relatively small and at times decorated with niello and gemstones; the later pieces are much larger and elaborately encrusted with oversize emeralds, diamonds, and other stones. The illustrations dating from this period show Süleyman, members of his court, and other personages wearing ornaments with aigrettes on their turbans as well as belts made of a series of plaques.

Among the sixteenth-century turban ornaments is a comparatively large example (**79**) found in the Mausoleum of İbrahim Paşa, who died in 1536 and was buried in a tomb erected in the courtyard of the Mosque of Şehzade Mehmed. The gold ornament is shaped as an ovoid disk with a large opening at the top, which still contains peacock feathers; flanking it are two small cylindrical sockets for additional plumes and a pair of rings, each bearing chains terminating with hooks. At the bottom of the disk is a tubular shaft used to stick the ornament into the folds of the turban; the ornament was secured by the hooked chains.

The front of the disk has a complicated design rendered in three superimposed planes. On the very top is a central roundel with a palmette finial enclosed by large leaves growing from a floral source. This element, which is an abstracted representation of a hatayi, is filled with saz motifs; a scroll with leaves, hatayis, peonies, and blossoms with swirling petals appears in the core, while blossoming branches and floral sprays decorate the leaves. A lobed medallion, its frame over-

79. Gold turban ornament with peacock feathers, second half sixteenth century (İstanbul, Türk ve İslam Eserleri Müzesi, 438)

laid by the large leaves, appears in the middle plane, under which is the lowest register of the disk; both are decorated with floral motifs. All components have raised outlines, the floral motifs are finely detailed, and ring matting is applied to the grounds. The back is incised with a series of lozenges composed of long leaves enclosing hatayi sprays amid leaves. Similar motifs appear in the sockets and the upper portion of the shaft.

The hatayi, with elaborate leaflike petals overlaid with floral sprays and lozenges created by thin long leaves (see also **61**), indicates that the sorguç was made during the second half of the sixteenth century. This striking ornament with its highly sophisticated composition and flawless execution must have been presented to the mausoleum by one of his devotees or descendants several decades after his death.

Another gold example (**80**), found in the Mausoleum of Hürrem Sultan, displays the simple elegance befitting a sorguç worn by a woman. At the top is a socket, incised with a saz scroll executed in relief against a ring-matted background. Below is a fluted globe encircled by two molded bands. The shaft is plain; at its top are rings, to which gold or jeweled chains must have been attached.

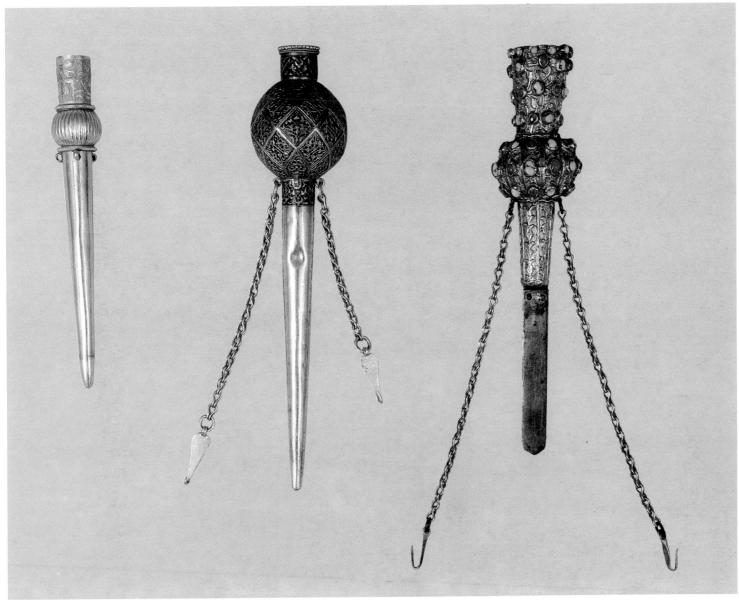

80 (left) and 81 (center). Gold turban ornaments, mid-sixteenth century (İstanbul, Türk ve İslam Eserleri Müzesi, 419 and 421)

82 (right). Jeweled gold turban ornament, second half sixteenth century (İstanbul, Türk ve İslam Eserleri Müzesi, 416)

There are no contemporary representations of Hürrem Sultan, and the paintings said to portray her all date from later periods. Several paintings of court ladies were made in the sixteenth century by European visitors; these were based on hearsay, however, since men could not have been permitted into the women's quarters. Some of these represent ladies wearing conical caps draped with scarves, decorated with headbands and gold cylindrical ornaments containing plumes.[59] Hürrem's headdress must have been similar but more elaborate. Also found in her mausoleum and transferred to the Museum of Turkish and Islamic Arts is a spray of gold flowers that may have been a hair ornament.

Housed in that museum are several other gold turban ornaments, which were found in the Mausoleum of Selim II. One of them (81) is an earlier and simpler piece, possibly worn by Selim when he was a crown prince. It has a socket, polyhedral head, circular band above the tubular shaft, and four rings; two of the rings have gold chains with hooks, while the others may have been used to attach additional ornaments. The socket, head, and band above the shaft are decorated with rumis placed on a nielloed ground. A rumi scroll decorates the socket, encircled by a granulated frieze and a molded braid; symmetrical elements radiating from a central motif embellish the flat planes of the head; the design on the socket is repeated on the band.

A second sorguç belonging to Selim II (82) has a slightly different shape and is encrusted with rubies and turquoises. It shows a high flaring socket, a ribbed head, and a conical section above the shaft, which is flat and made of silver. Hooked chains are attached to rings along the bottom of the head.

The socket and head are embellished with cabochon-cut gems, mounted into high collars joined by branches to the

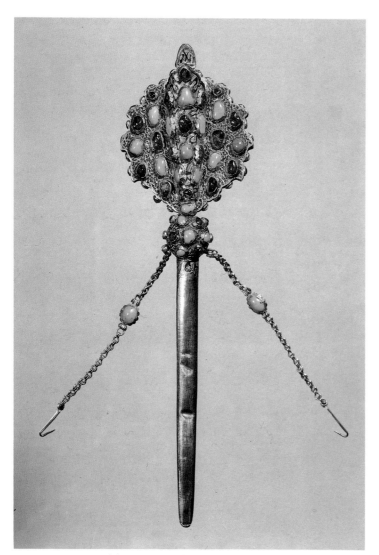

83. Jeweled and nielloed gold turban ornament (back), mid-sixteenth century (İstanbul, Topkapı Sarayı Müzesi, 2/2912)

decorated with floral and rumi scrolls placed on a niello ground. The same design is used on the sides of the palmette, the globe, and the upper edge of the shaft. The back has a large rounded socket affixed to the center, extending from the edge of the palmette to its tip. This component has nielloed cloud bands between the gems, while the remaining areas show the same design used on the face.

The use of niello, floral and rumi scrolls, and gems set into petaled mounts and prongs suggests a mid-sixteenth-century date. This ornament, which is at once robust and delicate, must have been made for a member of the royal family, possibly for Süleyman himself.

Detail of front, **83**

saz scrolls filling the interstices; the background is ring matted. The unit above the shaft shows vertical bars that alternate with branches bearing hatayis and leaves placed on a ring-matted ground. It is joined to the shaft by rivets.[60]

One of the largest turban ornaments in the Hazine of the Topkapı Palace (**83**) combines the techniques of the last two examples discussed above, employing niello inlaying as well as gem encrustation. Shaped as a flat lobed palmette with a finial, it has a globe above the shaft and a pair of hooked chains. Both faces of the palmette as well as its sides and the globe are encrusted with rubies and turquoises set in petaled mounts that rise high above the surface; each of the chains is set with a pair of addorsed turquoise stones that share the same pronged mount.

The front of the palmette contains a large sapphire in the center surrounded by four diamonds in addition to rubies and turquoises. A large ruby appears on the finial. The field is

Arms and Armor

Among the precious objects produced for the court, it is perhaps Ottoman arms and armor that are best represented in both the Topkapı Palace and in royal collections outside Turkey, such as those in Vienna, Kraków, and Budapest. The vast quantity of richly decorated weapons and military accoutrements that have been preserved is indicative of the size and wealth of the Ottoman army. Süleyman and his predecessors, proud of their rank as *serasker* (commander in chief of the armed forces), were superior military leaders and strategists. The greatest was Süleyman, who personally led more than a dozen campaigns. The sultans were involved with the training and performance of their men, which enabled them to undertake the victorious campaigns that extended the frontiers of their empire and enriched their treasuries. They were equally concerned with the impression made by superbly equipped and splendidly attired armies reflecting the majesty and power of their state at home and abroad.

Travelers and official visitors to the Ottoman world remarked on the high degree of regimentation of the Ottoman forces, their brilliantly colored battle dress and banners, and the impeccable quality of their weapons. Baron Busbecq, the Habsburg ambassador to the court of Süleyman, who witnessed the departure of the sultan from İstanbul in 1555, made the following observations:

> The Turkish horseman presents a very elegant spectacle
> mounted on a horse . . . with trappings and horsecloths of silver
> spangled with gold and precious stones. He is resplendent in
> raiment of cloth of gold and silver, or else of silk or satin, or at
> any rate the finest scarlet, or violet, or dark green cloth. At
> either side is a fine sheath, one to hold the bow, the other full
> of bright-colored arrows . . . [an] ornamented shield . . . is at-
> tached to the left arm . . . his right hand is encumbered by a
> light spear, usually painted green . . . and he is girt with a scim-
> itar studded with gems, while a steel club hangs from his horse-
> cloth or saddle.[61]

The Ottoman armed forces were highly structured and divided into corps, each of which served a different function, used specific weapons, and wore individualized garments and headdresses. The Ehl-i Hiref artists involved with producing arms and armor were just as specialized, and belonged to the societies that made swords, daggers, scabbards, bows, arrows, maces, shields, cannons, and rifles.[62] The swordmakers were divided into two units: the *şimşirgeran*, who made regular swords, and the *dimişkeran*, who produced watered steel blades. These artists were assisted by goldsmiths, gemstone carvers, gold inlayers, ivory carvers, tanners, and embroiderers, who also contributed to the manufacture of weapons. In addition there were hat makers who supplied the headdresses; weavers who produced the garments, saddlecloths, banners, and tents;[63] and musical instrument makers who provided the military band with drums, horns, and cymbals.

Ottoman arms and armor, originally kept in the Arsenal in the first courtyard of the palace, included a collection of weapons belonging to other Islamic dynasties, such as the Mamluks and Safavids.[64] All items were stamped with the mark of the arsenal. The ceremonial swords of the Ottoman sultans were carefully preserved in the Hazine, the most revered one belonging to Osman, the founder of the dynasty. As a part of their accession ceremonies, the sultans girded themselves with Osman's sword, professing to uphold the ancestral gazi spirit.

The largest collection of swords belonged to Süleyman; many of them were made by master sword makers who signed their names.[65] According to the published payroll registers,[66] the society during Süleyman's reign included native artists as well as individuals from Bosnia and Tabriz. The names inscribed on the existing swords made for Süleyman, however, are not listed in the registers. The inscriptions include the names of Ahmed Tekelü, the maker of the famous *yatağan* (sword) dated 1526/1527 (see **86**); Mehmed (possibly the Mehmed b. Hamza recorded in 1526), who made one sword; Hacı Murad b. Hoşkadem, whose name appears on five examples, two of which were made for Süleyman;[67] Seyyid Bayram, who made one sword in 1560/1561;[68] Hacı Yusuf, who made two swords;[69] and Hacı Sungur, whose name appears on forty pieces. The latter artist, who was from Cairo and worked for the last Mamluk sultans, appears to have come to İstanbul during the reign of Bayezid II and made two swords, one of which is dated 1506/1507. Since the signature "Hacı Sungur" appears on swords spanning more than a hundred years, there were either several men with the same name or it was used by a workshop. There are at least five examples dedicated to Süleyman, none of which are dated.[70]

The Ottoman sword, renowned for the elasticity and strength of its blade, was highly prized. The type called *kılıç* is slightly curved and has a unique blade that widens on the cutting edge two-thirds of the way toward the tip and forms a spur, thus concentrating weight of the weapon at its lower portion and increasing the effectiveness of the blow. The *kılıç* demanded agile wrist action rather than strength in the arm. Extensive training was required to achieve the proper technique. The shape of the blade, which became characteristic of Ottoman swords, appeared during the reign of Mehmed II, coexisting with the classical straight sword. Its distinctive curve evolved during the first quarter of the sixteenth century, achieving the perfect balance between weight, length, and shape during the reign of Süleyman.

Süleyman's functional swords (see **88–90**), made for use in the battlefield and on hunting expeditions, have flattened and slightly tilted hilts, which are generally covered with leather to provide a good grip.[71] The pommels and guards are frequently made of silver, at times gilded and inlaid with niello; in some examples these components are of blackened steel decorated with gold, employing a particular technique called *küftgari*, in which gold wire was hammered onto the roughened steel, resembling overlaying. The matching scabbards, covered with leather similar to the hilts, have silver or steel chapes, lockets, and sling mounts used for attaching the weapons to belts and decorated in the same manner as the pommels and guards. Some of the mid-sixteenth-century examples were also embellished with jeweled plaques. The steel blades are inlaid or overlaid with gold and at times embellished with gems. Many examples contain the figure of a fish placed on the hilt, which appears to be a talismanic symbol; its proper meaning is yet to be understood.

Also made for Süleyman was a different type of sword called *meç*, shaped like a skewer (see **87**). The weapon, which dates to the reign of Mehmed II, was produced in limited numbers and obviously functioned more as a piercing instrument than a cutting one, possibly to penetrate heavy armor.

Ceremonial swords dating from Süleyman's reign are dazzling works of art, richly inlaid with gold and encrusted with gems. They include the sword of Osman, which was redecorated in the mid-sixteenth century, its blade totally covered with gold inlay and its guard swooping down and terminating in dragon heads,[72] and the unique yatağan (see **86**) made for the sultan by Ahmed Tekelü.[73] The yatağan, obviously a display piece, with fantastic decoration of animated scrolls and combats between mythical creatures, is unique in its representation of figural themes associated with the saz style. Other ceremonial pieces reveal the same interest in gem encrustation found on the Hazine objects produced in the second half of the sixteenth century, and include helmets, parts of armor, maces, daggers, archer's rings, and shields.

Ottoman helmets (see **84**) were conical, with swelling sides tapering toward the apex, their shape resembling turbans; they were supplied with visors, neck guards, and movable nasals; some also had ear guards, sockets for plumes, and chain mail protecting the neck and shoulders. The majority are of steel, inlaid with gold and at times set with gems; there are also gilded-copper examples with incised decoration.[74]

There are extremely few complete suits of body armor,[75] although there exist a number of arm guards with gloves, leg guards, and breastplates decorated in the same fashion as the imperial helmets. Ottoman maces, with gold-sheathed iron (see **85**), rock-crystal, or jade heads, were beautifully fashioned, either simply carved or embellished with gems. These decorative pieces were also formidable weapons, their elegant shapes and surface embellishment belying their deadly purpose.

Süleyman was hardly ever represented wearing a dagger, even though a number of these weapons were produced during his reign (see **92–94**). Some of the daggers have carved rock-crystal and ivory hilts, while other hilts are made of jade or ivory inlaid with gold and set with gems. Most of these daggers appear to have been made as gifts or display pieces

and were not an integral part of the sultans' outfit as they were in Iran and India.

The most decorative and yet extremely functional Ottoman battle accoutrements were wicker shields (see **98–102**), embroidered with silk as well as silver and gold threads, lined with velvet and padded, and supplied with steel bosses, frequently decorated with gold inlays and gems. Their laborious technique involved wrapping long strands of twigs with silk and metal threads and stitching them into place to form the shields. Wicker, an extremely strong and resilient material, was also lightweight, an asset for cavalrymen and foot soldiers alike. Similar shields appear to have been used in India and Iran. Although extant Indian examples have not been published, warriors carrying shields with concentric lines, obviously representing wound wicker, are depicted in late-sixteenth-century Mughal manuscripts. A few Iranian examples have survived, the most interesting of which is decorated with a series of lions attacking bulls.[76]

Embroidery also adorned bow cases and quivers (see **103** and **104**) made of leather or of velvet lined with leather. A number of leather examples were appliquéd with leather pieces, some of which were gilded. Embroidered and appliquéd leather were also used for saddles, saddlecloths, riding boots, canteens, and caskets or boxes (see **105** and **106**).

Another technique applied to saddles, canteens, containers, bow cases, and quivers as well as to bows and arrows was lacquer in intricate designs painted on wood and leather and covered with a thick varnish. Their decorative repertoire reveals the hands of nakkaşhane artists who must have been employed to work on these items. Ottoman bows were world renowned, and archery was particularly favored by the sultans, especially by Bayezid II, who was an expert bow maker.

Although the Ottomans were preoccupied with military regalia and the representation of the power and wealth of the empire through a dazzling display of weapons, costumes, banners, and bands, no complete military outfit or full-horse armor has survived from the reign of Süleyman.[77] The best preserved banners, tents, and horse trappings, captured in 1683 during the second siege of Vienna, are in Kraków. The richness of these items is indicative of what must have accompanied Süleyman when he besieged Vienna at the height of Ottoman power 150 years earlier. There exist, however, several janissary headdresses, shields, and parts of horse trappings from the mid-sixteenth century, which provide clues to the splendor of the sultan's army.[78]

Ottoman arms and armor, as well as Hazine objects, had a strong impact on the artists of the neighboring countries, particularly on the Hungarians, Austrians, and Venetians who produced similar pieces decorated with Turkish designs.[79]

Among the most spectacular gold-inlaid and gem-encrusted helmets preserved in the Hazine of the Topkapı Palace is an example with a conical body that tapers toward the high finial (**84**), supplied with a nasal, visor, and neck guard. The

84. Jeweled and gold-inlaid steel helmet, mid-sixteenth century (İstanbul, Topkapı Sarayı Müzesi, 2/1187)

Detail of neck guard, **84**

steel surfaces have been blackened, inlaid with gold, and affixed with gold cartouches set with rubies, turquoises, and a
few lavender-colored and green stones. Gem-encrusted gold
bands encircle the edge, crown, and finial, as well as the visor and neck guard.

At the edge is a wide band with reciprocal double palmettes, which display alternating use of two different techniques of gold inlay. One shows rumis and blossoms inlaid
into the blackened ground, and lies flush with the surface;
the other has applied gold plaques with hatayi scrolls rendered in relief on a ring-matted ground, encrusted with gems
set into petaled mounts that rise high in the center. The combination of flat and raised inlays recalls the techniques used
on jades, creating a similar articulated surface.

The same alternating techniques are employed on the upper portion of the helmet, which has a series of raised gold
ovals and lobed oblongs decorated with gem-encrusted hatayi
scrolls; the interstices are filled with similar designs, but inlaid flush into the blackened ground and sprinkled with
petal-mounted gems deeply embedded into the surface. At
the tapering crown is a series of vertical panels embellished
with intersecting cloud bands rendered in reserve with gold

applied to the background, creating a faceted effect. Above is
another raised and gem-encrusted gold section, continuing
the faceted design and terminating in a finial with a large
lavender-colored stone set at the apex.

The nasal, inlaid with flat rumis as well as hatayis on a
blackened ground, has a large turquoise at its apex; it slides
through a jeweled loop and locks in place with a palmette-
headed screw. The visor, affixed by gold studs, repeats the
design found on the upper portion of the helmet—gem-
encrusted ovals and oblongs on a flatly inlaid floral ground.
The flexible neck guard, attached by three hinges, is also similarly decorated except that it has two sprays of tulips flanking a central oval. Naturalistic flowers were rarely employed
on Ottoman metalwork produced for the court, and the use
of these gem-encrusted gold tulips is unusual.

This helmet is a tour de force, employing several techniques, materials, and decorative themes. Datable to the mid-
sixteenth century, it could only have been made for the sultan. It belongs to a group of gold-inlaid and gem-encrusted
ceremonial helmets, some of which are decorated with inscriptions. None, however, mentions the owner, except a
gold-inlaid example in Vienna, which is inscribed with the

name of Sokollu Mehmed Paşa,[80] Süleyman's last grand vezir, who also served his son and grandson.

The style and technique of decoration employed on the applied components of the helmet were used also on a gold-sheathed mace (85), which has an iron or steel core. Its spherical head has a series of vertical panels separated by raised ribs enclosing hatayi scrolls on a ring-matted ground; the scrolls bear blossoms that rise high above the surface and are set with rubies or turquoises. The overall effect suggesting fluting is identical to the crown of the helmet. The apex of the mace, in contrast, was worked in a different technique: it has a gold medallion pierced with a scallop pattern and inlaid with thin sheets of turquoise in a technique called *firuzekari*.[81]

Attached to the very top is a multipetaled gold blossom rendered in relief, its central gem missing.

A molded band joins the head to the handle, which is divided into five zones separated by rings; the molded band, the rings between the zones, and the rounded terminal are set with gems. The upper four zones of the handle are subdivided into vertical panels by slightly raised ribs, each filled with delicately rendered saz scrolls; the ribs and panels in the lowest zone are placed diagonally, creating a twisted effect.

Ottoman maces were also made of rock crystal, jade, and silver; some have spherical or flanged heads, others show balls attached to chains.[82]

The most splendid piece produced during the reign of Sü-

Detail of head, **85**

85. Jeweled gold mace, mid-sixteenth century (İstanbul, Topkapı Sarayı Müzesi, 2/715)

leyman was the yatağan (**86**) made for him in 1526/1527 by Ahmed Tekelü, who employed diverse materials and techniques to display the full scope of the decorative vocabulary of the age in a work of art that is at once delicate and robust. In addition, he incorporated figural compositions that represent the eternal combat between the dragon and the senmurv in an enchanted forest, transforming the most characteristic saz theme found in album drawings into a three-dimensional composition.

The sword has an ivory hilt with a slightly rounded pommel, decorated with three superimposed designs: on the lowest register is a spiral floral vine inlaid with black; above it is a gold saz scroll bearing hatayis, peonies, and leaves; on the top register are gold cloud bands that create large volutes,

at times knotting together and forming loops. The gold-inlaid saz scroll and cloud bands are rendered in high relief and minutely detailed, with the elements standing above the surface. The pommel, once embellished with a large gold-petaled central gem (possibly a turquoise) set into a deeply carved socket, contains a black spiral vine under a gold saz scroll, which has tiny ruby-centered hatayis. The top of the pommel has a silver boss enclosed by a gold scroll set with turquoise. The gold guard is incised with saz scrolls placed on a ring-matted ground.

The slightly curving steel blade, which has a prominent spine and thickens toward the point, is decorated on both sides, each divided into three sections that contain similar designs. The upper sections represent a fire-breathing dragon

Detail of hilt, **86**

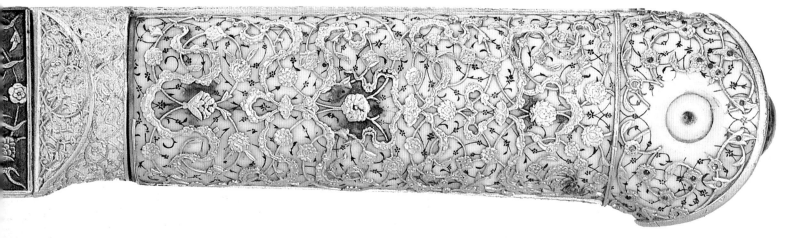

86. Jeweled and gold-inlaid yatağan made for Sultan Süleyman by Ahmed Tekelü in 1526/1527 (İstanbul, Topkapı Sarayı Müzesi, 2/3776)

with a scaly body intertwined with saz scrolls; its claws grasp the branches as it emerges from the foliage to attack a senmurv. The senmurv, which confronts the dragon with its mouth open and claws ready to tear into its opponent, has a scaly and feathered body and a tail with long and swirling plumes. The creatures were cast separately in steel or iron and affixed to the surface; the senmurv and the face and legs of the dragon are inlaid with gold, their eyes set with rubies. Gold inlay, which stands in relief, is also applied to the foliage enclosing the creatures. The metal in the background and on the visible portions of the dragon has been blackened. The two sides of the blade show variations in the floral scrolls and configurations of the protagonists, indicating that they were worked separately.

The central sections, which show a frieze of minute trefoils along the cutting edge of the blade, are filled by two versions of the same theme. One side displays a gold-inlaid animated scroll with large lion heads amid smaller ones belonging to dragons, monkeys, bears, and other animals; the other side reveals a scroll with hatayi blossoms and composite rumis. The longer and last sections of the blade have gold-inlaid sülüs inscriptions, that extend to the tip; the words on one side state that the piece was made for the Hazine of the sultan and praises him, and those on the other side give his name together with the date. A cartouche on the spine encloses the name of the maker.[83]

The yatağan is a unique piece that reaches the epitome of technical and artistic virtuosity, and includes a rich and un-

Detail of blade, **86**

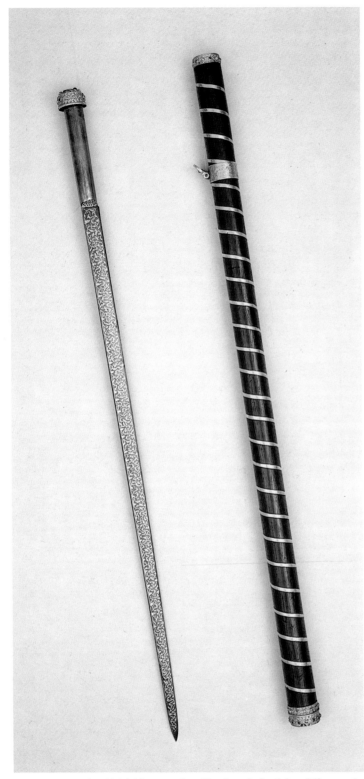

87. Jeweled and gold-inlaid meç and scabbard made for Sultan Süleyman in 1531/1532 (İstanbul, Topkapı Sarayı Müzesi, 1/74)

usual repertoire not used on other metal objects. The combat between the dragon and senmurv and the animated scrolls are exceptional, employing themes found in album drawings and manuscript illuminations. The animated scroll, popularly used in inlaid brasses produced in the central Islamic lands in the thirteenth and fourteenth centuries, became fashionable in fifteenth- and sixteenth-century illuminations made in Herat and Tabriz. Its appearance in volumes produced in the Ottoman court in the second quarter of the sixteenth century shows the impact of this tradition.[84] Ahmed Tekelü must have relied on manuscripts for his animated scrolls, since this theme had not been produced on metalwork for the preceding two centuries. This highly talented and creative artist is only known through the yatağan made for Süleyman; if he produced other pieces, they were either destroyed or await discovery.

Another unusual sword made for Süleyman is a meç (87), which has a cylindrical silver hilt with a gold pommel, the latter decorated with floral scrolls encrusted with rubies and turquoises set into plain collars and placed on a ring-matted ground. The semicircular section between the hilt and blade is embellished with rumis, executed in reserve on a gold ground. One side of the blade is covered with gold-inlaid cloud bands while the other has a long gold-inlaid inscription extending to the point. The inscription begins with the besmele, contains Koranic verses and prayers, states that it was made for the Hazine of the "greatest sultan, Süleyman Han bin Selim Han, may his victories be glorious," gives the name of the city as Kostantiniye (İstanbul), and concludes with the date 1531/1532. The name of the maker is not given. The cylindrical scabbard, which encases the sword up to the pommel, is made of wood and is diagonally wound with gold strips. Placed at the upper and lower edges are gold bands decorated with palmettes and set with gems in round collars. In the center is a wide gold sling mount, incised with floral scrolls and affixed with a ring used to attach the piece to the belt.

A more typical sword is the kılıç with its distinctive curved blade. Most of the examples in the Topkapı Palace bearing Süleyman's name were repaired and their handles and guards replaced in later periods. One of the few swords that retains its original components (88) has a faceted wood hilt covered with black leather, attached to the core with three gilded silver studs, and a gold-inlaid steel pommel and guard, the former bent out of shape during restoration. The edge of the pommel has a beaded band; cloud bands decorate the central panel and hatayi scrolls with additional cloud bands appear in the surrounding zones. The same scrolls, radiating from a multipetaled blossom enclosed by a quatrefoil cloud band, were used on the guard, which has relatively stout quillons and short prongs extending toward the handle and blade. The gold inlay is thickly applied and detailed with chasing and punching, while the steel ground is blackened. The blade,

which becomes double-edged toward the point, has gold-inlaid inscriptions on both sides. The inscriptions on one side contain the same Koranic verses used in the meç; those on the other side state that the weapon is entrusted to the will of God and to the guidance of the Prophet and his descendants, and that this noble *hüsam* (sword) is for the protection of the sultan of mankind, "Sultan Süleyman bin Selim, may God grant him victory."

The scabbard has a wooden core covered with black leather; it is embellished with gold-inlaid blackened steel upper and lower chapes as well as a pair of similarly constructed sling mounts with rings. These components are decorated in the same manner as the hilt and guard, with rumis in addition to hatayis and cloud bands.

The style of the floral motifs recalls that on the gilded silver jugs, suggesting that the sword dates from the early part of Süleyman's reign. The thickly inlaid gold motifs rendered in relief also point to the second quarter of the sixteenth century. Abrasions on the gold inlays indicate that this sword has seen considerable use.

88. Gold-inlaid kılıç and scabbard made for Sultan Süleyman, second quarter sixteenth century (İstanbul, Topkapı Sarayı Müzesi, 1/463)

Detail of hilt, 88

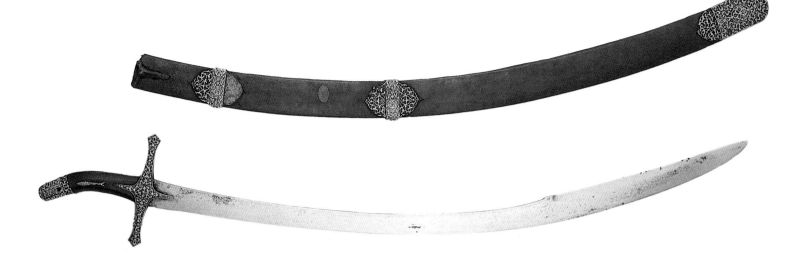

89. Gold-inlaid kılıç and scabbard, second quarter sixteenth century, (İstanbul, Topkapı Sarayı Müzesi, 1/294)

Another sword and scabbard dating from the same period (89) shows a variation in the technique of its decoration. Similar to the previous example, it has a faceted hilt covered with black leather and a gold-inlaid blackened steel pommel and guard with elongated quillons and pointed prongs. The blade is so heavily abraded that there is now only a trace of the original inscription and design. The scabbard, also covered with black leather, has a gold-inlaid steel lower chape and two sling mounts with rings; the upper chape and parts of the steel mounts are missing.

The hilt is original and slightly inclined, counterbalancing the curve of the blade. Its faceted pommel has a gold-inlaid rumi band along the edge; the central panel is inlaid with superimposed hatayi and rumi scrolls that lie flush with the surface; the flanking panels also have two layers of scrolls, the lower one bearing flattened blossoms and the upper one showing cloud bands in relief. The band encircling the upper edge of the pommel displays four cartouches inscribed with a pair of Persian couplets rendered in talik[85] and interspersed with small blossoms set with rubies. Stones were originally set into the deep sockets in the central panel of the hilt. The guard combines the motifs used on the handle and has a flat floral scroll over which are cloud bands and rumis executed in relief. On one side of the hilt is a gold-inlaid, scaly fish.

The gold-inlaid steel components of the scabbard also combine filigreed rumis, flat floral scrolls, and raised cloud bands. In some areas, more specifically the middle bars of the sling mounts and the back portion of the lower chape, the designs are rendered in reserve, contrasting the gold and blackened steel backgrounds. The combination of thin inlays flush with the surface and thickly applied raised elements with chased

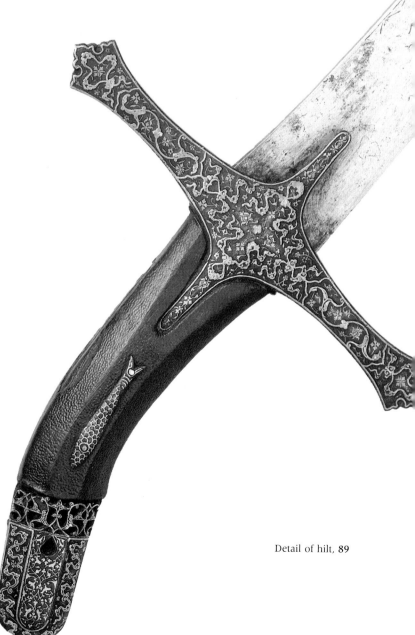

Detail of hilt, 89

156

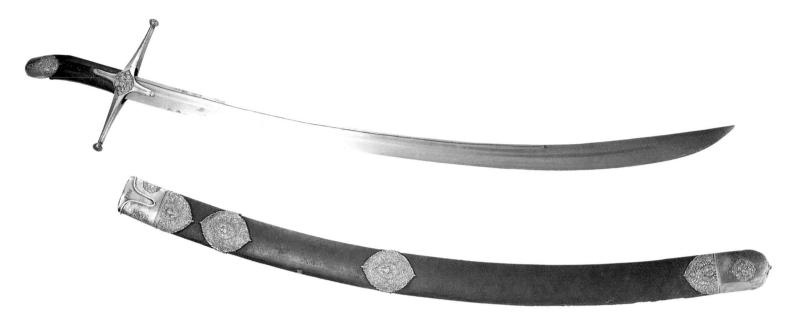

90. Kılıç and scabbard with gilded silver components, stamped with the seal of Sultan Süleyman, mid-sixteenth century (Vienna, Kunsthistorisches Museum, A. 1341)

details was observed in the helmet (see **84**); here, however, these two techniques are superimposed, creating a richly textured surface. The Topkapı Palace owns a number of swords decorated in this manner, some of which have rubies and turquoises set into the gold-inlaid steel components.

Among the more unusual swords produced for Süleyman in the mid-sixteenth century is an example in Vienna (**90**), recorded as having entered the collection of Archduke Ferdinand II at Ambras Castle in Tirol by 1583.[86] Its faceted wood hilt is covered with black leather and embellished with a gilded silver pommel and guard with elongated quillons that terminate in rounded elements. The steel blade is undecorated. The wood scabbard is also covered with black leather and affixed with gilded silver chapes and a pair of ovoid sling mounts. At the back of the lower chape is an assay stamp in the form of a tuğra identified as that of Süleyman.

The gilded silver components are chased with varied designs. The rounded elements at the tips of the quillon have reciprocal palmettes, and the smaller lobed ovals on the guard and upper and lower chapes contain saz scrolls on a ring-matted ground. The larger ovals on the scabbard show a more intricate composition. In the center of each is a cypress tree flanked by two pairs of tulips and encircled by a beaded band; the wide outer zone contains scrolls bearing multipetaled roses, enclosed by a remarkable frame composed of overlapping feathery leaves, each overlaid with a spray of rounded blossoms; ring matting decorates the background.

The sword and scabbard employ both the saz style and the naturalistic genre that were created in the nakkaşhane. This feature was observed on the gilded copper-alloy tankard, in the enameled portions of the black stone jug, and in the neck

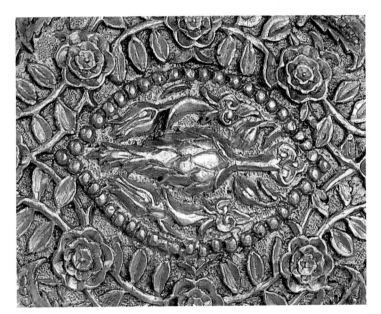

Detail of chape, **90**

guard of the helmet (see **53, 64,** and **84**). The overlapping feathery leaves were frequently employed in manuscript illuminations, bookbindings,[87] brocaded silks, and tiles. Their appearance on metalwork is unusual.

Some imperial swords of the period were ceremonial—such as the yatağan made for Süleyman and the refurbished examples belonging to Sultan Osman and the Prophet Muhammed—while others were functional, used in warfare and hunting. Imperial Ottoman daggers, on the other hand, appear to have been more decorative than ceremonial or functional, and were frequently presented as gifts. For instance, during bayram celebrations the sultan received daggers or dagger handles from goldsmiths, gold inlayers, gemstone carvers, and the members of the kündekari society. He must have also sent daggers as diplomatic gifts to neighboring states, for some superb examples are housed in European royal collections.

Most of the Ottoman daggers have a straight double-edged blade with a pierced central groove and are inlaid with gold scrolls, at times also with Persian or Turkish verses. The handles generally have a flattened grip with swelling sides and a lobed pommel; they are made of ivory, mother-of-pearl, jade, or other precious materials, often inlaid with gold and set with gems. Some daggers have matching scabbards, employing the same materials and designs as those used on the hilt.[88] There are also several daggers with slightly curving blades or cylindrical hilts. None of the known examples bears the signature of the maker or gives the name of the sultan and the year in which it was made except one.

The exception (91) is the dagger with a carved rock-crystal hilt and pierced steel blade, both inlaid with gold. The hilt has a lobed pommel with carved and gold-inlaid inscriptions. The upper lobe on the front contains the phrase "feth-i acem" (conquest of Iran); below it is a square, flanked by mirror-image inscriptions. The square is divided into sixteen compartments, each with a letter; the numerical values of the letters total sixty-six, the same as those in the word Allah. Written on either side in mirror-image is "malik ül-mülk" (sovereign of the land). The upper lobe on the back contains the words for year and date, below which is another square with its letters totaling 920 (that is, the year in the Islamic calendar that corresponds to A.D. 1514/1515), flanked by the same mirror-image phrase used on the front. Small turquoise stones with plain gold collars decorate the lobes of the pommel, while a larger ruby is mounted on the apex. The flattened grip with slightly swelling sides is carved with hatayi and rumi scrolls; the lower band shows a series of trefoils framed by heart-shaped elements.

Both sides of the blackened steel blade have cartouches with floral scrolls at the upper and lower portions and rumi braids applied to either side of the pierced center, which is partially divided in two by a thin strip with a palmette head. This decorative feature was commonly used on daggers produced in the first half of the sixteenth century.

This exceptional dagger must have been made for Selim I to commemorate his conquest of Tabriz. The style of hatayis and rumis used on the grip recalls that employed in the silver tray and jugs discussed earlier, prototypes of which can be traced to manuscripts produced in the second half of the fifteenth century.[89]

The shape of the rock-crystal hilt appears on several carved ivory examples dating from the mid-sixteenth century. They

91 (right). Gold-inlaid dagger with jeweled rock-crystal hilt made for Sultan Selim I in 1514/1515 (İstanbul, Topkapı Sarayı Müzesi, 2/254)

92 (left). Gold-inlaid dagger with carved ivory hilt, mid-sixteenth century (Riyadh, Rifaat Sheikh al-Ard Collection)

generally have angular sides and beaded bands encircling the rounded pommel, and a slightly swelling grip. One of these (92) has a lobed pommel, decorated with scrolls bearing hatayi blossoms and rumis; the lobes create ten convex panels along the upper edges, each filled with a blossom. The grip and its sides repeat the design used on the pommel. The floral elements are rendered in relief, their details finely incised. A silver band joins the hilt to the blade.

The curved steel blade has a blackened panel embellished with gold scrolls; the upper portion shows rumis flanking trefoils and the lower hatayis, with a cypress tree placed at the very tip. It has been suggested that the shape of the blade is typical of a date slightly later than the hilt;[90] however, the

158

motifs used in this portion, including the cypress tree, appear on other mid-sixteenth-century arms and armor, such as Süleyman's sword in Vienna (see **90**).

There are at least two other carved-ivory dagger hilts, now separated from their blades, that show the same style of decoration. One of them is in the British Museum,[91] and the second is in the Victoria and Albert Museum.[92] Ivory dagger hilts were sometimes dyed green, as is one in the Metropolitan Museum of Art.[93]

Ivory hilts were also inlaid with black organic material and gem-encrusted gold scrolls, as in Süleyman's yatağan. The same materials and techniques were used on daggers, the most outstanding of which is the example in Vienna (**93**). This dagger has a superbly crafted steel blade with a pierced central groove and a gilded silver guard that was cast in two pieces and joined in the center, forming a ridge. This component contains a lobed prong incised with palmettes and a pair of curved quillons that terminate in dragon heads. The ivory hilt with a rounded pommel and swelling grip is decorated with black-inlaid floral scrolls over which is a gold scroll, its blossoms set with turquoises and rubies in plain collars. The execution of the two scrolls is identical to that found on a

belt (see **76**), while the dragon heads with open jaws displaying long sharp teeth are similar to those used on gilded silver and gold vessels and containers (see **51**, **52**, **54**, and **61**). This type of quillon appears on daggers and swords dating from the second quarter of the sixteenth century, including the refurbished swords of the Prophet Muhammed and the orthodox caliphs.[94]

The Vienna dagger has a gilded silver scabbard, affixed with a plain silver central component with lobed edges. Palmettes with trefoil finials are incised into the upper and lower portions, repeating the design used on the prong. At the back is a swivel with a dragon-headed ring for attaching the piece to a belt.

A slightly later Ottoman dagger with matching scabbard (**94**) shows a different technique. The rounded hilt with an arched pommel and the tapering scabbard with a spherical terminal are made of jade and decorated with gold-inlaid scrolls bearing delicately incised leaves and blossoms with striated petals, in the centers of which are rubies set into high squared collars. A large ruby is mounted on the apex of the pommel. At one time the scabbard contained a ring set with rubies just above the tip.[95] The scrolls with gold wire inlays,

93. Dagger with jeweled ivory hilt and partially gilded silver scabbard, second quarter sixteenth century (Vienna, Kunsthistorisches Museum, C. 152a)

94. Dagger with jeweled jade hilt and scabbard, second half sixteenth century (Vienna, Kunsthistorisches Museum, C. 208)

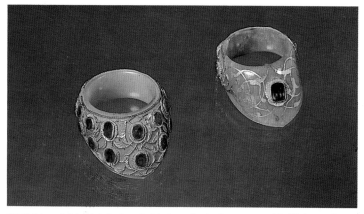

95 (left) and 96 (right). Jeweled jade archer's rings, second half sixteenth century (İstanbul, Topkapı Sarayı Müzesi, 2/74 and 2/83)

finely detailed leaves and blossoms, and gems set into floral mounts are identical to those used on several carved stone bookbindings, vessels, and containers discussed above, particularly the Koran covers, black stone jug, and jade cup and tankard (see 20, 21, and 64–66). The gold guard reveals an abstracted version of the dragon-headed curved quillons seen on the previous example. It is incised with floral scrolls and encrusted with rubies set into plain ring mounts.

The steel blade is also inlaid with gold and contains the same design on both sides, divided into two sections by a pair of palmettes. Saz scrolls are placed on the upper portions and talik inscriptions, separated by a central ridge and gold-inlaid cartouches, appear in the two convex compartments of the lower portions. One side of the blade has a Turkish poem and the other a Persian one.[96]

The same materials and techniques were used on jade plaques decorating swords, scabbards, shields, bow cases, and quivers in addition to archer's rings, called *zehgir*, which have a wide pointed edge to protect the thumb. One of these rings (95), made of pale green jade, is inlaid with gold and set with rubies, using the style discussed on the dagger and scabbard. It contains two rows of ruby-centered blossoms in the front and sides, and a large emerald at the back. The gems, set into high, slightly squared collars rising in the center of the blossoms, are surrounded by gold wire scrolls bearing rumis and feathery leaves with finely incised details. The floral elements, inlaid into shallow grooves, are rendered in relief and rise above the surface.

A second example (96), carved from jade of the same color, employs both the flatly inlaid rumi scrolls that lie flush with the surface and raised blossoms holding gems. A large emerald is set into a flower in the front, while rubies appear in the blossoms around the sides. The combination of flat and raised gold inlays, also observed in other jade examples, including Koran covers, was characteristic of the age.

The same techniques were applied to jade plaques decorating arms and armor as well as saddles and horse trappings. These plaques, generally shaped as lobed ovals and framed in gold, were affixed to leather, velvet, and metal pieces. An unusual example (97), executed in mother-of-pearl, was said to come from horse trappings. The plaque, backed and framed in gilded silver, is carved with two scrolls bearing blossoms and leaves; the lower one, rendered in a spiral design, is inlaid with black, and the upper one, which is in relief, is inlaid with gold and contains blossoms encrusted with rubies and turquoises set into plain round collars. The same materials, techniques, and designs were observed on an ivory belt and a dagger (see 76 and 93); mother-of-pearl, backed and framed with gilded silver, was also used on another belt (see 78).

Among the most decorative and yet functional arms and armor were embroidered wicker shields, which must have created a dazzling spectacle when the army marched to battle or paraded through cities. These extremely sturdy and lightweight shields have basically the same shape and size; they are 60 to 67 centimeters (about 23 to 26 inches) in diameter, with a slightly convex outer zone constructed of wound wicker. The central boss, rising to 15 or 16 centimeters (approximately 5 inches), was made of steel or iron and often inlaid with gold. The underside is padded and lined with velvet or other soft fabrics, has a square cushion in the center to protect the elbow, and is supplied with cord handles and fastenings that looped around the arm. The designs on the wicker portion are varied, combining saz scrolls, sprays of naturalistic flowers, cloud bands, and çintemani patterns.

Wicker shields, which appear to have been introduced in the first half of the sixteenth century, were used throughout the 1600s. There is little evidence that the practice continued beyond the eighteenth century; changes in warfare technology may have made them obsolete. These attractive shields,

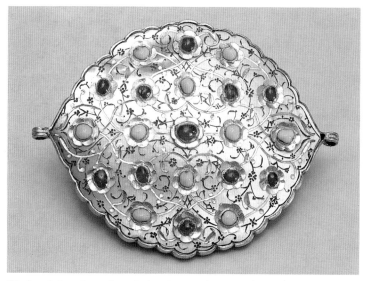

97. Jeweled mother-of-pearl plaque, second quarter sixteenth century (Vienna, Kunsthistorisches Museum, C. 152b)

along with other Ottoman weapons and hunting equipment, were collected by European royalty.

One of these shields (98) has four red cloud bands forming elaborate volutes, alternating with turquoise oblongs bearing inscriptions, placed on a golden-beige field. The cloud bands are superimposed with white, yellow, and silver blossoms, leaves, and triple balls; the oblongs contain a Persian poem written in silver talik with white flowers and leaves filling the interstices. Bands composed of red, white, and silver elements encircle the outer and inner edges. Silver used in the design has oxidized and appears black.

The central boss is sheathed in gold, covered with floral scrolls with ring matting applied to the background, and encrusted with rubies and turquoises, following the color scheme of the wicker portion. At the apex is a rounded element, now crushed, incised with a hatayi braid and set with a large ruby; it is enclosed by a radiating blossom with eight petals that terminate in lobed ovals. The blossom and ovals are decorated with two superimposed hatayi scrolls and a series of natural rubies and turquoises set into high circular collars. The zones between the ovals show the same scrolls but have in each a pair of deer or fox.

A thin band showing the same scrolls, alternately encrusted with rubies and turquoises, frames the boss. The wicker portion is attached to the core with several tiny nails. The underside of the shield is padded and lined with dark red velvet.

The verses, which exalt the virtues of the shield, and the representation of animals amid foliage are unusual. These were features of contemporary Safavid shields, which suggests that it was made by one of the Tabrizi artists in the court or inspired by Iranian models. Radiating blossoms enclosed by ovals and encrusted with rubies and turquoises recall the design of the gold-inlaid steel mirror (see 72), which is also datable to the second quarter of the sixteenth century.

An equally sumptuous shield (99) has a wide ruby-red outer zone decorated with ten large units composed of a pair of rumis flanking a central hatayi. Placed reciprocally with tips overlapping, the rumis are filled with branches bearing hatayi blossoms, buds, and leaves rendered in black, beige, pistachio-green, ruby red, and gold on alternating black and white grounds. The narrower pistachio-green inner zone is inscribed with Koranic verses written in black sülüs, interrupted by roundels with the word *Allah* rendered in reserve on a black ground. Thin braids frame the outer and inner zones. The wicker portion is attached to the back by eight gold or gilded studs shaped as multipetaled blossoms.

The blackened-steel central boss contains a swirling design with raised ribs radiating from a knob, once set with a large gem. Two gold floral scrolls, one bearing rounded blossoms and the other elongated rumis, are inlaid in alternating units. Placed around the edge of the boss is a pierced frame decorated with gold floral elements, echoing the design of the wicker portion.

The reciprocal design used on the outer zone of the shield reflects the traditional mode employed by the court artists. It was first used in manuscript illuminations and then applied to other materials, including textiles and ceramics. This particular theme originated in Herat during the late fifteenth century and was adapted by both Ottoman and Safavid artists.

A second feature that characterizes Ottoman decorative arts, the saz style, was employed on another shield (100) that also has a ruby-red ground. It is decorated with a bold scroll, its curving branches bearing four large hatayi blossoms surrounded by peonies, buds, and feathery leaves executed in cream, pistachio-green, blue, brown, and silver, now oxidized. Gilded floral studs join the outer and inner parts.

The blackened steel boss has a swirling design with raised ribs. Placed around the edge is a gold nesih inscription containing the famous Throne Verse from the Koran. Traces of gold inlay on the boss itself indicate that this portion was decorated in the same manner as the previous example and must have been affixed with a knob, which is also lost.

The third Ottoman decorative feature, sprays of naturalistic flowers growing amid leaves from a single source, is found on yet another ruby-red shield (101). Ten bunches springing from the outer edge alternately bear five carnations with a pair of tulips or three tulips with a pair of buds, their branches and blossoms overlapping one another. The branches and leaves are embroidered in pistachio-green, while the flowers are rendered in cream, pale blue, and silver outlined in black. The silver, which is oxidized, appears to have been wrapped around a yellow silk core to produce a golden tone. Zigzag bands encircle the outer and inner edges of the wicker portion, once again affixed to the back with floral studs. The blackened steel boss has a central, ten-pointed star rendered in relief. It was originally embellished with gold scrolls, of which only a trace remains.

The theme of symmetrically composed flowers springing from a central source was extremely popular, and was employed in diverse arts. Fan-shaped carnations with serrate-edged petals and elongated three-pronged tulips with curved tapering tips were particularly favored throughout the second half of the sixteenth century.

A slightly later shield (102) is decorated with three large hatayi blossoms alternating with cloud bands and triple balls, rendered in pistachio-green, cream, and silver outlined with black. Its blackened steel boss has a raised knob in the center, encircled with a gold-inlaid band alternately filled with hatayi

overleaf

98. Embroidered wicker shield with jeweled gold boss, second quarter sixteenth century (İstanbul, Topkapı Sarayı Müzesi, 1/2466)
99 to 101. Embroidered wicker shields with gold-inlaid bosses, mid-sixteenth century (İstanbul, Topkapı Sarayı Müzesi, 1/1930, 1/2441, and 1/2571)
102. Embroidered wicker shield with gold-inlaid boss, second half sixteenth century (İstanbul, Topkapı Sarayı Müzesi, 1/2597)

98

99

101

100

102

triple balls in the field, and encircling band are embroidered with gold, with the details rendered in blue, green, and red silks. The case has a pair of brocaded straps attached by gilded silver cartouches decorated with saz scrolls and ring matting. The stitches in the gold-embroidered areas create a texture that is remarkably similar to the ring matting used in the metal components.

Ottoman bow cases and quivers, used in battle as well as during peaceful activities such as hunts and athletic competitions, were elaborately decorated. Archery was ardently supported by the sultans and many, including Süleyman, not only practiced the sport but excelled in it. The society of the

103. Embroidered velvet bow case, mid-sixteenth century (İstanbul, Topkapı Sarayı Müzesi, 1/10989)

blossoms and rumis, surrounded by three similarly decorated oval medallions and framed by a pierced rumi band. This shield uses plain steel discs as studs.

Triple balls also appear on an embroidered dark red velvet bow case (103), which is lined and backed with leather dyed the same color. The velvet-covered front is decorated with a row of three lobed ovals with palmette pendants that are filled with rumi scrolls and decrease in size toward the lower edge; the field is sprinkled with triple balls, which are repeated in the wide band framing the edges. The central ovals,

104a and 104b. Appliquéd leather bow case (right) and quiver (left), second quarter sixteenth century (Vienna, Kunsthistorisches Museum, C. 5 and 5a)

archers was highly respected, and was headed by such important persons as Şeyh Hamdullah.

The majority of bow cases and quivers was made of embroidered velvet. There were also painted, embroidered, and appliquéd leather examples as well as those made of inlaid wood.[97] Similar to wicker shields, these cases were admired by European rulers and preserved in their treasuries.

One of the largest collections of Ottoman bow cases and quivers, many made as matching pairs, was assembled by Archduke Ferdinand II at Ambras Castle. It includes a superbly decorated set (**104a** and **104b**), appliquéd with red, tan, black, cream, and gilded leather, stitched with blue and red silk and gold thread. The bow case has a dark red border enclosing a tan field. The border has two superimposed scrolls rendered in cream with touches of black and gold: one bears hatayi blossoms, buds, and leaves; the other has large composite rumis. The field also shows the same two scrolls, which have larger flowers and are further embellished with cloud bands. The scrolls create spiral formations and overlap the two central red cartouches, the larger of which is placed in the wider upper portion of the case, and the smaller set toward the lower edge. There is an empty unit on the upper right that must have had a metal component similar to the gilded silver examples used on the case described above.

The quiver is similarly decorated, but has only one central red-ground cartouche, above which is a horizontal row of trefoils enclosed by roundels created by the scrolls. The two blank areas on projections on the right must have also been reserved for metal components.

The backs of both cases have wide borders made of black leather, framed with tan leather strips. The field is covered with dark blue satin and embellished with leather filigreed lobed ovals with axial pendants, decorated with two superimposed rumi scrolls. The bow case contains a pair of these ovals, while the quiver has a larger central one, flanked by cloud bands, following the format used on the exterior.

The decorative themes employing a combination of hatayis, rumis, and cloud bands suggest that the set was made in the second quarter of the sixteenth century, prior to the flowering of the saz style. This date is also supported by the spiral scrolls. The delicacy of design and the finesse of execution indicate that the cases were produced in the imperial workshop and presented as a diplomatic gift. The pieces are in impeccable condition and must have been used rarely, if at all, and preserved with care in the Ambras Castle treasury.

One of the leather appliquéd items in the same collection is a canteen (**105**) presented by Murad III to Rudolf II by 1581.[98] The shape of this piece is similar to that of the gold ceremonial matara (see **54**) except that it has a rounded base. On one side is a small spout fitted with an ivory stopper with a large finial. Another stopper, made of horn and surmounted by an ivory cap, appears in the mouth. The everted shoulders contain silver mounts with floral studs and rings; braided red

cords tied to the stoppers on the spout and mouth are looped through these rings and connected to a heavier cord that serves as the handle.

The bulbous body is covered with red leather and framed with white and grayish-blue bands accentuated by gold cording. The front and back bear superimposed scrolls with either grayish-blue rumis or stylized white blossoms, stitched along the edges with gold thread to create a beaded effect; gold thread is also used for the tiny triple balls sprinkled in the interstices. A series of white, black, and red pierced and overlapping collars appears above the body, decorated with exaggerated volutes, trefoils, and palmettes. The slender neck, covered with grayish-blue leather, overlays the upper collar with lobed edges. The flattened sides are appliquéd in the same fashion as the upper body but have at the top lobed ovals enclosing stars, stitched in gold on black leather. The sides curve into the rounded base, which contains a scroll bearing trefoils.

In spite of the intricate designs of the appliqués, the canteen projects a robust and sturdy feeling, most likely resulting from its simple utilitarian shape and subdued colors. The red used here is lighter and brighter than the deep ruby seen ear-

105. Appliquéd leather canteen presented by Sultan Murad III to Emperor Rudolf II c. 1580 (Vienna, Kunsthistorisches Museum, C. 28)

106. Appliqued leather boots made for Sultan Selim II, mid-sixteenth century (İstanbul, Topkapı Sarayı Müzesi, 2/4447)

lier and exemplifies the shade preferred in the latter part of the sixteenth century.

Leather appliqués were employed on a variety of riding equipment, including saddles, saddlecloths, coats, hats, gloves, and boots, including a pair worn by Selim II (**106**), according to the Topkapı Palace registers. Made of tan leather lined with pink satin, they are appliquéd with dark red scrolls bearing rumis and palmettes outlined with thick silver threads that create an effect not unlike twisted wire around the motifs. The soles, constructed of thick leather, are flat, and the toes are slightly pointed. This extraordinary pair of high boots is among the earliest examples of Ottoman footwear surviving from the sixteenth century.[99]

The appliqué technique used in the boots is different from that seen on the canteen. The red scrolls were not applied over the tan leather; the pieces were cut to fit together in jigsaw-puzzle or mosaic fashion, secured by zigzag stitches and covered by heavier silver overstitching. Most of the footwear made for the court employed this technique, which provided

flexibility. Overlaid appliqués were generally used for pieces that required stiffness, such as bow cases, quivers, and canteens. At times both techniques were combined on footwear, working into the design pieces that fit together where flexibility was desired and overlaid appliqués where the shape had to be more firm. Leather boots and shoes were also decorated with stamped designs, embroidered with silk and metallic threads, and encrusted with gems. Their stylistic features suggest that they were made in the second half of the sixteenth century.

Furniture

The Hazine collection also contained inlaid wood furnishings and accessories, which employed different techniques and materials than those used for precious objects and arms and armor. Most of the artists responsible for their production belonged to the kündekari society and were renowned for creating designs in which various panels with interlocking shapes were joined, the grain of woods and other materials placed in such a manner that they expanded and contracted in unison when exposed to fluctuations of humidity and heat, and remained intact for centuries. The kündekari technique was used primarily for geometric patterns, either totally covering the pieces or in combination with inlaid components. The latter were executed by hollowing out from the panels the required patterns and embedding into them precut wood, ivory, mother-of-pearl, and tortoiseshell plaques, which lay flush with the surface. Inlay was more adaptable for curving designs, and thus was employed for floral motifs and inscriptions. These two techniques had been practiced to some extent by Seljuk and Mamluk woodworkers.

Both kündekari and inlay were applied to thrones, chairs, chests, writing boxes, bow cases, and other secular pieces as well as to lecterns, Koran boxes, book stands, and storage caskets made for mosques and mausoleums. The same techniques and materials were used in doors, window shutters, and cupboards decorating secular and religious buildings.

Frequently the inlays were enhanced by silver, gold, and lead strips; the ivory tinted green; the tortoiseshell lined with gold foil; and the mother-of-pearl inlaid with black organic materials, gold, and gems. Diverse woods such as sandalwood, mahogany, walnut, and ebony were also combined, producing a rich and varied surface tonality and texture.

Carved and inlaid woodwork was produced throughout Ottoman history. Examples dating from the late-fifteenth and early-sixteenth centuries are inlaid with ivory and made of walnut or ebony. Mother-of-pearl appears to have been added to the repertoire by the 1550s, and tortoiseshell began to be widely used in the third quarter of the century. After the 1600s mother-of-pearl and tortoiseshell were the two most popular materials, surviving to the present day.

The series of objects that establishes this chronology begins with an ivory-inlaid walnut Koran box produced for Bayezid II in 1505/1506 by an artist named Ahmed b. Hasan.[100] A second piece, a small ebony box made for Selim I, is inlaid with white and green tinted ivory; it also employs silver strips and small units with minuscule mosaiclike inlays, indicating that this technique was practiced during his reign.[101] Another ivory-inlaid example dating from the second quarter of the sixteenth century is a hexagonal Koran box found in the mausoleum of Süleyman's son, Şehzade Mehmed, who died in 1543.[102] A related piece is a rahle (see 108), inlaid with ivory and ebony and decorated with mosaic units, found in the Mausoleum of Hürrem Sultan, who died in 1558. A fifth datable example comes from the Mausoleum of Selim II. This large Koran box (see 111) inlaid with ivory, mother-of-pearl, and mosaic panels indicates that by the third quarter of the sixteenth century the use of mother-of-pearl was fully established.

The most splendid pieces are those that incorporate tortoiseshell inlays. The earliest appearance of this material is on a bookbinding made for an imperial album around 1560 (see 49a). This shell must have been such a new and novel item at the time that it was employed in this unusual manner. By the last quarter of the sixteenth century, it was widely used and applied to architectural decoration. The most celebrated master of the following century was Sedefkar Mehmed Ağa, who produced dazzling pieces for his patron Ahmed I, including a Koran box for his mausoleum and furnishings and doors for his mosque in addition to the throne mentioned earlier (see fig. 17).[103]

Many of the inlaid-wood pieces were donated to the türbes. Although a number were produced and placed in the mausoleums shortly after the personages died, others were removed from older buildings and transferred to newly constructed tombs. Therefore not all the furnishings and objects found in the türbes can be dated to the time the owner died. For instance, the Koran box of Bayezid II, made in 1505/1506, came from the Mausoleum of Selim I; the Mausoleum of Ahmed I, the richest of all, contained fifteenth-century examples as well as mid-sixteenth-century pieces. Türbe items, nevertheless, are extremely valuable in studying the chronological sequence of styles and techniques as well as the tradition of presenting gifts for perpetuating the memory of the deceased, a concept that was unique to Turkish dynasties.

The Topkapı Palace contains two inlaid wood thrones, one of which was made for Ahmed I in the early seventeenth century. The date of the other is not fully established, but the use of ivory and mother-of-pearl inlay points to the mid-sixteenth century; the date is supported also by stylistic evidence, similar designs having been employed on inlaid wood furnishings from the mausoleums of Hürrem Sultan and Selim II.

The earlier throne (107), which must have been made for Süleyman, is shaped as a settee with four straight legs and a high triangular back. Constructed of five components that lock together (two pieces constitute the back, two the sides, and one the seat), it was conveniently dismantled and transported. This portable throne, made of walnut, is totally covered with ebony, ivory, and mother-of-pearl inlays; its legs, arms, and back are decorated with geometric and floral compositions. The seat is painted with an overall pattern of double wavy lines, an ingredient of the çintemani pattern, rendered in black on a dull-yellow ground. The outer panels of the arms and lower back contain inlaid-ivory geometric designs that radiate from twelve-pointed stars and create a series of polygons. The inner faces of these areas are decorated with alternating ovals and roundels enclosing ivory-inlaid rumis. Bands with meander patterns inlaid with thin strips of silver encircle these panels on both sides.

The high back employs the same design on both faces. A palmette crest rises above the sloping articulated edges composed of trefoils flanked by rumis, rendered in reserve on an inlaid-ivory background. In the center is a large lobed medallion inlaid with mother-of-pearl. It contains trefoils, palmettes, and leaves radiating from a blossom, in the core of which is a large turquoise set into a gold mount shaped like a multipetaled flower. The medallion is flanked by ivory-inlaid elements that consist of a pair of ovals with trefoil pendants and a series of triple balls. The ovals are composed of intersecting continuous bands that loop around a central blossom. Carved ivory finials, once surmounted by gems, are affixed to the front and back projections of the arms, the latter resting on triangular panels and thus rising higher. These triangles as well as those on the legs are decorated with ivory-inlaid cloud bands.

The throne was also inlaid with gemlike mosaic lozenges and hexagons containing microscopic bits of white ivory, green-dyed ivory, and silver. They appear on the frames around the seat, arms, and upper and lower sections of the back.

The same decorative vocabulary was employed on a rahle (108) found in the Mausoleum of Hürrem Sultan. This piece must have been made in the same workshop by the artists who produced the throne. With the exception of mother-of-pearl, it is inlaid with the same materials, ebony and ivory, with occasional silver strips highlighting the design.

The rahle consists of two pieces that join together by hinges. Each piece contains two components: the smaller upper panel, which cradles the book, and the larger lower panel, which supports the stand.

The outer surfaces of the upper panels are decorated with ivory-inlaid geometric designs radiating from a central star framed by a braid. The inner faces show a central oval with axial pendants, surrounded by corner quadrants, and enclosed by a wide meander-pattern frame. These elements are

107. Inlaid wood throne, mid-sixteenth century (Istanbul, Topkapı Sarayı Müzesi, 2/2879)

inlaid with ivory, with silver used sparingly in the frame. The composition of the inner faces recalls that of bookbindings, a feature seen on several other rahles and writing boxes.[104]

The outer surfaces of the lower panels are divided into four sections framed by silver-inlaid meander bands. The wide central portion repeats the design used on the exterior of the upper panels. The narrow oblongs above and below have lobed ovals with mosaic lozenges and hexagons inlaid with silver and white and green-dyed ivory. The lower section consists of lobed arches forming the legs, with triple balls inlaid into the spandrels. The inner surfaces of these panels are painted with an overall pattern of rumis, rendered in black on a golden-red ground. The hinges, painted with the same colors, bear triple balls set into lobes; the design becomes visible only when the stand is opened, since its parts are painted

on separate areas of the hinges, a most ingenious and pleasing device.

It is not surprising that the largest surviving group of inlaid wood furnishings consists of Koran boxes, which were presented to mosques, medreses, and mausoleums and thus carefully preserved through the ages. Some of these boxes were so highly regarded that they were removed from their original buildings and placed in newly-established edifices. This appears to have been the case with a sixteenth-century example (**109**), which was found in the library of the Aya Sofya Mosque built by Mahmud I more than two hundred years later. Unfortunately its patron and the building it originally occupied were not recorded. This Koran box is one of the earliest in the series, and contains an unusual and varied decorative repertoire. Inlaid with ebony and ivory, it also

168

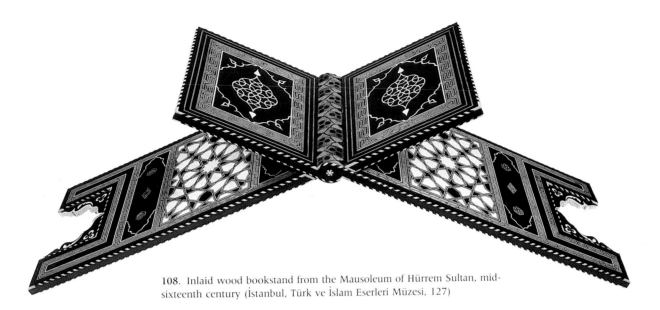

108. Inlaid wood bookstand from the Mausoleum of Hürrem Sultan, mid-sixteenth century (İstanbul, Türk ve İslam Eserleri Müzesi, 127)

109. Inlaid wood Koran box, second quarter sixteenth century (İstanbul, Türk ve İslam Eserleri Müzesi, 5)

contains silver, tortoiseshell, and a type of iridescent mother-of-pearl called *arusak* in addition to mosaic units composed of silver, white and green dyed ivories, and ebony. The decoration relies on floral motifs accentuated by geometric elements as well as inscriptions.

The piece, conceived as a cube resting on four stout legs, its lid surmounted by a large dome, resembles a funerary monument. Each of the side panels of the base has a lobed central oval attached to a pair of blossoms and palmettes with trefoil finials, surrounded by a pair of cloud bands and relatively large mosaic hexagons, and enclosed by lobed corner spandrels. The borders around the edges as well as the legs are alternately inlaid with rumi cartouches and small mosaic hexagons. All the motifs are inlaid with ivory, except the blossoms and the trefoil finials, which are rendered in mother-of-pearl with silver cores. Carved ivory hemispherical bosses are affixed to the cores of the central ovals.

The sides of the lid bear carved ivory oblongs with inscriptions interspersed with quatrefoils that enclose rumis and turn the corners. The rumis and the sülüs inscriptions, which contain the Throne Verse from the Koran together with additional prayers, are rendered in relief against a green-painted ground. An ivory band, decorated with mosaic lozenges, hexagons, and cartouches that turn the corners, frames the flat upper surface of the lid. On the same surface a circular ebony band, inlaid with ivory floral scrolls and mosaic hexagons, encircles the base of the dome. The triangular corners between these two bands show empty sockets that possibly held small hemispheres, echoing the architectural type that has a large central dome flanked by four smaller ones.

The dome is inlaid with alternating ivory and ebony bands that not only create a chevron design, but also produce a ribbed effect, intentionally stressing the seams between the panels. The scalloped collar at the top is inlaid with tortoiseshell. Above are a series of ebony and ivory bands with reciprocal palmettes, mosaic hexagons, and mother-of-pearl florals. The dome is superbly designed, showing different motifs that blend with those in the adjacent areas. The composition accelerates toward the top and must have terminated with a majestic finial.

The lid is attached to the base with a pair of hinges and two chains. The underside of the flat surface is painted with black rumis on a red ground; the dome, painted cream, has a gold central medallion surrounded by five black rumi cartouches. The composition recalls the decoration found in domed buildings. Inside the base are five compartments, with four oblongs placed around a small square. Books were obviously placed in the oblong compartments and notes and papers in the central unit. The interior, now bare, must have originally been lined.

Another Koran box produced in the second half of the sixteenth century (110) was found in the Mausoleum of Mehmed III, who died in 1603. This example, constructed as

110. Inlaid wood Koran box, second half sixteenth century (İstanbul, Türk ve İslam Eserleri Müzesi, 13)

a large dome with a faceted and relatively squat base resting on arches, is inlaid with dark and light woods, ivory, and mother-of-pearl. The twelve-sided base contains a continuous talik inscription, with a selection from the Hadis rendered in ivory on ebony.

The lid, edged with ivory and ebony strips, is composed of twelve triangles interspersed with elongated lozenges. Each triangle is further divided into a central lozenge flanked by smaller triangles. The smaller triangles are of dark brown wood and inlaid with rumi cartouches with trefoil finials rendered in ivory and ebony. The small lozenges, also of the same wood, have lobed ovals with pendants executed in ivory; at their centers are mother-of-pearl blossoms decorated with spiral floral scrolls inlaid with black. Empty sockets in the cores of the blossoms must have been set with gems. The large elongated lozenges, made of ebony framed with ivory, have central diamonds enclosed by mosaic bands; these diamonds are of mother-of-pearl and decorated in the same manner as the blossoms, with empty central sockets. The lozenges converge at the apex, which is missing its finial.

The interior of the lid has a gold central boss enclosed by a dark green medallion, its twelve trefoils projecting into the red field. The base, lined with pistachio-green silk, contains a central triangle surrounded by rectangular compartments.

This example also re-creates a miniature domed building inspired by contemporary architecture. A most remarkable effect is created by the optical play of inlays, which transform the smooth dome into an articulated structure and link it with the faceted base.

The Koran box from the Mausoleum of Selim II (111) establishes the classical format: a high pedestal resting on four legs supports a cubical container surmounted by a dome on a polygonal zone of transition. Its stylistic and technical features indicate that it was made for that building, either during Selim's lifetime or shortly after his death in 1574. It is inlaid with ebony, mahogany, ivory, and mother-of-pearl, with strips of lead and gold used sparingly in the bands framing the panels.

The ebony pedestal inlaid with ivory is decorated with panels composed of lobed central ovals with rumi palmettes and trefoil pendants, enclosed by corner spandrels employing the same design. These panels are framed by geometric bands inlaid with ebony, ivory, mahogany, and lead, and surrounded by a series of mosaic elements. Mosaic elements also extend to the arched legs, which repeat the theme used in the spandrels. A frieze with reciprocal palmettes encircles the upper edge.

The base reveals a geometric design radiating from a ten-pointed star, inlaid with ebony and mother-of-pearl and framed with the same band used on the pedestal. The central star has gold-inlaid scrolls bearing blossoms, the gem settings of which have been removed. A makili kufi band repeating the besmele appears on the upper edge.

111. Inlaid wood Koran box from the Mausoleum of Sultan Selim II, second half sixteenth century (İstanbul, Türk ve İslam Eserleri Müzesi, 2)

The hexagonal zone of transition to the dome shows mosaic stars and hexagons inlaid with ebony, and natural and green-dyed ivory. Above it is a frieze of overlapping triangles. The dome, rising from a band of intersecting ovals, has a series of diamonds and triangles inlaid with mother-of-pearl, ebony, and ivory. At the apex is a large pear-shaped finial decorated with ebony and ivory bands.

The interior of the dome is lavishly painted, and contains a central medallion decorated with black rumis on a red ground; enclosing it are four pairs of cartouches with gold rumis on a black ground. The red field is sprinkled with gold cloud bands; black rumis fill the corners. The base is also painted red and divided into a central square surrounded by four oblong compartments. The central square is covered and painted with black, gold, and ivory motifs.

This Koran box with its harmonious proportions, contrasting use of diverse materials and decorative themes, and infinitesimally detailed inlays represents the technical perfection of sixteenth-century inlaid woodwork.

NOTES

1. A list of the Hazine inventories was published in İstanbul 1940; for the 1505 inventory see Rogers 1986a.

2. These manuscripts are identified by ''H.,'' which stands for the Hazine, and ''H.S.,'' for the Hırka-i Saadet.

3. The same artist together with other Venetian jewelers had made a saddle, a saddlecloth, and a mechanical doll in the hope of selling them to the sultan. See Kurtz 1969.

4. Rogers 1983b, no. 81.

5. Kurtz 1969; and St. Clair 1973, no. 2.

6. Books on circumcision festivals of 1582 and 1720 not only record these gifts but also illustrate them. Hundreds of bayram gifts are listed in Meriç 1963. Contemporary historians also mentioned items presented during special occasions, including Arifi in his *Süleymanname*, Peçevi in his *Tarih*, and Ahmed Feridun Paşa in his account of the Szigetvár campaign.

7. Leithe-Jasper and Distelberger 1984, 24 and 25; and Çağman 1984, fig. 11.

8. Among them is the eighteenth-century Indian throne presented by the ruler of Iran; the Byzantine reliquary with the hand and arm of Saint John the Baptist; the famous ''Kaşıkcı'' diamond, thought to be the one identified as the ''Pigot'' gem once in the possession of Napoleon's mother; a pair of gold candlesticks, each weighing forty-six kilograms (101 pounds) and encrusted with more than six thousand diamonds, intended as gifts to Medina. Zinc vessels, steel belts, and a gold-inlaid jug made for Ismail were a part of Selim I's booty when he captured Tabriz in 1514.

9. The throne's dimensions are 108 x 178 cm (42½ x 70⅛ in.). The components of the bedlike throne are as follows: front, two panels; sides, two panels; side arms, two panels; back, two panels at lower portion and two panels at the triangular upper portion. These panels, covered on both sides with gem-encrusted gold plaques, fit together and are locked by the seat, which is made of walnut and usually covered by a cushion.

10. Another portable throne is an eighteenth-century Indian one, which may have been used by the sultans on some occasions.

11. Published in Çığ 1976.

12. Danışman 1969–1971, 2:265 and 266.

13. Çağman 1984, 68–72.

14. This document, mentioned earlier, has been partially published in Meriç 1953, no. LXXIV. The number of artists brought to İstanbul by Selim I, either émigrés from Herat or native Tabrizis, appears to be exaggerated as only a handful were eventually employed by the court. Of course they could have joined the local guilds, whose products are virtually unknown.

15. The works of this artist and his style are analyzed in Çağman 1984.

16. The chief in 1606 was another Bosnian by the name of Cafer.

17. Meriç 1963, no. IV.

18. Meriç 1963, no. V.

19. Close to 150 artists are listed as having presented gifts on different occasions in Meriç 1963, nos. I–III.

20. Several are published in A. U. Pope 1964–1965, pl. 1380; and Köseoğlu 1980, 7.

21. See a few objects illustrated in İstanbul 1983, E. 85, 96, and 215; and Atıl et al 1986, 37–38 and fig. 16.

22. Allan and Raby 1982, pl. 14.

23. There is a strange series of small silver- and copper-inlaid brass inkwells or containers representing human figures, inscribed with the names of the Ottoman sultans, which appear to have been produced in the nineteenth or twentieth century. The purpose, technique, and provenance of these require further study to establish when and where they were made. Several such examples were published in Paris 1977, no. 562; and Frankfurt 1985, vol. 2, nos. 6/6 and 6/8.

24. For a study of Ottoman jades see Skelton 1978. After this publication a number of other jade vessels, previously thought to be Indian, were identified as Turkish; see, for instance, Sotheby's 1982, nos. 330 and 331.

25. See, for instance, Allan and Raby 1982, pls. 23, 29, 30–33, 35–38, and 40–43.

26. Allan and Raby 1982, pl. 6; and İstanbul 1983, E. 21.

27. Allan and Raby 1982, pl. 21; see also İstanbul 1983, E. 23 for a pair of brass candlesticks made for the same sultan.

28. The men from the Balkans are listed as Kasım Bosna, Hızır Akkerman, Hasan Arnavud, all master goldsmiths; see Çağman 1984, 68.

29. For other similar pieces in Hungarian collections see a bowl dated 1537 (Fehér 1975, ill. 16) and two daggers made in 1543 and 1549 (Allan and Raby 1982, pl. 8a; and Sarre and Martin 1912, pl. 242).

30. Atıl et al 1985, no. 27.

31. Allan and Raby 1982, pl. 5.

32. For a study of this practice see Ünal 1963, where 269 pieces are listed as having been decorated in the court. See also İstanbul 1983, E. 255 and 271.

33. One example in the British Museum, decorated with rumi scrolls, was published in Frankfurt 1985, vol. 2, no. 11/4.

34. For a study of Timurid brass jugs see Atıl et al 1985, no. 25, where several pieces are illustrated and references to other publications are given. Ulugh Bey's jade jug, now in the Gulbenkian Foundation in Lisbon, might have also been a part of the Timurid collection in İstanbul; see Grube 1974, fig. 107.

35. In addition to the two examples discussed here, there is a lidded jug in the Hermitage, published in Miller 1959; and Allan and Raby 1982, pl. 7c. In Sotheby's 1985c, no. 126, there are references to others in the Serbian Monastery of Visoki Dečani, Old Orthodox Church in Sarajevo, and Benaki Museum in Athens. Another example was recently auctioned in London (Sotheby's 1986, no. 73).

36. See, for instance, a group of similar sixteenth-century silver objects in Hungarian collections discussed in Fehér 1965b.

37. It is identified as Selim b. Süleyman in Miller 1959 and as Süleyman b. Selim in Allan and Raby 1982, 218, n. 40. One of the more unusual gilded silver pieces, recently published in Sotheby's 1986, no. 128, is an ewer with a domical lid, single handle, dragon-shaped spout, and a high flaring foot; in addition to rumi, hatayi, and cloud band scrolls that decorate its surface, fantastic birdlike creatures with knotted tails appear on the handle; the neck and foot contain enameled cartouches. The vessel appears to be an experimental piece with odd proportions, as if the maker used the shape of a jug, to which he appended a high foot and an elaborate sculptural handle.

38. Fehér 1965a, figs. 3–5.

39. The lid was most likely a domical one topped by a knob. This type of lid can be seen on a gilded copper tankard decorated with vertical rows of cypress trees alternating with large tulips, using only naturalistic themes, as well as on one in tinned copper with a similar decorative repertoire. The gilded copper example, which is slightly larger, has black organic material applied to the background; it is published in Frankfurt 1985, vol. 2, no. 6/15. For the tinned copper piece see Sotheby's 1985b, no. 258.

40. One of these lobed plaques from a quiver is published in Skelton 1978, fig. 2; and Rogers 1983b, no. 413.

41. It is surprising that in the 1558 *Süleymanname* illustrations the Has Oda officials, who always accompany the sultan, are not represented with these two items. Nigari's c. 1560 portrait of Süleyman shows two attendants, one of whom carries only a sword. The matara began to be depicted in manuscripts produced after the 1568/1569 account of the Szigetvár campaign, which suggests that the canteen either became a part of the sultan's ceremonial effects during the last days of Süleyman's reign or its official usage was initiated by Selim II and continued by Murad III and his followers.

42. The inscription is published in Sourdel-Thomine 1971, no. 16.

43. For a study of these pieces and their inscriptions see Sourdel-Thomine 1971.

44. Sourdel-Thomine 1971, no. 18; and Çağman 1984, fig. 6.

45. See İstanbul 1983, E. 95 and 215; and Atıl et al 1986, fig. 16.

46. The other jade, called jadeite, is almost emerald-green and was not discovered until the eighteenth century. Therefore all jade objects produced earlier in the Ottoman court are nephrite.

47. The other box is published in İstanbul 1983, E. 82.

48. It has also been identified as "black amber," which seems an unlikely material to associate with Herat.

49. See, for example, Paris 1977, no. 672 for an archer's ring and nos. 674–676 for three cups, one of which is described here. The cups are recorded as having entered the royal French collection between 1684 and 1701.

50. This type of ewer was produced in China since the Yüan period, dating back to the first quarter of the fourteenth century.

51. This bookbinding, attributed to the chief goldsmith Mehmed, is published in İstanbul 1983, E. 202; and Çağman 1984, fig. 8.

52. A white porcelain vessel was also converted to a canteen by using gilded silver components; see İstanbul 1983, E. 130.

53. Berlin 1982, no. 109.

54. See Rogers 1983a, pl. 61.

55. This subject is discussed in Rogers 1983a; see also Rogers 1982, 292–294, where the glassmakers employed in the Süleymaniye are described. Rogers suggests that the Venetian ship that was wrecked in 1583 off the Dalmatian coast was headed for İstanbul with a cargo consisting mostly of glass window panes, vessels, and mirrors.

56. See Meriç 1953. It is interesting to note that the kündekari also presented items such as spoons and archer's rings made from other materials—mother-of-pearl, tortoiseshell, and rare woods—that they themselves may have produced.

57. An identical buckle with matching plaques is published in İstanbul 1983, E. 86. See also İstanbul 1983, E. 90 and 91 for other ivory buckles and plaques.

58. The production of small ivory vessels appears to have continued in Egypt, as observed on several examples dating from the sixteenth century, including a beaker made in Cairo in 1520/1521 by Muhammed or Mehmed Salih, now in the Victoria and Albert Museum. The same stylistic features appear on a portable pen case, called *divit*, its inscription stating that it was made in Egypt in 1671/1672 by the same artist. There is obviously something wrong in the dates on these two objects, which were made by the same man in the same style, but one hundred and fifty years apart. Further research is required to identify the production of ivory vessels in Egypt during the Ottoman period and to determine which date is correct.

59. Several of these ladies appear in an album, now in Vienna, published in Tuğlacı 1984, 101.

60. For a similar gem-encrusted piece inlaid with niello from the same mausoleum see İstanbul 1983, E. 83.

61. Forster 1968, 145 and 146.

62. The Ehl-i Hiref register of 1526, published in Öz 1950, 52–53, lists the following society members responsible for imperial arms and armor:

    18 sword makers (11 masters and 7 apprentices)
    18 dagger makers (12 masters and 6 apprentices)
    7 scabbard makers (4 masters and 3 apprentices)
    3 shield makers (all masters)
    17 mace makers (4 masters and 13 apprentices)
    14 arrow makers (11 masters and 3 apprentices)
    23 bow makers (18 masters and 5 apprentices)
    6 cannon makers (all masters)
    10 rifle makers (all masters)
    22 "damascene" sword makers (all masters)

These artists frequently presented their wares, particularly swords, to the sultan during bayram celebrations (Meriç 1963).

63. For one of the tents in Krakow see Mackie 1980, ill. 221; another in Budapest is published in Fehér 1975, pls. I, II, and ill. 1. For a study of Ottoman banners see Denny 1974b.

64. Part of this collection has now been moved to the Military Museum, while some ten thousand more valuable items constitute the arms and armor section of the Topkapı Palace, displayed in the former Inner Treasury building in the second courtyard.

65. For the arms and armor collection in the Topkapı Palace see Ü. Yücel 1970 and Tezcan 1983; for a study of known sword makers see Ü. Yücel 1964–1965; a group of Ottoman swords are also published in Tezcan 1982.

66. Ü. Yücel 1964–1965.

67. Ü. Yücel 1964–1965, figs. 16–19.

68. Ü. Yücel 1964–1965, figs. 23a and b.

69. Ü. Yücel 1964–1965, figs. 38 and 39.

70. Ü. Yücel 1964–1965, figs. 25–35. Yücel also states that there are a number of fake "Hacı Sungur" swords, most of which are dated 1550 and dedicated to "Sultan Mehmed," which makes no historical sense; see Ü. Yücel 1964–1965, fig. 35.

71. There are also examples with horn hilts, most of which appear to be later replacements.

72. Ü. Yücel 1970, fig. 3.

73. Slightly later examples just as splendidly decorated are in the Treasury of the Teutonic Knights (formerly the Knights of Malta) in Vienna. Other refurbished swords belonged to the Prophet Muhammed, their hilts and scabbards made during the reign of Ahmed I (E. Yücel 1982, 15).

74. For the early examples of the turban-shaped helmet see Alexander 1983; imperial Ottoman helmets are described in Tezcan 1975.

75. There are only two complete ones in the Topkapı Palace; they belonged to Mehmed II and Murad IV.

76. A. U. Pope 1964–1965, pls. 1421 and 1422.

77. There is an arm guard inscribed with Süleyman's name in the Waffensammlung of the Kunsthistorisches Museum in Vienna, published in Sacken 1855, 212 and 213; Grosz and Thomas 1936, 95, no. 8; and illustrated in Sarre and Martin 1912, no. 346.

78. See, for instance, the section on Ottoman arms and armor in Karlsruhe 1977; Copenhagen 1980, 63–75; Vienna 1983, 181–212; and Frankfurt 1985, 2:343–372. For gilded copper shields and horse's frontals see İstanbul 1983, E. 228–230.

79. Even Benvenuto Cellini, the renowned sixteenth-century goldsmith, attempted to imitate a gold-inlaid Ottoman dagger. See Allan and Raby 1982, 42.

80. This helmet, in the Waffensammlung in Vienna, was made around 1560–1570; it is published in Sacken 1855, 210 and 211; and Grosz and Thomas 1936, 93, no. 7 and pl. 11. Other examples are illustrated in Tezcan 1975.

81. This technique was popular in the late sixteenth century and was applied to mirrors, belts, handles of swords and daggers, scabbards, and even to such objects in the round as rose water sprinklers. See İstanbul 1983, E. 118 and 119.

82. See, for instance, Washington 1966, nos. 246–250; and İstanbul 1983, E. 221.

83. The inscription, published in İstanbul 1958, no. 69, is translated as follows:
Side 1 of the blade: "For the treasury of the greatest sultan, the just, the generous, lord of [the] necks of the nations, master of the Turkish kings and the Arabs and the non-Arabs, defender of the noble and the pure, conqueror of the infidels and the impious, protector of Islam."
Side 2 of the blade: "and the Muslims, shadow of God in the two worlds, ebu'l-gazi [father of the warrior of the faith], the sultan son of the sultan, the Sultan Süleyman bin Selim Han bin Bayezid Han, may his victory be glorious and his dominion be perpetual. In the year 933 [1526/1527]."
Spine: "Work of Ahmed Tekelü."

84. They appear, for instance, in the headings of the Şahname discussed above (32).

85. The poem reads: "May the world be as you wish and heaven be your friend. May the creator of the world be your protector."

86. Archduke Ferdinand II (1529–1595) purchased the Ambras Castle, near Innsbruck, in 1564, the year he inherited the province of Tirol upon the death of his father Ferdinand I, the former archduke of Austria who had been the Holy Roman Emperor since 1558. Ferdinand II's collection of Ottoman arms and armor, now housed in the Waffensammlung in Vienna, appears to have been started in the 1550s, incorporating items that were purchased or given as presents to his father and his ambassadors as well as objects captured during the Habsburg-Ottoman wars between 1556 and 1566. Although the earliest inventory of the Ambras collection compiled in 1564 does not seem to contain this and other sixteenth-century Ottoman pieces discussed here—such as the sword, a second dagger, and a plaque—further research is required to properly identify the items listed in the register with the existing ones. Part of the collection was published in Sacken 1855; and Grosz and Thomas 1936; the inventories, taken almost every ten years since 1564 and published in the nineteenth century, are compiled in Luchner 1958.

87. The same medallions decorate the frame of the exterior covers of the Süleymanname; reproduced in Atıl 1986, 81.

88. Among the most ornate examples are those in the Waffensammlung and the Treasury of the Teutonic Knights in Vienna, Württembergisches Landesmuseum in Stuttgart, Historisches Museum in Dresden, and the Hermitage in Leningrad. Some of these have been published in Sarre and Martin 1912, pl. 242; Glück and Diez 1925, 472 and 473; and Ivanov 1979, pls. 62–67, 70, and 71.

89. See, for example, the illumination and bookbinding of a work dated 1465 reproduced in Atıl 1980, ills. 65 and 66; and İstanbul 1983, E. 4. See also İstanbul 1983, E. 12 for similar designs in another manuscript produced during the reign of Bayezid II.

90. Geneva 1985, no. 315.

91. Frankfurt 1985, vol. 2, no. 10/2.

92. The size of these hilts is all about the same, about 12.7 to 13.0 cm (5 to 5⅛ in.) high, including the unit inserted into the guard; and 2.0 to 2.5 cm (¼ to 1 in.) thick.

93. Alexander 1983, fig. 1; the blade of this example has a Turkish poem composed by Necati, its mystical contents analyzed in that article. The same poem appears on a dagger in Edinburgh that has a beautifully decorated sixteenth-century blade and a later jade handle; this example is published in London 1976, no. 232.

94. See, for instance, the two examples reproduced in Zaky 1979, pls. 203 and 206.

95. Illustrated in Sarre and Martin 1912, pl. 242; and Glück and Diez 1925, 473.

96. The inscriptions, published in Sacken 1855, 158 and 159, no. 8, have been partially identified by Anatol Ivanov. The Persian poem reads:

Draw the dagger and pull the heart from our breast.
So that thou mayest see our heart among the lovers.
Every time that thy dagger talked of vengeance,
It brought the times into confusion by its shedding of blood.
By the elegance and purity of the stones which are on it
It recalled a willow leaf covered with dew.

The first verse, found on several other daggers, is published in Ivanov 1979, 75, type VIII; the other two verses, also found on daggers, appear in Ivanov 1979, 75, type VII. The Turkish poem has not been fully translated, but its first verse seems to be identical to that on another dagger, published in Ivanov 1979, pl. 70.

97. See, for instance, examples published in Paris 1977, no. 385; İstanbul 1983, E. 224 and 225; and Frankfurt 1985, vol. 2, no. 11/5.

98. This information was kindly provided by Christian Beaufort-Spontin, director of the Waffensammlung.

99. For a study of shoes and boots in the palace collection see Atasoy 1969. This article also names the shoemakers listed in the payroll register dated 1545. The nine-member society, headed by a Bosnian, included local artists as well as men from Bosnia, Hungary, Croatia, and Herzegovina.

100. İstanbul 1983, E. 19; and Frankfurt 1985, vol. 2, no. 8/2.

101. This chest also contained a silver ring with the seal of Selim I carved on a black stone. See İstanbul 1956, no. 5; and İstanbul 1983, E. 79.

102. İstanbul 1983, E. 147.

103. The lectern from this mosque is reproduced in Bates 1980, ill. 56.

104. See, for instance, the writing box with a rahle-type surface published in İstanbul 1983, E. 78. This example, which also dates from the mid-sixteenth century, came from the Mausoleum of Ahmed I.

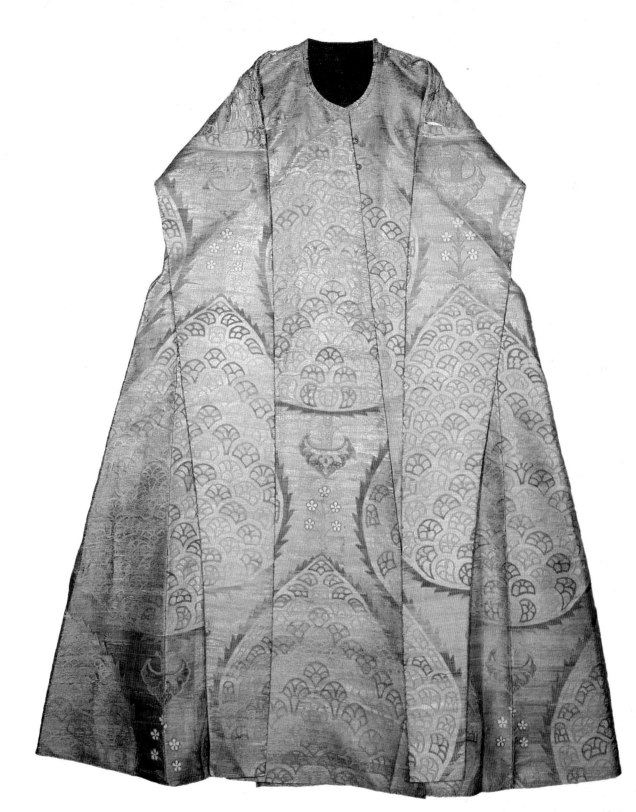

119. Seraser ceremonial kaftan with pinecone pattern, mid-sixteenth century (İstanbul, Topkapı Sarayı Müzesi, 13/9)

The fabric appears to have come into fashion in the middle of the sixteenth century. One of the earliest seraser ceremonial kaftans (119) is decorated with a series of large stylized silver pinecones enclosed by flamelike rose-colored borders and filled with pistachio-green and rose-colored scalloped motifs. Each cone has a spray of blossoms and leaves growing from its apex, while a stubby trunk with a scalloped cloud collar appears at its base. The gold field provides contrast to the main themes. Similar to all brocaded silks, the silver tone is created by strips of silver metal wrapped around a white silk core, while the gold tone is achieved either by gold or by gilded silver strips wrapped around a yellow silk core. In some examples of seraser the same golden effect is achieved by using silver strips on yellow silk.

120. Embroidered ceremonial kaftan made for Şehzade Mehmed, second quarter sixteenth century (İstanbul, Topkapı Sarayı Müzesi, 13/739)

Seraser was the most valued gift. One stunning kaftan, woven in gold and silver with only pistachio-green used to outline large peacock tails used as the main design, must have been presented to a foreign emissary as a hilat. It is now divided among three collections, with parts owned by the Textile Museum in Washington, the Metropolitan Museum of Art in New York, and the Museum of Fine Arts in Boston.[52]

Two of the most unusual kaftans in the Topkapı Palace are made of ruby-red satin, their necks, fronts, hems, side slits, and cuffs banded with wide panels embroidered in zerduz. In this technique the entire surface is covered with heavy gold thread couched with yellow silk, creating a twilled effect, while the design is rendered in colored silks. Both are ceremonial kaftans with long sleeves and were made for Şehzade

194

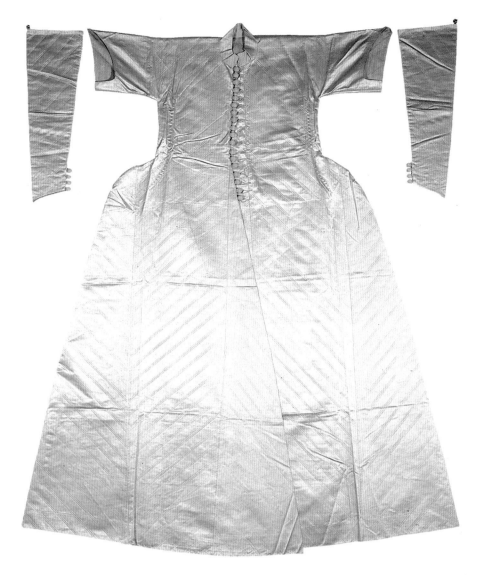

121a and 121b. Atlas kaftan with matching sleeves made for Sultan Süleyman, mid-sixteenth century (İstanbul, Topkapı Sarayı Müzesi, 13/100)

Mehmed. One is decorated with çintemani patterns,[53] while the other (120) has scrolls with hatayi blossoms and buds, cloud bands, and rumis, the characteristic motifs used in the court during the second quarter of the sixteenth century.

The embroidered panels of the latter kaftan are 21 centimeters (8¼ inches) wide. The gold is so heavy that it must have required assistants to place it over the shoulders of Şehzade Mehmed, who presumably wore it while standing up during official ceremonies. The superimposed scrolls, rendered mostly in blue with black and two shades of red used in the details, are extremely delicate, their design recalling the decoration used in the sultan's tuğras. These two embroidered kaftans, together with the two kemhas made for Şehzades Bayezid and Mustafa, are unique, and reflect the splendor of Süleyman's court.

Süleyman generally wore simple outfits, such as the entari with matching kolluk (121a and 121b) woven in an unusual color that can best be described as rosy beige or pale peach. Its style is identical to the robe he wore as a child, with a narrow stand-up collar and projecting hips. The front fastens with corded buttons and loops; the same fastenings are used on the cuffs of the separate sleeves that button into the shoulders of the robe. The compound satin is woven with a supplemental twill that creates a series of triple lines placed diagonally. The same weave is used on the pale green silk facings of the lining. Both the cut and fabric of this robe are typical of his garments.

As can be observed in this example, Süleyman was a slender man. Although it is difficult to determine his height, most of his robes are 145 to 150 centimeters (about 57 to 59 inches) long, suggesting that he was close to six feet tall, which was considerable for the age. When wearing his large imperial turban, the sultan must have presented an impressive figure.[54]

195

The Topkapı Palace collection also owns a large number of undergarments known as talismanic shirts (*tılsımlı gömlek*). Made of soft white cotton, linen, and occasionally cream or pink silks and painted with polychrome pigments, gold, and silver, these garments are decorated with Koranic verses, prayers, and magical squares with digits and letters (*vefk*) whose numerical values (*cefr*) were used in predicting the future. The shirts were worn next to the skin to protect the owner from a variety of mishaps, including illness, danger from enemies, and evil forces. These magical or talismanic shirts were also used in Iran and India.

The preparation of these garments was complicated, their proper time of execution determined by court astrologers and their designs worked out by specialists in numerology and onomancy. The inscriptions on a unique shirt made for Şehzade Cem, the son of Mehmed II, state that the work was begun on 30 March 1477 and completed on 29 March 1480, the text giving the exact minutes, hours, and configuration of the constellation in both dates.[55] With the exception of two examples, the owners of these garments are not identified, nor are they dated and signed by the makers. The two exceptions are shirts made for Şehzade Cem and Selim II (see **123**).

One of the unidentified shirts (**122**) is decorated with such finesse that it could only have been produced for Süleyman. Made of white linen and lined with white cotton with rose-colored silk facings, it is cut like a collarless, open-fronted,

122. Talismanic shirt, second quarter sixteenth century (İstanbul, Topkapı Sarayı Müzesi, 13/1150)

Detail, **122**

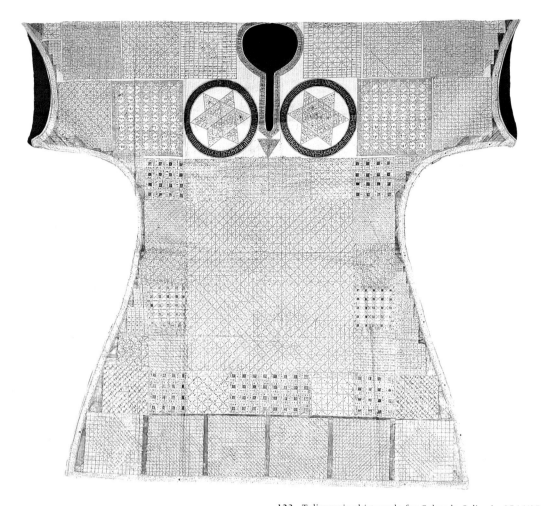

123. Talismanic shirt made for Şehzade Selim in 1564/1565 (İstanbul, Topkapı Sarayı Müzesi, 13/1133)

long-sleeved kaftan with slits at the sides. Wide bands at the shoulders, cuffs, underarm and side seams, hem, and front openings are decorated with rows of inscriptions alternately written in gold, blue, black, and red sülüs, enclosing a frieze of scrolls bearing hatayi blossoms and rumis that are composed entirely of microscopic gubari script.

The front of the shirt contains a pair of vertically placed, almost rectangular panels framed by additional rows of inscriptions. These panels as well as the surrounding areas are filled with rumi and hatayi scrolls that enclose medallions and cartouches painted with gold, blue, and red designs. Interspersed between them are gold and blue squares containing makili kufi inscriptions. Additional inscriptions written in different inks and scripts appear in the horizontal panels below the rectangles as well as along the hem. The back has a large central diamond filled with inscribed squares and a wide panel at the hem decorated with cartouches composed of rumis, cloud bands, and hatayi scrolls.

The inscriptions employing diverse scripts and styles would have been written by highly competent court calligraphers. The illuminations, on the other hand, show a close resemblance to tuğras and manuscript decorations dating from the second quarter of the sixteenth century, and probably

were executed by nakkaşhane members.[56]

A second talismanic shirt (123) is unusually cut: it is shorter, has a slit at the neck, and fastens along the underarms and sides with a series of ties. Made of white linen lined with red silk, its design consists of squares filled with magical numbers and letters painted in black, blue, and red inks in addition to gold and silver; Koranic verses and prayers written in gold sülüs appear in bands encircling the sides, sleeves, and hem.

The gold band around the neck is inscribed with Koranic verses rendered in black sülüs. The triangle below the slit contains a dedication giving the name "Selim Han bin el-Sultan Süleyman Han." On each side is a large medallion, framed in silver, enclosing a star containing black kufi inscriptions. The back of the shirt is also covered with magical squares. Written in a star-shaped unit in the middle of the lower edge are the name of the maker, Derviş Ahmed b. Süleyman, and the year 1564/1565.

The shirt, made for Selim a year before his accession to the throne, is the only talismanic shirt that is signed by the maker. Derviş Ahmed must have prepared the magical numbers, calculated the numerical values of the digits and letters used in the onomancy, and most likely produced the shirt.

198

Accessories and Embroideries

Another category of imperial Ottoman textiles consists of embroidered silks, velvets, cottons, linens, and wools which were fashioned into garments, accessories, and furnishings.[57] Embroidery using silk and metallic threads was also applied to wicker shields and to leather bookbindings, boxes, containers, riding and hunting equipment, shoes, boots, caps, jackets, and even floor coverings. Appliquéd and embroidered tents surrounded by fabric enclosures were part of the sultans' campaign regalia, as can be observed in historical manuscripts.[58]

Ceremonial kaftans, such as the one made for Şehzade Mehmed (see 120), handkerchiefs, sashes, portfolios, quivers, bow cases, and throne cushions and bolsters heavily embroidered with gold were produced by the society of the zerduz, while garments, accessories, and furnishings used on a daily basis were made by individuals, mostly by women who belonged to the court or worked at home. Domestic embroideries ranged from nightgowns and underwear to a variety of accessories, such as caps, shoes, handkerchiefs, scarves, headbands, and sashes. In addition, embroidery was used for turban covers, bohças, towels, napkins, quilt covers, sheets, and pillow cases as well as for prayer cloths and floor coverings.[59]

The decorative repertoire used in sixteenth-century embroideries closely followed the themes initiated by the nakkaşhane, relying on rumis, cloud bands, and çintemanis as well as saz-style hatayi blossoms and feathery leaves. In addition, there were naturalistic sprays of tulips, carnations, and hyacinths with occasional palms and cypress trees. Colors used were generally the popular pistachio-green, ruby red, and bright blue, supplemented at times by yellow and white, with brown and black outlines. Silver and gold were used on ceremonial and imperial pieces, while polychrome silks decorated others.

Similar to kaftans, embroidered items owned by the sultans and members of their families were traditionally placed in their mausoleums. Several handkerchiefs and headbands, found in the mausoleums of Şehzade Mehmed and Hürrem Sultan, must have been used by them during their lifetimes. Other items, such as ceremonial kaftans, sashes, and portfolios, were preserved in the palace.

Four handkerchiefs found in the Mausoleum of Şehzade Mehmed reveal an interesting technique. They are made of loosely woven cinnamon-colored linen, partially printed black, and decorated with embroidered borders. They are about 52 centimeters (20½ inches) square, and their borders are approximately 5 centimeters (2½ inches) wide.

One of them (124) has a black center with a reserved border decorated with interlacing bands that create two rows of hexagons, the centers of which are also printed black. The bands and hexagons are embroidered with geometric cartouches and stars rendered in polychrome silks and gold.

Embroidery techniques included zigzag stitch, satin stitch, pierced work, and *tel kırma*, in which metal foils are folded over to create a knotted effect.

A second example (125) also reveals a printed black center with black panels in the reserved border. The embroidered design is composed of two wide intersecting bands decorated with geometric motifs with sprays of stylized blossoms placed in the triangular interstices. The oblongs in the centers of the bands are filled with symbolic kufi inscriptions that repeat *elif* and *lam*, (the letters *a* and *l*), which had mystical connotations. These, as well as the squares in the corners, are printed black. The latter contains four stylized carnations interspersed with leaves. A thin cord encircles the embroidery, which is stitched in the traditional techniques. This example is unusual in its use of inscriptions.

In a third handkerchief (126) black was used only in the interstices of the border. This band has lobed medallions enclosing sprays of tulips and carnations that alternate with vases containing the same two flowers. A pair of red and black cords finishes the edges. There is also black on the border of a fourth piece (127), which is embellished with a chevron band rendered in reserve. The band is decorated with a floral scroll, while sprays of two large carnations flanked by small tulips and rounded blossoms appear in the black-ground triangles. Carnations and rounded blossoms also appear in the corner. A double cord finishes the edges. The techniques used on these four examples as well as the types of embroidery stitches and materials are identical, indicating that they were made in the same workshop.

Another handkerchief (128) came to the Topkapı Palace from the Mausoleum of Hürrem Sultan. Made of ivory-colored linen, it is bordered with a lattice pattern that creates a series of lozenges. Each lozenge encloses a star with four tulips radiating from its outer edges. Embroidered with blue, brown, pistachio-green, and ruby-red silks and gold, it displays the same stitches as the handkerchiefs made for Şehzade Mehmed. Hürrem Sultan's handkerchief is more delicate than her son's, its colors more suitable for a lady.

There are no handkerchiefs identifiable with Süleyman. The sultans used elaborately embroidered ceremonial handkerchiefs, similar to the three spectacular examples housed in the Topkapı Palace that are recorded as having come from the Mausoleum of Ahmed I. Their wide borders, embroidered with gold and silver using the zerduz technique, are so heavy that the central portions of the linens have been torn away by their weight.[60] The dating of this group of ceremonial handkerchiefs is difficult to determine, since embroideries made in the second half of the sixteenth and first half of the seventeenth centuries used similar techniques and designs. It is possible that some were made earlier and presented to Ahmed I's mausoleum at the time of his death.

The handkerchief was a traditional Islamic symbol of royalty and kingship, held by rulers during official functions. The

124

125

126

127

124 to **127** (left). Embroidered handkerchief made for Şehzade Mehmed (details), second quarter sixteenth century (İstanbul, Topkapı Sarayı Müzesi, 31/58, 31/60, 31/59, and 31/61)

128 (right). Embroidered handkerchief made for Hürrem Sultan (detail), second quarter sixteenth century (İstanbul, Topkapı Sarayı Müzesi, 31/1473)

Ottomans continued this practice, as seen in the portraits of the sultans dated between the fifteenth and eighteenth centuries; Süleyman was frequently depicted holding a handkerchief, for instance in the portrait by Nigari (see fig. 10) and several illustrations in the *Süleymanname*.[61]

These embroidered handkerchiefs were so highly valued that they were given as gifts or awards. According to Baron Busbecq, these items were the prizes in archery competitions: "The reward of victory is an embroidered towel [handkerchief], such as we use for wiping our faces."[62]

Also found in Hürrem Sultan's mausoleum were a number of embroidered headbands, which were worn by the women to hold their caps and headscarves in place. One of them (**129**) is covered with embroidery and decorated with rows of eight-petaled blossoms alternately rendered in blue, red, and silver on a gold ground. It is framed by a thin red-and-gold chevron border and finished with a gold cord. The tapering ends of the band were once attached to ribbons that tied behind the head.

A second headband from the same mausoleum (**130**) is

201

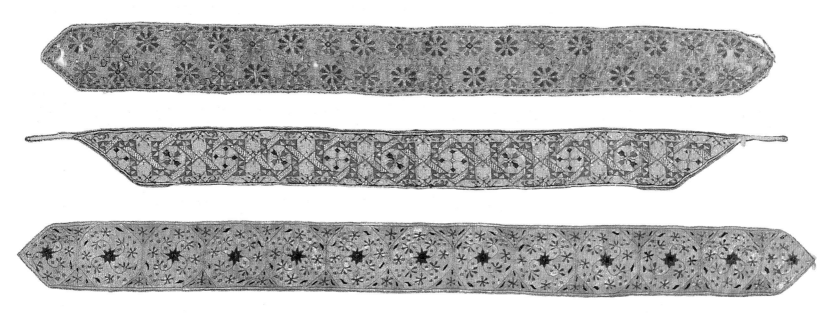

129 (above) and 130 (center). Embroidered headbands made for Hürrem Sultan, second quarter sixteenth century (İstanbul, Topkapı Sarayı Müzesi, 31/1478 and 31/1480)

131 (below). Embroidered headband, second half sixteenth century (İstanbul, Topkapı Sarayı Müzesi, 31/1477)

slightly smaller and has a pair of strips extending from its tapered ends. The design consists of a series of intersecting and connected squares that form eight-pointed stars and enclose tulips or other blossoms. Additional tulips and hyacinths appear in the interstices. Embroidered on beige linen in black, blue, cream, and ruby-red silks and gold, it is backed with plain cloth.

The largest group of ladies' caps, scarves, and headbands owned by the Topkapı Palace came from the Mausoleum of Ahmed I, where his wife Kösem Sultan is also buried.[63] A number of similar items were found in the Mausoleum of Murad III, including a headband (131) covered with gold and silver. The design consists of connected gold octagons, each decorated with a central blossom that sprouts swirling branches bearing flowers, buds, and leaves. The silver triangles between them have additional blossoms and leaves. This example is embroidered with black, blue, pistachio-green, and ruby red, the most popular colors of the age. It may have belonged to the wife of Murad III, Safiye Sultan, who was also buried there.

The Topkapı Palace owns four embroidered sashes in the superb zerduz technique that date from the mid-sixteenth century. These sashes, made of lightweight pale-cinnamon-colored linen, are about 28 centimeters (11 inches) wide, their ends embroidered on one side with bands approxi-

mately 12.5 centimeters (5 inches) high. Their lengths vary from 180 to 500 centimeters (71 to 200 inches, or 6 to 17 feet), which indicates that they were wound several times around the waist. The designs on the bands are mirror images so that when the sashes are folded in half the same decoration shows on both sides of the loose ends. Similar sashes were worn by high palace officials, including the members of the Has Oda, as represented in Nigari's portraits of Süleyman and Selim II (see figs. 10 and 11).

One of the sashes (132) is embroidered with six pastel colors, using heavy blue, green, pink, tan, white, and yellow silk thread on a gold ground. Its design is based on saz scrolls with large hatayi blossoms, buds, and leaves intermingled with cloud bands. The zerduz-embroidered ground creates a shimmering texture against which the motifs are rendered in satin and stem stitches. This example, which must be the earliest in the series, is remarkable for its wide range of colors.

A second sash (133) employs the same stitches in blue, pistachio-green, and ruby red with a limited use of brown. The design is in the naturalistic genre, with two large palm trees growing from pots amid bunches of flowers; on either side of the palms are vases with tulips and carnations, below which are sprays of diverse blossoms.

A third sash (134) has bands of ruby-red silk sewn onto its edges. These bands are embroidered with blue, pale green,

202

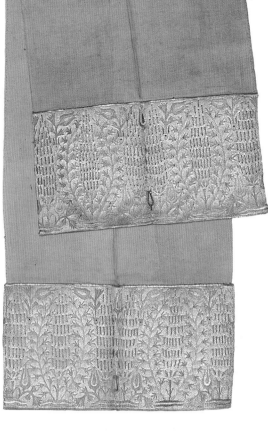

132 (left), 133 (center), and 134 (right). Embroidered sashes (details), mid-sixteenth century (İstanbul, Topkapı Sarayı Müzesi, 31/50, 31/49, and 31/1475)

and pink on a gold ground and decorated with two central cypress trees flanked by hyacinth sprays growing from a pair of double wavy lines. On either side of each hyacinth spray are two other cypresses flanked by three-pronged tulips rising from a similar source; the voids at the top contain sprays of tulips and leaves that grow from pots or vases. This example, found in the Mausoleum of Ahmed I, may date from a slightly later period although it is technically identical to the others in the series.

Gold and silver embroidery was also applied to cushion covers, one of the most refined examples showing a radiating design composed of floral scrolls and roosters on a ruby-red satin ground (135). In the center is a multipetaled blossom surrounded by small flowers and enclosed by a medallion with eight palmettes. The scalloped floral scroll around the medallion contains eight points that terminate in two alternating motifs. The motif at the four corners shows a large plane-tree leaf superimposed by a central blossom that sprouts smaller flowers; a pair of feathery leaves grows from its sides and swoops down; a rooster, shown in profile with its head turned back, perches on the branch below. The other motif is a large hatayi blossom with buds and leaves springing from its apex. The main elements are embroidered in gold and silver zerduz with three shades each of blue, green, and yellow applied to the flowers.

This example combines the *şemse* (radiating star or central medallion) motif found on manuscript illuminations with saz blossoms and leaves; in addition it employs the serrated plane-tree leaf, which was popular in textiles, particularly in velvets. The use of roosters is highly unusual for embroidered pieces, although birds do appear on the tiles and ceramic plates of the age.

This embroidered piece could have been made as a cushion for a throne or a sofa. Its design differs from other embroidered squares used as bohças, head scarves, and turban covers. Although bohças vary in size according to their function, they are generally decorated with wide borders. Borders also appear on head scarves and turban covers, which have a central medallion that was placed on the top of the head or headdress. These, however, are generally made of lightweight, finely woven linens or cottons and thus are much softer.[64]

Similar finely woven cloths were used for quilt covers *(yorgan örtüsü)*. They are possibly the best-known examples of Turkish embroidery, with large quantities of seventeenth- and eighteenth-century examples collected in European and American museums.[65] The covers have borders on all four sides; the centers are decorated either with overall patterns that repeat the same motifs, which are frequently placed in alternating rows, or have vertical-stem formations; a few also

203

135 (above). Embroidered cushion cover, mid-sixteenth century (Los Angeles County Museum of Art, M. 85.237.8)

136 (right). Embroidered quilt cover, mid-sixteenth century (Washington, The Textile Museum, 1.22)

show lattice or ogival compositions. Although their dimensions depended on the quilts, which were made for both children or adults, they averaged 240 by 170 centimeters (94½ by 67 inches), which is an ample size for today's double bed.

One of the earliest quilt covers (136) is embroidered in silk with an extraordinarily wide range of colors that includes thirteen shades. The piece has been cut in half, with possible losses in the center (its width must have been originally at least 158 centimeters, or 62¼ inches). Executed in a double running stitch on a plain-weave white cotton, it is decorated with a highly sophisticated vertical-stem pattern using two superimposed scrolls. One of the scrolls bears alternating tulips and carnations; the other is more complex, and has twisting saz leaves that lay over blossoms in addition to hatayis and several other types of flowers and buds, together with short branches that curve into the voids.

The border, framed by thin bands of trefoils, contains a series of crescents enclosing either tulips or carnations, flanked by pairs of small tulips, flowering branches, hatayi blossoms, various other flowers, and leaves. The crescents provide a restful frame to the overwhelming rhythm created in the central field. The complexity of the pattern, the masterful rendition of the design, and the extensive range of colors suggest that the piece was produced for the palace.

A second quilt cover (137) is embroidered with the more popular colors: bright blue, pistachio-green, and rose red. Its field consists of a repeat pattern with alternating large and small bunches of symmetrically composed flowers growing from stylized vases. The larger bunches contain three tulips with a pair of carnations and rosebuds; the smaller ones show one carnation flanked by two pairs of blossoms. They are arranged in alternating rows, creating an overall pattern.

The wide border displays a more complicated design. It is divided into lozenges separated by diagonal lines; the diagonals in the centers of the four sides converge to create triangles. The upper border has been incorrectly worked; one of the diagonals is missing, so there is a large off-center trapezoid instead of a triangle. Each of these units contains a variation of the bunches used in the field. Framing the border on both sides are narrower bands decorated with scrolls bearing the same flora. Similar to all the other quilt covers, the design of the field is directional, with the flowers growing from a clearly defined base. Those in the border alternate, facing all four corners.

The quilt covers described above represent highly refined workmanship. The laborious effort involved in producing

137. Embroidered quilt cover (detail), second half sixteenth century (İstanbul, Topkapı Sarayı Müzesi, 31/4)

205

138. Embroidered velvet portfolio, second half sixteenth century (İstanbul, Topkapı Sarayı Müzesi, 31/168)

Embroidery was also applied to leather cases and containers. One of the novelty leathers employed in the sixteenth century was sharkskin; it was used on a bookbinding (see 19), as well as a tankard[67] and a rectangular box (140). Since all three pieces employ the same materials and techniques, they must have been made in one workshop.

The box, which has a wooden core, contains a flat lid with sloping sides and a narrow edge. The top of the lid and sides of the base are decorated in the same fashion: in the center is a large blossom surrounded by symmetrically arranged scrolls bearing hatayi blossoms, diverse flowers, buds, and leaves, rendered in gold with details stitched in blue, green, and red. The sloping sides of the lid and its narrow edges display a scroll with hatayi blossoms and buds. The main motifs are embroidered in three layers: red and blue stitches appear at the bottom, cream is used on the middle, and gold on the top, with the underlayers of different colored silks appearing as minute dots. This unusual technique renders the design in relief, giving it a three-dimensional quality, and creates an in-

139. Embroidered and appliquéd velvet portfolio, second half sixteenth century (İstanbul, Topkapı Sarayı Müzesi, 31/1891)

these large embroideries is reflected in an undated document that states that, when several quilt covers were ordered by the palace, it was difficult to find women who were willing to undertake the task, many refusing the work because the designs were too refined and delicate.[66]

Embroidery was applied to various cloth bags and cases, some of which protected spoons (kaşıklık), while others contained money, keys, tobacco, pocket watches, documents, and Korans (collectively called kese). One such case (138) is made of burgundy-colored velvet embroidered with gold, silver, and blue, using zerduz, satin, and stem stitches. The design consists of large cloud bands creating symmetrical volutes, surrounded by palmettes, blossoms, and long feathery leaves rendered in gold and silver. The cloud bands are overlaid with trefoils and leaves executed in blue silk. The front and back panels, as well as the lobed flap, are banded with silver and gold strips. The case, which is thought to have been used for a Koran, is lined with green silk.

Another case (139), made of dark-ruby-red velvet, employs a different technique. It is decorated with a series of triple balls executed in silver seraser and appliquéd with silver thread. Each ball has an off-center void that is oriented toward the center of the clusters. Smaller versions of the same balls line the edge, their voids alternately facing in and out; thin strips of silver frame the border.

This example, which is not sewn at the sides, would have been folded in three, making an oblong portfolio about 37 by 73 centimeters (14½ by 28¾ inches). Its fairly large size suggests it was planned for documents and fermans.

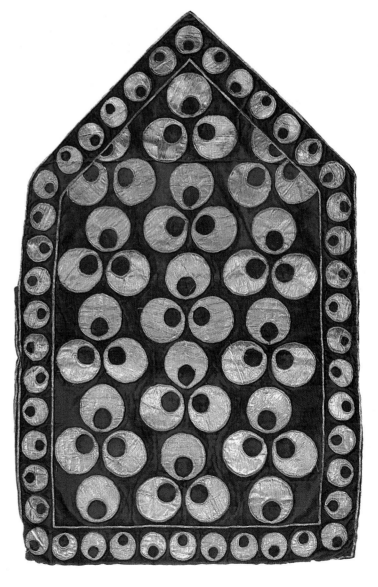

140. Embroidered sharkskin box, second half sixteenth century (İstanbul, Topkapı Sarayı Müzesi, 31/268)

teresting texture that matches the stippled surface of the leather. The palmette-shaped brackets, hinges, and clasp of the box are made of gold. Its interior is lined with ruby-red silk and contains a removable compartment. This meticulously designed and executed box must have been made for the imperial wardrobe and used to store precious items, such as jewelry.

Textiles and Furnishings

Ottoman textiles were in great demand in Europe, and were purchased in large quantities to be fashioned into royal and ecclesiastical garments or used as decorative wall hangings and covers for tables and altars. Some of these, together with hilats presented by sultans as gifts, were later cut up and acquired by various collections.

The decorative repertoire of Ottoman weavers can best be studied by the lengths of fabrics preserved in European and American collections. The majority are kemhas and çatmas made for export, most likely produced in Bursa. A large number of the kemhas were intended for garments, while the çatmas include both dress fabrics and upholstery goods designed to cover bolsters and cushions or to be spread on the floor. Although decorations of these export wares are not as refined as those made for the court by the imperial weavers, they are of the highest quality and had to meet strict regulations imposed by the state before being sold.

Their designs fall into three general groups: overall patterns; latticework, generally composed of connected ogival medallions with rare examples showing a double-ogival design; and vertical-stem motifs with undulating branches bearing overlapping floral or composite elements.

The decorative themes range from çintemani patterns, palmettes, trefoils, rumi scrolls, cloud bands, and hatayi blossoms and leaves to naturalistic flowers. The main themes are frequently superimposed with additional motifs and, with the exception of some overall patterns, the design is directional, with a distinct source from which the elements spring. Even though overall, ogival, and vertical-stem patterns as well as certain individual motifs, such as roundels enclosing crescents, rumis, and cloud bands, can be traced to thirteenth- and fourteenth-century Seljuk and Mamluk silks,[68] these formal devices were reinterpreted and combined with native themes, including saz elements and naturalistic flora, to create designs that were unique to the Ottoman world and that characterized its textile production.

Colors used in the kemhas reflect the taste of the age, with ruby red being the most popular shade; also included are bright blue, pistachio-green, cream, pink, and brown, at times purple and yellow as well, with ample use of gold, gilded silver, or plain silver strips wrapped around yellow silks, producing shimmering golden tones. The velvets have a more limited palette. The majority have a ruby-red-pile ground with the same color and weave used to define the motifs; the main elements are rendered in pistachio-green (at times pale-olive-green or bluish-green) pile as well as ivory, gold, and

207

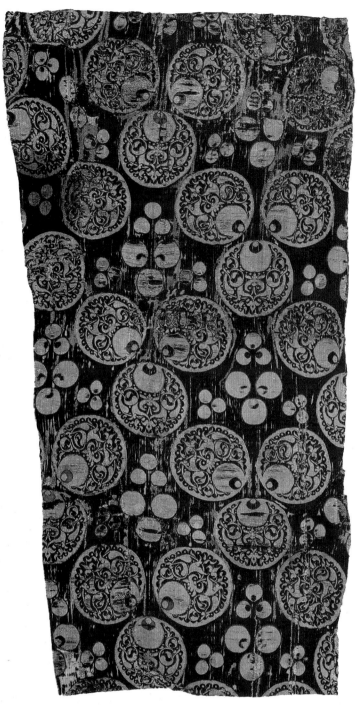

141. Kemha fragment with triple-ball pattern, mid-sixteenth century (Los Angeles County Museum of Art, M. 85.237.1)

of a series of triple balls rendered in three different sizes. The largest balls are composed of three concentric crescents oriented toward the centers of the clusters. The innermost crescent encloses an off-center roundel; the middle one is plain; and the outer one is filled with an elaborate rumi scroll. Alternating with these large clusters are medium-size balls flanked by three sets of smaller triple balls. The medium balls contain two concentric crescents; the outer is plain, the inner encloses a tiny roundel. The smallest balls have a single crescent with a roundel. The increase in the number of concentric crescents according to the size of the balls is masterfully conceived.

The fabric is worn and frayed, indicating that it was once part of a kaftan. Four pieces were used to construct this example; other fragments from the same garment are in the Museum of Fine Arts in Boston and in the Victoria and Albert Museum.[69]

Balls enclosing concentric crescents, employed in threes or singly, were also combined with double wavy lines, rumis, or scrolls bearing naturalistic flowers, frequently creating ogival patterns, which were by far the most popular designs on Ottoman textiles.[70]

Among the more delicate and unusual ogival kemhas is a gold-ground piece with scrolls bearing large rosebuds and tiny leaves rendered in ruby red with touches of pale blue and green (142). Hanging from the tip of each curved lozenge is a multipetaled blossom, possibly a peony, sprouting a single leaf. In the center of the ogival medallions are two large alternating floral motifs. One is a serrated plane-tree leaf superimposed by a spray of tulips, carnations, and small blossoms amid leaves; the flowers grow from a single source and surround a central pomegranate. The second is a stylized flower and contains long petals interspersed with trefoils; in its core is a large carnation, while tulips overlay the long petals and other blossoms appear on the trefoils.

This fabric includes the most characteristic textile motifs: serrate-edged plane-tree leaves and stylized hatayis overlaid with sprays of naturalistic blossoms, rosebuds rendered in three compartmented vertical units, three-pronged tulips, fan-shaped carnations, multipetaled peonies, and abstracted pomegranates.

A more common lattice pattern is composed of undulating bands that meet to create alternately placed ogival medallions filled with a variety of floral motifs. One of these fabrics (143) has ruby red ogival medallions formed by gold bands outlined in blue serrate-edged strips. The bands are overlaid with ivory branches that alternately knot or sprout red tulips. The ogival medallions contain gold lobed ovals framed by ivory trefoils with pendants; in the center is an ivory plane-tree leaf overlaid by a spray of gold carnations, tulips, and leaves flanking a central rosebud; surrounding it is a pair of blue knotted cloud bands and a series of red blossoms.

This example contains the same plane-tree leaf with natu-

silver satin weave. The pile was always cut uniformly, unlike European velvets, which were at times looped (uncut) or in varied heights. The metal strips, generally gilded silver wrapped on a yellow silk core and plain silver on a white core, are more pliable than the European examples and thus less likely to break and unravel.

One of the earliest kemhas (141) has a ruby-red ground with a blue, ivory, yellow, and gold overall pattern consisting

142 (above). Kemha fragment with lattice pattern, second half sixteenth century (Kuwait National Museum, LNS 105 T)

143 (right). Kemha fragment with ogival pattern, second half sixteenth century (Washington, The Textile Museum, 1.70)

144. Kemha fragment with ogival pattern (detail), second half sixteenth century (New York, The Metropolitan Museum of Art, 49.32.79)

ralistic flowers seen in the previous kemha; in addition, it displays the trefoils with pendants, cloud bands, and knotted branches frequently employed in manuscript illuminations.

The same weave and pattern appear on a rare purple-ground fragment (**144**), which might have been a part of a chasuble. The gold bands forming the ogival medallions are decorated with scrolls bearing purple and red tulips and rose-buds, and are framed by articulated ivory strips outlined in red. The ogival medallions enclose gold lobed ovals bordered by flamelike ivory bands; in the center of each is a spray with a central tulip flanked by a variety of spring flowers growing from a central source. The flowers used on this textile include irises and narcissi in addition to the more common rosebuds, carnations, and tulips; its purple ground is also uncommon.[71]

A variation of the same pattern (**145**) shows bright blue bands enclosing gold ogival medallions with ivory and rosy beige used to accentuate certain elements. The bands are dec-orated with two superimposed gold scrolls; one bears pome-

145. Kemha fragment with ogival pattern, second half sixteenth century (New York, The Metropolitan Museum of Art, 52.20.22)

210

granates shown in cross section, the other has tulips. The lobed ovals contain three concentric units: the central one encloses a single tulip flanked by a profusion of thin and long overlapping leaves, rendered in gold and placed on a blue ground embellished with dots; the second oval has a series of serrated trefoils growing inward from the lobed frame, woven in rosy beige on a gold ground; and the outer unit contains sprays of blue hyacinths separated by large feathery leaves on a gold ground.

Another fragment from the same bolt is in Lyons.[72] The Victoria and Albert Museum owns a piece with an identical pattern woven with blue, red, cream, and gold on a green ground, thought to be the back of a chasuble.[73]

A more sophisticated design is found on a kemha composed of two superimposed scrolls that create a fine lattice-work of ogival patterns (146), rendered in gold with touches of bright blue and ruby red, originally outlined in black (now

146. Kemha fragment with double ogival pattern, second half sixteenth century (New York, The Metropolitan Museum of Art, 52.20.18)

disintegrated) on a ruby-red ground. One of the scrolls contains oversize blossoms at the intersecting points of the ogees, connected by thick curving branches that cut through the flowers of the second scroll. These oversize blossoms have a central roundel enclosed by five concentric zones in which plain gold alternates with red or blue. A pomegranate growing from the top of each blossom provides a direction to the otherwise overall pattern.

The second scroll, which has split leaves, trefoils, composite rumis, and branches sprouting from its sides, bears four different hybrid flowers. The larger examples, their centers filled with red blossoms enclosed by blue roundels, are placed at the intersecting points of the medallions. The remaining types are composed of various lobed layers enclosing blue, red, and gold central roundels, using multiples of threes and sixes. This fragment, originally attached to four other small pieces that were later removed, appears to have belonged to a kaftan. Another piece from the same garment is in the Victoria and Albert Museum.

A less-common pattern is composed of parallel rows of undulating stems bearing floral motifs, which create diagonals and horizontals that counterbalance the strong vertical thrust of the design. This pattern appears on a fragment from a kemha kaftan in the Metropolitan Museum of Art (**147**). The stems are decorated with chevrons and bordered with articulated bands. They sprout alternating branches that bear large leaves, delicate tulips, and large tulips or hatayis. The branches split into two; one section has a large leaf growing diagonally toward the left or the right, accompanied by a tulip; the other section pierces the stem, terminating in a blossom facing the opposite direction, and has a small rounded leaf overlapping the stem. The large leaves are overlaid with sprays of carnations and tulips or five-petaled flowers, hatayi blossoms, and buds. The large tulips, oriented to the left, contain polychrome hatayi blossoms and buds; the large hatayis, oriented right, contain tulips flanking a central carnation with overlapping leaves around their outer petals.

The undulating stems, curving branches, and alternating orientation of leaves and blossoms create a softly swaying movement as if the plants are caught in the wind. The combination of saz elements (hatayi blossoms and buds, serrate leaves, and piercing branches) with naturalistic flowers (sprays of tulips and carnations) is most skillfully conceived and executed, harmoniously blending the two traditions.

There are relatively few kemhas with vertical-stem patterns. One sixteenth-century piece, bearing alternating pinecones and pomegranates, was made into a large portfolio;[74] others were fashioned into kaftans.[75] There are also seventeenth-century examples using the same design.[76] The pattern was employed on an embroidered quilt cover (see **136**).

Vertical stems were also used in a type of fabric called çatma, a brocaded and voided velvet that combines satin weave with cut pile. Velvet weave was applied either to the main themes or to the background, with the design rendered in metallic threads. One of these çatmas, combining green velvet-outlined gold tulips and pinecones on a ruby-red ground, was found in the Mausoleum of Hürrem Sultan;[77] another, employing ruby-red velvet tulips on a silver ground, was made into a ceremonial kaftan for Murad III.[78]

A group of çatmas is decorated with superimposed scrolls that form an ogival pattern. One of the earlier examples in the series (**148**) has a highly complex design rendered in gold on a ruby-red velvet ground with details executed in cut pile. It contains two sets of vertically placed overlapping ogival medallions superimposed on a spiral scroll that radiates from a central hatayi enclosed by a scalloped ring of cloud bands. The hatayi is at once within the core of one ogival medallion and constitutes the upper and lower points of the second. In addition, the scrolls that form these medallions are overlaid with blossoms and cartouches, sprout branches bearing blossoms and buds, and terminate with a pair of large rumis that join the central hatayi. The spiral scroll, which creates symmetrical volutes around the central hatayi and under the composite rumis, bears tiny blossoms, buds, leaves, and hooked extensions.

The large rumis and hatayis, as well as the spiral scroll, recall the designs employed on Süleyman's tuğras. Similar motifs were used to decorate the tiles in the Mausoleum of Selim I (1522/1523),[79] and the painted wood panels in the Mausoleum of Şehzade Mehmed (1548),[80] which indicates that the designs formulated in the nakkaşhane were quickly applied to the other arts. This velvet should be dated to the second quarter of the sixteenth century, based on the stylistic features of the period.

Some of the çatmas with ogival patterns employ both gold and voided superimposed scrolls on a pile ground; others use one set of connected ogival medallions without overlapping. The chronological sequence of these examples has yet to be determined. Although it is tempting to attribute the more complex designs to the earlier half of the sixteenth century and the simpler examples, which frequently incorporated such Italianate elements as crowns, to a later period, these features may reflect different workshops and markets (some velvets woven for the palace, others for domestic consumption and export) rather than a chronological sequence. Even the products of the court workshops must have varied depending on the uses of the çatmas; the ones made for imperial garments and furnishings were more refined than those used elsewhere in the palace.

The decoration of a refined çatma fragment (**149**) appears at first to employ a complex overall pattern. Its design is actually based on a vertical-stem pattern that contains two alternating medallions. The motifs were executed on a dark green ground in pistachio-green and pale ruby red as well as silver, which was wrapped around ivory, yellow, and orange silks to create three different metallic tones.

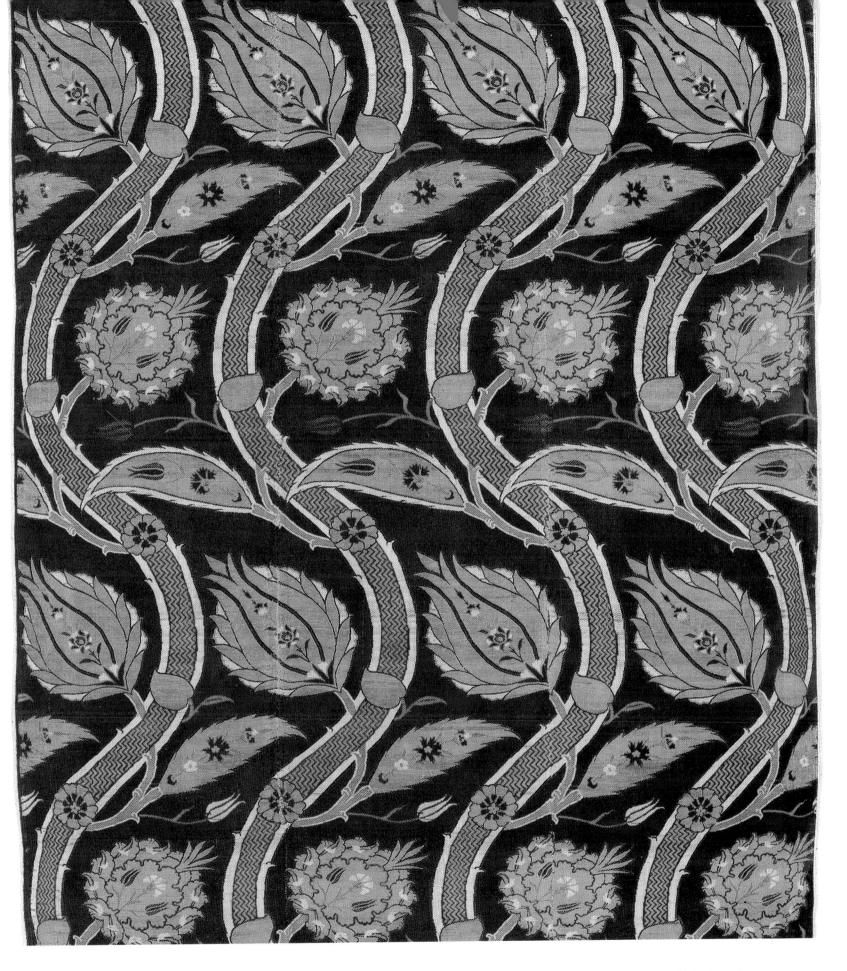

147. Kemha fragment with vertical-stem pattern, second half sixteenth century (New York, The Metropolitan Museum of Art, 52.20.21)

One of the medallions is composed of three sets of overlapping and intersecting circular bands that radiate from a central roundel. The other medallion shows a swirling pattern with two sets of crescents, its alternating elements overlaid with leaves; extending from the sides are a pair of thick curved leaves.

This fragment, which has lost most of its pile and metallic strips, still creates a vibrant and almost psychedelic composition with its swirling, intersecting, and twisting elements. Another fragment of almost the same size is in the Binney Collection.[81] The worn condition of both pieces suggests that the textile received heavy use, perhaps on a bench or divan.

In the Ottoman court richly brocaded satins and velvets were spread on the ground covering pillows and floor cushions, creating comfortable and opulent settings. Baron Busbecq, narrating one of his meetings with Süleyman, described the scene: "The sultan was seated on a rather low sofa, not more than a foot from the ground and spread with many costly coverlets and cushions embroidered [most likely brocaded] with exquisite work."[82] Representations of the sultan in the historical manuscripts also show him sitting on cushion-covered thrones, with large textiles spread on the ground. Some of these have overall patterns, while others show central medallions.

One of the existing kemha floor coverings (**150**) has the same format as a rectangular rug, with a wide border enclosing central medallions and corner quadrants. Decorated with ruby red, gold, and silver motifs on a rich blue ground, it is constructed of three widths woven on a special loom 100 centimeters (38¾ inches) wide. Now cut in half, it was originally 800 centimeters (26 feet 3 inches) long and had three central medallions. Each of the slightly flattened lobed medallions with trefoil pendants contains a central blossom surrounded by sprays of carnations and round flowers resembling sweet alyssum radiating from the center; two of the sprays extend into the finials with tulips. One quarter of the same medallion appears in each corner.

The blue border has a scrolling branch with hybrid blossoms, flanked at the top or at the bottom by two leaves that create a reciprocal pattern. The two thin guard stripes are decorated with a scroll bearing trefoils and blossoms.

Nihale designs based on compositions used in medallion rugs, which in turn reflect the impact of bookbindings, were also executed in voided velvets woven with metallic threads. One of the çatma coverings dating from the sixteenth century is remarkably similar to a rug with an overall pattern of geometric patterns decorated with floral motifs. Woven with four

148 (left). Çatma fragment with ogival pattern (detail), second quarter sixteenth century (New York, The Metropolitan Museum of Art, 12.49.5)

149 (right). Çatma fragment with swirling roundels, mid-sixteenth century (Kuwait, Kuwait National Museum, LNS 99 T)

150 (left and right). Kemha floor
covering (details), second half sixteenth
century (İstanbul, Topkapı Sarayı
Müzesi, 13/1783)

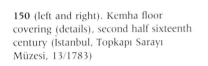

Reconstruction, 150

151. Çatma fragment, second half sixteenth century (Washington, The Textile Museum, 1.55)

Reconstruction, **151**

colors of pile in addition to gold and silver, it represents a rare and sumptuous type of velvet used in the court.[83]

The composition of another piece (**151**) recalls that of medallion rugs, with additional half medallions on the sides, creating an ogival pattern in the field. This voided velvet, woven in dark ruby red, ivory, and gold, is a fragment of a larger fabric. It was originally constructed of two loom widths, with the missing half composed as the mirror image of the existing piece; the complete piece most likely contained at least two or three central medallions, making its

length at minimum 312 centimeters (10 feet 2⅞ inches) or 430 centimeters (14 feet 1¼ inches).[84]

The central medallion with pendants contains a multi-petaled blossom framed by roundels and encircled by a lobed scroll that bears small trefoils alternating with large tulips; carnations appear between the tulips and hyacinths fill the pendants. The motifs are rendered in red with touches of gold on an ivory ground. The same scheme is followed in the quarter medallions on the corners and the half medallions on the sides; these have rosebuds and blossoms with serrated

152. Çatma floor covering (details), second half sixteenth century (The Detroit Institute of Arts, 48.137)

petals (possibly forget-me-nots) instead of tulips and carnations. The wide band between the medallions contains blossoms rendered in gold on red.

The wide red border contains a series of lobed ivory medallions linked by a pair of scrolling branches bearing tulips and other blossoms. In the centers of the medallions are quatrefoils filled with flowers, while sprays of carnations and tulips grow at its corners. Braided guard stripes enclose the border.

The harmonized balance between velvet and voided areas and the employment of ivory, red, and gold as the background and in the main themes create a lively and vibrant composition. The masterful design and superb technique of execution suggest that the piece was made for the court. It was either used as a long runner spread on the floor or as a barricade held up by attendants during official parades, as represented in the *Şahname-i Mehmed III*.[85]

A çatma nihale of an extraordinary size, 490 by 268 centimeters (16 feet 1 inch by 8 feet 9½ inches), was constructed of four loom widths with a border on four sides (**152**). Its field is decorated with an overall grid pattern composed of pairs of palm trees that create crosses; between them are

219

highly stylized large eight-petaled blossoms enclosing rose-buds alternating with carnations. Ruby-red pile appears in the background of the main motifs, which are voided and woven in ivory; bluish-green and red pile are used to outline the motifs and to render the floral elements, which radiate from golden cores. The golden metallic effect is achieved with silver strips wrapped around yellow threads.

The border, enclosed by ivory guard stripes outlined in red, reveals an ivory ground with a series of large eight-petaled blossoms that enclose tulips and hyacinths. These blossoms are connected by diamonds flanked by carnations and curving leaves. Red and bluish-green pile are used to outline the large blossoms and render the flowers, while golden metallic threads appear in the centers and in the connecting diamonds.

Similar to the previous example, red and ivory are employed both as the background and as the main design elements, producing a vibrating composition. The pile of two adjoining loom widths faces one direction while the remaining two face the other, further enhancing the shimmer of the surface.

The overall pattern creates an effect not unlike that used on contemporary Uşak rugs, particularly in the types called ''small-pattern Holbeins'' or ''Lottos.'' This pattern, which can be traced to thirteenth-century Anatolian rugs, was used on star-and-cross wall tiles dating from the Seljuk period. It appears in the frontispiece of a Koran dated 1523/1524 (see 8), which suggests that nakkaşhane themes might have also influenced the weavers.

This impressive piece, owned by the Detroit Institute of Arts, is in an impeccable state of preservation and has a fascinating history. It is recorded as having belonged to Andrea Doria (1466–1560), the famous admiral of the Habsburg emperor Charles V, and was in the Villa Doria-Pamphili in Rome until 1918. The nihale was said to be the one that hung behind the throne used by the emperor when he first visited Andrea Doria's splendid flagship, the *Capitana*, in March 1533.[86] Both Charles V and Prince Philip were received on the ship on subsequent occasions and sat on a throne set up in front of the velvet hanging. It is thought to have remained on the *Capitana* after Andrea Doria's death and moved to Rome in the seventeenth century when the Villa Doria-Pamphili was built by one of his descendants.

It is doubtful that the Detroit nihale is the same velvet that hung behind the throne of Charles V when he first visited the *Capitana* in 1533. Naturalistic sprays of carnations, hyacinths, rosebuds, and tulips as well as palm trees made their appearance in manuscripts produced in the 1540s, as represented in the lacquered doublures of the Hadis dedicated to Şehzade Mehmed (see 18a), and would not have spread to textiles and ceramics until the next decade.

The earliest date in which the nihale could have been woven is in the 1550s. This particular overall pattern with its stylized version of spring flowers was popularly employed on a series of velvets with the same colors produced in the second half of the sixteenth century. If the Detroit nihale was used in Andrea Doria's flagship during his lifetime, it is one of the earliest in the series. Though its date cannot be securely established, the velvet is of superb quality and was treasured by his descendants.

An equally refined example combines saz elements with naturalistic floral sprays (153) and employs a different technique, the tapestry weave associated with *kilims* (flat-woven rugs). The fragment contains a wide border flanked by guard stripes that join together in a stepped formation. In the field is a large hatayi flanked by a pair of saz leaves that overlap the smaller hatayis and leaves sprouting from its top. The hatayi has in its core a blossom enclosed by rumis and trefoils, placed on a gold oval framed by a wide silver zone with floral scrolls. The flanking silver saz leaves are overlaid by hyacinth sprays; the blossoms and leaves sprouting from the hatayi are rendered in silver and overlaid by additional floral elements. In the corner is a silver cartouche enclosing rumis, leaves, and blossoms. The interstices between these elements are filled with hatayis, blossoming branches, and other types of flowers placed on the gold field.

The border contains two superimposed scrolls, also on a gold ground; one bears silver hatayis and the other has blue hatayis with additional blossoms and leaves. The red guard stripes are decorated with a series of stars interspersed with pairs of triangles that create hexagons.

The silver flora in both the field and border are outlined in black with red, blue, and green (now much faded) used for the details. The same colors are applied to the other elements. Metallic threads are constructed of silver wrapped around ivory silk or gilded silver wound around golden beige.

The piece, which has lost a portion of its edge, must have been used as a saddlecloth; similar coverings are depicted on late-sixteenth-century manuscript illustrations. There is a complete tapestry-woven example with the same joined guard stripes and large central oval flanked by floral motifs in the Benaki Museum in Athens.[87]

The tapestry weave of this piece is unusual for Ottoman textiles used as furnishings. Its superb execution and sophisticated composition indicate that it was made for the palace, employing the designs formulated in the nakkaşhane. Tapestry-woven floor coverings with floral themes were produced from the mid-fifteenth century onward, flourishing in the late sixteenth and early seventeenth centuries. Their decorative repertoire differs from the folk traditions of Anatolia, and is closely associated with imperial textiles and rugs. It has been suggested that a number of these court-style kilims were made to be used as floor coverings in tents.[88]

The largest group of sixteenth-century Ottoman furnishings housed in European and American collections are covers for bolsters called yastık, which were generally made of voided

153. Tapestry-woven saddlecloth, second half sixteenth century
(Washington, The Textile Museum, 1.38)

Reconstruction, 153

velvets, although embroidered and seraser examples were also used. Among the most popular çatma yastık designs were overall çintemanis, fan-shaped carnations, series of eight-petaled blossoms, and plane-tree leaves superimposed by naturalistic flowers. These cushions, made of single loom widths of 65 to 66 centimeters (25⅝ to 26 inches), range in length from 106 to 123 centimeters (41¾ to 48½ inches) and are traditionally finished at either end with six arch-shaped elements called lappets.

One of the exceptions is a çintemani-patterned example (154) woven on an exceptionally wide 78.1 centimeter (30¾ inch) loom. Although its ends are missing, enough remains to indicate that it was finished with five lappets. In addition, the sides have bands composed of reciprocal tulips; the use of side bands is an unusual feature in yastık design. The field shows three repeats of tripartite triple balls and a pair of double wavy lines with cloud bands filling the interstices. The motifs, rendered in silver on a ruby-red ground, are outlined

154. Çatma cushion cover, mid-sixteenth century (Cambridge, Mass., Harvard University Art Museums, 85.295)

155. Çatma cushion cover, second half sixteenth century (Boston, Museum of Fine Arts, 77.256)

and detailed in red or pale bluish-green pile. The same color scheme is employed in the borders, where the tulips are alternately outlined in red and bluish green, and in the lappets, which appear to have been decorated with cloud bands.

The same pattern is found on a number of velvet fragments used as covers for bolsters or floor cushions.[89] It was also used on kemha, serenk (see 113), and block-printed silks fashioned into garments, as discussed earlier. Kaftans and bolster covers with çintemani designs are frequently represented in manuscripts dating from the mid-sixteenth century, attesting to the immense popularity of this theme during Süleyman's reign.

An equally popular motif was fan-shaped carnations filled with additional flowers, generally employed as an overall repeat pattern. One of its earlier and more lively renditions is on a çatma yastık (155) that employs the same technique and

color scheme as the one described above. The field contains a spray with five large carnations, a pair of leaves, and two small tulips growing symmetrically from the base. The carnations are overlaid by tulips, five-petaled flowers, hyacinths, and rosebuds, while the two feathery saz leaves are overlaid by rosebuds. The main themes are rendered in silver, outlined and detailed in red and green pile on a red velvet ground. The six silver lappets at each end contain lobed medallions.

The compartmented fan-shaped carnation was one of the most characteristic motifs on furnishings produced between the mid-sixteenth and mid-seventeenth centuries. It frequently appears on velvet nihales and cushion and bolster covers as well as on embroideries and brocaded silks. Bolster covers also employed overall patterns of blossoms and plane-tree leaves superimposed by floral sprays in addition to centralized compositions with radiating elements.[90] The yastık

156. Seraser cushion cover, second half sixteenth century (Washington, The Textile Museum, 1.65)

157. Çatma cover, late sixteenth century (The Art Institute of Chicago, 1949.300)

design with a radiating composition in the field and lappets at each end served as the model for a mid-seventeenth-century embroidered cover.[91]

The more sumptuous yastıks were embroidered or made of seraser. One of the rare seraser examples (156), woven with pistachio-green silk, contains a central gold oval framed by a band of serrated leaves enclosing a symmetrical scroll with blossoms and rosebuds surrounding a central flower. Stems bearing similar blossoms, carnations, and feathery leaves overlaid with sprays of flowers decorate the corners of the silver field. Four complete and two half lappets filled with floral sprays appear at one edge. The reddish-gold tone used in this fabric was produced by gilded silver wound on orange silk. This cover is one of a pair; its mate is in Warsaw.[92]

The quality of weaving is not as refined as the serasers used for imperial kaftans (see 119), which suggests that upholstery fabrics were not as carefully designed and executed, or that the yastık was not produced in the palace workshops but was made for public consumption or for export.

One type of large velvet cover is constructed of two loom widths, each approximately 65 centimeters (25⅝ inches) wide and about 170 to 180 centimeters (some 67 to 71 inches) long. Most of these pieces have overall patterns—eight-petaled blossoms, fan-shaped carnations, or plane-tree leaves[93]—with a pseudo border defined by several thin lines laid over the motifs. These cloths were either spread on the floor in small chambers that projected out from the walls and were surrounded by windows, or were used as covers for fairly large floor cushions.

One of these velvets is decorated with a series of concentric balls flanked by a pair of incurving leaves (157). The pattern consists of six horizontal rows placed on alternating axes. A

223

thin band frames the piece, cutting off the elements along the edges, while another band is laid over the field, forming an artificial border. Ruby-red pile is used for the background and for defining the details of the main motifs, which are rendered in gilded metal.

Each ball contains a central roundel with a blossom, enclosed by two concentric crescents. The two flanking leaves are joined at the base and embellished with sprays of flowers; those on alternating rows show a slightly different configuration and terminate with rosebuds. The design, which combines formalized çintemani motifs with naturalistic elements and employs only red and gold, creates a bold and striking effect.

Incurving leaves or floral sprays flanking a central element was a popular theme, applied to book decoration, metalwork, textiles, rugs, ceramics, and tiles (see **53**, **90**, **158**–**162**, **189**, **194**, and **207**). It was particularly favored on textiles and tiles and used as an overall pattern with the motifs placed on alternating axes.[94]

Rugs

Although there has been extensive research devoted to the study of Ottoman rugs, their dates and production centers are still debated. Without doubt the finest examples woven with silk warps and wefts and wool and cotton piles, using designs created in the nakkaşhane, were produced in the imperial workshops in İstanbul. Two other major centers, generally associated with all-wool examples, are Cairo and Uşak, both of which manufactured splendid rugs in the sixteenth century. Cities such as Bergama, Gördes, Karapınar, Konya, Kula, and Milas are also thought to have been active during this period.

Rugs produced in the imperial workshops employ saz elements in addition to naturalistic flora and use the asymmetrical knot, which is far more suitable for weaving intricate floriated designs than the symmetrical knot. Clues to the chronological development of these rugs are provided by the nakkaşhane designs as well as tile panels in dated or datable buildings, which help to determine at least the termini a quo for their composition. The decorative themes employed on rugs were fully established in the nakkaşhane in the mid-sixteenth century and applied to all the imperial arts, including tiles.

Tiles on the facade of the Sünnet Odası (see fig. 21), produced at the height of the saz period in the 1550s, show the finest application of the nakkaşhane themes on ceramics. Those in the Mosque of Rüstem Paşa and in the mausoleums of Hürrem Sultan, Selim II, and Murad III (see figs. 23 and 25), indicate that the saz style, incorporated with naturalistic elements, became a part of the tile makers repertoire by 1560. The rectangular panels in the porticoes of these structures use the same format found on prayer rugs: a pair of

spandrels at the top creating a mihrab niche. Although it is not possible to determine whether the format was first devised by rug weavers or tile makers, Ottoman tiles depicting mihrab niches, at times with lamps hanging in the centers, date back to the fifteenth century,[95] while the earliest extant prayer rugs were made in the second half of the sixteenth century.

The most refined court-style examples are small seccades, or prayer rugs, that are distinguished by their wide borders that use both saz and naturalistic scrolls and have a central field framed at the top by horseshoe, or "Bursa," arches. In a group of these rugs columns support the central niche; there are either single columns placed at the sides or additional double columns dividing the field into three. Six prayer rugs are known to belong to this unusual group: four of them, in Kuwait (see **158**), Budapest,[96] Cincinnati,[97] and East Berlin,[98] have single columns flanking the niche; and two, in New York (see **159**) and Bucharest,[99] have fields divided into three. A mosque lamp hangs from the center of the niche in the Kuwait, Cincinnati, and New York rugs; sprays of naturalistic blossoms grow between the columns in the foreground of those in New York and Bucharest. The columns on all these seccades are similar: they have acanthuslike capitals and decorated slender shafts that rise from hexagonal buildings resting on arched pedestals. The architectural bases are unique to this group of prayer rugs. The New York seccade (and possibly the damaged one in Bucharest) has additional hexagonal domed buildings in the panel above the niche. The structures employed here and on the bases of the columns are identical to the types used in the manuscripts dating from the 1530s and 1540s.

The same format was used on rugs made as torah curtains for synagogues, the most well-known of which is in Washington.[100] This example has a Hebrew inscription that states "this is the Gate of the Lord through which the righteous enter," indicating that the niche was not meant to be a mihrab but an arched gateway to paradise. Two other torah curtains woven in the style of prayer rugs are in Padua and Jerusalem.[101] They were commissioned either by the synagogues or by wealthy patrons who presented them as gifts to their temples.

A second group of prayer rugs contains only a horseshoe arch defining the niche and quarter medallions on the lower two corners; the field is filled with a profusion of symmetrically growing saz blossoms and leaves with sprays of flowering fruit-tree branches. Only three examples of this extraordinary type, in Vienna (see **160**), Baltimore,[102] and the McMullan Collection,[103] are datable to the sixteenth century. This group with the dense floral field shows the same border as the examples with columns.

A related type with the same border, niche formation, and pair of quadrants in the lower corners has a single large floral element in the field.[104] There are, in addition, similar prayer rugs with empty niches.[105] The Ottomans also produced large prayer rugs, called *saf*, which contained a series of mihrabs. Made for imperial mosques, they are thought to have been woven in Uşak, following the patterns used on the seccades made in the court workshops. Several fragments of saf rugs were found in the Selimiye Mosque in Edirne, while others are in American and European collections.[106]

Rugs produced for secular use vary in size and are generally rectangular, although a few square ones were also woven. Some of these rugs, most preserved in American and European collections, are of superb quality and suggest court manufacture; others, which apply court designs to mass-produced examples made for domestic consumption or for export, appear to have been made in several centers, including Cairo and Uşak. Among the rectangular rugs are a small example in Paris (see **161**) and a larger one in New York,[107] both woven in fine wool using the asymmetrical knot without the silk and cotton normally associated with court manufacture. The quality of these two rugs is comparable to the seccades, which indicates that all-wool rugs were also produced for the court.

The same material and technique appear in an unusual series of identical rugs whose format is similar to bookbindings. Four of these, once in the Palazzo Corsi in Florence, are now housed in London, Berlin, Budapest, and Paris;[108] a fifth example is in New York (see **162**). There are also ivory-ground wool rugs woven with symmetrical knots decorated with overall çintemani patterns.[109] Although wool rugs with symmetrical knots are assigned to Anatolia, generally to Uşak, those with more refined designs using asymmetrical knots are traditionally given a Cairene provenance, which is by no means firmly established. It has been suggested that the earlier rugs produced in the imperial workshops used the fine luminous wool found in the Egyptian examples, while those made after the third quarter of the century incorporated silk and cotton.[110]

Ottoman rug weavers also produced unusually shaped examples, such as long panels, octagonal spreads, and cruciform table covers. A narrow and long panel in the Textile Museum in Washington[111] appears to have been designed to be used as an overhanging edge on a canopy erected in front of an imperial tent. Similar canopies are frequently represented in manuscript illustrations. Two octagonal or circular court-style examples are known to exist from the sixteenth century.[112] These pieces, thought to have been made as table covers, were more likely spread on the floor and used for dining. Guests seated on the ground around rectangular or circular floor spreads are represented in manuscripts and described by Baron Busbecq: "An oblong leather coverlet closely crowded with dishes is spread on the ground over a rug."[113] In Europe, however, these rugs were most likely used to cover round tables, adapting to western custom. The cruciform rugs, in contrast, must have been made for export, ordered by

Europeans as table or chest covers. Two sixteenth-century examples have been published: one of them, in San Gimignano Museum, is embellished with a European coat of arms, and the other is in the Victoria and Albert Museum.[114]

The most magnificent Ottoman court-style rugs are seccades, which are characterized by their small size and were meant to be used by one person either in private devotion or as part of a group. They all have mihrab niches, which are sometimes clearly identified by arches supported by columns or by a pair of spandrels. The niche, frequently supplied with a hanging lamp, was used to orient the seccade—and the worshiper—toward the Kaaba in Mecca. Since the seccade traditionally was spread on the floor before prayer and folded in fourths to be stored, the materials used had to be soft and pliable. These included knotted pile rugs woven in wool, silk, and cotton as well as embroidered, appliquéd, and brocaded satins and velvets. The format of the Ottoman individual prayer rug as well as that of the safs was imitated in other Islamic societies, particularly in the Muslim courts in India.[115]

One of the earliest court prayer rugs (**158**), which is in Kuwait, has a ruby-red field with an ivory horseshoe arch supported by a pair of columns and a wide pale blue border. The spandrels of the arch are filled with dark green scrolls bearing polychrome naturalistic flowers; the columns, decorated with a series of lozenges, rise from architectural structures composed as domed multistoried hexagonal buildings, minutely detailed with arcades, doorways, and windows. The columns are surmounted by acanthus capitals, which join the spandrels with an entablature embellished with smaller hexagonal domed structures. Above the arch is a rectangular panel divided into two lobed oblongs filled with floral motifs. Suspended by three chains between the spandrels is a blue mosque lamp decorated with naturalistic blossoms.

The wide border is flanked by a pair of guard stripes composed of blossoms separated by strips, framed on either side by thin bands with rumi scrolls. The border itself is decorated with a scroll that creates reciprocal volutes and bears alternating peonies or hatayis flanked by pairs of long feathery saz leaves. Sprouting from these blossoms are branches with tulips, carnations, hyacinths, jasmine, sweet alyssum, and a multitude of other spring flowers, which spread into the adjacent zones and overlap or intersect the other elements. Rendered on a pale blue ground, this fantastic scroll harmoniously blends the saz style with the naturalistic genre.

The incorporation of elements inspired by local architecture is unique to this series of prayer rugs. Columns decorated with similar lozenge-patterned tiles can be found in Ottoman structures dating from the second half of the sixteenth century. The more common capital, however, employs the *mukarnas* (stalactite formation), and not acanthus. Carved marble Corinthian-type capitals made for pre-Ottoman structures and reused in a few Ottoman buildings may have served as models for the ones in the prayer rugs. The blue-ground

158. Prayer rug with a pair of columns, second half sixteenth century (Kuwait National Museum, LNS 29 R)

159. Prayer rug with three pairs of columns, second half sixteenth century (New York, The Metropolitan Museum of Art, 22.100.51)

mosque lamp with polychrome floral motifs, suspended by three chains, has parallels in ceramic examples, particularly the pair of lamps made for the Mosque of Sokollu Mehmed Paşa in the 1570s (see **195**). The mihrab niche with a hanging lamp that symbolizes celestial light, employed in religious buildings, is incorporated into the repertoire of the rugs. The iconography and design of the seccades are specifically conceived for ritual prayer with references to life hereafter, possibly for the souls of the deceased. The fact that two of the examples in İstanbul were found in imperial mausoleums suggests that they were intended as donations to türbes.[116]

The same format and decoration, with minor variations in the colors used for the motifs and their backgrounds, appear in the Cincinnati rug, formerly in the Moore Collection. It is

about the same size (168 by 128 centimeters, or 66⅛ by 50⅜ inches) and may have been made as a companion piece using the same cartoon.

A more complex field was employed on the Metropolitan Museum seccade (**159**), which has almost the same dimensions as the one discussed above as well as an identical border flanked by the same guard stripes. Its field, however, is divided into three compartments by additional pairs of columns. Their pedestals, shafts, capitals, and the miniature domical buildings above the entablatures at the bases of the arches follow the format of the Kuwait rug. The central compartment, rendered in deep emerald green, has a rounded arch with a mosque lamp; the side arches are pointed and the spandrels are filled with rumis, cartouches, and blossoms.

Growing between the pedestals of the columns below are sprays of carnations, tulips, roses, five-petaled blossoms, and other flora. The rectangular panel above the arches has a series of palmette crenellations interspersed with cypress trees flanked by naturalistic blossoms; seen behind the crenellations above the central arch are four hexagonal buildings with ribbed domes.

This exquisite seccade is decorated with a profusion of delicate and harmoniously balanced curvilinear designs that rival the saz drawings and illuminations of the masters working in the nakkaşhane. Its composition symbolizes the gardens of paradise, with perpetually blossoming spring flowers growing at its threshold.[117] The four buildings in the upper panel, protected by a row of trees and palmettes, represent heavenly pavilions, possibly even the domiciles of the souls of the righteous. Symbolizing the serene and exuberant beauty and the perpetuity of paradise, the seccade provides the proper setting and mood for prayer.

The theme of paradise gardens is even more evident in the second type of prayer rug, with an abridged version of the mihrab niche, a lobed arch at the upper corners, and quarter medallions at the lower corners. The most spectacular example in this series is the one in Vienna (160), its field densely covered with a variety of floral elements. Its border is identical to the columned examples in Kuwait and the Metropolitan Museum, using the same motifs and color scheme.

The ruby-red field is decorated with a symmetrical composition that sprouts from the base and contains a central row of hatayis surrounded by overlapping, intersecting, curving, and twisting saz and naturalistic elements. The spandrels at the top are filled with rumi scrolls and cartouches. These cartouches as well as the flowers in the field are cut off by the frame, extending the design beyond the borders. Cloud bands with rumis fill the quarter medallions in the lower corners.

Traditional rumis and cloud bands used in the spandrels and lower corners provide a contrast to the saz elements employed in the field and border, which in turn are contrasted by the naturalistic blossoming branches and sprays incorporated into the design. The composition, with its almost overwhelming efflorescence, recalls the equally dazzling designs employed in the tiles of the period, particularly the famous panel from the portico of the Mosque of Rüstem Paşa, datable to 1561 (see fig. 25).[118]

There are two other almost identical seccades; one is in the Walters Art Gallery and the other was formerly in the McMullan collection. Although the field in these examples follows the design and color scheme used in the Vienna rug, their borders differ. The Walters piece has a cloud-scroll band with hatayis and naturalistic flowers, interspersed with cartouches, and the other has a narrower frame with a different type of hatayi scroll. These two examples must have used the same cartoon for the field but relied on other designs for the borders.

Among the smaller secular rugs produced in the court workshops is a rectangular piece in a format identified with bookbindings, that is, a central medallion with corner quadrants enclosed by a frame (161). The composition of the field is an elaboration of that employed on the Vienna seccade; growing from each end toward the center are lush florals extending from a central row of hatayis, flanked by saz leaves and branches of blossoming fruit trees. These elements, joined to the central medallion, form a strong central axis and are flanked by repeats of the same configurations cut off by the borders. Supplementing them are four sprays that grow in the interstices, surround the central medallion, and join together at the sides. The dark blue field, thus filled with a profusion of saz elements, is accentuated by axial motifs that create staggered horizontal formations. The central medallion has sprays of tulips, rosebuds, hyacinths, and naturalistic flowers and leaves radiating from a multipetaled blossom, placed on a red ground. One quarter of the same medallion appears in the corners.

The red-ground border follows the reciprocal design seen in the prayer rugs with branches bearing alternating peonies and hatayis flanked by saz leaves or hyacinths, tulips, carnations, and roses. The stylistic features of this example, such as the density of the design and the abstraction of the motifs, suggest that it is from a slightly later period than the prayer rugs, and was produced toward the end of the sixteenth century. Dating from the same period and possibly manufactured in the same workshop is a larger all-wool rug in the Metropolitan Museum of Art that displays an expanded version of the composition with additional axial elements and medallions.[119]

Another small secular rug, its format even more closely related to bookbindings, was woven entirely of wool (162). Its red field is covered with horizontal rows of ivory balls alternating with yellow-outlined green wavy lines, creating an abridged çintemani pattern. The lobed blue central medallion with trefoil pendants encloses a large rumi cartouche, flanked by sprays of blossoms overlapped by leaves in the saz fashion; the cartouches and sprays grow from a hatayi, providing a direction to the otherwise overall design. The articulated corner quadrants do not repeat the design of the central medallion but bear rumi cartouches and scrolls on the same blue ground.

The red border has two superimposed scrolls, one with hatayis and the other peonies, creating a flowing rhythm around the comparatively static and directional field. The ivory guard stripes, bordered by thin bands (the outer of which is missing), contain a scroll with yellow and red blossoms.

This example belongs to a group of four identical rugs. The existence of a series of matching rugs is unusual and suggests that they were mass-produced for export in a noncourt workshop, either in the capital or in one of the provincial centers.

160 (left). Prayer rug with saz design,
second half sixteenth century (Vienna,
Österreichisches Museum für
Angewandte Kunst, T. 8327)

161 (right). Rug with saz design,
second half sixteenth century (Paris,
Musée des Arts Décoratifs, A. 7861)

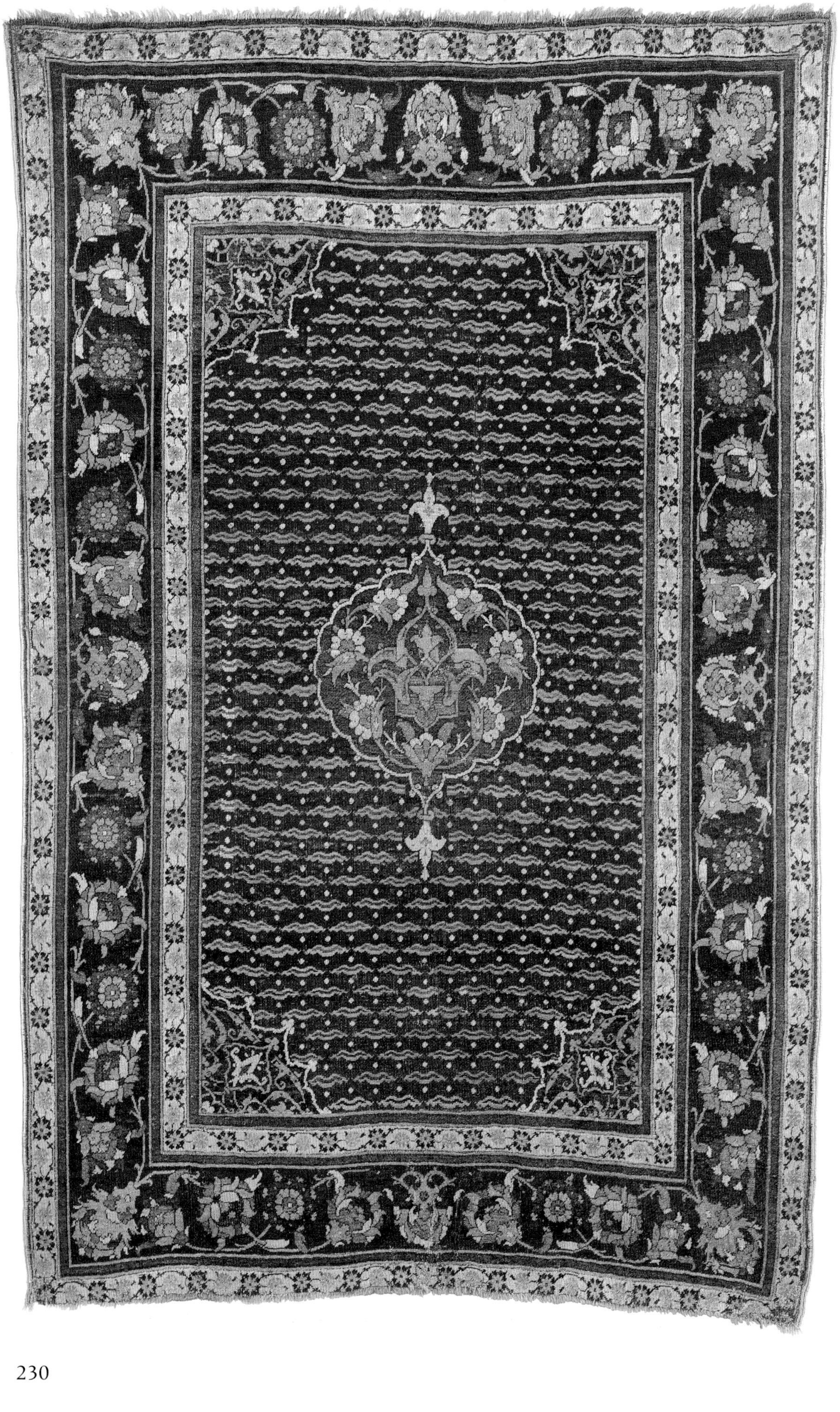

162. Rug with
çintemani pattern,
second half sixteenth
century (New York, The
Metropolitan Museum of
Art, 1971.263.2)

NOTES

1. For the significance of silk in the Ottoman Empire see İnalcık 1971. Commercial and industrial developments of Bursa are studied in Dalsar 1960 and Çizakca 1980. Documents related to the status of Bursa in the fifteenth century are published in İnalcık 1960.

2. These decrees are published in Barkan 1942.

3. An important document dated 1502, published in Öz 1950, 48–51, describes in detail the types of materials used and the techniques employed in production. Here one thousand weavers were reprimanded for the use of defective materials; there may have been at least that many more innocent artisans.

4. This inventory is published in İstanbul 1940; the section on textiles is discussed in Öz 1950, 26–45. For a recent study and the analyses of the terminology see Rogers 1986b.

5. Öz 1950, 51.

6. See, for instance, those published in Geijer 1951.

7. See Öz 1950, 56–59. Although some of the types, such as seraser, kemha, and atlas, are recognized, the words used for other fabrics are yet to be properly interpreted.

8. Published in Barkan 1979, 281–295. The terms used in the 1540/1541 list are *kadife-i benek-i müzehheb*, which appears to mean velvet decorated with spots or medallions; under this heading are *döşeme-i ala*, high quality upholstery, and *döşeme-i bi-zemin*, floor covering. Another heading uses *kadife-i çatma-i döşeme-i Bursa*, which suggests the velvet used in this type of upholstery fabric included gold and silver threads. The following terminology was employed to identify quality, technique, and usage in 1586: *ala* (high), *evzat* (medium), and *edna* (low); *çatma* (woven with gold and silver), *benek* (woven with silver ?), and *hav* (pile or plain velvet); *ba-zemin* (floor), *döşeme* (upholstery), and *nümune* (sample), which suggests that samples were woven according to designs provided by the court and sent back for approval before processing the order.

9. Danışman 1969–1971, 2:293.

10. Danışman 1969–1971, 2:278.

11. Öz 1950, 55–56.

12. This document and payroll registers related to the court weavers are published in Öz 1950, 52–54.

13. One of the longest pieces of velvet, decorated with fan-shaped carnations, is 60 cm (23⅝ in.) wide and 279 cm (109 in., or 9 ft. 1 in.) long. This example may have been made to upholster a divan (Denny 1982, pl. 131).

14. Terms used in costumes, mixed with twentieth-century vocabulary, are published in Koçu 1969. For a study of Ottoman headdress see Kumbaracılar n.d.

15. See, for instance, the officials represented in the accession ceremonies of the sultan in the *Süleymanname* published in Atıl 1986, 91–93.

16. See, for instance, the one worn by Osman II in the *Şekayik-i Numaniye* of c. 1619 reproduced in Atıl 1980, pl. 30.

17. Atıl 1986, figs. 29 and 31. Representations of several sixteenth-century Ottoman ladies are published in Tuğlacı 1984, 97–103. A costume book dated 1587, which was copied by Rubens, also contains studies of women; see Kurz and Kurz 1973. Many European representations, however, are based on hearsay and therefore fanciful.

18. Some of these caps, kerchiefs, and headbands were found in royal mausoleums, particularly in that of Ahmed I. See İstanbul 1983, E. 126–129.

19. Atıl 1986, 149.

20. The woodcut showing Siegmund Freiherr von Herberstein in his kaftan, identified as being made of Italian velvet, is studied in Wearden 1985.

21. Mackie 1980, ill. 211.

22. Meriç 1963, nos. IV and V.

23. See Çağman 1973. The most interesting painting, showing bolts of brocades and large rugs carried on the shoulders of several men, is in the *Şahinşahname* of 1581; see Atasoy and Çağman 1974, pl. 18.

24. London 1976, no. 73.

25. One of the largest collections of these vestments is in Poland; a number of these are published in Warsaw 1983. There is also an extensive collection in Moscow.

26. For two studies of Ottoman-Italian interaction of textile designs see Reath 1927 and Schmidt 1933.

27. The most famous scenes appear in the c. 1582 *Surname* with Şehzade Mehmed riding on lengths of brocaded silks on his way to At Meydanı; and in the c. 1596 *Şahname-i Mehmed III* where officers form barricades for the procession of the sultan by holding up textiles. See Öz 1950, pls. VII and XVII.

28. For a study of Ottoman banners see Denny 1974b. Although no banners dating from Süleyman's reign have survived, there is a tomb cover in the Topkapı Palace inscribed with his name, published in Öz 1950, pl. XXVII.

29. Forster 1968, 61.

30. For the works attributed to Gentile Bellini as well as other Europeans in the court during the 1480s see Atıl 1973b, figs. 21–23. Pinturrichio's frescoes in the Borgia apartments in the Vatican, datable to 1492–1494, and those in the cathedral of Siena, datable to 1500–1510, are published in Sakisian 1925; Babinger 1959; and Denny 1972, fig. 10.

31. Denny 1982, pl. 126; and Rogers 1983b, no. 83.

32. Kühnel and Bellinger 1957, 57.

33. London 1983, no. 56.

34. Fifteen were listed in 1526, ten in 1545, six in 1557–1558, and ten in 1566. Membership in the society rose to sixteen in 1596. These registers and artists are studied in Çetintürk 1963.

35. Both documents are published in Barkan 1972–1979, 2: 194, nos. 496 and 497; and discussed in Rogers 1982, 306–308, where possible Safavid gifts of rugs are also mentioned. Rogers suggests that Küre may not be the town near Kastamonu on the Black Sea, but a city somewhere close to Tire in western Anatolia, since the kadı of Tire was asked to supervise the order.

36. Danışman 1969–1971, 2:293.

37. Ellis 1969, fig. 12; and İstanbul 1983, E. 239. It was found in the türbe of Selim II in 1885, transferred first to the Çinili Köşk, then to the Topkapı Palace.

38. These kaftans have not yet been properly studied. Five of them together with parts of twenty-six others were given to the Royal Scottish Museum in Edinburgh. A few were published in London 1950, nos. 12 and 13.

39. Many important examples, together with several from the Benaki Museum, were published in Öz 1950 and 1951. This study should not be consulted without Denny 1971, where the identifications of a number of early kaftans are questioned and their dating revised.

40. Documents list Bursa, Bilecik, Ankara, Karaman, and Denizli, which specialized in velvets, silks, wools, and other materials. It is still not possible to determine which goods were produced in which cities.

41. This is indicated by a letter sent in 1554 from the Ottoman governor of Cairo to the Venetian representative, which states that the fabrics were to be produced according to the designs provided; see Gökbilgin 1964, 219, no. 99. In a letter dated 1589 Murad III requested from the doge of Venice 2,000 pieces of brocaded fabrics of "the same type woven in the past for the Ottoman court;" see Turan 1968, 252.

42. Öz 1950, 16.

43. Öz 1950, pl. XXV; and Altay 1979, 9.

44. Öz 1950, pl. XXVI.

45. Rogers 1986c, pl. 62.

46. Öz 1950, pl. XXII; see also pl. XXIII for a variation of the design in which ogival medallions enclose the triple dots.

47. One of the earliest çintemani-patterned velvet kaftans is thought to be that of Mehmed II; see Öz 1950, pl. V.

48. İstanbul 1983, E. 116.

49. It was once thought to have belonged to Mustafa I (1617–1618 and 1622–1623) or Mustafa II (1695–1703), the confusion arising from the label "Sultan Mustafa." The title sultan, however, was used by both the rulers and the princes, as well as by the wives of the monarchs; when used by women it was placed after their given names, as in "Hürrem Sultan." This extremely fragile kaftan has been published a number of times including Öz 1950,

pl. XXI; Mackie 1980, pl. 59; İstanbul 1983, E. 103; and Frankfurt 1985, vol. 2, no. 5/1. The identification of this kaftan with Şehzade Mustafa was established by Filiz Çağman, who also suggested that the black-ground example discussed here must have been for Şehzade Bayezid, not Sultan Bayezid II. See İstanbul 1983, E. 103.

50. Atıl 1980, ill. 87; and İstanbul 1983, E. 107.

51. Öz 1950, pl. X; and İstanbul 1983, E. 136.

52. The Textile Museum piece is published in Denny 1972, fig. 17; and Mackie 1973, no. 11. The Museum of Fine Arts also owns a seraser fragment woven with red and blue silk in addition to a seraser cream and mustard-yellow ceremonial kaftan; the designs of both contain large palmettes flanked by a pair of incurving leaves. The kaftan must have been made for Osman II in the second decade of the seventeenth century.

53. Berker 1981, 19; Mackie 1980, pl. 64; Denny 1982, pl. 135; and Rogers 1986c, pl. 91.

54. Some of the kaftans identified as Süleyman's range between 120 and 140 cm (roughly 47 to 55 in.); others, mostly wool overcoats, are 160 to 167 cm (about 61 to 63 in.). There are also a few jackets 72 to 80 cm (about 28 to 31 in.) long. The shorter kaftans could have been worn when he was a young man, and the long overcoats might have dragged on the ground. It is not known whether the robes stopped at the ankles or touched the ground. His portraits made by Lorichs and Nigari, however, suggest that the hems of the robes rested on the tops of his shoes.

55. İstanbul 1983, E. 25.

56. The same collaboration of calligraphers and illuminators appears on another shirt, which may have been made several years earlier; published in İstanbul 1983, E. 27.

57. For a study of Ottoman embroidery techniques see Gönül 1969.

58. A large number of these tents are housed in the Military Museum in İstanbul, while a few are in the Wawel Castle in Kraków and the National Museum in Budapest. See Mackie 1980, ill. 221; and Fehér 1975, pls. I, II, and ill. 1.

59. For a remarkable large early-seventeenth-century embroidered floor covering measuring 548 × 212 cm (almost 17 × 7 ft.) see Denny 1982, pl. 130; and İstanbul 1983, E. 241. For prayer cloths see İstanbul 1983, E. 238; and Frankfurt 1985, vol. 2, no. 5/22.

60. Two of these are published in Berker 1981, 52; and Mackie 1980, ill. 216. See also Berker 1978 for a study of handkerchiefs owned by the Topkapı Palace.

61. See, for instance, Atıl 1980, ills. 68, 85, 98, 103, and 117 and pls. 19 and 21. For illustrations in the *Süleymanname* see Atıl 1986, 144, 152, 162, 168, 178, and 180.

62. Forster 1968, 134.

63. Some of these are published in İstanbul 1983, E. 126–129.

64. See, for instance, the bohças, head scarves, and turban covers published in Gönül n.d.; Berker 1981; Denny 1982, pls. 144, 145, 148, and 149; and İstanbul 1983, E. 146 and 245. One of the early turban covers in the Topkapı Palace belonged to Selim II. Decorated with sprays of spring flowers and blossoming trees, it shows a superb rendition of the naturalistic style.

65. The largest collections of these covers are in the Victoria and Albert Museum, the Textile Museum, Washington, and the Art Institute of Chicago. Several other examples were published in Mackie 1980, ill. 217; Denny 1982, pls. 138, 141–143, 146, 147, 151, 153, 155, and 156.

66. See İstanbul 1983, E. 144; the same document states that 450 to 500 dirhems (almost one and a half kilos or more than three pounds) of silk thread were used for each of seven sheets ordered.

67. See Berker 1981, 32 and 33.

68. See, for instance, Falke 1936, figs. 285 and 286; Schmidt 1958, figs. 96 and 130; Mackie 1980, ills. 198 and 199; Atıl 1981b, nos. 114–116 and 118; and İstanbul 1983, D. 175a and b.

69. The Boston fragment is 112 × 60 cm (44⅛ × 23⅝ in.) while the London piece is 124 × 65.5 cm (48¹³⁄₁₆ × 25¾ in.) and contains the full loom width. These may have been cut from the front and back panels of the kaftan, while the Binney Collection example appears to have been pieced from the other parts. The Victoria and Albert piece is published in London 1950, no. 10; and Rogers 1983b, fig. 4. A similar pattern with only large and small triple balls, the former filled with crosshatching, cloud bands, and rumis, was made into a chasuble; see Warsaw 1983, pl. IX.

70. See, for instance, the fragment illustrated in London 1950, no. 7; and the kemha said to come from the Mausoleum of Selim II, published in Öz 1950, pl. XXX.

71. A piece from the same fabric is in the Museum of Fine Arts, Boston, where there are two other purple-ground kemhas.

72. Lyons 1976, no. 67. This example with the same width is 143 cm (56¼ in.) long.

73. See London 1950, no. 1; this fragment is 147.3 × 66 cm (58 × 26 in.).

74. İstanbul 1983, E. 140.

75. See Mackie 1973, no. 9 for a fragment. For kaftans see Öz 1950, pl. XVIII; Altay 1979, 4 and 5; Mackie 1980, ill. 204; İstanbul 1983, E. 141; and Frankfurt 1985, vol. 2, no. 5/6.

76. Mackie 1973, no. 22.

77. Öz 1950, pl. XXVIII.

78. Altay 1979, 15; and İstanbul 1983, E. 135.

79. Öz 1957, pl. XXIX.

80. One of these panels, removed from the mausoleum, is in the Victoria and Albert Museum.

81. Binney 1981, Textile 1A; this piece measures 146 × 55.9 cm (57½ × 22 in.).

82. Forster 1968, 58 and 59.

83. This example, owned by the Corcoran Gallery of Art, Washington, was cut from a larger piece and made into a small nihale by reusing its original borders (Corcoran 1948, no. T. 3).

84. A similar red and ivory velvet woven with metallic thread shows the complete design constructed of two loom widths, but contains only a portion of its entire length. It is published in Lisbon 1963, no. 101. It measures 126 × 175 cm (49⅝ × 68⅞ in.) and has a field identical to this example, but the border is composed of a scroll bearing plane-tree leaves.

85. See Öz 1950, pl. XVII, where similarly patterned textiles are illustrated.

86. Weibel 1948.

87. Öz 1951, pl. XCIV; and Denny 1972, fig. 23.

88. For studies of court-style kilims see Yetkin 1971; Balpınar 1983; and Petsopoulos 1979, 52–54.

89. See, for instance, Jenkins 1983, pl. 152; and Leth 1975, 118.

90. One of the carnation-patterned velvet yastıks was made into a chasuble in Poland, published in Warsaw 1983, pl. XI. For others with central medallions see Lisbon 1963, no. 109; and Mackie 1980, ill. 207. For a remarkable velvet saddlecloth using the same themes see Mackie 1980, ill. 208; and Frankfurt 1985, vol. 2, no. 11/25a.

91. This example, 118 × 116 cm (46½ × 45⅝ in.), must have been made as a cover for a child's quilt; it is illustrated in İstanbul 1983, E. 247.

92. Warsaw 1983, pl. II.

93. See, for instance, Riyadh 1985, no. 161.

94. See, for instance, the velvet reproduced in Dimand 1944, 216; and the tile panel from the Mosque of Rüstem Paşa illustrated in Denny 1977, fig. 79. This motif was used in an oversize format on kaftans during the seventeenth and eighteenth centuries; see Öz 1950, pls. I and II; and İstanbul 1983, E. 289.

95. See, for instance, the c. 1421 tiled mihrab from the Mosque of Mehmed I in Bursa illustrated in Denny 1980, pl. 36. Tiles on the Sünnet Odası and Mausoleum of Murad III are published in Denny 1980, pls. 44–45 and ill. 162. Tiles with mihrabs were also made in Iran as early as the twelfth century.

96. This fragment is published in Ellis 1969, fig. 9.

97. Ellis 1969, fig. 10.

98. See Ellis 1969, fig. 3; and London 1983, no. 55.

99. This example, also a fragment, is published in Beattie 1968, fig. 3; and Ellis 1969, fig. 20.

100. This rug, which is in the Textile Museum, was published a number of times, including Kühnel and Bellinger 1957, pls. XXX and XXXI; Beattie 1969, fig. 2; Ellis 1969, fig. 19; and Washington 1974, no. V.

101. The Padua example is illustrated in Landsberger 1945–1946, fig. 4. This and the Jerusalem rug are discussed in Denny 1986.

102. Published in several studies, including Ellis 1969, fig. 6; Washington 1974, no. II; and London 1983, no. 54.

103. The present location of this rug, published in Ellis 1969, fig. 7, is not known.

104. One of these, in İstanbul, was found in the Mausoleum of Selim II. In the past it was thought erroneously to have come from the Mausoleum of Ahmed I. See Ellis 1969, fig. 12; and İstanbul 1983, E. 239. A second rug, in Washington, has a lamp suspended in the niche. Ellis 1969, fig. 13; and Washington 1974, no. III.

105. One such example in İstanbul was found in the Mausoleum of Ahmed I and another, in West Berlin, bears a chronogram giving the date 1610/1611. Both are published in Ellis 1969, figs. 2 and 8. Also dating from late sixteenth or early seventeenth century are a number of seccades with densely decorated fields, following the style seen in the second group of prayer rugs. Several of these are published in Ellis 1969, figs. 14–18; and Washington 1974, no. IV.

106. See Ellis 1969, figs. 21–24; Washington 1974, no. XI; and İstanbul 1983, E. 233 and 234. The same type of rug was woven in Cairo during the seventeenth century, as indicated in the 1674 inventory of the Yeni Cami in İstanbul, which lists several Egyptian safs that contained 10 to 132 niches as well as examples from Uşak. See Sakisian 1931.

107. Mackie 1980, ill. 184.

108. The Berlin rug is published in Bode and Kühnel 1958, pl. III; and the Paris rug is illustrated in Beattie 1968, fig. 4.

109. See Mackie 1976 for a study of one at the Textile Museum, with related examples.

110. See Yetkin 1981, 101–127, for a survey of Ottoman court rugs.

111. Mackie 1973, no. 33.

112. One of these, in the Corcoran Gallery of Art, is published in Yetkin 1981, ill. 63. According to Erdmann 1970, 198, there is another one in the Archbishop's Palace in Kremsier, Czechoslovakia. See London 1983, no. 24 for a third almost circular sixteenth-century example decorated in the Mamluk style. The same format was executed in appliquéd leather; one such example, in the Topkapı Palace Museum, is published in Gönül n.d., pl. 28.

113. Forster 1968, 220.

114. For the San Gimignano rug see Yetkin 1981, ill. 64. The other is published in London 1983, no. 52; this entry also mentions a third example in Berlin.

115. For Mughal seccades and safs, in addition to later Ottoman examples, see Ellis 1969, 18–20.

116. One from the Mausoleum of Selim II and the other from that of Ahmed I are published in İstanbul 1983, E. 239; and Ellis 1969, fig. 2.

117. The niches in these prayer rugs may symbolize both the mihrab and the gateway to paradise; thus their format was easily adapted for synagogue hangings, where the representation of the latter was desired.

118. See Denny 1977 for an expert study of the tiles of this mosque; see also Denny 1980, ill. 161 for this panel.

119. See note 107 above.

The Royal Kilns

The production of ceramics during the age of Süleyman was extremely prolific and creative, developing new styles and techniques that not only revolutionized the tradition of Ottoman pottery, but had a profound and long-lasting impact for centuries to come, both within the empire and abroad. This era witnessed a diversity of styles that show the strong influence of designs formulated in the nakkaşhane. Decorative themes used in manuscript illuminations (and even figural illustrations) were expertly applied to pottery and tiles and rendered with the same finesse, revealing the hands of master painters or designers.

The construction of a large number of religious, charitable, and educational architectural compounds sponsored by the sultans, members of the royal family, and high-ranking administrators resulted in an unprecedented need for tiles. Ceramic vessels were also highly regarded by the court and kept in the Hazine; furthermore, they were commissioned and purchased by wealthy Ottomans and Europeans. Imperial patronage and domestic and foreign markets promoted a demand for high-quality wares, to which the potters responded by creating some of the most distinguished objects in the history of ceramics.

Sixteenth-century Ottoman ceramics are technically unsurpassed: the compact, hard, and white body was covered with an engobe (thin coating of fine white slip), which produced a smooth surface; the designs were painted with clear and brilliant colors, which were frequently shaded and outlined by darker lines; the glaze was crystal-clear, even, and close-fitting. These technical features enabled the potters to produce an extraordinary range of themes, at times rivaling the works of the nakkaşhane masters. They employed traditional motifs, saz designs, and naturalistic flowers in addition to inscriptions and figural compositions. They also produced copies as well as adaptations of Yüan and Ming dynasty Chinese porcelain[1] and translated contemporary metalwork shapes and designs into pottery.

Detail, 180

The four types of Ottoman pottery[2] all evolved and flourished during the age of Süleyman. The first type is underglaze painted in blue, or blue-and-white ware, which relied heavily on the nakkaşhane for design and metalwork for shapes, and incorporated selected motifs from Chinese porcelain. The second type, which is less coherent, employed two tones of blue—blue and turquoise—and reveals a larger repertoire of nakkaşhane themes, representing saz designs, spiral scrolls, naturalistic flora, and figural elements in addition to Chinese-inspired compositions. The third type expanded the palette by incorporating green, which ranges from sage (similar to the pistachio-green found on textiles) to olive, and purple, which varies between pale mauve and violet. The designs in this group display spontaneity and expert drawing. The fourth type, which replaced the weaker greens and purples with a brilliant emerald green and a bright, true red, established the classical style of Ottoman pottery with an exuberant display of all the decorative themes practiced by the court artists.

The chronological sequence of these four types of İznik ceramics is generally established by tiles found in dated or datable buildings and a few objects inscribed with dates. Although these sources are useful for determining the years in which the types flourished, they are by no means indicative of the beginning or, more significantly, the end of each, since the groups overlapped and coexisted for some decades. The blue-and-white and blue-and-turquoise survived well into the seventeenth century; the type with the pale green and purple also continued beyond the sixteenth century, particularly in such provinces as Syria. It was, however, the polychrome ware with the bright green and red that came to characterize Ottoman ceramics after the 1550s.

It is useful to turn to the nakkaşhane to establish the termini a quo for the designs that were employed in all four types. Traditional floral scrolls, rumis, and cloud bands as well as themes inspired by Yüan and Ming dynasty porcelain were well within the decorative vocabulary of the artists by the middle of the fifteenth century. The saz style, established in the İstanbul nakkaşhane in the 1530s, and the naturalistic genre, which developed fully by the 1540s, were applied to ceramics by the middle of the sixteenth century.

Ottoman pottery produced during the first half of the fifteenth century was buff- or red-bodied and underglaze-painted in blue, green, and sometimes purple. Tiles produced in Bursa reveal the reddish body and employ *cuerda seca,* or "dry cord," in which a greasy material was placed between the colors to prevent them from running, and tile-mosaic, a laborious technique that involved cutting patterns from tile slabs glazed in monochrome colors and fitting them together.[3]

The same two techniques appear in Edirne and continue in the monuments built in İstanbul. After the middle of the fifteenth century, however, Ottoman tiles are white-bodied. In İstanbul this body appears in the tile-mosaic panels used on the facade of the Çinili Köşk, built in 1473 by Mehmed II within the Topkapı Palace complex;[4] and in the cuerda seca tiles in the Mosque of Selim I (1522/1523), the Medrese of Hürrem Sultan (1538/1539),[5] the Mausoleum of Şehzade Mehmed (1548),[6] and the Mosque of Kara Ahmed Paşa (1554), where this technique was employed for the last time.

The first use of white-bodied underglaze-painted tiles is in the Muradiye Mosque in Edirne. The structure, built for Murad II in 1435/1436, was originally decorated with wall paintings and sometime later, possibly in the mid-fifteenth century, a dado of hexagonal blue-and-white tiles was added to the sanctuary.[7] It is not known when these tiles were made or whether they were intended for this building or removed from another. Their decoration incorporates Chinese-inspired themes (such as floral bouquets and scrolls) as well as designs employed in late-fifteenth-century manuscripts produced in the Edirne court. The same body appears in the underglaze-painted blue, turquoise, and purple lunettes made for the Üç Şerefeli Mosque in Edirne, built for Murad II between 1437 and 1447.[8]

Tiles used in the monuments constructed during the first half of the fifteenth century in Bursa and Edirne, which were the capitals of the empire prior to the conquest of İstanbul, must have been made locally. Imperial kilns in İznik appear to have been set up soon after the court settled in the new capital, most likely by the potters of Edirne who moved there. This city, which had been producing pottery since the fourteenth or fifteenth century, had ample supplies of white clay and sand, together with water, wood, and minerals needed by the ceramists. The first commission of the İznik potters must have been the tiles used in the Çinili Köşk, which were executed in the tile-mosaic technique, relying on the style employed in Edirne. This laborious method was soon abandoned in favor of underglaze-painted tiles.

The earliest datable underglaze-painted blue-and-white tiles made in İznik appear to be those decorating two mausoleums in Bursa, which was the traditional site for the tombs of princes. One of them was made for Şehzade Mustafa (died 1474/1475), and another for Şehzade Mahmud (died 1507/

Fig. 19. Blue-and-white ewer dated 1510 (London, The British Museum, G. 1983.1)

1508). Since the tiles in both structures are almost identical, they must have been produced at the same time, possibly in the 1510s or the 1520s when the royal mausoleums in Bursa were redecorated.[9] The same style of decoration appears on a series of mosque lamps found in the Mausoleum of Bayezid II (c. 1512) in İstanbul and in the tiles of the Yeni Valide Mosque in Manisa (1522/1523) and those in the Mausoleum of Çoban Mustafa Paşa in Gebze (1528/1529).[10]

Another date is presented by a ceramic ewer (fig. 19) inscribed 1510.[11] This famous piece, now in the British Museum as a part of the Godman Bequest, copies the shape of a metal ewer and contains an Armenian inscription in the foot ring, which states that it was made for "Abraham of Kütahya," a term which came to be used to identify the entire series. İznik ware is also mentioned in the Hazine inventories dated 1505, which list ewers *(ibrik),* basins *(leğen* or *liğen),* and footed bowls *(ayak tası,* presumably meaning *ayaklı tas).*[12]

This evidence demonstrates that İznik was producing underglaze-painted blue-and-white pottery by the turn of the sixteenth century. The decorative repertoire of this ware relies heavily on manuscript illuminations, using scrolls with hatayis, rumis, and cloud bands as well as inscriptions, employing tight compositions with clearly defined zones, painted either in blue on white or with the motifs reserved in white against a blue-painted background.

This style, characterized by elaborate blossoms with curling petals rendered in a painterly manner, was applied to large bowls, mosque lamps, plates, and jars as well as candlesticks, ewers, jugs, and pen boxes that follow the angular and articulated shapes of metalwork. In addition, there are series of plates decorated with floral scrolls, bouquets of blossoms, or three bunches of grapes that copy the themes and compositions found on Yüan and Ming dynasty wares. In some examples Chinese prototypes were faithfully followed, while in others certain motifs were selected and at times combined with indigenous themes.

Chinese-inspired motifs in blue-and-turquoise ware reveal a greater freedom of execution, abandoning the rigid designs and compact compositions found in the blue-and-white group. Blue-and-turquoise ware, which includes the same range of vessels and plates, is datable by a few monuments and objects. Tiles with these two colors were used in revetments, as seen in the Mausoleum of Çoban Mustafa Paşa in Gebze. They were also applied to the tightly-wound spiral scrolls seen on objects popularly known as Golden Horn

Fig. 20. Blue-and-white fragmentary bottle dated 1529 (London, The British Museum, G. 1983.16)

ware, because a group of shards and small vessels with this design was discovered in 1905 when the foundations of the post office building were dug in Sirkeci, a district in İstanbul where the Golden Horn flows into the Sea of Marmara.[13] This design, employed on the early tuğras of Süleyman, appears on extremely few tiles.[14] It is also found on a number of vessels, the most important of which is a broken bottle dated 1529, now in the British Museum (fig. 20). The ambiguous inscriptions around the neck and inside the foot ring of this piece state that it was ordered as an "object" from Kütahya by a bishop named Ter Martiros for the Monastery of the Holy Mother of God in Ankara.[15] The British Museum bottle indicates that the spiral scroll was well within the repertoire of the potters by 1530.

The most splendid blue-and-turquoise wares are the five large rectangular tiles on the facade of the Sünnet Odası, which were probably made in the mid-sixteenth century and moved to the fourth courtyard of the palace a hundred years later. Their decoration shows the perfected saz style with an exuberant growth of overlapping, intersecting, twisting, and turning composite hatayis and feathery leaves, recreating the enchanted forests associated with this genre. Drawn with the assurance of a saz master, possibly by Şahkulu himself, their designs parallel the magnificent kemhas used in the kaftans made for Şehzades Mustafa and Bayezid in the 1550s.

These tiles, thought to have been made for one of Süleyman's pavilions, contain two different compositions. Four of them, measuring 127 by 48 centimeters (50 by 18⅞ inches), were pounced from the same cartoon[16] that was reversed in two panels, creating two pairs of mirror-image compositions. Each panel represents luxuriant foliage with two fantastic chilins at the bottom; hidden among the foliage are five birds, their eyes once set with precious stones (fig. 21). The fifth panel replaces the chilins with a large double-handled vase from which the flora emerges.[17] These two compositions were so admired that they were copied a century later and used to decorate the Bağdad Köşkü, built in 1639 in the fourth courtyard of the palace. In contrast to the large single-tile format used in the mid-sixteenth century, these later versions are composed of several rectangular pieces.

Saz themes including animals appear to have been used on hexagonal tiles as well, since there exists a series with a pair of ducks swimming among the foliage.[18] The same floral themes were applied to vessels and plates, some of which represent human figures and animals. Three fragments from a vessel, thought to have been a tankard, show a princely entertainment scene with two men with turbans and beards, a wine steward holding a bottle, and several animals and birds, including a cheetah and a parakeet.[19] An equally unusual blue-and-turquoise piece is a fragment of a plate, its center decorated with a crane or heron engulfed by saz blossoms and leaves.[20] The impact of album drawings and manuscript illustrations also is evident on other examples produced in

237

Fig. 21. (above and left) Tile panels on the facade of the Sünnet Odası in the fourth courtyard of the Topkapı Palace, c. 1550

the second quarter of the sixteenth century, some of which show narrative cycles, such as a snake attacking a bird or a fleet of ships with sails billowing in the wind (see **176** and **177**).

A piece of cardinal importance for the dating of blue-and-turquoise ware is a mosque lamp in the British Museum (fig. 22) that bears an inscription around its foot stating that it was made in 1549 in İznik; it also gives the name of its maker, Musli, and evokes the name of Eşrefzade, a local saint. The decoration, painted in blue, turquoise, and black, is highly conservative and relies on rumi scrolls and cloud bands.[21] Thin bands placed below the neck, however, contain sprays of spiked blue tulips, which were popularly used in the group painted with pale green and purple. The lamp was made for the Dome of the Rock in Jerusalem, which was re-decorated by Süleyman in the mid-sixteenth century. The exterior of the structure was covered with tile-mosaic, cuerda seca, and underglaze-painted panels; the inscription below the drum contains the date 1545/1546, while that on the north porch gives the year 1551/1552. It has been suggested that the tiles were made on the premises; the mosque lamps, in contrast, were shipped to Jerusalem.[22]

Musli's lamp forms a link between the blue-and-turquoise ware and the third type, in which black outlines frequently define the motifs. Tiles produced in this type appear in the Mosque of Hadım İbrahim Paşa in İstanbul, built in 1551, and in the Yeni Kaplıca Bath in Bursa, which was redecorated by the grand vezir İbrahim Paşa in 1552/1553.[23] Four-color ware using pale green and purple appears to have flourished in the mid-sixteenth century, skillfully combining the saz style with the naturalistic genre.

The majority of the pieces employing pale green and purple are large bowls or plates; there are a few smaller bowls, jars, and jugs. The decoration is almost always floral—stylized and/or naturalistic—with rare examples showing birds or busts. The latter appear in plates with wide flattened rims and relatively deep central wells, using the *tondino* shape that was popular in Italy in the first quarter of the sixteenth century. One of these has the bust of a European youth in the center, its rim decorated with sprays of tulips and triple balls; another a woman with a headscarf, presumably representing an Ottoman lady.[24] It should be mentioned that Ottoman figures were also depicted in Italian ceramics, one of which, a Deruta lusterware datable to 1520–1540, shows a turbaned man, who may have been intended to represent Süleyman.[25]

Each piece in this type was created as an individual work by a master painter. The objects, which display exquisite brushwork, subdued color schemes, and a refined sense of aesthetics, constitute an aristocratic group of İznik pottery and suggest exclusive patronage. Süleyman may have been one of their most ardent supporters. This type ceased to be popular after his death and was soon replaced with the ware decorated with vivid blue, turquoise, emerald green, and thick bright red.

The fourth and last group of İznik ware, which coexisted with the third type in the mid-sixteenth century, displays the epitome of the technical and aesthetic achievements of Ottoman ceramics. The designs are remarkably varied and include the full range of the decorative vocabulary of the age.

The earliest dated appearance of the celebrated Turkish red, which was applied in relief, is in the Süleymaniye Mosque, completed in 1557. Here it was used in selected areas, noticeably around the mihrab, and appears relatively subdued. Panels with the same palette that decorate the porticoes of the mausoleums of Hürrem Sultan and Süleyman in the same

complex indicate that the true red was perfected within a few years (figs. 23 and 24). The technique was fully exploited in the Mosque of Rüstem Paşa, built in 1561 (fig. 25). This structure is almost a pattern book of decorative themes and includes every single design developed in the nakkaşhane, displaying a lavish use of tiles that totally cover the interior of this otherwise insignificant structure.[26] A more restrained usage representing the fully established classical style is found in the 1570s in the Sokollu Mehmed Paşa Mosque in İstanbul (fig. 26), Selimiye Mosque in Edirne,[27] and the tiles commissioned by Murad III for the hall leading to the baths in the Harem of the Topkapı Palace (see **210**).

Tiles dating from the second half of the sixteenth century reveal a harmonious collaboration between the architects, nakkaşhane artists, and ceramists. The structures mentioned above were created by Sinan, the imperial architect responsible for scores of buildings in the capital and the provinces, who might have been responsible also for determining where the tiles were to be placed.

Fig. 22. Mosque lamp from the Dome of the Rock in Jerusalem, made by Musli in İznik in 1549 (London, The British Museum, 87 5-16 1)

Fig. 23. Tile panel on the portico of the Mausoleum of Hürrem Sultan, c. 1558

Fig. 24. Tile panel on the portico of the Mausoleum of Sultan Süleyman, c. 1566

Fig. 25. Tile panel on the portico of the Mosque of Rüstem Paşa, c. 1561

There are extremely few datable objects that use the brilliant red. The earliest appears to be a lamp from the Süleymaniye Mosque (see 191) and shows the same restrained red seen in the tiles of the building.[28] Two others, found in the Mosque of Sokollu Mehmed Paşa built fifteen years later, reveal the full development of the color and must have been contemporary with the structure (see 195). Only one polychrome plate bears a date and the name of the owner; inscribed in the foot ring is a notation that states it was made in 1606/1607 and purchased by Mehmed Şah, a person otherwise unknown.[29] There also exist several other dated pieces made in the second half of the seventeenth century, some of which reflect folk traditions and are decorated with buildings or figures.[30] A few other vessels contain inscriptions of poetry without giving dates or names of makers or owners. One of these is a tankard with a Turkish poem encircling its body;[31]

another is a lidded bowl decorated with panels containing stanzas by Hayati and Revani, two popular sixteenth-century Turkish poets.[32]

Polychrome İznik ware—which includes a variety of bottles, jugs, jars, ewers, tankards, vases, bowls, plates, pen boxes, mosque lamps, and spherical hanging ornaments, all predominantly decorated with saz themes and naturalistic flowers, with select examples incorporating birds—were valued in the court and collected by foreigners. Several examples have drilled holes, suggesting that they were once encrusted with gems in gold mounts, similar to the decoration applied to Chinese porcelains.[33] Some were enhanced by gilding, such as the lamps from the Mosque of Sokollu Mehmed Paşa; the gilding has flaked off and only traces are now visible.

Pottery and tiles were also commissioned by synagogues, since there are at least two lamps with Hebrew inscriptions,[34] and by Greek churches and monasteries, including those in İstanbul and Mount Athos.[35]

Over the centuries Europeans purchased large quantities of İznik ceramics, which are now housed in public and private collections in various countries.[36] The value attached to Turkish ceramics is attested to by the metal mounts added to some of these pieces, frequently in an effort to restore broken spouts, handles, and rims.[37] Objects were also commissioned by foreign diplomats, including a series of plates decorated with the coat of arms of the Mocenigo family of Venice.[38] Items commissioned by the Europeans caused concern in the palace, as they forestalled the delivery of the tiles needed for the imperial buildings. Fermans issued in the late sixteenth century attempted to curtail the production of wares for foreigners and ordered the potters to work on the tiles required by the court.[39] Prices fixed by the state had forced the potters to seek other markets and take on outside commissions, which were far more profitable.

Price-fixing is usually given as the cause for the decline of İznik workshops in the seventeenth century.[40] However, the construction of imperial compounds had also diminished and the demand for tiles was greatly reduced. İznik's primary function was to provide tiles to decorate both the religious complexes and the Topkapı Palace pavilions. Once this came to a halt, the potters sought other clients, who purchased vessels and plates. When imperial patronage stopped, quality declined, and İznik potters started mass-producing wares for domestic use and for export. Evliya Çelebi commented on this sad state of affairs and mentioned that in the mid-seventeenth century İznik had only nine workshops in contrast to around three hundred at the beginning of the century.

Although İznik was the site of the royal kilns in the sixteenth century, ceramics were also produced in other centers. The potters who made the tiles of the Dome of the Rock in Jerusalem worked on location and moved to Damascus after their project was completed, thus helping to reestablish the Syrian industry, which had stopped production after the mid-fifteenth century. Their first commission was the decoration of the Süleymaniye Complex in Damascus, which was completed in 1554. The tiles of this edifice reflect the provincial applications of the nakkaşhane themes and employ blue, turquoise, black, purple, green, and a weak pink under a crackled glaze, the workers being unable to duplicate the brilliant red and superior glaze of İznik.[41] A similar provincial production is seen in Diyarbakır, where the local potters were also unable to produce the bright red.[42] Kütahya, a flourishing pottery center today, was also active in the sixteenth century and is thought to have produced at least one vessel—the broken bottle dated 1529—for the Armenian monastery in Ankara.[43] The manufacture of ceramics in Cairo has not yet been studied in detail, although there exist several objects datable to the sixteenth century that appear to have been made there.

İstanbul also had a local production which, according to Evliya Çelebi, consisted of one hundred shops with three hundred potters in the seventeenth century.[44] There is no reason to doubt that a number of the so-called Golden Horn pieces, especially the group found during the excavations of the post office building, was not made locally. Their quality is inferior to İznik wares and indicates a nonimperial workshop.

The Ehl-i Hiref registers also include tile makers (kaşiciler); one master and eleven apprentices are listed in 1526,[45] four appear in the 1557–1558 register, and three are recorded in 1566. The limited number of tile makers and the reduction of their number from twelve to three between 1526 and 1566 indicate that there was no great need for their services and that these men were obviously not producing tiles for the imperial structures in the capital; they may have been responsible for making cartoons sent to İznik and involved with the installation of the panels after the tiles arrived in İstanbul.

Ottoman pottery appears to have been more popular in Europe than within the empire, since the largest collections of sixteenth-century objects are outside Turkey. They were cherished as works of art and not used on a daily basis, which may explain the survival of such large quantities in England, France, Austria, and Italy. It should be mentioned that a substantial percentage of these collections was amassed in Turkey during the nineteenth century, when there was no local interest in İznik wares. Although these wares were all func-

Fig. 26. Tile panels from the mihrab of the Mosque of Sokollu Mehmed Paşa, c. 1572

tional (with the possible exception of mosque lamps and spherical pieces used for symbolic and decorative purposes), they have remained in pristine condition due to their high quality and the care with which they were handled by their owners.

The popularity of İznik products led to Italian copies in the second half of the sixteenth century.[46] European copies were revived in the nineteenth century, following the enthusiasm for orientalism that swept Europe, with excellent imitations (and even forgeries) of sixteenth-century Ottoman ceramics made in France, England, Hungary, Austria, and Italy, particularly in Florence by Cantagalli.[47] A similar revival took place in Turkey in the twentieth century with the Yıldız Palace studios in İstanbul and workshops in Kütahya actively reproducing the types of pottery and tiles initiated in İznik.

White Ware

Ottoman potters, whose copies of blue-and-white Yüan and Ming dynasty porcelain are well known, were thought to have been oblivious to Chinese white ware and celadon. The recent publication of a white plate with molded decoration in the Topkapı Palace indicates that İznik potters also produced monochrome wares.[48] The artists must have experimented with green glazes as well, since objects with this color were recorded in the documents, and fragments have been found in İznik; some of the so-called Iranian celadons in the Topkapı Palace may have been made by Ottoman potters.

The white plate in the Topkapı Palace (163) has an exceptional decorative repertoire that employs two or more different traditions and styles. A Chinese-inspired scroll with split leaves recalling rumis appears on the flattened rim foliated with eight points; the cavetto contains six isolated cloud-band cartouches; and the center shows a large hexagon that has at its corners small trefoils with sprays of fine lines that extend into the voids between the cloud bands of the cavetto. The exterior shows six floral sprays painted in white slip, while the design on the interior was produced by molding. The use of a mold suggests that there were other examples, none of which has yet come to light.

The hexagon in the center reproduces compositions used on blue-and-white or blue-and-turquoise tiles (see 180). A scroll with six large hatayis alternates with six cartouches formed by a pair of rumis growing from a central peony; the scroll links with the small blossoms in the centers of the cartouches, creating a twelve-pointed star. The unit is banded by blossoms cut in half.

An identical composition is found on a blue-and-white tile with the same shape and dimensions, indicating that the cartoon for the tile was reemployed to make the mold for the plate.[49] The frame with cut-off blossoms makes far more sense on tiles, since the blossoms become completed when several tiles are joined together.

The same cartoon was used on another plate, which is underglaze-painted in blue, turquoise, green, and purple.[50] This example belongs to the third type of İznik ware and is thus datable to the second quarter of the sixteenth century, suggesting that the molded white plate and the blue-and-white tile were also produced during these years.

The Topkapı Palace plate is obviously an experimental piece, using Chinese-inspired scrolls and cloud bands that were already a part of the decorative vocabulary of İznik ware and combining them with a composition used on tiles produced in the same locality. One wonders why a hexagonal tile pattern was chosen among all the available compositions. The experiment was not very successful, which may explain the absence of other pieces produced from the same mold.

A more typical white ware incorporates restrained underglaze-painted blue designs, as observed in the jug in Kuwait (164). It has a thin blue band at the rim, decorated with a scroll similar to that on the plate. A simplified blue braid and a wider band composed of connected trefoils encircle the neck; another blue braid appears at the lower edge of the body. The handle is defined by two wide vertical blue lines, with a series of horizontal strokes filling the outer surface; a lobed cartouche and a blossom embellish the upper and lower ends.

The remaining decoration is rendered in slip and consists of a series of "lotus" panels, or rectangles surmounted by trefoil arches. A frieze of these panels appears around the neck and lower body, each filled with trefoil blossoms with additional trefoils sprinkled between the arches. The upper body contains a variation of the same theme; the panels are upside-down, joined together, and filled either with a long stroke or a row of four trefoils.

The simplicity of the decoration suggests that it was produced in the second quarter of the sixteenth century, revealing an understatement similar to that found on engraved and incised silver vessels. The same limited use of blue on a white body appears in a mosque lamp found in the Mausoleum of Selim I and on a spherical ornament in the Walters Art Gallery, both of which contain only bands of inscriptions.[51] A shard of a molded plate decorated with floral scrolls and sprays with thin blue bands defining its rim, cavetto, and center was unearthed in İznik during the 1983 excavations. These examples appear to belong to a small group of İznik pieces produced around the same time.

Blue-and-White Ware

The earliest type of İznik ceramics is blue-and-white ware. There are two fairly distinct groups; in the first metalwork shapes and nakkaşhane designs were used. In the second

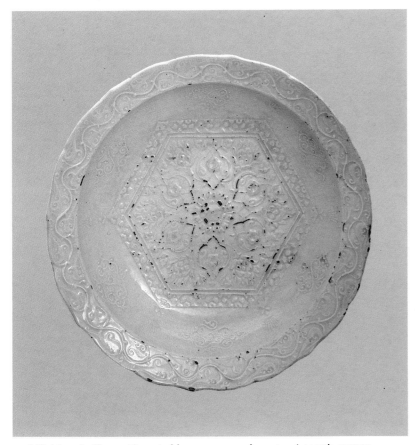

163 (above). Plate with central hexagon, second quarter sixteenth century (İstanbul, Topkapı Sarayı Müzesi, 15/6086)

164 (right). Jug with slip-painted decoration, second quarter sixteenth century (Kuwait National Museum, LNS 174 C)

Chinese porcelains were reproduced in a most liberal manner by abstracting certain themes and fusing them with nakkaş-hane elements, thus creating individual compositions.

The first group consists of large bowls, mosque lamps, candlesticks, jars, ewers, and plates with a few pen boxes, spherical ornaments, and pilgrim flasks. Compositions are generally compartmentalized, with white and blue grounds used in alternating units. The designs are tightly drawn, concise, and frequently cut off by a frame, suggesting that a fragment of a larger composition was employed. The decorative repertoire relies on superimposed scrolls bearing rumis, cloud bands, hatayis, peonies, and inscription panels, separated by bands with braids, scrolls, and chevrons, creating highly elaborate but rigidly structured compositions.

The motifs are frequently defined by darker lines, detailed with light and dark strokes, and shaded, producing a vibrant three-dimensional effect. In a number of examples dots were used in the background, reproducing the ring matting in metalwork. Metalwork shapes are particularly noticeable in several articulated and angular ewers and jugs, some of

which were later restored with metal fittings.[52] Metalwork shapes can also be found in large bowls, mosque lamps, candlesticks,[53] spherical ornaments, pen boxes, and even plates. The plates have everted flattened rims that are rarely foliated. The composition is generally concentric panels, recalling both fifteenth-century metal examples and Chinese porcelains, which were themselves based on Islamic metal shapes, further complicating the sources of İznik pieces. Among the more rarely produced shapes are small bowls,[54] jars, pilgrim flasks, and tankards,[55] which seem to have survived as single examples.

This early blue-and-white group contains an unusually large number of pieces decorated with kufi or sülüs inscriptions. Because items made for religious monuments, such as mosque lamps and spherical ornaments, were traditionally inscribed with Koranic verses and prayers, their incorporation into the decorative repertoire of ceramic examples is understandable. Inscriptions on pen boxes, plates, and jugs produced for secular use are not as easily explained, unless the models used were inscribed metal pieces. Another explana-

243

165. Large bowl with reciprocal design (profile), first quarter sixteenth century (Paris, Musée du Louvre, 7880-92)

tion could be the strong impact of nakkaşhane illuminations, which frequently included titles of books and chapter headings. Inscriptions on the majority of blue-and-white objects have not been deciphered, since they were written without diacritics, leading to the assumption that they were purely decorative. It seems unlikely that meaningless decorative scripts would have been tolerated in a society that valued calligraphy as highly as the Ottomans. The content of these inscriptions awaits study and proper analysis.

Blue-and-white ceramics, which had a universal appeal and were produced by many civilizations, were revived by the potters of Kütahya in the eighteenth century, the shapes and styles of their pieces reflecting contemporary traditions.[56]

Among the most remarkable achievements of İznik potters were large bowls, which were executed in blue-and-white, blue-and-turquoise, as well as in four-color ware with green and purple until the mid-sixteenth century. No examples employing the thick red are known to exist. Most of these bowls have the same dimensions and shape; some are slightly smaller and rest on a higher foot. More than twenty such pieces are known, one half of which belong to the first group of blue-and-whites.

A representative example is the splendid bowl in the Louvre (**165**), which is 42.5 centimeters (16¾ inches) in diameter. The interior contains a central medallion decorated with radiating rumi and hatayi scrolls executed in reserve on a blue ground. Enclosing the medallion is an eight-pointed star; around the inner walls is a band composed of eight blue-ground arch-shaped elements that create a reciprocal pattern with the voided white areas, which are embellished with large quatrefoils. Minute blue triple balls are sprinkled on the white areas of the walls as well as in the star.

The exterior is decorated with large volutes of connected cloud bands placed over two scrolls, one bearing composite rumis, the other hatayis. Rendered on a blue ground, the composition totally engulfs the walls, with its elements cut off at the rim and base. The overall design with a marked horizontal movement on the exterior contrasts with the strong radiating composition on the interior. The cylindrical and relatively low foot contains a rumi scroll, painted in reserve above a plain white band.

The decoration used inside the bowl derives from manuscript illuminations that contain radiating star-shaped central medallions and rectangular frames with reciprocal designs.

Interior, 165

These two features have been combined, creating a most effective circular composition. The motifs used on the exterior also follow those employed in manuscripts.

The artist who produced this bowl was a highly skilled potter who was able to throw a large and perfect piece. One wonders whether he was also responsible for the decoration, which shows masterful brushwork, employing light and dark cobalt blue to shade and accentuate the elements. It is possible that the shape was produced by one specialist and the design painted by another, who not only relied on nakkaşhane themes but adapted them to suit a three-dimensional object.

An almost identical piece is in the Victoria and Albert Museum.[57] This example shows another band around the foot and a slightly different handling of motifs, indicating that it was produced as an individual piece. There are several other large bowls with similar reciprocal panels on the inner walls, their exteriors decorated with simpler hatayi scrolls rendered in blue on a white ground.[58] These oversize bowls must be the ones mentioned in the 1505 inventory of the Hazine. Unfortunately none have survived in Turkish collections and all

245

the known examples are in European museums.[59]

Another series in this group of blue-and-white ware consists of mosque lamps. Five of them share the same shape and are fairly squat. Three were found in the Mausoleum of Bayezid II, one comes from the Mosque of Sokollu Mehmed Paşa, and another is now in the British Museum.[60]

A different shape with a high flaring neck and a more elongated body is seen on four other lamps: one of them was found in the Mausoleum of Bayezid II, another came from in the Mosque of Sokollu Mehmed Paşa, and two are in the British Museum.[61] Three of these contain panels on the body inscribed with the words "Allah, Muhammed, Ali," and one has no inscription panels on its body; the inscriptions on the necks of all four pieces vary. Although they were produced at the same time and follow the same shape and proportions, each displays a different composition.

The lamp found in the Mosque of Sokollu Mehmed Paşa (166) has three lobed medallions on the neck interspersed with cloud bands. The medallions, which extend to the rim and neck with interlacing bands, are inscribed "ya emana ali, keennebi allah ali, kulullah ali," (Oh, trustworthy Ali; you, the prophet of God, Ali; the slave of God, Ali) rendered in white kufi on a blue ground sprinkled with tiny blue dots. A beaded band with surface gilding encircles the lower edge of the neck.

The inscriptions on the body, placed in three lobed rectangles that also extend vertically by interlacing bands, repeat the phrase "Allah, Muhammed, Ali," rendered in white sülüs on a blue ground. Between the rectangles are three small handles surrounded by cloud bands and quatrefoils; the interstices are filled by rumi scrolls. The lower portion of the body has a wide zone decorated with a hatayi scroll. The foot contains a beaded band and a braid, both painted in reserve. The white areas of the neck and body are sprinkled with minuscule triple dots.

The underside of the lamp is also decorated. Trefoils encircle the inner edge of the foot ring and a circular design radiating from an eight-pointed star appears at the base. All the lamps in the series have radiating designs inside the foot ring.

The same vocabulary, motifs cut off at the edges and triple dots filling the background, was used in the Louvre bowl; the dotted grounds of the inscription panels re-create the effect of the ring matting. The shape of the lamp also follows contemporary examples made of silver, copper, and brass. This shape was used in fourteenth- and fifteenth-century glass lamps produced in Mamluk Syria and Egypt that may have served as models for the Ottoman metal examples.

The lamp, produced in the second quarter of the sixteenth century, must have been transferred to the Mosque of Sokollu Mehmed Paşa sometime after it was completed in 1571/ 1572; lamps contemporary with the mosque follow the style of the period and are painted with polychrome colors including the bright red (see 195).

Ceramic mosque lamps were nonfunctional objects and suspended in mosques and mausoleums to symbolize the celestial light allegorized in the famous Koranic verse that likens the light of the heavens to a mihrab in which there is a lamp. The production of these ceramic lamps appears to be a sixteenth-century Ottoman phenomenon with very few examples dating from the later periods. More than a dozen blue-and-white pieces are known to exist.[62] None are dated or inscribed with the names of their makers or patrons.

The inscriptions on this lamp, as well as the others in the series, are puzzling with their repeated evocations of Ali, the fourth orthodox caliph and the founder of the Shia branch of Islam. The traditional inscriptions on mosque lamps were Koranic verses, particularly the Verse of Light, although Ottoman examples also use selections from the Hadis, the names of the four orthodox caliphs, or the kelime-i tevhid (the profession of faith). The repeated use of Ali's name on mosque lamps produced for Ottoman patrons, who were Sunni, not Shiite, has yet to be satisfactorily explained.

Another symbolic object with an equally problematic inscription is a spherical ornament, which was used in both religious and secular buildings. Identified as yumurda (egg) in inventories and lists of gifts presented to the sultan during bayrams, these spherical ornaments, executed in metalwork, ceramics, possibly even in glass, were suspended over thrones or hung from the vaulted ceilings in ceremonial chambers, mosques, and mausoleums, as represented in manuscript illustrations. A number of precious metal pieces, some decorated with gems, are preserved in the Hazine; others were found in mausoleums. The same ornaments were used in churches, symbolizing universality and rebirth. The Ottoman examples appear to have more secular connotations, reflecting imperial power and justice, similar to the orb. Ceramic balls are relatively few in number, with less than a dozen blue-and-white and polychrome examples known to exist.

One of the rare blue-and-white balls (167), a slightly flattened sphere in shape, has a nipple at the bottom and a hole at the top that served a dual function: it allowed air to escape during firing and was used to attach a hook for suspension. The top has a blue frame around the hole, followed by a blank white zone. A second zone, framed by beaded bands, contains an elaborate foliated kufi inscription on a blue ground with blossoms and triple dots sprinkled in the voids. The inscription, which has not been deciphered, contains several vertical letters that terminate with large rumis. An abbreviated form of "Allah" appears above the letters. The zone at the bottom, also painted in reserve, is divided into three sections by knotted bands that evolve from a star enclosing the nipple. Each has a crescent-shaped cloud band and central blossom flanked by rumis. The same abbreviated form of "Allah" appears in the bands between these sections.

Another blue-and-white example has a totally different design. It is decorated only with a band of sülüs inscriptions

and once had gilded motifs, now visible only in traces.[63] Its sparse decoration and style of writing resemble the ceramic lamp found in the Mausoleum of Selim I.[64]

Among the unique early blue-and-white objects is a rectangular pen box with rounded corners (168). This shape was frequently used in metalwork and precious materials (see 62

166 (left). Mosque lamp with inscribed panels, first quarter sixteenth century (İstanbul, Arkeoloji Müzesi, 41/2)
167 (above). Spherical hanging ornament with inscriptions, first quarter sixteenth century (London, Victoria and Albert Museum, 337-1903)
168 (below). Pen box with inscriptions, first quarter sixteenth century (London, The British Museum, G. 1983.7)

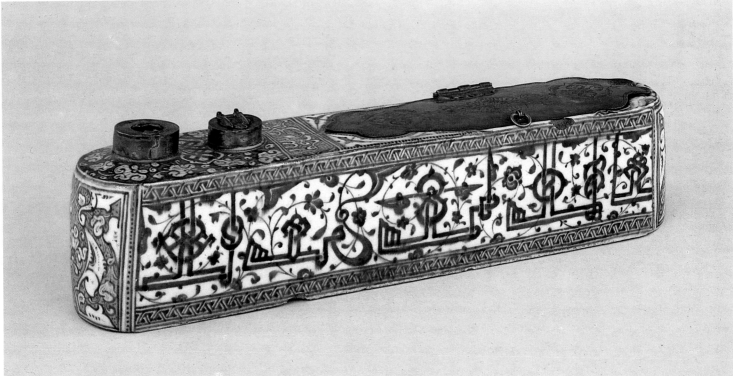

and **68**) as well as Chinese porcelains that copied Islamic prototypes.[65] The long sides of the pen box, framed at the top and bottom with interlacing bands executed in reserve, contain kufi inscriptions with knotted and intertwined vertical letters on a delicate hatayi scroll. The curved short sides have large rumis and hatayis in white on a blue ground. The top shows an open oblong compartment for pens and a covered section with a panel of nesih inscriptions and two cylindrical containers for inks. The inscriptions, written in white on a pale blue ground, contain the words "help from God and speedy victory," a part of a Koranic verse. The unit with the cylindrical pots is decorated in reserve with hatayi scrolls and a central knotted cartouche. The bottom of the open compartment is painted with a series of lozenges forming a diaper pattern. The underside of the pen box is embellished with four large cloud bands placed over a hatayi scroll.

This exquisitely designed and produced pen box was restored in the late eighteenth or early nineteenth century at which time an engraved silver lid was attached to the open compartment and the two cylindrical containers were added.

The plaited kufi inscriptions on the sides have not been successfully deciphered. It has been suggested that they repeat the words "salah sifr ve sad selam," which could be translated as "competent (or expedient) writing and manifold (or prosperous) perfection," most suitable good wishes for the calligrapher who owned the box.

In contrast to the single blue-and-white pen box that has survived from the early sixteenth century, there exist a dozen contemporary plates, which are composed of concentric panels and have flattened rims. The interior panels are decorated in reserve, while the exteriors of the cavetti have a blue floral scroll and at times scalloped lines around the rims. Only one example, which is in İstanbul, appears to have a foliated rim,[66] and some show blank interior cavetti.[67]

The only plate in the group that contains an inscription is in the Louvre (**169**). It has a dense hatayi scroll on the rim, an inscription panel with a version of the same scroll in the cavetto, and a band around the central medallion that is identical to that on the rim. Each zone is defined by blue and white lines. The central medallion contains a radiating pattern, in the core of which is a blossom enclosed by scrolls bearing rumis that form an eight-pointed star. The radial design provides a focus to the composition, which consists of revolving bands of scrolls that move clockwise, following the direction of the script. The movement is highly sophisticated, suggesting a perpetual flow that recalls the mystic interpretation of the harmony and rhythm of the universe frequently represented in Koranic illuminations.

169. Plate with concentric panels, first quarter sixteenth century (Paris, Musée du Louvre, 6321)

170. Plate with peony scroll, second quarter sixteenth century (İstanbul, Arkeoloji Müzesi, 41/155)

On the exterior, thin blue lines define the rim, cavetto, and foot. A scalloped blue line encircles the rim while a large and freely drawn hatayi scroll decorates the cavetto. This looser scroll, painted with light and dark tones of blue, contrasts with the tightly executed hatayi scroll inside the plate. The painter created positive and negative versions of the same theme, using white on blue on the interior and blue on white on the exterior.

In the second group of early blue-and-white ware the themes found on Chinese porcelains were reproduced with considerable flexibility. The shapes of the plates adhere to the Chinese prototypes, with clearly defined rims, cavetti, and central medallions. Scrolls or wave patterns appear on the rims, which are at times foliated or plain with a lobed line suggesting foliation; floral scrolls or sprays are placed in the cavetto; and peony scrolls, lotus bouquets, or three bunches of grapes are used in the center. The exterior repeats the composition found on the interior cavetto. The design is always painted in blue on white and never executed in reserve. In contrast to Chinese ware, the points of the foliated rims seldom align with the sprays in the cavettos or the points of the scalloped lines framing the central medallion. The themes used on the rims and cavetti are chosen at random and do not follow the rigidity seen in blue-and-white Chinese porcelains.

Peony scrolls and lotus bouquets inspired by Yüan or Ming dynasty ceramics were employed in mid-fifteenth-century bowls and plates as well as in the hexagonal tiles of the Muradiye Mosque in Edirne. The sudden interest in producing exact copies of Chinese porcelain most likely resulted from the expansion of the imperial kitchens of the palace, which created a demand for a substantial stock of serving pieces. Since it was not always possible to acquire large quantities of Chinese plates with the same design, İznik potters were called upon to complete the sets. As usual, the taste of the court set the precedent and İznik copies of Chinese porcelain became popular among the wealthy citizens.

The most frequently reproduced design was the peony scroll that faithfully copied the formal arrangement used in early Ming dynasty prototypes.[68] In İznik versions there is generally a high cylindrical foot, light and dark shades of blue, and a reinterpretation of the floral elements within the overall composition. One of the examples in the Çinili Köşk Collection (170) has a thirteen-lobed rim filled with a scroll bearing hatayis and peonies intermingled with rounded fruit resembling pomegranates. The cavetto has thirteen ribbed panels, each containing a floral spray. The central medallion encloses a scrolling branch that has four large and four small blossoms revolving around a central peony. In contrast to the majority of Chinese-inspired İznik plates, the number of lobes in the rim and the floral sprays in the cavetto is the same. The cavetto is identical on the interior and the exterior.

Although at first glance the plate appears to be a reason-able facsimile of a Chinese blue-and-white porcelain, examination reveals that the painter exercised a considerable amount of artistic freedom, individualizing his piece. The same individualization is found on each plate with this design. In contrast to Chinese examples, which retain a consistent execution and design, İznik blue-and-white shows a variation of hands and often a disregard for duplication.

Another group of blue-and-white objects displays the same stylistic idiosyncrasies, with floral scrolls that have hybrid hatayis and peonies, elongated feathery leaves, and hooked trefoils. The elements sway and turn, creating a lively composition. This particular style appears to belong to a single workshop that flourished in the mid-sixteenth century and made both blue-and-white and polychrome examples for one or two generations. Some pieces show animated floral compositions with birds or creatures hidden among the foliage.

One of the blue-and-white plates made by this studio (171) has a wave pattern on its rim. This pattern, based on Chinese models, was absorbed into the vocabulary of İznik potters. The theme of waves crashing on rocks and producing sprays of water was abstracted, becoming a series of spiral roundels and vertical bars alternating with lobed white areas filled with strokes and triple roundels.

The center of this plate, which disregards the cavetto, has a

171. Plate with floral scroll, mid-sixteenth century (Copenhagen, The David Collection, 27/1978)

172. Plate with floral bouquet, second quarter sixteenth century (New York, The Metropolitan Museum of Art, 29.33)

politan Museum of Art (**172**) shows the adaptation of this theme to a high-footed plate. Its foliated rim bears a wave pattern. The deep cavetto is decorated with lotus panels terminating with trefoil arches, each enclosing a small trefoil; additional trefoils appear in interstices between the arches. The center shows a spray with a large lotus, flanked by symmetrically arranged stylized blossoms with leaves, growing from a horizontal strip. The exterior of the cavetto has a series of abutted lotus panels, alternately filled with bold vertical strokes or a row of three trefoils. On the high foot are separated lotus panels like those inside the cavetto.

The execution of the blossoms, which display delicate brushwork and employ shading and voiding to define the details, contrasts with the stylized designs used in the cavetto and rim. The painter appears to have been exercising artistic freedom in the representation of the floral spray, while relying on established formulas for the remaining areas. The same motifs are used in the cavetto and rim of another plate that shows a variation in the flowers.[77] The lotus bouquet framed by arched panels was also rendered in the four-color ware with red.[78]

The third Chinese theme reproduced by İznik potters was three bunches of grapes amid scrolling vines and leaves, which became popular after the second quarter of the sixteenth century. Several plates with this design were made in blue and white, although the majority incorporated blue and turquoise.

Blue-and-Turquoise Ware

The second type of İznik ware shows that not only was the palette expanded to include a greenish-turquoise, but the themes represented by the potters became extremely diversified, ranging from spiral scrolls, saz motifs, and naturalistic flowers to figural compositions. The execution is painterly and the designs are freely drawn, revealing an uninhibited experimentation with themes and compositions. Some examples continued Chinese porcelain designs, while others show vestiges of motifs used in the blue-and-white ware. Most of the pieces are single examples that attempted to re-create on pottery the extraordinarily rich artistic vocabulary of the age. The diversity of decorative themes employed in objects belonging to this type makes it difficult to determine stylistic groupings and chronological development. The second color, introduced in the 1520s, continued to be used with the blue beyond the turn of the next century and was periodically revived in the ensuing years.

The popular theme of three bunches of grapes was frequently rendered in blue and turquoise, with the latter color used in the leaves and certain motifs, as represented on a large plate in the Metropolitan Museum of Art (**173**). The foliated rim reveals a different interpretation of the wave pat-

scroll with six hatayis, feathery leaves, and hooked buds revolving around a peony in a counterclockwise movement. The exterior of the cavetto has six rounded blossoms alternating with the same number of hooked trefoils. Blue lines around the rim are lobed, although the rim itself is plain. The motifs are shaded with reserved details, producing a painterly effect. Black is used only to define the spiral roundels of the wave pattern on the rim.

The style of blossoms and hooked buds evokes a distant resemblance to Chinese peonies and spiked and lobed leaves, which may have stimulated the development of these features.[69] The same motifs appear in different configurations on a number of other blue-and-white plates,[70] a pair of large jars decorated with peony scrolls or hatayis enclosed by four leaves that create lozenges,[71] as well as on a rare ewer with an overlapping ogival pattern composed of leaves,[72] two small jars,[73] and a unique candlestick inscribed with the name of its owner, Hacı Mehmed b. Süleyman.[74] There are also blue and turquoise-green examples, such as a tankard;[75] and polychrome lamps[76] and plates, in which the blossoms have become animated, containing heads of lions or sprouting stems terminating with birds.

The Chinese-derived theme of a lotus bouquet was not as widespread as the floral scroll and was produced in a limited number of pieces. The blue-and-white example in the Metro-

173. Plate with three bunches of grapes, second quarter sixteenth century (New York, The Metropolitan Museum of Art, 66.4.10)

tern, employing calligraphic lines with soft washes and delicate strokes. The number of points on the rim is ignored in the two types of floral sprays decorating the cavetto. Three bunches of grapes with scrolling vines and large leaves fill the central medallion. Turquoise, used sparingly in the rim and cavetto, is applied to the upper portions of the grape leaves and the loops of the scrolling vine, playfully disregarding the concept of full and void. The exterior of the cavetto repeats the design used on the interior.

Grapes with dark blue "eyes" and leaves detailed with linear or reserved veins are characteristic of this series of plates, as are the wave patterns on the rims and the floral sprays in the cavetti. Although the theme was most frequently rendered in blue-and-white[79] and blue-and-turquoise ceramics,[80] there are also plates with green, purple, or red bunches of grapes.[81] In some examples floral scrolls were used in the cavetto instead of sprays[82] and one of the more innovative plates added a tree to the center, its branches interwined with

251

174. Plate with diaper pattern, second quarter sixteenth century (New York, The Metropolitan Museum of Art, 14.40.727)

grape vines.[83] This fruit was also used on polychrome tile panels dating between the last quarter of the sixteenth and the first quarter of the seventeenth centuries.

A highly celebrated blue-and-turquoise plate is the example bequeathed by Benjamin Altman to the Metropolitan Museum of Art (174). The design in the center is thought to be a translation of the diaper pattern found in fourteenth-century Chinese celadons, employing blue and turquoise to paint a theme that had been molded on the monochromatic Chinese pieces.[84] The diaper pattern was also employed on contemporary inlaid woodwork, and a different version was painted inside a blue-and-white pen box (see 168). Another configuration with rectangular elements placed horizontally and vertically, displaying a bolder pattern, appears in the center of a blue-and-white plate.[85] It was used even earlier on a blue-and-black underglaze-painted plate made in Syria during the fourteenth century.[86] This pattern, therefore, was a part of the artistic repertoire of the age and already produced on İznik wares; its use as the central theme of a blue-and-white example may have been inspired by Chinese celadons assembled in the imperial kitchens. The border, on the other hand, is definitely derived from nakkaşhane designs.

The Altman plate is a masterpiece of pottery painting, using voided details and controlled brushstrokes to contour and shade the motifs, creating an exquisitely vibrant and three-dimensional composition. The wide blue-ground band around the plain rim contains a scroll composed of oversize rumis that divide this zone into ten reciprocal lobes. Sprouting from the scroll and filling each lobe is a hatayi surrounded by leaves and buds; the blossoms show two types and sizes, with larger, more naturalistic examples placed within the lobes and smaller, more stylized ones in the interstices along the rim. The center of the plate has a plain white band enclosing the diaper-patterned medallion framed by trefoils. The diaper motifs are outlined in blue and alternate between turquoise and white, producing yet another reciprocal pattern.

The exterior walls are embellished with a dense scroll bearing hatayis and peonies. In contrast to the interior, which is painted turquoise with dark blue outlines on a blue ground, the exterior is decorated in blue on white but employs the same shaded and voided detailing. The delicate brushwork and strength of design indicate that a master painter produced this plate.

A group of blue-and-turquoise plates combines floral motifs employed in the earlier blue-and-whites with naturalistic flowers, frequently vases filled with blossoms, in the central medallions. The composition in these medallions is directional, with a clearly defined top and bottom, while repetitive and circular designs are employed in the cavetti and rims.

In the central medallion of one of these (175) a semicircular panel supports the vase and a large lobed arch encloses it. The double-handled vase is decorated with a rumi cartouche enclosing a trefoil, flanked by a pair of pots. Sprays of tulips,

175. Plate with vases, second quarter sixteenth century (London, The British Museum, G. 1983.52)

carnations, hyacinths, rounded blossoms, buds, and feathery leaves on broken branches grow from the containers; two large hatayis enclosed by cloud bands and cloud collars fill the lateral lobes of the arch.

There are sprays of rounded blossoms alternating with cloud bands in the cavetto. The foliated rim has a series of lobed blue oblongs, each with a pair of leaves flanking a blossom, creating S-shaped motifs. One of the oblongs is considerably smaller than the others, indicating that the painter drew the design freehand without relying on a cartoon. The exterior of the cavetto shows a blue scroll rendered in the style of the earlier blue-and-white ware.

Other blue-and-turquoise plates with a similar combination of styles depict single-handled bottles and jugs placed on low taborets or scrolls evolving from a source placed at the bottom of the central medallion.[87] A large vase with hatayi blossoms and leaves is represented on one of the blue-and-turquoise tile panels facing the Sünnet Odası. This theme, which was employed on textiles and embroideries as well as other types of İznik pottery and tiles produced in the sixteenth century,[88] first appeared in manuscript illustrations dating from the 1520s, such as the *Divan-ı Selimi* (see 28a).

A plate with a similar lobed blue arch in its central medallion represents a narrative episode (176). In it a snake entwined around the trunk of a large tree approaches an unsuspecting bird perched in the branches. The theme recalls saz drawings in which ferocious dragons emerge from dense foliage to attack birds. A mid-sixteenth-century drawing, thought to have been made either in Tabriz or İstanbul, shows a similar episode with a snake approaching a bird's nest, set in an idyllic landscape with peris and demons.[89] The theme used here is abstracted from saz drawings and rendered in a more prosaic manner.

Growing from the foot of the tree is a bush with several blossoms that recall the type used in one of the sprays decorating the cavetto of the grape plate (see **173**). The foliated rim is embellished with a series of ovals enclosing rounded blossoms that resemble those on the plate with vases (see **175**). The cavetto is plain except for a thin garland of hatayi blossoms and leaves. The exterior has a floral scroll, following the blue-and-white style.

Narrative episodes and figural representations are rare on sixteenth-century İznik wares; these designs, taken from al-
bum drawings and manuscript illustrations, appear only on a few blue-and-turquoise plates. In one of them, a fleet of ships sails around a large galleon (**177**). The style of the galleon with a U-shaped hull, cantilevered fore and aft decks, fully rigged masts, and billowing sails recalls those used in the paintings of Piri Reis and Nasuh (see **35**, **36**, **38**, and **40**). Large and small galleys enclose the flagship and advance toward the center and the left with their sails catching the wind, creating an energetic and sweeping movement across the circular plate. The ships, with carefully defined sails and rigging, float on a sea decorated with dots. Several are cut off at the edges of the composition, indicating that what is captured on the plate is a portion of an even larger design.

Double blue lines together with a band of small roundels frame the central composition, which is encircled by a plain white cavetto. A braid decorates the slightly raised rim. The exterior shows a floral scroll. The plate, which has no foot

176. Plate with snake, second quarter sixteenth century (London, Victoria and Albert Museum, C.2019-1910)

177 (above). Plate with ships, second quarter sixteenth century (London, Victoria and Albert Museum, 713-1902)

178 (right). Bottle with spiral scroll, second quarter sixteenth century (London, The British Museum, 78 12-30 519)

ring, resembles a flat tray, a shape that became widely used in the second half of the sixteenth century. Ships were also rendered on later polychrome ware, generally depicting only a single galleon (see **201**).

An entirely different theme—thin spiral scrolls bearing minute blossoms and leaves, frequently overlaid with trefoil rumi cartouches and palmettes—appears on another group of blue-and-turquoise pieces. This design, which was also used on Süleyman's tuğras and manuscript illuminations,[90] was applied to bottles, jugs, ewers, small and large bowls, and plates with plain or foliated rims, as well as to a rare group of tiles. Some of the scrolls were painted in a dark blackish-green.[91] A few bowls show the tightly-wound spiral scroll on

the interior and a looser floral one reminiscent of earlier blue-and-white ware on the exterior. On one small jar, found in İstanbul, there is a bolder and cruder version of the spiral scroll with pale red blossoms.[92] These examples suggest that the group overlaps the earlier blue-and-white and the later polychrome types. Among the more unusual pieces employing this design are two mosque lamps,[93] and several tondino bowls with wide flattened rims and small lidded ewers with attached spouts that reflect Italianate shapes.[94]

The only dated example in this group is the British Museum bottle made in 1529 (see fig. 20). A second bottle in the same collection (**178**) has a more elongated shape with its tall neck embellished with a bold ring. The neck is divided

179 (above). Plate with spiral scroll, second quarter sixteenth century
(Kuwait National Museum, LNS 231 C)

180 (right). Panel with hexagonal tiles, second quarter sixteenth century
(İstanbul, Arkeoloji Müzesi, 41/515 and 41/1121)

in two by the ring, which is framed on both sides by turquoise strips. Braided bands appear at the edge of the slightly flaring rim and below the ring. Continuous scrolls bearing tiny buds and leaves, accentuated by turquoise and blue lozenges, revolve around the neck. A plain white band appears at the base of the neck.

The zone around the shoulder contains a different application of the same scroll, which creates seven spiraling circles; similar lozenges are placed at the points of intersection and cut off by the frames at the top and bottom. The swelling body repeats the same design, employing six large volutes with larger lozenges composed of turquoise and blue rumis. A crosshatched small diamond is placed in the center of each circle. A scroll with cloud bands encircles the lower body, while a pair of thin turquoise lines and a chevron band were painted on the foot.

Bottles with thick rings on their necks were popularly produced in sixteenth-century İznik ceramics, some of which were decorated with naturalistic blossoms in blue and turquoise or polychrome.[95]

The themes on the bottle reappear on a large plate (**179**), which has a foliated rim decorated with a scroll bearing small turquoise blossoms and blue S-shaped motifs. The cavetto has a series of blue cloud bands enclosing turquoise flowers. The central medallion contains spiral scrolls that create five volutes around a central one that has a blossom in its core and thickly painted leaves defining its perimeter. Trefoil cartouches with rumis appear between the outer volutes; cartouches and blossoms, cut off by the frame, line the outer edge. The exterior repeats the design used on the interior of the cavetto, with small sprays of blossoms and leaves added to the interstices.

Other plates with similar scrolls in the central medallion have variations in the cavetto and rim, incorporating floral sprays, garlands, or wave patterns; a few incorporate hatayi scrolls and bunches of tulips. Some have foliated rims while others are shaped as flat trays.

Blue and turquoise were also used on tiles, including small hexagonal pieces decorated with identical radial compositions, indicating that they were mass-produced from the same cartoons. One design used in these tiles consists of a central blossom enclosed by a six-pointed star; from alternate points a pair of branches evolves and creates three large ogival cartouches (**180**). Each cartouche is flanked by large rumis and

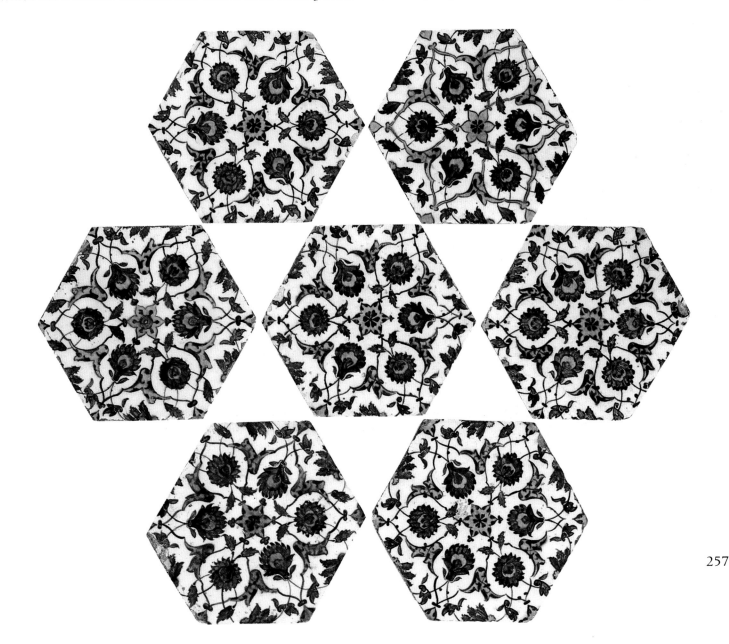

257

encloses a hatayi blossom. The interstices between the cartouches are filled with additional hatayis, which appear to be attached to the tip of another cartouche beyond the edge of the tile, creating an alternating pattern.

A group of these hexagonal tiles was affixed to the facade of the Sünnet Odası, and similar examples are housed in Turkish, European, and American collections.[96] Other hexagons use a variation of the radiating and overlapping patterns with ogival cartouches.[97] One such tile served as a model for a white molded plate (see **163**) as well as an underglaze-painted example.

The repertoire of blue-and-turquoise ware includes saz themes that were employed on large tile panels and diverse objects, such as mosque lamps,[98] jugs, plates, and jars, some of which were rendered in reserve on a blue ground and mixed with naturalistic flora.[99] Others rely solely on naturalistic elements, the most beautifully painted examples being a series of blue-ground tiles that represent large blossoming fruit trees with hyacinths and tulips growing at their bases. These panels, removed from their original structure, are now housed in Copenhagen and Lisbon.[100] A characteristic of the designs used in these examples is the central source from which the flora springs, a feature that was fully exploited in the four-color ware using pale green and purple.

Four-color Ware with Purple

The most exquisite type of İznik ware is painted with two tones of blue (cobalt blue and greenish- or bluish-turquoise), green (which ranges from sage, or pale pistachio-green, to olive), and purple (appearing frequently as pale mauve or violet), often using greenish black to define the motifs. The designs reveal the strong impact of the nakkaşhane, and include elaborate saz scrolls and sprays of naturalistic flora, at times used together and mixed with rumi cartouches and cloud bands. This ware, with its highly refined brushwork and harmonious compositions, must have been produced by master painters who conceived each piece as an original work of art. Even when a theme is repeated on a series of plates or bowls, the configuration of elements varies, showing an attempt to individualize the objects.

Examples of this ware include a limited number of large footed bowls, some of which have saz scrolls on the exteriors but diversify the interiors by employing different combinations of floral sprays, rumis, and cloud bands.[101] Similar compositions appear on a large group of plates[102] as well as several jars, jugs, ewers, and small bowls with a relatively high foot, some of which have domical lids;[103] a few pieces are rendered on a deep-blue ground.[104] Included in this type are the tondino-shaped examples with portrait busts and an unusual jug decorated with Maltese crosses, its pinched rim forming a spout, based on Italian prototypes.[105] These pieces

appear to have been commissioned by foreign patrons, most likely Italians.

Some of the plates in green and purple reflect Chinese-inspired compositions and themes, with three bunches of grapes or floral scrolls that evolve from a single source in the central medallion. One such example (**181**) has a lobed rim decorated with a floral scroll. The cavetto contains sprays of the same flora, and the central medallion depicts scrolling branches with hatayis and peonies amid small leaves and buds growing from a tuft of leaves placed at the bottom. Touches of pale green and purple appear in the blossoms. The exterior of the cavetto repeats the design used on the interior.

181. Plate with floral spray, mid-sixteenth century (London, The British Museum, G. 1983.33)

This plate exemplifies the freedom with which İznik potters adapted and interpreted the compositions and themes of Chinese porcelain. Although the same tripartite division is employed, the lobes defining the zones vary and do not conform with the number of sprays decorating the cavetto; the scrolls and sprays are rendered in the style and color scheme of the period, particularly noticeable in the orientation of the central design and the insistence on showing the source from which the flora grows.

One of the most outstanding examples of this type reveals the same orientation (**182**). On this plate a single branch springs from a pair of twisted leaves and turns, breaks, and

182. Plate with saz spray, mid-sixteenth century (Private collection)

revolves in a counterclockwise direction, creating a circular movement that accentuates the shape of the object. In the center is a large compound hatayi surrounded by peonies and other hatayis that sprout buds and feathery leaves, which overlap, intersect, and pierce one another. Another large leaf springs from the same source and twists over the scrolling branch, sprouting sprays of tiny blossoms. The extraordinary movement produced by the revolving branch, the feeling of depth created by the overlapping of the elements, and the painterly use of pigments with shaded and textured components are rarely matched.

In contrast to the movement depicted on the interior, the exterior shows a subdued and conservative design. A blue chevron encircles the rim, while the cavetto contains bunches of blue tulips alternating with turquoise and green blossoms. Bunches of pointed tulips, which are almost a trademark of this ware, were also used on blue-and-turquoise examples, their first datable appearance being on the neck of the mosque lamp made in 1549 for the Dome of the Rock.

The saz scroll employed on the plate could only have been executed by a great draftsman and painter. The plate was cherished through the centuries and has been repaired with metal staples after having been broken into three pieces. The design is compatible with those on the flyleaves of an album compiled around 1560 and the two kemhas made into kaftans for Şehzades Mustafa and Bayezid (see **116**).

The same scroll appears on a blue-and-turquoise hexagonal tile in the Victoria and Albert Museum[106] and two other similar fragments in Hamburg.[107] The most exuberant rendition of this theme is found on the Sünnet Odası tiles (see fig. 21). It seems, therefore, that the ultimate manifestation of the saz style in ceramics took place in the mid-sixteenth century and was simultaneously rendered both in blue-and-turquoise and four-color ware with purple.

One of the rare jars employing these four colors is decorated with saz scrolls that encircle its neck and body (**183**). The rim contains a band with a series of small roundels and strokes, reminiscent of the wave pattern. The neck has a scroll with six large hatayis surrounded by smaller blossoms and feathery leaves that are linked together by small crescent-shaped cloud collars. The hatayis are almost in cross section: a ring of petals encloses three pods amid leaves. A chevron band and a blue frieze composed of roundels join the neck to the shoulder. The body bears a larger version of the saz scroll, its hatayis sprouting several podlike buds. The band at the lower edge of the body contains a scroll with the same small blossoms used on the neck. A blue and white braid appears around the foot.

Although the blue used on the jar is a deep cobalt, the other three pigments are pastel in tone, and include a pale greenish turquoise, a grayish green, and a pinkish mauve. Blue and turquoise are applied to the blossoms, green is used primarily on the leaves, and purple appears in the center of

183. Jar with saz scroll, mid-sixteenth century (London, The British Museum, 78 12-30 513)

the leaves, blossoms, buds, and cloud collars. The sinuous movement created by the long leaves that swoop and overlap the other elements is similar to the compositions found in album paintings. The revolving movement of the scrolls is opposed by the leaves, which create their own rhythm.

Another outstanding example of this ware is the famous plate in the Louvre (**184**), which presents the most innovative approach to pottery painting, totally disregarding the shape of the object and extending the composition beyond the confines of its rim. It is almost as if the painter produced a large painting, the center of which was cut out in a circular format and transferred onto a plate with a lobed and everted rim. Painted in deep and pastel blues, bright turquoise, grayish green, and pinkish mauve, the composition radiates from

184. Plate with peacock, mid-sixteenth century (Paris, Musée du Louvre, 3449)

185. Plate with floral spray, mid-sixteenth century (London, The British Museum, G. 1983.21)

a cluster of leaves placed at the lower edge held together by a turquoise crescent. Growing from the center of the cluster is a trunk with a large pinecone or artichoke, sprouting buds and a curving branch; flanking it are two other branches bearing a variety of hybrid hatayis, peonies, blossoms, pods, buds, and small and large leaves that revolve around the plate, overlapping and intersecting one another. Another branch winds up the trunk of the tree, its blossom overlaying the pinecone; shorter branches with tulips and possible jasmines grow around the base. The elements along the edge are cut off by the rim and include several bisected cloud bands. Striding calmly in this exuberant flora is a pale-blue peacock, rendered in profile with its head turned back. The curvature of its neck, body, and tail echoes the rhythm of the saz leaves.

The exterior, similar to the previous plate with the saz scroll, follows the formulaic scheme: bunches of blue tulips alternate with turquoise and green blossoms.

The combination of saz elements with a peacock recalls the tile panels of the Sünnet Odası, in which various birds appear on branches. Luxuriant gardens with fabulous creatures reflect the impact of saz drawings on ceramics, recreating similar enchanted settings with imaginary vegetation and inhabitants. Peacocks and other birds were also depicted on four-color ware with the brilliant red, showing vestiges of the saz tradition (see **192** and **199**).

The majority of the four-color ware with purple are plates which depict in their central medallions sprays of hatayis and naturalistic flowers growing from a clearly defined source, encircled by rims decorated with diverse motifs. On the rim of one of these plates is a highly abstracted version of the wave pattern (**185**). The central medallion has branches that bear large hatayis overlaid by cloud bands and flanked by hyacinths, bell-shaped flowers (perhaps fuchsias), and tulips. The flora springs from a lobed turquoise crescent surrounded by two cloud bands; similar lobed crescents embellish some of the branches. A serrate-petaled blossom (possibly a forget-me-not) growing on the left provides an unexpected asymmetry to the composition. The motifs are freely drawn and show variation in size and placement, further disrupting symmetry. The exterior contains pairs of blue tulips alternating with single blossoms.

The combination of stylized and naturalistic motifs appears on almost all four-color plates with purple, each in a different configuration. In some examples the division between rim and cavetto was disregarded,[108] as seen in the Louvre plate; in others the rims were decorated with abstract wave patterns, bunches of flowers, or a series of blossoms. Among the more popular designs are large central hatayis flanked by sprays of hyacinths and leaves, encircled by wave-patterned rims. This composition is found on several four-color plates with purple as well as on those painted with red (see **189**).

There are also examples that employ as their main theme the pinecone/artichoke, including the plate in the British Museum (**186**) that has a dense and intricate composition filled with an unusually rich variety of naturalistic and stylized flora. The source here is clusters of leaves, which knot together and sprout branches. The central branches bear two round pinecones, one painted blue and the other green with contrasting details. They are flanked by branches with large blossoms, small buds or pods, and leaves that join at the top and create an ogival arch. Other branches loop around them, their long feathery leaves overlapping the blossoms. Between the pinecones are cloud bands, from which sprays of blossoms spring.

The composition creates an overall effect of streams of branches that burst from the central source and curve, twist, overlap, and intersect one another, producing an energetic movement. The flowers resemble roses and rosebuds, fruit-tree blossoms, and stylized peonies. Once again, the symmetry of the composition is intentionally opposed by the rose and two rosebuds growing at the base. The lobed blue rim contains blossoms alternating with tulips flanked by cloud bands. The exterior shows pairs of tulips interspersed with cloud bands encircling small blossoms.

The decorative repertoire of four-color ware with purple was diversified, frequently combining traditional, saz, and naturalistic elements on the same piece.[109] There are also examples that employ only saz scrolls or naturalistic flowers. The latter is represented on a jug (**187**) that is decorated with blossoms and buds similar to the naturalistic ones seen on the plate. The rim contains a green band with spiral roundels; another green band decorated with chevrons and a thick blue line appears at the lower edge of the neck. The neck is adorned with two alternating sprays of flowers: one has a purple blossom drawn frontally, the other a blue flower drawn in profile, both flanked by buds and leaves. The same combination, with larger elements, is repeated on the body; here, the purple sprays have additional pairs of blue buds.

The stems on both the neck and body form softly curving diagonals as if swaying in the wind, similar to the effect produced in vertical-stem-pattern textiles (see **147**). This simple format with alternating views and colors creates a most attractive and lively composition. The band above the foot has a braid pattern, while a simple greenish-black line encircles the foot. The handle is defined by two thick blue lines filled with horizontal strokes.

Single-handle jugs, based on metal prototypes, were executed in blue-and-white as well as polychrome painted wares (see **164**, **194**, and **198**). The smaller ones, such as this example, might have been used as individual serving pieces for liquids as well as containers for flowers, whereas the larger ones functioned as pitchers.

Four-color Ware with Red

The classical type of İznik pottery was established in the mid-sixteenth century after the development of the thick brilliant red first used in the Süleymaniye Mosque, which was completed in 1557. Within a decade it was employed on a variety of objects and tiles, which represented the full range of decorative repertoire of the age. There was hardly any shape or design that escaped the attention of the potters, who created freely drawn, impeccably painted, and flawlessly glazed examples both for the court and for domestic and foreign markets.

The decoration, drawn in black and painted with blue, turquoise, emerald green, and bright red, shows an exuberance of themes and original compositions with very little duplication. The artists were able to paint any given surface, ranging from spherical ornaments to immense tile panels that covered the walls of buildings. This ware also includes a rare group painted with tinted slips.

Four-color İznik ware with red reveals a joyous celebration of nature. Stylized and naturalistic flora in perpetual bloom, representing paradise gardens and symbolizing eternal bliss, sacred and profane love, and good wishes for life on earth and hereafter, blend mystical concepts with more prosaic and

186. Plate with pinecones and blossoms, mid-sixteenth century (London, The British Museum, G. 1983.48)

187. Jug with floral sprays, mid-sixteenth century (Paris, Musée du Louvre, 7257)

188. Lid with rumi scroll, mid-sixteenth century (Paris, Musée du Louvre, A.O. 5960)

easily understood themes. The decorative repertoire includes formal designs, such as rumi scrolls, cloud bands, and çinte-mani and scale patterns as well as saz elements and a variety of naturalistic flowers and trees, including hatayi blossoms, long feathery leaves, roses, tulips, carnations, hyacinths, blossoming fruit trees, and cypresses. Figural compositions are limited to birds.[110] Sailboats and ships, on the other hand, became a popular theme toward the end of the sixteenth century and appear on plates, tankards, and jugs made for popular consumption. Inscriptions were, with the exception of mosque lamps, very few.[111]

The shapes include plates with plain or foliated rims, flat traylike circular pieces, vases, bottles, tankards, jugs, lidded bowls, mosque lamps, spherical ornaments, and even pen boxes and tombstones, at times rendered on blue, green, or red grounds. Large footed bowls, produced in other İznik types, appear to have been omitted from the repertoire of the four-color wares with red. On the other hand there are a number of new shapes, including a few jarlike vases with shoulders pierced to hold flowers, their bases painted with signs resembling an "S" superimposed by a "T," possibly made for Europeans and imitating maiolica marks.[112]

Because there are no signed and dated examples the chronological development of this type of ware is difficult to establish. The potters worked for a mixed clientele and produced both high-quality pieces and mass-produced examples.

Pale and washed out reds in one group of objects suggest that they were among the earlier examples exhibiting the new color. Among these is a circular lid with a short straight edge and a central boss (188), presumably once a part of a

covered cylindrical box or bowl. The boss, painted blue and encircled by a green band, shows intersecting rumi scrolls revolving around a six-petaled blossom, in reserve and accented with touches of red. Similar rumi scrolls appear on the flattened portion of the lid, painted in blue and red on white. The scrolls overlap, knot, and loop around one another and create three large and three small cartouches. The design of the central boss appears on the edge of the lid.

A second example belonging to the early experimental group is a plate with a central hatayi enclosed by a pair of incurving saz leaves that spring from a cluster at the bottom (189). The hatayi grows from a pair of thin branches that meet to form an ogival arch, held together by a cloud collar. Two other thin and long branches, bearing blossoms at their tips, cross under the hatayi, break at the top, and swoop down along the sides. Growing at the base are additional leaves and flowers. The leaves at the base and around the central blossom overlay sprays of red blossoms; touches of red also appear in the other blossoms and leaves as well as in the trefoil at the lower tip of the hatayi and in its central pods. Emerald green was employed in the smaller leaves, replacing the weaker grayish sage used in the previous group. The foliated rim contains a wave pattern, while the exterior is decorated with sprays of tulips that alternate with roundels.

The compositions used in the central medallion, rim, and exterior were employed on four-color ware with purple[113] as well as on early four-color ware with red.[114] The appearance of the same theme on two different types of ceramics suggests that they were produced contemporaneously.

A floral motif that was used in the scrolls decorating a group of mid-sixteenth-century blue-and-whites (see 171) appears as the main theme in a plate rendered in blue, turquoise, and pale red (190), which indicates that pottery painted with a single color also was contemporaneous with polychrome examples. In the center of this plate is an elaborate cartouche composed of trefoils, split leaves, and floral elements sprouting two large lateral leaves that swing back and join the main unit with buds. The tendrils at the base terminate in a pair of bird heads with crownlike cloud bands placed over them. Additional cloud bands appear in the voids around the edges. A stylized wave pattern encircles the plain rim; the exterior shows six sketchily drawn cloud bands alternating with circular motifs.

The transformation of a floral element into a zoomorphic one, initiated by saz drawings, is found on other Ottoman ceramics. In some examples the blossoms are animated and represent faces of animals;[115] in others the flowers are made to resemble fish or insects.[116] This fanciful conflation of animal and floral elements appears on a limited number of pieces and represents a little-known but fascinating aspect of İznik pottery.

Among the rare datable early pieces using red is the famous lamp in the Victoria and Albert Museum (191), reputed

189. Plate with central hatayi, mid-sixteenth century (London, The British Museum, 78 12-30 502)

190. Plate with central cartouche and pair of birds, mid-sixteenth century (Paris, Musée du Louvre, 7880-83)

to have come from the Süleymaniye Mosque. This large lamp has a high flaring neck, low foot, and a bulbous body divided into two by a band, each half decorated with several quatrefoil cartouches cut in half. Affixed to the upper half are three large hemispherical bosses with serpentine handles between them. The base, also decorated, has a small central hole.

The lamp was constructed in three pieces, neck, upper body, and lower body; handles and bosses were produced separately. Broken in the past, one of the handles and a section of the rim are missing. The misalignment of the two halves of the body indicates that they became separated and were incorrectly reattached. In spite of its thin red and runny blue pigments, the lamp is carefully designed and painted, combining hatayis and rumis. It must have been one of a series made for Süleyman's mosque and mausoleum.

A turquoise band with a black rumi scroll encircles the rim. The neck bears a portion of the Verse of Light containing the words ''God is the light of the heavens and the earth,'' in white sülüs outlined in black on a blue ground filled with hatayi scrolls. A white band appears between the neck and the upper edge of the body.

The upper half of the body shows bisected quatrefoils composed of white rumis that extend either down toward the bosses or grow up and engulf the handles. The quatrefoils are painted red and filled with large black hatayis. The interstices, which contain floral scrolls, are painted blue and create a zig-zag pattern around the quatrefoils. The motifs in both the red-ground and blue-ground areas are connected by intersecting stems, producing an intricate network with elements overlapping one another. The lower half of the body employs the same composition.

The bosses exhibit a similar design with red cartouches formed by white rumis enclosing black hatayis radiating from a central star. Three handles, decorated with overlapping blue petals, emerge from the centers of the hatayis in the quatrefoils and attach to the shoulder. Chains, which would normally have looped around the handles, are affixed by metal plugs inserted in holes drilled into the body. It is possible that these plugs were made after the lamp was broken and one of the handles was lost.

The base, painted turquoise, contains a red and white blossom around the central hole, surrounded by cloud bands. The red used in the base is bright and thickly applied, contrasting with the weak tone used elsewhere in the lamp. It appears that the technique was just being perfected.

The shape of this lamp differs from the blue-and-white examples (see **166**). This large format with hemispherical bosses was repeated in a pair of lamps found in the Mosque of Sokollu Mehmed Paşa (see **195**).

192. Plate with hatayi scroll and peafowl, mid-sixteenth century (London, Victoria and Albert Museum, C.2005-1910)

A better, but not totally perfected, application of the red is found on a plate decorated with a central medallion enclosing a long-tailed bird amid sprays of hatayi blossoms, buds, and feathery leaves (**192**). The flora revolve around the plate without a clearly defined source of origin, which is unusual in İznik wares. The only element growing from the edge is a thin blue leaf placed above the head of the bird, which lacks the crest of the peacock and may represent a peahen. The motifs, outlined in black and painted in red and blue as well as reserved in white, appear on a deep green ground.

The plate has a red and white braid on its flattened rim, plain cavetto, and a series of red leaves enclosing the central medallion. The exterior contains sprays of rounded blossoms alternating with roundels. The theme used in the central medallion with composite blossoms and overlapping elements is characteristic of saz drawings which frequently depict birds hidden among fantastic foliage.

The same theme was represented on an earlier example with pale green and purple (see **184**). An identical design on a red ground appears in the center of another plate,[117] while similar peafowl engulfed with saz scrolls and/or naturalistic flora are shown on a number of later plates and tiles.[118] The most remarkable tiles employing this theme were used to face the interior of the Has Oda in the Topkapı Palace in the 1570s.[119] There is also a series of small tiles representing parrots flanking fountains, in American and European collec-

267

193 (above). Pen box with saz scroll, third quarter sixteenth century (Paris, Musée du Louvre, 4048)

194 (right). Large jug with hatayis and leaves, third quarter sixteenth century (London, The British Museum, G. 1983.121)

tions, which must have been removed from a late-sixteenth-century building.[120]

The potters soon mastered the red, which after the 1560s was used on virtually all the vessels and tiles produced in İznik. The elaborate floral compositions employed on tiles were applied to diverse objects, including such rare pieces as rectangular pen boxes, of which only two are known to have survived. One of them, in the Louvre, has lost its lid (193). The piece is decorated with red rumis that create cartouches in the center of the long sides and around the corners. The rumis are overlaid by scrolls bearing large polychrome hatayis, peonies, buds, and leaves that fill the cartouches and the interstices. Although thin red lines encircle the upper and lower edges of the box, the design appears to have been taken from a larger composition, possibly a tile panel, wrapped around the sides and cut off at the top and bottom. The recessed ledge at the rim suggests that the lid had straight sides and fitted snugly over the opening. The interior is empty and undecorated.

A slightly larger example in the Victoria and Albert Museum, similarly painted with rumis and hatayis, also lacks its lid. It has a long open compartment and a small unit pierced with two circular holes to hold cylindrical ink pots. The edges

of this box are grooved, indicating that its lid was flat and slid into place. Pen boxes with lids or sliding covers were produced in more precious materials, such as jade, rock crystal, and gold (see 59 and 62). These may have provided the models for the ceramic examples, which were also executed in blue and white (see 168).

Many polychrome objects share designs used on brocaded silks and velvets, their common source being the nakkaşhane. Large hatayi blossoms flanked by saz leaves and floral sprays that join at the top and form ogival medallions, employed on ceramic plates (see 189) and tiles and on textiles, appear on a large jug in the British Museum (194). The neck of this example, which contains a braided band on its rim, has four hatayis enclosed by sprays of fruit blossoms and saz leaves. The bands below are decorated with lobed rectangles bearing rounded flowers and a row of bisected blossoms.

Motifs on the neck were repeated on the body, with larger elements and extra leaves and blossoms to accommodate the wider surface. An attempt was made to extend the composition by cutting off the motifs at the lower edges of the neck and body as well as to join the ogival medallions by orienting their tips toward one another on either side of the neckband. Thus the design creates a series of small and large ovals, em-

195 (left). Lamp from the Mosque of Sokollu Mehmed Paşa, c. 1572 (İstanbul, Arkeoloji Müzesi, 41/16)

196 (right). Spherical hanging ornament with saz design, second half sixteenth century (London, The British Museum, G. 1983.120)

phasizing the swell of the sides of the body.

Hatayis also decorate a pair of large lamps that were found in the Mosque of Sokollu Mehmed Paşa, built by Sinan in 1571/1572. The building was commissioned by Esmahan Sultan, the daughter of Selim II, for her husband, Sokollu Mehmed, who served as grand vezir between 1565 and 1579. The mosque contains some of the most outstanding examples of İznik tiles.[121] The lamps made for this structure are equally refined, painted in reserve on a dark blue ground and embellished with large hemispherical bosses, following the shape of the lamp identified with the Süleymaniye Mosque (see 191).

One lamp from Sokollu Mehmed Paşa's mosque (195) contains on its neck the kelime-i tevhid, "la ilahe illallah Muhammed rasulullah" (there is no god but God, Muhammed is his Prophet), written in white sülüs on a blue ground. The last word, which did not fit around the neck, was written above the others. Two thin braids encircle the rim and the lower edge of the neck.

The body, which was produced separately, shows the same thickening at the joint with the neck as the lamp from the Süleymaniye Mosque. Its upper edge contains a thin turquoise line and a band of trefoils. Three hemispherical turquoise bosses, affixed to the middle of the body between the handles, are framed by the same band and decorated with black rumis placed around a central blossom. These bosses were originally gilded and now show only traces of gold. A scroll with three large and three smaller blossoms fills the areas below the handles and bosses; pairs of leaves, superimposed with sprays of flowers and overlapping buds, extend up and flank the handles. The base contains a central hole surrounded by a medallion embellished with large blossoms.

Polychrome lamps produced after the mid-sixteenth century appear to have similar holes inside their foot rings, which may have been a technical necessity when producing almost spherical pieces that are more than 30 centimeters (12 inches) in diameter. They also served to attach spherical ornaments, or "eggs," that were suspended below the lamps.

A variation of the same design appears on the other lamp from the Mosque of Sokollu Mehmed Paşa, which is similarly constructed and supplied with a hole inside its foot ring.[122] The pierced base is also found on the example made in 1549 for the Dome of the Rock in Jerusalem (see fig. 22). It appears that the group of large lamps made after the middle of the sixteenth century began to employ this feature, which served both functional and decorative purposes.

Polychrome mosque lamps were often paired with spherical ornaments, similar to blue-and-white examples (see 167). These ornaments are generally divided into two halves with the decoration applied to the hemisphere facing down while a blank zone encircled the top. They are supplied with two axial holes used for attaching suspension cords or chains as well as decorative tassels.

One of the largest polychrome balls (196) has around its lower hole a turquoise quatrefoil composed of red rumis, each lobe enclosing a hatayi. Surrounding the quatrefoil are four white cartouches that fill the triangular voids between its lobes and create a medallion. Branches evolving from the tips of the quatrefoil form another group of four white cartouches framed by red rumis that extend to the widening sides of the globe. This zone, painted blue, is filled with additional hatayis linked by stems to the central blossoms. The complex design produces not only a series of overlapping and intersecting elements, but skillfully juxtaposes primary and secondary

271

themes. The upper hemisphere is blank, with a thin blue line and a row of trefoils lining its perimeter.

There are several equally large hemispherical ornaments, each decorated with a different composition.[123] Similar to the large polychrome mosque lamps, they appear to have been popular in the second half of the sixteenth century. The production of these ceramic lamps and ornaments reflects a trend in decorating the structures as well as the flowering of İznik workshops.

Ceramic objects with intricate saz scrolls, fantastic foliage, and sophisticated designs coexisted with another group which relied on simpler compositions and motifs, frequently representing sprays of roses and rosebuds intermingled with carnations, tulips, and blossoming fruit-tree branches. A characteristic of this group is a red rose in full bloom, shown in profile with its layered petals detailed in reserve, accompanied by buds and ovoid leaves.

This flower appears on a variety of objects, including a lidded bowl with a high foot in the British Museum (**197**). The lid surmounted by a large knob repeats the shape of the rounded body, creating a flattened globe with two axial extensions, one forming the knob, the other the slender flaring foot. The knob, surmounted by a red blossom, joins the lid

198 (above). Jug with sprays of roses, second half sixteenth century (Paris, Musée du Louvre, 7595)

199 (right). Plate with floral spray and two birds, second half sixteenth century (New York, The Metropolitan Museum of Art, 59.69.1)

197. Covered bowl with sprays of roses, second half sixteenth century (London, The British Museum, Fb. Is. 5)

with a series of bands decorated with overlapping petals and braids. Growing from the outer band and radiating toward the edge of the lid are four blue cypress trees alternating with sprays containing a pair of large roses and a rosebud amid leaves and two small crocuslike flowers; at the base of the spray is a lobed crescent. A blue band with bisected blossoms facing down encircles the lid.

An identical band, with its half blossoms facing up, appears around the rim of the bowl. The walls show the same design used on the lid with a pair of additional red tulips flanking the roses. The flora grow up from the base of the bowl, counteracting the downward orientation of the motifs on the lid. The foot contains tulips alternating with crocuses, which grow down, following the direction on the lid. Inside the bowl is a medallion with a multipetaled blossom.

Covered bowls, also produced in four-color ware with purple, were at times painted in reserve on blue or red grounds.

They all have central medallions inside the base; in some the foot ring is also embellished. A few are symmetrical; the lid is identical in shape and decoration to the bowl and the foot ring is used as a knob. These examples served a double function; they were used as covered containers and, when separated, as two individual pieces.

Roses, mixed with other types of blossoms, also appear on a jug (198). The rim of this example has the same band with the bisected blossoms. The neck contains four stems with red flowers flanked by crocuses alternating with sprays bearing blue blossoms. A sketchy braid and a frieze of overlapping petals encircle the lower edge of the neck.

The pear-shaped body is decorated with four rosebushes, each with two branches; one branch is upright and bears a large rose and the other bends over, breaks, and curves downward, its blossom placed at the bottom. Leaves and small crocuses grow from the same cluster. One of the bushes

deviates from the scheme and shows a multipetaled red blossom instead of a rose at its base. Between the roses are three sprays with blue flowers. The central spray, which grows higher, has serrate-petaled flowers, while the lateral ones repeat the type used on the neck. The flaring foot is encircled by a series of black lines. The curving handle has two bold vertical lines with horizontal strokes applied to the outer surface, following the formula used on ceramic jugs.

The flowers, which grow upward from the base of the neck and the body, sway in alternating directions and create a movement that enhances the rounded shape of the jug. This movement is countered by the swirling and bent branches, which provide additional interest and enliven the composition.

The bent or broken branch that counteracts the energetic growth of sprays was a common device used in polychrome wares and appears on an unusual plate representing two tiny birds amid oversize blossoms (199). The foliate rim of this ex-

200. Plate with rumi scroll, late sixteenth century (New York, The Metropolitan Museum of Art, 66.4.13)

201. Plate with galleon, late sixteenth century (Copenhagen, The David Collection, 24/1975)

ample exhibits the wave pattern, which in the second half of the sixteenth century became a formulaic decorative theme; here it is painted in blue and accentuated with green and red. The center contains stems that spring from a cluster of leaves, curve around the plate, and bear different flowers: a branch from a fruit tree, a small crocus, a large tulip, a rose, an iris, and a spray of hyacinths. The stem with the tulip breaks at the edge of the composition, its blossom, flanked by two large leaves, overlaying the other elements. Perched on this stem is a handsome long-tailed bird with a crest facing a smaller bird, which stands on a leaf on the other side of the central rose. The birds seem to represent the male and female of the same species with blue feathers, green wings, and red beaks and feet. The exterior of the plate shows pairs of tulips alternating with blossoms.

Confronting male and female birds separated by a large rose, a flower associated with unrequited love, appear to contain a specific meaning. The iconography of flowers on İznik ceramics has not been properly studied, although Ottoman society was deeply involved with their meaning, and produced volumes devoted to such flowers as tulips and hyacinths.

İznik potters also made plates decorated with traditional designs in addition to those employing saz themes and naturalistic flora. One of these is painted blue and decorated with a bold rumi scroll reserved in white and accentuated by red and green (200). The symmetrical composition evolves from two large rumis that grow from the base and rejoin to form a trefoil; their stems loop through a cartouche placed in the center, fan out, and come together to create an ogival medallion at the top as well as large volutes at the sides. Additional stems spring from a stylized blossom placed in the trefoil, intersect, overlap, or join the first scroll, their elements filling the voids. The familiar wave pattern appears on the rim and

the equally stereotyped alternating bunches of tulips and rounded blossoms are on the exterior.

The design in the center is taken from tiles with scrolling rumis that have an airy and rhythmic flow and cover large surfaces. The most outstanding examples rendered with delicate rumis were used in the Harem suite built by Sinan for Murad III in 1578. A fragment of a border in the British Museum displays a bolder treatment of the same motif, which resembles that of this plate.[124]

A different effect is achieved in another late-sixteenth-century plate, which represents a galleon caught in a turbulent storm (201) with crested waves crashing against its hull and violent gusts of wind whipping the sails and flags, creating a dramatic composition. The galleon has a black hull, blue and red decks decorated with blossoms and crosshatching, and fully rigged masts with plain, striped, or speckled sails. Two sets of cloud bands appear at the top, while sea monsters and large fish jump menacingly around the ship. The wave pattern in the everted rim unifies the composition by repeating the turbulence of the sea.

The style of the galleon can be traced to an earlier blue-and-turquoise plate (see 177), which in turn was inspired by contemporary manuscript illustrations. Sailboats and galleons were frequently depicted on late-sixteenth- and early-seventeenth-century plates, as well as jugs, jars, and bottles.[125]

A group of polychrome-painted ware dating from the second half of the sixteenth century employs a different technique, and shows a predominance of naturalistic flowers. The objects are covered with an engobe tinted various shades of blue and red and underglaze-painted in polychrome slips. One of these slip-painted objects is a high-footed bowl with a coral-colored engobe (202). A blue-and-white braid encircles the rim and the lower edge of the flaring foot. Decorating the

202. Bowl with carnations, second half sixteenth century (Paris, Musée du Louvre, 6325)

275

203. Plate with tulips, second half sixteenth century (Kuwait National Museum, LNS 323 C)

body are eight bushes, each with stems bearing a white and red carnation, a white tulip, and a spray of blue blossoms. The stems and leaves are rendered in black, with white dots added to the bases of the leaves. The stems with the tulips revolve around the bushes, bend at the top, and swoop down and across, their blossoms overlaying the other elements; this feature has been observed on several other İznik examples (see **189, 198,** and **199**). Small black cloud bands, cut off by the rim band, appear between each spray. The foot contains white carnations alternating with blue blossoms, repeating the scheme on the body; the blossoms here, however, grow down toward the edge. The interior, also covered with engobe, has a central medallion enclosing the same bush depicted on the exterior. The bowl may have had a domical lid, similar to another polychrome example (see **197**).

One of the slip-painted plates has a pinkish mauve engobe and a radiating design in its center (**203**). Its lobed rim contains blue and white tulips alternating with blue leaves overlaid by sprays of red blossoms. In the center is a blue blossom surrounded by white flowers that recall sweet alyssum. Radiating from this core are eight sprays alternately bearing blue and white tulips or blue leaves superimposed with red sprays, repeating the theme used on the rim. One of the leaves swoops under the other, crosses over, and lies on top of

the stems, producing a counterclockwise movement. White hyacinths that evolve from the same spray lean over in the opposite direction, providing contrary motion. Black cloud bands, intersected by the foliate band around the central medallion, fill the voids between the sprays.

The double swirling pattern is extremely effective and enlivens the otherwise static design. Although there are several slip-painted plates with concentric or circular designs, the radiating and revolving movement depicted in this example is extraordinary. Tulips decorated with blue and white chevrons are also unusual.

Most slip-painted plates follow the classical composition with sprays of blossoms springing from a central source,[126] as exemplified by a blue-ground plate in Ecouen (**204**). Its plain rim defined by foliated lines shows red carnations alternating with bunches of white blossoms. The same flowers appear in the sprays decorating the center, growing from a cluster of leaves. The branch in the middle begins with a pair of white blossoms, splits into two, extends to the sides with additional white blossoms, and terminates with red carnations. The lateral branches bear white sweet alyssum; one has an additional flower growing in the center, while the other sprouts a pair of carnations. The remaining branches swing down along the lower edges and bear large white flowers.

The symmetry of the composition is relieved by the carefree placement of the blossoms, producing an airy and flowing design. The exterior of the plate shows the traditional scheme of pairs of tulips alternating with multipetaled blossoms.

The same blue engobe appears on a tankard (**205**), a cylindrical vessel with an angular handle also produced in metal as well as in jade (see **53** and **66**). The bands at the rim and base employ the çintemani pattern with clusters of triple white dots separated by diagonal black wavy lines arranged in a chevron pattern. The body depicts four large swooping saz leaves that alternate with curving branches bearing blossoms with serrated petals, carnations, oversize irises, and tiny crocuses. The branches cross over one another behind the leaves, creating a delightfully vibrant contrapuntal composition. The sides of the handle have sketchy leaves, while the upper edge bears horizontal strokes commonly found on the handles of ceramic jugs and tankards.

The iris with linear petals and the crocus were represented on the plate with two birds (see **199**). These motifs, once within the repertoire of the potters, were applied to various objects executed in different techniques.

Some of the slip-painted pieces depict the main themes in white on a blue ground or use polychrome on a coral-colored engobe.[127] A more unusual example is a red-ground bottle decorated with rumis painted in a wider range of colors that includes blue, white, lavender, and purple. The body is pierced with regularly spaced holes, presumably to hold gems set into mounts,[128] recalling the practice applied to a group of porcelains. The embellishment of a slip-painted object with precious materials indicates that the court valued these products as highly as Chinese pieces.

The production of slip-painted ware did not extend beyond the sixteenth century. Although this technique was also applied to tiles, it was not very successful, since painting with polychrome pigments on a smooth white surface offered greater freedom to the potters.

One of these tiles painted with polychrome pigments is a relatively large single piece decorated with a saz scroll (206). Designed as an independent panel, it is framed by a row of trefoils with additional braids placed along its sides. The saz scroll, with its highly detailed compound hatayis, leaves, buds, and blossoms that overlay, intersect, and pierce one another, represents the ultimate expression of this style. A series of branches radiate from a large central hatayi filled with a multitude of small flowers and pods; they bear curving feathery leaves and smaller hatayis that are superimposed by

204 (left). Plate with carnations and sweet alyssum, second half sixteenth century (Ecouen, Musée de la Renaissance, C1. 8549)

205 (above). Tankard with floral sprays, second half sixteenth century (Paris, Musée du Louvre, A.A. 403)

277

206 (above). Tile with saz scroll, second half sixteenth century (Paris, Musée du Louvre, 3919/2/287)

207 (right). Tombstone with floral spray (both sides), second half sixteenth century (London, Victoria and Albert Museum, 862-1901)

sprays, sprout buds and blossoms, and overlap and/or pierce one another. The cutting of the elements by the frame suggests that the scroll extends beyond the panel and that what is captured here is only a portion of an infinitely larger design.

The sinuous rhythm of the composition and the self-assurance, power, and virtuosity of brushwork indicate that a master painter conceived it. An identical piece, in the Harvard University Art Museums in Cambridge, suggests that the design was reproduced on several panels used to decorate an unidentified building.[129]

Another single tile is shaped as a small flat tombstone with a pointed arch at the top and a wider articulated base (207). Each side is outlined by a red band and contains a central lobed oval flanked by two different floral arrangements that grow symmetrically from leaves and pods placed at the bottom. The narrow edges are painted green. The blue oval, framed in green and supplied with a pair of axial trefoils, is inscribed in four lines of white sülüs. The text begins with the kelime-i tevhid and concludes with a prayer for the soul of the deceased: ''la ilahe illallah Muhammed rasulullah rahmetullah aliye'' (there is no god but God, Muhammed is his Prophet, may God show mercy to him). The shape of the

lobed medallion with pendants recalls those used both in bookbindings and dedicatory pages in manuscripts.

On the lower portion on one of the sides are pairs of roses, tulips, and sprays of hyacinth; two long rosebushes filled with buds and pods grow around the central oval and terminate at the top with large blossoms. Cloud bands appear along the edges and a rumi cartouche enclosing a blossom appears at the apex of the arch. On the other side are the same roses and tulips at the base; the hyacinths are omitted and the rosebushes are replaced with two flowering fruit-tree branches.

The kelime-i tevhid, which declares the unity of God, is frequently used in mausoleums and on objects made for religious monuments, including mosque lamps (see 195). It also appears on carved tombstones. This tile could not have been intended as a tombstone since the name of the deceased is not given in the inscription. Yet its shape, which re-creates the mihrab niche, and its wording indicate a religious context. The tile may have been made as a commemorative plaque for a mausoleum and placed on a wall to represent the mihrab.

Naturalistic flora also decorate a series of tiles shaped as spandrels, which were used in pairs over doorways, win-

278

dows, or niches, as represented in contemporary manuscripts (see **28a**). Their triangular shapes with articulated inner sides resemble the corner quadrants employed in bookbindings. One pair of these decorative architectural elements (**208**) is painted with three sprays that grow from the lobed edges and extend toward the top, overlapping one another. The one springing from the lowest lobe bears a rose and a small crocus that swings back toward the stem. Another grows from the next lobe, sprouts several rosebuds and pods, and terminates with a large blossom with swirling petals. The third, which has at its base a beautifully drawn pair of twisted saz leaves, contains several stems that bear roses, rosebuds, crocuses, fruit tree flowers, and large blossoms with swirling petals. Tiny cloud bands appear along the sides while rumis fill the facing corners of the upper lobes. The spandrels are framed with blue lines, their edges painted green.

The delicate interplay of twisting, turning, and overlapping stems with flowers of diverse types growing in opposite directions produces a fanciful and exhilarating composition that projects a sense of vitality and endless springtime. A pair of spandrels with a tighter and more static composition employing similar blossoms with swirling petals is in the Victoria and Albert Museum; another pair with blue fruit-tree blossoms is in the Metropolitan Museum of Art and a second identical pair is divided between the Çinili Köşk and Kuwait.[130]

The majority of the tile panels produced during the second half of the sixteenth century were constructed from a number of square pieces, which were affixed to the walls next to one another and completed the design. Areas with specific shapes, such as those around the mihrabs and over doors and windows, required greater care in devising compositions that fit the requirements of the architects. The ingenuity of İznik potters is observed in a series of lunettes with pointed arches thought to have come from a palace built next to the Mosque of Piyale Paşa constructed in 1573.[131]

These panels, decorated with identical saz scrolls and cloud bands, are composed of sixteen tiles, one half of which are

208. Pair of spandrels with floral sprays, second half sixteenth century (Copenhagen, The David Collection, 2/1962)

square while the remaining are shaped to fit the lunette. As seen in the example in Boston (209), each panel is framed by a blue band with blossoms joined to a pair of curving leaves, which overlap other blossoms and are themselves overlaid with tulips, and form reciprocal S-shaped motifs. In the central field is a trefoil created by red cloud bands that knot at the base and swirl out to the sides. Inside the trefoil is a composite hatayi with branches growing from its outer petals and forming at the sides spiral scrolls bearing blossoms, buds, and leaves. Other branches evolve from the knot and develop similar formations. The elements overlap, twist, turn, and

pierce one another in the characteristic saz manner. Although the design was reproduced from a cartoon and copied on a series of panels, each shows a fresh rendition.

Piyale Paşa, who served as the grand admiral of the Ottoman fleet between 1554 and 1568, was married to Hace Gevheri Mülük, the daughter of Selim II. His mosque was once part of a complex thought to have been designed by Sinan. Other tiles in this building show the same high quality observed in the lunettes, and are composed of similar saz scrolls.[132] The lunettes, made for one of the buildings in the complex or for Piyale Paşa's residence, were most likely

209. Lunette with saz scroll from the Palace of Piyale Paşa, c. 1573 (Boston, Museum of Fine Arts, 06.2437)

placed over windows or doors, or used to decorate the porticos, as observed in several contemporary mosques.[133]

Among the most renowned sixteenth-century tiles are three panels originally commissioned by Murad III for the chamber adjacent to the imperial baths in the Harem of the Topkapı Palace. These panels, later moved to an area known as the Golden Passage (Altın Yol), are constructed of forty-five square tiles and decorated with Persian verses placed above the arches, each of which has a different composition.[134]

One of them (**210**) is framed with a turquoise and red band decorated with white rumis; the same band appears below the narrow panel with the inscriptions at the top, and

defines the central arch. The inscriptions, in white talik on a blue ground, fill two oval cartouches within the panel. A few floral elements grow from the letters, and one daring tulip even pierces a horizontal stroke. The spandrels of the arch are filled with white cloud bands on a red ground. The deep blue field encloses a glorious flowering fruit tree, its turquoise branches bearing red and white blossoms and buds. Growing at its base is a rich cluster of leaves overlaid by floral sprays and surrounded by bunches of tulips, hyacinths, and buds. Two other bushes with tulips, carnations, and roses flank the foot of the tree with additional small sprays placed between.

The verses in the oblongs state that the *şahnişin* of the ex-

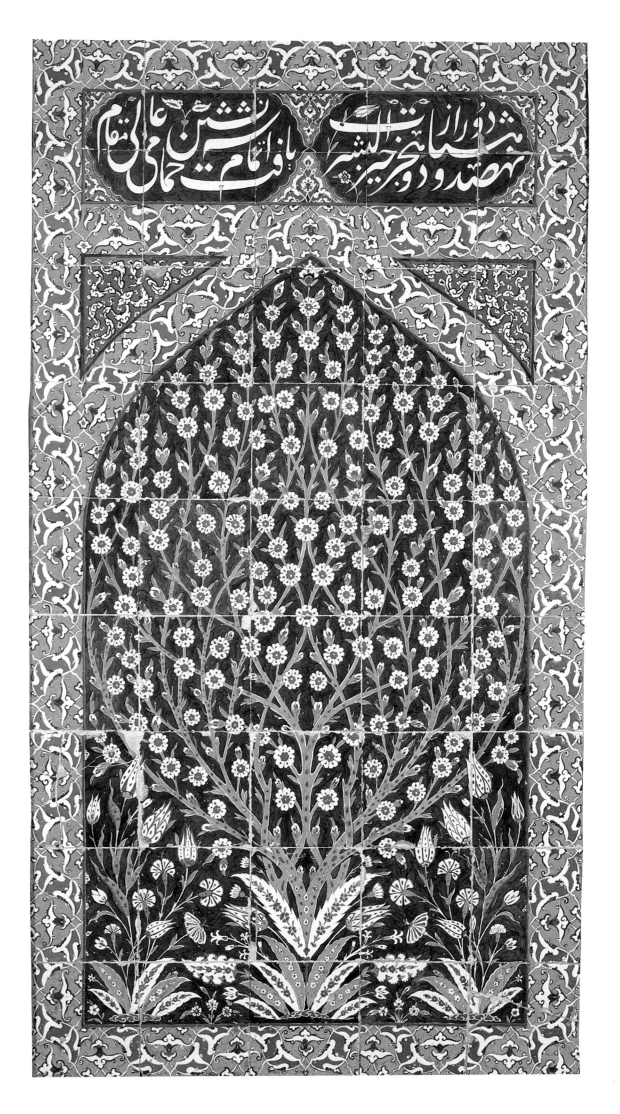

alted bath was completed in the auspicious year 1574/1575. This word, generally applied to bay windows in enclosed balconies, must refer to the arches in the tiles used to face the walls of this chamber. There must have been a series of these panels that created the illusion of an arcade, beyond which was a paradise garden filled with fantastic foliage. The scheme of using a row of tile panels decorated with arches was also employed in the Harem suite dating from the same period, showing painted marble columns, capitals, and voussoirs.[135] It also appears in the Mausoleum of Murad III and in the Mosque of Ahmed I.[136]

The impact of nakkaşhane designs is evident in the composition of this panel; blossoming fruit trees placed on a blue ground was a favorite theme employed in the illuminations of the most celebrated manuscripts produced during the reign of Süleyman, including the 1546/1547 Koran of Ahmed Karahisari and the 1558 biography of the sultan (see **9a** and **41a–41d**).

This design was popularly applied to tiles, including those decorating the Mausoleum of Hürrem Sultan,[137] the Mosque of Rüstem Paşa,[138] the facade of the Sünnet Odası,[139] the Selimiye Mosque in Edirne,[140] the Aya Sofya Library,[141] and the Mosque of Sultan Ahmed I,[142] surviving into the seventeenth century.

The overwhelming influence of the nakkaşhane on all the imperial arts was due to the collaborative genius of scores of talented and conscientious artists. Guided by Süleyman, a demanding patron with an impeccably refined sense of aesthetics and connoisseurship, they left a splendid legacy for future generations.

210. Tile panel from the Harem of the Topkapı Palace, dated 1574/1575 (İstanbul, Topkapı Sarayı Müzesi, 8/1067)

NOTES

1. For a study of Chinese porcelains in İstanbul see Zimmerman 1930; and J.A. Pope 1972. A thorough study of the history of this collection appears in Raby and Yücel 1986.

2. This classification was established by Arthur Lane in *Later Islamic Pottery* (published in 1957 and revised in 1971) and elaborated in his article on Iznik ware in 1957. See also Denny 1980 and Carswell 1982 for excellent studies on Ottoman ceramics.

3. The most famous of the Bursa buildings using these techniques are the Green Mosque and Mausoleum built between 1419 and 1424. See Denny 1980, ills. 139–141 and pls. 35 and 36; and Carswell 1982, pls. 56a, 57, and 58a.

4. See Öz 1957, pls. XXII–XXVI; and Öney 1976, 65.

5. For one of the lunettes from this structure see İstanbul 1983, E. 51.

6. The tiles of this building are studied in Yenişehirlioğlu 1980.

7. See Riefstahl 1937 for a study of the tiles in this building; see Gasparini 1985 for a recent publication of the wall paintings.

8. See Denny 1980, pl. 38 for a reproduction of one of these lunettes.

9. See Denny 1980, ills. 151 and 152, where they are dated to c. 1525.

10. For a study of the mosque lamps see Ünal 1969, 82–89. The decorations of the Gebze and Manisa structures have not been properly investigated. For illustrations of these tiles see Carswell 1980, pls. 61a and 62.

11. This piece has been published a number of times. For a detailed study of the ewer and its inscriptions see Carswell 1972, 78, 79, and 81. The date 959 is written out in the Armenian calendar, which corresponds to A.D. 1510. It has been suggested that the ewer was made in Kütahya, which is possible since it appears to be a provincial copy with an awkward shape and relatively crude drawing.

12. Lane 1957, 254.

13. These pieces are now in the Victoria and Albert Museum.

14. See Düsseldorf 1973, no. 304 for rare fragments in Berlin.

15. Carswell 1972, 79–81; the year 978 (A.D. 1529) is written out and rendered in the Armenian calendar, similar to the ewer dated 1510.

16. Denny 1980, pls. 44 and 45; and Mahir 1986, figs. 20 and 21.

17. Mahir 1986, fig. 22.

18. Several in the Victoria and Albert and the British Museum are published in Lane 1957, fig. 36; Denny 1977, fig. 143; Rogers 1983b, no. 140; and Frankfurt 1985, vol. 2, no. 2/66. Meant to be set on their points, they measure 28 cm (11 in.) from top to bottom.

19. These fragments, which are in Berlin, are published in Lane 1957, fig. 32; and Zick-Nissen 1976, fig. 10.

20. This example, which is in Vienna, is published in Rogers 1983b, fig. 8.

21. This famous piece is published many times, including in Lane 1957, fig. 42; Ünal 1969, pl. II; Lane 1971, pl. 38; Denny 1980, ill. 153; and Carswell 1982, pl. 87.

22. There is another fragmentary lamp in the British Museum that is thought to have come from the same building; this example is decorated in an identical manner but does not contain inscriptions giving the date, city, and name of the maker.

23. Carswell 1984. See also Carswell 1982, pl. 78; and Paris 1977, no. 587 for similar tiles.

24. See Rackham 1934/1935, pls. 17a and b. The example with the young man is also published in Lane 1957, fig. 41; and Frankfurt 1985, vol. 2, no. 2/12.

25. This piece is in the Victoria and Albert Museum.

26. See Denny 1977 for an analysis of the tiles in this building.

27. See Denny 1980, pls. 46, 47, and 49 for reproductions of these tiles.

28. This lamp was mentioned as being in the Süleymaniye Mosque in Fortnum 1869, 396.

29. Published in Ennès and Kalus 1979; and Frankfurt 1985, vol. 2, no. 2/42.

30. See, for instance, those illustrated in Frankfurt 1985, vol. 2, nos. 2/48 and 2/49.

31. London 1976, no. 419.

32. Rogers 1984, figs. 4 and 5.

33. See, for instance, two examples published in İstanbul 1983, E. 165; and Rogers 1984, pl. IX.

34. One of these, in the Kuyaş Collection in İstanbul, is published in Ünal 1969, fig. 25; another is mentioned as having been in the market in New York in Lane 1957, 278.

35. See Lane 1957, 277 and 278; and Carswell 1966.

36. See Lane 1957, 279 for Venetian purchases in 1573–1578.

37. See Lane 1957, figs. 29 and 30, and note 96 on 280; and Rogers 1983b, nos. 109, 110, 128, and 134.

38. See Lane 1957, 279 and fig. 46.

39. See Otto-Dorn 1941, 165–195 for these edicts.

40. See Raby 1976 for a study of İznik in this period.

41. See Lane 1957, fig. 48; and Carswell 1982, pls. 106–110 for Damascus tiles. Other Syrian tiles are discussed in Carswell 1978.

42. See Carswell 1982, pls. 111–114. A thorough study of the Diyarbakır tile industry appears in Raby 1977–1978.

43. For a historical survey of the Kütahya industry, especially in the eighteenth century, see Carswell 1972; see also Şahin 1979–1980.

44. Danışman 1969–1971, 2: 283.

45. Öz 1950, 52 and 53.

46. See, for instance, the group of maiolica vessels published in Lane 1957, fig. 45; see also Lane 1957, 280 for references to other copies made in Florence and Padua.

47. Cantagalli workshops used the mark of a rooster on the base of the pieces. Two large Cantagalli pieces decorated with saz scrolls, a polychrome vase painted with red and a high-footed bowl employing pale green and purple, were auctioned in London recently. See Sotheby's 1983, no. 161; and Sotheby's 1985a, no. 372. This workshop produced such fine copies that they were frequently mistaken for sixteenth-century İznik ware. There are two large polychrome vases in Florence (published in Öz 1957, pl. LXXI, no. 131) and in Seattle (illustrated in J. A. Pope 1972, fig. 15), which are identical to the one sold in London in 1983.

48. Raby and Yücel 1983.

49. Raby and Yücel 1983, fig. 15.

50. Raby and Yücel 1983, fig. 14.

51. The mosque lamp is illustrated in Ünal 1969, fig. 15.

52. See Lane 1957, figs. 27–30 for three of these ewers and fig. 31 for one of the jugs. A second jug, which has lost its handle, has a most unusual decoration with a landscape and a group of buildings that recall those in the illustrations by Piri Reis and by Nasuh; see İstanbul 1983, E. 39.

53. Only one candlestick belonging to this group is known; see Carswell 1982, pl. 70. Another, published in Frankfurt 1985, vol. 2, no. 2/5, seems to be problematic.

54. Carswell 1985, nos. 72 and 74.

55. See Lane 1957, figs. 3 and 5 for the jar and flask; for the others, page 261.

56. For a study of Kütahya production see Carswell 1972. See Carswell 1985 for the long-lasting and wide-ranging popularity of the blue-and-white ceramic tradition in Asia, Europe, and America.

57. Lane 1957, fig. 11.

58. See, for example, Fehérvári 1973, no. 192; Lisbon 1983, no. 38; and Rogers 1983b, no. 107.

59. Lane 1957 lists twelve blue-and-white or blue-and-turquoise examples, two with spiral scrolls, and five painted with green and purple. Most of these are in British and French museums.

60. Ünal 1969, figs. 2–6. See also Lane 1957, figs. 16–19; İstanbul 1983, E. 35 and 36; and Rogers 1983b, no. 108.

61. Ünal 1969, figs. 7–10. See also Lane 1957, figs. 20 and 21; Lane 1971, pl. 25a; London 1976, no. 409; İstanbul 1983, E. 37; and Frankfurt 1985, vol. 2, no. 2/7.

62. Two other related pieces are in Berlin and Paris; see Lane 1957, fig. 22; and Paris 1977, no. 582.

63. This example, in the Walters Gallery of Art, has holes at the top and bottom; inside the ball is a metal chain with a wooden tulip painted red, which suggests a post-1540s date. Another blue-and-white ball was recently sold in London (Sotheby's 1983, no. 160).

64. Illustrated in Ünal 1969, fig. 15.

65. The same shape appears in an eighteenth-century blue-and-white example, most likely produced in Kütahya. For a reproduction of this piece see Ünal 1965, fig. 9.

66. Lane 1957, fig. 6; and İstanbul 1983, E. 31.

67. Lane 1959, fig. 24; Paris 1977, nos. 583 and 584; Denny 1980, ill. 40; and İstanbul 1983, E. 32.

68. For a study of this group see Denny 1974a; for other examples see Paris 1971, no. 92; Düsseldorf 1973, nos. 311–313; Fehérvári 1973, no. 194; and İstanbul 1983, E. 34.

69. A small bowl in İstanbul, which combines these features with Chinese-inspired themes, appears to be the earliest in the series (İstanbul 1983, E. 38).

70. See, for instance, plates reproduced in Mustafa 1961, fig. 16; Düsseldorf 1973, no. 327; Fehérvári 1973, no. 196; Denny 1974a, figs. 15 and 16; and İstanbul 1983, E. 48.

71. J.A. Pope 1972, figs. 14 and 17.

72. Frankfurt 1985, vol. 2, no. 2/24.

73. Carswell 1982, no. 99; and Rogers 1983b, no. 126.

74. Carswell 1982, no. 98.

75. Frankfurt 1985, vol. 2, no. 2/28.

76. A. Welch 1979, no. 31; for a detail of the lamp, see Denny 1974a, fig. 18.

77. See Fehérvári 1973, no. 195. See also Denny 1974a, fig. 8 for a different handling of the same theme.

78. Rogers 1983b, no. 123.

79. See, for example, J.A. Pope 1972, figs. 8 and 9; Atıl 1973a, no. 80; Copenhagen 1973, 100; and Carswell 1982, pls. 76 and 77.

80. For some of these examples see Lane 1971, pl. 32B; and Fehérvári 1973, no. 193.

81. For an example with purple grapes see Paris 1977, no. 591; one of the plates with red grapes is published in J.A. Pope 1972, fig. 3.

82. See, for instance, the plates in J.A. Pope 1972, fig. 2; Atıl 1973a, no. 83; and İstanbul 1983, E. 47.

83. Published in Carswell 1982, pl. 75; and Riyadh 1985, no. 128.

84. Its celadon prototype is discussed in J.A. Pope 1972.

85. Paris 1977, no. 584.

86. See Atıl 1981b, no. 72.

87. See, for instance, Atıl 1973a, no. 81; and Carswell 1982, pl. 64b.

88. A plate painted in four colors including purple was published in İstanbul 1983, E. 50.

89. For a reproduction of this album page see Atıl 1978b, no. 13.

90. See, for example, the dedication pages in the 1558 *Süleymanname* reproduced in Atıl 1986, 84 and 85.

91. See the large footed bowl in the Victoria and Albert Museum published in Denny 1980, ill. 154; and İstanbul 1983, E. 49. In the same collection is another large bowl, the foot of which has been cut down. See Lane 1957, 271, n. 34.

92. This piece is mentioned in Lane 1957, 270.

93. One, in the Metropolitan Museum of Art, is published in Ünal 1969, fig. 11; and Denny 1977, fig. 3. Another, which is in İstanbul, was damaged during firing; it is reproduced in Ünal 1969, fig. 12.

94. See, for example, Metropolitan 1968, no. 20; Lane 1971, pl. 29A; and Edwards and Signell 1982, 33.

95. See, for instance, Lane 1971, pl. 34A; Copenhagen 1975, 103; Rogers 1983b, nos. 138 and 139; and Frankfurt 1985, vol. 2, no. 2/27.

96. See, for instance, Paris 1977, no. 588 for identical pieces.

97. See İstanbul 1983, E. 45; and Carswell 1982, pls. 83 and 84.

98. See the large example in Copenhagen 1975, 99.

99. Rogers 1983b, nos. 112 and 120.

100. See Copenhagen 1975, 114; Lisbon 1963, no. 64; and Frankfurt 1985, vol. 2, no. 2/68.

101. See, for instance, the example in the British Museum published in Lane 1957, fig. 44; and London 1976, no. 413. For another piece in the Victoria and Albert Museum, see Denny 1977, fig. 167.

102. For a study of this style and reproductions of several of these plates see Rogers 1985a.

103. Frankfurt 1985, vol. 2, no. 2/13.

104. Frankfurt 1985, vol. 2, no. 2/14.

105. Lane 1971, pl. 35A.

106. Denny 1981, fig. 4.

107. One of these is illustrated in Frankfurt 1985, vol. 2, no. 2/65.

108. See, for example, Lane 1971, pl. 36A; Atıl 1973a, no. 82; and Rogers 1985a, figs. 6, 7, 20, and 23.

109. For another plate that uses the same combination see Paris 1977, no. 593. This plate has a wave pattern on the rim and hatayis and pinecones in the central medallion.

110. A group of early seventeenth-century pieces with diverse animals and human figures, generally painted on a green ground, represents a folk tradition and is crudely painted. Whether they were made in İznik or not is speculative.

111. See, for instance, the tankard with a Turkish poem illustrated in London 1976, no. 419; and the covered bowl with verses by Hayati and Revani in Rogers 1984, figs. 4 and 5.

112. One of these, formerly in the Godman Collection, is published in Lane 1971, pl. 41A; and London 1976, no. 415. Another, in the British Museum, is illustrated in Hobson 1932, pl. 39a. A third example is in a private collection in New York. In Lane 1957, 279 and 280, n. 92, a fourth example is mentioned.

113. See, for instance, Paris 1953, no. 302; Denny 1977, fig. 172; Carswell 1982, pl. 81; Rogers 1983b, no. 114; and Rogers 1985a, fig. 24.

114. Similar pieces are illustrated in Rackham 1969, nos. 114 and 116; and Atıl 1973a, no. 84.

115. See, for example, the "lion" face on the polychrome mosque lamp published in Denny 1974a, fig. 18; and A. Welch 1979, no. 31.

116. One of these plates, painted blue, is in the Victoria and Albert Museum; another, in polychrome, was formerly in the Godman Collection, now bequeathed to the British Museum.

117. This piece, in the Musée National de Céramique in Sèvres, is reproduced in Erdmann 1963, fig. 43; Süslü 1976, fig. 3; and Denny 1981, fig. 5.

118. See Erdmann 1963, figs. 44 and 46; Süslü 1976, figs. 2 and 5–7; and Lane 1960, pl. 17a. A slightly different style is represented on an example published in İstanbul 1983, E. 163.

119. This chamber, now housing the sacred items associated with the Prophet Muhammed and called Hırka-i Saadet Odası, is not easily accessible. A few of these panels are reproduced in Öz 1957, pl. XLVIII; and Süslü 1976, figs. 8 and 9.

120. See Atıl 1973a, no. 88.

121. See Denny 1980, pl. 49.

122. Ünal 1969, fig. 21. For other polychrome lamps see Ünal 1969, figs. 22–25; A. Welch 1979, no. 31; and Rogers 1985b, figs. 1 and 5. One of these, published in Ünal 1969, fig. 25, contains a Hebrew inscription and must have been commissioned for a synagogue.

123. Two in Cairo are published in Mustafa 1961; another in the Benaki Museum is illustrated in Frankfurt 1985, vol. 2, no. 2/16; for a fourth, in the Brooklyn Museum, see Travelstead 1982.

124. Rogers 1983b, no. 133.

125. See, for example, Rackham 1959, pls. 205–211; Lane 1971, pl. 46B; Atıl 1973a, no. 86; Copenhagen 1975, 103; and Frankfurt 1985, vol. 2, no. 2/46.

126. For other examples of slip-painted plates using the same design see Lane 1971, pl. 44B; Denny 1974, fig. 7; and Rogers 1983b, nos. 130 and 135.

127. See, for instance, Lane 1971, pl. 45A; and İstanbul 1983, E. 167.

128. This bottle, the neck of which is broken, is illustrated in İstanbul 1983, E. 165.

129. This tile, which is not published, is registered under number 1960.17.

130. For the Çinili Köşk example see İstanbul 1983, E. 170. The others have not been published. The pair in the Metropolitan Museum of Art is registered under 02.5.89 and 02.5.90.

131. Close to a dozen of these lunettes are known to exist in Paris, Lisbon, London, Cologne, Berlin, Hamburg, Vienna, Kuwait, and Boston. Some are published in Lisbon 1963, no. 52; Paris 1971, no. 102; Düsseldorf 1973, no. 343; London 1973, no. 420; Vienna 1977, no. 55; and Frankfurt 1985, vol. 2, no. 2/70, where additional references are listed.

132. See Öz 1957, pl. XLIV. Fragments of a frieze from this mosque are now in Lisbon and Berlin; one of these is published in Frankfurt 1985, vol. 2, no. 2/75. Two other panels with Koranic inscriptions said to be from the same mosque show a totally different style; these are illustrated in Jenkins 1983, 117; and Frankfurt 1985, vol. 2, no. 2/67.

133. See, for instance, those in the Mosque of Takkeci İbrahim Ağa built in 1592, illustrated in Öz 1957, pl. LIII. For other lunettes see Denny 1977, figs. 38–43.

134. For color illustrations, see Yücel 1978, 2 and 3. See also Öz 1957, pls. XLVI and XLVII; and İstanbul 1983, E. 155–157.

135. Öz 1957, pl. LI; and Öney 1976, frontispiece.

136. Öz 1957, pls. LV and LVI; and Öney 1976, 54.

137. Öz 1957, pl. XXXIII; and Denny 1977, fig. 201.

138. Öz 1957, pl. XXXVIII; and Denny 1977, figs. 52, 104, and 215.

139. Öney 1976, 86; and Denny 1977, figs. 136 and 220.

140. Öney 1976, 88.

141. Otto-Dorn 1957, fig. 68.

142. Öney 1976, 54.

Appendixes

Appendix 1

Vakfiye of Hürrem Sultan

The vakfiye for Hürrem's endowment in the Aksaray district of İstanbul,[1] called the Külliye of Haseki Hürrem, lists the salaries and duties of the personnel in this complex as well as those in a mosque in Ankara. The Külliye, which comprised a mosque, imaret, medrese, elementary school, hospital, and fountain, was built in the section then called Avrat Pazarı, later named Haseki in Hürrem's honor.[2] It was the first monument constructed in the capital by Sinan after he was appointed the chief royal architect. Completed in 1538/1539, the complex is the third largest in the capital; the larger ones were established by Mehmed II (Fatih) and Süleyman (Süleymaniye). The mosque, which is across the street from the rest of the buildings, was enlarged in 1612; the medrese was restored in later years and its cuerda seca lunettes were removed to the Çinili Köşk;[3] the imaret was functioning until recently, providing meals to some five hundred persons a day; the hospital is still used as a medical center for women.

The vakfiye relates only to the mosque, medrese, and imaret in İstanbul and to the mosque in Ankara. It also states that the income is to be provided by the lands assigned to Hürrem Sultan. The following is a summary of the conditions set forth by the donor.

Conditions of endowment relating to the mosque:
  per diem of fifteen dirhems to an imam to read the Koran every day;
  per diem of eight dirhems to a *hatib* (preacher) to pray during Fridays and bayrams;
  per diem of eight dirhems to a *müezzin* (person who calls for prayer);
  per diem of one and a half dirhems each to six persons to continually read the Koran;
  per diem of four dirhems to one person to teach the recitation of the Koran;
  per diem of one dirhem each to seven persons to read the Koran in memory of Hürrem Sultan after her death;
  monthly salary of a quarter dirhem to one person to read at least ten verses from the Koran after each evening prayer;
  per diem of three dirhems to as many persons as required to open and close the doors and light and extinguish the lamps;
  per diem of two dirhems to as many persons as required to provide water (for ablutions);
  and adequate water for other essential personnel, their salaries to be determined by their duties.

Conditions of endowment relating to the medrese:
  per diem of fifty dirhems to a virtuous *müderris* (professor);
  per diem of five dirhems to his chief assistant;
  per diem of two dirhems to his second assistant.

Conditions of endowment relating to the imaret:
  per diem of eight dirhems to a şeyh;
  per diem of five dirhems to a supervisor of the storehouse;
  per diem of four dirhems to the recorder of the goods in the storehouse;
  per diem of three dirhems to a handyman to undertake the necessary repairs;
  two meals, including one meat dish, will be distributed each day;
  Fridays during Kandil (four feasting days commemorating Prophet Muhammed's birth, revelation, ascent, and the Night of Power) and Ramazan (month of fasting), rice pilav and honey will be distributed; on the Prophet's, birthday *zerde* pilav (pilav with saffron) will be prepared;
  meals distributed in the imaret will also be made available to the students in the medrese; to the imam, hatib, müezzin, caretaker of the mosque; and to all other personnel employed in the Külliye;
  during Kurban Bayramı (Festival of Sacrifice in the month of Zilhicce) ten rams will be slain and their meat distributed to the poor; candles will be lit in the Zaviye (Dervish Lodge) of Toklu Dede (which must be the Toklu İbrahim Dede Mescidi dating from the Byzantine period, converted into a mosque by Mehmed II, and later used as a dervish lodge).

Conditions of endowment relating to the mosque in Ankara:
  per diem of four dirhems to an imam to lead prayers five times a day and present the hutba on Fridays;
  per diem of three dirhems each to two müezzin;
  per diem of two dirhems each to six reciters of the Koran;
  per diem of one dirhem each to the caretakers, lamp lighters, and other necessary personnel.

Babüssade Ağası was appointed as the *nazır* (administrator) of the endowment and Mehmed Bey b. Abdürrahman was the *mütevelli* (trustee). The vakfiye was signed on 18 Receb 947 (18 November 1540) in the presence of witnesses.

NOTES

1. See 6.
2. Goodwin 1971, 204–206.
3. One of these lunettes was published in İstanbul 1983, E. 51.

Appendix 2

Palace Expenses

A. Expenses for the *şahname-i hassa* 960 (1552/1553) to 963 (1555/1556): TOTAL 21,056 akçes.[1]

1.	gold leaf (*varak-ı zer*) for sprinkling, 178 packs	2,805
2.	ink (*mürekkeb*)	209
3.	paper (*devlet-abadi*), 356 pieces (*kıta*)	3,392
4.	paper (*semerkandi*), 192 pieces	800
5.	gold leaf and lapis lazuli (*laciverd*) for the chief grinder	200
6.	lapis lazuli, indigo blue (*çivid*), resin (?, *aşı*), vermilion (*zencefre*), white lead (*isfidaç*), red lead (*sülüngen*), yellow (*zerd*), green (*sebz*), camel (*lök*), soot black (*dude*) for the paintings (*tasvirat*)	185
7.	salary of Mustafa, *katib-i şahname*, 962 (1554/1555) to 963 (1555/1556), fifteen months and 12 days	4,620
8.	subsistence (*nafaka*) for thirty katiban, 343 days	1,826
9.	subsistence for fifteen nakkaşan for 58 days	558
10.	wages (*ücret*) for katiban for writing 45,000 verses	4,200
	a) 15,000 verses at 600	
	b) 30,000 verses at 3,600	
11.	wages for the chief grinder of the katiban	200
12.	wages for the bookbinder, cardboard, and chemicals	20
13.	wages for the katib for final copying of the text (*beyaz-ı şahname*)	1,880
14.	wages for the carpenters for constructing partitions in the chamber of the katiban in the quarters (*derhane*) of Fethullah Çelebi, the şahnameci	161

B. Expenses for the *mesahif-i şerife* (Korans) for the *cami-i şerif* (Süleymaniye ?) 960 (1552/1553) to 963 (1555/1556): TOTAL 88,489 akçes.[2]

1.	paper (*devlet-abadi*), 2,653 pieces (*kıta*)	26,624
	a) 168 pieces at 8	
	b) 436 pieces at 8.5	
	c) 101 pieces at 9	
	d) 336 pieces at 9.5	
	e) 627 pieces at 10	
	f) 144 pieces at 10.5	
	g) 275 pieces at 11	
	h) 252 pieces at 11.5	
	i) 314 pieces at 12	
2.	high-quality leather (*sağrıha-i ala*), 14 pieces at 30	420
3.	cardboard and chemicals for bindings, 16 pieces at 20	320

4.	leather (*sahtiyan*) for bindings, 12 pieces at 20		240
5.	wages for katiban		7,600
	a) Ahmed, katib and nakkaş, for transcribing and illuminating two volumes	4,500	
	b) Emir Efendi, for transcribing one volume	1,200	
	c) Sofi, one volume	1,900	
6.	expenses (*harc*) for the works of nakkaşan for illuminations, serlevhas, drawing of text lines		44,703
	a) Şah Mehmed, five volumes	6,300	
	b) Mehmed Eyyubi, six volumes	5,000	
	c) Ali b. Bayram, three volumes	2,900	
	d) Abdülgani nakkaş, one volume	4,000	
	e) Kara Mehmed, one volume	6,000	
	f) Evrenos, two volumes	2,215	
	g) İsmail, eight volumes	15,788	
	h) Hacı Abi, katib and nakkaş, chemicals, for one volume	2,500	
7.	expenses for bookbindings		3,050
	a) Hüseyin Çelebi, seven volumes	1,350	
	b) Mustafa Çelebi, eight volumes	1,300	
	c) Hürrem Çelebi, one volume	200	
	d) Hacı Hasan Çelebi, one volume	200	
8.	expenses for inks and other items for the katiban		5,532
	a) Mehmed b. Şükrullah	450	
	b) Ali b. Husam	360	
	c) Korucuzade	490	
	d) Abdültayyib	120	
	e) Kadı Mahmud	1,200	
	f) Kasım Bey	810	
	g) Derviş Çelebi	400	
	h) Ahmed, brother of above	300	
	i) Hüsam Rumi	200	
	j) Hamdi b. Mustafa Şahzade	400	
	k) Piri b. Hızır	322	
	l) Mahmud Macar	100	
	m) Behram katib	380	

NOTES

1. This document, pertaining to the expenses accrued by the palace, is published in Barkan 1979, 69, no. l.

2. Barkan 1979, 69 and 70, no. m.

Appendix 3

Society of Painters and Bookbinders

The dates of the earliest payroll registers of the Ehl-i Hiref coincide with those of the reign of Süleyman. The Ehl-i Hiref documents were drawn four times a year and listed the members in ranking order, giving their names and daily wages in akçes. A number of these registers recording the nakkaşan and the mücellidan have been published[1] together with documents related to gifts presented from the artists to the sultan and special bonuses awarded by the sultan to the artists. The information presented in this appendix is a compilation of the registers dated between 1526 and 1566 together with related documents.

The following is a brief description of these payroll registers.

1. Undated register drawn before 1526:[2] lists forty-one members of the Cemaat-i Nakkaşan and nine members of the Cemaat-i Mücellidan.

   The nakkaşan were divided into twenty-nine masters and twelve apprentices, headed by Şahkulu, called ressam. Included in it are three men from Tabriz, two called Rumi, suggesting that they came from Rumelia, or the western provinces of the empire; and one each from Circassia (Çerkes) and Moldavia (Buğdan).

   The mücellidan included six masters and three apprentices, headed by Alaeddin-i Kullei. Two of the men are listed as being Circassians.

2. Document dated Rebiülahir 932[3] (15 January–12 February 1526): lists the same forty-one nakkaşan and eight of the mücellidan, giving information on their backgrounds and dates of entry into the society.

   Among the masters in the nakkaşhane were three men (including Şahkulu) who were exiled from Tabriz, went to Amasya, and then entered the imperial society in İstanbul; two others have appended to their names the word "Tebrizi," indicating that they too came from that city. Another "Tebrizi" master is definitely recorded as having originated from "Acem," that is, Azerbaijan or Iran; and finally there are four men who are mentioned as being the sons of "Acem" masters. Four others are listed as being the sons of former imperial painters with no indication of their origin; one was the son of the imperial gatekeeper; six were former slaves, purchased or given as gifts; seven others were gifts of various pages and officials; and three were assigned to the Edirne Palace.

   In addition to the ten members who are recorded as having come from Iran or being the sons of Iranians, the register contains two Circassians, an Albanian, and a Moldavian. Another breakdown indicates that nine members were recorded during the reign of Bayezid II, thirteen under Selim I, and nine entered the studio under Süleyman. The dates of entry of the others are not given. One of the apprentices in the mücellidan group, Cafer-i Çerkes, was omitted from this list. It is either an oversight or this man was no longer employed in 1526.

3. Register dated Muharrem, Safer, and Rebiülevvel 952[4] (15 March–11 June 1545): includes fifty-nine nakkaşan and twelve mücellidan.

   The nakkaşan were divided into two corps: the Bölük-i Rumiyan, headed by Şahkulu-i Bağdadi, consisted of twenty-four masters with twenty apprentices; and the Bölük-ı Aceman had eleven masters with four apprentices. The Rumiyan corps include four men from Bosnia (Bosna); three from Austria (Nemçe); two from Circassia; and one each from Albania (Arnavud), Moldavia, and Rumelia. The Aceman corps included ten masters from Tabriz and one apprentice from Isfahan.

   The mücellidan, headed by Mehmed b. Ahmed, had four Rumelian apprentices and one Austrian.

4. Document dated Rebiülevvel, Rebiülahir, and Cumadeyn 965[5] (22 December 1557–20 March 1558): lists thirty-four nakkaşan and ten mücellidan.

   The nakkaşan register consisted of only the Rumiyan corps, headed by Mehmed Şah. It included twenty-six masters and ten apprentices of which six were from Bosnia; two from Albania, Hungary (Macar), and Rumelia; and one each from Austria, Circassia, Georgia (Gürci), and Moldavia. It is possible that this is a partial listing of the society and the Aceman section was lost.

   The mücellidan document, headed by the same Mehmed b. Ahmed, contained only the names of the masters, with two from Rumelia and one from Bosnia.

5. Register drawn between Muharrem 965 and Muharrem 966[6] (24 October 1557–14 October 1558): included thirty-nine nakkaşan and ten mücellidan.

   The nakkaşan were once again divided into Rumiyan and Aceman corps. The former, headed by Kara Memi, consisted of twenty masters and six apprentices, five of whom came from Bosnia and one each from Albania, Georgia, Moldavia, and Rumelia. The latter had seven masters with six apprentices; five of them were from Tabriz, one each from Europe (Freng), Hungary, and Isfahan.

   The mücellidan, still headed by Mehmed b. Ahmed, included the same two men from Rumelia and one Bosnian.

6. Document drawn in Muharrem, Safer, and Rebiülevvel 974[7] (19 July–15 October 1566): listed thirty-eight nakkaşan and ten mücellidan.

   The nakkaşan in the Rumiyan corps, headed by Mehmed Sinan, consisted of twenty-two masters with ten apprentices. Six originated from Bosnia and one each from Albania, Georgia, Hungary, Moldavia, and Rumelia. Among the six Aceman members were four masters from Tabriz and one European.

   The mücellidan continued to be headed by Mehmed b. Ahmed and contained the same men listed in 1557–1558.

The next document is dated Receb, Şaban, and Ramazan 1005[8] (2 March–29 May 1596) and listed 124 nakkaşan equally divided into sixty-two masters and sixty-two apprentices without being separated into Rumiyan and Aceman corps. Almost all of the artists appear to be of local origin, with the exception of one man each from Albania, Bosnia, Europe, and Georgia. One of the apprentices by the name of Toma Manol must have been a foreigner, but his country of origin was not given. Two masters were listed as being from Edirne and Bursa. The society was headed by Lutfi Abdullah, sernakkaşan; below him are Cafer Abdullah, kethüda, and Yahya Abdullah, serbölük.

The mücellidan now had thirty-eight members, of whom twenty-three were masters. The group was headed by Süleyman b. Mehmed, the son of the former chief, and includes a kethüda, Hürrem-i Rum.

The register that followed, dated Muharrem, Safer, Rebiülevvel

1005[9] (26 August–22 November 1596) had 129 nakkaşan and thirty-nine mücellidan headed by the same artists. These two registers contained the largest number of salaried men in the history of the Ehl-i Hiref. Membership in the society showed a decrease in the ensuing years.

The charts below are based on the registers dated between 1526 and 1566, and list the artists in alphabetical order. Recorded under the dated registers are their daily wages, given in akçes. The section under Corps designates the groups to which they belonged, that is, Rum for Rumiyan and Acem for Aceman; *M* is used for master and *A* for apprentice. It should be noted that the divisions between Rumiyan and Aceman did not exist in 1526. The section on comments includes their titles (serbölük, sernakkaş, ressam, nakkaş, and so forth) together with information gathered from other sources, such as dates of entry into the societies and gifts exchanged between the sultan and the artists. Also included in this section is the information published on the expenses accrued by the Topkapı Palace relating to Korans made for the Süleymaniye between 1552/1553 and 1555/1556;[10] this document, marked with an asterisk (*), is translated in Appendix 2b.

A. Cemaat-i Nakkaşan (Society of Painters)

Name of Artist	1526	1545	1557/1558	1557–1558	1566	Corps	Comments
		Date of Register with Daily Wages				Corps	Comments
Abdülali-i Tebrizi		20		20		Acem M	nakkaş; gave gifts to the sultan c. 1555
Abdülfettah-i Tebrizi		12				Acem M	nakkaş; came from Tabriz in 1514; gave gifts to the sultan c. 1555
Abdülgani							musavvir and nakkaş; came from Tabriz in 1514; gave gifts to the sultan c. 1555; received from the sultan 2,000 akçes in 1555/1556; listed in 1552/1553–1555/1556 as having illuminated one Koran and paid 4,000 akçes*
Abdülhalik-i Tebrizi		12				Acem M	nakkaş; came from Tabriz in 1514; gave gifts to the sultan c. 1555
Abdülhamid-i Tebrizi		10.5		16		Acem M	nakkaş; gave gifts to the sultan c. 1550–1555
Abdülkerim b. Hasan Çelebi		2				Rum A	
Abdülmecid-i Tebrizi							nakkaş; received from the sultan 2,000 akçes in 1555/1556
Abdülvehhab b. Fazlullah	8.5					M	became apprentice when father, an imperial master, died during reign of Selim I
Abdürrahman							called cedvelkeş (one who draws margin lines) nakkaş; received from the sultan 2,000 akçes c. 1535
Ahi Bey-i Tebrizi		10		10	10	Acem M	nakkaş; came from Tabriz in 1514; gave gifts to the sultan c. 1550–1555; received from the sultan 1,000 akçes in 1555/1556
Ahmed	1.5					A	apprentice of İbrahim; former slave; registered 25 Zilkade 930 (15 October 1524)
Ahmed							katib and nakkaş; listed in 1552/1553–1555/1556 as having transcribed and illuminated two Korans and paid 4,500 akçes*
Ahmed Bey-i Tebrizi					10	Acem M	
Ahmed b. Kasım		6	6	6.5	7.5	Rum M	
Ahmed-i Firuz Bey	15	16				Rum M	nakkaş; slave of Firuz Bey; registered when master died during reign of Selim I; received from the sultan 1,500 akçes c. 1535
Ahmed-i Rumi	10					M	
Alaeddin Mehmed (Muhammed)							nakkaş; came from Tabriz in 1514; gave gifts to the sultan c. 1550–1555 together with his father (Muhammed ?) and brother Kemal
Ali	2	1				Rum A	apprentice of Hüseyin-i Rumi; registered 15 Şevval 925 (10 October 1519); sent to the Edirne Palace

	1526	1545	1557/1558	1557–1558	1566		
Ali							nakkaş; received from the sultan 1,000 akçes in 1511; given to Şehzade Mehmed in 1542
Ali Bey-i Tebrizi		11				Acem M	nakkaş; came from Tabriz in 1514; gave gifts to the sultan c. 1555
Ali b. Bayram			8	8	9.5	Rum M	listed in 1552/1553–1555/1556 as having illuminated three Korans and paid 2,900 akçes*
Ali b. Ferruh		1				Rum A	
Ali, brother of Abdülkerim		1	2	2		Rum A	
Ali, brother of Mehmed b. Bayram	7	8				Rum M	
Ali, brother of Mehmed b. Melek Ahmed	8	9				Rum M	
Ali-i Çerkes		2.5				Rum M	
Ali-i Macar			6			Rum M	
Ali-i Nemçe		1				Rum A	
Alikulu-i Tebrizi		3.5		4	6.5	Acem M	called *ama* (blind); nakkaş; came from Tabriz in 1514
Aliyyüddin-i Tebrizi		15				Acem M	
Ayas-ı Arnavud	3					M	gift of a page; registered during the reign of Selim I
Bayram b. Derviş[11]	13	17	17	17		Rum M	nakkaş; registered during reign of Bayezid II; gave gifts to the sultan c. 1545–1555; received from the sultan 2,000 akçes c. 1535 and 1555/1556; died 23 Muharrem 966 (5 November 1558)
Cafer b. Ali (Şerif)		1	8	8.5		Rum A-M	
Cafer b. Nasuh			4	4	6.5	Rum A-M	
Cafer-i Macar			5			Rum M	
Derviş Bey							musavvir; came from Tabriz in 1514
Derviş Mehmed					3	Acem A	nakkaş; gave gifts to the sultan c. 1550–1555
Derviş Mehmed b. Kasım					10.5	Acem M	
Derviş Mehmed-i İsfahani		1		1		Acem A	
Durmuş	2					A	nakkaş; received from the sultan 1,000 akçes c. 1535
Durmuş b. Hayreddin	15	16.5				Rum M	father imperial master; registered during reign of Bayezid II
Durmuş b. Hızır							nakkaş; received from the sultan 1,000 akçes 1511
Durmuş Mehmed							nakkaş; received from the sultan 1,000 akçes in 1555/1556
Emir Cafer				8.5		Rum M	

	1526	1545	1557/1558	1557–1558	1566		
Evrenos	10	11				Rum M	nakkaş; former slave; relative of Yahya; registered as apprentice during reign of Bayezid II; gave gifts to the sultan c. 1550–1555; received from the sultan 1,000 akçes c. 1535; listed in 1552/1553–1555/1556 as having illuminated two Korans and paid 2,215 akçes*
Fazullah[12]							nakkaş; received from the sultan 500 akçes in 1505
Ferhad-ı Bosna		5.5	9	9.5	11.5	Rum M	
Ferruh-ı Çerkes	3					M	given to the sultan by a page; registered Muharrem 927 (December 1520–January 1521)
Hace Bey-i Tebrizi	10.5					M	gave gifts to the sultan c. 1545; received 1,000 akçes from the sultan c. 1535
Hacı Abdi							katib and nakkaş; listed in 1552/1553–1555/1556 as having illuminated one Koran and paid 2,500 akçes*
Hacı Bey-i Tebrizi	10.5					M	
Hamza-i Nemçe		1				Rum A	apprentice of Kara Memi
Hasan b. Abdülcelil	20.5					M	ressam and nakkaş; also called Hasan Çelebi, Hasan Bey, or Küçük Hasan Çelebi; father an Iranian master; registered during reign of Bayezid II; first mentioned in 1504, this artist is listed as being a nakkaşbaşı after 1510 with a daily salary of 25–35 akçes; gave gifts to the sultan c. 1545–1555; received from the sultan 1,000–3,000 akçes together with brocaded garments 1504–c. 1555
Hasan b. Ahmed							received from the sultan 2,000 akçes c. 1535
Hasan b. Hızır	3.5	6.5	7	7.5	9	Rum M	father imperial Iranian master; registered during reign of Selim I
Hasan b. Kemal		2				Rum A	
Hasan b. Mehmed	20	22				Rum M	nakkaş; called Büyük Hasan Çelebi; father Iranian master; registered during reign of Bayezid II; gave gifts to the sultan c. 1545–1555
Hasan-ı Bosna			5			Rum M	
Haydar-ı Arnavud			9			Rum M	
Hızır		1		1		Acem A	apprentice of Sultan Ali
Hızır b. Ali		8.5				Rum M	
Hürrem-i Bosna					4.5	Rum A	apprentice of serbölük Mehmed Sinan
Hürrem-i Nemçe		1		2		Rum A	

	1526	1545	1557/1558	1557–1558	1566		
Hüseyin	1.5					A	apprentice of Hasan Bey; given to the sultan by a page; registered 27 Cemazilevvel 927 (6 May 1521)
Hüseyin b. Hasan Çelebi	2.5					A	registered as apprentice when father, an imperial master, died during reign of Selim I
Hüseyin-i Bosna		1	6	6	8.5	Rum A-M	apprentice of Yusuf
Hüseyin-i Rumi	12.5					M	nakkaş; exiled from Tabriz to Amasya; registered Rebiülahir 929 (November–December 1522); gave gifts to sultan c. 1545; received from the sultan 1,000 akçes c. 1535
Hüseyin Üngürüs	1.5						apprentice of Hasan Çelebi; employed by Sinan Paşa, then by Hüdavendigar; registered Receb 924 (January–February 1518)
İbrahim b. Ahmed	8.5	12.5				Rum M	nakkaş; received from the sultan 700 akçes c. 1535
İskender							nakkaş; received from the sultan 1,000 akçes in 1511
İskender	2					A	registered 6 Rebiülevvel 926 (25 February 1520); given to Edirne Palace
İskender-i Bosna		1		1.5	5	Rum A	recorded in 1596 as ranking eighth with salary of 13 akçes per day; listed as deceased in August–November 1596
İsmail							listed in 1552/1553–1554/1555 as having illuminated eight Korans and paid 15,788 akçes*
Kara Memi (Mehmed-Siyah or Kara Mehmed)[13]		16.5		25.5		Rum M	nakkaşbaşı in 1557–1558; gave gifts to the sultan c. 1550–1555; listed in 1552/1553–1555/1556 as having illuminated one Koran and paid 6,000 akçes*
Kasım-ı Arnavud		5	7	7.5	10.5	Rum M	sent to Edirne with the sultan (n.d.)
Kasım-ı Bosna		1				Rum A	
Kasım-ı Çerkes			6			Rum M	
Kasım-ı İsfahani	12.5					M	exiled from Tabriz to Amasya; registered Rebiülahir 929 (November–December 1522)
Kaytaş		1		2		Acem A	apprentice of Abdülhamid
Kaytaş-ı Frengi				2.5	4.5	Acem A-M	recorded in 1596 as ranking eleventh with salary of 10.5 akçes per day; listed as deceased August–November 1596
Kemal Abdullah					4	Rum A	
Mahmud	2					A	purchased as a slave; registered during reign of Selim I
Mahmud b. Mahmud					4.5	Rum A	

	1526	1545	1557/1558	1557–1558	1566		
Mahmud-ı Gürci			1	1	3	Rum A	apprentice of Mustafa-ı Buğdan in 1557/1558 and 1566; recorded in 1596 and 1605 as ranking twelfth with salary of 6.5 akçes per day
Mahmud-ı Tebrizi							nakkaş; received from the sultan 2,000 akçes in 1510
Mansur Bey							nakkaş; came from Tabriz in 1514; gave gifts to the sultan c. 1555
Mehmed		1				Rum A	apprentice of Şah Hüseyin
Mehmed					5.5	Rum A	
Mehmed b. Abdurrahman	4.5	5.5	6	6.5		Rum M	father an imperial master; registered during reign of Selim I
Mehmed b. Abdülevvel			2	3	6	Rum M	
Mehmed b. Bayram	8.5					M	nakkaş; registered 25 Şevval 904 (5 June 1499); gave gifts to the sultan c. 1545–1555; received from the sultan 800 akçes c. 1535
Mehmed b. Hasan		3	5	5.5	9	Rum M	
Mehmed b. Hasan Çelebi	3.5					M	
Mehmed b. Mehmed					6	Rum M	
Mehmed b. Melek Ahmed	7.5	9	10			Rum M	nakkaş; registered during reign of Bayezid II; called Hacı; received from sultan 1,000 akçes 1555/1556; listed as deceased in the register of 1557/1558
Mehmed Eyyübi							listed in 1552/1553–1555/1556 as having illuminated six Korans and paid 5,000 akçes*
Mehmed Ferhad					3	Rum A	
Mehmed-i Bosna		1	1	1.5	3	Rum A	sent to Edirne in 1557/1558
Mehmed Sinan				34.5		Rum M	nakkaş; also called Mehmed Çelebi Sinan; serbölük in 1566; received from the sultan 1,600 akçes in 1555/1556
Mehmed Şah-ı Tebrizi (Şah Mehmed)		19	25	19.5	25.5	Acem M Rum M	musavvir and nakkaş; came from Tabriz in 1514; gave gifts, including binding of the *Guy ve Çevgan*, to the sultan c. 1545; received from the sultan 1,400 akçes c. 1560; listed in Aceman corps in 1545, 1557–1558, and 1566 but as the serbölük of the Rumiyan corps in 1557/1558; listed in 1552/1553–1555/1556 as having illuminated five Korans and paid 6,300 akçes*
Melek Ahmed-i Tebrizi	24					M	nakkaş; came from Iran during reign of Bayezid II; gave gifts to the sultan c. 1545; received from the sultan 400 to 2,000 akçes between 1503 and c. 1535

	1526	1545	1557/1558	1557–1558	1566		
Mir Aka-ı Tebrizi (Hacı Mir)		5		7	12.5	Acem M	nakkaş; came from Tabriz in 1514; gave gifts to the sultan c. 1555
Mirza Bey							nakkaş; came from Tabriz in 1514; gave gifts to the sultan, c. 1555
Mustafa		1				Rum A	
Mustafa		1				Rum A	apprentice of Mir Aka
Mustafa b. Yusuf	3.5	5.5	5	5.5		Rum A	registered 4 Cumadelahir 926 (12 February 1520)
Mustafa b. Yusuf		2				Rum A	apprentice of Kara Memi
Mustafa Divane			2	2	4	Rum A	
Mustafa-ı Buğdan	6.5	11	13	14	14.5	Rum M	former slave given to Hüdavendigar; registered 2 Zilkade 919 (30 December 1513)
Mustafa Müzehhib					8	Rum M	
Mustafa Sarmaşık							nakkaş; received from the sultan 1,300 akçes in 1555/1556
Nasuh	2					A	apprentice of Bayram b. Derviş; purchased as a slave; registered 3 Cemaziyelahir 924 (13 May 1518)
Nazar							nakkaş; came from Tabriz in 1514
Nebi					13	Rum M	it is possible that he is the same person as Nebi b. Bali, Nebi Çelebi, and Nebi-i Kara Memi, who started as an apprentice in 1545 and became a master after 1557–1558
Nebi b. Bali		1				Rum A	
Nebi Çelebi			9			Rum M	
Nebi-i Kara Memi				10		Rum M	
Osman[14]					6	Rum M	recorded in 1596 as ranking seventh with salary of 31 akçes per day
Pervane		2		2		Acem A	apprentice of Abdülali in 1545 and 1557–1558
Pervane-i Bosna			2	3	9	Rum M	
Pervane-i Macar				4	8.5	Acem M Rum M	
Pervane-i Nevrekob			5			Rum M	
Pir Çelebi			5			Rum M	
Piri b. Abdülevvel		2				Rum A	
Piri b. Ahmed		1				Rum A	apprentice of Rumi
Rum			6			Rum A	apprentice of serbölük Şah Mehmed (Mehmed Şah-ı Tebrizi)
Sekban Veyz				4.5		Rum M	
Seydi Nakkaş				4		Rum M	
Sultan Ali-i Basmai	9.5	12.5				Acem M	nakkaş; also called Ali Sultan; gave gifts to the sultan c. 1550–1555
Şah Hüseyin b. Ressam Husam	6					M	registered 14 Cemaziyelahir 930 (20 April 1524) after death of father, an Iranian master

	1526	1545	1557/1558	1557–1558	1566		
Şahkulu-ı Bağdadi[15]	22	25				Rum M	nakkaş and ressam; exiled from Tabriz to Amasya; registered Muharrem 927 (December 1520–January 1521); highest rank in 1526 and serbölük in 1545; gave gifts, including a representation of a peri on paper, to the sultan c. 1545; received from the sultan 2,000 akçes and a brocaded kaftan c. 1535; 3,000 akçes and a brocaded Bursa velvet designated for him in 1555/1556, could not be given since he had died
Şeref							nakkaş; came from Tabriz in 1514
Şeyh Han							nakkaş; came from Tabriz in 1514
Şeyh Kemal							nakkaş; came from Tabriz in 1514
Üveys b. Ahmed	12.5	13	14	14	15	Rum M	father imperial gatekeeper; registered during reign of Bayezid II
Yahya							nakkaş; received from the sultan 2,000 akçes in 1508
Yunus							nakkaş; received from the sultan 700 akçes in 1511
Yusuf		1				Rum A	
Yusuf	3					A	apprentice of Küçük Hasan Çelebi; former slave of Yunus Paşa
Yusuf	2					A	apprentice of Kasım; registered during reign of Selim I; given to Edirne Palace
Yusuf-ı Çerkes	2.5	7				Rum A-M	apprentice of Abdülevvel; given to the sultan by a page; registered during reign of Selim I
Yusuf-ı Nemçe			6			Rum A	
Yusuf-ı Rum		7	11	11	13	Rum M	

B. Cemaat-i Mücellidan (Society of the Bookbinders)

Name of Artist	Date of Register with Daily Wages					Corps	Comments
	1526	1545	1557/1558	1557–1558	1566		
Alaeddin-i Kullei	15.5					M	father retired from Janissary Corps and assigned to Yedikule fortress; registered 4 Cemaziyevvel 924 (14 June 1518); head of society in 1526
Ahmed			9	10	11	M	called "mücellidan-ı katiban-ı divan-ı ali" (bookbinder of the secretaries of the Divan-ı Hümayun); given 9 akçes per day in 1557/1558 although normal daily wage was 2 akçes; sent to Edirne with the sultan (n.d.)
Ahmed b. Kamil		5				M	his two sons, Abdi and Mustafa, employed from 1595 to 1617
Ali							gave gifts to the sultan c. 1545–1555
Bali b. Ali	4.5					M	apprentice of Alaeddin; registered 14 Rebiülahir 927 (24 March 1521)
Cafer-i Çerkes	2					A	apprentice of Mehmed
Cafer-i Rum		1				A	apprentice of Mustafa
Davud-ı Çerkes	11.5					M	given by Ahmed during reign of Bayezid II
Hasan b. Ahmed (Hacı Hasan Çelebi)	2	4.5	5	5.5	6	A-M	registered same date as Hüseyin b. Ahmed; son Ahmed employed in the society 1596 to 1623; listed in 1552/1553–1555/1556 as having bound one Koran and paid 200 akçes*
Hasan b. Taş(zade)		1.5	2	2	2	A-M	apprentice of Ahmed in 1545; master after 1557/1558
Hürrem-i Rum (Hürrem Çelebi)		1	6	7.5	10	A-M	apprentice of Hasan in 1545; master after 1557/1558; kethüda with salary of 20.5 akçes per day in 1596; sent to Edirne with the sultan (n.d.); son Mehmed employed in the society in 1596–1597; listed in 1552/1553–1555/1556 as having bound one Koran and paid 200 akçes*
Hüseyin b. Ahmed (Hüseyin Çelebi)	3	10	10	13.5		M	registered as apprentice in 4 Cemaziyelahir 924 (14 June 1518) when father, an imperial master, died; listed in 1552/1553–1555/1556 as having bound seven Korans and paid 1,350 akçes*
Hüseyin-i Nemçe		2				A	apprentice of Mehmed
İsmail	13					M	slave of Firuz Bey; registered during reign of Selim I
Mahmud-ı Rum		1	1			A	apprentice of Hüseyin
Mehmed b. Abdülvehhab					4		

	1526	1545	1557/1558	1557–1558	1566		
Mehmed b. Ahmed[16]	13.5	16	16	17	17	M	father imperial master; registered during reign of Selim I; head of the society between 1545 and 1566; received from the sultan 1,000 akçes c. 1535; brothers Mustafa, Hasan, and Hüseyin also employed in the society; sons Süleyman, Mahmud, Kara Mehmed, and their sons and grandsons employed in the society until after 1623
Mustafa b. Ahmed (Mustafa Çelebi)	2	6.5	9	9.5	13	M	registered same date as Hüseyin b. Ahmed; received from the sultan 700 akçes in 1555/1556; ranked twelfth with salary of 15 akçes per day in 1596; sons, Bekir and Mehmed, employed in the society 1596 and 1605; listed in 1552/1553–1555/1556 as having bound eight Korans and paid 1,300 akçes*
Osman		1				A	
Osman Bosna			5	5	7	M	
Süleyman b. Mehmed			3	3.5	5	M	registered 6 Muharrem 965 (29 October 1557); head of the society with 18 akçes per day in 1596
Yusuf-ı Rum		1	5	5.5	7	A-M	apprentice in 1545; master after 1557/1558

NOTES

1. Meriç 1953, 1954, and 1963.

2. Meriç 1953 no. I; and Meriç 1954, no. I.

3. Meriç 1953, no. II; and Meriç 1954, no. II.

4. Meriç 1953, no. III; and Meriç 1954, no. III.

5. Meriç 1953, no. IV; and Meriç 1954, no. IV.

6. Meriç 1953, no. V; and Meriç 1954, no. V.

7. This unpublished document is in İstanbul, Başvelaket Arşivi, D. 6196.

8. Meriç 1953, no. VI; and Meriç 1954, no. VI.

9. Meriç 1953, no. VII; and Meriç 1954, no. VII.

10. Barkan 1979, 69 and 70, no. m.

11. Bayram b. Derviş illuminated the Koran transcribed by Abdullah b. İlyas in 1523/1524. See 8.

12. This artist may be the same person as Fadlullah b. Arab who illuminated two copies of the Enam Suresi in 1506/1507. See Yağmurlu 1973, no. XVIII.

13. Kara Memi's name appears in two manuscripts: the Koran transcribed by Abdullah Sayrafi in 1344/1345 and illuminated by Kara Memi in 1554/1555; and the Divan-ı Muhibbi transcribed by Mehmed Şerif in February–March 1566. See 14 and 26.

14. Ahmed Feridun Paşa's Nuzhet el-Esrar el-Ahbar der Sefer-i Sigetvar dated 1568/1569 and Lokman's Tarih-i Sultan Süleyman of 1579/1580 are attributed to Osman. See 42 and 43.

15. Şahkulu's name appears on two album drawings. See figs. 8 and 9.

16. This artist's name appears in the refurbished Koran transcribed by Abdullah Sayrafi in 1344/1345; a note in the beginning of the volume states that Mehmed Çelebi made the new binding in 1555/1556. The binding was later removed from the work and cannot be identified. See 14.

Appendix 4

Genealogical Tables

Süleyman and His Family

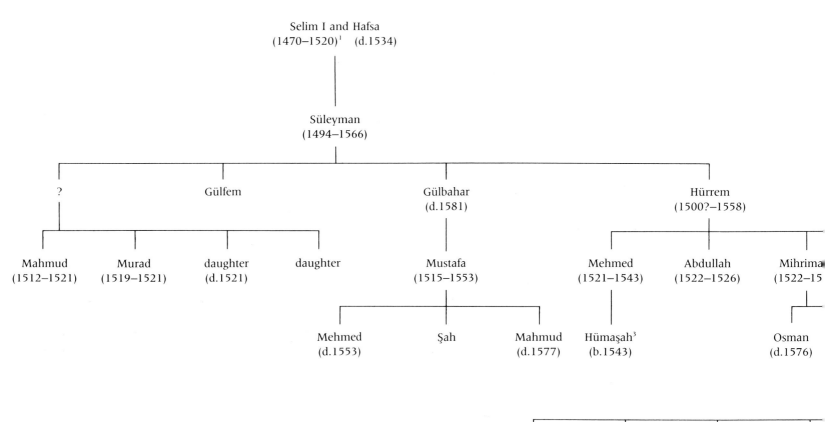

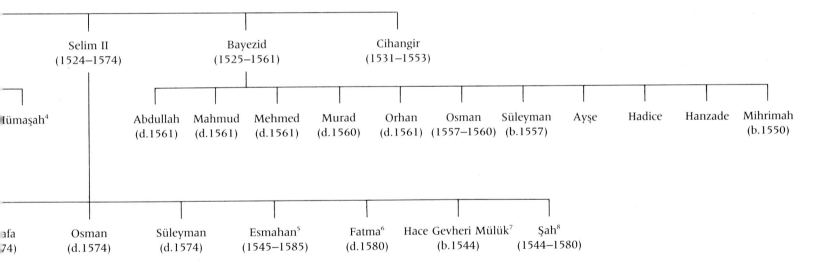

Selim II
(1524–1574)

Bayezid
(1525–1561)

Cihangir
(1531–1553)

Mümaşah[4]

Abdullah
(d.1561)

Mahmud
(d.1561)

Mehmed
(d.1561)

Murad
(d.1560)

Orhan
(d.1561)

Osman
(1557–1560)

Süleyman
(b.1557)

Ayşe

Hadice

Hanzade

Mihrimah
(b.1550)

afa
74)

Osman
(d.1574)

Süleyman
(d.1574)

Esmahan[5]
(1545–1585)

Fatma[6]
(d.1580)

Hace Gevheri Mülük[7]
(b.1544)

Şah[8]
(1544–1580)

The Ottoman Sultans

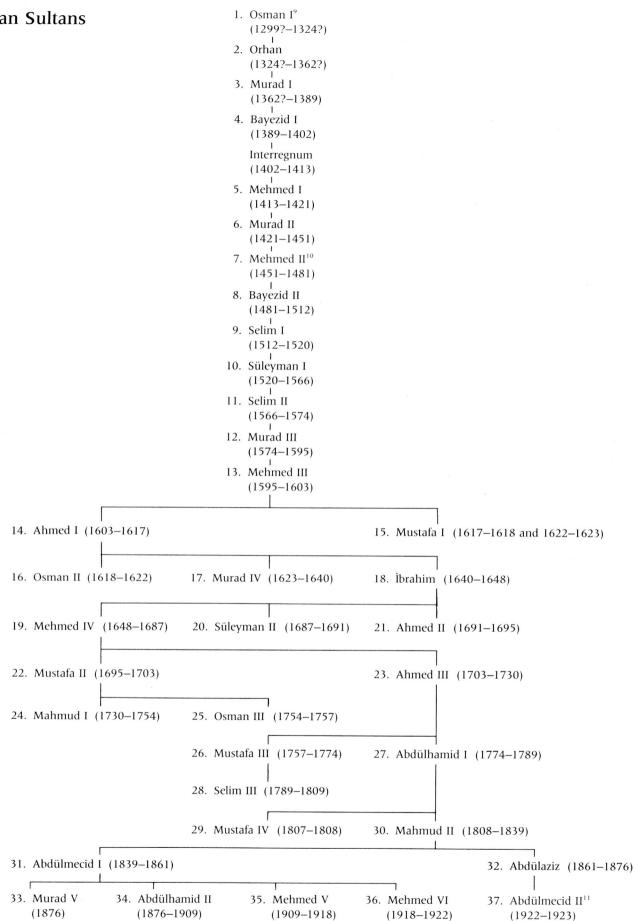

1. Osman I[9]
(1299?–1324?)

2. Orhan
(1324?–1362?)

3. Murad I
(1362?–1389)

4. Bayezid I
(1389–1402)

Interregnum
(1402–1413)

5. Mehmed I
(1413–1421)

6. Murad II
(1421–1451)

7. Mehmed II[10]
(1451–1481)

8. Bayezid II
(1481–1512)

9. Selim I
(1512–1520)

10. Süleyman I
(1520–1566)

11. Selim II
(1566–1574)

12. Murad III
(1574–1595)

13. Mehmed III
(1595–1603)

14. Ahmed I (1603–1617)   15. Mustafa I (1617–1618 and 1622–1623)

16. Osman II (1618–1622)   17. Murad IV (1623–1640)   18. İbrahim (1640–1648)

19. Mehmed IV (1648–1687)   20. Süleyman II (1687–1691)   21. Ahmed II (1691–1695)

22. Mustafa II (1695–1703)   23. Ahmed III (1703–1730)

24. Mahmud I (1730–1754)   25. Osman III (1754–1757)

26. Mustafa III (1757–1774)   27. Abdülhamid I (1774–1789)

28. Selim III (1789–1809)

29. Mustafa IV (1807–1808)   30. Mahmud II (1808–1839)

31. Abdülmecid I (1839–1861)   32. Abdülaziz (1861–1876)

33. Murad V
(1876)
34. Abdülhamid II
(1876–1909)
35. Mehmed V
(1909–1918)
36. Mehmed VI
(1918–1922)
37. Abdülmecid II[11]
(1922–1923)

302

NOTES

1. Dates used here refer to the birth and death of the individuals.

2. Mihrimah married in 1539 Rüstem Paşa.

3. Hümaşah married in 1566 Ferhad Paşa and in 1575(?) Mehmed Paşa.

4. Hümaşah married in 1580 Semiz Ahmed Paşa and in 1582 Ahmed Feridun Paşa.

5. Esmahan married in 1562 Sokullu Mehmed Paşa and in c. 1580 Kalaylıkoz Ali Paşa.

6. Fatma married in 1574 Kanijeli Siyavuş Paşa.

7. Hace Gevheri Mülük married in 1566 Piyale Paşa and in 1578 Mehmed Paşa.

8. Şah married in 1562 Çakır.

9. Dates given refer to the reigns of the sultans.

10. Mehmed II also reigned 1444–1446 after Murad II abdicated in his favor.

11. Since the sultanate was abolished in 1922, Abdülmecid II served only as caliph.

List of Objects

Dimensions are given in centimeters, with inches in parentheses, height or length before width; in the case of three-dimensional objects, height before width before depth, or height before diameter. Bibliographic references are given in parentheses at the end of each entry.

1. Illuminated tuğra of Sultan Süleyman

c. 1550
158 × 240 (62³⁄₁₆ × 94½)
İstanbul, Topkapı Sarayı Müzesi, G.Y. 1400
(İstanbul 1983, E. 53)

2. Ferman with illuminated tuğra of Sultan Süleyman

c. 1530–1540
Turkish text; 12 lines written in divani; end missing
164.0 × 40.0 (64⁹⁄₁₆ × 15¾)
İstanbul, Türk ve İslam Eserleri Müzesi, 2238
Transferred from the Evkaf Müessesatı, İlmiye Dairesi, 1914
(Safadi 1978, fig. 148; Lowry 1982, no. 185)

3. Ferman with illuminated tuğra of Sultan Süleyman

Dated 21 Rebiülahir 959 (19 April 1552)
Turkish text; 13 lines written in divani
168.0 × 41.0 (66⅛ × 16⅛)
İstanbul, Topkapı Sarayı Müzesi, E. 7816/2
(Umur 1980, fig. 119)

4. Illuminated tuğra of Sultan Süleyman

c. 1555–1560
Removed from the ferman
52.0 × 64.5 (20½ × 25⅜)
New York, The Metropolitan Museum of Art, Rogers Fund, 1938, 38.149.1
Purchased from Beghian, 1938
(McAllister 1938, 247; Dimand 1958, fig. 45; Dimand 1944, 211; Metropolitan 1968, no. 36; Indianapolis 1970, no. 87)

5. Ferman with illuminated tuğra of Sultan Selim II

Dated 13 Receb 976 (1 January 1569)
Turkish text; 38 lines written in divani
372.0 × 46.0 (146½ × 18⅛)
İstanbul, Türk ve İslam Eserleri Müzesi, 4125
Purchased, 1968
(Umur 1980, fig. 128)

6. Illuminated serlevha from the *Vakfiye* of Hürrem Sultan

Transcribed in 18 Receb 947 (18 November 1540)
Original stamped and gilded leather binding with filigree doublures. Arabic text; 73 folios with 9 lines written in nesih; illuminated serlevha (fols. 1b–2a), tuğra of Sultan Süleyman (fol. 7a), and verse stops; date and signatures of witnesses on folio 72a
25.3 × 17.3 (9¹⁵⁄₁₆ × 6¹³⁄₁₆)
İstanbul, Türk ve İslam Eserleri Müzesi, 2191, folios 1b–2a
Transferred from the Evkaf Evamir Kalemi, 1919
(Çığ 1971, no. VII)

7. Illuminated folios from a Koran

Transcribed by Şeyh Hamdullah in 901 (1495/1496) in İstanbul
Original stamped and gilded leather binding. Arabic text; 337 folios with 14 lines written in nesih; illuminated frontispiece (fols. 1b–2a), serlevha (fols. 2b–3a), chapter headings, marginal ornaments, and verse stops; colophon with date, name of calligrapher, and city on folio 337b
28.2 × 20.0 (11⅛ × 7⅞)
İstanbul, Topkapı Sarayı Müzesi, E.H. 72, folios 327b–328a
Formerly in the Emanet Hazinesi of the Topkapı Palace
(Karatay 1962–1969, no. 798)

8. Illuminated frontispiece from a Koran

Transcribed by Abdullah b. İlyas and illuminated by Bayram b. Derviş Şir in 930 (1523/1524)
Dedicated to Sultan Süleyman
Original stamped and gilded binding with filigree doublures. Arabic text; 477 folios with 11 lines written in nesih; illuminated frontispiece (fols. 1b–2a), serlevha (fols. 2b–3a), chapter headings, marginal ornaments, and verse stops; dedication on folio 477a; colophon with date and names of artists on folio 477b
25.5 × 17.0 (10¹⁄₁₆ × 6⅞)
İstanbul, Topkapı Sarayı Müzesi, E.H. 58, folios 1b–2a
Formerly in the Emanet Hazinesi of the Topkapı Palace
(Karatay 1962–1969, no. 810; Derman 1970, figs. 7 and 8; Yağmurlu 1973, figs. 11 and 12; İstanbul 1983, E. 57; Atıl 1986, fig. 11)

9a. Illuminated serlevha from a Koran

Transcribed by Ahmed Karahisari in 953 (1546/1547)
Modern stamped and gilded binding. Arabic text; 238 folios with 15 lines written in nesih; illuminated serlevha (fols. 1b–2a), chapter headings, marginal ornaments, and verse stops; gold marginal drawings on folios 233b–234a; chapter titles and concluding prayers on folios 234b–235a written in sülüs; colophon with date, name of calligrapher, and seal of Sultan Süleyman, with the date 1012 (1603) added later on folio 235b; additional prayers on folios 236b–238a
29.1 × 18.5 (11⁷⁄₁₆ × 7⁵⁄₁₆)
İstanbul, Topkapı Sarayı Müzesi, Y.Y. 999, folios 1b–2a
Formerly in the Hazine of the Topkapı Palace
(Washington 1966, no. 180; Atıl 1980, ill. 91; Rome 1980; Atıl 1986, fig. 35)

9b. Gold binding for Karahisari's Koran (**9a**); pasteboard core covered with silver seraser; set with rubies, turquoises, and pearls

Second half seventeenth century
29.3 × 18.2 (11⁹⁄₁₆ × 7³⁄₁₆)
İstanbul, Topkapı Sarayı Müzesi, 2/2097

Formerly in the Hazine of the Topkapı Palace
(İstanbul 1983, E. 269)

10. Frontispiece from a collection of religious texts
Transcribed by Ahmed Karahisari c. 1540−1550
Original stamped and gilded binding with paper-lined doublures.
Arabic text; 15 folios with 13 lines written in gold and black
muhakkak, nesih, and sülüs; contains the Enam Suresi from the
Koran (VI: 1−165; fols. 2b−12a), prayers (fol. 12b); selections from
the Hadis (fols. 13a−13b), and the *Kaside-i Burda* (fols. 14b−15a);
signatures of Karahisari on folios 12b and 15a
50.0 × 35.0 (19¹¹⁄₁₆ × 13¹³⁄₁₆)
İstanbul, Türk ve İslam Eserleri Müzesi, 1443, folios 1b−2a
Transferred from the Library of the Aya Sofya Mosque, 1914
(Ünver 1948; Akurgal et al 1966, 218; Washington 1966, no. 179;
Yazır 1972−1974, vol. 2, figs. 181 and 182; Aksoy 1977, 125, 128,
and 129; Safadi 1978, fig. 149; Lowry 1982, no. 183; İstanbul 1983,
E. 60; Frankfurt 1985, vol. 2, no. 1/76)

11. Two folios from an album of calligraphy
Transcribed by Ahmed Karahisari in 960 (1552/1553)
Original stamped and gilded leather binding. Arabic text; 22 folios
with 3 lines written sideways in gold and black nesih and sülüs;
prayers at the beginning (fols. 1b−2a); alphabetic studies (fols. 3b−
18a); backs of folios blank; colophon with name of calligrapher on
folio 20a; date on folio 22a; seal of Ahmed III on folio 1b
38.0 × 26.2 (15 × 10⁵⁄₁₆)
İstanbul, Topkapı Sarayı Müzesi, A. 3654, folios 1b−2a
Formerly in the Library of Ahmed III in the Topkapı Palace
(*Sanat* 1982, 132)

12. Illuminated serlevha from a book of daily prayers (*Evrad el-Usbu*)
Transcribed by Hasan b. Ahmed Karahisari in 974 (1566/1567)
Dedicated to Sultan Selim II
Modern binding. Arabic text; 7 folios with 9 to 14 lines written in
alternating muhakkak, nesih, and sülüs; gold-speckled margins;
illuminated dedication (fols. 1b−2a), serlevha (fols. 2b−3a), chapter
headings, panels inserted into the text, and verse stops; colophon
with date and name of calligrapher on folios 6b and 7a
36.2 × 25.7 (14¼ × 10⅛)
İstanbul, Topkapı Sarayı Müzesi, E.H. 1077, folios 2b−3a
Formerly in the Emanet Hazinesi of the Topkapı Palace
(Karatay 1962−1969, no. 5636; Derman 1970, fig. 18; Derman
1982, pls. 9 and 10)

13. Illuminated serlevha from part two of a Koran (II:142−252)
Transcribed by Yakut el-Mustasimi in 681 (1282/1283); illuminated
and bound mid-sixteenth century
Stamped and gilded leather binding with filigree doublures. Arabic
text; 50 folios with 5 lines written in muhakkak; illuminated
serlevha (fols. 1b−2a) and field around the text; gold marginal
drawings on all folios; colophon with date and name of calligrapher
on folio 50a
34.0 × 23.2 (13⅜ × 9⅛)
İstanbul, Topkapı Sarayı Müzesi, E.H. 227, folios 1b−2a
Formerly in the Emanet Hazinesi of the Topkapı Palace
(Karatay 1962−1969, no. 99)

14. Two folios from a Koran
Transcribed by Abdullah Sayrafi in 745 (1344/1345); illuminated by
Kara Memi in 962 (1554/1555); bound by Mehmed Çelebi in 963
(1555/1556); additional text written by Hasan in 984 (1556/1557);
prepared for the treasury of Rüstem Paşa
Modern binding. Arabic text; 330 folios with 15 lines written in
nesih; illuminated folios at beginning and end (fols. 1a, 1b−2a, 2b−
3a, 329−330a, and 330b), chapter headings, marginal ornaments,
and verse stops; gold marginal decorations on folios 3b−4a;
notation on first folio gives dates and names of artists and patron
22.7 × 16.0 (8¹⁵⁄₁₆ × 6⁵⁄₁₆)
İstanbul, Topkapı Sarayı Müzesi, E.H. 49, folios 329b−330a
Formerly in the Emanet Hazinesi of the Topkapı Palace
(Karatay 1962−1969, no. 141; Yağmurlu 1973, figs. 23 and 24; Atıl
1986, fig. 9; Tanındı 1986, figs. 1−8)

15. Stamped and gilded leather binding from a Tefsir (*Tefsir-i Mevahıb-ı Aliye*)
Manuscript transcribed by İbn Refieddin Fazlullah et-Tebrizi in 20
Receb 925 (18 July 1519) in İstanbul
Persian text; 380 folios with 27 lines written in talik; illuminated
serlevha (fol. 1b) and section headings; colophon with date, name
of artist, and city on folio 380a
32.7 × 24.0 (12⅞ × 9⁷⁄₁₆)
İstanbul, Topkapı Sarayı Müzesi, A. 21
Formerly in the Library of Ahmed III in the Topkapı Palace
(Karatay 1961a, no. 5)

16. Stamped and gilded leather binding from a Koran
Manuscript transcribed by Argun Kamili in 706 (1306/1307);
illuminated and bound mid-sixteenth century
Arabic text; 102 folios with 5 lines written in sülüs; contains
chapters I, VI, XVIII, XXXIV, and XXXV; illuminated serlevha
(fols. 1b−2a), field around the text on all folios, chapter headings,
and verse stops
32.5 × 25.8 (12¾ × 10¹⁄₁₆)
İstanbul, Topkapı Sarayı Müzesi, E.H. 222
Formerly in the Emanet Hazinesi of the Topkapı Palace
(Karatay 1962−1969, no. 135; Tanındı 1986, figs. 12 and 13)

17. Stamped and gilded leather binding from a small Koran
Manuscript transcribed mid-sixteenth century
Arabic text; unpaginated, 16 lines written in gubari; illuminated
serlevha
5.7 × 5.0 (2¼ × 2)
İstanbul, Topkapı Sarayı Müzesi, E.H. 522
Formerly in the Emanet Hazinesi of the Topkapı Palace
(Karatay 1962−1969, no. 638; İstanbul 1983, E. 66)

18a. Lacquered binding from a Hadis
Manuscript transcribed by Abdülhayf Ali c. 1540
Dedicated to Şehzade Mehmed
Persian text; 8 folios with 13 lines written in kaatı tevkii and talik;
illuminated serlevha (fols. 1b-2a), panels within text, verse stops,
and diacritics; gold-speckled marbled margins; colophon with
dedication and name of calligrapher on folio 8b
24.5 × 15.0 (9⅝ × 5¹⁵⁄₁₆)
İstanbul, Topkapı Sarayı Müzesi, E.H. 2851
Formerly in the Emanet Hazinesi of the Topkapı Palace
(*Sanat* 1982, 134; İstanbul 1983, E. 61; Tanındı 1984, figs. 13 and
14; Atıl 1986, fig. 36)

18b. Illuminated serlevha from the Hadis (**18a**)

Folios 1b–2a

19. Sharkskin binding from a Koran; exterior embroidered with black and blue silk and gold; stamped and gilded leather doublures

Second half sixteenth century
Arabic text; 373 folios with 15 lines written in nesih; illuminated serlevha (fols. 1b–2a), marginal ornaments, and verse stops
14.5 × 9.5 (5¾ × 3¾)
İstanbul Üniversite Kütüphanesi, A. 6570
Transferred from the Yıldız Palace (originally from the Topkapı Palace)
(İstanbul 1983, E. 181)

20. Jade and gold binding from a Koran; inlaid with niello and set with emeralds and rubies

Inscribed cartouche on the spine added later; fore-edge flap on interior inscribed with a Koranic verse (LVI: 77–80)
Second half sixteenth century
17.8 × 10.7 (7 × 4¼)
İstanbul, Topkapı Sarayı Müzesi, 2/2121
Topkapı Palace Collection
(İstanbul 1983, E. 200; Çağman 1984, fig. 7)

21. Hexagonal jade binding from a small Koran; set with emeralds and rubies

Manuscript transcribed by Mehmed Tahir in 978 (1570/1571)
Arabic text; unpaginated, written in gubari; illuminated serlevha (fols. 1b–2a), chapter headings, and verse stops; colophon with date and name of calligrapher on last page
5.0 × 5.0 (2 × 2)
İstanbul, Topkapı Sarayı Müzesi, 2/2896
Topkapı Palace Collection

22. View of the Mescid-i Haram in Mecca from the *Futuh el-Harameyn* of Muhyi Lari

c. 1540
Original stamped and gilded leather binding. Persian text; 58 folios with 12 lines in 2 columns written in talik; 13 illustrations; illuminated serlevha (fol. 1b)
22.2 × 14.8 (8¾ × 5¹³⁄₁₆)
İstanbul, Topkapı Sarayı Müzesi, R. 917, folio 14a
Formerly in the Revan Pavilion of the Topkapı Palace
(Karatay 1961a, no. 772; Tanındı 1983a, figs. 3–5)

23. View of the Aksa Mosque and the Dome of the Rock in Jerusalem from a pilgrimage scroll *(Hac Vekaletnamesi)*

Transcribed by Mehmed Ebu Fadl Sincari in 951 (1544/1545)
Prepared by Hacı Piri b. Seyyid Ahmed for Şehzade Mehmed
Turkish text; verses from the Koran written in nesih and sülüs enclosing 15 illustrations
524.0 × 46.0 (206½ × 18⅛)
İstanbul, Topkapı Sarayı Müzesi, H. 1812
Formerly in the Hazine of the Topkapı Palace
(Karatay 1961b, no. 668; Tanındı 1983a, figs. 11–14; Tanındı 1983b)

24. Folio from the *Divan-ı Muhibbi*

Written by Sultan Süleyman mid-sixteenth century
Original stamped and gilded leather binding. Turkish and Persian verse; 120 folios in 8 to 14 lines written in talik; some with gold marginal drawings
21.2 × 14.0 (8⅜ × 5½)
İstanbul, Topkapı Sarayı Müzesi, H. 1132, folio 94a
Formerly in the Hazine of the Topkapı Palace
(Karatay 1961b, no. 2331)

25. Illuminated serlevha from the *Divan-ı Muhibbi*

Transcribed by Mehmed Şerif in 973 (1565/1566) in İstanbul
Original binding with stamped and gilded binding. Turkish and Persian verse; 205 folios with 6 lines in 2 columns written in talik; illuminated serlevhas for Persian poems (fols. 5b–6a) and Turkish poems (fols. 39b–40a); each folio illuminated and decorated with gold marginal drawings; colophon with date and name of calligrapher on folio 203a; last three odes on folios 203b–205a written by Sultan Süleyman; several empty or unfinished folios
20.4 × 13.0 (8¹⁄₁₆ × 5⅛)
İstanbul, Topkapı Sarayı Müzesi, R. 738 mük., folios 39b–40a
Formerly in the Revan Pavilion of the Topkapı Palace
(Karatay 1961b, no. 2330; Atıl 1986, fig. 34)

26. Two folios from the *Divan-ı Muhibbi*

Transcribed by Mehmed Şerif in Şaban 973 (February/March 1566) in İstanbul; illuminated by Kara Memi
Modern binding. Turkish and Persian verse; 370 folios with 13 lines in 2 columns written in talik; illuminated dedication (fols. 1b–2a), serlevha (fols. 2b–3a), section headings, and panels between verses on all folios; gold marginal drawings on each page after folio 3b; colophon with date and name of calligrapher on folio 366b; name of illuminator on folios 360b and 367a
26.3 × 16.7 (10⅜ × 6⁹⁄₁₆)
İstanbul, İstanbul Üniversite Kütüphanesi, T. 5467, folios 359b–360a
Transferred from the Yıldız Palace (originally from the Topkapı Palace)
(Ünver 1951; Derman 1970, fig. 21; İstanbul 1983, E. 62; Atıl 1986, fig. 10)

27. Stamped and gilded leather binding from the *Divan-ı Muhibbi*

c. 1560
Turkish and Persian verse; 252 folios with 13 lines in 2 columns written in talik; illuminated serlevha (fols. 1b–2a) and section headings on the first seven folios
25.5 × 16.0 (10¹⁄₁₆ × 5⁵⁄₁₆)
İstanbul, Türk ve İslam Eserleri Müzesi, 1962
Transferred from the Library of the Mosque of Mehmed II, 1914
(Çığ 1953, figs. X and XI; Washington 1966, no. 182; Atıl 1980, ill. 92; Atıl 1986, fig. 33)

28a. Sultan Selim I in his library (left) and riding with his court (right) from the *Divan-ı Selimi*

Transcribed by Şahsuvar Selimi c. 1520
Modern binding. Persian verse; 68 folios with 11 lines in 2 columns written in talik; two double-folio paintings; illuminated serlevha (fols. 1b–2a) and section headings; gold marginal drawings on all folios; many folios with representation of angels and animals

inserted into the text; colophon with name of calligrapher on folio 67a
19.6 × 12.0 (7¾ × 4¾)
İstanbul Üniversite Kütüphanesi, F. 1330, folios 27b–28a
Transferred from the Yıldız Palace (originally from the Topkapı Palace)
(Edhem and Stchoukine 1933, no. VII; Atıl 1980, ill. 19; İstanbul 1983, E. 56; Atıl 1986, fig. 15)

28b. Two folios from the *Divan-ı Selimi* (**28a**)
Folios 25b–26a

29. Polo players from the *Divan-ı Nevai*
c. 1530–1540
Original stamped, gilded, and lacquered leather binding with lacquered doublures. Turkish verse; 214 folios with 17 lines in 2 columns written in talik; 8 paintings, including a double frontispiece (fols. 1b–2a); illuminated serlevha (fols. 2b–3a) and section headings; gold marginal drawings on all folios
26.5 × 17.0 (10⁷⁄₁₆ × 6¹¹⁄₁₆)
İstanbul, Topkapı Sarayı Müzesi, R. 804, folio 89b
Formerly in the Revan Pavilion of the Topkapı Palace
(Karatay, 1961b, no. 2293; Stchoukine 1966, pls. XIV and XV; Atasoy and Çağman 1974, pl. 4; İstanbul 1983, E. 58; Tanındı 1984, figs. 9 and 10; Rogers 1986b, pls. 133 and 134)

30. Illuminated serlevha from the *Guy ve Çevgan* of Arifi
Transcribed by Mehmed b. Gazanfer in 946 (1539/1540)
Modern binding covered with marbled paper. Persian verse; 35 folios with 10 lines in 2 columns written in kaatı talik; double-folio illustration at end (fols. 34b–35a); illuminated serlevha (fols. 1b–2a), single folio resembling a bookbinding (fol. 34a), section headings, and panels inserted into the text; gold marginal drawings; colophon with date and name of calligrapher on folio 33b
24.2 × 15.0 (9⁹⁄₁₆ × 5¹⁵⁄₁₆)
İstanbul, Topkapı Sarayı Müzesi, H. 845, folios 1b–2a
Formerly in the Hazine of the Topkapı Palace
(Karatay 1961a, no. 666; Stchoukine 1966, pl. XVI; Çağman and Tanındı 1979, no. 132; İstanbul 1983, E. 59; Frankfurt 1985, vol. 2, no. 1/13; Rogers 1986b, pl. 140)

31. Polo game (left) and entertainment of prince (right) from the *Divan-ı Jami*
c. 1520
Original stamped, gilded, and lacquered leather binding. Persian verse; 201 folios with 12 lines in 2 columns written in talik; 10 illustrations, including a double frontispiece (fols. 1b–2a); illuminated serlevha (fol. 2b) and section headings
25.5 × 16.0 (10¹⁄₁₆ × 6⁵⁄₁₆)
İstanbul, Topkapı Sarayı Müzesi, H. 987, folios 1b–2a
Formerly in the Hazine of the Topkapı Palace
(Karatay 1961a, no. 687; Çağman 1978, fig. 23; Atıl 1980, ill. 73)

32. Court of Gayumars from the *Şahname* of Firdausi
c. 1520–1530
Original stamped and gilded binding with filigree doublures. Persian verse; 575 folios with 25 lines in 4 columns written in talik; 57 illustrations, including one spread to double folios (fols. 9b–10a); illuminated serlevhas (fols. 1b–2a and 10b–11a), unfinished dedication (fol. 9a), section headings, and occasional panels inserted

into the text; seal of Sultan Süleyman on folio 1a
35.0 × 24.5 (13¹³⁄₁₆ × 9¹¹⁄₁₆)
İstanbul, Topkapı Sarayı Müzesi, H. 1499, folio 14a
Formerly in the Hazine of the Topkapı Palace
(Karatay 1961a, no. 341; Atıl 1980, pl. 18)

33a. Capture of Ferhad by Hüsrev from the *Hamse-i Nevai*
Transcribed by Pir Ahmed b. İskender in 937 (1530/1531)
Original lacquered bookbinding with stamped and gilded leather doublures. Turkish verse; 309 folios with 23 lines in 4 columns written in talik; 16 illustrations; illuminated dedication (fol. 1a), serlevha (fols. 1b–2a), and section headings; colophon with date and name of calligrapher on folio 309b
29.5 × 18.5 (11⅝ × 7⁵⁄₁₆)
İstanbul, Topkapı Sarayı Müzesi, H. 802, folio 99a
Formerly in the Hazine of the Topkapı Palace
(Karatay 1961b, no. 2299; Stchoukine 1966, pls. X and XI; Atasoy and Çağman 1974, pl. 3; Çağman and Tanındı 1979, no. 136; Atıl 1980, ill. 74; Grube 1981, figs. 14–16; Tanındı 1984, fig. 18; Atıl 1986, figs. 6 and 12; Rogers 1986b, pls. 135–139)

33b. Lacquered binding from the *Hamse-i Nevai* (**33a**)

34. Royal couple in a courtyard from the *Ravzat el-Uşak* of Arifi
c. 1560
Original stamped and gilded leather binding. Persian verse; 64 folios with 12 lines in 2 columns written in talik; 3 illustrations; illuminated serlevha (fol. 1a) and section headings
25.1 × 17.1 (9⅞ × 6¾)
Cambridge, Mass., Harvard University Art Museums, The Edwin Binney, 3rd Collection of Turkish Art, 85.216, folio 23a
Formerly in the Michel Onou Collection, Russian Embassy, İstanbul
(Binney 1979, pp. no. 13 and 164–165; Atıl 1986, figs. 39–41)

35. Parchment map of the Atlantic Ocean with portions of Europe, Africa, and Central and South America
Made by Piri Reis in Muharrem 919 (March–April 1513) in Gelibolu
Presented to Sultan Selim I in 1517 in Cairo
Turkish text and commentaries; fragment of a world map
90.0 × 63.0 (35⁷⁄₁₆ × 24¹³⁄₁₆)
İstanbul, Topkapı Sarayı Müzesi, R. 1633 mük.
Formerly in the Revan Pavilion of the Topkapı Palace
(Kahle 1932; Akçura 1966; İnan 1974; Hapgood 1979; Washington 1966, no. 188; İstanbul 1983, E. 73)

36. View of Çanakkale from the *Kitab-ı Bahriye* of Piri Reis
Transcribed in 932 (1525/1526)
Dedicated to Sultan Süleyman
Original stamped and gilded leather binding with marbled paper doublures. Turkish text; 421 folios with 15 lines written in nesih; 215 illustrations; illuminated serlevha (fol. 1b) and section headings; two unnumbered folios at the beginning with the table of contents; seal of Sultan Süleyman on folio 2a; statement that material compiled by Piri Reis and written down by Muradi on folio 292b
31.8 × 22.0 (12½ × 8¹¹⁄₁₆)
İstanbul, Topkapı Sarayı Müzesi, H. 642, folio 44a
Formerly in the Hazine of the Topkapı Palace
(Kahle 1929; Karatay 1961b, no. 1336; Akalay 1969, figs. 9 and 10; Soucek 1973; Atıl 1986, fig. 19)

37. Sultan Selim I at the Battle of Çaldıran from the *Selimname* of Şükrü Bitlisi

c. 1525
Original stamped, gilded, and lacquered leather cover on the front; back cover and spine modern. Turkish verse; 277 folios with 11 lines in 2 columns written in talik; 24 illustrations, including frontispiece on folio 1a (right half missing); illuminated serlevha (fols. 1b–2a) and panels inserted into selected folios of the text
26.0 × 18.0 (10¼ × 7⅛)
İstanbul, Topkapı Sarayı Müzesi, H. 1597–1598, folio 113a
Formerly in the Hazine of the Topkapı Palace
(Karatay 1961b, no. 639; Çağman 1978, fig. 20; Atıl 1980, ill. 77; Tanındı 1984, fig. 8; Rogers 1986b, pl. 150)

38. View of Lepanto from the *Tarih-i Sultan Bayezid* of Matrakcı Nasuh

Transcribed and illustrated by the author c. 1540
Original stamped and gilded leather binding. Turkish text; 82 folios with 13 lines written in nesih; 10 illustrations, including two spread to double folios; illuminated serlevha (fol. 1b)
26.8 × 18.3 (10⁹⁄₁₆ × 7³⁄₁₆)
İstanbul, Topkapı Sarayı Müzesi, R. 1272, folios 21b–22a
Formerly in the Revan Pavilion of the Topkapı Palace
(Karatay 1961b, no. 624; Yurdaydın 1963, figs. 41–48; Akalay 1969, figs. 7 and 10; Rogers 1986b, pls. 145 and 146)

39a. View of İstanbul from the *Beyan-ı Menazil-i Sefer-i Irakeyn* of Matrakcı Nasuh

Transcribed and illustrated by the author c. 1537
Modern binding. Turkish text; 179 folios with 17 lines written in nesih; 128 illustrations, many spread to double folios; illuminated serlevha (fol. 1b)
31.6 × 23.3 (12⁷⁄₁₆ × 9³⁄₁₆)
İstanbul Üniversite Kütüphanesi, T. 5964, folios 8b–9a
Transferred from the Yıldız Palace (originally from the Topkapı Palace)
(Gabriel 1928; Akurgal et al 1966, 200 and 201; Denny 1970; Atasoy and Çağman 1974, pl. 6; Yurdaydın 1976; Atıl 1980, ill. 78; İstanbul 1983, E. 74; Atıl 1986, fig. 17)

39b. View of Sultaniye from the *Beyan-ı Menazil-i Sefer-i Irakeyn* (**39a**)

Folios 32b–33a

40. View of Genoa from the *Tarih-i Feth-i Siklos, Estergon, ve Estonibelgrad* of Matrakcı Nasuh

Transcribed and illustrated by the author c. 1545
Modern binding. Turkish text; 146 folios with 13 lines written in nesih; 32 illustrations including several spread to double folios; illuminated serlevha (fol. 1b)
26.1 × 17.5 (10⁵⁄₁₆ × 6⅞)
İstanbul, Topkapı Sarayı Müzesi, H. 1608, folios 32b–33a
Formerly in the Hazine of the Topkapı Palace
(Karatay 1961b, no. 667; Yurdaydın 1963, figs. 19–40; Akalay 1969, figs. 2–4, 6, and 8; Fehér 1976, pls. XXIII–XXVI; Çağman and Tanındı 1979, no. 142; Çağman 1976, fig. 14; Atıl 1980, ill. 79; Çağman 1980, pl. 161; Grube 1982, pl. 211; İstanbul 1983, E. 72; Atıl 1986, fig. 18; Rogers 1986b, pls. 147 and 148)

41a. Siege of Belgrade from the *Süleymanname* of Arifi

Transcribed by Ali b. Emir Bey Şirvani mid-Ramazan 965 (late June–early July 1558)
Original stamped and gilded binding. Persian verse; 617 folios with 15 lines in 4 columns written in talik; 69 illustrations, including four spread to double folios; illuminated dedication (fols. 1b–2a), serlevha (fols. 2b–3a), section headings, and panels inserted into selected folios; colophon with date and name of calligrapher on folio 617b
36.5 × 25.4 (14⅜ × 10)
İstanbul, Topkapı Sarayı Müzesi, H. 1517, folios 108b–109a
Formerly in the Hazine of the Topkapı Palace
(Karatay 1961a, no. 160; Stchoukine 1966, pls. XIX–XXII; Akalay 1970; Atasoy 1970; Atasoy and Çağman 1974, pls. 7–9; Akalay 1978; Atıl 1980, ills. 80–83; Çağman 1980, pls. 162–164; Fehér 1976, pls. VII–XII, XIV, XV, XVII, XVIII, XXI, XXVII, XXXI, and XXXV; İstanbul 1983, E. 70 and 71; Atıl 1986; Rogers 1986b, pls. 152–154)

41b. Battle of Mohács from the *Süleymanname* (**41a**)

Folios 219b–220a

41c. Sultan Süleyman with Barbaros Hayreddin Paşa from the *Süleymanname* (**41a**)

Folio 360a

41d. Sultan Süleyman arriving at Kasr-ı Şirin from the *Süleymanname* (**41a**)

Folio 367a

42a. Sultan Süleyman receiving Stephen Zápolya from the *Nuzhet el-Esrar el-Ahbar der Sefer-i Sigetvar* of Ahmed Feridun Paşa

Transcribed in 976 (1568/1569)
Modern binding. Turkish text; 305 folios with 15 lines in 4 columns written in nesih; 20 illustrations, including six spread to double folios; illuminated serlevha (fol. 1b)
39.0 × 25.0 (15⅜ × 9⅞)
İstanbul, Topkapı Sarayı Müzesi, H. 1339, folio 16b
Formerly in the Hazine of the Topkapı Palace
(Karatay 1961b, no. 692; Stchoukine 1966, pls. XXVI and XXVIII; Atasoy and Çağman 1974, pl. 11; Fehér 1976, pls. XXXVII, XL–XLII, and XLIV–XLVII; Akalay 1978, figs. 8, 16, 18, and 20; Çağman and Tanındı 1979, nos. 148 and 149; Atıl 1980, ill. 84; Çağman 1980, pl. 165; İstanbul 1983, E. 172; Atıl 1986, fig. 21; Rogers 1986b, pls. 157)

42b. View of Szigetvár from the *Nuzhet el-Esrar el-Ahbar der Sefer-i Sigetvar* (**42a**)

Folios 32b–33a

43a. Süleyman praying at the Mausoleum of Eyüb Ensari from the *Tarih-i Sultan Süleyman* of Lokman

Transcribed by Kasım el-Hüseyni el-Aridi el-Kazvini in 987 (1579/1580)
Original stamped and gilded leather binding with lacquered doublures. Persian verse; 121 folios with 17 lines in 4 columns written in talik; 32 illustrations, including six spread to double folios; illuminated dedication (fol. 1a), serlevha (fol. 1b), section headings, and panels inserted into select folios; colophon with date

and name of calligrapher on folio 121a
37.8 × 26.0 (14⅞ × 10¼)
Dublin, The Trustees of the Chester Beatty Library, MS. 413, folio 38a
Purchased, 1920s
(Minorsky 1958, no. 413; Stchoukine 1966, pls. XXXI–XXXVII; Ünver 1970; Atasoy and Çağman 1974, pls. 12 and 13; James 1981, nos. 33a and b; Grube 1982, pl. 207; Rogers 1983b, nos. 76–78; Vienna 1983, nos. 2/9 and 12/6)

43b. Army marching with Sultan Süleyman's coffin from the *Tarih-i Sultan Süleyman* (**43a**)
Folios 113b–114a

43c. Sultan Selim II praying outside Belgrade from the *Tarih-i Sultan Süleyman* (**43a**)
Folios 116b–117a

43d. Burial of Sultan Süleyman from the *Tarih-i Sultan Süleyman* (**43a**)
Folio 115b

44. View of Lepanto
Mid-sixteenth century
57.5 × 75.7 (22⅝ × 29¹³⁄₁₆)
İstanbul, Topkapı Sarayı Müzesi, 17/348
Topkapı Palace Collection
(İstanbul 1983, E. 75)

45a. Saz leaves from an album
Mid-sixteenth century
32 folios with Akkoyunlu, Safavid, and Ottoman calligraphy, paintings, and drawings
30.3 × 20.8 (11¹⁵⁄₁₆ × 8³⁄₁₆)
İstanbul, Topkapı Sarayı Müzesi, H. 2147, folio 22b
Formerly in the Hazine of the Topkapı Palace
(Grube 1961b, fig. 25; Grube 1962a, fig. 4; Denny 1983, pls. 11)

45b. Hatayi blossoms from an album (**45a**)
Folio 23a
(Grube 1961b, fig. 28; Grube 1962c, fig. 6; Denny 1983, pl. 18)

45c. Floral composition with senmurv and chilin from an album (**45a**)
Folio 21a
(Grube 1961b, fig. 29; Grube 1962c, fig. 7; Atıl 1980, ill. 88)

45d. Combat between dragon and lion from an album (**45a**)
Folio 32b
(Grube 1961b, fig. 38; Grube 1962b, fig. 18)

46. Dragon in foliage from an album
Mid-sixteenth century
Stamped with a seal bearing a Koranic verse (XL:44)
17.5 × 40.0 (6⅞ × 15¾)
The Cleveland Museum of Art, Purchase from the J. H. Wade Fund, 44.492
Formerly in the Charles Ricketts Collection; purchased 1944
(Martin 1912, pl. 271; Kühnel 1923, pl. 98; Grube 1961b, fig. 6a;

Grube 1962a, no. 77; Grube 1962b, fig. 14; Denny 1979b, 8; Grube 1982, pl. 191; Denny 1983, pls. 1 and 7; Frankfurt 1985, vol. 2, no. 1/14; Maher 1986, figs. 3 and 4)

47. Composite page with saz leaves and peri from an album
Mid-sixteenth century
43 folios with Safavid, Shaybanid, and Ottoman paintings and drawings
35.4 × 22.0 (13¹⁵⁄₁₆ × 8¹¹⁄₁₆)
İstanbul, Topkapı Sarayı Müzesi, H. 2168, folio 10b
Formerly in the Hazine of the Topkapı Palace

48a. Peri with a lute from an album
Mid-sixteenth century
34 folios with Safavid, Shaybanid, Mughal, and Ottoman paintings and drawings
36.0 × 25.0 (14³⁄₁₆ × 9⅞)
İstanbul, Topkapı Sarayı Müzesi, H. 2162, folio 9a
Formerly in the Hazine of the Topkapı Palace

48b. Seated peri from an album (**48a**)
Attributed to Velican
Second half sixteenth century
Folio 8b
(Denny 1983, pl. 20; İstanbul 1983, E. 176)

49a. Tortoiseshell and silver binding from an album; stamped and gilded leather doublures
c.1560
Arabic and Persian verse; 49 folios in diverse lines and columns written in talik; illuminated flyleaves, unfinished dedication (fols. 1b–2a), frontispiece with the Fatiha Suresi from the Koran (I:1–7; fols. 2b–3a), and panels inserted into the text; gold marginal drawings on all folios; calligraphic drawing of a lion (fol. 46a); calligraphic exercise (fol. 46b); kaatı garden (fol. 47a); and drawings of animals and flowers (fols. 47b–48a)
35.2 × 23.3 (13⅞ × 9³⁄₁₆)
İstanbul Üniversite Kütüphanesi, F. 1426
Transferred from the Yıldız Palace (originally from the Topkapı Palace)

49b. Illuminated frontispiece with the Fatiha Suresi (I:1–7) from an album (**49a**)
Transcribed by Şah Mahmud Nişapuri c. 1530–1540 and illuminated c. 1560
Folios 2b–3a
(İstanbul 1983, E. 64)

49c and 49d. Two folios from an album (**49a**)
Transcribed by Şah Mahmud Nişapuri c. 1530–1540 and illuminated c. 1560
Folios 22b and 27a

49e and 49f. Drawings of a dragon (left) and hatayi blossoms (right) from an album (**49a**)
Mid-sixteenth century
Folios 47b–48a
(İstanbul 1983, E. 63; Atıl 1986, fig. 8; Maher 1986, figs. 6 and 18)

50. Silver plate; spun and hammered
Second quarter sixteenth century
Stamped with the seal of Sultan Süleyman
2.0 × 29.0 (¹³/₁₆ × 11⁷/₁₆)
İstanbul, Topkapı Sarayı Müzesi, 23/1625
Topkapı Palace Collection
(*Sanat* 1982, 94; İstanbul 1983, E. 94)

51. Gilded silver jug with lid; cast and hammered
Second quarter sixteenth century
16.0 × 12.7 (6⁵/₁₆ × 5)
London, The Board of Trustees of the Victoria and Albert Museum,
158–1894
Acquired, 1894
(London 1931, pl. 26; Lane 1957, fig. 4; London 1976, no. 163;
Allan and Raby 1982, pl. 18; İstanbul 1983, E. 93; Frankfurt 1985,
vol. 2, no. 6/23)
Shown in Washington only

52. Gilded silver jug; cast and hammered
Second quarter sixteenth century
Stamped with the seal of Sultan Selim I (?)
10.1 × 6.3 (4 × 2½)
London, Her Royal Highness Princess Esra Jah
Purchased 1985
(Sotheby's 1985a, no. 126)

53. Gilded copper alloy tankard; cast, hammered, and
incised; lined with tin
Second quarter sixteenth century
Three cartouches on body inscribed in Arabic written in sülüs
13.5 × 8.0 (5⁵/₁₆ × 3⅛)
Baltimore, The Walters Art Gallery, 54.512
Acquired before 1931
(Melikian-Chirvani 1975, figs. 7 and 8; Allan and Raby 1980, pl. 4)

54. Gold canteen; hammered, inlaid with niello, and set with
jade plaques, emeralds, rubies, and pearl
Second half sixteenth century
27.5 × 23.0 × 14.3 (10¹³/₁₆ × 9¹/₁₆ × 5⅝)
İstanbul, Topkapı Sarayı Müzesi, 2/3825
Topkapı Palace Collection
(Raby and Allan 1982, pl. 28; *Sanat* 1982, 117; İstanbul 1983,
E. 206)

55. Gold-sheathed silver Kaaba lock; cast and hammered
Made for Sultan Süleyman in 973 (1565/1566)
Inscribed on one side of the finial with the name and titles of the
sultan and the date rendered in eight lines written in nesih
75.0 × 10.5 (29⁹/₁₆ × 4⅛)
İstanbul, Topkapı Sarayı Müzesi, 2/2274
Topkapı Palace Collection
(İstanbul 1958, no. 67; Sourdel-Thomine 1971, no. 16)

56. Zinc jug with lid; cast and hammered, inlaid with gold,
and set with emeralds, rubies, turquoises, and pearls
Second quarter sixteenth century
13.5 × 11.4 (5⁵/₁₆ × 4½)
İstanbul, Topkapı Sarayı Müzesi, 2/2873

Topkapı Palace Collection
(İstanbul 1983, E. 96)

57. Zinc jug with lid; cast and hammered, inlaid with gold,
and set with rubies, turquoises, diamonds, and peridots
Second quarter sixteenth century
İstanbul, Topkapı Sarayı Müzesi, 2/2856
18.0 × 12.7 (7⅛ × 5)
Topkapı Palace Collection

58. Rock-crystal jug; carved
Second quarter sixteenth century
İstanbul, Topkapı Sarayı Müzesi, 2/467
14.0 × 7.5 (5½ × 2¹⁵/₁₆)
Topkapı Palace Collection
(İstanbul 1983, E. 92)

59. Rock-crystal pen box; carved, framed with gold, and set
with emeralds and rubies
Second half sixteenth century
12.0 × 30.5 × 11.5 (4¾ × 12 × 4⁹/₁₆)
İstanbul, Topkapı Sarayı Müzesi, 2/479
Topkapı Palace Collection
Not in exhibition

60. Rock-crystal and gold canteen; carved, hammered, and
set with diamonds, rubies, and emeralds
Second half sixteenth century
İstanbul, Topkapı Sarayı Müzesi, 2/484
32.2 × 15.7 (12¹¹/₁₆ × 6³/₁₆)
Topkapı Palace Collection
(İstanbul 1983, E. 212; Türkoğlu 1985, 17)
Not in exhibition

61. Rock-crystal and gold jug with lid; set with emeralds and
rubies, and lined with illuminated paper
Second half sixteenth century
20.0 × 15.5 (7⅞ × 6⅛)
İstanbul, Topkapı Sarayı Müzesi, 2/8
Topkapı Palace Collection
(*Sanat* 1982, 115; İstanbul 1983, E. 211; Türkoğlu 1985, 12)

62. Rock-crystal and gold pen box; set with emeralds and
rubies, and lined with illuminated paper
Second half sixteenth century
8.5 × 40.0 × 11.0 (3⅜ × 15¾ × 4⁵/₁₆)
İstanbul, Topkapı Sarayı Müzesi, 2/22
Topkapı Palace Collection
(Washington 1966, no. 222; Preyger 1970, pl. III; İstanbul 1983,
E. 209; Türkoğlu 1985, 13)

63. Jade box with nielloed gilded silver brackets; inlaid with
gold and set with rubies and turquoises
Second quarter sixteenth century
7.0 × 16.0 × 6.0 (2¾ × 6⁵/₁₆ × 2⅜)
İstanbul, Topkapı Sarayı Müzesi, 2/2085
Topkapı Palace Collection

64. Black stone jug with lid; inlaid with gold and set with rubies, amethysts (?), and turquoises
Second half sixteenth century
Filter inside neck inscribed with Koranic verse (LXXVI:21) written in sülüs
19.0 × 14.0 (7½ × 5½)
İstanbul, Topkapı Sarayı Müzesi, 2/3831
Topkapı Palace Collection
(Washington 1966, no. 219; Köseoğlu 1980, 27; Skelton 1978, fig. 1; Türkoğlu 1985, 14)

65. Jade cup; inlaid with gold and set with rubies
Second half sixteenth century
4.5 × 8.5 (1¹³⁄₁₆ × 3⅜)
Paris, Musée du Louvre, Section Islamique, M.R. 202
Registered in the royal French collection between 1684 and 1701
(Paris 1791, no. 109; Barbet de Jouy 1867, E. 181; A.U. Pope 1964–1965, pl. 1456C; Paris 1977, no. 676)

66. Jade tankard with lid; inlaid with gold and set with amethysts (?), emeralds, peridots, and rubies
Second half sixteenth century
17.7 × 10.2 (7 × 4)
İstanbul, Topkapı Sarayı Müzesi, 2/3832
Topkapı Palace Collection
(İstanbul 1983, E. 207)

67. Jasper (?) pen case; inlaid with gold and set with emeralds and rubies
Second half sixteenth century
3.0 × 27.0 × 3.8 (1³⁄₁₆ × 10⅝ × 1½)
İstanbul, Topkapı Sarayı Müzesi, 2/2111
Topkapı Palace Collection
(İstanbul 1983, E. 205)

68. Blue-and-white porcelain pen box; inlaid with gold and set with emeralds and rubies
Fifteenth-century Chinese ware decorated second half sixteenth century
7.0 × 27.0 × 8.0 (2¾ × 10⅝ × 3³⁄₁₆)
İstanbul, Topkapı Sarayı Müzesi, 2/894
Topkapı Palace Collection
(David 1933–1934, pl. IX; Ünal 1963, fig. 9)

69. Covered white porcelain bowl with rock-crystal dome; inlaid with gold, set with emeralds and rubies, and lined with illuminated paper
Made of two mid-sixteenth-century Chinese bowls decorated second half sixteenth century
Inscribed in the foot ring of the bowl "shih-fu chih tso" in Chinese in a square format, giving the name of the maker
17.5 × 15.0 (6⅞ × 5¹⁵⁄₁₆)
İstanbul, Topkapı Sarayı Müzesi, 15/2767
Topkapı Palace Collection
(Zimmerman 1930, pl. 70; Ünal 1963, fig. 10; Misugi 1981, T. 109; İstanbul 1983, E. 214)

70. White porcelain ewer with gold lid; set with emeralds and turquoise
Early-fifteenth-century Chinese ware refurbished second half sixteenth century
33.0 × 10.0 (13 × 3¹⁵⁄₁₆)
İstanbul, Topkapı Sarayı Müzesi, 15/2944
Topkapı Palace Collection
(Ünal 1963, fig. 2; Misugi 1981, T. 69)

71. Celadon canteen with gilded silver spouts and cover; set with coral
Late-fourteenth- or early-fifteenth-century Chinese ware refurbished second half sixteenth century
20.5 × 15.0 (18¹⁄₁₆ × 5¹⁵⁄₁₆)
İstanbul, Topkapı Sarayı Müzesi, 15/668
Topkapı Palace Collection
(İstanbul 1983, E. 131)

72. Steel mirror with jade handle; inlaid with gold and niello, and set with rubies and turquoises
Second quarter sixteenth century
Inscribed with three Persian couplets written in talik
30.0 × 14.1 (11¹³⁄₁₆ × 5⁹⁄₁₆)
İstanbul, Topkapı Sarayı Müzesi, 2/1801
Topkapı Palace Collection
(İstanbul 1983, E. 81)

73. Ivory mirror with ebony handle; carved and inlaid with black organic material and gold
Made for Sultan Süleyman by Gani in 950 (1543/1544)
Inscribed with three Turkish couplets written in sülüs
30.2 × 12.2 (11⅞ × 4¹³⁄₁₆)
İstanbul, Topkapı Sarayı Müzesi, 2/2893
Topkapı Palace Collection
(Konyalı 1950; Öz n.d., 61; İstanbul 1958, no. 73; Paris 1953, no. 188; Akurgal et al 1966, 210; Washington 1966, no. 216; Köseoğlu 1980, 20; İstanbul 1983, E. 88)

74. Ivory mirror; carved and set with turquoise in a gold mount
Second quarter sixteenth century
31.0 × 10.3 (12³⁄₁₆ × 4¹⁄₁₆)
İstanbul, Topkapı Sarayı Müzesi, 2/1804
Topkapı Palace Collection
(Arseven n.d., fig. 528; İstanbul 1983, E. 89; Frankfurt 1985, vol. 2, no. 10/1)

75. Ivory buckle; carved
Second quarter sixteenth century
6.0 × 5.6 × 1.4 (2⅜ × 2³⁄₁₆ × ¼)
Kuwait National Museum, Dar al-Athar al-Islamiya, LNS 46 I
Purchased
(Sotheby's 1983, no. 143; Keene 1984a, 26; Keene 1984b, no. 38)

76. Ivory belt; inlaid with black organic material and gold, and set with rubies and turquoises
Second quarter sixteenth century
78.8 × 6.5 (31¹⁄₁₆ × 2⁹⁄₁₆)
İstanbul, Topkapı Sarayı Müzesi, 2/539

Topkapı Palace Collection
(Washington 1966, no. 215; İstanbul 1983, E. 87)

77. Ivory belt; inlaid with black organic material and gold, and set with rubies and turquoises
Mid-sixteenth century
65.5 × 4.5 (25¹³/₁₆ × 1¹³/₁₆)
İstanbul, Türk ve İslam Eserleri Müzesi, 482
Transferred from the Mausoleum of Sultan Selim II, 1915

78. Mother-of-pearl belt; inlaid with black organic material and gold
Mid-sixteenth century
91.0 × 2.7 (35¹³/₁₆ × 1¹/₁₆)
İstanbul, Topkapı Sarayı Müzesi, 2/575
Topkapı Palace Collection
(İstanbul 1983, E. 120)

79. Gold turban ornament with peacock feathers; hammered and chased
Second half sixteenth century
Ornament, 14.3 × 6.5 (5⅝ × 2⁹/₁₆)
İstanbul, Türk ve İslam Eserleri Müzesi, 438
Transferred from the Mausoleum of İbrahim Paşa, 1914
(Washington 1966, no. 213; Tapan 1977, 150; İstanbul 1983, E. 216)

80. Gold turban ornament; chased
Mid-sixteenth century
Height, 12.0 (4¾)
İstanbul, Türk ve İslam Eserleri Müzesi, 419
Transferred from the Mausoleum of Hürrem Sultan, 1911

81. Gold turban ornament; chased and inlaid with niello
Mid-sixteenth century
Height, 16.5 (6½)
İstanbul, Türk ve İslam Eserleri Müzesi, 421
Transferred from the Mausoleum of Sultan Selim II, 1915

82. Gold turban ornament; chased and set with rubies and turquoises
Second half sixteenth century
Height, 14.5 (5¾)
İstanbul, Türk ve İslam Eserleri Müzesi, 416
Transferred from the Mausoleum of Sultan Selim II, 1915

83. Gold turban ornament; inlaid with niello and set with rubies, turquoises, sapphires, and diamonds
Mid-sixteenth century
19.4 × 5.7 (7⅝ × 2¼)
İstanbul, Topkapı Sarayı Müzesi, 2/2912
Topkapı Palace Collection
(İstanbul 1983, E. 84)

84. Steel helmet; inlaid with gold and set with rubies, turquoises, and amethysts(?)
Mid-sixteenth century
28.0 × 23.5 (11¹/₁₆ × 9¼)
İstanbul, Topkapı Sarayı Müzesi, 2/1187

Topkapı Palace Collection
(Öz n.d., 58; Tezcan 1975, 22; İstanbul 1983, E. 219)

85. Gold-sheathed mace; set with rubies and turquoises
Mid-sixteenth century
Length, 72.0 (28⅜)
İstanbul, Topkapı Sarayı Müzesi, 2/715
Topkapı Palace Collection

86. Yatağan; ivory hilt inlaid with black organic material and gold, and set with rubies and turquoises; gold guard; steel blade inlaid with gold, affixed with partially gilded cast steel or iron elements and set with rubies
Made for Sultan Süleyman by Ahmed Tekelü in 933 (1526/1527)
Inscribed on both sides of the blade in Arabic with praises to the sultan, and the date written in sülüs; the name of the maker inscribed on the spine
Length, 66.0 (26)
İstanbul, Topkapı Sarayı Müzesi, 2/3776
Topkapı Palace Collection
(Sarre and Martin 1912, no. 248; İstanbul 1958, no. 69; Mayer 1962, 19; A. U. Pope 1964–1965, pl. 1424 D; İstanbul 1983, E. 85)

87. Meç and scabbard; silver hilt with gold pommel set with rubies and turquoises; steel blade inlaid with gold; wood scabbard with gold bands, chapes, and sling mounts inlaid with rubies and turquoises
Made for Sultan Süleyman in İstanbul in 938 (1531/1532)
Inscribed on one side of the blade in Arabic with Koranic verses (LXV:2–3), prayers, the name of the sultan, the city, and the date written in sülüs
Length of sword, 73.0 (28¾); length of scabbard, 73.5 (28¹⁵/₁₆)
İstanbul, Topkapı Sarayı Müzesi, 1/74
Topkapı Palace Collection
(Paris 1953, no. 51)

88. Kılıç and scabbard: leather-covered hilt with steel pommel and guard inlaid with gold; steel blade inlaid with gold; leather-covered scabbard with steel chapes and sling mounts inlaid with gold
Made for Sultan Süleyman second quarter sixteenth century
Inscribed on both sides of the blade in Arabic with Koranic verses (LXV:2–3), praises, and the name of the sultan written in sülüs
Length of sword, 93.8 (36¹⁵/₁₆); length of scabbard, 87.8 (34⁹/₁₆)
İstanbul, Topkapı Sarayı Müzesi, 1/463
Topkapı Palace Collection
(İstanbul 1958, no. 51)

89. Kılıç and scabbard; leather-covered hilt with steel pommel and guard inlaid with gold and set with turquoises; steel blade; leather-covered scabbard with steel chapes and sling mounts inlaid with gold
Second quarter sixteenth century
Inscribed on the hilt with two Persian couplets written in talik; inscription on blade too damaged to be deciphered
Length of sword, 95.8 (37¹¹/₁₆); length of scabbard, 84.0 (33⅛)
İstanbul, Topkapı Sarayı Müzesi, 1/294
Topkapı Palace Collection

90. Kılıç and scabbard; leather-covered hilt with gilded silver pommel and guard; steel blade; leather-covered scabbard with gilded silver chapes and sling mounts

Mid-sixteenth century
Back of lower chape stamped with the seal of Sultan Süleyman
Length of sword, 96.0 (37⅞); length of scabbard, 86.0 (33⅞)
Vienna, Kunsthistorisches Museum, Waffensammlung, A. 1341
Registered in the Ambras Castle Collection in Tirol 1583
(Grosz and Thomas 1936, 99, no. 21)

91. Dagger; carved rock-crystal hilt inlaid with gold and set with ruby and turquoises; steel blade with pierced central groove inlaid with gold

Made for Sultan Selim I in 920 (1514/1515)
Inscribed on both sides of hilt in ebced
Length, 31.5 (12⅞₆)
İstanbul, Topkapı Sarayı Müzesi, 2/254
Topkapı Palace Collection
(Washington 1966, no. 237; İstanbul 1983, E. 80)

92. Dagger; carved ivory hilt; silver guard; steel blade inlaid with gold

Mid-sixteenth century
Length, 36.0 (14³⁄₁₆)
Riyadh, Rifaat Sheikh al-Ard Collection
Formerly in the Earls of Warwick Collection
(Geneva 1985, no. 315)

93. Dagger and scabbard; ivory hilt inlaid with black organic material and set with rubies and turquoises; gilded silver guard; steel blade with pierced central groove; silver scabbard partially gilded

Second quarter sixteenth century
Length of dagger, 49.4 (19⁷⁄₁₆); length of scabbard, 38.0 (14¹⁵⁄₁₆)
Vienna, Kunsthistorisches Museum, Waffensammlung, C. 152a
Registered in the Ambras Castle Collection in Tirol in 1603
(Sacken 1855, 297, no. 27; Grosz and Thomas 1936, 95, no. 7; Thomas 1963–1964, fig. 6)

94. Dagger and scabbard; jade hilt and scabbard inlaid with gold and set with rubies; gold guard set with rubies; fluted steel blade inlaid with gold

Second half sixteenth century
Inscribed on one side of blade with three Persian couplets and on the other three Turkish couplets, both written in talik
Length of dagger, 31.6 (12⁷⁄₁₆); length of scabbard, 21.6 (8½)
Vienna, Kunsthistorisches Museum, Waffensammlung, C. 208
Registered in the Ambras Castle Collection in Tirol in 1603
(Sacken 1855, 158 and 159, no. 8; Sarre and Martin 1912, nos. 321 and 322; Glück and Diez 1925, 473; Grosz and Thomas 1936, 95, no. 10; Ivanov 1979, no. 67)

95. Jade archer's ring; inlaid with gold and set with rubies and emerald

Second half sixteenth century
Diameter, 4.0 (1⁹⁄₁₆)
İstanbul, Topkapı Sarayı Müzesi, 2/74
Topkapı Palace Collection
(İstanbul 1983, E. 217)

96. Jade archer's ring; inlaid with gold and set with rubies and emerald

Second half sixteenth century
Diameter, 4.0 (1⁹⁄₁₆)
İstanbul, Topkapı Sarayı Müzesi, 2/83
Topkapı Palace Collection
(İstanbul 1983, E. 218)

97. Mother-of-pearl plaque; inlaid with black organic material and gold, and set with rubies and turquoises

Second quarter sixteenth century
6.5 × 8.5 (2⁹⁄₁₆ × 3⁵⁄₁₆)
Vienna, Kunsthistorisches Museum, Waffensammlung, C. 152b
Registered in the Ambras Castle Collection in Tirol in 1603
(Sacken 1855, 292 and 293; Grosz and Thomas 1936, 101, no. 15)

98. Wicker shield; embroidered with red, tan, turquoise, white, and yellow silk and silver; gold-sheathed central boss set with rubies and turquoises

Second quarter sixteenth century
Inscribed with two Persian couplets written in talik
Diameter, 59.5 (23⁷⁄₁₆)
İstanbul, Topkapı Sarayı Müzesi, 1/2466
Topkapı Palace Collection

99. Wicker shield; embroidered with beige, black, green, red, and white silk and gold metallic threads; steel central boss pierced and inlaid with gold

Mid-sixteenth century
Inscribed with Koranic verses (XLVIII:1-3) written in sülüs
Diameter, 59.0 (23¼)
İstanbul, Topkapı Sarayı Müzesi, 1/1930
Topkapı Palace Collection
(Arseven n.d., fig. 592; Paris 1953, no. 18; İstanbul 1983, E. 104)

100. Wicker shield; embroidered with cream, blue, brown, green, and red silk and silver; steel central boss inlaid with gold

Mid-sixteenth century
Inscribed with Koranic verse (II:255) written in nesih
Diameter, 62.0 (24⁷⁄₁₆)
İstanbul, Topkapı Sarayı Müzesi, 1/2441
Topkapı Palace Collection
(İstanbul 1983, E. 105)

101. Wicker shield; embroidered with black, blue, cream, green, and red silk and silver; steel central boss inlaid with gold

Mid-sixteenth century
Diameter, 64.0 (25³⁄₁₆)
İstanbul, Topkapı Sarayı Müzesi, 1/2571
Topkapı Palace Collection
(Washington 1966, no. 234; Mackie 1980, ill. 220; Tezcan 1983, back cover; İstanbul 1983, E. 227)

102. Wicker shield; embroidered with black, cream, green, and red silk and silver; steel central boss, pierced and inlaid with gold

Second half sixteenth century

Diameter, 67.0 (26⅜)
İstanbul, Topkapı Sarayı Müzesi, 1/2597
Topkapı Palace Collection
(İstanbul 1983, E. 226)

103. Velvet bow case; embroidered with blue, green, and red silk and gold; affixed with gilded silver studs to leather lining
Mid-sixteenth century
74.0 × 34.0 (29⅛ × 13⅜)
İstanbul, Topkapı Sarayı Müzesi, 1/10989
Topkapı Palace Collection
(Gönül n.d., pl. 22; Paris 1953, no. 23; Rogers 1986c, pl. 92)

104a and 104b. Leather bow case and quiver; embroidered and appliquéd
Second quarter sixteenth century
Bow case, 68.0 × 35.0 (26¾ × 13¾); quiver, 42.0 × 26.0 (16½ × 10¼)
Vienna, Kunsthistorisches Museum, Waffensammlung, C. 5 and C. 5a
Registered in the Ambras Castle Collection in Tirol in 1603
(Sacken 1855, 280; Grosz and Thomas 1936, 97, no. 7; Thomas 1963–1964, fig. 5)

105. Leather canteen; embroidered and appliquéd; ivory, silver, and horn components
Second half sixteenth century
29.5 × 26.0 × 13.5 (11⅝ × 10¼ × 5⁵⁄₁₆)
Vienna, Kunsthistorisches Museum, Waffensammlung, C. 28
Given by Sultan Murad III to Emperor Rudolf II before 1581
(Vienna 1932, no. 147; Grosz and Thomas 1936, 92, no. 7; Thomas 1963–1964, fig. 8)

106. Leather boots; embroidered and appliquéd
Made for Sultan Selim II mid-sixteenth century
Height, 53.0 (20⅞)
İstanbul, Topkapı Sarayı Müzesi, 2/4447
Topkapı Palace Collection
(Paris 1953, no. 488; Atasoy 1969, fig. 1; Denny 1982, pl. 137; İstanbul 1983, E. 108)

107. Wood throne; inlaid with ebony, ivory, mother-of-pearl, and silver strips; set with turquoise in a gold mount; painted seat; constructed of five interlocking pieces
Mid-sixteenth century
129.0 × 163.5 × 75.0 (50¹³⁄₁₆ × 64³⁄₁₆ × 29⁹⁄₁₆)
İstanbul, Topkapı Sarayı Müzesi, 2/2879
Topkapı Palace Collection
(Arseven n.d., fig. 570; Öz n.d., 54; Kerametli 1961, fig. 10; İstanbul 1983, E. 77; Frankfurt 1985, vol. 2, no. 8/1)

108. Wood bookstand; inlaid with ebony, ivory, and silver strips; painted hinges and underside
Mid-sixteenth century
Closed, 82.3 × 28.8 (32½ × 11⅜)
İstanbul, Türk ve İslam Eserleri Müzesi, 127
Transferred from the Mausoleum of Hürrem Sultan, 1926
(Çulpan 1968, fig. 11; Yücel 1977, 62)

109. Wood Koran box; inlaid with ebony, ivory, mother-of-pearl, tortoiseshell, and silver; interior of dome painted
Second quarter sixteenth century
Inscribed with Koranic verse (II:255) and prayers written in sülüs
78.0 × 50.7 × 50.7 (30¾ × 19¹⁵⁄₁₆ × 19¹⁵⁄₁₆)
İstanbul, Türk ve İslam Eserleri Müzesi, 5
Transferred from the Library of the Aya Sofya Mosque, 1918
(İstanbul 1983, E. 76)

110. Wood Koran box; inlaid with ebony, ivory, mother-of-pearl, and tortoiseshell; originally set with gems or gold blossoms; interior of dome painted and base lined with silk
Second half sixteenth century
Inscribed with selections from the Hadis (Concordance VI:62) written in talik
76.0 × 66.0 (29¹⁵⁄₁₆ × 26)
İstanbul, Türk ve İslam Eserleri Müzesi, 13
Transferred from the Mausoleum of Sultan Mehmed III, 1915
(İstanbul 1983, E. 148)

111. Wood Koran box; inlaid with ebony, mahogany, ivory, mother-of-pearl, and lead; interior of dome painted
Inscribed with the besmele written in makili kufi
Second half sixteenth century
Inscribed with the besmele written in makili kufi
166.0 × 52.8 × 52.8 (65⅜ × 20⅞ × 20⅞)
İstanbul, Türk ve İslam Eserleri Müzesi, 2
Transferred from the Mausoleum of Sultan Selim II, 1914
(İstanbul 1983, E. 149; Frankfurt 1985, vol. 2, no. 8/4)

112a and 112b. Child's kaftan with matching pants; green silk; compound satin with supplemental twill (atlas); white cotton lining bordered with mauve silk
Made for Sultan Süleyman c. 1510
Length of kaftan, 72.0 (28⅜); length of pants (including socks), 70.0 (27⁹⁄₁₆)
İstanbul, Topkapı Sarayı Müzesi, 13/92 and 13/93
Topkapı Palace Collection

113a and 113b. Child's kaftan with matching detachable sleeves; red and yellow silk; compound satin with supplemental twill (serenk); beige cotton lining bordered with blue silk
Second quarter sixteenth century
Length of kaftan, 72.5 (28⁹⁄₁₆); length of sleeves, 47.3 (18⅝)
İstanbul, Topkapı Sarayı Müzesi, 13/1015
Topkapı Palace Collection
(İstanbul 1961, no. 17)

114. Kaftan with reciprocal pattern; light blue, green, and red silk and gold; compound satin with supplemental twill (kemha); quilted; beige cotton lining bordered with green silk
Second quarter sixteenth century
Length, 124.0 (48¹³⁄₁₆)
İstanbul, Topkapı Sarayı Müzesi, 13/46
Topkapı Palace Collection
(Öz 1950, pl. XXIV; Sevin 1975, 17; Mackie 1980, ill. 201 and pl. 60; İstanbul 1983, E. 102; Rogers 1986c, pl. 7)

115. Pair of detachable sleeves; dusty-rose silk with gold; compound satin with supplemental twill (kemha); white cotton lining bordered with green silk

Made for Sultan Süleyman, second quarter sixteenth century
Length, 95.0 (37⅜)
İstanbul, Topkapı Sarayı Müzesi, 13/72
Topkapı Palace Collection

116. Ceremonial kaftan with saz pattern; blue, blackish-brown, peach, green, red, and white silk and gold; compound satin with supplemental twill (kemha); yellow silk lining bordered with red silk

Made for Şehzade Bayezid, mid-sixteenth century
Length, 148.0 (58¼)
İstanbul, Topkapı Sarayı Müzesi, 13/37
Topkapı Palace Collection
(Öz 1950, pl. XX; Akurgal et al 1966, 207; Sevin 1975, 16; Altay 1979, 7 and 19; Öney 1980, pl. 138; Sanat 1982, 102; Rogers 1986c, pl. 36)

117. Kaftan with star pattern; blue, cream, and red silk and gold; compound satin with supplemental twill (kemha); dark red silk lining bordered with yellow silk

Mid-sixteenth century
Length, 138.5 (54⁵⁄₁₆)
İstanbul, Topkapı Sarayı Müzesi, 13/21
Topkapı Palace Collection
(Öz 1950, pls. VIII and IX; Paris 1953, no. 457; Schmidt 1958, fig 286; Sevin 1975, 15; Altay 1979, 2; Mackie 1980, ill. 200; Öney 1980, pl. 137)

118. Ceremonial kaftan with ogival pattern; blue, green, red, white, and yellow silk; compound satin with supplemental twill (serenk); lined with sable

Mid-sixteenth century
Length, 135.0 (53³⁄₁₆)
İstanbul, Topkapı Sarayı Müzesi, 13/932
Topkapı Palace Collection
(Öz 1951, pl. XCV; Sevin 1975, 18; Washington 1966, no. 205; Altay 1979, 20; İstanbul 1983, E. 106)

119. Ceremonial kaftan with pinecone pattern; green and red silk, gold and silver; compound satin (seraser); white cotton lining bordered with dark red silk

Mid-sixteenth century
Length, 157.0 (61¹³⁄₁₆)
İstanbul, Topkapı Sarayı Müzesi, 13/9
Topkapı Palace Collection
(Mackie 1980, ill. 210; Frankfurt 1985, vol. 2, no. 5/2; Rogers 1986c, pl. 48)

120. Embroidered ceremonial kaftan; red compound satin with supplemental twill (atlas); appliquéd bands embroidered with black, blue, and two shades of red silk and gold (zerduz); yellow silk lining bordered with purple silk

Made for Şehzade Mehmed, second quarter sixteenth century
Length, 149.0 (58¹¹⁄₁₆)
İstanbul, Topkapı Sarayı Müzesi, 13/739
Topkapı Palace Collection

(Sevin 1975, 19; Altay 1979, 26; Berker 1981, 18; Barışta 1981, no. 1; Sanat 1982, 142; İstanbul 1983, E. 101; Frankfurt 1985, vol. 2, no. 5/4; Rogers 1986c, pl. 86)

121a and 121b. Kaftan with matching detachable sleeves; rosy-beige silk; compound satin with supplemental twill (atlas); white cotton lining bordered with green silk

Made for Sultan Süleyman, mid-sixteenth century
Length of kaftan, 146.0 (57½); length of sleeves, 49.0 (19⁵⁄₁₆)
İstanbul, Topkapı Sarayı Müzesi, 13/100
Topkapı Palace Collection

122. Talismanic shirt; white linen painted with black, blue, red, and gold; white cotton lining bordered with rose-colored silk

Second quarter sixteenth century
Inscribed with verses from the Koran (XLVIII, XXXVI–XLVI, and XVIII) written in sülüs, gubari, and makili kufi
Length, 122.5 (48¼)
İstanbul, Topkapı Sarayı Müzesi, 13/1150
Topkapı Palace Collection
(İstanbul 1983, E. 54)

123. Talismanic shirt; white linen painted with black, blue, red, gold, and silver; lined with red silk

Made by Derviş Ahmed b. Süleyman for Şehzade Selim in 972 (1564/1565)
Inscribed with verses from the Koran (XVIII, XXXVI–XLVI, and XLVIII) written in sülüs, gubari, and makili kufi
Length, 106.0 (41¾)
İstanbul, Topkapı Sarayı Müzesi, 13/1133
Topkapı Palace Collection
(Gökyay 1976, 101)

124. Handkerchief; cinnamon-colored linen printed black; borders embroidered with blue, brown, green, red, white, and yellow silk and gold

Second quarter sixteenth century
55.0 × 53.0 (21¹¹⁄₁₆ × 20⅞)
İstanbul, Topkapı Sarayı Müzesi, 31/58
Transferred from the Mausoleum of Şehzade Mehmed
(Arseven n.d., fig. 600; Barışta 1981, no. 12; Berker 1981, 48 and 49; İstanbul 1983, E. 98)

125. Handkerchief; cinnamon-colored linen printed black; borders embroidered with pale blue, brown, green, pink, red, and yellow silk and gold

Second quarter sixteenth century
52.0 × 52.0 (20½ × 20½)
İstanbul, Topkapı Sarayı Müzesi, 31/60
Transferred from the Mausoleum of Şehzade Mehmed
(Gönül n.d., pl. 20; Barışta 1981, no. 13; İstanbul 1983, E. 99; Rogers 1986c, pl. 88)

126. Handkerchief; cinnamon-colored linen printed black; borders embroidered with light blue, brown, green, red, white, and yellow silk and gold

Second quarter sixteenth century
52.5 × 50.5 (20¹¹⁄₁₆ × 19⅞)

İstanbul, Topkapı Sarayı Müzesi, 31/59
Transferred from the Mausoleum of Şehzade Mehmed
(Arseven n.d., fig. 102; İstanbul 1983, E. 97; Rogers 1986c, pl. 88)

127. Handkerchief; cinnamon-colored linen printed black; borders embroidered with light blue, brown, green, red, white, and yellow silk and gold

Second quarter sixteenth century
53.5 × 52.8 (21¹/₁₆ × 20¹⁵/₁₆)
İstanbul, Topkapı Sarayı Müzesi, 31/61
Transferred from the Mausoleum of Şehzade Mehmed
(Gönül n.d., pl. 18; Barışta 1981, no. 8)

128. Handkerchief; ivory-colored linen; borders embroidered in blue, brown, green, and red silk and gold

Second quarter sixteenth century
52.3 × 51.5 (20⁵/₈ × 20³/₈)
İstanbul, Topkapı Sarayı Müzesi, 31/1473
Transferred from the Mausoleum of Hürrem Sultan
(Berker 1978, fig. 6; Gönül 1969, fig. 12; Barışta 1981, no. 6; Rogers 1986c, pl. 90)

129. Headband; beige linen embroidered with blue and red silk, gold and silver

Second quarter sixteenth century
55.5 × 5.0 (21⁷/₈ × 2)
İstanbul, Topkapı Sarayı Müzesi, 31/1478
Transferred from the Mausoleum of Hürrem Sultan
(Arseven n.d., fig. 58; Gönül n.d., pl. 17c; Barışta 1981, no. 15; Berker 1983, figs. 18a and b; İstanbul 1983, E. 100)

130. Headband; beige linen embroidered with black, blue, cream, and red silk and gold

Second quarter sixteenth century
56.5 × 4.5 (22¼ × 1¾)
İstanbul, Topkapı Sarayı Müzesi, 31/1480
Transferred from the Mausoleum of Hürrem Sultan
(Gönül n.d., pl. 17a; Vienna 1932, no. 26; Berker 1981, 22; Frankfurt 1985, vol. 2, no. 5/7a)

131. Headband; beige linen embroidered with black, blue, green, and red silk, gold and silver

Second half sixteenth century
55.0 × 5.0 (21¹¹/₁₆ × 2)
İstanbul, Topkapı Sarayı Müzesi, 31/1477
Transferred from the Mausoleum of Sultan Murad III
(Berker 1981, 22; Frankfurt 1985, vol. 2, no. 5/7b)

132. Sash; cinnamon-colored linen embroidered with light blue, green, pink, tan, white, and yellow silk and gold

Mid-sixteenth century
177.0 × 29.0 (69¹¹/₁₆ × 11⁷/₁₆)
İstanbul, Topkapı Sarayı Müzesi, 31/50
Topkapı Palace Collection
(Arseven, n.d. fig. 575; Gönül n.d., pl. 21a; İstanbul 1983, E. 109)

133. Sash; cinnamon-colored linen embroidered with blue, light brown, green, and red silk and gold

Mid-sixteenth century
217.0 × 28.0 (85⁷/₁₆ × 11¹/₁₆)
İstanbul, Topkapı Sarayı Müzesi, 31/49
Topkapı Palace Collection
(Arseven n.d., fig. 576; Gönül n.d., pl. 21b; İstanbul 1983, E. 110)

134. Sash; cinnamon-colored linen banded with red satin embroidered with blue, green, and pink silk and gold

Mid-sixteenth century
520.0 × 28.5 (204¾ × 11¼)
İstanbul, Topkapı Sarayı Müzesi, 31/1475
Transferred from the Mausoleum of Sultan Ahmed I

135. Cushion cover; red compound satin embroidered with three shades of blue, three shades of green, and three shades of yellow silk, gold and silver

Mid-sixteenth century
86.7 × 83.8 (34⅛ × 33)
Los Angeles County Museum of Art, The Edwin Binney, 3rd Collection of Turkish Art, M. 85.237.8
Purchased
(Binney 1981, Textile 2A; Denny 1982, pl. 150)

136. Quilt cover; off-white cotton embroidered with seven colors and thirteen shades, including black, blue, five shades of tan ranging from beige to brown, two shades of green, two shades of red, white, and yellow silk; fragment

Mid-sixteenth century
231.0 × 79.0 (90¹⁵/₁₆ × 31⅛)
Washington, The Textile Museum, 1.22
Purchased before 1940
(Mackie 1973, no. 10 and pl. II; Mackie 1980, ill. 219 and pl. 62)

137. Quilt cover; white linen embroidered with blue, green, and red silk; constructed of three loom widths

Second half sixteenth century
232.0 × 170.0 (91⁵/₁₆ × 66¹⁵/₁₆)
İstanbul, Topkapı Sarayı Müzesi, 31/4
Topkapı Palace Collection
(Arseven n.d., fig. 565; Gönül n.d., pl. 27; Öz 1942, 35; Barışta 1981, no. 43; İstanbul 1983, E. 144)

138. Portfolio; dark red velvet embroidered with blue silk, gold, and silver; lined with green silk

Second half sixteenth century
Closed, 19.0 × 41.0 (7½ × 16⅛)
İstanbul, Topkapı Sarayı Müzesi, 31/168
Topkapı Palace Collection
(Gönül n.d., 24; Berker 1981, 3; Denny 1982, pl. 136; İstanbul 1983, E. 122)

139. Portfolio; red velvet appliquéd with silver seraser; stitched with silver

Second half sixteenth century
Extended, 112.0 × 73.0 (44⅛ × 28¾)
İstanbul, Topkapı Sarayı Müzesi, 31/1891

Topkapı Palace Collection
(İstanbul 1983, E. 123)

140. Sharkskin box; wooden core; exterior embroidered with blue, cream, green, red silk and gold; interior covered with red silk; gold brackets, hinges, and clasp
Second half sixteenth century
17.0 × 27.0 × 14.0 (6⅝ × 10⅝ × 5½)
İstanbul, Topkapı Sarayı Müzesi, 31/268
Topkapı Palace Collection
(Berker 1981, 32; *Sanat* 1982, 144; İstanbul 1983, E. 117; Rogers 1986c, pl. 94)

141. Fragment with triple ball pattern; blue, ivory, red, and yellow silk and gold; compound satin with supplemental twill (kemha); constructed of four pieces
Mid-sixteenth century
112.0 × 60.0 (44⅛ × 23⅝)
Los Angeles County Museum of Art, The Edwin Binney, 3rd Collection of Turkish Art, M. 85.237.1
Purchased
(Binney 1979, Textile 2)

142. Fragment with lattice pattern; light blue, pale green, and red silk and gold; compound satin with supplemental twill (kemha)
Second half sixteenth century
132.8 × 64.0 (52¼ × 25³⁄₁₆)
Kuwait National Museum, Dar al-Athar al-Islamiya, LNS 105 T
Purchased
(Jenkins 1983, 153)

143. Fragment with ogival pattern; blue, ivory, and red silk and gold; compound satin with supplemental twill (kemha)
Second half sixteenth century
161.0 × 67.0 (63⅜ × 26⅜)
Washington, The Textile Museum, 1.70
Formerly in the Kelekian Collection; purchased 1952
(Guiffrey and Migeon 1908, pl. 38; Denny 1982, fig. 5; Mackie 1973, no. 5; Mackie 1980, ill. 202)

144. Fragment with ogival pattern; ivory, purple, and red silk and gold; compound satin with supplemental twill (kemha)
Second half sixteenth century
125.7 × 67.0 (49½ × 26⅜)
New York, The Metropolitan Museum of Art, Anonymous gift, 1949, 49.32.79
Acquired 1949
(Dimand 1935, fig. 25; Day 1950, 117)

145. Fragment with ogival pattern; blue, ivory, and rosy beige silk and gold; compound satin with supplemental twill (kemha)
Second half sixteenth century
60.0 × 67.0 (23⅝ × 26⅜)
New York, The Metropolitan Museum of Art, Purchase, Joseph Pulitzer Bequest, 52.20.22
Formerly in the Kelekian Collection; purchased 1952

(Guiffrey and Migeon 1908, 43; Berlin 1982, no. 111)

146. Fragment with double ogival pattern; black, blue, and red silk and gold; compound satin with supplemental twill (kemha)
Second half sixteenth century
Maximum, 127.0 × 65.0 (50 × 25⅝)
New York, The Metropolitan Museum of Art, Purchase, Joseph Pulitzer Bequest, 52.20.18
Formerly in the Kelekian Collection; purchased 1952
(Guiffrey and Migeon 1908, pl. 44; Metropolitan 1968, no. 46)

147. Fragment with vertical-stem pattern; blue, ivory, green, and red silk and gold; compound satin with supplemental twill (kemha); constructed of three pieces
Second half sixteenth century
121.9 × 67.3 (48 × 26½)
New York, The Metropolitan Museum of Art, Purchase, Joseph Pulitzer Bequest, 52.20.21
Formerly in the Kelekian Collection; purchased 1952
(Metropolitan 1952, 103; Dimand 1958, fig. 243; Metropolitan 1968, no. 45; Metropolitan 1975; Mackie 1980, ill. 206; Berlin 1982, no. 113)

148. Fragment with ogival pattern; red silk and gold; compound satin and velvet (çatma)
Second quarter sixteenth century
260.4 × 63.5 (102½ × 25)
New York, The Metropolitan Museum of Art, Rogers Fund, 1912, 12.49.5
Purchased 1912
(St. Clair 1973, fig. 30)

149. Fragment with swirling roundels; two shades of green and red silk and silver; compound satin and velvet (çatma)
Mid-sixteenth century
145.5 × 55.0 (57¼ × 21⅞)
Kuwait National Museum, Dar al-Athar al-Islamiya, LNS 99 T
Purchased

150. Floor covering; dark blue and red silk, gold and silver; compound satin with supplemental twill (kemha); fragment constructed of three loom widths
Second half sixteenth century
400.0 × 300.0 (157½ × 118⅛)
İstanbul, Topkapı Sarayı Müzesi, 13/1783
Topkapı Palace Collection
(Öz 1951, pl. LXVIII; İstanbul 1983, E. 235)

151. Fragment with medallions; ivory and red silk and gold metal; compound satin and velvet (çatma)
Second half sixteenth century
174.0 × 66.5 (68½ × 26¼)
Washington, The Textile Museum, 1.55
Purchased 1951
(Denny 1972, fig. 18; Mackie 1973, no. 16)

152. Floor covering; ivory, bluish-green, and red silk and silver; compound satin and velvet (çatma); constructed of four loom widths

Second half sixteenth century
490.0 × 268.0 (193 × 105½)
The Detroit Institute of Arts, Gift of Mr. and Mrs. Eugene H. Welker, 48.137
Formerly in the Doria Collection at Villa Doria-Pamphili, Rome (until 1918); Giorgio Sangiorgi and Adolph Loewi Collections; acquired 1948
(Weibel 1948)

153. Saddlecloth; black, blue, green, and red silk, gold and silver; tapestry-woven fragment

Second half sixteenth century
85.5 × 55.0 (33½ × 21⅝)
Washington, The Textile Museum, 1.38
Purchased 1931
(Denny 1972, fig. 22; Mackie 1973, no. 13)

154. Cushion cover; pale bluish-green and red silk and silver; compound satin and velvet (çatma); fragmentary

Mid-sixteenth century
97.8 × 76.1 (38½ × 30)
Cambridge (Mass.), Harvard University Art Museums, The Edwin Binney, 3rd Collection of Turkish Art, 85.295
Purchased
(Binney 1979, Textile 1)

155. Cushion cover; bluish-green and red silk and gold; compound satin and velvet (çatma)

Second half sixteenth century
123.5 × 66.0 (48⅝ × 26)
Boston, Museum of Fine Arts, 77.256
Gift of Martin Brimmer, 1877

156. Cushion cover; green silk, and gold and silver; compound satin (seraser)

Second half sixteenth century
106.0 × 67.0 (41¾ × 26⅜)
Washington, The Textile Museum, 1.65
Purchased 1951
(Mackie 1973, no. 12)

157. Cover; red silk and gold; compound satin and velvet (çatma); constructed of two loom widths

Late sixteenth century
163.9 × 128.2 (64½ × 50½)
The Art Institute of Chicago, 1949.300
Gift of Burton Y. Berry, Chicago, 1949

158. Prayer rug with a pair of columns; two shades of blue, two shades of green, ivory, red, and golden tan; silk warp and weft with wool and cotton pile

Second half sixteenth century
172.5 × 128.5 (67¹⁵⁄₁₆ × 50⅝)
Kuwait National Museum, Dar al-Athar al-Islamiya, LNS 29 R
Formerly in the Aberley Collection; purchased
(Herrmann 1982, no. I; Jenkins 1983, 157)

159. Prayer rug with three pairs of columns; three shades of blue, two shades of green, ivory, red, and tan; silk warp and weft with wool and cotton pile

Second half sixteenth century
172.7 × 127.0 (68 × 50)
New York, The Metropolitan Museum of Art, Gift of James F. Ballard, 1922, 22.100.51
Formerly in the James F. Ballard Collection; acquired 1922
(Dimand 1944, 215; Dimand 1958, fig. 204; Bode and Kühnel 1958, fig. 53; Schlosser 1963, no. 14; Lukens 1965, no. 58; Beattie 1968, fig. 1; Metropolitan 1968, no. 28; Ellis 1969, fig. 4; Dimand 1973, no. 105; Washington 1974, no. I; Mackie 1980, ill. 192)

160. Prayer rug with saz design; black, two shades of blue, brown, two shades of green, ivory, red, and yellow; silk warp and weft with wool and cotton pile

Second half sixteenth century
181.0 × 127.0 (71¼ × 50)
Vienna, Österreichisches Museum für Angewandte Kunst, T. 8327
Formerly in the royal Austrian collection at Schönbrunn Palace
(Riegl 1892, vol. 2, pl. XIV; Martin 1908, vol. 1, fig. 331; Sarre and Martin 1912, no. 155; Sarre and Trenkwald 1926, pl. 56; Ellis 1969, pl. I; Dimand 1973, 200; Erdmann 1960, pl. VII; Schlosser 1963, pl. II; London 1976, no. 45; Vienna 1977, no. 42; Denny 1979a, no. 19; Mackie 1980, pl. 55; Frankfurt 1985, vol. 2, no. 3/8)
Shown in Washington only

161. Rug with saz design; two shades of blue, green, ivory, red, and yellow; cotton warp and wool weft and pile

Second half sixteenth century
223.0 × 188.0 (87¹³⁄₁₆ × 74)
Paris, Musée des Arts Décoratifs, A. 7861
Formerly in the Sichel Collection; purchased 1894
(Martin 1908, vol. 1, fig. 327; Erdmann 1960, fig. 137; Bode and Kühnel 1958, fig. 50; Schlosser 1963, no. 18; Paris 1971, no. 5; Paris 1977, no. 311; Mackie 1980, ill. 183; Yetkin 1981, ill. 78; İstanbul 1983, E. 240; Frankfurt 1985, vol. 2, no. 3/9)

162. Rug with çintemani pattern; black, blue, two shades of green, ivory, red, golden tan, and yellow; wool warp, weft, and pile

Second half sixteenth century
200.6 × 121.9 (78¾ × 48)
New York, The Metropolitan Museum of Art, Gift of Joseph V. McMullan, 1971, 1971.263.2
Acquired 1971
(McMullan 1965, no. 6; Frankfurt 1969, no. 5; Metropolitan 1970, no. 7; McMullan 1972, no. 6; Dimand 1973, fig. 194; Yetkin 1981, pl. 75)

163. Plate with central hexagon; molded white ware

Second quarter sixteenth century
9.0 × 42.5 (3⁹⁄₁₆ × 16¾)
İstanbul, Topkapı Sarayı Müzesi, 15/6086
Topkapı Palace Collection
(Raby and Yücel 1983, figs. 11–13)

164. Jug; underglaze painted in white slip and blue
Second quarter sixteenth century
25.4 × 16.5 (10 × 6½)
Kuwait National Museum, Dar al-Athar al-Islamiya, LNS 174 C
Purchased
(Jenkins 1983, 119)

165. Large bowl; underglaze painted in blue
First quarter sixteenth century
23.2 × 46.2 (9⅛ × 18³⁄₁₆)
Paris, Musée du Louvre, Section Islamique, 7880-92
Transferred from Musée de Cluny, 1926
(Lane 1957, fig. 12; Paris 1971, no. 93; Paris 1977, no. 589)

166. Mosque lamp; underglaze painted in blue
First quarter sixteenth century
Three cartouches on neck inscribed with pious evocations to Ali;
those on the body inscribed with "Allah, Muhammed, Ali," written
in kufi and sülüs
27.6 × 18.2 (10⅞ × 7³⁄₁₆)
İstanbul, Arkeoloji Müzesi, Çinili Köşk, 41/2
Transferred from the Mosque of Sokollu Mehmed Paşa, 1885
(Öz 1957, no. 120; Washington 1966, no. 262; Ünal 1969, fig. 8;
Kolsuk 1976, 82 and 83; Tuncay 1978, fig. 2)

167. Spherical hanging ornament; underglaze painted in blue
First quarter sixteenth century
Inscriptions written in kufi undeciphered
Diameter, 17.0 (6¹¹⁄₁₆)
London, The Board of Trustees of the Victoria and Albert Museum,
337-1903
Purchased 1903
(Lane 1957, 261)
Shown in Washington only

168. Pen box; underglaze painted in blue; silver lid and
containers added later
First quarter sixteenth century
Inscriptions written in kufi on sides undeciphered; panel on top
inscribed with a portion of Koranic verse (LXI:13) written in nesih;
seal of Sultan Selim III on silver components
6.3 × 29.6 × 6.0 (2½ × 11¹¹⁄₁₆ × 2⅜)
London, The Trustees of the British Museum, G. 1983.7
Godman Bequest, 1983
(Lane 1957, fig. 23; Lane 1971, pl. 25B; London 1976, no. 411;
Rogers 1984, pl. XII; Frankfurt 1985, vol. 2, no. 2/3; Rogers 1985c,
56)

169. Plate with concentric panels; underglaze painted in blue
First quarter sixteenth century
Inscriptions written in kufi undeciphered
7.3 × 40.0 (2⅞ × 15¾)
Paris, Musée du Louvre, Section Islamique, 6321
Piet Lataudrie Bequest, 1909
(Lane 1957, fig. 8; Paris 1971, no. 90; London 1976, no. 407;
Denny 1977, fig. 2; Paris 1977, no. 581; İstanbul 1985, E. 30;
Frankfurt 1985, vol. 2, no. 2/2)

170. Plate with peony scroll; underglaze painted in blue
Second quarter sixteenth century
9.4 × 36.5 (3¹¹⁄₁₆ × 14⅜)
İstanbul, Arkeoloji Müzesi, Çinili Köşk, 41/155
Transferred from the Yıldız Palace, 1912
(Munich 1965, no. 118; İstanbul 1983, E. 33)

171. Plate with floral scroll; underglaze painted in blue and
black
Mid-sixteenth century
7.5 × 35.5 (2¹⁵⁄₁₆ × 14)
Copenhagen, The David Collection, 27/1978
Purchased 1978
(Carswell 1982, pl. 97)

172. Plate with floral bouquet; underglaze painted in blue
Second quarter sixteenth century
10.2 × 31.7 (4 × 12½)
New York, The Metropolitan Museum of Art, Rogers Fund, 1929,
29.33
Purchased 1929
(Grube 1961a, fig. 4; Denny 1974a, fig. 10)

173. Plate with three bunches of grapes; underglaze painted
in blue and turquoise
Second quarter sixteenth century
6.7 × 38.4 (2⅝ × 15⅛)
New York, The Metropolitan Museum of Art, Harris Brisbane Dick
Fund, 1966, 66.4.10
Formerly in the Adda Collection; purchased 1966
(Rackham 1959, no. 62; Denny 1977, fig. 30; J. A. Pope 1972, fig.
1; Denny 1980, ill. 155; Carswell 1985, no. 76)

174. Plate with diaper pattern; underglaze painted in blue
and turquoise
Second quarter sixteenth century
7.7 × 39.4 (3¹⁄₁₆ × 15½)
New York, The Metropolitan Museum of Art, Bequest of Benjamin
Altman, 1913, 14.40.727
Formerly in the Henry G. Marquand Collection; acquired 1914
(Marquand 1903, no. 1191; Metropolitan 1930, fig. 104; Dimand
1958, fig. 144; Lane 1957, figs. 25 and 26; Grube 1961a, fig. 1;
Metropolitan 1968, no. 17; Lane 1971, pl. 29B; Denny 1977, figs. 7,
32, 33, and 34; J. A. Pope 1972, figs. 21 and 27; Denny 1980,
ill. 41)
Shown in New York only

175. Plate with vases; underglaze painted in blue and
turquoise
Second quarter sixteenth century
5.5 × 34.8 (2³⁄₁₆ × 13⅝)
London, The Trustees of the British Museum, G. 1983.52
Godman Bequest, 1983
(Lane 1957, fig. 39; Rogers 1984, fig. 3; Rogers 1985a, fig. 12)

176. Plate with a snake; underglaze painted in blue and
turquoise
Second quarter sixteenth century
5.7 × 33.7 (2¼ × 13¼)

London, The Board of Trustees of the Victoria and Albert Museum, C. 2019-1910
Formerly in the Louis Huth Collection; George Salting Bequest, 1910
(Christie's 1905, no. 244; London 1907, no. 10; Lane 1957, fig. 38; Lane 1971, pl. 30B; Miller 1972, 85; Öney 1976, 99)
Shown in Washington only

177. Plate with ships; underglaze painted in blue and turquoise
Second quarter sixteenth century
4.0 × 32.6 (1⁹⁄₁₆ × 12¹³⁄₁₆)
London, The Board of Trustees of the Victoria and Albert Museum, 713-1902
Formerly in the Godman Collection; purchased 1902
(Lane 1957, fig. 40)
Shown in Washington only

178. Bottle; underglaze painted in blue and turquoise
Second quarter sixteenth century
43.5 × 20.3 (17⅛ × 8)
London, The Trustees of the British Museum, 78 12-30 519
Acquired in Italy by Eugene Piot (died c. 1832); Henderson Bequest, 1878
(Hobson 1932, fig. 110; Carswell 1982, pl. 73; İstanbul 1983, E. 41; Rogers 1985c, 53)

179. Plate with spiral scroll; underglaze painted in blue and turquoise
Second quarter sixteenth century
7.5 × 44.0 (2¹⁵⁄₁₆ × 17⁵⁄₁₆)
Kuwait National Museum, Dar al-Athar al-Islamiya, LNS 231 C
Purchased
(Sotheby's 1981, no. 218; Carswell 1982, pl. 74; Rogers 1983b, fig. 15)

180. Panel with seven hexagonal tiles; underglaze painted in blue and turquoise; blue-glazed triangular tiles modern
Second quarter sixteenth century
Diameter of each, 17.5 to 18.5 (6⅞ to 7⁵⁄₁₆)
İstanbul, Arkeoloji Müzesi, Çinili Köşk, 41/515 (three tiles) and 41/1121 (two tiles)
Purchased 1943
(Öney 1975, pl. 46; İstanbul 1983, E. 44)

181. Plate with floral spray; underglaze painted in blue, green, and purple
Mid-sixteenth century
7.6 × 38.9 (3 × 15¹⁵⁄₁₆)
London, The Trustees of the British Museum, G. 1983.33
Godman Bequest, 1983
(Denny 1974a, fig. 6; Rogers 1985a, fig. 11)

182. Plate with saz spray; underglaze painted in blue, turquoise, green, and purple
Mid-sixteenth century
4.3 × 27.6 (1¹¹⁄₁₆ × 10⅞)
Private collection
Formerly in F. A. White, E. L. Paget, and Adda Collections
(Rackham 1959, no. 69; S. C. Welch 1972, figs. 7 and 8; Denny 1974a, fig. 12; Denny 1977, figs. 169 and 170; Denny 1980, ill. 39; Denny 1981, fig. 3)
Shown in Washington and New York only

183. Jar; underglaze painted in blue, green, and purple
Mid-sixteenth century
33.5 × 23.7 (13³⁄₁₆ × 9⅜)
London, The Trustees of the British Museum, 78 12-30 513
Henderson Bequest, 1878
(Lane 1971, pl. D)

184. Plate with peacock; underglaze painted in blue, turquoise, green, and purple
Mid-sixteenth century
7.5 × 37.5 (2¹⁵⁄₁₆ × 14¾)
Paris, Musée du Louvre, Section Islamique, 3449
Koechlin Bequest, 1932
(Paris 1903, no. 377; Paris 1953, no. 242; Kiefer 1956, fig. 10; Paris 1971, no. 95; Paris 1977, no. 590; Rogers 1983b, fig. 10; Frankfurt 1985, vol. 2, no. 2/15)

185. Plate with floral spray; underglaze painted in blue, turquoise, green, and purple
Mid-sixteenth century
7.0 × 37.4 (2¾ × 14¾)
London, The Trustees of the British Museum, G. 1983.21
Godman Bequest, 1983

186. Plate with pinecones and blossoms; underglaze painted in blue, turquoise, green, and purple
Mid-sixteenth century
7.0 × 38.8 (2¾ × 15⁵⁄₁₆)
London, The Trustees of the British Museum, G. 1983.48
Godman Bequest, 1983
(Rogers 1985a, fig. 4)

187. Jug; underglaze painted in blue, turquoise, green, and purple
Mid-sixteenth century
20.0 × 14.0 (7⅞ × 5½)
Paris, Musée du Louvre, Section Islamique, 7257
Gift of Jeuniette, 1919

188. Lid; underglaze painted in blue, turquoise, and red
Mid-sixteenth century
2.5 × 20.3 (1 × 8)
Paris, Musée du Louvre, Section Islamique, A.O. 5960
Gift of Auguste Chabrière, 1904
(Migeon 1922, vol. 2, no. 215; Denny 1977, fig. 187; Kühnel 1977, pls. 14 and 24a; Paris 1977, no. 594; Frankfurt 1985, vol. 2, no. 2/19)

189. Plate with central hatayi; underglaze painted in blue, green, and red
Mid-sixteenth century
6.5 × 29.8 (2⁹⁄₁₆ × 11¾)
London, The Trustees of the British Museum, 78 12-30 502
Henderson Bequest, 1978
(Hobson 1932, fig. 98; Rogers 1983b, no. 142)

190. Plate with central cartouche and a pair of birds; underglaze painted in blue, turquoise, and red
Mid-sixteenth century
6.2 × 31.2 (2⁷/₁₆ × 12⁵/₁₆)
Paris, Musée du Louvre, Section Islamique, 7880-83
Transferred from Musée de Cluny, 1926
(Paris 1977, no. 605; Rogers 1983b, fig. 11; Frankfurt 1985, vol. 2, no. 2/32)

191. Mosque lamp; underglaze painted in blue, turquoise, black, and red
c. 1557
Inscribed on the neck with the Ayet el-Nur (XXIV:35) written in sülüs
48.2 × 31.5 (19 × 12⁷/₁₆)
London, The Board of Trustees of the Victoria and Albert Museum, 131-1885
From the Süleymaniye Mosque; acquired 1885
(Rackham 1934/1935, pl. 19; Lane 1957, fig. 43; Ünal 1969, fig. 19; Lane 1971, pl. 39; Denny 1977, fig. 190)
Shown in Washington only

192. Plate with hatayi scroll and peafowl; underglaze painted in blue, green, and red
Mid-sixteenth century
3.8 × 30.3 (1½ × 11¹³/₁₆)
London, The Board of Trustees of the Victoria and Albert Museum, C. 2005-1910
George Salting Bequest, 1910
(Christie's 1899, no. 91; London 1907, no. 3; Rackham 1934/1935, pl. 20a; Erdmann 1963, fig. 45; Süslü 1976, fig. 4; Denny 1981, fig. 6)
Shown in Washington only

193. Pen box; underglaze painted in blue, green, and red
Third quarter sixteenth century
9.0 × 28.5 × 11.6 (3⁹/₁₆ × 11¼ × 4⁹/₁₆)
Paris, Musée du Louvre, Section Islamique, 4048
Purchased 1897
(Paris 1971, no. 97)

194. Large jug; underglaze painted in blue, green, and red
Third quarter sixteenth century
31.5 × 10.8 (12⁷/₁₆ × 4⅜)
London, The Trustees of the British Museum, G. 1983.121
Godman Bequest, 1983

195. Mosque lamp; underglaze painted in blue, green, and red
c. 1572
Inscribed on the neck with kelime-i tevhid written in sülüs
47.5 × 29.0 (18¹¹/₁₆ × 11⁷/₁₆)
İstanbul, Arkeoloji Müzesi, Çinili Köşk, 41/16
Transferred from the Mosque of Sokollu Mehmed Paşa, 1885
(Kühnel 1938, pl. 26; Öz 1957, no. 124; Munich 1965, no. 129; Ünal 1969, fig. 20; Denny 1977, fig. 191; Tuncay 1978, fig. 8; Tuncay 1980, 11; İstanbul 1983, E. 154)

196. Spherical hanging ornament; underglaze in blue, green, and red
Second half sixteenth century
Height, 24.5 (9⅝)
London, The Trustees of the British Museum, G. 1983.120
Godman Bequest, 1983
(Rogers 1984, fig. 6; Rogers 1985b, figs. 7 and 7a)

197. Covered bowl; underglaze painted in blue, green, and red
Second half sixteenth century
22.5 × 19.1 (8⅞ × 7½)
London, The Trustees of the British Museum, F.B. Is. 5
A.W. Franks Bequest, 1897
(Lane 1971, pl. E)

198. Jug; underglaze painted in blue, green, and red
Second half sixteenth century
25.5 × 15.6 (10⅛ × 6³/₁₆)
Paris, Musée du Louvre, Section Islamique, 7595
Salomon de Rothschild Bequest, 1922

199. Plate with floral spray and two birds; underglaze painted in blue, green, and red
Second half sixteenth century
6.7 × 28.6 (2⅝ × 11¼)
New York, The Metropolitan Museum of Art, Gift of James J. Rorimer in appreciation of Maurice S. Dimand's curatorship, 1933–1959, 59.69.1
Purchased 1959
(Metropolitan 1968, no. 21; Metropolitan 1972, fig. 25; Jenkins et al. 1977, pl. 271)

200. Plate with rumi scroll; underglaze painted in blue, green, and red
Late sixteenth century
5.4 × 29.9 (2⅛ × 11¾)
New York, The Metropolitan Museum of Art, Harris Brisbane Dick Fund, 1966, 66.4.13
Formerly in the Adda Collection; purchased 1966
(Rackham 1959, no. 184; Berlin 1981, no. 103)

201. Plate with galleon; underglaze painted in black, blue, turquoise, green, and red
Late sixteenth century
7.0 × 36.0 (2¾ × 14³/₁₆)
Copenhagen, The David Collection, 24/1975
Purchased 1975
(Frankfurt 1985, vol. 2, no. 2/47)

202. Bowl with carnations; underglaze painted in black, blue, red, and white on coral-colored engobe
Second half sixteenth century
13.3 × 20.3 (5¼ × 8)
Paris, Musée du Louvre, Section Islamique, 6325
Piet Lataudrie Bequest, 1910
(Migeon 1922, vol. 2, no. 213; Paris 1971, no. 106; Paris 1977, no. 603)

203. Plate with tulips; underglaze painted in blue, black, red, and white on pinkish-mauve engobe
Second half sixteenth century
6.5 × 32.0 (2⁹⁄₁₆ × 12⅝)
Kuwait National Museum, Dar al-Athar al-Islamiya, LNS 323 C
Purchased

204. Plate with carnations and sweet alyssum; underglaze painted in blue, red, and white on blue engobe
Second half sixteenth century
6.2 × 30.4 (2⁷⁄₁₆ × 12)
Ecouen, Musée de la Renaissance, Cl. 8549
Formerly in the Saltzmann Collection; acquired by Musée de Cluny, 1866; formerly in the Musée du Louvre, Section Islamique (7880-90); transferred from Musée de Cluny
(Denny 1977, fig. 192; Denny 1980, pl. 43; İstanbul 1983, E. 166)

205. Tankard; underglaze painted in black, red, and white on blue engobe
Second half sixteenth century
21.8 × 13.0 (8⁹⁄₁₆ × 5⅛)
Paris, Musée du Louvre, Section Islamique, A.A. 403
Gift of Chompret, 1939
(Paris 1971, no. 105; Paris 1977, no. 601)

206. Tile with saz scroll; underglaze painted in blue, green, and red
Second half sixteenth century
34.5 × 62.0 (13⁹⁄₁₆ × 24⁷⁄₁₆)
Paris, Musée du Louvre, Section Islamique, 3919/2/287
Formerly in the Sorlin-Dorigny Collection; acquired 1895
(Migeon 1922, vol. 2, no. 246)

207. Tombstone; underglaze painted in blue, green, and red
Second half sixteenth century
Inscribed on both sides with the kelime-i tevhid and a prayer for the soul of the deceased, written in sülüs
42.0 × 29.0 (16⁹⁄₁₆ × 11⁷⁄₁₆)
London, The Board of Trustees of the Victoria and Albert Museum, 862-1901
Purchased 1901
(Öney 1976, 103)
Shown in Washington only

208. Pair of spandrels; underglaze painted in blue, green, and red
Second half sixteenth century
Each, 56.0 × 29.5 (22⅛ × 11⅝)
Copenhagen, The David Collection, 2/1962
Formerly in the M.S. Savadjian Collection; purchased 1962
(Copenhagen 1975, 106; Frankfurt 1985, vol. 2, no. 2/74)

209. Lunette; underglaze painted in blue, green, and red; composed of sixteen tiles
c. 1573
71.0 × 141.5 (27¹⁵⁄₁₆ × 55¹¹⁄₁₆)
Boston, Museum of Fine Arts, Bequest of Mrs. Martin Brimmer, 06.2437
From the Palace of Piyale Paşa; acquired 1906
Shown in Washington only

210. Tile panel; underglaze painted in blue, green, and red; composed of forty-five square tiles
Dated 982 (1574/1575)
Two panels at the top inscribed with a Persian couplet terminating with the date, written in talik
218.0 × 122.0 (85¹³⁄₁₆ × 48¹⁄₁₆)
İstanbul, Topkapı Sarayı Müzesi, 8/1067
Formerly installed in the Harem of the Topkapı Palace
(Arseven n.d., pl. 6; Aslanapa n.d., pl. VIIIa; Öz 1957, pl. XLVI; Denny 1977, fig. 219; E. Yücel 1978, 2; *Sanat* 1982, 64 and 65; İstanbul 1983, E. 157)

Concordance

Collection	Accession Number	Catalogue Number
Baltimore, The Walters Art Gallery	54.512	53
Boston, Museum of Fine Arts	06.2437	209
	77.256	155
Cambridge, Mass., Harvard University Art Museums	85.216	34
	85.295	154
The Art Institute of Chicago	1949.300	157
The Cleveland Museum of Art	44.492	46
Copenhagen, The David Collection	2/1962	208
	24/1975	201
	27/1978	171
The Detroit Institute of Arts	48.137	152
Dublin, The Chester Beatty Library	MS. 413	43a-d
Ecouen, Musée de la Renaissance	Cl. 8549	204
İstanbul, Arkeoloji Müzesi, Çinili Köşk	41/2	166
	41/16	195
	41/155	170
	41/515	180
	41/1121	180
İstanbul Üniversite Kütüphanesi	A. 6570	19
	F. 1330	28a-b
	F. 1426	49a-f
	T. 5467	26
	T. 5964	39a-b
İstanbul, Topkapı Sarayı Müzesi	1/74	87
	1/294	89
	1/463	88
	1/1930	99
	1/2441	100
	1/2466	98
	1/2571	101
	1/2597	102
	1/10989	103
	2/8	61
	2/22	62
	2/74	95
	2/83	96
	2/254	91
	2/467	58
	2/479	59
	2/484	60
	2/539	76
	2/575	78
	2/715	85
	2/894	68
	2/1187	84
	2/1801	72
	2/1804	74
	2/2085	63
	2/2097	9b

Accession Number	Catalogue Number
2/2111	67
2/2121	20
2/2274	55
2/2856	57
2/2873	56
2/2879	107
2/2893	73
2/2896	21
2/2912	83
2/3776	86
2/3825	54
2/3831	64
2/3832	66
2/4447	106
8/1067	210
13/9	119
13/21	117
13/37	116
13/46	114
13/72	115
13/92	112a
13/93	112b
13/100	121a-b
13/739	120
13/932	118
13/1015	113a-b
13/1133	123
13/1150	122
13/1783	150
13/1891	139
15/668	71
15/2767	69
15/2944	70
15/6086	163
17/348	44
23/1625	50
31/4	137
31/49	133
31/50	132
31/58	124
31/59	126
31/60	125
31/61	127
31/168	138
31/268	140
31/1473	128
31/1475	134
31/1477	131
31/1478	129
31/1480	130
31/1891	139
A. 21	15
A. 3654	11

Collection	Accession Number	Catalogue Number	Collection	Accession Number	Catalogue Number
	E. 7816/2	3		G. 1983.52	175
	E.H. 49	14		G. 1983.120	196
	E.H. 58	8		G. 1983.121	194
	E.H. 72	7	London, Princess Esra Jah Collection		52
	E.H. 222	16	London, Victoria and Albert Museum	131-1885	191
	E.H. 227	13		158-1894	51
	E.H. 522	17		337-1903	167
	E.H. 1077	12		713-1902	177
	E.H. 2851	18a-b		862-1901	207
	G.Y. 1400	1		C.2005-1910	192
	H. 642	36		C.2019-1910	176
	H. 802	33a-b	Los Angeles County Museum of Art	M. 85.237.8	135
	H. 845	30		M. 85.237.1	141
	H. 987	31	New York, The Metropolitan Museum of Art	12.49.5	148
	H. 1132	24		14.40.727	174
	H. 1339	42a-b		22.100.51	159
	H. 1499	32		29.33	172
	H. 1517	41a-d		38.149.1	4
	H. 1597-1598	37		49.32.79	144
	H. 1608	40		52.20.18	146
	H. 1812	23		52.20.21	147
	H. 2147	45a-d		52.20.22	145
	H. 2162	48a-b		59.69.1	199
	H. 2168	47		66.4.10	173
	R. 738 mük.	25		66.4.13	200
	R. 804	29		1971.263.2	162
	R. 917	22	Paris, Musée des Arts Décoratifs	A. 7861	161
	R. 1272	38	Paris, Musée du Louvre	3449	184
	R. 1633 mük.	35		3919/2/287	206
	Y.Y. 999	9a		4048	193
İstanbul, Türk ve İslam Eserleri Müzesi	2	111		6321	169
	5	109		6325	202
	13	110		7257	187
	127	108		7595	198
	416	82		7880-83	190
	419	80		7880-92	165
	421	81		A.A. 403	205
	438	79		A.O. 5960	188
	482	77		M.R. 202	65
	1443	10	Private collection		182
	1962	27	Riyadh, Rifaat Sheikh al-Ard Collection		92
	2191	6	Vienna, Kunsthistorisches Museum	A. 1341	90
	2238	2		C. 5	104a
	4125	5		C. 5a	104b
Kuwait National Museum	LNS 29 R	158		C. 28	105
	LNS 46 I	75		C. 152a	93
	LNS 99 T	149		C. 152b	97
	LNS 105 T	142		C. 208	94
	LNS 174 C	164	Vienna, Österreichisches Museum für Angewandte Kunst	T. 8327	160
	LNS 231 C	179			
	LNS 323 C	203	Washington, The Textile Museum	1.22	136
London, The British Museum	78 12-30 502	189		1.38	153
	78 12-30 513	183		1.55	151
	78 12-30 519	178		1.65	156
	Fb. Is. 5	197		1.70	143
	G. 1983.7	168			
	G. 1983.21	185			
	G. 1983.33	181			
	G. 1983.48	186			

Shortened References

Adıvar 1970 — Adıvar, Adnan A. *Osmanlı Türklerinde İlim*. İstanbul, 1970.

Akalay 1969 — Akalay, Zeren. "Tarihi Konularda İlk Osmanlı Minyatürleri." *Sanat Tarihi Yıllığı* 2 (1969): 102–115.

Akalay 1970 — Akalay, Zeren. "Tarihi Konularda Türk Minyatürleri." *Sanat Tarihi Yıllığı* 3 (1970): 151–166.

Akalay 1973 — Akalay, Zeren. "Topkapı Sarayı Müzesi Kütüphanesi Hazine 753 no.'lu Nizami Hamsesi'nin Minyatürleri." *Sanat Tarihi Yıllığı* 5 (1973): 389–409.

Akalay 1978 — Akalay, Zeren. "The Forerunners of Classical Turkish Miniature Painting." In *Fifth International Congress of Turkish Art*, edited by Géza Fehér, 31–47. Budapest, 1978.

Akalay 1979 — Akalay, Zeren. "XVI. Yüzyıl Nakkaşlarından Hasan Paşa ve Eserleri." In *I. Milletlerarası Türkoloji Kongresi. 3: Türk Sanat Tarihi*, 607–625. İstanbul, 1979.

Akçura 1966 — Akçura, Yusuf. *Piri Reis Haritası*. İstanbul, 1966.

Aksoy 1977 — Aksoy, Şule. "Hat Sanatı." *Kültür ve Sanat* 5 (1977): 115–137.

Akurgal et al 1966 — Akurgal, Ekrem; Mango, Cyril; and Ettinghausen, Richard. *Treasures of Turkey*. Geneva, 1966.

Alexander 1983 — Alexander, David G. "Two Aspects of Islamic Arms and Armor." *Metropolitan Museum Journal* 18 (1983): 97–109.

Allan and Raby 1982 — Allan, James, and Raby, Julian. "Metalwork." In *Tulips, Arabesques and Turbans*, edited by Yanni Petsopoulos, 17–53. London, 1982.

Altay 1970 — Altay, Fikret. "The Vestments of the Sultans." *Apollo* 92, no. 101 (July 1970): 62–63.

Altay 1979 — Altay, Fikret. *Topkapı Sarayı Müzesi. 3: Kaftanlar*. İstanbul, 1979.

Anafarta 1969 — Anafarta, Nigar. *Hünername: Minyatürleri ve Sanatçıları*. İstanbul, 1969.

Arseven n.d. — Arseven, Celal Esad. *Les Arts Décoratif Turc*. İstanbul, n.d.

Aslanapa n.d. — Aslanapa, Oktay. *Turkish Arts: Seljuk and Ottoman Carpets, Tiles and Miniature Paintings*. İstanbul, n.d.

Atasoy 1969 — Atasoy, Nurhan. "Shoes in the Topkapı Palace Museum." *Journal of the Regional Cultural Institute* 2, no. 1 (Winter 1969): 5–31.

Atasoy 1970 — Atasoy, Nurhan. "1558 Tarihli Süleymanname ve Macar Nakkaş Pervane." *Sanat Tarihi Yıllığı* 3 (1970): 167–196.

Atasoy 1972 — Atasoy, Nurhan. "Nakkaş Osman'ın Padişah Portreleri Albümü." *Türkiyemiz* 6 (February 1972): 2–14.

Atasoy and Çağman 1974 — Atasoy, Nurhan, and Çağman, Filiz. *Turkish Miniature Painting*. İstanbul, 1974.

Atıl 1973a — Atıl, Esin. *Ceramics from the World of Islam*. Washington, 1973.

Atıl 1973b — Atıl, Esin. "Ottoman Miniature Painting Under Sultan Mehmed II." *Ars Orientalis* 9 (1973): 103–120.

Atıl 1973c — Atıl, Esin. *Turkish Art of the Ottoman Period*. Washington, 1973.

Atıl 1978a — Atıl, Esin. "Ahmed Nakşi: An Eclectic Painter of the Early Seventeenth Century." In *Fifth International Congress of Turkish Art*, edited by Géza Fehér, 103–121. Budapest, 1978.

Atıl 1978b — Atıl, Esin. *The Brush of the Masters: Drawings from Iran and India*. Washington, 1978.

Atıl 1980 — Atıl, Esin. "The Art of the Book." In *Turkish Art*, edited by Esin Atıl, 137–238. Washington and New York, 1980.

Atıl 1981a — Atıl, Esin. *Kalila wa Dimna: Fables from a Fourteenth-Century Arabic Manuscript*. Washington, 1981.

Atıl 1981b — Atıl, Esin. *Renaissance of Islam: Art of the Mamluks*. Washington, 1981.

Atıl 1984 — Atıl, Esin. "Mamluk Painting in the Late Fifteenth Century." *Muqarnas* 2 (1984): 159–171.

Atıl 1986 — Atıl, Esin. *Süleymanname: The Illustrated History of Süleyman the Magnificent*. Washington and New York, 1986.

Atıl et al 1985 — Atıl, Esin; Chase, W.T.; and Jett, Paul. *Islamic Metalwork in the Freer Gallery of Art*. Washington, 1985.

Babinger 1959 — Babinger, Franz. "Dschem-Sultan im Bilde des Abendlands." In *Aus der Welt der islamischen Kunst*, edited by Richard Ettinghausen, 255–266. Berlin, 1959.

Balpınar 1983 — Balpınar, Belkıs. "Classical Kilims." *Hali* 6, no. 1 (Spring 1983): 13–20.

Barbet de Jouy 1867 — Barbet de Jouy, H. *Galerie d'Apollon, Notice des Gemmes et Joyaux*. Paris, 1867.

Barışta 1981   Barışta, Örcün. *Osmanlı İmparatorluk Dönemi Türk İşlemelerinden Örnekler.* Ankara, 1981.

Barkan 1942   Barkan, Ömer Lütfi. "Kanunname-i İhtisab-ı Bursa." *Tarih Vesikaları Dergisi* 7 (1942): 15–40.

Barkan 1972–1979   Barkan, Ömer Lütfi. *Süleymaniye Cami ve İmareti İnşaatı (1550–1557).* 2 vols. Ankara, 1972–1979.

Barkan 1979   Barkan, Ömer Lütfi. "İstanbul Saraylarına Ait Muhasebe Defterleri." *Belgeler* 13 (1979): 1–380.

Bates 1980   Bates, Ülkü. "Architecture." In *Turkish Art,* edited by Esin Atıl, 43–136. Washington and New York, 1980.

Beattie 1968   Beattie, May H. "Coupled-Column Prayer Rugs." *Oriental Art* 14, no. 4 (Winter 1968): 243–258.

Berker 1973   Berker, Nurhayat. "Kaşbastı (Diadem)." *Türk Etnoğrafya Dergisi* 13 (1973): 9–23.

Berker 1978   Berker, Nurhayat. "Saray Mendilleri." In *Fifth International Congress of Turkish Art,* edited by Géza Fehér, 173–181. Budapest, 1978.

Berker 1981   Berker, Nurhayat. *Topkapı Sarayı Müzesi. 6: İşlemeler.* İstanbul, 1981.

Berkovits 1964   Berkovits, Ilona. *Illuminated Manuscripts from the Library of Matthias Corvinus.* Budapest, 1964.

Berlin 1982   *The Arts of Islam: Masterpieces from the Metropolitan Museum of Art.* Berlin, 1982.

Binney 1979   Binney, Edwin, 3rd. *Turkish Treasures from the Collection of Edwin Binney, 3rd.* Portland, Ore., 1979.

Binney 1981   Binney, Edwin, 3rd. *Turkish Treasures from the Collection of Edwin Binney, 3rd: 1981 Supplement to the 1979 Catalogue.* San Diego, 1979.

Bode and Kühnel 1958   Bode, Wilhelm von, and Kühnel, Ernst. *Antique Rugs from the Near East.* Braunschweig and Berlin, 1958.

Bombaci 1965   Bombaci, Alessio. "Les Toughras Enluminés de la Collection de Documents Turcs des Archives d'État de Venise." In *Atti del Secondo Congresso Internazionale di Arte Turca,* 26–29. Naples, 1965.

Carswell 1966   Carswell, John. "Pottery and Tiles on Mount Athos." *Ars Orientalis* 6 (1966): 77–90.

Carswell 1972   Carswell, John. *Kütahya Tiles and Pottery from the Armenian Cathedral of St. James, Jerusalem.* 2 vols. Oxford, 1972.

Carswell 1978   Carswell, John. "Syrian Tiles from Sinai and Damascus." In *Archaeology in the Levant: Essays for Kathleen Kenyon,* edited by R. Moorey and P. Parr, 269–296. Warminster, 1978.

Carswell 1982   Carswell, John. "Ceramics." In *Tulips, Arabesques and Turbans,* edited by Yanni Petsopoulos, 73–119. London, 1982.

Carswell 1984   Carswell, John. "The Tiles in the Yeni Kaplica Baths at Bursa." *Apollo* 120, no. 269 (July 1984): 36–43.

Carswell 1985   Carswell, John. *Blue and White: Chinese Porcelain and Its Impact on the Western World.* Chicago, 1985.

Christie's 1899   Christie's. *Old Dresden Porcelain.* London, 9 February 1899.

Christie's 1905   Christie's. *Oriental Porcelain, Rhodian and Damascus Ware, Objects of Art and Decorative Furniture.* London, 17 and 22 May 1905.

Copenhagen 1975   The David Collection. *Islamic Art.* Copenhagen, 1975.

Copenhagen 1980   Dammikkelsen, Bente, and Lundbaek, Torben, eds. *Ethnographic Objects in the Royal Danish Kunstkammer 1650–1800.* Copenhagen, 1980.

Corcoran 1948   Corcoran Gallery of Art. *Carpets for the Great Shah.* Washington, 1948.

Çağman 1973   Çağman, Filiz. "Şahname-i Selim Han ve Minyatürleri." *Sanat Tarihi Yıllığı* 5 (1973): 411–442.

Çağman 1974–1975   Çağman, Filiz. "Sultan Mehmet II Dönemine Ait Bir Minyatürlü Yazma: Külliyat-ı Katibi." *Sanat Tarihi Yıllığı* 6 (1974–1975): 333–346.

Çağman 1976   Çağman, Filiz. "The Place of the Turkish Miniature in Islamic Art." In *Turkish Contribution to Islamic Arts,* 90–117. İstanbul, 1976.

Çağman 1978   Çağman, Filiz. "The Miniatures of the *Divan-ı Hüseyni* and the Influence of Their Style." In *Fifth International Congress of Turkish Art,* edited by Géza Fehér, 231–259. Budapest, 1978.

Çağman 1980   Çağman, Filiz. "Turkish Miniature Painting." In *The Art and Architecture of Turkey,* edited by Ekrem Akurgal, 222–248. Oxford, 1980.

Çağman 1984   Çağman, Filiz. "Serzergeran Mehmet Usta ve Eserleri." In *Kemal Çığ'a Armağan,* 51–88. İstanbul, 1984.

Çağman and Tanındı 1979   Çağman, Filiz, and Tanındı, Zeren. *Topkapı Saray Museum: Islamic Miniature Painting.* İstanbul, 1979.

Çetintürk 1963   Çetintürk, Bige. "İstanbul'da XVI. Asır Sonuna Kadar Hassa Halı Sanatkarları." *Türk Sanatı Tarihi: Araştırma ve İncelemeleri* 1 (1963): 715–731.

Çığ 1959   Çığ, Kemal. "Türk ve İslam Eserleri Müzesindeki Minyatürlü Kitapların Kataloğu." *Şarkiyat Mecmuası* 3 (1959): 50–90.

Çığ 1971   Çığ, Kemal. *Türk Kitap Kapları.* İstanbul, 1971.

Çığ 1976   Çığ, Kemal. "The Decoration on the Ceiling of the Throne Which Belongs to Mehmet III in the Reception Room of the Topkapı Palace." In *IVème Congrès International d'Art Turc*, 47–48. Aix-en-Provence, 1976.

Çizakça 1980   Çizakça, Murat. "A Short History of the Bursa Silk Industry (1500–1900)." *Journal of the Economic and Social History of the Orient* 23, parts 1 and 2 (1980): 142–153.

Çulpan 1968   Çulpan, Cevdet. *Türk-İslam Tahta Oymacılık Sanatından Rahleler.* İstanbul, 1968.

Dalsar 1960   Dalsar, F. *Türk Sanayi ve Ticaret Tarihinde Bursa'da İpekçilik.* İstanbul, 1960.

Danışman 1969–1971   Danışman, Zuhuri. *Evliya Çelebi Seyyahatnamesi.* 15 vols. İstanbul, 1969–1971.

David 1933–1934   David, Sir Percival. "Chinese Porcelain at Constantinople." *Transactions of the Oriental Ceramic Society* 11 (1933–1934): 15–21.

Day 1950   Day, Florence E. "Silks of the Near East." *Metropolitan Museum of Art Bulletin* n.s. 9, no. 4 (December 1950): 108–117.

Demiriz 1977   Demiriz, Yıldız. "16. Yüzyıla Ait Tezhipli bir Kuran." *Sanat Tarihi Yıllığı* 7 (1977): 41–58.

Denny 1970   Denny, Walter B. "A Sixteenth-Century Architectural Plan of Istanbul." *Ars Orientalis* 8 (1970): 49–63.

Denny 1971   Denny, Walter B. "Book Reviews." *Textile Museum Journal* 3, no. 2 (December 1971): 38–42.

Denny 1972   Denny, Walter B. "Ottoman Turkish Textiles." *Textile Museum Journal* 3, no. 3 (December 1972): 55–66.

Denny 1973   Denny, Walter B. "Anatolian Rugs: An Essay on Method." *Textile Museum Journal* 3, no. 4 (December 1973): 7–25.

Denny 1974a   Denny, Walter B. "Blue-and-White Islamic Pottery on Chinese Themes." *Boston Museum Bulletin* 72, no. 368 (1974): 76–98.

Denny 1974b   Denny, Walter B. "A Group of Silk Islamic Banners." *Textile Museum Journal* 4, no. 1 (December 1974): 67–81.

Denny 1976   Denny, Walter B. "Ceramic Revetments of the Mosque of the Ramazan Oğlu in Adana." In *IVème Congrès International d'Art Turc*, 57–65. Aix-en-Provence, 1976.

Denny 1977   Denny, Walter B. *The Ceramics of the Mosque of Rüstem Pasha and the Environment of Change.* London and New York, 1977.

Denny 1978   Denny, Walter B. "Islamic Textiles and Urban Life: The Ottoman Turks." In *The Warp and Weft of Islam*, edited by Jere L. Bacharach and Irene A. Bierman, 17–24. Seattle, 1978.

Denny 1979a   Denny, Walter B. *Oriental Rugs.* New York, 1979.

Denny 1979b   Denny, Walter B. "The Origin of the Designs of Ottoman Court Carpets." *Hali* 2, no. 1 (Spring 1979): 6–12.

Denny 1980   Denny, Walter B. "Ceramics." In *Turkish Art*, edited by Esin Atıl, 239–297. Washington and New York, 1980.

Denny 1981   Denny, Walter B. "Turkish Ceramics and Turkish Painting: The Role of the Paper Cartoon in Turkish Ceramic Production." In *Essays in Islamic Art and Architecture*, edited by Abbas Daneshvari, 29–36. Malibu, 1981.

Denny 1982   Denny, Walter B. "Textiles." In *Tulips, Arabesques and Turbans*, edited by Yanni Petsopoulos, 121–168. London, 1982.

Denny 1983   Denny, Walter B. "Dating Ottoman Turkish Works in the Saz Style." *Muqarnas* 1 (1983): 103–121.

Denny 1985   Denny, Walter B. "Early Turkish Carpets" and "Mamluk and Ottoman Carpets." In *The Macmillan Atlas of Rugs and Carpets*, edited by David Black, 48–59 and 60–65. New York, 1985.

Denny 1986   Denny, Walter B. "The Origin and Development of Ottoman Court Carpets." *Oriental Carpets and Textile Studies* 2 (1986) (forthcoming).

Derman 1970   Derman, M. Uğur. "Kanuni Devrinde Yazı Sanatımız." In *Kanuni Armağanı*, 269–289. Ankara, 1970.

Derman 1982   Derman, M. Uğur. *Türk Hat Sanatının Şaheserleri.* İstanbul (?), 1982.

Dickson and Welch 1981   Dickson, Martin Bernard, and Welch, Stuart Cary. *The Houghton Shahname.* 2 vols. Cambridge, Mass. and London, 1981.

Dimand 1935   Dimand, Maurice S. *Guide to and Exhibition of Oriental Rugs and Textiles.* New York, 1935.

Dimand 1944   Dimand, Maurice S. "Turkish Art of the Muhammadan Period." *Metropolitan Museum of Art Bulletin* n.s. 2, no. 7 (March 1944): 211–217.

Dimand 1958 — Dimand, Maurice S. *Handbook of Muhammadan Art*. New York, 1958 (revised edition).

Dimand 1973 — Dimand, Maurice S. *Oriental Rugs in the Metropolitan Museum of Art*. New York, 1973.

Duda 1983 — Duda, Dorothea. *Islamische Handschriften. I: Persische Handschriften*. 2 vols. Vienna, 1983.

Düsseldorf 1973 — Hetjens-Museum. *Islamische Keramik*. Düsseldorf, 1973.

Edhem and Stchoukine 1933 — Edhem, Fehmi, and Stchoukine, Ivan. *Les manuscrits orientaux illustrés de la Bibliothèque de l'Université de Stamboul*. Paris, 1933.

Edwards and Signell 1982 — Edwards, Holly, and Signell, Carl. *Patterns and Precision: The Arts and Sciences of Islam*. Washington, 1982.

Eldem and Akozan 1982 — Eldem, Sedad H., and Akozan, Feridun. *Topkapı Sarayı: Bir Mimari Araştırma*. İstanbul, 1982.

Ellis 1969 — Ellis, Charles G. "The Ottoman Prayer Rugs." *Textile Museum Journal* 2, no. 4 (December 1969): 5–22.

Ennès and Kalus 1979 — Ennès, Pierre, and Kalus, Ludvik. "Un plat d'Iznik à inscription turque." *Revue du Louvre et des Musées de France* 29, no. 4 (1979): 258–260.

Erdmann 1938 — Erdmann, Kurt. "Kairener Teppiche. I: Europäische und islamische Quellen des 15–18 Jahrhunderts." *Ars Islamica* 5 (1938): 179–206.

Erdmann 1959 — Erdmann, Kurt. "Die Fliesen am Sünnet odasi des Topkapı Sarayı in İstanbul." In *Aus der Welt der Islamischen Kunst*, edited by Richard Ettinghausen, 144–153. Berlin, 1959.

Erdmann 1960 — Erdmann, Kurt. *Oriental Carpets: An Essay on Their History*, translated by Charles G. Ellis. New York, 1960.

Erdmann 1963 — Erdmann, Kurt. "Neue Arbeiten zur türkischen Keramik." *Ars Orientalis* 5 (1963): 191–219.

Eyice 1970 — Eyice, Semavi. "Avrupalı Bir Ressamın Gözü ile Kanuni Sultan Süleyman." In *Kanuni Armağanı*, 129–170. Ankara, 1970.

Falke 1936 — Falke, Otto von. *Decorative Silks*. New York, 1936.

Fehér 1965a — Fehér, Géza. "L'influence turque sur les arts décoratifs populaires hongrois." In *Atti del Secondo Congresso Internazionale di Arte Turca*. 119–122. Naples, 1965.

Fehér 1965b — Fehér, Géza. "Quelques problèmes des objets d'art métalliques turc-osmanlis mis au jour en Hongrie." In *Atti del Secondo Congresso Internazionale di Arte Turca*, 123–128. Naples, 1965.

Fehér 1975 — Fehér, Géza. *Craftsmanship in Turkish-Ruled Hungary*. Corvina, 1975.

Fehér 1976 — Fehér, Géza. *Türkische Miniaturen aus den Chroniken der Ungarischen Feldzüge*. Budapest, 1976.

Fehérvári 1973 — Fehérvári, Géza. *Islamic Pottery: A Comprehensive Study Based on the Barlow Collection*. London, 1973.

Fischer 1962 — Fischer, E. *Melchior Lorch*. Copenhagen, 1962.

Forster 1968 — Forster, Edward S., trans. *The Turkish Letters of Ogier Ghiselin de Busbecq*. Oxford, 1968 (reprint).

Fortnum 1869 — Fortnum, C.D.E. "On a Lamp of Persian Ware Made for the Mosque of Omar at Jerusalem in 1549." *Archaeologia* 42 (1869): 387–397.

Frankfurt 1969 — *Islamische Teppiche*. Frankfurt, 1969.

Frankfurt 1985 — Museum für Kunsthandwerk. *Türkische Kunst und Kultur aus osmanischer Zeit*. 2 vols. Frankfurt, 1985.

Gabriel 1928 — Gabriel, Albert. "Les étapes d'une campagne dans les deux Irak." *Syria* 9 (1928): 327–349.

Gasparini 1985 — Gasparini, Elisabetta. *Le Pitture Murali della Muradiye di Edirne*. Padova, 1985.

Geijer 1951 — Geijer, Agnes. *Oriental Textiles in Sweden*. Copenhagen, 1951.

Glück and Diez 1925 — Glück, Heinrich, and Diez, Ernst. *Die kunst des Islam*. Berlin, 1925.

Goodwin 1971 — Goodwin, Godfrey. *A History of Ottoman Architecture*. London, 1971.

Gökbilgin 1964 — Gökbilgin, Tayyip. "Venedik Devlet Arşivindeki Vesikalar Külliyatında Kanuni Sultan Süleyman Devri Belgeleri." *Belgeler* 1, no. 2 (July 1964): 119–120.

Gökyay 1976 — Gökyay, Orhan Şaik. "Tılsımlı Gömlekler." *Türk Folkloru Araştırmaları Yıllığı* 3 (1976): 93–112.

Göl 1970 — Göl, Hülya. "Calligraphy through the Ages." *Apollo* 92, no. 101 (July 1970): 38–40.

Gönül n.d. — Gönül, Macide. *Turkish Embroideries: XVI–XIX Centuries*. İstanbul, n.d.

Gönül 1969 — Gönül, Macide. "Some Turkish Embroideries in the Collection of the Topkapı Sarayı Museum in İstanbul." *Kunst des Orients* 6, no. 1 (1969): 43–76.

Grosz and Thomas 1936 — Grosz, August, and Thomas, Bruno. *Katalog der Waffensammlung in der Neuen Burg*. Vienna, 1936.

Grube 1961a   Grube, Ernst J. "Masterpieces of Turkish Pottery in the Metropolitan Museum of Art and in the Private Collection of Mr. James J. Rorimer in New York." In *First International Congress of Turkish Arts*, 153–175. Ankara, 1961.

Grube 1961b   Grube, Ernst J. "A School of Turkish Miniature Painting." In *First International Congress of Turkish Arts*, 176–209. Ankara, 1961.

Grube 1962a   Grube, Ernst J. *Miniature islamische dal XIII al XIX secolo*. Venice, 1962.

Grube 1962b   Grube, Ernst J. "Miniatures in Istanbul Libraries. I." *Pantheon* 20 (1962): 213–226.

Grube 1962c   Grube, Ernst J. "Miniatures in Istanbul Libraries. II." *Pantheon* 20 (1962): 306–313.

Grube 1974   Grube, Ernst J. "Notes on the Decorative Arts of the Timurid Period." In *Gururajamanjarika*, 233–269. Naples, 1974.

Grube 1981   Grube, Ernst J. "Notes on Ottoman Painting in the 15th Century." In *Essays in Islamic Art and Architecture*, edited by Abbas Daneshvari, 51–62. Malibu, 1981.

Grube 1982   Grube, Ernst J. "Painting." In *Tulips, Arabesques and Turbans*, edited by Yanni Petsopoulos, 193–212. London, 1982.

Guiffrey and Migeon 1908   Guiffrey, M. Jules, and Migeon, M. Gaston. *La Collection Kelekian: Etoffes et Tapis d'Orient et de Venice*. Paris, 1908.

Halman 1979   Halman, Talat Said. "Rapture and Revolution: Poetry of the Islamic Middle East." *The Poetry Society of America Bulletin* 69 (Autumn 1979): 3–22.

Hapgood 1979   Hapgood, Charles H. *Maps of the Ancient Sea Kings*. Philadelphia, 1979 (revised edition).

Herrmann 1982   Herrmann, Eberhart. *Seltene Orientteppiche/Rare Oriental Carpets: IV*. Munich, 1982.

Hobson 1932   Hobson, R.L. *A Guide to the Islamic Pottery of the Near East*. London, 1932.

Indianapolis 1970   Indianapolis Museum of Art. *Treasures from the Metropolitan*. Indianapolis, 1970.

Islamic Art 1981   *Islamic Art* 1 (1981). Special issue on İstanbul albums.

Ivanov 1979   Ivanov, Anatol A. "A Group of Iranian Daggers of the Period from the Fifteenth Century to the Beginning of the Seventeenth." In *Islamic Arms and Armour*, edited by Robert Elgood, 64–77. London, 1979.

İnalcık 1960   İnalcık, Halil. "Bursa: XV. Asır Sanayi ve Ticaret Tarihine Ait Vesikalar." *Belleten* 24, no. 93 (1960): 45–102.

İnalcık 1969   İnalcık, Halil. "Süleyman the Lawgiver and Ottoman Law." *Archivum Ottomanicum* 1 (1969): 105–138.

İnalcık 1971   İnalcık, Halil. "Harir, silk. II: The Ottoman Empire." *Encyclopedia of Islam*, new edition, 3: 211–218. Leiden and London, 1971.

İnan 1974   İnan, Afet. *Piri Reis'in Hayatı ve Eserleri: Amerika'nın En Eski Haritaları*. Ankara, 1974.

İpşiroğlu 1964   İpşiroğlu, M. Ş. *Saray-Alben*. Wiesbaden, 1964.

İstanbul 1940   Topkapı Sarayı Müzesi. *Topkapı Sarayı Müzesi Arşiv Kılavuzu*. İstanbul, 1940.

İstanbul 1956   Topkapı Sarayı Müzesi. *Eski Çekmeceler*. İstanbul, 1956.

İstanbul 1958   Topkapı Sarayı Müzesi. *Kanuni Sultan Süleyman Sergisi*. İstanbul, 1958.

İstanbul 1961   Topkapı Sarayı Müzesi. *Çocuk Elbiseleri Sergisi*. İstanbul, 1961.

İstanbul 1983   Turkish Ministry of Culture and Tourism. *The Anatolian Civilisations. III: Seljuk/Ottoman*. İstanbul, 1983.

James 1981   James, David. *Islamic Masterpieces of the Chester Beatty Library*. London, 1981.

Jenkins 1983   Jenkins, Marilyn, ed. *The al-Sabah Collection: Islamic Art in the Kuwait National Museum*. London, 1983.

Jenkins et al 1977   Jenkins, Marilyn; Meech-Pekarik, Julia; and Valenstein, Suzanne. *Oriental Ceramics: The World's Great Collections. 12: The Metropolitan Museum of Art*. Tokyo, 1977.

Kahle 1926   Kahle, Paul. *Piri reis Bahrije. Das türkisches Segelhandbuch für das Mittelländische Meer von Jahre 1521*. Berlin and Leipzig, 1926.

Kahle 1929   Kahle, Paul. "Piri Reis und seine Bahrije." In *Beiträge zur historischen Geographie, Kulturgeographie, Ethnographie und Kartographie, vornehmlich des Orients*, edited by Hans Mzik, 60–76. Leipzig and Vienna, 1929.

Kahle 1932   Kahle, Paul. *Die Verschollene Columbus-Karte von Amerika von Jahre 1498 in einer türkischen Weltkarte von 1513*. Berlin and Leipzig, 1932.

Karatay 1961a   Karatay, Fehmi E. *Topkapı Sarayı Müzesi Kütüphanesi Farsça Yazmalar Kataloğu*. İstanbul, 1961.

Karatay 1961b   Karatay, Fehmi E. *Topkapı Sarayı Müzesi Kütüphanesi Türkçe Yazmalar Kataloğu*. 2 vols. İstanbul, 1961.

Karatay 1962–1969   Karatay, Fehmi E. *Topkapı Sarayı Müzesi Kütüphanesi Arapça Yazmalar Kataloğu.* 4 vols. İstanbul, 1962–1969.

Karlsruhe 1977   Badischen Landesmuseums. *Die Türkenbeute.* Karlsruhe, 1977.

Keene 1984a   Keene, Manuel. "Al-Sabah Collection: Recent Acquisitions." *Arts and Islamic World* 2, no. 2 (Summer 1984): 23–26.

Keene 1984b   Keene, Manuel. *Selected Recent Acquisitions.* Kuwait, 1984.

Kerametli 1961   Kerametli, Can. "Osmanlı Devri Ağaç İşleri, Tahta Oyma, Sedef, Bağ ve Fildişi Kakmalar." *Türk Etnoğrafya Dergisi* 4 (1961): 5–13.

Kiefer 1956   Kiefer, Charles. *Les Cahiers de la Céramique. No. 4: Les Céramiques musulmanes d'Anatolie.* Paris, 1956.

Koçu 1969   Koçu, Reşat Ekrem. *Türk Giyim, Kuşam ve Süsleme Sözlüğü.* Ankara, 1969.

Kolsuk 1976   Kolsuk, A. "Osmanlı Devri Çini Kandilleri." *Türk Etnoğrafya Dergisi* 15 (1976): 73-91.

Konyalı 1950   Konyalı, İbrahim H. "Atatürk'ü Büyüleyen İki Tarihi Ayna." *Tarih Hazinesi* 2 (1950): 80–82.

Koşay and Fehér 1964–1965   Koşay, Hamit Z., and Fehér, Géza. "Macaristan'daki Türk Kuyumculuk Yadigarları, Balkanlardaki Kuyumculuğa Türk Tesiri." *Türk Etnoğrafya Dergisi* 7–8 (1964–1965): 19–37.

Köseoğlu 1980   Köseoğlu, Cengiz. *Topkapı Sarayı Müzesi. 5: Hazine.* İstanbul, 1980.

Kumbaracılar n.d.   Kumbaracılar, İzzet. *Serpuşlar.* İstanbul, n.d.

Kuran 1978   Kuran, Aptullah. "The Mosques of Sinan." In *Fifth International Congress of Turkish Art*, edited by Géza Fehér, 559–568. Budapest, 1978.

Kurz 1969   Kurz, Otto. "A Gold Helmet made in Venice for Sultan Sulayman the Magnificent." *Gazette des Beaux-Arts* 74 (1969): 249–258.

Kurz and Kurz 1973   Kurz, Otto, and Kurz, Hilde. "The Turkish Dresses in the Costume Book of Rubens." *Nederlands Kunsthistorisch Jaarboek* 23 (1973): 240–247.

Kühnel 1923   Kühnel, Ernst. *Miniaturmalerei im Islamischen Orient.* Berlin, 1923.

Kühnel 1938   Kühnel, Ernst. *İstanbul Arkeoloji Müzelerinde Şaheserler. III: Çinili Köşk'de Türk ve İslam Eserleri Koleksiyonu.* Berlin and Leipzig, 1938.

Kühnel 1955   Kühnel, Ernst. "Die Osmanische Tughra." *Kunst des Orients* 2 (1955): 69–82.

Kühnel 1977   Kühnel, Ernst. *Die Arabeske: Sinn und Wandlung eines Ornaments.* Graz, 1977 (revised edition).

Kühnel and Bellinger 1957   Kühnel, Ernst, and Bellinger, Louisa. *Cairene Rugs and Others Technically Related: 15th–17th Century.* Washington, 1957.

Kürkçüoğlu 1962   Kürkçüoğlu, Kemal E. *Süleymaniye Vakfiyesi.* Ankara, 1962.

Landsberger 1945–1946   Landsberger, Franz. "Old-time Torah Curtains." *Hebrew Union College Annual* 19 (1945–1946): 353–387.

Lane 1957   Lane, Arthur. "The Ottoman Pottery of Isnik." *Ars Orientalis* 2 (1957): 247–281.

Lane 1960   Lane, Arthur. *A Guide to the Collection of Tiles. Victoria and Albert Museum.* London, 1960.

Lane 1971   Lane, Arthur. *Later Islamic Pottery.* London, 1971 (revised edition).

Leithe-Jasper and Distelberger 1984   Leithe-Jasper, Manfred, and Distelberger, Rudolf. *Le Kunsthistorisches Museum-Vienna: Trésor et Collection des sculptures et des objets d'art.* London, 1984.

Lisbon 1963   Calouste Gulbenkian Foundation. *Oriental Islamic Art.* Lisbon, 1963.

London 1907   Burlington Fine Arts Club. *Faience of Persia and the Nearer East.* London, 1907.

London 1931   Royal Academy of Arts. *Catalogue of the International Exhibition of Persian Art.* London, 1931.

London 1950   Victoria and Albert Museum. *Brief Guide to Turkish Woven Fabrics.* London, 1950.

London 1976   Arts Council of Great Britain. *The Arts of Islam.* London, 1976.

London 1983   Arts Council of Great Britain. *The Eastern Carpet in the Western World.* London, 1983.

Lowry 1982   Lowry, Heath. "Calligraphy—Hüsn-i Hat." In *Tulips, Arabesques and Turbans*, edited by Yanni Petsopoulos, 169–191. London, 1982.

Luchner 1958   Luchner, Laurin. *Denkmal eines Renaissance fürsten: Versuch einer Rekonstruktion des Ambraser Museums von 1583.* Vienna, 1958.

Lukens 1965   Lukens, Marie G. *The Metropolitan Museum of Art: Guide to the Collections: Islamic Art.* New York, 1965.

Lyons 1976   Musée Historique des Tissus. *Etoffes Merveilleuses.* Lyons, 1976.

McAllister 1938   McAllister, Hannah E. "Tughras of Sulaiman the Magnificent." *Metropolitan Museum of Art Bulletin* 34, no. 11 (January 1939): 247–248.

Mackie 1973   Mackie, Louise W. *The Splendor of Turkish Weaving.* Washington, 1973.

Mackie 1976   Mackie, Louise W. "A Turkish Carpet with Spots and Stripes." *Textile Museum Journal* 4, no. 3 (1976): 5–20.

Mackie 1980   Mackie, Louise W. "Rugs and Textiles." In *Turkish Art*, edited by Esin Atıl, 299–393. Washington and New York, 1980.

McMullan 1965   McMullan, Joseph V. *Islamic Carpets.* New York, 1965.

McMullan 1972   McMullan, Joseph V. *Islamic Carpets from the Collection of Joseph V. McMullan.* London, 1972.

Mahir 1986   Mahir, Banu. "Saray Nakkaşhanesinin Ünlü Ressamı Şah Kulu ve Eserleri." *Topkapı Sarayı Müzesi: Yıllık* 1 (1986): 113–130.

Marquand 1903   Marquand, Henry G. *Catalogue of the Art and Literary Property Collected by the Late Henry G. Marquand,* edited by Thomas E. Kirby. New York, 1903.

Martin 1908   Martin, F. R. *A History of Oriental Carpets Before 1800.* 2 vols. Vienna, 1908.

Martin 1912   Martin, F. R. *The Miniature Paintings and Painters of Persia, India, and Turkey.* London, 1968 (reprint).

Mayer 1962   Mayer, L. A. *Islamic Armourers and Their Works.* Geneva, 1962.

Melikian-Chirvani 1975   Melikian-Chirvani, Assadullah Souren. "Recherches sur l'école du bronze ottoman au XVIe siècle." *Turcica* 6 (1975): 146–167.

Meredith-Owens 1962   Meredith-Owens, Glynn M. "Turkish Miniatures in the Selim-name." *The British Museum Quarterly* 26, nos. 1–2 (September 1962): 33–35.

Meriç 1953   Meriç, Rıfkı Melul. *Türk Nakış Sanatı Tarihi Araştırmaları. I: Vesikalar.* Ankara, 1953.

Meriç 1954   Meriç, Rıfkı Melul. *Türk Cild Sanatı Tarihi Araştırmaları. I: Vesikalar.* Ankara, 1954.

Meriç 1963   Meriç, Rıfkı Melul. "Türk Sanatı Tarihi Vesikaları: Bayramlarda Padişahlara Hediye Edilen Sanat Eserleri ve Karşılıkları." *Türk Sanatı Tarihi: Araştırma ve İncelemeleri* 1 (1963): 764–786.

Metropolitan 1930   Metropolitan Museum of Art. *Handbook of Mohammedan Decorative Arts.* New York, 1930.

Metropolitan 1952   "Recent Accessions." *Metropolitan Museum of Art Bulletin* n.s. 11, no. 3 (November 1952): 100–104.

Metropolitan 1968   "The Ottoman Empire." *Metropolitan Museum of Art Bulletin* n.s. 26, no. 5 (January 1968).

Metropolitan 1970   "Islamic Carpets." *Metropolitan Museum of Art Bulletin* 28, no. 10 (June 1970).

Metropolitan 1972   Metropolitan Museum of Art. *Guide to the Metropolitan Museum of Art.* New York, 1972.

Metropolitan 1975   "Islamic Art." *Metropolitan Museum of Art Bulletin* n.s. 33, no. 1 (Spring 1975).

Migeon 1922   Migeon, Gaston. *Musée du Louvre: L'Orient Musulman.* 2 vols. Paris, 1922.

Miller 1959   Miller, Yuri. "Turetski Serebryani Kuvschinchik XVI.v (petit cruche turque en argent du XVIe siècle)." *Soobscheniya Gosudarstvennogo Ermitazha* 15 (1959): 52–54.

Miller 1972   Miller, Yuri. *Chudozestvennaja keramika Turcii.* Leningrad, 1972.

Miller 1978   Miller, Yuri. "Artistic Contacts of Turkey with Other Countries in the Sixteenth and Seventeenth Centuries." *Trudy Gosudarstvennogo Ermitazha* 19 (1978): 106–114.

Minorksy 1958   Minorsky, V. *The Chester Beatty Library: A Catalogue of the Turkish Manuscripts and Miniatures.* Dublin, 1958.

Misugi 1981   Misugi, T. *Chinese Porcelain Collections in the Near East. II: The Topkapı Palace Museum.* Hong Kong, 1981.

Mustafa 1961   Mustafa, Mohammed. "Meisterwerke türkischer Kunst aus Sammlungen in Kairo." In *First International Congress of Turkish Arts,* 266–269. Ankara, 1961.

Munich 1965   Mathildenhöhe (Darmstadt). *Türkische Kunst: Historische Teppiche und Keramik eine Ausstellung des Deutschen Kunstrales.* Munich, 1965.

Oberhummer 1902   Oberhummer, Eugen. *Konstantinopel unter Sultan Suleiman dem Grossen: Aufgenommen im Jahre 1559 durch Melchior Lorichs.* Munich, 1902.

Otto-Dorn 1941   Otto-Dorn, Katharina. *Das Islamische Iznik.* Berlin, 1941.

Otto-Dorn 1957   Otto-Dorn, Katharina. *Türkische Keramik.* Ankara, 1957.

Öğütmen 1970   Öğütmen, Filiz. "A Wealth of Miniatures." *Apollo* 92, no. 101 (July 1970): 28–37.

Öney 1975   Öney, Gönül. *Turkish Ceramic Tile Art.* Tokyo, 1975.

Öney 1976   Öney, Gönül. *Türk Çini Sanatı/Turkish Tile Art.* İstanbul, 1976.

Öney 1980   Öney, Gönül. "Architectural Decoration and the Minor Arts." In *The Art and Architecture of Turkey,* edited by Ekrem Akurgal, 170–207. Oxford, 1980.

Öz n.d.   Öz, Tahsin. *The Topkapı Saray Museum: 50 Masterpieces.* İstanbul, n.d.

Öz 1942   Öz, Tahsin. "Türk El İşlemeleri ve Resim Dairesi." *Güzel Sanatlar* 4 (1942): 29–52.

Öz 1950   Öz, Tahsin. *Turkish Textiles and Velvets: XIV–XVI Centuries.* Ankara, 1950.

Öz 1951 Öz, Tahsin. *Türk Kumaş ve Kadifeleri. II: XVII–XIX Yüzyıl ve Kumaş Süslemesi.* İstanbul, 1951.

Öz 1957 Öz, Tahsin. *Turkish Ceramics.* Ankara, 1957.

Özbay 1970 Özbay, Jale. "Chinese and Japanese Porcelain." *Apollo* 92, no. 101 (July 1970): 54–57.

Paris 1791 *Inventaire des Bijoux de la Couronne.* Paris, 1791.

Paris 1903 L'Union Centrale des Arts Décoratifs. *Exposition des Arts musulmans.* Paris, 1903.

Paris 1953 Musée des Arts Décoratifs. *Splendeur de l'Art Turc.* Paris, 1953.

Paris 1971 Réunion des Musées Nationaux. *Arts de l'Islam des Origines à 1700.* Paris, 1971.

Paris 1977 Réunion des Musées Nationaux. *L'Islam dans les collections nationales.* Paris, 1977.

Petsopoulos 1979 Petsopoulos, Yanni. *Kilims.* Fribourg, 1979.

Pitcher 1972 Pitcher, Donald Edgar. *An Historical Geography of the Ottoman Empire.* Leiden, 1972.

A.U. Pope 1964–1965 Pope, A.U., ed. *A Survey of Persian Art.* 12 vols. London and New York 1964–1965 (reprint).

J.A. Pope 1970 Pope, John Alexander. *Fourteenth-Century Blue-and-White: A Group of Chinese Porcelains in the Topkapu Sarayi Müzesi, Istanbul.* Washington, 1970.

J.A. Pope 1972 Pope, John Alexander. "Chinese Influence on Iznik Pottery: A Re-examination of an Old Problem." In *Islamic Art in the Metropolitan Museum of Art,* edited by Richard Ettinghausen, 125–139. New York, 1972.

Preyger 1970 Preyger, Firuze. "The Imperial Treasury." *Apollo* 92, no. 101 (July 1970): 41–45.

Raby 1976 Raby, Julian. "A Seventeenth-Century Description of Iznik/Nicea." *Istanbuler Mitteilungen* 26 (1976): 149–188.

Raby 1977/1978 Raby, Julian. "Diyarbakır: A Rival to Iznik." *Istanbuler Mitteilungen* 27/28 (1977/1978): 429–459.

Raby and Yücel 1983 Raby, Julian, and Yücel, Ünsal. "Blue-and-White, Celadon and White Wares: İznik's Debt to China." *Oriental Art* 29, no. 1 (Spring 1983): 38–48.

Raby and Yücel 1986 Raby, Julian, and Yücel, Ünsal. "Chinese Porcelain at the Ottoman Court" and "The Archival Documentation." In vol. 1 of *Chinese Ceramics in the Topkapı Saray Museum, Istanbul,* edited by John Ayers. London, 1986 (forthcoming).

Rackham 1934/1935 Rackham, Bernard. "Turkish Pottery." *Transactions of the Oriental Ceramics Society* 1934/1935: 35–48.

Rackham 1959 Rackham, Bernard. *Islamic Pottery and Italian Maiolica.* London, 1959.

Reath 1927 Reath, Nancy Andrews. "Velvets of the Renaissance, from Europe and Asia Minor." *Burlington Magazine* 50 (1927): 298–304.

Renda 1973 Renda, Günsel. "Topkapı Sarayı Müzesindeki H. 1321 no.'lu Silsilename'nin Minyatürleri." *Sanat Tarihi Yıllığı* 5 (1973): 443–495.

Renda 1976 Renda, Günsel. "New Light on the Painters of the Zubdet al-Tawarikh in the Museum of Turkish and Islamic Arts in Istanbul." In *IVème Congrès International d'Art Turc,* 183–200. Aix-en-Provence, 1976.

Riefstahl 1937 Riefstahl, R.M. "Early Turkish Tile Revetments in Edirne." *Ars Islamica* 4 (1937): 249–281.

Riegl 1892 Riegl, Alois. *Oriental Carpets.* 4 vols. Vienna, 1892.

Riyadh 1985 King Faisal Foundation. *The Unity of Islamic Art.* Riyadh, 1985.

Rogers 1982 Rogers, J. Michael. "The State and the Arts in Ottoman Turkey. Part 2: The Furniture and Decoration of the Süleymaniye." *International Journal of Middle East Studies* 14 (1982): 283–313.

Rogers 1983a Rogers, J. Michael. "Glass in Ottoman Turkey." *Deutsches Archäologisches Institut Abteilung Istanbul* 33 (1983): 239–266.

Rogers 1983b Rogers, J. Michael. *Islamic Art & Design. 1500/1700.* London, 1983.

Rogers 1984 Rogers, J. Michael. "The Godman Bequest of Islamic Pottery." *Apollo* 120, no. 269 (July 1984): 24–35.

Rogers 1985a Rogers, J. Michael. "A Group of Ottoman Pottery in the Godman Bequest." *Burlington Magazine* 127, no. 984 (March 1985): 134–155.

Rogers 1985b Rogers, J. Michael. "An Iznik Mosque-Lamp and a Globe in the Godman Bequest, British Museum." *Orientations* 16, no. 9 (September 1985): 43–49.

Rogers 1985c Rogers, J. Michael. "İznik Pottery in the British Museum." *Hali* 7, no. 2 (April–June 1985): 50–57.

Rogers 1986a Rogers, J. Michael. "An Ottoman Palace Inventory of the Reign of Bayazid II." *Proceedings of the Congrès International des Etudes Ottomanes et pré-Ottomanes.* İstanbul, 1986 (forthcoming).

Rogers 1986b Rogers, J. Michael, ed. *Topkapi Saray Museum: 1. The Albums and Illustrated Manuscripts* by Filiz Çağman and Zeren Tanındı. London and New York, 1986.

Rogers 1986c Rogers, J. Michael, ed. *Topkapi Saray Museum: 2. The Costumes, Embroideries, and Other Textiles* by Hülya Tezcan and Selma Delibaş. London and New York, 1986.

Rome 1980 *The Holy Qur'an Manuscript in 953/1546 by Ahmed Karahisari for Sultan Süleyman the Magnificent.* Rome, 1980 (facsimile edition).

Rosenzweig 1978–1979 ''Stalking the Persian Dragon: Chinese Prototypes for the Miniature Representations.'' *Kunst des Orients* 12, no. 1/2 (1978–1979): 151–176.

Sacken 1855 Sacken, Eduard Freiherr von. *Die K.K. Ambraser-Sammlung.* Vienna, 1855.

Safadi 1978 Safadi, Yasin Hamid. *Islamic Calligraphy.* London, 1978.

Sakisian 1925 Sakisian, Arménag. ''Djem Sultan et les Fresques de Pinturicchio.'' *Revue de l'Art* 47, no. 263 (February 1925): 81–91.

Sakisian 1931 Sakisian, Arménag. ''L'Inventaire des tapis de la mosquée Yeni-Djami de Stamboul.'' *Syria* 12 (1931): 368–373.

Sanat 1982 *Sanat* 7 (1982). Special issue on the Topkapı Palace Museum.

Sarre 1939 Sarre, Friedrich. ''Die Fayencen von Nicaea und ihr Export nach dem Abendland.'' *Pantheon* 24 (1939): 341–345.

Sarre and Martin 1912 Sarre, Friedrich, and Martin, F.R. *Die Ausstellung von Meisterwerken muhammedanischer Kunst in München 1910.* 4 vols. Berlin, 1912.

Sarre and Trenkwald 1926 Sarre, Friedrich, and Trenkwald, Hermann. *Ancient Oriental Carpets. I,* translated by A.F. Kendrick. Vienna and Leipzig, 1926.

Schlosser 1963 Schlosser, Ignaz. *The Book of Rugs: Oriental and European.* New York, 1963.

Schmidt 1933 Schmidt, Heinrich J. ''Turkish Brocades and Italian Imitations.'' *Art Bulletin* 15 (1933): 374–383.

Schmidt 1958 Schmidt, Heinrich J. *Alte Seidenstoffe.* Brunswick, 1958.

Selen 1937 Selen, H. Sadi. ''Piri Reis'in Şimali Amerika Haritası.'' *Belleten* 1/2 (1937): 515–523.

Sertoğlu 1975 Sertoğlu, Midhat. *Osmanlı Türklerinde Tuğra.* İstanbul, 1975.

Sevin 1975 Sevin, Nurettin. ''Saray Kaftanları.'' *Sanat Dünyamız* 3, no. 3 (January 1975): 14–23.

Skelton 1978 Skelton, Robert. ''Characteristics of Later Turkish Jade Carving.'' In *Fifth International Congress of Turkish Art,* edited by Géza Fehér, 795–807. Budapest, 1978.

Sotheby's 1981 Sotheby's. *Fine Oriental Miniatures, Manuscripts and Islamic Works of Art.* New York, 21 May 1981.

Sotheby's 1982 Sotheby's. *Catalogue of Important Chinese and Islamic Jade Carvings.* London, 8 June 1982.

Sotheby's 1985a Sotheby's. *Islamic Works of Art, Carpets and Textiles.* London, 16–17 April 1985.

Sotheby's 1985b Sotheby's. *Islamic Works of Art, Carpets and Textiles.* London, 15–16 October 1985.

Sotheby's 1985c Sotheby's. *Fine Oriental Manuscripts and Miniatures.* London, 21–22 November 1985.

Sotheby's 1986 Sotheby's. *Islamic Works of Art, Carpets and Textiles.* London, 16 April 1986.

Soucek 1973 Soucek, Svat. ''A propos du livre d'instructions nautiques de Piri Reis.'' *Revue des Etudes Islamiques* 41, no. 2 (1973): 241–255.

Sourdel-Thomine 1971 Sourdel-Thomine, Janine. ''Clefs et serrures de la Kaba: notes d'épigraphie arabe.'' *Revue des Etudes Islamiques* 39, no. 1 (1971): 29–86.

Sözen 1975 Sözen, Metin, ed. *Türk Mimarisinin Gelişimi ve Mimar Sinan.* İstanbul, 1975.

Söylemezoğlu 1974 Söylemezoğlu, Nerkis. ''An Illustrated Copy of Hamdi's *Yusuf we Züleykha* dated A.H. 921/1515 A.D. in the Bayerische Staatsbibliothek in Munich.'' In *Near Eastern Numismatics, Iconography, Epigraphy and History,* edited by D.K. Kouymjian, 469–478. Beirut, 1974.

Stchoukine 1966 Stchoukine, Ivan. *La peinture turque d'après les manuscrits illustrés. Ire partie: de Suleyman Ier à Osman II. 1520–1622.* Paris, 1966.

Stchoukine 1967 Stchoukine, Ivan. ''Miniatures turques du temps de Mohammad II.'' *Ars Asiatiques* 15 (1967): 47–50.

Stchoukine 1972 Stchoukine, Ivan. ''La Khamseh de Nizami, H. 753, du Topkapı Sarayı Müzesi d'Istanbul.'' *Syria* 49 (1972): 240–246.

St. Clair 1973 St. Clair, Alexandrine N. *The Image of the Turk in Europe.* New York, 1973.

Stockholm 1985 Statens Historiska Museum. *Islam: Konst och Kultur.* Stockholm, 1985.

Süslü 1976 Süslü, Özden. ''Le Motif du paon dans la céramique ottoman du XVIe siècle.'' *IVème Congrès International d'Art Turc,* 237–247. Aix-en-Provence, 1976.

Şahin 1979-1980 Şahin, Faruk. ''Kütahya Çini Keramik Sanatı ve Tarihinin Yeni Buluntular Açısından Değerlendirilmesi.'' *Sanat Tarihi Yıllığı* 9–10 (1979–1980): 259–286.

Tanındı 1983a   Tanındı, Zeren. "İslam Resminde Kutsal Kent ve Yöre Tasvirleri." *Journal of Turkish Studies (Orhan Şaik Gökyay Armağanı. II)* 7 (1983): 407–437.

Tanındı 1983b   Tanındı, Zeren. "Resimli Bir Hac Vekaletnamesi." *Sanat Dünyamız* 9, no. 28 (1983): 2–6.

Tanındı 1984   Tanındı, Zeren. "Rugani Türk Kitap Kaplarının Erken Örnekleri." In *Kemal Çığ'a Armağan*, 223–253. İstanbul, *Topkapı Sarayı Müzesi: Yıllık* 1 (1986): 140–152. 1984.

Tanındı 1986   Tanındı, Zeren. "13–14. Yüzyılda Yazılmış Kuranların Kanuni Döneminde Yenilenmesi." *Topkapi Sarayi Müzesi: Yillik* 1 (1986): 140–152.

Tapan 1977   Tapan, Nazan. "Sorguçlar." *Sanat* 6 (1977): 99–107.

Tezcan 1975   Tezcan, Turgay. "Topkapı Sarayı Müzesindeki Türk Miğferleri." *Sanat Dünyamız* 2, no. 5 (September 1975): 21–27.

Tezcan 1982   Tezcan, Turgay. "15. Yüz Yılda Değişik Form Gösteren Türk Kılıçlar." *Sanat Dünyamız* 9, no. 25 (1982): 23–26.

Tezcan 1983   Tezcan, Turgay. *Topkapı Sarayı Müzesi. 9: Silahlar.* İstanbul, 1983.

Thomas 1963/1964   Thomas, Bruno. "Aus der Waffensammlung in der Neuen Burg zu Wien: Orientalische Kostbarkeiten." *Bustan* 4/5 (1963/1964): 121–126.

Titley 1981   Titley, Norah M. *Miniatures from Turkish Manuscripts.* London, 1981.

Travelstead 1982   Travelstead, Brooke. "An Ornamental Ceramic Globe from the Ottoman Period." *Apollo* 115, no. 242 (April 1982): 237.

Tuğlacı 1984   Tuğlacı, Pars. *Women in Turkey: Women of İstanbul in Ottoman Times.* İstanbul, 1984.

Tuncay 1978   Tuncay, Hülya. "Topkapı Sarayı Müzesindeki Çini Kandiller." *Sanat Dünyamız* 4, no. 12 (January 1978): 10–16.

Tuncay 1980   Tuncay, Hülya. *Topkapı Sarayı Müzesi. 4: Çinili Köşk.* İstanbul, 1980.

Turan 1968   Turan, Şerafettin. "Venedikte Türk Ticaret Merkezi." *Belleten* 32, no. 126 (1968): 247–283.

Türkoğlu 1985   Türkoğlu, Sabahattin. "Saray Kuyumculuğu." *Sanat Dünyamız* 11, no. 34 (1985): 12–17.

Uluçay 1970   Uluçay, Çağatay. "Kanuni Sultan Süleyman ve Ailesi ile İlgili Bazı Notlar ve Vesikalar." In *Kanuni Armağanı*, 227–257. Ankara, 1970.

Umur 1980   Umur, Suha. *Osmanlı Padişah Tuğraları.* İstanbul, 1980.

Uzunçarşılı 1986   Uzunçarşılı, İsmail Hakkı. "Osmanlı Sarayında Ehl-i Hiref 'Sanatkarlar' Defterleri." *Belgeler* 15 (1986): 23–76.

Ünal 1963   Ünal, İsmail. "Çin Porselenleri Üzerindeki Türk Tarsiatı." *Türk Sanatı Tarihi: Araştırma ve İncelemeleri* 1 (1963): 677–714.

Ünal 1965   Ünal, İsmail. "Les poteries de faience appartenant aux collections des Messieurs Hüseyin Kocabaş and Tevfik Kuyaş." In *Atti del Secondo Congresso Internazionale di Arte Turca*, 265–271. Naples, 1965.

Ünal 1969   Ünal, İsmail. "Çini Cami Kandilleri." *Türk Sanatı Tarihi: Araştırma ve İncelemeleri* 2 (1969): 74–111.

Ünver 1946   Ünver, A. Süheyl. *Ressam Nigari: Hayatı ve Eserleri.* Ankara, 1946.

Ünver 1948   Ünver, A. Süheyl. *Hattat Ahmet Karahisari.* İstanbul, 1948.

Ünver 1951   Ünver, A. Süheyl. *Müzehhib Karamemi: His Life and Works.* İstanbul, 1951.

Ünver 1970   Ünver, A. Süheyl. "Kanuni Sultan Süleyman'ın Son Avusturya Seferinde Hastalığı, Ölümü, Cenazesi ve Defni." In *Kanuni Armağanı*, 301–306. Ankara, 1970.

Vienna 1932   *Türkische Kunst aus sieben Jahrhunderten.* Vienna, 1932.

Vienna 1977   Schloss Halbturn. *Kunst des Islam.* Vienna, 1977.

Vienna 1983a   Historischen Museums der Stadt Wien. *Die Türken vor Wien: Europa und die Entscheidung an der Donau 1683.* Vienna, 1983.

Vienna 1983b   Österreichischen Nationalbibliothek. *Österreich und die Osman.* Vienna, 1983.

Warsaw 1983   Muzeum Narodowe w Warszawie. *Tkanina turecka XVI–XIX w. ze zbiorów polskich.* Warsaw, 1983.

Washington 1966   Smithsonian Institution. *Art Treasures of Turkey.* Washington, 1966.

Washington 1974   Textile Museum. *Prayer Rugs.* Washington, 1974.

Wearden 1985   Wearden, Jennifer. "Siegmund von Herberstein: An Italian Velvet in the Ottoman Court." *Costume* 19 (1985): 22–29.

Weibel 1948   Weibel, Adele Coulin. "A Turkish Velvet Hanging." *Bulletin of the Detroit Institute of Arts* 27, no. 2 (1948): 80–83.

A. Welch 1979   Welch, Anthony. *Calligraphy in the Arts of the Muslim World.* New York, 1979.

S.C. Welch 1972 — Welch, Stuart Cary. "Two Drawings, a Tile, a Dish, and a Pair of Scissors." *Islamic Art in the Metropolitan Museum of Art*, edited by Richard Ettinghausen, 291–298. New York, 1972.

Welch and Welch 1982 — Welch, Anthony, and Welch, Stuart Cary. *Arts of the Islamic Book: The Collection of Prince Sadruddin Aga Khan.* Ithaca and London, 1982.

Woodhead 1983 — Woodhead, Christine. "An Experiment in Official Historiography: the Post of Şehnameci in the Ottoman Empire, c. 1555–1605." *Wiener Zeitschrift für die Kunde des Morgenlandes* 75 (1983): 157–182.

Yağmurlu 1970 — Yağmurlu, Haydar. "Relics of the Prophet Muhammed." *Apollo* 92, no. 101 (July 1970): 50–53.

Yağmurlu 1973 — Yağmurlu, Haydar. "Topkapı Sarayı Müzesi Kütühanesinde İmzalı Eserleri Bulunan Tezhip Ustaları." *Türk Etnoğrafya Dergisi* 13 (1973): 79–131.

Yazır 1972–1974 — Yazır, Mahmud B. *Medeniyet Aleminde Yazı ve İslam Medeniyetinde Kalem Güzeli.* 2 vols. İstanbul, 1972–1974.

Yenişehirlioğlu 1980 — Yenişehirlioğlu, Filiz. "Şehzade Mehmet Türbesi Çinileri Üzerinde Gözlemeler." In *Bedrettin Cömert'e Armağan*, 449–465. İstanbul, 1980.

Yetkin 1971 — Yetkin, Şerare. "Türk Kilim Sanatında Yeni Bir Gurup: Saray Kilimleri." *Belleten* 35, no. 138 (1971): 217–227.

Yetkin 1981 — Yetkin, Şerare. *Historical Turkish Carpets.* İstanbul, 1981.

Yurdaydın 1963 — Yurdaydın, Hüseyin G. *Matrakçı Nasuh.* Ankara, 1963.

Yurdaydın 1964 — Yurdaydın, Hüseyin G. "Matrakçı Nasuh'un Minyatürlü İki Yeni Eseri." *Belleten* 28, no. 110 (1964): 229–233.

Yurdaydın 1965 — Yurdaydın, Hüseyin G. "Matrakçı Nasuh'un Hayatı ve Eserleri ile İlgili Yeni Bilgiler." *Belleten* 29, no. 114 (1965): 329–354.

Yurdaydın 1976 — Yurdaydın, Hüseyin G. *Nasuhü's-Silahi (Matrakçı), Beyan-ı Menazil-i Sefer-i Irakeyn-i Sultan Süleyman Han.* Ankara, 1976.

E. Yücel 1978 — Yücel, Erdem. "Altın Yol ve Takkeci Camii Çinileri." *Türkiyemiz* 6, no. 18 (February 1978): 2–6.

E. Yücel 1982 — Yücel, Erdem. *Topkapı Sarayı Müzesi. 7: Hırka-ı Saadet.* İstanbul, 1982.

Ü. Yücel 1964–1965 — Yücel, Ünsal. "Türk Kılıç Ustaları." *Türk Etnoğrafya Dergisi* 7–8 (1964–1965): 59–99.

Ü. Yücel 1970 — Yücel, Unsal. "Thirteen Centuries of Islamic Arms." *Apollo* 92, no. 101 (July 1970): 46–49.

Zaky 1979 — Zaky, A.R. "Medieval Arab Arms." In *Islamic Arms and Armour*, edited by Robert Elgood, 202–211. London, 1979.

Zich-Nissen 1976 — Zich-Nissen, Johanna. "Some Rare Pieces of Ottoman Blue-and-White Ceramics: A Study in Style and Technique in View to Yüan and Early Ming Porcelain." In *IVème Congrès International d'Art Turc*, 249–256. Aix-en-Provence, 1976.

Zimmermann 1930 — Zimmermann, Ernst. *Altchinesische porzellane im Alten Sarai.* Berlin and Leipzig, 1930.

Select Bibliography

Historical Setting

Alderson, A. D. *The Structure of the Ottoman Dynasty*. Reprint. Westport, 1982.

Altınay, Ahmet Refik. *On Altıncı Asırda İstanbul Hayatı*. İstanbul, 1935.

Bradford, Ernle. *The Great Siege*. London, 1961.

Bradford, Ernle. *The Sultan's Admiral: Life of Barbarossa*. London, 1969.

Braudel, Fernand. *The Mediterranean and the Mediterranean World in the Age of Philip II*. 2 vols. New York, Hagerstown, San Francisco, and London, 1972–1973.

Bridge, Antony. *Suleiman the Magnificent*. New York, 1983.

Brockman, Eric. *The Two Sieges of Rhodes: 1480–1522*. London, 1969.

Coecke van Aelst, Pieter. *Ces moeurs et fachons de faire de Turcs*. Antwerp, 1553.

Coles, Paul. *The Ottoman Impact on Europe*. London, 1968.

Fischer-Galati, S. *Ottoman Imperialism and German Protestantism, 1521–1555*. Cambridge (Mass.), 1959.

Forster, Edward S., trans. *The Turkish Letters of Ogier Ghiselin de Busbecq*. 1927. Reprint. Oxford, 1968.

Göllner, Carl. *Turcica: die europäischen Türkendrucke des XVI. Jahrhunderts*. 2 vols. Bucharest and Baden-Baden, 1961–1968.

Historischen Museum. *Wien 1529: Die erste Türkenbelagerung*. Vienna, 1979.

İnalcık, Halil. "Süleyman the Lawgiver and Ottoman Law." *Archivum Ottomanicum* 1 (1969): 105–138.

İnalcık, Halil. *The Ottoman Empire: The Classical Age 1300–1600*. London, 1973.

Käldy-Nagy, Gyula. "Rural and Urban Life in the Age of Sultan Süleyman." *Acta Orientalia* 32 (1978): 285–319.

Kappert, Petra. *Geschichte Sultan Süleyman Kanunis von 1520 bis 1567 (oder "Tabakat ül-Memalik ve Derecat ül-Mesalik" von Celalzade Mustafa genannt Koca Nişancı)*. Wiesbaden, 1981.

Lewis, Bernard. *İstanbul and the Civilization of the Ottoman Empire*. Norman, 1963.

Lewis, Raphaela. *Everyday Life in Ottoman Turkey*. London and New York, 1971.

Lybyer, Albert Howe. *The Government of the Ottoman Empire in the Time of Suleiman the Magnificent*. Cambridge (Mass.), 1913.

Mantran, Robert. *La vie quotidienne à Constantinople au temps de Soliman le Magnifique et de ses successeurs*. Paris, 1965.

Miller, Barnette. *Beyond the Sublime Porte: The Grand Seraglio of Stambul*. New Haven, 1941.

Miller, Barnette. *The Palace School of Muhammad the Conqueror*. Reprint. New York, 1973.

Oberhummer, Eugen. *Konstantinopel unter Sultan Suleiman dem Grossen: Aufgenommen im Jahre 1559 durch Melchior Lorichs*. Munich, 1902.

Parry, V. J. "The Ottoman Empire, 1520–1566." In *New Cambridge Modern History*, 2:510–533. Cambridge (Mass.), 1958.

Pitcher, Donald Edgar. *An Historical Geography of the Ottoman Empire*. Leiden, 1972.

Reyhanlı, Tülay. *İngiliz Gezginlerine Göre XVI. Yüzyılda İstanbul'da Hayat (1582–1599)*. Ankara, 1983.

Rouillard, Clarence Dana. *The Turk in French History, Thought, and Literature (1520–1660)*. Paris, 1938.

Shaw, Stanford J. *History of the Ottoman Empire and Modern Turkey*. 2 vols. Cambridge, 1976.

Stripling, G.W.F. *The Ottoman Turks and the Arabs, 1511–1574*. Reprint. Urbana, 1942.

Stuminger, W. *Bibliographie und Ikonographie der Türkenbelagerungen Wiens 1529 und 1683*. Graz and Cologne, 1955.

Tauer, Félix. *Histoire de la Campagne du Sultan Süleyman Ier contre Belgrade en 1521*. Prague, 1924.

Turan, Şerafettin. *Kanuni'nin Oğlu Şehzade Bayezid Vakası*. Ankara, 1961.

Türk Tarih Kurumu. *Kanuni Armağanı*. Ankara, 1970.

Uraz, Murat, trans. *Peçevi Tarihi*. 2 vols. İstanbul, 1968.

Vaughan, Dorothy. *Europe and the Turk: A Pattern of Alliances, 1350–1700*. Liverpool, 1954.

Woodhead, Christine. "An Experiment in Official Historiography: The Post of Şehnameci in the Ottoman Empire, c. 1555–1605." *Wiener Zeitschrift für die Kunde des Morgenlandes* 75 (1983): 157–182.

Yurdaydın, Hüseyin G. *Kanuni'nin Cülusu ve İlk Seferleri*. Ankara, 1961.

Art and Architecture (surveys and general studies)

Akurgal, Ekrem, ed. *The Art and Architecture of Turkey*. Oxford, 1980.

Akurgal, Ekrem; Mango, Cyril; and Ettinghausen, Richard. *Treasures of Turkey*. Geneva, 1966.

Apollo 92, no. 101 (July 1970). Special issue on the Topkapı Palace Museum.

Arseven, Celal Esad. *Les Arts Décoratif Turc*. İstanbul, n.d.

Arseven, Celal Esad. *Türk Sanatı*. İstanbul, 1970.

Aslanapa, Oktay. *Turkish Art and Architecture*. London, 1971.

Atıl, Esin. *Turkish Art of the Ottoman Period*. Washington, 1973.

Atıl, Esin, ed. *Turkish Art*. Washington and New York, 1980.

Binney, Edwin, 3rd. *Turkish Treasures from the Collection of Edwin Binney, 3rd*. Portland (Ore.), 1979.

Binney, Edwin, 3rd. *Turkish Treasures from the Collection of Edwin Binney, 3rd: 1981 Supplement to the 1979 Catalogue.* San Diego, 1981.

Demiriz, Yıldız. "Türk Sanatında Bahar Açmış Meyve Ağacı Motifi." In *I. Milli Türkoloji Kongresi,* 382–400. İstanbul, 1980.

Denny, Walter B. "Dating Ottoman Turkish Works in the Saz Style." *Muqarnas* 1 (1983): 103–121.

Diez, Ernst, and Aslanapa, Oktay. *Türk Sanatı.* İstanbul, 1955.

Eyice, Semavi. "Avrupalı Bir Ressamın Gözü ile Kanuni Sultan Süleyman." In *Kanuni Armağanı,* 129–170. Ankara, 1970.

Fehér, Géza. "L'influence turque sur les arts décoratifs populaires hongrois." In *Atti del Secondo Congresso Internazionale di Arte Turca,* 119–122. Naples, 1965.

Fehér, Géza. "Macar Sanatında Görülen Türk Etkisi." *Türk Sanatı Tarihi: Araştırma ve İncelemeleri* 2 (1969): 205–213.

Fischer, E. *Melchior Lorichs.* Copenhagen, 1962.

Karabacek, Josef von. *Abendländische Künstler zu Konstantinopel im XV. und XVI. Jahrhundert. 1: Italienische Künstler am Hofe Muhammads II., des Eroberers 1451–1481.* Vienna, 1918.

Kurz, Otto. *The Decorative Arts of Europe and the Islamic East.* London, 1977.

Meriç, Rıfkı Melul. "Türk Sanatı Tarihi Vesikaları: Bayramlarda Padişahlara Hediye Edilen Sanat Eserleri ve Karşılıkları." *Türk Sanatı Tarihi: Araştırma ve İncelemeleri* 1 (1963): 764–786.

Miller, Yuri. "Artistic Contacts of Turkey with Other Countries of the Sixteenth and Seventeenth Centuries." *Trudy Gosudarstvennego Ermitazha* 19 (1978): 106–114.

Museum für Kunsthandwerk. *Türkische Kunst und Kultur aus osmanischer Zeit.* 2 vols. Frankfurt, 1985.

Petsopoulos, Yanni, ed. *Tulips, Arabesques and Turbans.* London, 1982.

Raby, Julian. *Venice, Dürer, and the Oriental Mode.* London, 1982.

Sanat 7 (1982). Special issue on the Topkapı Palace Museum.

Smithsonian Institution. *Art Treasures of Turkey.* Washington, 1966.

St. Clair, Alexandrine N. *The Image of the Turk in Europe.* New York, 1973.

Titley, Norah M. *Dragons in Persian, Mughal, and Turkish Art.* London, 1981.

Turkish Ministry of Culture and Tourism. *The Anatolian Civilisations. III: Seljuk/Ottoman.* İstanbul, 1983.

Welch, Stuart Cary. "Two Drawings, a Tile, a Dish, and a Pair of Scissors." In *Islamic Art in The Metropolitan Museum of Art,* ed. Richard Ettinghausen, 291–298. New York, 1972.

Yapı ve Kredi Bankası. *Turkish Contribution to Islamic Arts.* İstanbul, 1976.

Architecture

Barkan, Ömer Lütfi. *Süleymaniye Cami ve İmareti İnşaatı (1550–1557).* 2 vols. Ankara, 1972–1979.

Bates, Ülkü. "Architecture." In *Turkish Art,* ed. Esin Atıl, 43–136. Washington and New York, 1980.

Bates, Ülkü. "The Patronage of Sultan Süleyman: The Süleymaniye Complex in İstanbul." *Edebiyat Fakültesi Araştırma Dergisi (Memoriam A.L. Gabriel),* 1978, 65–76.

Eldem, Sedad H., and Akozan, Feridun. *Topkapı Sarayı: Bir Mimari Araştırma.* İstanbul, 1982.

Gasparini, Elisabetta. *Le Pitture Murali della Muradiye di Edirne.* Padova, 1985.

Goodwin, Godfrey. *A History of Ottoman Architecture.* London, 1971.

Kuran, Aptullah. "The Mosques of Sinan." In *Fifth International Congress of Turkish Art,* ed. by Géza Fehér, 559–568. Budapest, 1978.

Kuran, Aptullah. *Sinan: The Grand Old Man of Ottoman Architecture.* İstanbul, 1987. Forthcoming.

Kürkçüoğlu, Kemal E. *Süleymaniye Vakfiyesi.* Ankara, 1962.

Necipoğlu-Kafadar, Gülru. "The Süleymaniye Complex in Istanbul: An Interpretation." *Muqarnas* 3 (1985): 92–117.

Rogers, J. Michael. "The State and the Arts in Ottoman Turkey. Part 1: The Stones of the Süleymaniye," and "Part 2: The Furniture and Decoration of the Süleymaniye." *International Journal of Middle East Studies* 14 (1982): 71–86 and 283–313.

Sözen, Metin, ed. *Türk Mimarisinin Gelişimi ve Mimar Sinan.* İstanbul, 1975.

Stierlin, Henri. *Soliman et d'Architecture ottomane.* Fribourg, 1985.

Turan, Şerafettin. "Osmanlı Teşkilatında Hassa Mimarları." *Tarih Araştırmaları Dergisi* 1 (1963): 157–202.

Tuğras

Bombaci, Alessio. "Les Toughras Enluminés de la Collection de Documents Turcs des Archives d'Etat de Venise." In *Atti del Secondo Congresso Internazionale di Arte Turca.* 26–29, Naples, 1965.

Kühnel, Ernst. "Die Osmanische Tughra." *Kunst des Orients* 2 (1955): 69–82.

McAllister, Hannah E. "Tughras of Sulaiman the Magnificent." *Metropolitan Museum of Art Bulletin,* 34, no. 11 (January 1939): 247–248.

Sertoğlu, Midhat. *Osmanlı Türklerinde Tuğra.* İstanbul, 1975.

Umur, Suha. *Osmanlı Padişah Tuğraları.* İstanbul, 1980.

Arts of the Book

Akalay, Zeren. "Tarihi Konularda İlk Osmanlı Minyatürleri." *Sanat Tarihi Yıllığı* 2 (1969): 102–115.

Akalay, Zeren. "Tarihi Konularda Türk Minyatürleri." *Sanat Tarihi Yıllığı* 3 (1970): 151–166.

Akalay, Zeren. "Topkapı Sarayı Müzesi Kütüphanesi Hazine 753 no.'lu Nizami Hamsesi'nin Minyatürleri." *Sanat Tarihi Yıllığı* 5 (1973): 389–409.

Akalay, Zeren. "The Forerunners of Classical Turkish Miniature Painting." In *Fifth International Congress of Turkish Art,* ed. Géza Fehér, 31–47. Budapest, 1978.

Akalay, Zeren. "XVI. Yüzyıl Nakkaşlarından Hasan Paşa ve Eserleri." In *I. Milletlerarası Türkoloji Kongresi. 3: Türk Sanat Tarihi,* 607–625. İstanbul, 1979.

Aksoy, Şule. "Hat Sanatı." *Kültür ve Sanat* 5 (1977): 115–137.

Anafarta, Nigar. *Hünername: Minyatürleri ve Sanatçıları.* İstanbul, 1969.

And, Metin. *Turkish Miniature Painting: The Ottoman Period.* Revised edition. İstanbul, 1982.

Aslanapa, Oktay. "Osmanlı Devri Cilt Sanatı." *Türkiyemiz* 38 (October 1982): 12–17.

Atasoy, Nurhan. "1558 Tarihli Süleymanname ve Macar Nakkaş Pervane." *Sanat Tarihi Yıllığı* 3 (1970): 167–196.

Atasoy, Nurhan. "Nakkaş Osman'ın Padişah Portreleri Albümü." *Türkiyemiz* 6 (February 1972): 2–14.

Atasoy, Nurhan, and Çağman, Filiz. *Turkish Miniature Painting.* İstanbul, 1974.

Atıl, Esin. "Ottoman Miniature Painting under Sultan Mehmed II." *Ars Orientalis* 9 (1973): 103–120.

Atıl, Esin. "The Art of the Book." In *Turkish Art,* ed. Esin Atıl, 137–238. Washington and New York, 1980.

Atıl, Esin. *Süleymaniye: The Illustrated History of Süleyman the Magnificent.* Washington and New York, 1986.

Çağman, Filiz. "Şahname-i Selim Han ve Minyatürleri." *Sanat Tarihi Yıllığı* 5 (1973): 411–442.

Çağman, Filiz. "Sultan Mehmet II Dönemine Ait Bir Minyatürlü Yazma: Külliyat-ı Katibi." *Sanat Tarihi Yıllığı* 6 (1974–1975): 333–346.

Çağman, Filiz. "XV.yy. Kağıt Oymacılık (Kaatı) Eserleri." *Sanat Dünyamız* 3, no. 8 (September 1976): 22–27.

Çağman, Filiz. "The Place of the Turkish Miniature in Islamic Art." In *Turkish Contribution to Islamic Arts,* 90–117. İstanbul, 1976.

Çağman, Filiz. "The Miniatures of the *Divan-ı Hüseyni* and the Influence of Their Style." In *Fifth International Congress of Turkish Art,* ed. Géza Fehér, 231–259. Budapest, 1978.

Çağman, Filiz, and Tanındı, Zeren. *Topkapı Saray Museum: Islamic Miniature Painting.* İstanbul, 1979.

Çığ, Kemal. *Türk Kitap Kapları.* İstanbul, 1971.

Demiriz, Yıldız. "16. Yüzyıla Ait Tezhipli Bir Kuran." *Sanat Tarihi Yıllığı* 7 (1977): 41–58.

Denny, Walter B. "A Sixteenth-Century Architectural Plan of Istanbul." *Ars Orientalis* 8 (1970): 49–63.

Derman, M. Uğur. "Kanuni Devrinde Yazı Sanatımız." In *Kanuni Armağanı,* 269–289. Ankara, 1970.

Derman, M. Uğur. *Türk Hat Sanatının Şaheserleri.* İstanbul(?), 1982.

Duda, Dorothea. "Ein Beispiel der Tabrizer Buchkunst am Osmanenhof." *Kunst des Orients* 12, nos. 1–2 (1978–1979): 61–78.

Duda, Dorothea. *Islamische Handschriften. I: Persische Handschriften.* 2 vols. Vienna, 1983.

Ettinghausen, Richard. *Turkey: Ancient Miniatures.* New York, 1961.

Ettinghausen, Richard. *Turkish Miniatures from the 13th to the 18th Century.* New York, 1965.

Fehér, Géza. *Türkische Miniaturen aus den Chroniken der Ungarischen Feldzüge.* Budapest, 1976.

Fisher, Allan W., and Garrett Fisher, Carol. "A Note on the Location of the Royal Ottoman Painting Ateliers." *Muqarnas* 3 (1985): 118–120.

Gabriel, Albert. "Les étapes d'une campagne dans les deux Irak." *Syria* 9 (1928): 327–349.

Goodrich, Thomas D. "Ottoman Americana: The Search for the Sources of the Sixteenth-Century Tarih-i Hind-i Garbi." *Bulletin of Research in the Humanities* 87, no. 3 (Autumn 1982): 269–294.

Grube, Ernst J. "A School of Turkish Miniature Painting." In *First International Congress of Turkish Arts,* 176–209. Ankara, 1961.

Grube, Ernst J. "Miniatures in Istanbul Libraries. I." *Pantheon* 20 (1962): 213–226.

Grube, Ernst J. "Miniatures in Istanbul Libraries. II." *Pantheon* 20 (1962): 306–313.

Grube, Ernst J. "Herat, Tabriz, Istanbul: The Development of a Pictorial Style." In *Paintings from Islamic Lands,* ed. R. Pinder-Wilson, 85–109. Oxford, 1969.

Grube, Ernst J. "Notes on Ottoman Painting in the 15th Century." In *Essays in Islamic Art and Architecture,* ed. Abbas Daneshvari, 51–62. Malibu, 1981.

Grube, Ernst J. "Painting." In *Tulips, Arabesques and Turbans,* ed. Yanni Petsopoulos, 193–212. London, 1982.

Halbout du Tanney, Dominique. "Un chef-d'oeuvre de la peinture ottomane: La Couronne des Chroniques au musée Jacquemart André." In *Revue du Louvre et des Musées de France* 29, no. 3 (1979): 187–198.

Lowry, Heath. "Calligraphy—Hüsn-i Hat." In *Tulips, Arabesques and Turbans,* ed. Yanni Petsopoulos, 169–191. London, 1982.

Mahir, Banu. "Saray Nakkaşhanesinin Ünlü Ressamı Şah Kulu ve Eserleri." *Topkapı Sarayı Müzesi: Yıllık* 1 (1986): 113–130.

Meredith-Owens, Glynn M. "Turkish Miniatures in the Selimname." *The British Museum Quarterly* 26, nos. 1–2 (September 1962): 33–35.

Meredith-Owens, Glynn M. "A Persian Manuscript of the Reign of Bayezid II with Ottoman Miniatures." *Bulletin of the Prince of Wales Museum of Western India* 10 (1967): 27–31.

Meriç, Rıfkı Melul. *Türk Nakış Sanatı Tarihi Araştırmaları. I: Vesikalar.* Ankara, 1953.

Meriç, Rıfkı Melul. *Türk Cild Sanatı Tarihi Araştırmaları. I: Vesikalar.* Ankara, 1954.

Rado, Şevket. *Türk Hattatları.* İstanbul, 1984.

Renda, Günsel. "Topkapı Sarayı Müzesindeki H. 1321 no.'lu Silsilename'nin Minyatürleri." *Sanat Tarihi Yıllığı* 5 (1973): 443–495.

Renda, Günsel. "New Light on the Painters of the Zubdet al-Tawarikh in the Museum of Turkish and Islamic Arts in Istanbul." In *IVème Congrès International d'Art Turc,* 183–200. Aix-en-Provence, 1976.

Sevin, Muhiddin. *Hat Sanatımız.* İstanbul, 1982.

Söylemezoğlu, Nerkis. "An Illustrated Copy of Hamdi's *Yusuf we Züleykha* dated A.H. 921/1515 A.D. in the Bayerische Staatsbibliothek in Munich." In *Near Eastern Numismatics, Iconography, Epigraphy and History,* ed. D.K. Kouymjian, 469–478. Beirut, 1974.

Stchoukine, Ivan. *La peinture turque d'après les manuscrits illustrés. Ire partie: de Suleyman Ier à Osman II. 1520–1622.* Paris, 1966.

Stchoukine, Ivan. "Miniatures turques du temps de Mohammad II." *Ars Asiatiques* 15 (1967): 47–50.

Stchoukine, Ivan. "Un manuscrit illustré de la Bibliothèque de la Bayazid II." *Ars Asiatiques* 24 (1971): 9–22.

Stchoukine, Ivan. "La Khamseh de Nizami, H. 753, du Topkapı Sarayı Müzesi d'Istanbul." *Syria* 49 (1972): 240–246.

Tanındı, Zeren. "İslam Resminde Kutsal Kent ve Yöre Tasvirleri." In *Journal of Turkish Studies (Orhan Şaik Gökyay Armağanı. II)* 7 (1983): 407–437.

Tanındı, Zeren. "Resimli Bir Hac Vekaletnamesi." *Sanat Dünyamız* 9, no. 28 (1983): 2–6.

Tanındı, Zeren. "Rugani Türk Kitap Kaplarının Erken Örnekleri." In *Kemal Çığ'a Armağan,* 223–253. İstanbul, 1984.

Tanındı, Zeren. "13–14. Yüzyılda Yazılmış Kuranların Kanuni Döneminde Yenilenmesi." *Topkapı Sarayı Müzesi: Yıllık* 1 (1986): 140–152.

Titley, Norah M. "Istanbul or Tabriz?: The Question of Provenance of Three 16th century Neva'i Manuscripts in the British Library." *Oriental Art* 24, no. 3, (Autumn 1978): 292–296.

Titley, Norah M. *Miniatures from Turkish Manuscripts.* London, 1981.

Uzunçarşılı, İsmail Hakkı. "Osmanlı Sarayında Ehl-i Hiref 'Sanatkarlar' Defterleri." *Belgeler* 15 (1986): 23–76.

Ünver, A. Süheyl. *Ressam Nigari: Hayatı ve Eserleri.* Ankara, 1946.

Ünver, A. Süheyl. *Hattat Ahmet Karahisari.* İstanbul, 1948.

Ünver, A. Süheyl. *Müzehhib Karamemi: His Life and Works.* İstanbul, 1951.

Ünver, A. Süheyl, and Meşara, Gülbün. *Türk İnce Oyma Sanatı: Kaatı.* İstanbul and Ankara, 1980.

Yağmurlu, Haydar. "Topkapı Sarayı Müzesi Kütüphanesinde İmzalı Eserleri Bulunan Tezhip Ustaları." *Türk Etnoğrafya Dergisi* 13 (1973): 79–131.

Yazır, Mahmud B. *Medeniyet Aleminde Yazı ve İslam Medeniyetinde Kalem Güzeli.* 2 vols. İstanbul, 1972–1974.

Yurdaydın, Hüseyin G. *Nasuhü's-Silahi (Matrakçı), Beyan-ı Menazil-i Sefer-i Irakeyn-i Sultan Süleyman Han.* Ankara, 1976.

Metalwork and Other Precious Materials

Alexander, David G. "Two Aspects of Islamic Arms and Armor." *Metropolitan Museum Journal* 18 (1983): 97–109.

Allan, James, and Raby, Julian. "Metalwork." In *Tulips, Arabesques and Turbans,* ed. Yanni Petsopoulos, 17–53. London, 1982.

Bikkul, Ahat Ural. "Topkapı Sarayı Müzesindeki Türk Kılıçları Üzerinde Bir İnceleme." *Türk Etnografya Dergisi* 4 (1962): 20–28.

Çağman, Filiz. "Serzergeran Mehmet Usta ve Eserleri." In *Kemal Çığ'a Armağan,* 51–88. İstanbul, 1984.

Çığ, Kemal. "Coffrets turcs anciens pour les versets coraniques; étuis pour la conservation de la barbe du Prophète et leurs artisans." In *First International Congress of Turkish Arts,* 83–84. Ankara, 1961.

Çulpan, Cevdet. *Türk-İslam Tahta Oymacılık Sanatından Rahleler.* İstanbul, 1968.

Erginsoy, Ülker. "Turkish Contributions to the Art of Islamic Metalwork." In *Turkish Contribution to Islamic Arts,* 192–204. İstanbul, 1976.

Erginsoy, Ülker. "Turkish Metalwork." In *The Art and Architecture of Turkey,* ed. Ekrem Akurgal, 208–221. Oxford, 1980.

Fehér, Géza. "Contribution au problème de l'orfèverie turque à l'époque de l'empire ottoman." In *Acta Orientalia* 17 (1964): 113–127.

Fehér, Géza. "Quelques problèmes des objets d'art métalliques turc-osmanlis mis au jour en Hongrie." In *Atti del Secondo Congresso Internazionale di Arte Turca,* 123–128. Naples, 1965.

Fehér, Géza. *Craftsmanship in Turkish-ruled Hungary.* Corvina, 1975.

Ivanov, Anatol A. "A Group of Iranian Daggers of the Period from the Fifteenth Century to the Beginning of the Seventeenth." In *Islamic Arms and Armour,* ed. Robert Elgood, 64–77. London, 1979.

Kerametli, Can. "Osmanlı Devri Ağaç İşleri, Tahta Oyma, Sedef, Bağ ve Fildişi Kakmalar." *Türk Etnoğrafya Dergisi* 4 (1961): 5–13.

Koşay, Hamit Z., and Fehér, Géza. "Macaristan'daki Türk Kuyumculuk Yadigarları, Balkanlardaki Kuyumculuğa Türk Tesiri." *Türk Etnoğrafya Dergisi* 7–8 (1964–1965): 19–37.

Köseoğlu, Cengiz. *Topkapı Sarayı Müzesi. 5: Hazine.* İstanbul, 1980.

Melikian-Chirvani, Assadullah Souren. "Recherches sur l'école du bronze ottoman au XVIe siècle." *Turcica* 6 (1975): 146–167.

Miller, Yuri. "Turetski Serebryani Kuvschinchik XVI.v (petit cruche turque en argent du XVIe siècle)." *Soobscheniya Gosudarstvennogo Ermitazha* 15 (1959): 52–54.

Preyger, Firuze. "Bayram Tahtı." *Türk Etnoğrafya Dergisi* 13 (1973): 71–77.

Rice, D.S. "Studies in Islamic Metalwork. IV." *Bulletin of the School of Oriental and Asian Studies* 15/3 (1953): 489–503.

Rogers, J. Michael. "Glass in Ottoman Turkey." *Deutsches Archäologisches Institut Abteilung Istanbul* 33 (1983): 239–266.

Skelton, Robert. "Characteristics of Later Turkish Jade Carving." In *Fifth International Congress of Turkish Art,* ed. Géza Fehér, 795–807. Budapest, 1978.

Sourdel-Thomine, Janine. "Clefs et serrures de la Kaba: notes d'épigraphie, arabe." *Revue des Études Islamiques* 39, no. 1 (1971): 29–86.

Tapan, Nazan. "Sorguçlar." *Sanat* 6 (1977): 99–107.

Tezcan, Turgay. "Topkapı Sarayı Müzesindeki Türk Miğferleri." *Sanat Dünyamız* 2, no. 5 (September 1975): 21–27.

Tezcan, Turgay. *Topkapı Sarayı Müzesi. 9: Silahlar.* İstanbul, 1983.

Türköğlu, Sabahattin. "Saray Kuyumculuğu." *Sanat Dünyamız* 11, no. 34 (1985): 12–17.

Ünal, İsmail. "Çin Porselenleri Üzerindeki Türk Tarsiatı." *Türk Sanatı Tarihi: Araştırma ve İncelemeleri* 1 (1963): 677–714.

Yücel, Erdem. "Osmanlı Ağaç İşçiliği." *Kültür ve Sanat* 5 (1977): 58–71.

Yücel, Ünsal. "Türk Kılıç Ustaları." *Türk Etnoğrafya Dergisi* 7−8 (1964−1965): 59−99.

Costumes, Textiles, and Embroideries

Altay, Fikret. *Topkapı Sarayı Müzesi. 3: Kaftanlar.* İstanbul, 1979.

Atasoy, Nurhan. "Shoes in the Topkapı Palace Museum." *Journal of the Regional Cultural Institute* 2, no. 1 (Winter 1969): 5−31.

Barışta, Örcün. *Osmanlı İmparatorluk Dönemi Türk Işlemelerinden Örnekler.* Ankara, 1981.

Bassana, Luigi. *I costumi et i modi particolari de la vita de'Turchi. Ristampa fotomeccanica dell'ed. originale (Roma 1545).* Monaco di Baviera, 1963.

Berker, Nurhayat. "Kaşbastı (Diadem)." *Türk Etnoğrafya Dergisi* 13 (1973): 9−23.

Berker, Nurhayat. "Saray Mendilleri." In *Fifth International Congress of Turkish Arts,* ed. Géza Fehér, 173−181. Budapest, 1978.

Berker, Nurhayat. *Topkapı Sarayı Müzesi. 6: Işlemeler.* İstanbul, 1981.

Berker, Nurhayat, and Durul, Yusuf. *Türk Işlemelerinden Örnekler.* İstanbul, 1971.

Denny, Walter B. "Ottoman Turkish Textiles." *Textile Museum Journal* 3, no. 3 (December 1972): 55−66.

Denny, Walter B. "A Group of Silk Islamic Banners." *Textile Museum Journal* 4, no. 1 (December 1974): 67−81.

Denny, Walter B. "Islamic Textiles and Urban Life: The Ottoman Turks." In *The Warp and Weft of Islam,* ed. Jere L. Bacharach and Irene A. Bierman, 17−24. Seattle, 1978.

Denny, Walter B. "Textiles." In *Tulips, Arabesques and Turbans,* ed. Yanni Petsopoulos, 121−168. London, 1982.

Ettinghausen, Richard. "An Early Ottoman Textile." In *First International Congress of Turkish Arts* 134−140. Ankara, 1961.

Gervers, Veronika. *The Influence of Ottoman Turkish Textiles and Costumes in Eastern Europe.* Toronto, 1982.

Gökyay, Orhan Şaik. "Tılsımlı Gömlekler." *Türk Folkloru Araştırmaları Yıllığı* 3 (1976): 93−112.

Gönül, Macide. *Turkish Embroideries: XVI−XIX Centuries.* İstanbul, n.d.

Gönül, Macide. "Some Turkish Embroideries in the Collection of the Topkapı Sarayı Museum in İstanbul." *Kunst des Orients* 6, no. 1 (1969): 43−76.

Johnstone, Pauline. *Turkish Embroideries in the Victoria and Albert Museum.* London, 1986.

King, Donald, and Goedhuis, Michael. *Imperial Ottoman Textiles.* London, 1980.

Koçu, Reşat Ekrem. *Türk Giyim, Kuşam ve Süsleme Sözlüğü.* Ankara, 1969.

Kumbaracılar, İzzet. *Serpuşlar.* İstanbul, n.d.

Kurz, Otto, and Kurz, Hilde. "The Turkish Dresses in the Costume Book of Rubens." *Nederlands Kunsthistorisch Jaarboek* 23 (1973): 240−247.

Mackie, Louise W. *The Splendor of Turkish Weaving.* Washington, 1973.

Mackie, Louise W. "Rugs and Textiles." In *Turkish Art,* ed. Esin Atıl, 299−393. Washington and New York, 1980.

Menavino, G.A. *Trattato de costumi et vita de'Turchi.* Florence, 1548.

Muzeum Narodowe w Warszawie. *Tkanina turecka XVI−XIX w. ze zbiorow polskich.* Warsaw, 1983.

Öz, Tahsin. *Turkish Textiles and Velvets: XIV−XVI Centuries.* Ankara, 1950.

Öz, Tahsin. *Türk Kumaş ve Kadifeleri. II: XVII−XIX Yüzyıl ve Kumaş Süslemesi.* İstanbul, 1951.

Schmidt, Heinrich J. "Turkish Brocades and Italian Imitations." *Art Bulletin* 15 (1933): 374−383.

Süslu, Özden. "İstanbul Üniversitesi Kitaplığı Müzesindeki 16ıncı Yüzyıla Ait Osmanlı Minyatürlerindeki Kumaş Desenleri Üzerine Bir Deneme." *Sanat Tarihi Yıllığı* 5 (1973): 547−578.

Süslü, Özden. "Topkapı Sarayı ve Türk İslam Eserleri Müzelerinde Bulunan XIV. Yüz Yıla Ait Osmanlı Minyatürlerindeki Kumaş Desenlerinin İncelenmesi." *Sanat Tarihi Yıllığı* 6 (1976): 215−278.

Victoria and Albert Museum. *Brief Guide to Turkish Woven Fabrics.* London, 1950.

Wace, A.J.B. "The Dating of Turkish Velvets." *Burlington Magazine* 64 (1934): 167−170.

Wearden, Jennifer. "Siegmund von Herberstein: An Italian Velvet in the Ottoman Court." *Costume* 19 (1985): 22−29.

Rugs

Aslanapa, Oktay. "Die Frage der osmanischen Palastteppiche." In *First International Congress of Turkish Arts,* 25−26. Ankara, 1961.

Balpınar, Belkıs. "Classical Kilims." *Hali* 6, no. 1 (Spring 1983): 13−20.

Beattie, May H. "Coupled-Column Prayer Rugs." *Oriental Art* 14, no. 4 (Winter 1968): 243−258.

Bilgin, Ülkü. "Saf Seccadeler." *Sanat* 6 (1977): 47−57.

Çetintürk, Bige. "İstanbul'da XVI. Asır Sonuna Kadar Hassa Halı Sanatkarları." *Türk Sanatı Tarihi: Araştırma ve İncelemeleri* 1 (1963): 715−731.

Denny, Walter B. "Anatolian Rugs: An Essay on Method." *Textile Museum Journal* 3, no. 4 (December 1973): 7−25.

Denny, Walter B. *Oriental Rugs.* New York, 1979.

Denny, Walter B. "The Origin of the Designs of Ottoman Court Carpets." *Hali* 2, no. 1 (Spring 1979): 6−12.

Denny, Walter B. "Early Turkish Carpets" and "Mamluk and Ottoman Carpets." In *The Macmillan Atlas of Rugs and Carpets,* ed. David Black, 48−59 and 60−65. New York, 1985.

Denny, Walter B. "The Origin and Development of Ottoman Court Carpets." *Oriental Carpet and Textile Studies* 2 (1986). Forthcoming.

Ellis, Charles G. "The Ottoman Prayer Rugs." *Textile Museum Journal* 2, no: 4 (December 1969): 5−22.

Enderlein, Volkmar. "Zwei agyptische Gebetsteppiche im Islamischen Museum." *Forschungen und Berichte* 13 (1971): 7−15.

Erdmann, Kurt. "Kairener Teppiche. I: Europäische und islamische Quellen des 15−18. Jahrhunderts." *Ars Islamica* 5 (1938): 179−206.

Erdmann, Kurt. "Kairener Teppiche II: Mamluken und Osmanen-Teppiche." *Ars Islamica* 7 (1940): 121–191.

Erdmann, Kurt. *Der Türkische Teppich des 15. Jahrhunderts.* İstanbul, 1957.

Erdmann, Kurt. *Oriental Carpets: An Essay on Their History,* trans. Charles G. Ellis. New York, 1960.

Erdmann, Kurt, "Neure Untersuchungen zur Frage der Kairener Teppiche." *Ars Orientalis* 4 (1961): 65–105.

Kühnel, Ernst, and Bellinger, Louisa. *Cairene Rugs and Others Technically Related: 15th–17th Century.* Washington, 1957.

Mackie, Louise W. "A Turkish Carpet with Spots and Stripes." *Textile Museum Journal* 4, no. 3 (1976): 5–20.

Mackie, Louise W. "Rugs and Textiles." In *Turkish Art,* ed. Esin Atıl, 299–393. Washington and New York, 1980.

Textile Museum. *Prayer Rugs.* Washington, 1974.

Yetkin, Şerare. "Türk Kilim Sanatında Yeni Bir Gurup: Saray Kilimleri." *Belleten* 35, no. 138 (1971): 217–227.

Yetkin, Şerare. "Osmanlı Saray Halılarından Yeni Örnekler." *Sanat Tarihi Yıllığı* 7 (1977): 143–164.

Yetkin, Şerare. *Historical Turkish Carpets.* İstanbul, 1981.

Ceramics

Aslanapa, Oktay. *Anadolu'da Türk Çini ve Keramikleri Sanatı.* İstanbul, 1965 (also published in German as *Türkische Fliesen und Keramik in Anadolien.* İstanbul, 1965).

Aslanapa, Oktay. "İznik Kazılarında Ele Geçen Keramikler ve Çini Fırınları." *Türk Sanatı Tarihi: Araştırma ve İncelemeleri* 2 (1969): 62–73.

Aslanapa, Oktay. "Pottery and Kilns from the İznik Excavations." In *Forschungen zur Kunst Asiens,* ed. Oktay Aslanapa and Rudolf Naumann. İstanbul, 1970.

Carswell, John. "Pottery and Tiles on Mount Athos." *Ars Orientalis* 6 (1966): 77–90.

Carswell, John. *Kütahya Tiles and Pottery from the Armenian Cathedral of St. James, Jerusalem.* 2 vols. Oxford, 1972.

Carswell, John. "Six Tiles." In *Islamic Art in the Metropolitan Museum of Art,* ed. Richard Ettinghausen, 99–124. New York, 1972.

Carswell, John. "Some Fifteenth-Century Hexagonal Tiles from the Near East." *Victoria and Albert Museum Yearbook* 3 (1972): 59–75.

Carswell, John. "Syrian Tiles from Sinai and Damascus." In *Archaeology in the Levant: Essays for Kathleen Kenyon,* ed. R. Moorey and P. Parr, 269–296. Warminster, 1978.

Carswell, John. "Ceramics." In *Tulips, Arabesques and Turbans,* ed. Yanni Petsopoulos, 73–119. London, 1982.

Carswell, John. "The Tiles in the Yeni Kaplica Baths at Bursa." *Apollo* 120, no. 269 (July 1984): 36–43.

Crowe, Yolande. "İznik and the Chinese Manner: Waves and Vines." In *Fifth International Congress of Turkish Art,* ed. Géza Fehér, 207–214. Budapest, 1978.

Çorum, Bengi. "Bursa Müzesi Tarafından Müsadere Edilen İznik Keramikleri." *Sanat Tarihi Yıllığı* 4 (1974–1975): 280–288.

Denny, Walter B. "Blue-and-White Islamic Pottery on Chinese Themes." *Boston Museum Bulletin* 72, no. 368 (1974): 76–98.

Denny, Walter B. "Ceramic Revetments of the Mosque of the Ramazan Oğlu in Adana." In *IVème Congrès International d'Art Turc,* 57–65. Aix-en-Provence, 1976.

Denny, Walter B. *The Ceramics of the Mosque of Rüstem Pasha and the Environment of Change.* New York and London, 1977.

Denny, Walter B. "Ceramics." In *Turkish Art,* ed. Esin Atıl, 239–297. Washington and New York, 1980.

Denny, Walter B. "Turkish Ceramics and Turkish Painting: The Role of the Paper Cartoon in Turkish Ceramic Production." In *Essays in Islamic Art and Architecture,* ed. Abbas Daneshvari, 29–36. Malibu, 1981.

Ennès, Pierre, and Kalus, Ludvik. "Un plat d'Iznik à inscription turque." In *Revue du Louvre et des Musées de France* 29, no. 4 (1979): 258–260.

Erdmann, Kurt. "Die Fliesen am Sünnet odasi des Topkapı Sarayı in İstanbul." In *Aus der Welt der Islamischen Kunst,* ed. Richard Ettinghausen, 144–153. Berlin, 1959.

Erdmann, Kurt. "Neue Arbeiten zur türkischen Keramik." *Ars Orientalis* 5 (1963): 191–219.

Grube, Ernst J. "Masterpieces of Turkish Pottery in the Metropolitan Museum of Art and in the Private Collection of Mr. James J. Rorimer in New York." In *First International Congress of Turkish Arts,* 153–175. Ankara, 1961.

Kolsuk, Asuman. "Osmanlı Devri Çini Kandilleri." *Türk Etnografya Dergisi* 15 (1976): 73–91.

Kolsuk, Asuman. "Haliç İşi Denilen İznik Çinileri." *Kültür ve Sanat* 5 (1977): 52–57.

Lane, Arthur. *Later Islamic Pottery.* 1957. Revised Edition. London, 1971.

Lane, Arthur. "The Ottoman Pottery of Isnik." *Ars Orientalis* 2 (1957): 247–281.

Miller, Yuri. *Chudozestvennaja keramika Turcii.* Leningrad, 1972.

Otto-Dorn, Katharina. *Das Islamische Iznik.* Berlin, 1941.

Otto-Dorn, Katharina. *Türkische Keramik.* Ankara, 1957.

Öney, Gönül. *Turkish Ceramic Tile Art.* Tokyo, 1975.

Öz, Tahsin. *Turkish Ceramics.* Ankara, 1957.

Pope, John Alexander. "Chinese Influence on Iznik Pottery: A Re-examination of an Old Problem." In *Islamic Art in the Metropolitan Museum of Art,* ed. Richard Ettinghausen, 125–139. New York, 1972.

Raby, Julian. "A Seventeenth-Century Description of İznik/Nicea." *Istanbuler Mitteilungen,* 26 (1976): 149–188.

Raby, Julian. "Diyarbakir: A Rival to Iznik." *Istanbuler Mitteilungen* 27/28 (1977/1978): 429–459.

Raby, Julian, and Yücel, Ünsal. "Blue-and-White, Celadon and White Wares: Iznik's Debt to China." *Oriental Art* 29, no. 1 (Spring 1983): 38–48.

Riefstahl, R. M. "Early Turkish Tile Revetments in Edirne." *Ars Islamica* 4 (1937): 249–281.

Rogers, J. Michael. "The Godman Bequest of Islamic Pottery." *Apollo* 120, no. 269 (July 1984): 24–35.

Rogers, J. Michael. "A Group of Ottoman Pottery in the Godman Bequest." *Burlington Magazine* 127, no. 984 (March 1985): 134–155.

Rogers, J. Michael. "Iznik Pottery in the British Museum." *Hali* 7, no. 2 (April–June 1985): 50–57.

Rogers, J. Michael. "An Iznik Mosque-Lamp and a Globe in the Godman Bequest, British Museum." *Orientations* 16, no. 9 (September 1985): 43–49.

Sarre, Friedrich. "Der Import orientalischer Keramik nach Italien im Mittelalter und in der Renaissance." *Forschungen und Fortschritte* 9 (1933): 423–424.

Sinemoğlu, Nermin. "Kanuni Çağı Duvar Çinilerinin Kompozisyon Düzeni Açısından Üslup Tahlili." *Sanat Tarihi Yıllığı* 5 (1973): 241–259.

Süslü, Özden. "Le motif du paon dans la céramique ottomane du XVIe siècle." In *IVème Congrès International d'Art Turc*, 237–247. Aix-en-Provence, 1976.

Şahin, Faruk. "Kütahya Çini Keramik Sanatı ve Tarihinin Yeni Buluntular Açısından Değerlendirilmesi." *Sanat Tarihi Yıllığı* 9–10 (1979–1980): 259–286.

Travelstead, Brooke. "An Ornamental Ceramic Globe from the Ottoman Period." *Apollo* 115, no. 242 (April 1982): 237.

Ünal, İsmail. "Les Poteries de faience appartenant aux collections des Messieurs Hüseyin Kocabaş and Tevfik Kuyaş." In *Atti del Secondo Congresso Internazionale di Arte Turca*, 265–271. Naples, 1965.

Ünal, İsmail. "Çini Cami Kandilleri." *Türk Sanatı Tarihi: Araştırma ve İncelemeleri* 2 (1969): 74–111.

Yenişehirlioğlu, Filiz. "Şehzade Mehmed Türbesi Çinileri Üzerinde Gözlemeler." In *Bedrettin Cömert'e Armağan*, 449–456. İstanbul, 1980.

Yetkin, Şerare. "Türk Çini Sanatından Bazı Önemli Örnekler ve Teknikleri." *Sanat Tarihi Yıllığı* 1 (1964–1965): 60–102.

Glossary

aba heavy wool cloth; also used to identify a coat made from this fabric

Acem an Iranian, a non-Arab, a Shiite Turk residing in Iran (especially in Azerbaijan), or a foreigner

akçe silver coin used in the Ottoman Empire; during Süleyman's reign, an akçe weighed ⅓ of a dirhem (or ⅔ of a gram) and contained 85 percent silver

Arz Odası Reception Room in the third courtyard of the Topkapı Palace where foreign ambassadors were received and petitions submitted to the sultan

atlas monochrome compound-weave silk fabric

bayram religious holiday

besmele phrase placed at the beginning of a Koranic chapter, translated "In the name of God, the Merciful, the Compassionate"

Birun Outer Service of the palace institution, which included the artists and craftsmen whose facilities were located in the first courtyard of the Topkapı Palace

bohça square fabric, generally embroidered, used to wrap clothing as well as gifts

celi large-format writing, frequently used in architectural inscriptions

cemaat society, as in Cemaat-i Nakkaşan, Society of Painters

chilin four-legged mythical creature used in saz-style representations

cloud band decorative motif resembling a thin and curving cloud

cloud collar crescent-shaped motif composed of cloudlike formations

cuerda seca Spanish term, meaning "dry cord," applied to a technique of decorating tiles in which a greasy material was placed between the glazes to prevent them from running into one another; when the piece was fired, this material burned off, leaving a dark outline

çakşır pants with attached socks worn under a kaftan

çatma voided silk velvet woven with gold, gilded silver, and silver metallic threads

çintemani design composed of a series of triple balls and double wavy lines, originally symbolizing tiger stripes and leopard spots

devşirme tribute children recruited by the state from the non-Muslim provinces and educated in the palace, provincial courts, or armed forces to fill posts in administrative and military ranks

dirhem silver coin generally used in pre-Ottoman times; also a measure of weight equivalent to approximately three grams

divan upholstered benches placed along the walls of a chamber; the word derives from the Divan-ı Hümayun, the members of which sat on such couches

Divan a collection of poems written by one author

Divan-ı Hümayun Imperial Council of Ministers

divani a style of cursive script, frequently used in fermans

Ehl-i Hiref Society of the Talented; a special group of artists, artisans, and craftsmen employed by the court. Provincial courts and the residences of the princes also had their own Ehl-i Hiref corps

Enderun Inner Service of the palace institution, the members of which occupied the third courtyard of the Topkapı Palace and were trained to serve the state

entari inner kaftan

ferman imperial edict with the tuğra of the sultan placed at the top, validating its contents

grand vezir chief of the vezirs and the executive representative of the sultan in administrative and military affairs; the highest rank attainable in the devşirme system

gubari minuscule format of writing, frequently used in small Korans suspended from banners

Hadis Traditions, or the record of sayings and deeds of the Prophet Muhammed as handed down by his companions; study of the Traditions

hakkak gemstone carver; plural, hakkakin

347

hanap	tankard, a cylindrical vessel with a single handle used as a drinking vessel
Harem	sacred or protected place; name given to the quarters in the Topkapı Palace occupied by the family of the sultan
Has Oda	Throne Room in the third courtyard of the Topkapı Palace used during the ceremonial activities; also called the Hırka-ı Saadet Odası (Chamber of the Holy Mantle) since it housed the sacred relics, including the mantle and banner of the Prophet Muhammed and the swords of the four orthodox caliphs
haseki	favorite; highest rank in the Harem among the women of the sultan
hatayi	stylized lotus blossom; frequently accompanied by buds and leaves and used in decorative scrolls
Hazine	Treasury in the third courtyard of the Topkapı Palace, where the sultans' valuable objects were kept
hilat	robe of honor; following the Islamic tradition of presenting sumptuous robes as gifts to deserving dignitaries, the Ottoman sultans gave one or more hilats to foreign ambassadors, court officials, and esteemed artists
hutbe	sermon given in the name of the ruling sultan that follows the traditional prayer on Friday, the Islamic day of rest and worship
imaret	soup kitchen distributing free meals to the needy, frequently a part of an architectural compound endowed by a patron
janissary	anglicized version of yeniçeri, meaning new recruits; this corps, recruited from the devşirme children, constituted the most highly disciplined branch of the infantry
kaatı	découpage; calligraphy employing letters cut out of paper and pasted onto a sheet; a technique also applied to producing three-dimensional paintings
kadı	judge in Ottoman courts who administered the şeriat and kanun

kaftan	collarless, long- or short-sleeved garment used both as an outer robe and an inner robe by men and women. The ceremonial outer kaftan was open in the front and had long sleeves that hung at the back; the arms of the wearer would pass through the slits in the shoulders and expose the inner kaftan. The inner kaftan, called entari, was held at the waist by a jeweled belt or an embroidered sash and usually had short sleeves, to which separate sleeves, called kolluk, would be attached
kanun	secular law issued by the sultan in the form of fermans on topics not covered by the şeriat
katib	scribe or calligrapher; plural, katiban
kelime-i tevhid	"There is no god but God and Muhammed is his prophet," the profession of Muslim faith and declaration of God's unity
kemha	compound-weave fabric using polychrome silks together with gold, gilded silver, and silver metallic threads
kethüda	lieutenant, or second-in-charge
kılıç	characteristic Ottoman sword with a curving blade
kolluk	detachable sleeves buttoned to the shoulders of a short-sleeved inner kaftan, or entari
kufi	angular script
kursi	lectern
küftgari	inlay work using gold wire hammered into a roughened metal surface
kündekari	woodworkers who also carved and cut ivory, mother-of-pearl, and tortoiseshell and inlaid them on wooden objects; also applied to the technique of constructing woodwork by interlocking panels
maşrapa	jug with a single handle used as a drinking vessel
makili	angular script written in a checkerboard format
matara	ceremonial canteen used by the sultan, carried by the head of the Has Oda
medrese	university; frequently a part of an architectural compound endowed by a patron
meç	sword with a straight, thin blade
muhakkak	a style of cursive script
musavvir	painter; word used to denote a painter of figures

mücellid	bookbinder; plural, mücellidan
mülkname	property deed that assigns income from designated lands to support an endowment
müselsel	type of writing in which the letters are joined together
müzehhib	illuminator
nakkaş	designer, decorator, or painter; plural, nakkaşan
nakkaşbaşı	head nakkaş; see also sernakkaş
nakkaşhane	building or institution where the nakkaşan worked
nesih	a style of cursive script
nişancı	chancellor in the Divan-ı Hümayun responsible for affixing the sultan's tuğra on fermans
nihale	woven or embroidered floor covering
paşa	title given to high-ranking officials, particularly to vezirs, governors-general, and military commanders
peri	angel, more specifically a fairy or a beautiful female spirit inhabiting a fantastic world
rahle	folding bookstand
ressam	painter
Rumi	one from Rumelia, or the European provinces of the empire. Originally the word Rum was applied to the lands of the Eastern Roman Empire, hence to Anatolia as well
rumi	decorative element consisting of elongated leaves with pointed tips, frequently employed in scrolls; at times the leaves were split and paired to create a cartouche or joined by an undulating branch
saf	large multiniche prayer rug used in mosques
sancak	banner or standard; also a district in a province. The most prestigious sancaks were assigned to the princes at an early age, where they were trained in administrative and military affairs
saz	an enchanted forest of hatayis, long feathery leaves, and abstract flora inhabited by peris, dragons, and other fantastic creatures, applied to a style of representation that re-creates this world, as well as to a decorative scroll in which the elements intertwine, overlap, and intersect one another
seccade	small prayer rug with a mihrab niche
senmurv	fantastic bird resembling a phoenix

seraser	compound-weave fabric woven with silver and gold metallic threads
serbölük	head of a corps
serenk	compound-weave fabric using two or three colors of silk
serlevha	illuminated title page in a manuscript
sernakkaş	head nakkaş; see also nakkaşbaşı
sikkezan	maker of molds used in stamps, coins, or seals
sorguç	jeweled gold turban ornament with sockets for plumes
sülüs	a style of cursive script
şah	king; title used by Muslim rulers, also used as a given name or a part of a name
şahname	book of kings; biography of the sultan
şahnameci	official biographer or historian of the sultan
şalvar	loose pants gathered at the ankles with buttons or loops
şehzade	prince; son of the sultan
şeriat	religious law of Islam based on the Koran
şeyh	spiritual leader
şeyhülislam	leader of Islam and the head of the ulema; title of the chief judge and enforcer of the Islamic laws and the representative of the sultan's religious authority
talik	a style of cursive script used mainly for transcribing literary and epic texts; also called nastalik
Tefsir	text devoted to the explanation and interpretation of the Koran
tevkii	a style of cursive script
tile-mosaic	technique used in tiles in which the individual motifs were cut from ceramic slabs glazed in monochrome colors and fitted together to form the design
tombak	gilded copper
tondino	Italian word for a bowl with a deep well and wide flattened rim
tutya	zinc
tuğra	monogram of the sultan affixed to a ferman, legalizing its contents
tuğrakeş	person who draws the tuğra
türbe	mausoleum, frequently a part of an architectural compound endowed by the patron where he, together with the members of his immediate family, was buried

ulema	learned men, scholars, clergymen, or professors of theology
vakfiye	record listing sources of income, activities, and expenditures to maintain religious, social, and charitable institutions included in an endowment
vakıf	endowment or foundation trust established by the donor for the maintenance of religious, charitable, and social edifices
valide sultan	queen mother; woman whose son was the reigning sultan
vezir	governor-general or commander in chief in charge of a major province of the empire who had the privilege to use the title paşa
yastık	bolster or cushion
yatağan	sword that is shorter than a kiliç and has a slightly curving blade
zahriye	dedicatory pages, usually placed at the beginning of a manuscript, in which the text was enclosed by a medallion
zerduz	embroidery using gold thread that totally covers the surface
zerger	goldsmith; plural, zergeran
zernişani	gold inlayer

Index

Special Acknowledgments for Reference Photographs

The author and publishers would like to express their sincere thanks to the following persons and institutions for granting permission to reproduce the photographs and drawings used as references in this volume.

Walter B. Denny	Figs. 12, 23, 24, and 26
Zeki Fındıkoğlu	150, 151, and 153 (reconstructions)
Reha Günay	Fig. 21
Banu Mahir	Fig. 8
Suha Umur	Fig. 14
Mohamed U. Zakariya	Fig. 13
İstanbul, Topkapı Sarayı Müzesi	Figs. 10, 11, and 16–18
London, the Trustees of the British Museum	Figs. 7, 15, 19, 20, and 22
Munich, Alte Pinakothek	Fig. 4
New York, The Metropolitan Museum of Art, Harris Brisbane Dick Fund, 1928	Fig. 3
Paris, Réunion des Musées Nationaux	Fig. 5
Vienna, Kunsthistorisches Museum	Fig. 1
Vienna, Österreichische Nationalbibliothek	Fig. 6
Washington, Architect of the Capitol	Fig. 2
Washington, Smithsonian Institution, Freer Gallery of Art	Fig. 9